Psychology in Perspective

Psychology in Perspective

James Hassett

Boston University

HARPER & ROW, PUBLISHERS, New York
Cambridge, Philadelphia, San Francisco,
London, Mexico City, São Paulo, Sydney

This book is dedicated to

—My editors, past and present,

*Without their help, guidance, support, and friendship,
this book could easily have been mediocre;*

—And my wife, Pat,

Without her, my life could have been too.

Sponsoring Editor: Susan Mackey
Development Editor: Johnna Barto
Project Editor: Ronni Strell
Designer: Robert Sugar
Production Manager: Jeanie Berke
Photo Researcher: June Lundborg
Compositor: York Graphic Services, Inc.
Printer and Binder: R. R. Donnelley & Sons Company
Art Studio: Vantage Art, Inc.

Psychology in Perspective

Library of Congress Cataloging in Publication Data

Hassett, James.
   Psychology in perspective.

  Bibliography: p.
  Includes index.
  1. Psychology. I. Title.
BF121.H26   1984   150   83-18461
ISBN 0-06-042688-8

Credits

Illustrations and Photographs

(continued on p. 617)

Contents

3   Biology and Human Behavior

4   Sensation and Perception

7   Thought and Language

8   Childhood

Preface

In 10 years of teaching introductory psychology, I have never been able to find a satisfactory textbook. The problem is certainly not a lack of books to choose from: According to a recent count there are 113 introductory psychology texts in print (Rogers & Bowie, 1983), and countless others have gone out of print in my decade of teaching. At various times, I have tried several of the more widely respected texts. Each provided students with a reasonable list of concepts and technical terms. Some were well written and tried to relate these concepts to everyday life. But none of these successful texts taught students to think clearly and objectively about behavior and experience.

After reading these books, my students knew many terms but very little about what a scientific approach to human behavior really means. When methodological issues and critical analyses were mentioned, they were isolated in separate chapters or boxes, which were almost always packed with abstract details that were boring and difficult to remember. On the basis of reading these introductory texts, students would not be likely to notice the difference between a claim based on a strong study, a weak study, or no study at all.

I became particularly aware of the result of this educational failure when I took a leave from Boston University to work for one year as an associate editor at *Psychology Today* magazine. Most of our readers had some background in psychology. Yet the letters they wrote and the questions they asked revealed many fundamental misunderstandings about the nature of this infant science. Too many thought that their own experiences and biases held the key to understanding all behavior. If a 10-year program of research challenged a conclusion they had drawn over one evening and six beers, they were more likely to question the research than to doubt their own idle speculations.

Therefore, I decided to write an introductory psychology text that would consciously try to educate students to think critically about behavior and experience. A book that would present psychology not as a list of facts to be memorized, but rather as an ongoing process of trying to gain insights into the awe-inspiring complexity of human thought and action.

Goals of the Book

More specifically, the book that I began to outline in 1978 had three major goals: to promote critical thinking, to make the scientific method accessible, and to emphasize depth over breadth.

PROMOTE CRITICAL THINKING

The most obvious feature of this text that promotes critical thinking is a series of boxes entitled "Becoming a Critical Consumer." Each presents a passage from a popular account of psychology—ranging from *Walden Two* and the *New York Times* to Doctor Spock and Doctor Joyce Brothers—and asks students to compare these claims with material presented elsewhere in the text. Perhaps less obvious, but equally important in pedagogical terms, are the frequent discussions of the failures of "common sense," particularly in the description of the effects of biases and expectations on everyday observation (Chapter 1), and the discussion of misunderstandings about face validity and psychological tests (Chapter 12).

MAKE SCIENTIFIC METHOD ACCESSIBLE

The second goal—to make the scientific method accessible—is approached by frequent descriptions of the human side of science: How Skinner accidentally discovered extinction when a food dispenser broke (Chapter 5), how Piaget studied his own children (Chapter 8), and how Freud analyzed his own dreams (Chapter 11). While this type of background material sets the tone, the real work of integrating methodology with content occurs in another series of boxes, entitled "How Do They Know?" For example, case-study techniques are discussed in the story of Phineas Gage and what this unfortunate victim of brain damage can teach us about the relation of biology to behavior (Chapter 2). Similarly, the notion of replication is presented not in an isolated list of scientific methods, but as a way of understanding possible sex differences in fear of success (Chapter 10).

EMPHASIZE DEPTH OF COVERAGE

Finally, this book was designed to emphasize depth over breadth. Clearly, any student who takes a course in introductory psychology should be exposed to certain basic facts and phenomena, such as classical and operant conditioning, attribution theory, and psychoanalysis. All such central principles are covered in this book, as in virtually every other. But too many introductory texts seem concerned with packing in as many theories, names, and details as possible. This strategy often overwhelms students with so many facts that they fail to understand where those "facts" came from.

This book was written in the belief that it is far more important for the introductory student to have a firm grip on the nature of the psychoanalytic approach than to memorize the differences between Freud, Jung, Adler, and Horney. The resulting emphasis on depth over breadth can be seen throughout the text. For example, Chapter 11, on personality, focuses on a detailed overview of a single theorist for each of the major theoretical approaches. Similarly, Chapter 13, on abnormal diagnosis, provides some detail on four major categories of disorders (personality, anxiety, affective, and schizophrenic) rather than devoting the available space to a laundry list of DSM-III's 17 major categories and hundreds of subdivisions.

OTHER DISTINGUISHING FEATURES

In addition to the three major features of promoting critical thinking, making the scientific method accessible, and emphasizing depth over breadth, this book is also unusual in its analysis of the historical forces that shaped psychology and its practical applications in society.

Historical Perspective. Most introductory texts cover history by defining structuralism and functionalism in the first chapter and never mentioning them again. This text has attempted to weave historical background throughout the narrative, as in the analysis of the evolution of studies of forgetting from the associative theories of decay and interference to the cognitive approach of cue-dependent forgetting (Chapter 6).

Applications. Most chapters include a section entitled "Applied Psychology," which shows how theoretical advances have been applied to such problems as noise (Chapter 4), behavioral medicine (Chapter 3), and eyewitness memory (Chapter 6).

Psychology as a Living Science. But this list of features and boxes is less important than the overall orientation of the book: To inspire students to learn more about psychology. While the questions that psychologists study have been fascinating enough to motivate thousands of people to devote their lives to this field, introductory texts lack this excitement. Many use outside devices—newspaper articles, flashy graphics, or even short stories—as if psychology were not interesting enough on its own terms. In contrast, this text emphasizes the drama of the scientific approach from the excitement of each new discovery to the inevitable frustration of discovering that behavior is always more complex than it first seems.

Scholarly and Readable Style. Many teachers now believe that there is an inverse correlation between scholarship and writing style: The introductory texts that students most enjoy reading are also the most likely to be slightly misleading or even downright wrong. *Psychology in Perspective* was written in the firm belief that students will learn best from a clear and sometimes humorous writing style that describes conclusions accurately and with appropriate scholarly caution.

This goal is certainly ambitious; it may even be a bit naive. In a 1980 study, J. Scott Armstrong simplified the writing style of conclusions from several articles that had appeared in scholarly journals in the field of management. His changes were designed to leave the substance of each conclusion intact; he simply broke long sentences into shorter ones, substituted simpler words, and so on. He then asked faculty members from leading graduate programs in management to rate the "competence of the research" reported in the original versions. Other faculty members rated the more directly written accounts of the same research. Distressingly, Armstrong found significantly lower ratings for the versions that were simple and straightforward. Armstrong's research, and my own experience as a textbook and magazine writer, leads me to wonder whether there is a comparable phenomenon in the intellectual world: "If I can understand this book easily, it must be overly simplistic."

While this book was written with ease of understanding as a major goal, every effort was made to avoid being simplistic. Readers who wonder whether this book succeeds in communicating sophisticated concepts in a straightforward manner are invited to compare the accounts in this text with other accounts on heritability (see Chapter 3), or the difference between fairness and cultural bias (see Chapter 12), or any other topic. I hope that readers who perform this test or who simply read a chapter will find that this book succeeds as a sophisticated attempt to put *Psychology in Perspective* for the introductory student.

Supplements

Psychology in Perspective is accompanied by a complete learning and teaching package. For the underprepared or busy student, the *Study Guide* provides a review of the text. Prepared by John Hummel, John Hall, and John Capeheart, University of Houston, Downtown College, this guide includes chapter outlines, short-answer study questions, applications sections, chapter reviews, and self-tests of multiple-choice and true-false questions.

The *Instructor's Manual* will ease the burdens of new teachers and harried veterans. William Smotherman, Oregon State University, has provided teaching resources, lecture notes, film lists, and suggested class activities for each chapter. In addition, I have written a special section for instructors who teach psychology majors or a very intensive introductory course. In these settings, it may be useful to supplement this text with extra readings designed to teach students how to use journals and other primary sources. Guidelines for this additional coverage and an annotated list of possible readings are provided.

William Dwyer, Memphis State University, generated approximately 1800 multiple-choice questions for the *Test Bank*. There are two forms of test items for each chapter. The questions test applications of concepts as well as knowledge of facts. This test bank is also available in a microcomputer format.

The instructor who wants even more support material can ask the local Harper & Row representative about a set of slides for introductory psychology.

Acknowledgments

After devoting 5 years of my life to this book, I am convinced that an author must begin a project of this sort with at least two major characteristics: stubbornness and ignorance. Stubbornness is required to continue on and on despite the inevitable obstacles and to overcome the sheer exhaustion induced by writing about so many different bodies of research and theory. Ignorance is even more important. If, at the beginning, I had understood how much I would be required to learn—about both psychology and writing—I would never have had the audacity to start writing.

More than 60 reviewers and editors share the credit for the content of this text. Editors rarely get the recognition they deserve for shaping the form and substance of their books. Among those who contributed to the book are Kathy Robinson, who guided my book over two years. Her enthusiasm and helpfulness never wavered through all the hard work. Johnna Barto not only offered countless helpful suggestions, but presented them so diplomatically that I sometimes came to think they were my own ideas. She was also the final arbiter of which jokes simply did not belong in this book.

Ronni Strell was the project editor who somehow transformed all the typed pages, galleys, illustrations, tables, bibliographies, permissions, and old notes scrawled on napkins into a coherent textbook. Robert Sugar is responsible for the elegant and sophisticated design and for putting up with my constant amateur meddling. B. F. Emmer copyedited the text, and June Lundborg researched the many photographs that help give this book its character. Jim Brennan reminded me to think about marketing before the book was even written, and Elisa Barouh helped get my bills paid on time.

And then there are the research assistants who spent literally years seeking out obscure references, proofreading my drafts, sending out permissions, and going beyond the call of duty to water my plant. Wendy Heath wins the award for the longest time ever spent trying to keep track of a shifting bibliography. I will give her full credit for the accuracy of these sources if she will let me try to blame her if there are any errors. Chris Chin and Vicky Abate each worked for a full year, getting overwhelmed by the details so that I wouldn't be. Among the others who made major contributions, I am particularly grateful to Sheree Dukes Kohak, Andrea Sterste, and Deb Nelson.

Many typists slaved over these words, but the biggest slaves were Nobi Yonekura for the first draft and Michele Murray for the second, third, and sometimes even the fourth.

The main reason that I went through so many drafts was that reviewers questioned every word and punctuation mark in every manuscript. The process was often frustrating; but in the end, this dialectic produced a far stronger book than I could have written alone.

I am particularly grateful to the four special consultants who obsessively reviewed the various drafts for accuracy, balance, and style:

Richard Kasschau, University of Houston
Frances McSweeney, Washington State University
Christopher Monte, Manhattanville College
Sandra Scarr, University of Virginia

Numerous reviewers offered helpful suggestions on chapter drafts. Some might be considered my coauthors; I thank them all:

Robert Arkin University of Missouri	Pietro Badia Bowling Green University	David Bolocofsky University of Northern Colorado
Joel Arnoff Michigan State University	Susan Belmore University of Kentucky	Michael Brailoff College of Marin

Gwen Broude
Vassar College

Larry Brown
Oklahoma State University

James Coyne
University of California

Gerald C. Davison
University of Southern
California

Nancy Denney
University of Kansas

Paul Ellen
Georgia State University

Bruce Fretz
University of Maryland

Meg Gerrard
University of Kansas

Alan Glaros
Wayne State University

Leonard Goodstein
University Associates

Bernard Gorman
Nassau Community College

Kenneth Green
California State University,
Long Beach

Richard Griggs
University of Florida

Therese Herman-Sissons
Montclair State College

Annette Hiedemann
West Virginia Wesleyan
College

Gladys Hiner
Oscar Rose State College

James Howell
Portland Community
College

Michael Hughmanick
West Valley College

James J. Johnson
Illinois State University

Chadwick Karr
Portland State University

Wright Killian
Pembroke State University

John M. Knight
Central State University

Edward Krupat
Massachusetts College of
Pharmacy

Robert Levy
Indiana State University

Kenneth Livingston
Vassar College

William Mackavey
Boston University

Donald McBurney
University of Pittsburgh

Douglas Mook
University of Virginia

Bert Moore
University of Texas at
Dallas

Nora Newcomb
Temple University

Edward O'Day
San Diego State
University

David Pomerantz
SUNY, Stony Brook

William Ray
Pennsylvania State
University

Marylou Robins
San Jacinto College

Billy B. Rose
San Antonio College

Richard Schuberth
Rice University

Jonathan Segal
Trinity College

Charles Sheridan
University of Missouri,
Kansas City

Joan Sieber
California State University,
Hayward

Charlotte Simon
Montgomery College

Mary Helen Spear
Prince George's Community
College

James R. Speer
Stephen F. Austin State
University

Ronald D. Taylor
University of Kentucky,
Fort Knox

Rodney Triplet
Middlebury
College

Jeffrey Turner
Mitchell College

Norris Vestre
Arizona State University

Michael Wessels
Randolph Macon
College

Robert L. Williams
Washington University

I would also like to thank my own students who read portions of this manuscript to provide a student's view. Dr. Bruce Steinberg also tested several chapters in his psychology classes at Curry College. I thank him and his students for their valuable comments about my book.

And, of course, I must thank Mom and Dad. It is only now that I have a child of my own that I am beginning to realize just how much they did for me.

Finally, I would like to thank you the reader for wading through this list of acknowledgments.

James Hassett

Psychology
in Perspective

1
Introduction: Psychology in Perspective

What is psychology?
A Variety of Questions
A Variety of Theoretical Perspectives
A Variety of Professional Activities
Some Common Goals

The need for a scientific approach to behavior
A Test of Common Beliefs
When Common Sense Fails

An introduction to scientific methods
Observational Methods
Correlational Methods
Experimental Methods
The Human Side of Science
The Scientific Method in Action

Summary

HOW DO THEY KNOW?
Statistical significance: When do teachers' expectations make a difference?

BECOMING A CRITICAL CONSUMER
Teacher expectations and IQ

My older brother was the first to tell me the truth about psychology. We were waiting for the Q36 bus on Hillside Avenue in Queens, New York. The subject came up because one of his college friends had just decided to major in psychology. I knew nothing about this mysterious subject.

"What do psychologists do?" I asked.

"Well," my brother replied, "they try to predict how people will act."

"What does that mean?"

"A psychologist might try to predict what a person will do when he walks into a room."

"They can't do that, can they?" I asked uneasily. Like many eighth-graders, I had a number of habits that I preferred to keep to myself.

"Of course not," he replied, with the total intellectual assurance that only college sophomores can master. "It's supposed to be a science, but they really don't know anything yet."

Thus, my first reaction to psychology consisted of equal parts of awe and skepticism—awe that scientists might someday know what I would do even before I did and skepticism that they would ever be able to pull it off.

Many years, countless psychology credits, and several degrees later, I still react to psychology with awe and skepticism. And like most teachers, I secretly want you to feel the same way I do. So throughout this book, I will try to amaze you with all the things that psychologists know—without ever losing sight of all the things that still remain to be learned.

I must admit that it was neither awe nor skepticism that led me to major in psychology. I was trying to impress a girl who was breathlessly thrilled at the prospect of understanding what makes people tick. I went along because psychology didn't seem too difficult and majoring in it only required one year of French.

When I lined up to register as a psychology major in my freshman year, I found myself standing next to a shelf of books with forbidding titles such as *Journal of Experimental Psychology*, Volume 67, 1964, and *Journal of Abnormal and Social Psychology*, Volume 28, 1933. I took one of these hefty volumes off the shelf and opened it at random to an article entitled "The Robustness of the Chi-Square Statistic." I looked again at the cover of the book to make sure it said psychology. It did. I turned to another article. And another. Though some of the articles seemed to have some vague relation to people, none of them made a lot of sense to me. If I had not already been waiting in line for one-and-a-half hours, I might have headed for the history department.

I have since learned that psychology is an incredibly diverse field that raises hundreds of questions I had never thought about—from the way nerve cells in the eye distinguish between red and orange to the mental processes involved in understanding a joke. I can't say that I came to psychology to learn about all these things, but I can say that most of them proved to be pretty interesting.

For example, because I now know a bit about human memory, I know that the anecdotes I've been writing are probably only partly true. The bus my brother and I were waiting for might have been the Q1 or the Q43, or maybe we were discussing sociology while waiting for the subway in Brooklyn. As we shall see in Chapter 6, human memory is constructive—we tend to fill in the details of a story. In time, we may remember these manufactured details as vividly as we remember the original events.

At least one more psychological phenomenon relates to these anecdotes. Most people tend to assume that their experiences are typical and that other people are generally like them. Thus I assume that you may be like me, that you come to your first psychology course with only a vague idea of what this subject is all about. And so the obvious place to begin this text is with a brief description of what psychology is and what it is not.

What Is Psychology?

Psychology may be defined as the scientific study of behavior and mental processes. The first people to wonder about the mysteries of human behavior were probably Adam and Eve. In a more formal sense, psychology's intellectual roots can be traced back at least as far as Aristotle, the Greek philosopher who analyzed the nature of thought and memory more than three centuries before the birth of Christ.

For more than 2,000 years, scholars have tried to understand human nature. From Homer's *Odyssey* to Chaucer's *Canterbury Tales*, from the *Analects* of Confucius to Machiavelli's *The Prince*, philosophers and theologians, playwrights and politicians have explored the workings of the human mind. But it was only a little over a century ago that psychology emerged as a distinct discipline.

Because the Greek philosopher Aristotle (384–322 B.C.) wrote widely on such topics as memory, thought, sensation, and perception, he is sometimes referred to as the "first psychologist." This painting by Ferdinand Delacroix is entitled *Aristotle Describing the Animals.*

Wilhelm Wundt (1832–1920) founded the first laboratory of experimental psychology in 1879 at the University of Leipzig in Germany. Many of his studies were based on **introspection**—the careful, rigorous, and disciplined analysis of one's own thoughts by highly trained observers. At first, university administrators were unenthusiastic about Wundt's laboratory because they feared that "prolonged use of [his] introspection techniques by psychology students was likely to drive them insane" (Fancher, 1979, p. 134). It did not, but neither did it have the impact on the development of psychology Wundt had hoped for. The behaviorists later rejected the introspectionists' study of internal mental processes.

According to most historians, psychology was born in 1879 when Wilhelm Wundt founded the first psychological laboratory at the University of Liepzig in Germany. But in a larger sense, psychology was one of several social sciences that emerged from nineteenth-century philosophy partly as a result of that discipline's growing involvement with the scientific method. Other social sciences that were born at about the same time include **sociology**—the study of society, groups, and social institutions—and **anthropology**—the study of the origins and characteristics of different cultures.

Thus, psychologists do not hold a monopoly on the study of human behavior. The boundaries between psychology and other sciences are often blurred. Sociologists, anthropologists, biologists, physicians, and others sometimes pursue the same problems from similar perspectives. In this section, we shall not attempt to define the precise compartments into which every scientist and nonscientist can be fitted. Rather, we shall try to convey a sense of the vast scope of psychology—the wide range of topics that psychologists study, the variety of their theoretical orientations, and the different professional activities they engage in. Only after reviewing this diversity shall we summarize the goals that all psychologists share.

A VARIETY OF QUESTIONS

One way to get a feeling for the wide range of topics that psychologists have studied is simply to preview some of the research that will be described in this text.

For example, *Are children's thought processes qualitatively different from those of adults?* In the chapter on childhood, we review Jean Piaget's studies suggesting that a rational child is not merely a miniature version of a rational adult; children may actually think and perceive the world in a different way.

Why do women get drunk more easily than men? It is not simply because they weigh less. A 140-pound woman who has three drinks in one hour will ordinarily feel the effects more than a 140-pound man who drinks the same amount in the same time. The chapter on biology and human behavior explains how physical differences between the sexes affect the psychological response to alcohol.

Can lie detectors really determine when people are telling the truth? In the chapter on motivation and emotion, we examine how lie detectors work and review the evidence concerning their accuracy.

Why do tape recordings of your own voice so often sound odd or unfamiliar? The answer lies partly in the physical structure of the ear, as explained in the chapter on sensation and perception.

Will pets learn faster if they are rewarded for good behavior or punished for being bad? The chapter on learning provides relevant data and describes many other general principles that apply to both animals and humans.

When is depression normal and when does it cross the line into mental illness? What can be done to cure depression? Some tentative answers appear in the two chapters on abnormal psychology.

As you read this text you will learn about these topics and many more. Any student who is still reluctant to abandon the stereotype that psychologists deal only with personal problems should simply turn to the table of contents. The chapters cover everything from learning to language, attitudes to adolescence, and personality to perception. In short, psychologists study a wide range of topics that can be applied to every aspect of human behavior and experience.

A VARIETY OF THEORETICAL PERSPECTIVES

In dealing with such a wide range of problems, psychologists have developed several theoretical perspectives. This can sometimes be confusing for introductory students. When people hear that psychology is a science, they often expect it to consist of a series of well-established facts of the sort one might learn in physics or astronomy. However, psychology is one of the younger sciences, and there are still disputes over some fundamental questions.

In his influential book *The Structure of Scientific Revolutions*, Thomas Kuhn (1970)* used the word **paradigm** to refer to a common set of beliefs and assumptions shared by a particular group of scientists. In a young, dynamic, and changing science like psychology, several contradictory paradigms may coexist. In this section, we introduce five major psychological paradigms—psychoanalytic, behavioral, humanistic, cognitive, and biological. Each provides a different way of looking at the

---

*In psychology, references are usually cited by listing the name of the author and the year of publication. See the bibliography for complete references.

complexity of behavior and experience. The influence of these paradigms on the development of psychology will be examined throughout the text.

The Psychoanalytic Approach.   The first complete and systematic theory of human behavior was proposed around the turn of the century by a Viennese neurologist named Sigmund Freud. Based on his experience in treating people with emotional problems, Freud developed the **psychoanalytic approach**, which stresses the importance of unconscious conflicts and biological instincts in the determination of complex human behavior.

Freud believed that inborn sexual and aggressive instincts could be transformed in the course of development to determine everything from a man's relationships with his parents to his choice of a career and a spouse. Freud argued further that people are not ordinarily aware of the actual causes of their behavior; the critical transformations of instinctual energy ordinarily remain hidden in the unconscious mind. He was also one of the first to stress the importance of early childhood experiences in shaping adult personality.

Freud and his followers—including Carl Jung, Alfred Adler, and Erik Erikson—developed rich, complex, and ambitious theories that attempted to explain every aspect of human behavior from trivial events such as slips of the tongue to the highest artistic and cultural achievements of the human race. All these psychoanalytic theories were **deterministic** because they implied that every act and feeling is the inevitable result of natural forces and previous events.

The Behavioral Approach.   Like psychoanalysis, behaviorism assumes that every act is caused by natural forces. But this determinism is virtually the only point of agreement. The **behavioral approach** focuses on the systematic study of observable behavior. While Freud was willing to speculate about the internal workings of the unconscious mind, the first behaviorists limited themselves to that which can be observed and measured directly—physical stimuli and behavioral responses. Thus behaviorism was sometimes referred to as S-R psychology.

John Watson, the most influential of the pioneer behaviorists, argued that psychology's early studies (by Wundt and others) of the nature of mental life had produced only confusion and inconsistency. In his presidential address to the American Psychological Association in 1915, Watson also argued that virtually all behavior was learned. Therefore, psychologists should seek to discover the basic laws of learning that apply to both animals and humans and provide the foundation for a natural science of behavior.

The behavioral approach dominated American psychology at least until the 1950s and, in modified form, is still influential. Perhaps most important, the behaviorists established a strong tradition of laboratory research with humans and lower animals. The most famous of Watson's intellectual descendants is B. F. Skinner, who is known both for his pioneering laboratory research on animal learning and for his more speculative writings, such as the novel *Walden Two* in which he described a utopian community designed on scientific behavioral principles.

The Humanistic Approach.   While Freud saw human choices as an inevitable result of hidden instinctual forces and the early behaviorists portrayed humans as mechanically responding to stimuli and rewards, humanistic psychology provided a more optimistic view. Instead of accepting determinism, this theory argued that free will allows people to make conscious choices to grow and become better human beings. Thus the **humanistic approach** is concerned with human values, subjective experience, and the uniqueness of each individual. Abraham Maslow, for example, studied the characteristics of people who used all their talents to achieve their full potential as human beings; he called these people *self-actualized.*

Many humanistic psychologists believe that science will never be able to comprehend fully the infinite complexity of human behavior and experience.

The Cognitive Approach.   The **cognitive approach** emphasizes the active internal nature of higher mental processes involved in such areas as attention, perception, memory, language, imagery, and reasoning. When behaviorists first focused on the stimuli that produced certain responses, they were unwilling to speculate about what went on inside the organism to form an intermediate link. For example, a strict behaviorist would study the way a child learned to speak only by considering the words and symbols the child was exposed to (stimuli) and the child's actual utterances (responses). A cognitive psychologist would use the same observations to try to deduce the internal linguistic rules the child had learned. Hearing a 2-year-old say, "You breaked it," a cognitive psychologist would infer that this error tells us something about a rule the child had deduced to form the past tense. Twenty-five years ago, few researchers favored such a cognitive approach; today, it may be the most influential paradigm in psychology.

In a way, a cognitive psychologist is like an engineer who tries to understand an automobile engine by studying the performance of the car. Inferences about internal structures are indirect, based on what can be seen. In contrast, the biological approach to psychology is roughly analogous to opening the hood and trying to take the engine apart.

The Biological Approach.   The **biological approach** to psychology analyzes the physiological events associated with behavior and experience. For example, a biological psychologist might study patients with brain injuries to determine the psychological implications of damage to a physical structure in the brain. Although the human brain contains billions of nerve cells and trillions of interconnections, recent advances in medical technology offer tremendous promise for future research.

The Value of Multiple Perspectives.   To understand the implications of these five approaches, it is helpful to consider how each might try to understand the problems of a college student who is anxious about grades. From a psychoanalytic perspective, this anxiety might reflect an unconscious conflict caused by an aggressive impulse that has been channeled into competition with other people over grades. From a behavioral perspective, the origins of this anxiety are likely to seem more straightforward—perhaps the student was severely punished for poor performance in the first grade and has learned to fear the results of tests. From a humanistic perspective, the problem may revolve around self-concept, the gap between what a person would like to be and how she perceives herself. From a biological perspective, this problem may be caused partly by a genetic predisposition to become anxious. Finally, the cognitive approach might explore the way this person interprets the meaning of a grade.

These different explanations might be useful for understanding different people—not everyone worries about grades for the same reason. Different types of psychotherapy are associated with these paradigms, and the type that actually works may depend on both the problem and the person. For this reason, most psychotherapists call themselves eclectic, implying that they do not always use the same approach (see Chapter 14).

Thus, each of the five paradigms provides a different way of looking at a person or situation, and each has proved its value in research and clinical practice (see Table 1.1). As psychology continues to develop, we can expect new paradigms to offer further insights.

TABLE 1.1
A Preview of Research Based on Five Theoretical Paradigms

The Paradigm	*The Research*
Psychoanalytic approach: stresses how unconscious conflicts and biological instincts determine complex human behavior	Freud and Breuer analyzed the case of Anna O., a disturbed young woman whose symptoms included visual problems that were not caused by physical illness. They discovered that one evening when Anna was caring for her dying father he asked what time it was, but the tears in her eyes prevented her from seeing her watch. Anna didn't want to upset her father by crying, so she tried to strangle her powerful emotions. This conflict was buried in her unconscious mind, and later led to visual problems (from Chapter 11).
Behavioral approach: systematically studies observable behavior	Ayllon and Azrin created a token economy to change the behavior of seriously disturbed mental patients. Desirable behaviors (such as getting dressed alone or making a bed) were systematically rewarded with tokens that could be redeemed for cigarettes, candy, etc. (from Chapter 5).
Humanistic approach: studies human values, subjective experience, and the uniqueness of each individual	Maslow studied extremely well-adjusted individuals, such as Eleanor Roosevelt and Albert Einstein, to try to discover the general characteristics of self-actualized people who used their talents to live up to their full potential (from Chapter 11).
Cognitive approach: emphasizes active internal nature of higher mental processes	Bartlett studied the way people remembered stories they had heard hours, days, or months before. He found that people often remembered a limited number of details and invented new material to fill in for what they had forgotten. He called this phenomenon *constructive memory* (from Chapter 6).
Biological approach: analyzes physiological events associated with behavior and experience	Broca studied the brains of patients who developed severe language problems. He consistently found damage in the same area on the left side of the brain (from Chapter 2).

A VARIETY OF PROFESSIONAL ACTIVITIES

Another way to demonstrate the diversity of psychology is to consider the different activities in which psychologists engage and the impact of their work on our society.

Sooner or later psychology touches your life. For example, almost everyone who goes to school in the United States takes aptitude and achievement tests designed by psychologists. The popularity of these tests can be traced to World War I, when psychologists were called on to develop simple exams to screen out draftees who were not intelligent enough to function in the armed forces. The Army Alpha Test (for those who could read) and the Army Beta Test (for those who could not) were so successful that mass mental testing became an accepted feature of American society.

One group of experts who had worked on the Army intelligence tests went on to develop a short objective test to evaluate college applicants. This test was introduced in June 1926 and became known as the Scholastic Aptitude Test (SAT). Every year, millions of students take the SAT and its many offspring, including the Graduate Record Examination, the Law School Admissions Test, and the Medical College Admissions Test.

Figure 1.1
The first mass testing program in history took place in World War I when the U.S. Army used intelligence tests to screen out recruits who were intellectually unable to perform as soldiers. This photograph shows recruits taking the Army intelligence test in 1917 at Camp Lee.

Psychologists have also worked behind the scenes to help shape twentieth-century technology. In one famous example (Lachman, Lachman, & Butterfield, 1979), psychologists helped discover why a particular airplane designed in the 1940s had a long history of crash landings. When engineers could find nothing wrong with the mechanical function of the plane, psychologists analyzed the cockpit design to try to determine the errors a human operator might make under stress. The psychologists discovered that the brake lever was located near a similar lever that raised the landing gear. Tragically, when pilots were unable to take their eyes off the runway during stressful landings, they sometimes identified the wrong control by touch, retracted the landing gear when they wanted to put on the brakes, and crashed the belly of the plane into the runway at top speed.

Once this flaw in design had been located, the solution was obvious—cockpit controls were redesigned so that completely different arm motions were required to put on the brakes and to retract the landing gear. Since then, in order to avoid such flaws, psychologists have worked closely with engineers on the design of many new machines.

Even the humanities have been touched by psychology. F. Scott Fitzgerald studied Freudian psychoanalysis before writing *Tender is the Night* (Hoffman, 1945), and Thomas Mann, when writing *The Magic Mountain,* was heavily influenced by Freud's theories (Brennan, 1942).

Our legal system, too, has been affected by psychology. In *Brown v. The Board of Education of Topeka,* the 1954 landmark decision that called for the desegregation of public schools, the Supreme Court cited studies of the effects of segregation on personality (Rosen, 1972). In a more recent Supreme Court case on the ideal size for juries, the majority opinion drew so heavily on research about small groups that at times it sounded more like an article in a social psychology journal than a legal document (Tanke & Tanke, 1979).

Thus psychology has influenced our laws, our literature, and even the way we live. In some cases this influence has been immediate and intentional; in other cases the impact has been less direct.

In every science, including psychology, there is a distinction between basic and applied research. **Basic research** uses the scientific method to try to understand fundamental laws of the mind and behavior; **applied research** tries to solve specific problems by applying scientific principles and knowledge. The percentage of psychologists working in various specialties within these two categories is summarized in Figure 1.2.

Applied Psychology.   As you can see in Figure 1.3, more than 3 out of every 4 psychologists work in applied areas. **Clinical psychology** involves the diagnosis and treatment of abnormal behavior. It is closely related to **counseling psychology**, which specializes in helping people solve everyday problems such as marital difficulties. As we shall see later, it is not always easy to draw a firm line between the normal and the abnormal, so these specialties are not always easy to differentiate. More than half of all psychologists identify themselves as specialists in the clinical or counseling fields. (These groups often work closely with **psychiatrists**, licensed physicians who are trained in medicine before they specialized in the treatment of mental and emotional problems.)

There are several other applied specialties in which large numbers of psychologists work. **School psychologists** provide advice and guidance in school systems. For example, they conduct testing programs to identify and help people with special needs, such as students with learning disabilities or those with unusually high intelligence. **Educational psychologists** work in the same general area but tend to be more concerned with ways of increasing teacher effectiveness. **Industrial psychologists** apply research findings to the world of work. They might help to select personnel, for example, or to restructure jobs to increase worker satisfaction.

Most psychologists who work in these areas have completed advanced postgraduate training and have received a PhD, EdD, MA, or similar degree. Undergraduate training in psychology almost always focuses on the basic scientific foundations of these specialties.

In this textbook, many chapters include a short section titled "Applied Psychology," which describes a particular practical problem such as noise pollution, eyewitness memory, or mental retardation. But most of the book focuses on basic research.

Basic Research. Basic research tries to answer fundamental questions about behavior, such as How is stress related to disease? or What brain areas are related to thirst? The answers may at times lead to practical applications. For example, we shall see that the study of personality characteristics associated with heart disease has led to therapeutic programs that are designed to promote healthier lifestyles. But basic research is not designed to solve practical problems; rather, it seeks knowledge for its own sake.

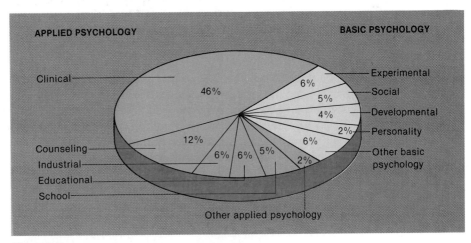

Figure 1.2
Most psychologists work in applied areas, particularly clinical psychology. This graph summarizes the distribution of full-time psychologists who are members of the American Psychological Association and hold doctoral degrees.

Since basic research provides the scientific foundation for practical applications, specialists in these areas exert more influence than their numbers might suggest. According to Figure 1.2, fewer than 1 out of 4 psychologists is involved in basic research. Yet virtually all of this book—and most other introductory psychology texts—is devoted to these specialties.

Basic researchers who call themselves **experimental psychologists** typically conduct laboratory studies in such areas as learning, human memory, and sensation and perception. **Physiological psychologists** study the biological bases of behavior—how the structure of the brain is related to experience, for example, or how genetics influences behavior. **Developmental psychologists** focus on the physical, intellectual, and emotional changes associated with aging. **Personality psychologists** focus on the problem of individual differences—how we come to be different from one another. **Social psychologists** are concerned with the way people respond to other human beings and how they interact with one another. A quick review of the table of contents reveals that each of these specialties is described in one or more chapters.

SOME COMMON GOALS

Thus far, this introduction to the nature of psychology has stressed diversity in research questions, theoretical approaches, and professional activities. Given all these differences, what do psychologists have in common?

The most obvious basis for unity is the nearly universal belief that the scientific method is a useful way to *understand, predict,* and *control* behavior. In one way or another, all scientists share these three major goals. A physicist, for example, may try to understand the principles involved in rocket propulsion, to predict how a certain rocket will take off, and to control the forces that can propel a rocket to the moon. Similarly, a psychologist might try to understand the laws of social interaction so that he might predict in advance how a certain group will make a decision. And ultimately he too might try to apply his knowledge to control behavior—suggesting, for example, what types of groups would be most efficient at making certain types of decisions.

Most people agree that it is useful for scientists to understand and predict natural phenomena. But as soon as scientists use this knowledge to change the physical or social environment, value judgments and ethical issues become involved.

Behavior control can raise especially difficult problems. Indeed, the very expression *behavior control* has a rather ominous tone. Few people object to psychologists' attempts to change abnormal or troublesome behavior, as when a therapist helps a business executive overcome a fear of flying. But, as we shall see later, when psychologists recommend how prisons should be organized or how parents should raise their children, the ethical issues become more complex.

Before such issues can be addressed, however, we must understand what the scientific method really involves. The next section explains how valuable a scientific approach to behavior can be and why common sense and casual observations are often misleading. Then we shall describe the scientific method in some detail.

The Need for a Scientific Approach to Behavior

Of course, psychologists are not the only ones who try to understand, predict, and control behavior. At one time or another, each of us has tried to understand why a friend seemed upset, to predict what Dad would say when he found out, or to change the bad habits of a loved one. To solve these ordinary problems in living, the "man in the street" uses common sense—some combination of lessons learned from the past and intuitions about the future. Unfortunately, common sense and personal experience can be misleading. This creates unique problems for both teachers and students of psychology.

If a physics teacher tells a class that force equals mass times acceleration, few students are likely to object that this goes against common sense, that in their experience force equals mass times acceleration squared. Similarly, students of basic chemistry usually accept the periodic chart of elements without debate. But by the time you read your first psychology book, you will have dealt with people for many years and, in all probability, you will have developed strong opinions about human nature.

For example, consider the following study. Researchers who followed 231 Boston couples for two years found that it was usually the woman who decided if and when a relationship should end (Hill, Rubin, & Peplau, 1976). Men tended to want to maintain the relationship and to feel more depressed and lonely after the breakup. Do you think it is true that men find it more difficult to end an affair? To answer this question you will probably turn to your own experience. If you happen to know three men who cheerfully dumped their women in the past month, you probably will doubt the study, even though it involved a much larger and more representative group studied for several years. Thus, when scientific findings conflict with common sense or personal experience, people often reject the scientific conclusion rather than question whether their experiences are typical and their observations accurate.

A TEST OF COMMON BELIEFS

To see whether students do indeed come to psychology classes with many misconceptions, psychologist Eva Vaughan developed the Test of Common Beliefs, which included 80 statements about behavior. Eight of these items are listed here: Before reading on, decide whether you think each is true or false.

1. A schizophrenic is someone with a split personality.
2. Boys and girls exhibit no behavioral differences until environmental influences begin to produce such differences.
3. Genius is closely akin to insanity.
4. To change people's behavior toward members of ethnic minority groups, we must first change their attitudes.
5. The basis of a baby's love for its mother is the fact that the mother meets the baby's physiological needs for food, water, and so on.
6. Children's IQ scores have very little relationship to how well they do in school.
7. The best way to ensure that a behavior will persist after training is to reward the

behavior every single time it occurs through training rather than reward it only once in a while.

8. Under hypnosis people can perform feats of physical strength that they could never do otherwise (adapted from Vaughan, 1977).

In Vaughan's original study, each of these eight statements was accepted by at least half of a group of 119 college students. If you are like most people, you probably believe that at least some of these statements are true. In fact, however, scientific research has shown that every one of them is false.

To make matters worse, incorrect opinions like these are often hard to change. In one study, Lamal (1979) compared students' scores on a modified version of the Test of Common Beliefs before and after they took an introductory psychology course. Although there was some improvement at the end of the course, the average student still accepted 38% of the false statements. Education can gradually correct mistaken beliefs, but the process is often slower than we might hope.

WHEN COMMON SENSE FAILS

Why are such misconceptions so difficult to correct? Part of the answer involves the way the human mind works or, as a psychologist might say, the way people process information. Many people rely heavily on common sense, but there are a number of ways in which common sense is systematically wrong.

Expectations and Bias.   The ability of the human mind to distort the facts is awe-inspiring. For example, a few weeks after Arthur Bremer shot presidential candidate George Wallace, *Life* magazine interviewed Bremer's mother to see what evil influences could have led to this assassination attempt. His mother explained, "I still think it was something he ate that didn't agree with him. Why else would he do such a thing? He didn't care about politics, at least not that I know of . . . It *had* to be something he ate" (quoted in Wittner, 1972, p. 32).

Perhaps the mothers of Hitler, Mussolini, and Jack the Ripper had similar explanations for their sons' lapses. While few psychologists would have the nerve to attack motherly love, it is quite clear that in this case, Mrs. Bremer was not being entirely objective.

Many psychologists have studied how expectations and bias influence what we perceive and remember. In one classic study of subjectivity, psychologists asked undergraduates from Dartmouth and Princeton to review films of a controversial football game between the two schools (Hastorf & Cantril, 1954). Sports fans will not be surprised to learn that Princeton students thought the Dartmouth team deserved more penalties for breaking the rules, whereas Dartmouth students noticed more infractions by the Princeton team. Two other classic demonstrations of the effect of expectations are illustrated in Figures 1.3 and 1.4.

Biases and expectations shape people's beliefs in a number of different ways. For one thing, people tend to seek out information that agrees with what they already believe and to ignore or avoid information that disagrees with their perceptions. In one ingenious experiment (Block & Balloun, 1967), people were asked to listen to two tape-recorded speeches about cigarette smoking. One speech summarized the evidence that smoking causes cancer; the other argued that this was a myth. Each subject was told that unfortunately the speeches had been recorded under poor conditions and were sometimes hard to hear unless the listener pressed a button to reduce static. Interestingly, nonsmokers tended to press the button to hear the antismoking message clearly, and smokers were more likely to press the button to listen to the prosmoking speech.

Not only do our biases and expectations affect what we pay attention to in the first place, but they can even change what we remember. In one study (Snyder & Uranowitz, 1978), 212 students read the fictitious life story of Betty K. After they

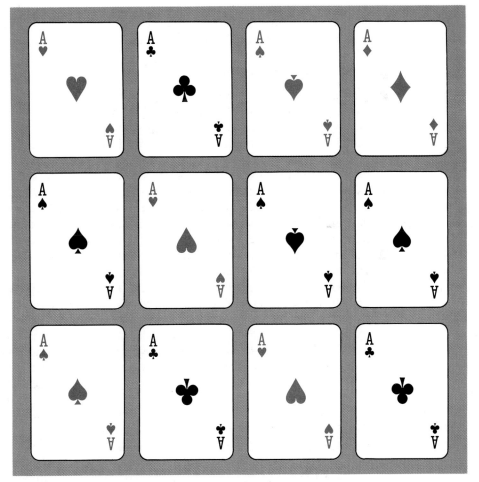

Figure 1.3
How many aces of spades do you see? For most people, a quick glance yields three. If you agree, go back and count again. Expectations can influence perception. Because you expect an ace of spades to be black, you can easily miss the two red ones. The correct total is five.

Figure 1.4
This picture of an argument was used in a classic study of the psychology of rumors. One person saw this picture and described it to a second person; the second described it to a third; and so on. As the story was repeated, the details were altered to fit the cultural stereotypes of the 1940s, when the study was performed. More than half the time, the sixth person in the rumor chain said that the black man, not the white man, held the razor.

had spent a few minutes thinking about what Betty was like, some were told she was a lesbian; others heard that she was heterosexual. A week later people from the second group described Betty as an attractive woman who had had a steady boyfriend in high school and a tranquil childhood. Although they had read the same life history, the people who had been told that Betty was a lesbian said she was rather unattractive, had never had a steady boyfriend, and had an abusive father. Sexual stereotypes had actually changed the way people remembered this fictional young woman.

Further complicating casual observations of behavior are **self-fulfilling prophecies**—expectations that come true partly because people believe them. If everyone believes that inflation is here to stay, they will spend more and increase inflation. If you think your new roommate is inconsiderate, you may treat her in such an unpleasant way that she will retaliate by behaving inconsiderately. Numerous studies have shown that one person's expectations can influence another's behavior (Snyder, 1982).

Self-fulfilling prophecies can be important not just in dealing with others but even in dealing with ourselves. Psychologists have shown that people who expect to fail often do; those with higher opinions of themselves are more likely to succeed (Jones, 1977). Thus, biases and expectations can influence not just what people attend to and remember but even what happens to them.

The Impact of Vivid Examples.   Still another problem with common sense is the fact that people are often overly impressed by vivid examples. Imagine how you might react in the following situation:

Let us suppose that you wish to buy a new car and have decided that on grounds of economy and longevity you want to purchase one of those solid, stalwart, middle-class Swedish cars—either a Volvo or a Saab. As a prudent and sensible buyer, you go to *Consumer Reports*, which informs you that the consensus of their experts is that the Volvo is mechanically superior, and the consensus of the readership is that the Volvo has the better repair record. Armed with this information, you decide to go and strike a bargain with the Volvo dealer before the week is out. In the interim, however, you go to a cocktail party where you announce this intention to an acquaintance. He reacts with disbelief and alarm: "A Volvo! You've got to be kidding. My brother-in-law had a Volvo. First, the fancy fuel injection computer thing went out. 250 bucks. Next he started having trouble with the rear end. Had to replace it. Then the transmission and the clutch. Finally sold it in three years for junk" (Nisbett, Borgida, Crandall & Reed, 1976, p. 129).

If you are totally rational and logical, this alarming report should not have a major impact on your plans. After all, if the *Consumer Reports* survey summarized the experiences of 900 Volvo owners, you now have information on 901. The averages still look very good. But you may not be totally rational and logical. Abstract averages lack the dramatic impact of one concrete, vivid case and often seem less convincing (Nisbett & Ross, 1980).

How many cigarette smokers have argued that no matter what the Surgeon General says, "I know a man who smoked three packs a day and lived to be 86"? Common sense may tell us that all of the scientist's fancy charts and technical reports are less convincing than a case you can see with your own eyes. But in this respect common sense is extremely misleading. The fact that one heavy smoker lives to be 86 does *not* disprove the general rule—on the average, smokers still die younger than nonsmokers. This vivid example merely reminds us that statistical predictions about large groups do not apply to every individual, that there are often exceptions to the rule.

In a systematic demonstration of the impact of vivid examples, Borgida and Nisbett (1977) directly contrasted the influence of abstract and concrete information on students' course choices. One group of psychology majors was given course evaluations based on the average ratings of large groups of students who had taken the courses. When the psychology majors later indicated what courses they themselves planned to take, they apparently ignored these abstract recommendations. In contrast, another group heard individual students describe what they had liked or disliked about specific courses. Although this concrete information only reflected the opinion of two or three individuals, students were more likely to follow this advice.

Even highly sophisticated observers may be fooled by common sense. In a discussion of the history of medicine, Crichton (1970) notes that nineteenth-century surgeons resisted change in operating-room procedures long after researchers had provided statistical proof that the sterilization of instruments reduced the risk of infection. One reason was that every surgeon could cite many examples of patients he had successfully operated on without washing his hands or sterilizing his instruments. These vivid examples seemed more convincing than abstract surveys showing that on the average more patients recovered when sterile procedures were observed. Many patients died because these surgeons based their practice on common sense.

Joseph Stalin hinted at a similar phenomenon when he said, "The death of a single Russian soldier is a tragedy. A million deaths is a statistic."

Psychology students should try to avoid this error in reasoning. A particular claim about human behavior should always be carefully evaluated in terms of the evidence on which it is based. The fact that you know someone who is an exception does not disprove the rule.

20/20 Hindsight. Sometimes, students have the opposite problem. Instead of arguing that a specific research conclusion goes against common sense and therefore must be wrong, they complain that a certain study simply confirms common sense and therefore seems trivial—they knew it all along. This criticism says as much about the way the human mind works as it does about psychology. No one should be surprised if some psychological research agrees with common sense. Sometimes common sense is right and sometimes it is wrong, and one goal of psychology is to find out which times are which. But when we say we could easily have predicted how an experiment would turn out, it may just be the wisdom of hindsight.

Most people tend to overrate their own success in predicting the future. If your best friend announces that he is getting married, you are likely to say to yourself, "I knew this would be the one." But if he announces instead that the relationship has ended, you would probably say to yourself, "I knew it wouldn't last." No matter what happens, we tend to think we knew it all along. Everybody is an expert in hindsight. Every sports fan can tell you what the coach should have done—after the game is over.

Many studies have shown that after people hear the results of a scientific experiment, a historical conflict, or a medical diagnosis (Arkes, Wortman, Saville, & Harkness, 1981), they think they could easily have predicted the results on the basis of common sense. But when other people were asked to *predict* the same results beforehand, they were not particularly successful. The answer was obvious only after the fact.

In this section, we have seen a number of reasons to beware of casual observations. We tend to filter the world through our biases, paying attention to and remembering facts that are consistent with our prior beliefs. Self-fulfilling prophecies can cause our false beliefs to become true. We are overly impressed by concrete evidence. And we tend to think we knew something all along even when we did not.

These and other deficiencies suggest that at least one proverb should be rewritten. Experience is the best teacher only after we have learned to become good students. A psychologist must learn to observe behavior systematically and to resist her own biases.

As you read the findings of a specific study, you will sometimes be tempted to say to yourself, "That's so true, I've felt that way myself" or "Horse feathers! I know that's not right." Such personal experiences may be convincing, but we must remember that, by themselves, they have little scientific validity. Whatever happened to you is just one person's experience, and there is an excellent chance that you are not able to be objective about it anyway. Intuitive opinions must be verified by a more systematic and objective approach to behavior and experience. And that is precisely what the scientific method provides.

An Introduction to Scientific Methods

There is no single set of procedures called *the scientific method*. Rather, science is an attitude—a rational and skeptical approach to knowledge. Because scientists are skeptical, psychologists are not willing to accept any generalization on faith or because an expert seems trustworthy. They insist that every claim must be tested against observable evidence.

If a psychologist hears someone say, "Did you know that happy infants always develop into optimistic adults?" or "Time after time, I have seen that American women are afraid to succeed at their careers," her response is always the same: How do they know? It is this critical questioning of every claim—even if it is made by another scientist—that lies at the very heart of science and of psychology.

Throughout this text, the emphasis is on evaluating the claims of the experts, on examining the evidence to reach your own conclusion. Inevitably this means learning about research methodology. Students are sometimes impatient with scientific controversies; they are more interested in learning conclusions than understanding how the conclusions were reached. Or as George Miller put it, methodological issues that are "bread and butter to the working scientist can be spinach to everyone else" (Lachman, Lachman, & Butterfield, 1979, p. 13).

But every student should learn to become a critical consumer of psychological knowledge. The very nature of psychology as an ongoing process of discovery demands that students learn not just what the experts have said but also why they said all those things in the first place.

As psychologists have grown in number and influence, almost every American has become a "consumer" of psychological knowledge and services. Many people learn about psychology primarily through newspaper and magazine articles that tell them how to develop more satisfying friendships, fulfill their potential, and determine if their pet goldfish is neurotic. Some of these articles are accurate and some are not. In this text, the sections titled "Becoming a Critical Consumer" encourage you to read some sample selections carefully to try to determine their strengths and weaknesses.

This book also emphasizes methodological issues, particularly in the sections titled "How Do They Know?" Each of these explains how a particular technique has led to greater understanding of such topics as the effects of punishment, the fear of success, and the nature of madness.

Before reading further, you need a general idea of the methods available to psychologists and how these methods are typically used. The next few pages provide a brief outline of the procedures that serve as the foundation for psychological knowledge—observational, correlational, and experimental methods.

Developmental psychologist Jean Piaget is shown here using the method of naturalistic observation to learn how children's cognitive abilities are revealed in the games they play.

OBSERVATIONAL METHODS

Partly because many important psychological phenomena are difficult to bring into a laboratory, psychologists sometimes turn to **naturalistic observation**—careful observation, recording, and analysis of everyday behavior. For example, many of Jean Piaget's influential ideas about developmental changes in cognitive abilities were stimulated by his naturalistic observations of his own three children.

Since casual observations of behavior can be distorted by expectations, bias, and the limitations of common sense, psychologists often take systematic steps to ensure the accuracy of naturalistic observations. For example, several observers may be asked to rate the same behavior simultaneously to see if independently they arrive at the same conclusions. In technical terms, an observation is said to be *reliable* if it can be reproduced consistently (see Chapter 12).

When direct forms of observation are impractical, psychologists may use techniques that ask people to report on their own attitudes and behavior. Sometimes, they **interview** people, systematically asking them questions about their experiences and feelings. A **questionnaire**—a written list of questions to which people respond—is closely related to the interview technique but is a bit more formal and more practical for questioning large groups of people in a short time.

Data from interviews, questionnaires, and other sources may be summarized in a **case history**, a detailed description of the life experiences and behavior patterns of a single individual. Clinical psychologists often find the case-history method helpful in understanding the problems of their clients. In Chapter 2, we describe one of the most famous case histories in psychology, that of Phineas Gage, an accident victim whose personality changed dramatically after specific areas in his brain were damaged.

While case histories focus on a single individual, **surveys** measure the behavior of large groups of people, usually by summarizing information from many interviews or questionnaires. In Chapter 9, we contrast several famous surveys of sexual behavior to illustrate the importance of beginning with a **representative sample**, a group in which subjects are systematically chosen to represent some larger population.

CORRELATIONAL METHODS

Data from surveys and other sources are often analyzed to identify precise relationships between two or more **variables**, factors that are measured or controlled in a scientific study. This often involves computation of a **correlation coefficient**, a precise statistical expression of the relationship between two variables. Correlation coefficients range in absolute value from 0 (implying no relationship) to 1 (implying that one variable predicts another perfectly).

Correlation coefficients and other correlational methods play an important role in psychological research; they are described more thoroughly in two "How Do They Know?" sections. In Chapter 3, we discuss interpretations of the magnitude of correlations by describing a quantitative study of how closely twins resemble each other. In Chapter 12, we explain the most common error in interpreting correlations—the belief that two variables that are correlated are *causally* related.

For example, if you read that people who smoke two packs of cigarettes per day die younger than nonsmokers, you might conclude that cigarette smoking causes death. By itself, this study does not prove this cause-effect link; other interpretations are possible. Perhaps chronic anxiety causes people to smoke, and anxiety causes early death. If this were the case, stopping smoking would not increase these people's life-span.

Other data, however, have shown that this interpretation is incorrect. Smoking does increase the risk of death. One way this causal relationship has been supported is through another research procedure—the experiment.

EXPERIMENTAL METHODS

An **experiment** is a scientific study in which a researcher tries to establish a causal link between two variables by manipulating one variable and observing changes in the other. The factor that the experimenter manipulates is called the **independent variable;** the **dependent variable** is the factor that may be affected. It is called *dependent* because the experiment is set up so that any changes that occur in this factor depend on changes in the independent variable.

For example, suppose you wanted to know whether alcohol influences memory. In one simple experiment, the independent variable could be the amount of vodka you gave subjects to drink, and the dependent variable could be how long it took them to memorize a shopping list of 25 grocery items.

To perform this simple study, you would assign people randomly to two groups—an **experimental group,** who received a particular treatment (in this case, perhaps 3 ounces of vodka), and a **control group,** who did not receive any special experimental treatment. It is very important that people be assigned to these two groups on a random basis. If you chose the experimental subjects from a high school scholarship class and the control subjects from a group of working-class adults, the resulting memory differences might reflect other variables as well as the effects of the alcohol. If, however, the groups were chosen randomly and the experimental group did indeed take a much longer time to learn the grocery list, it would be reasonable to conclude that the alcohol caused an impairment in memory.

Experimental methods are described in considerable detail in later chapters.

THE HUMAN SIDE OF SCIENCE

In reading a textbook, it is easy to forget that the principal actors in the drama of science are themselves living, breathing human beings. Like lawyers, accountants, and bus drivers, psychologists come in a variety of sizes, shapes, and temperaments. Some are driven by a desire for fame, some by financial pressures, some by an idealistic determination to improve the world, some by all this and more. And the way a researcher pursues a given problem may depend on his personality as well as his training.

Trying to understand science simply by memorizing its rules is a bit like trying to understand how Congress works by studying the U.S. Constitution and Robert's Rules of Order. To understand Congress, one must also know about lobbyists, political deals, and the nature of power. To understand a scientific result, one must also know about the historical events and the human background—the egotistical desire for fame, the spark of genius, and the fortunate accident. One of the goals of this textbook is to take you behind the scenes to glimpse the people and the cultural forces that have shaped psychology.

An introductory text must teach you the meaning of key terms such as *correlation* and *case history,* but abstract definitions can make science seem rather dry and boring. Nothing could be further from the truth. A scientist is like a detective in a murder novel, trying to solve the mysteries of nature by carefully analyzing its cryptic clues. We end this chapter with two examples of the scientific method in action in order to provide a more realistic picture of how psychology works.

THE SCIENTIFIC METHOD IN ACTION

The Case of Clever Hans. Around 1900, the Berlin press discovered Clever Hans. Hans was a trotting horse who could add, subtract, multiply, divide, and more. Or could he?

Every day around noon a retired mathematics teacher named Herr von Osten gave a free demonstration of his favorite horse's astounding abilities. "How much is $\frac{2}{5}$ and $\frac{1}{2}$?" Hans's trainer might ask. Hans would pause thoughtfully, tap his front right foot 9 times, pause again, and tap 10 times for the answer, $\frac{9}{10}$. "If the eighth day of the month comes on a Tuesday, what is the date of the following Friday?" While some members of the audience were still trying to figure that one out, Hans would tap 11 times and stop. "Which of these cards says *horse,* Hans?" Hans would carefully examine the printed cards placed before him and point to the correct card with his nose. (Naturally the card said *Pferd,* since Hans spoke only German.)

"Which hand is that gentleman raising, Hans?" Hans correctly moved his head to the right. And so on.

Hans could count the number of men or women in the audience or the number of people wearing eyeglasses. He answered questions by shaking his head *yes* or *no,* solved simple algebra problems, and could tell time. He could even spell out words using an elaborate code of foot taps developed by Herr von Osten. German educators concluded that Hans had the intelligence of a 13- or 14-year-old human.

Clever Hans became the rage of Germany and then of the world. His story was told in newspapers, magazines, and books. There were Clever Hans postcards and Clever Hans toys. In the meantime, the experts debated whether Hans was a miraculous freak, a fraud, or a living example of what horses everywhere could achieve with proper education.

Some experts believed that Hans really was a thinking horse. Others argued that he wasn't really intelligent, he just had a fantastic memory. A few said that Hans was stupid but telepathic—he got the answers from "thought waves which radiate from the brain of his master" (Pfungst, 1911, p. 28).

But human nature being what it is, many people suspected Herr von Osten of trickery. An informal commission was appointed to investigate the charge. In September 1904, thirteen experts (including a circus manager, a veterinarian, a teacher, and several zoologists and psychologists) reported that Herr von Osten was not guilty of using intentional signals or "unintentional signals of the kind which are presently familiar" (Pfungst, 1911, p. 254).

Clever Hans is tapping his hoof to answer an arithmetic problem during a test performed in Berlin in 1904.

But Oskar Pfungst, an associate of one of the psychologists on the committee, was not convinced. He proceeded to plan a series of experiments under more carefully controlled conditions. Clever Hans was high-strung and moody and had a tendency to bite his new trainers whenever he got excited. But the horse gradually learned to answer questions posed by the psychologist, and the research went on for two hours each day, four days a week.

Pfungst planned to vary systematically the conditions under which Hans was tested. First, he would ask Hans questions when Herr von Osten was not around. Later, Hans would wear large blinders so he could not receive visual cues. Cotton would be stuffed in Hans's ears to avoid unintentional auditory cues. Pfungst even considered obscuring the horse's sense of smell. The ultimate test of Hans's reasoning ability would be somehow to give him a problem to which no one present knew the answer. Throughout all this, conditions were to be kept as natural as possible, and each test would be repeated many times.

This type of careful, systematic observation gradually revealed Hans's secret. When the horse had to read a number from a card, he was right 98% of the time if the experimenter had looked at the card first, but only 8% of the time if he had not. Tests with written words yielded the same result. When the experimenter knew the answer, Hans had no trouble; when all around him were ignorant, so was Clever Hans. Later tests revealed the importance of visual cues. Hans became very upset when he had to wear blinders and spent much of his time trying to get a peek at his inquisitors. When he could not see the questioner, he could not get the right answer.

Armed with this information, Pfungst began watching Hans's performances more closely. He noticed that whenever anyone asked Hans a question, there was a natural tendency for the questioner to lean forward very slightly to watch the horse's foot. When Hans reached the right number of taps, the questioner would involuntarily jerk his head slightly upward. After Pfungst discovered this, he could make Hans tap as many times as he wanted by consciously leaning forward and then subtly jerking his head back. Other unintentional cues could explain Hans's other tricks.

Oskar Pfungst succeeded where so many had failed not because he was smarter than others who had studied Clever Hans or even because he was a more astute observer of animal behavior. Pfungst's advantage was his careful application of the scientific method.

He began by identifying variables that might affect Hans's performance, such as the presence of visual or auditory cues, and he went on to perform a series of experiments to test the importance of each variable. For example, in one of Pfungst's experiments, the independent variable was the presence or absence of auditory cues, which he manipulated by placing cotton in the horse's ears; the dependent variable was the percentage of problems that Clever Hans solved correctly.

When Pfungst compared Hans's performance with and without auditory cues, the dependent variable was not affected; so this experiment suggested that auditory cues were not a critical factor. But when visual cues were eliminated by putting blinders on Hans, the percentage of correct answers was much lower than when Hans did not wear blinders. This dramatic change in the dependent variable suggested that visual cues caused Hans to respond correctly.

In this way, systematic observation solved the mystery of Clever Hans. Herr von

Osten was innocent of trickery but guilty of not being careful enough. When it became clear that the psychologists were going to issue an unfavorable report, von Osten flew into a rage and forbade further experiments. He continued to believe in Hans and to exhibit him, apparently to his dying day. Pfungst went back to his laboratory and experimented with an elaborate device that measured very small movements of people's heads. And Clever Hans, we might guess, was left to wonder whatever happened to all those pompous men who used to ask him questions and why he was no longer on the front pages of *Frankfurter Zeitung.*

The Case of the Biased Teachers. Although the case of Clever Hans provides an excellent introduction to the application of scientific methods, psychologists usually study more general questions than whether a particular horse can talk. Our second case explores one of the most famous experiments in the recent history of psychology to show how the results of one study may be challenged—or even disproved—by another.

As noted earlier, psychologists have long been interested in the effects of self-fulfilling prophecies—predictions that come true partly because people believe them. In 1968, Robert Rosenthal and Lenore Jacobson published a book called *Pygmalion in the Classroom,* which seemed to prove that teachers' high expectations can raise students' IQs. The cautious phrase *seemed to prove* is quite intentional; as we shall see, other researchers found that teacher expectations have an effect, but not on IQ.

Rosenthal and Jacobson's research had begun several years earlier, in the spring

Many studies have shown that teachers' expectations can influence the way they act toward pupils.

of 1964, when they administered the "Harvard Test of Inflected Acquisition" to every student at a public elementary school. Teachers were told that this test would identify children who could be expected to show a sudden improvement in their academic work. Although the classroom performance of these late-bloomers might now seem quite ordinary or even below average, they would soon improve dramatically.

On the first day of the next semester, each teacher in the first through sixth grades was given a list of the pupils who had been identified by the test. But this list was purposely misleading. In fact, the Harvard Test of Inflected Acquisition was simply an IQ test. And the late-bloomers had not been identified by their test scores—their names had been picked randomly out of a hat.

The independent variable in this study involved teachers' expectations. Out of every 5 students, 1 was randomly identified as a late-bloomer. These made up the experimental group—subjects who had received a critical treatment to determine its effects. In contrast, the remaining children formed the control group—subjects who had not received any special experimental treatment.

The dependent variable in this study was performance on a similar test 12 months later. The control group provided a baseline estimate of how children from this elementary school changed in a year under normal conditions. Results for the experimental group should have been different only if teachers' expectations really had an effect on IQ.

As Figure 1.5 shows, the effects on first- and second-graders were quite dramatic. In both grades the gains in IQ for the late-bloomers were more than double those for the rest of the class. Because the only difference between the groups was

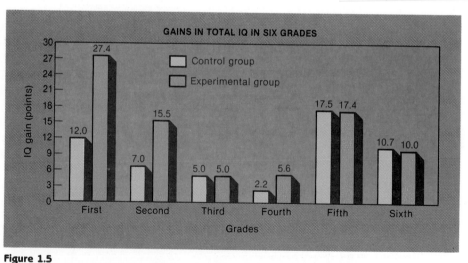

Figure 1.5

IQ gains of children identified as late-bloomers compared with normal controls (Rosenthal & Jacobson, 1968). Although this study showed dramatic gains in the first two grades, later replications led to more moderate conclusions.

what their teachers expected of them, these expectations seemed to be a very important factor. But what about the fourth grade, where the difference between the groups was only a few points, or the fifth and sixth grades, where there was even a slight tendency for the control group to do better? Do these small differences really mean something, or are they too small to have any importance? To answer such questions, psychologists turn to the study of statistics to determine whether a particular result is **statistically significant**, that is, if it is unlikely to have occurred by chance according to some predetermined criterion, usually a probability of less than 5%. The details of this criterion and of Rosenthal and Jacobson's results are described in "How Do They Know?" Statistical analysis revealed that there was a significant difference between the experimental and control groups in the first and second grades but not in the third, fourth, fifth, or sixth grades.

The general conclusion was widely reported in the press (for one example, see "Becoming a Critical Consumer"), and many experts speculated that low teacher expectations were often responsible for students' problems in school. The scientific community, however, was far more cautious.

Like many dramatic reports, the Rosenthal and Jacobson study created a tremendous amount of controversy. Other researchers examined the details closely and discovered many flaws that led to serious doubts. One critic (Thorndike, 1968, p. 708) charged that the study was "so defective technically that one can only regret that it ever go beyond the eyes of the original investigators!"

In 1971, Janet Elashoff and Richard Snow published *Pygmalion Reconsidered*, a critical analysis of technical and statistical details that was almost as long as the original report. They raised doubts about whether the IQ test Rosenthal and Jacobson used provided valid results for young children—a particularly damaging criticism because only the youngest group had shown gains in IQ.

One of the most important checks on the accuracy of research is **replication**— the repetition of a study to see whether the results are similar. In one chapter of *Pygmalion Reconsidered*, Baker and Christ summarized the attempts of other investigators to replicate the original study. If many researchers had been able to show that teacher expectations had raised IQs in many different settings, that would have implied that Rosenthal and Jacobson's conclusions were not the result of some idiosyncrasy of the original study. But the nine studies that measured IQs all found that positive teacher expectations failed to raise IQ.

Other researchers, however, showed that high teacher expectations can have more subtle effects. In one typical follow-up study (Rubovits & Maehr, 1971), 26 college students taught sample lessons to groups of four grade-school children. Each group consisted of two children who were identified as gifted and two who were described as nongifted (though all children were actually similar in ability). A neutral observer carefully recorded the teachers' behavior according to a precise rating system and discovered that the student teachers asked the supposedly gifted students more questions and praised their answers more often.

Most of the studies of teacher behavior reviewed by Baker and Christ (14 of 17) revealed that expectations did make a difference. And some studies of student performance (6 of 12) found that high teacher expectations could indeed improve

Statistical Significance: When Do Teachers' Expectations Make a Difference?

Whenever psychologists quantify psychological variables, they are faced with the problem of interpreting the observed numbers. In most cases this begins with a **test of statistical significance** to determine whether a particular mathematical result is likely to have occurred by chance.

Although many students are intimidated by the very word *statistics*, each of us intuitively applies certain laws of probability in everyday life. This is particularly true for people who spend a lot of time in casinos in Las Vegas or Atlantic City. Gamblers are continually faced with the problem of figuring the odds to choose a good bet.

Suppose that I bet you $10 on the flip of a coin: If heads comes up, I pay you $10; if it's tails, you pay me $10. I flip the coin and it comes up tails. You mumble something about bad luck and ask if I'd like to go for double or nothing. I do and it's tails again, and a third time, and a fourth time. By now you are down $80 and beginning to wonder if I take credit

cards. In your desperation you decide to keep doubling the bet until you win.

But suppose we bet 20 more times and the coin comes up tails every time. One tails is bad luck, 4 in a row is very bad luck, but 24 in a row sounds suspiciously like cheating. (A statistician could tell you that 24 tails in a row would occur by chance—that is, by accident—less than 1 out of every 10 million times.) You form a new theory: I offered to bet in the first place because I am a coin shark, a man who cheats unwitting opponents out of their money with trick coin flips. Note that it is possible that you are wrong—I may just be lucky. But you believe that this is far less likely than some other explanation, and you will probably be willing to act on this estimate of probability—possibly asking several large friends over to discuss my success in detail.

The psychologist who is trying to decide what to conclude on the basis of certain numerical results is faced with a similar problem in probabilities. In the Rosenthal and Jacobson

performance on non-IQ tests such as classroom examinations. Baker and Christ (1971) concluded, "The question for future research is not whether there are expectancy effects, but how they operate in school situations" (p. 64).

But the controversy did not end. In 1978, Robert Rosenthal and Donald Rubin published a summary of the literature on self-fulfilling prophecies, "Interpersonal Expectancy Effects: The First 345 Studies." These studies went far beyond teacher expectations; they documented the effects of expectations on the behavior of such groups as employers, therapists, and scientific researchers. After reviewing the wide range of methods used in these studies and the consistency of the effects, Rosenthal and Rubin concluded that expectations do indeed affect behavior.

experiment, IQs were measured before some children were identified as late-bloomers and then again one year later. It is not surprising that changes in the two groups were not identical. The question is, how big a difference would you expect to see by chance, even if the two groups were basically the same.

To answer this question psychologists use statistical procedures to determine the precise odds that a particular result did not occur by chance. For a variety of reasons, psychologists have agreed to accept findings that could be expected to occur by chance no more than 5 times out of every 100 (Cowles & Davis, 1982). This is often symbolized by the expression $p < .05$, which means that the probability that something will occur by chance is less than 5%. Psychologists who wish to be more conservative and take a smaller chance of accepting incorrect research results often use a cutoff point of 1 out of every 100 times ($p < .01$). Thus, a particular finding is said to be **statistically significant** if the odds against its occurrence by chance exceed some predetermined criterion, usually $p < .05$.

Thus, the first step Rosenthal and Jacobson took after collecting the data shown in Figure 1.5 was to perform a series of standard calculations (called an *analysis of variance*) to see whether the overall results were statistically significant. They were. The probability was less than .02 that the observed differences in IQ between experimental and control groups would have occurred by chance. They then did a separate analysis (using a different statistical procedure called a *t-test*) for each grade. For the first grade, the difference between the experimental and control groups was highly significant ($p < .002$). The results were also signficant for second-graders ($p < .02$). But the smaller differences observed in the third, fourth, fifth, and sixth grades might have resulted from random variation; none of these probabilities met the criterion of $p < .05$. Thus statistical analyses of the Rosenthal and Jacobson data revealed that teacher expectations affected performance only in the first and second grades.

Tests of statistical significance like this are a critical element in most psychological studies. A survey of journals published by the American Psychological Association found that more than 9 out of every 10 articles included significance tests (Eddington, 1974). The vast majority of the research findings described in this book were subjected to tests of statistical significance to be certain that they should not be attributed to chance.

But even this impressive summary did not settle the issue. Twenty-nine criticisms and commentaries by other experts were published along with this article, challenging many of the details and conclusions.

Some students are distressed by continuing controversies of this sort; they would like to know the truth and not be bothered with the details. But human behavior is extremely complex, and science often progresses by controversy. Psychology does not have a final set of answers to every question; it is a continuing process of searching for the truth.

If there is one lesson to be learned from this review of the Rosenthal and Jacobson research, it is that no single study ever settles an issue. Journalists often make

BECOMING A CRITICAL CONSUMER:

Teacher Expectations and IQ

On September 20, 1968, *Time* magazine (p. 62) published an article describing Rosenthal and Jacobson's research. As you read the excerpt, compare it to our description of the same research. Does the article accurately describe the major findings? Do you agree with the final conclusion? (A short discussion of these issues appear after the "Summary" at the end of this chapter.)

TEACHERS

Blooming by Deception

Critics of the public schools, particularly in urban ghettos, have long argued that many children fail to learn simply because their teachers do not expect them to. That proposition is effectively documented in a new book called *Pygmalion in the Classroom.* . . . [The authors] told the teachers that a new test could predict which slow-learning students were likely to "show an unusual forward spurt of academic and intellectual functioning." The exam, actually a routine but unfamiliar intelligence test, was given to all pupils. Teachers were then told which students had displayed a high potential for improvement. The names were actually drawn out of a hat.

When tested later, the designated late bloomers showed an average IQ gain of 12.22 points, while the rest of the student body gained 8.42 points. The gains were most dramatic in the lowest grades. First-graders whose teachers expected them to advance intellectually jumped 27.4 points, second-graders 16.5 points. There were similar gains in reading ability. One young Mexican American, who had been classified as mentally retarded with an IQ of 61, scored 106 after his selection as a late bloomer.

Rosenthal and Jacobson politely refrain from moralizing, suggesting only that "teachers' expectations of their pupils' performance may serve as self-fulfilling prophecies." But the findings raise some fundamental questions about teacher training. They also cast doubt on the wisdom of assigning children to classes according to presumed ability, which may only mire the lowest groups into self-confining ruts. If children tend to become the kind of students their teachers expect them to be, the obvious need is to raise the teachers' sights. Or, as Eliza Doolittle says in Shaw's Pygmalion, "The difference between a lady and a flower girl is not how she behaves, but how she's treated."

this mistake, reporting the latest finding by a psychologist (or a sociologist or a cancer researcher) as if this one study provided the answer the human race has been searching for since the dawn of time. Life is not this simple. A well-designed study tells us more than a poorly designed one, and any study at all provides more information than an unconfirmed or biased opinion. But there is always more to be learned and more data to be collected.

You cannot understand psychology unless you understand what constitutes trustworthy evidence. You must learn to tell the difference between conclusions based on a strong study, on a weak study, and on no study at all. Whenever you hear a wondrous new claim about an advance in understanding human behavior, your reaction should always be the same—How do they know? Only when you understand the evidence that lies behind the claim will you be able to make an intelligent assessment of its value and validity.

Throughout this text, there will be a strong emphasis on research methods. Hopefully, this exposure to scientific methods will teach you to think more clearly and objectively about people. And along the way, it will also help you to understand the most fascinating organisms on the face of the earth—you and me.

Summary

1. Psychology may be defined as the scientific study of behavior and mental processes.
2. Psychologists conduct research on a wide range of topics including the brain, learning and memory, thought, sensation and perception, normal and abnormal personality, and social psychology.
3. Psychologists take many different theoretical approaches to these problems. A **paradigm** is a common set of beliefs and assumptions shared by a particular group of scientists. In a young, dynamic, and changing science like psychology, several contradictory paradigms may coexist.
4. **Psychoanalysts** emphasize the role of unconscious processes and biological instincts in motivating behavior. **Behaviorists** emphasize systematic studies of observable behavior. **Humanistic psychologists** are particularly concerned with human values, subjective experience, and the uniqueness of the individual. **Cognitive psychologists** study the active internal nature of higher mental processes involved in attention, perception, memory, language, imagery, and reasoning. **Biological psychologists** analyze the physiological events associated with behavior and experience.
5. Psychologists also engage in a wide variety of professional activities. There is an important distinction between **basic research**, which uses the scientific method to try to understand fundamental laws of the mind and behavior, and **applied research** which tries to solve specific problems by applying scientific principles and knowledge. In practice, many psychologists are involved in both types of activities.
6. Psychologists use the scientific method to achieve three common goals—the understanding, prediction, and control of behavior.
7. Common sense and casual observations of behavior are often misleading. Expectations and bias can influence what people perceive, what they pay attention to, and even what they remember. **Self-fulfilling prophecies** are expectations that come true partly because people believe in them. People are often overly impressed by vivid information, even when abstract information is more trustworthy. Further, people often feel that they knew something all along, even when they did not.
8. Psychologists consequently distrust common sense and casual observations and rely instead on scientific methods to provide a more rational and skeptical ap-

proach to knowledge. Specific techniques are described in the sections titled "How Do They Know?" The procedures can be grouped according to observational, correlational, and experimental methods.

9. Observational methods in psychology include **naturalistic observation**—the careful observation, recording, and analysis of behavior. In **interviews**, psychologists systematically ask people questions about their experiences and feelings. **Questionnaires** are written lists of question to which people respond. Data from these and other sources may be summarized in a **case history**, a detailed description of the life experiences and behavior patterns of a single individual.

10. Psychologists often try to identify precise relationships between two or more **variables**, factors that are measured or controlled in a scientific study. This may involve computing a **correlation coefficient**, a precise statistical expression of the relationship between two variables.

11. **Experiments** are scientific studies in which a researcher can establish causal relationships by manipulating the **independent variable** and observing changes in the **dependent variable**. Subjects are randomly assigned to an **experimental group**, which receives some special treatment, and a **control group**, which does not.

12. The case of Clever Hans, a "talking" horse who was actually responding to nonverbal cues, illustrates the value of scientific observations of behavior.

13. In the widely publicized book *Pygmalion in the Classroom*, two researchers reported an experiment that seemed to show that teachers' high expectations could actually raise students' IQs. In this study, an experimental group of students were falsely identified to their teachers as late-bloomers, children who could be expected to show a spurt of intellectual development within a few months. Analysis of the results showed that IQ increases in the experimental group were indeed greater than those in the control group. These differences between the groups were **statistically significant** (that is, unlikely to have occurred by chance) only for first- and second-graders; no significant differences were detected for third-, fourth-, fifth-, and sixth-graders.

14. However, critics attacked many procedural details of this study. Further, nine other **replications** (repetitions of the study to see whether results would be similar) failed to find that teacher expectations could raise IQ. Other studies showed that teachers' expectations could influence their behavior and student performance on non-IQ tests. This illustrates why psychologists are reluctant to draw strong conclusions from a single study.

Discussion of "Becoming a Critical Consumer"

The Time *article presents a clear picture of the research design. However, it could easily create the wrong impression about the results. For example, while stating correctly that "the gains were most dramatic in the lowest grades," it does not note that teachers' expectations did* not *have significant effects in the third, fourth, fifth, and sixth grades.*

In the last paragraph, the sweeping conclusions for educational reform are premature. A cautious scientist would not change the entire educational system after conducting a single study.

Interestingly, most newspapers and magazines that enthusiastically reported this study did not report on later challenges. As noted in the text, subsequent studies revealed that expectations can influence teacher behavior but that they do not affect IQ.

To Learn More*

A Career in Psychology. If this chapter convinced you to devote the rest of your life to this field, write for this free booklet to: American Psychological Association, 1200 17 Street, N.W., Washington, D.C. 20036.

Nisbett, R., & Ross, L. *Human Inference: Strategies and Shortcomings of Social Judgment.* Englewood Cliffs, N.J.: Prentice-Hall, 1980. Research on the failures of common sense and much more.

Fancher, R. E. *Pioneers of Psychology.* New York: W. W. Norton, 1979. The historical origins of psychology, from René Descartes to B. F. Skinner.

*The references at the end of each chapter are listed in the order of recommendation, not alphabetically.

2
The Nervous System

The human brain is profoundly mysterious. How could this soggy mess of tissue create the pyramids and the Mona Lisa, the Roman Empire and the Russian Revolution, nuclear weapons and the Big Mac? How does this tangled network of cells regulate our heartbeat, our breathing, and the temperature of our bodies? And, as it oversees the thankless task of keeping us alive, where does the brain find time to marvel at the beauty of a sunset or wonder at the mystery of itself?

As psychologists have tried to develop a science of behavior and experience, they have often found themselves asking basic biological questions about how the nervous system works. In later chapters, when we discuss the nature of memory or sensation or motivation or abnormal behavior, we too shall often return to a discussion of the brain. Thus, it seems sensible to begin the study of psychology here, by showing how the biological paradigm tries to understand human thought and action on the physiological level.

Most of the time, people fumble along through life without paying much attention to their biological natures. But if a friend is paralyzed after his spinal cord is damaged in an auto accident or a relative has difficulty speaking after a stroke, we are all too grimly reminded of how truly fragile and intricate are the relationships between brain, behavior, and experience.

One way that scientists learn how the brain relates to behavior is by studying cases in which something goes wrong. For example, a **stroke** (technically known as a cerebrovascular accident) occurs when a blood vessel in the brain is blocked or broken. When brain tissue is deprived of the oxygen and nutrients carried in the blood, it dies. Depending on the location and the amount of dead tissue, the effects of a stroke can range from a mild passing dizziness or disorientation to death. Students of brain function are most interested in those intermediate cases in which permanent damage to the brain produces behavioral changes.

The term **aphasia** refers to a disturbance in the ability to speak or understand language caused by damage to the brain. There are many different types of aphasia, and a casual visitor to an aphasia clinic would probably be bewildered by the many different ways in which language can go wrong. For example, when a stroke victim with one type of aphasia was asked what he did on a typical day in the hospital, he replied: "Me go, er, uh, P.T. nine o'cot, speech . . . two times . . . read . . . wr . . . ripe, er, rike, er, write . . . practice . . . get-ting better" (Gardner, 1974, p. 61). In contrast to this slow and labored speech, some aphasia patients speak fluently but do not make any sense. When one such patient was asked why he was in the hospital, he replied: "Boy I'm sweating, I'm awful nervous, you know, once in a while I get caught up, I can't mention the tarripoi, a month ago, quite a little I've done a lot well, I'm pose a lot, while, on the other hand, you know what I mean" (Gardner, 1974, p. 68).

To a person who knows nothing about the structure and organization of the brain, the contrast between these patients is baffling. Why did the strokes affect their language abilities in such dramatically different ways?

Before the nineteenth century, scientists knew very little about strokes and aphasia. The French physician Paul Broca opened the door to a solution with an

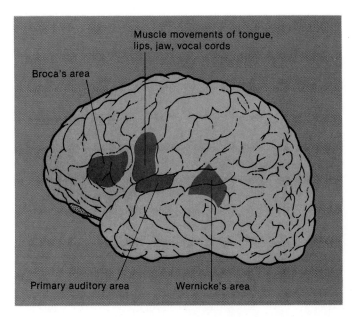

Muscle movements of tongue, lips, jaw, vocal cords

Broca's area

Primary auditory area

Wernicke's area

Figure 2.1

For most people, the left side of the brain controls language. Damage to specific areas produces different types of aphasia. Broca's area is adjacent to the motor strip that controls movement of muscles involved in speaking; damage here produces Broca's aphasia, which involves difficulty coordinating these muscles in speech. Wernicke's area is adjacent to the area in which information from the ear is first analyzed by the cortex; damage here produces Wernicke's aphasia, characterized by difficulties in understanding speech.

insight that now seems simple: He studied the brains of aphasia victims after they died. Beginning in 1861, Broca published a series of papers that described the results of his autopsies on the brains of aphasia patients. In every case, Broca found that damage was located near the front of the brain on the left side. This part of the brain is now called Broca's area (Figure 2.1) and is located next to brain areas that control the movements of muscles involved in speaking, such as the lips, jaw, tongue, and vocal cords. Broca's area seems to be responsible for coordinating these muscles during speech. When brain tissue in this area is damaged, the result is likely to be **expressive aphasia** (also known as Broca's aphasia), in which a person understands what others say but has difficulty speaking himself. Obviously, this was the problem of the gentleman described above who had so much trouble explaining that he went to P.T. (physical therapy) every day.

In 1874, a few years after Broca's discovery, Carl Wernicke published a paper describing how autopsies of another group of patients revealed that damage to a different area on the left side of the brain led to a different type of linguistic problem. Wernicke's area, as this part of the brain became known, is closer to the back of the brain and is located near areas involved with hearing. Damage here produces **receptive aphasia** (or Wernicke's aphasia), a syndrome involving difficulties in understanding speech. A patient with receptive aphasia can speak fluently but has problems using the right words and phrases. In extreme cases, speech becomes totally nonsensical, as it did for the second gentleman described above.

Today, more than a century after the pioneering efforts of Broca and Wernicke, advances in medical technology have substantially improved diagnosis. One hundred years ago, the site of brain damage could be precisely determined only after a

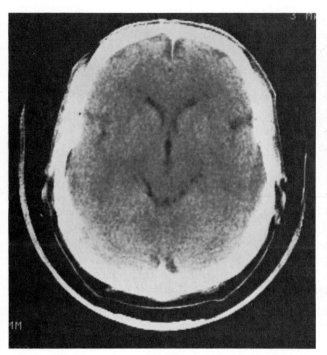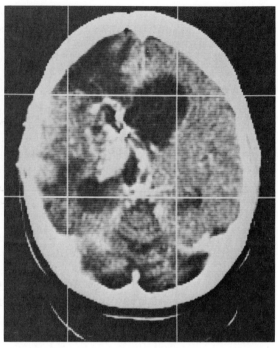

Figure 2.2
The CAT scan on the left shows a normal brain; the one on the right, a brain with a tumor. These images were generated by a computer that analyzed numerous X-rays taken from many different angles.

patient had died and the brain could be dissected in a laboratory. Aside from its macabre overtones, this procedure implied that diagnosis in living patients was based largely on guesswork.

Now, in the 1980s, there are a number of techniques to pinpoint damage in the living brain. For example, many hospitals are now equipped with elaborate devices to perform CAT scans (short for *computed axial tomography*).

For many years, neurologists have studied brain damage by taking X-rays of the head (typically, dyes are injected into the circulatory system of the brain to make blood vessels more visible). However, since a person's head is about 6 inches wide from ear to ear and at least as long from front to back, the flat, two-dimensional picture yielded by a traditional X-ray can be extremely confusing. In **CAT scans,** X-rays are taken from many different angles, and a computer analyzes these X-rays to generate a three-dimensional picture of the brain. The researcher or clinician can then ask the computer for a picture of any slice of tissue within the brain (see Figure 2.2). CAT scans now routinely help neurologists diagnose such problems as brain tumors, cerebral blood clots, and multiple sclerosis.

Technological advances have helped scientists learn a great deal more about the structure and function of both damaged and undamaged brains. For example, later researchers have verified Broca's observation that when brain damage produces permanent language disabilities, the problem is almost always on the left side of the brain. But in a few cases (roughly about 3%), damage to the right side of the brain produces similar problems, particularly among people who are left-handed. This observation has led brain scientists to study differences between righties and lefties, as described near the end of this chapter.

But despite the many advances in technique and knowledge, much remains to be learned. Brain scientists know little about how nerve cells in Broca's and Wernicke's areas perform their functions or even precisely what these functions are. On a more practical level, there is no known cure for aphasia. Some patients may improve dramatically as a result of speech therapy, but others respond less well to this treatment. This disparity between the progress that has been made in the last century and the mysteries that remain is a theme that recurs throughout this chapter and, indeed, throughout this book.

In any case, the study of aphasia leaves no doubt that if we want fully to understand human behavior and experience, we must learn about its biological basis. In this chapter, we focus on the structure of the nervous system and its many functions. In the following chapter we provide some examples of how complex and intricate are the relationships between biology and behavior by considering such topics as behavioral genetics, biological rhythms, stress, and drugs.

How Scientists Study the Brain

The clinical studies of aphasia patients described here provide a good introduction to the brain because the effects of damage are vivid and undeniable. But, from a scientific point of view, such clinical cases are limited in a number of ways. For example, a stroke may affect several brain structures at once, making it hard to determine which brain areas are responsible for specific behaviors. Further, there are a number of reasons why it is dangerous to generalize from a case study of a single individual. (See "How Do They Know?" on page 42.) Thus, it seems reasonable to begin our introduction to the nervous system with an overview of other techniques now available to study the brain, what they can tell us, and how they have evolved over the centuries.

NEUROANATOMICAL STUDIES

Neuroanatomical studies focus on the structure of the nervous system. The earliest brain scientists began on this level, by describing what the brain looked like and how it was put together. Removed from the skull, the brain looks a little like a 3-pound walnut composed of very soft cream-colored clay. It is covered with wrinkles and, like a walnut, can be neatly split down the middle into two symmetrical halves, called *cerebral hemispheres*.

When anatomists began to cut into the brain, they soon realized that it is not a uniform structure but is composed of a number of separate parts. Names we use today for these structures are often derived from the Latin or Greek terms that

The Case Study: Phineas Gage, a Man Who Nearly Lost His Head

A **case study** is an intensive study of a single individual. A biographer might focus on the most dramatic events in a person's life; a researcher doing a case study is engaged in a more systematic search for the patterns and causes of behavior.

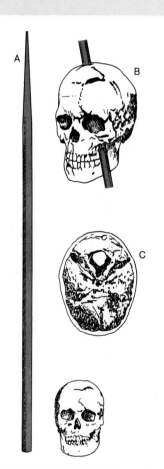

In a scientific sense, the study of a single individual cannot be taken as proof of any general psychological law. But a case study can provide valuable insights that can be tested on large groups. And it may provide valuable information on questions that would otherwise be impossible to study, such as how damage to the human brain affects behavior.

One of the most famous victims of accidental brain injury was a 25-year-old laborer named Phineas Gage. On September 13, 1848, Gage was blasting rock on a railroad construction project in Cavendish, Vermont. Gage's job was to pack down the explosive charge with an iron bar. In the middle of this delicate process, he was distracted and turned suddenly. The iron bar struck rock, a spark ignited the gunpowder, and the bar—roughly $3\frac{1}{2}$ feet long, 1 inch in diameter, and weighing 13 pounds—rocketed upward. It passed through Gage's left cheek, went right through the top of his head, and flew high into the air.

According to eyewitnesses, Gage was thrown to the ground and had a few minor convulsions but was up and talking within a few minutes. His men carried him to an ox cart, and the laborer sat erect for the $\frac{3}{4}$ mile ride into the village. He got out of the cart and walked up a long flight of stairs into his hotel room

One of the physicians who treated Phineas Gage drew these sketches to show the extent of skull damage and the relative size of the iron bar that had passed through his head.

with a little assistance. When a physician arrived a few minutes later, Gage greeted him cheerily and proceeded to describe how he had been injured. At first, the doctor refused to believe that an iron bar could pass completely through a man's skull and leave him alive to tell the tale. But "An Irishman standing nearby said, 'Sure it was so, sir, for the bar is lying in the road below, all blood and brains'" (Bigelow, 1850, p. 16). Other eyewitnesses later provided less graphic verifications.

Although Gage bled profusely and was quite sick for a few weeks, he remained rational throughout his illness and recovered quickly (Harlow, 1848). About a year later, Gage visited Boston and was examined at the Harvard Medical School. Doctors there verified the nature of the wound. (Admittedly, a few surgeons in other cities remained skeptical and referred to the case as a "Yankee invention." Harlow, 1868, p. 19)

The physicians who studied this case seemed more interested in the fact that a man could have survived such a massive injury than in relatively subtle effects on behavior. But they did notice a change. Phineas Gage was described as efficient, capable, and likable before the injury. Afterward, he became restless, irreverent, and profane. He devised one wild scheme after another. Sometimes he had trouble making up his mind; at other times he became extremely stubborn and paid little attention to the advice of others. In the words of his physician:

> A child in his intellectual capacity and manifestations, he has the animal passions of a strong man. Previous to his injury, though untrained in the schools, he possessed a well-balanced mind, and was looked upon by those who knew him as a shrewd, smart business man, very energetic and persistent in executing all his plans of operation. In this regard his mind was radically changed, so decidedly that his friends and acquaintances said he was "no longer Gage" (Harlow, 1869, p. 14).

Gage traveled throughout New England, carrying his iron bar wherever he went. He apparently even spent a short time in a freak show (at Barnum's in New York). Four years after the injury, Gage traveled to South America to start a coach line in Chile. He became ill and returned to San Francisco in 1860. He died soon after, $12\frac{1}{2}$ years after the accident. Gage's family donated his skull and the iron bar to science, and both ended up in the Harvard Medical School museum.

The story of Phineas Gage illustrates some of the strengths and weaknesses of the case-study approach. A person's life story provides a rich source of data that may suggest many more ideas than a limited scientific study that focuses on one aspect of behavior. But it is hard to know how Gage's behavior was affected by unique aspects of his personality, his experience, and the precise nature of his brain injury. This makes it very difficult to draw general conclusions about the function of the frontal lobes. It is also disconcerting that we must depend so heavily on the observational powers of Gage's physician. Perhaps if he had spoken to more of Gage's friends, for example, a different picture of the preaccident personality would have emerged.

Ultimately, it is this lack of objectivity that leads most psychologists to be cautious about case studies. Case studies can be informative, but they may also be misleading. Whenever possible, they must be supplemented by other types of research.

described their appearance. One structure deep inside the brain was called the *amygdala* because it looked like an almond; another is known as the *hippocampus* because its shape reminded some ancient anatomist of a seahorse. These and other basic structures of the human brain have been known since the time of Galen, a famous physician who lived about one-and-a-half centuries after Christ.

The next major advances in understanding the anatomy of the brain came after the invention of the microscope made it possible to magnify tissue many hundreds of times. Under the microscope, a plain, untreated slice of tissue taken from the brain reveals little; everything is packed so tightly together that one hardly sees more than a smear. But in 1875, Camillo Golgi discovered that when nerve tissue is treated with silver nitrate, a very small proportion of the cells become clearly visible under the microscope. Golgi thus discovered that **neurons**—or nerve cells—are the fundamental building blocks of the nervous system. The Golgi stain revealed that many neurons had a rather oddly shaped cell body with a number of long branches.

Although no one has discovered how or why the Golgi stain works, this technical advance enabled the Spanish anatomist Santiago Ramón y Cajal to chart the connections between cells in every part of the nervous system. (Golgi and Cajal shared a Nobel Prize for this work in 1906.) In the late 1800s, biologists had believed that the nervous system was composed of tubes through which electricity flowed, just as blood flowed through the arteries and veins. But Cajal believed that the nervous system was discontinuous, that there were very small gaps between neighboring cells. It was not until the early 1950s that Cajal was finally proved correct. The gap between neurons is only about 100 angstroms wide (an angstrom is 1 ten-billionth of a meter) and could be seen only by means of the incredible magnification of the electron microscope.

These are exciting times for neuroanatomists, as advances in technology such as the CAT scan allow them to probe ever more deeply into the structure of the brain. This knowledge provides the foundation on which psychologists build when they study the function of various brain structures.

ABLATION STUDIES

One way to try to understand how the brain actually works is to observe the effects of damage to certain structures. We have already seen how this applies to aphasia patients: Specific linguistic problems have been linked to different types of brain damage, suggesting that these structures play an important role in normal language use.

A similar rationale applies in **ablation studies,** which involve surgically removing or destroying brain tissue and observing the effects on behavior. For obvious reasons, this type of research should never be practiced on humans. But scientists have learned a great deal about the nervous system by performing ablation studies on animals. The resulting knowledge has contributed to human welfare and the saving of human lives.

Pierre Flourens pioneered this technique in the 1820s, when he removed thin slices of tissue from the cerebellum (located near the back of the brain) of birds, rabbits, and dogs. After he nursed the animals back to health, Flourens found that most lacked muscular coordination and had a poor sense of balance. Since this appeared to be the only effect of the operation, Flourens concluded that under normal conditions the cerebellum played an important role in muscular coordination and balance. Later studies using a variety of other techniques verified this.

The basic logic of ablation studies is still the same today, but surgical techniques have advanced considerably. Very small and precisely localized areas of the brain can be removed with miniaturized vacuum pumps, cauterized with heated probes, destroyed by electrical stimulation, or damaged by drugs that affect only one type of neuron. Regardless of the technique used, ablation studies allow researchers to study specific brain *lesions* (wounds or injuries) in a way that would not be possible if they were able to study only diseased or accidentally damaged brains.

Of course, human brain surgery is sometimes performed to treat medical problems such as brain tumors and certain types of epilepsy. Brain surgery patients are often followed carefully by research teams who are interested in side effects on behavior. For example, later in this chapter we discuss a group of epileptics who volunteered for an experimental operation in which the two sides of the brain were surgically separated so that, in a way, they had two minds in a single skull. We also examine the use of frontal lobotomy (in which portions of the frontal cortex are destroyed) to treat mental illness. Although such operations were motivated by a desire to help particular patients, research on the behavioral results can be seen as a kind of ablation study of the human brain.

ELECTRICAL STIMULATION

Another way to study brain function is to activate specific structures in the brain. In **electrical stimulation studies,** brain tissue is stimulated by an electric current while the effects on behavior are observed. The rationale for such studies can be traced to 1786, when Luigi Galvani discovered that a mild electric shock could contract the muscle in a dead frog's leg and cause the leg to twitch. Galvani believed that he had discovered the vital life force, and some observers predicted that scientists would soon be able to bring the dead back to life. They were wrong.

But in 1870, two German physiologists, Gustav Fritsch and Eduard Hitzig, were able to produce specific movements in living animals by applying a weak electric current to electrodes inserted in specific sites in the brain. (An **electrode** is simply a conductor of electrical activity that is placed in contact with biological tissue.) Although the electrical stimulation they used was not identical to the normal electrical and chemical signals of the brain, it was close enough to elicit specific muscular responses. For example, they found that stimulation of one spot on a dog's brain led to a leg twitch, another spot to a facial movement, a third spot to the contraction of a muscle in the neck, and so on. In this way, they were able to draw an early map of brain functions, relating specific anatomic areas to particular muscle movements.

As electrical stimulation techniques have become more sophisticated in the century since these observations, they have provided a great deal of information about the workings of the brain. In a few cases, electrical stimulation devices have been experimentally implanted in human patients to treat otherwise incurable conditions. For example, Gol (1967) reported the case of a man who was dying from cancer and suffered from such acute pain that he groaned continuously. After all other treatments failed, electrical stimulation of the brain relieved this man's continual pain. The value of this extreme and unorthodox treatment is still being tested in further research.

ELECTRICAL RECORDING

Electrical recording studies involve measuring the normal electrical activity of the brain. Both ablation and electrical stimulation are invasive techniques: they interfere with brain processes in the hope of understanding normal function. In contrast, electrical recording studies try to monitor the ordinary electrical activity of the brain with as little interference as possible.

An **electroencephalogram,** or **EEG,** is a recording of the electrical activity at the surface of the brain or on the skull. In 1929, an Austrian psychiatrist named Hans Berger announced that he had recorded the electrical activity of the human brain through electrodes attached to the skull. At first, many believed it would be possible to study the physical correlates of human thought. This led to tremendous excitement: scientists hurried to build EEG machines of their own, and science-fiction writers plotted about learning to read people's minds by studying their brain waves.

EEG recordings proved to be very useful in the diagnosis of certain medical conditions, particularly epilepsy. Epileptic seizures involve disordered bursts of electrical activity throughout the brain, and the electrical signs of even very minor seizures were quite dramatic (see Figure 2.3). As we shall see in Chapter 3, EEG recordings also help to identify several stages of sleep and provide insights into the hidden world of dreams.

But early EEG researchers soon discovered they would not be reading minds for quite some time. Recordings from the surface of the skull reflected the simultaneous activity of millions of neurons and were quite difficult to interpret. Some researchers therefore looked for more sophisticated recording techniques. One involved **micro-**

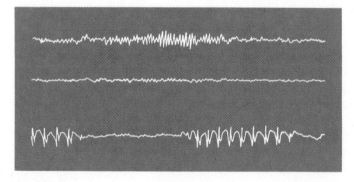

Figure 2.3
Typical EEG recordings. The first two were recorded at the same time from two different spots on the skull of a relaxed adult. The third was recorded during a petit mal epileptic seizure and shows dramatic spiking.

electrodes, wires small enough to record the electrical activity of a single nerve cell at a time. The diameter of the tip of a microelectrode is measured in microns (millionths of a meter), and it can detect an electrical charge of one-millionth of a volt. Single-cell recordings of this sort have provided many insights, particularly into the workings of the visual system. But since microelectrodes must be inserted into the brain and can destroy brain tissue, these studies have ordinarily been limited to animals.

CHEMICAL STUDIES

In this context, **chemical studies** involve introducing a chemical into the brain to determine its behavioral and physiological effects. Some of the most exciting work now being done depends on new chemical techniques for studying the structure and function of the brain.

For example, Louis Sokoloff and his colleagues at the National Institute of Mental Health recently developed a new way of tracing anatomic pathways in the brain. Active neurons consume glucose (a form of sugar) more rapidly than inactive neurons. In Sokoloff's procedure, 2-deoxyglucose, a type of sugar, is produced in a radioactive form. An animal is required to perform a certain task, such as visually distinguishing between a circle and a square, soon after an injection of radioactive 2-deoxyglucose. Brain cells involved in making this visual distinction consume more sugar, and radioactivity builds up in them. The animal is then sacrificed, the brain is frozen, and very thin slices of brain tissue are pressed against a piece of photographic film (which is sensitive to radioactivity). The developed photograph thus provides a picture of the brain cells that are especially active during performance of the task.

Another new technique will help researchers pinpoint the areas of the brain involved in normal human activities. A person inhales a slightly radioactive gas; radioactivity is passed from the lungs into the blood; and for the next 15 minutes or so this radioactive blood flows through the circulatory system. The circulation of blood to different brain areas provides a general index of the activation of neurons, and sophisticated devices to measure radioactivity have made it possible literally to watch blood flow to the front of a person's brain while she considers an abstract problem and then flow to speech centers in the left hemisphere as she begins to talk about it (Ingvar & Lassen, 1975).

For our purposes, the details of these procedures are less important than the fact that new techniques are constantly being developed to examine the brain in new ways.

CONVERGING LINES OF EVIDENCE AND CEREBRAL LOCALIZATION

Each method described in this section looks at the brain from a slightly different perspective. Scientists look for several lines of evidence that all lead to, or converge on, a single conclusion.

A good example of the way different scientific methods gradually lead to the same conclusion can be seen in the historical controversy over cerebral localization. According to the theory of **cerebral localization,** different areas of the brain are responsible for different psychological functions. The alternative theory, **holism,**

Franz Joseph Gall (1758–1828) was a brilliant anatomist; he was the first to trace fibers through the central nervous system to show how information crossed from one side of the body to the opposite side of the brain. But Gall is best remembered for **phrenology**—his attempts to relate character to the shape of the skull. In his autobiography, Gall traced this curious idea to an observation he had made as a schoolboy. Students who got better grades than he often did not seem brighter, but they did have protruding eyes, which he later attributed to overdeveloped verbal memories in the front of the skull. Unfortunately, the evidence behind phrenology rarely rose above this level. According to one nineteenth-century scientist's joke, after Gall's death, measurements of his own skull revealed that it was twice as thick as average.

claims that each psychological function is controlled by a wide variety of cells throughout the entire brain rather than being concentrated in a few discrete areas.

Medical historians usually trace the idea of cerebral localization to a controversial German physician named Franz Joseph Gall. Around 1800, Gall proposed the theory of **phrenology,** which held that the brain consists of a number of separate organs, each responsible for a specific human trait. Unusual growth of any of these organs creates a bump on the skull; the pattern of bumps reveals a person's character. According to one phrenological chart (see Figure 2.4), a woman with a bump on one spot near the top of her head would have an overdeveloped organ of imitation; she could therefore be expected to study religiously the latest fashions in *Vogue* magazine so that she would always know what clothes she was supposed to wear. If the bump were a little farther back, it would indicate an overactive organ of hope, and she might be a Chicago Cubs fan, believing every spring that this was the year that unfortunate team would finally win the pennant.

We now know that this theory is quite wrong. Skull shape does not conform to brain shape, and Gall's entire classification scheme has been discredited. But, as Edmund G. Boring (1950, p. 57) stated in *A History of Experimental Psychology,* phrenology was "an instance of a theory which, while essentially wrong, was just enough right to further scientific thought." Many of the landmark discoveries that we described earlier in this section can be traced back to Gall.

When Pierre Flourens refined the technique of ablation in the 1820s, he was trying to refute Gall's claim that the cerebellum was the "organ of amativeness."

Since removal of this area of the brain affected animals' coordination and balance rather than their sexual activities, Flourens felt that he had disproved at least this one claim of phrenology.

When Flourens went on to remove larger portions of the brain, he found little evidence of specific deficits. Thus he came to favor the view now known as holism. But later researchers, using other methods, disagreed. Broca's findings of specific deficits in the brains of aphasia patients supported the theory of cerebral localization. So did Fritsch and Hitzig's report that electrical stimulation of specific brain areas caused a dog to move particular muscles. The controversy over which theory was correct—cerebral localization or holism—went on for more than a century.

Gradually, however, various lines of evidence converged on the same conclusion. Basic sensory and motor functions are localized in the brain. But a rule of thumb might be that the more complex the psychological function, the less likely it is to be located in only one area of the brain. Thus, a sensory impression of a spot of light is highly localized in one area of the brain; the larger perception of a pattern of light and dark areas that leads you to recognize a photograph of the Osmond brothers is less clearly localized; and a reaction of sexual excitement to this picture involves still more complex interactions between different brain areas.

In the case of vision, simple sensations are localized in an area near the back of the brain called the occipital cortex (described later.) This conclusion is based on

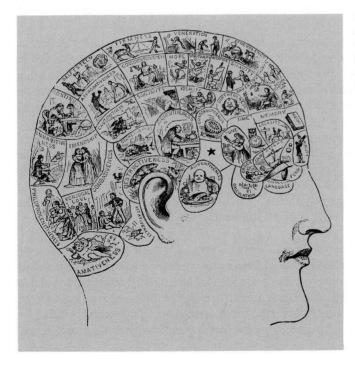

Figure 2.4
A phrenologist's chart illustrating one nineteenth-century theory about localization of personality traits in the brain. Although phrenology helped set the stage for early brain research, it was quite wrong.

several converging lines of evidence. When a particular area of the occipital cortex is destroyed, through surgery or accident, a person or animal becomes partially blind. EEGs and other electrical recordings from the occipital area change systematically when a person looks at a stimulus. Simple electrical stimulation of the occipital cortex produces a sensation of a light flashing in a particular spot. Since these and other studies all led to the same conclusion, scientists accepted the idea that simple visual sensations were located in a particular area of the brain.

But scientific agreement has come more slowly on whether complex psychological functions—such as hunger, aggression, and sexuality—are localized. In part, that is because various lines of evidence have not yet converged on a single conclusion; there is still a great deal of controversy over studies of these more complicated behavior patterns.

For example, in one of the most famous experiments on electrical stimulation of the brain, Dr. José Delgado implanted electrodes deep in the brain of a bull that had been bred for bullfighting and charging human beings. A special radio receiver attached to the bull's horns provided electrical stimulation through the electrodes to the bull's brain whenever Delgado pressed a button on a small transmitter. Dr. Delgado went into the bullring armed only with a cape and his transmitter. As the bull charged, Dr. Delgado pressed his button. Happily, the electrical stimulation caused the animal to stop his charge and turn aside. This demonstration was cited widely as proof that Dr. Delgado had located an aggressive center in the bull's brain (for an example, see "Becoming a Critical Consumer"). Electrical stimulation was believed to inhibit the activity of this brain center and thus curb aggressive responses.

But other brain scientists disagreed. Eliot Valenstein (1973) examined a film of this demonstration and noted that whenever the bull stopped its charge, it turned in one direction. He concluded that the electrical stimulation actually activated a brain area that controlled muscular movement. The bull turned aside not because its aggressiveness was curbed but because the electrical stimulation produced a turning movement.

Given the ambiguity of most complex behavior patterns and the fact that they can be influenced by such a wide variety of external stimuli, controversies over the localization of complex psychological functions are likely to continue. But, over time, scientific consensus should result as evidence from many sources and types of studies gradually converges on a single conclusion. In the meantime, it is important to remember that there is still considerable controversy over the localization of complex functions.

As we review brain structures in the next section, it may be hard to resist the temptation to ask which psychological function is regulated by the hippocampus, or the cerebellum, or the frontal cortex. Because introductory textbooks are required to simplify complex material, they sometimes may make the brain seem more localized and simple than it really is. As you read the next section, try to remember that the brain is an extremely sophisticated system that we are just beginning to comprehend.

Of Electrical Brain Stimulation and Bull

Compare this description of advances in brain research from an article in the *New York Times* (Rensberger, 1971), to the textbook account of the same research on page 50. How is this selection inaccurate or misleading? (A short discussion appears after the "Summary" at the end of this chapter.)

> Over the last few years, [scientists] have been learning to tinker with the brains of animals and men and to manipulate their thoughts and behavior.
>
> Though their methods are still crude and not always predictable, there can remain little doubt that the next few years will bring a frightening array of refined techniques for making human beings act according to the will of the psychotechnologist. . . .

Perhaps the most famous demonstration of the potential of psychotechnology was an experiment carried out several years ago by Yale University's José M. R. Delgado.

Dr. Delgado implanted a radio-controlled electrode deep within the brain of a "brave bull," a variety bred to respond with a raging charge when it sees any human being. But when Dr. Delgado pressed a button on a transmitter, sending a signal to a battery-powered receiver attached to the bull's horns, an impulse went into the bull's brain and the animal would cease his charge.

After several stimulations, the bull's naturally aggressive behavior disappeared. It was as placid as Ferdinand.

The Structure and Function of the Nervous System

THE NEURON AND THE SYNAPSE

As mentioned earlier, a *neuron* is an individual nerve cell. Although no two neurons look exactly alike, they do tend to come in a few basic shapes and sizes.

A neuron consists of three major parts. **Dendrites** are the parts of a neuron that usually receive electrical and chemical messages from other neurons. As you can see in Figure 2.5, dendrites look like a series of bushy trees clustered around the cell body. The **cell body** is usually shaped roughly like a pyramid or a sphere. Finally, a single **axon** usually transmits electrical impulses away from the cell body to other neurons. As Figure 2.5 suggests, the axon tends to be much longer and thinner than the dendrites. Electrical messages ordinarily travel in only one direction: Information comes into the cell via a dendrite, continues through the cell body, and passes along the axon until it reaches a synapse with the next cell. In some cases, axons transmit information directly to a cell body rather than through a dendrite. Thus, a **synapse** may be defined as the point where the axon of one neuron is connected to the dendrite or cell body of another neuron. The synapse includes a presynaptic

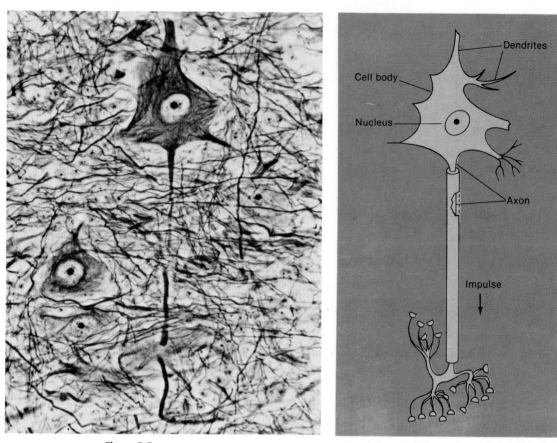

Figure 2.5
This typical neuron has been stained to increase visibility and enlarged through a microscope.
The schematic drawing shows major structures.

terminal on the axon, a small gap or space between the two neurons, and a postsynaptic membrane on the dendrite.

Neurons communicate with one another in an electrical and chemical code. When a neuron transmits an impulse, or fires, a small electrical charge passes along its length.

Neurons are said to operate by the *all-or-none principle* because at any given moment, a neuron transmits either its maximum electrical charge or nothing at all. Some have compared the firing of a neuron to the firing of a rifle. If you pull the trigger, the rifle either fires or it does not. There is no middle ground.

Neurons send their messages by changing the patterns and rate of this firing. In one study of the visual system of the frog (Muntz, 1964), for example, a particular color-sensitive neuron fired about 20 times per second when the frog looked at a blue stimulus, 7 times per second for a blue-green stimulus, and 3 times per second for a green stimulus.

Each time the neuron fires, a small electrical impulse passes down the length of its axon. When this impulse reaches the presynaptic terminals at the tip of the axon, it causes the release of thousands of molecules of a chemical called the neurotransmitter into the gap between the two cells. This produces a change in the postsynaptic membrane of the second neuron.

Thus a **neurotransmitter** is a chemical released at the synapse by the electrical action of one neuron that influences the electrical activity of another neuron. Until the 1960s, only three different chemicals were widely recognized as neurotransmitters (acetylcholine, norepinephrine, and serotonin). But an explosion of research in neurotransmitter chemistry has led to many new discoveries. In 1980, one expert put the number of neurotransmitters already discovered at "about two dozen" and predicted that the final total "may exceed 200" (Snyder, 1980, p. 979). In Chapter 3, we discuss how such drugs as amphetamines and heroin seem to work by changing the neurotransmitter chemistry of the brain.

In summary, while the signals that travel down axons are primarily electrical, the communication between cells is a chemical process. Synapses connect the axon of one neuron with the dendrite or cell body of another, and it is here that information is transferred.

A typical neuron may receive information from about 1,000 other cells; some motor neurons are connected by synapses with as many as 10,000 other cells. Stimulation at some synapses increases the likelihood that the next neuron in line will transmit an electrical charge of its own; stimulation at other synapses decreases the likelihood. At any given moment, the electrical state of a neuron is determined by the activity at all of its many synapses.

When you consider the fact that there are billions of neurons in the brain, and trillions of interconnections, you can begin to understand the complexity of trying to trace neural pathways through the nervous system.

THE ORGANIZATION OF THE NERVOUS SYSTEM

Usually, when we think of the nervous system we think of the brain. The brain is indeed the control center of our highest ideals and our basest passions. But a brain without eyes cannot see, and a brain without lips cannot speak. Other parts of the nervous system connect the brain with sensory receptors, muscles, and internal organs.

One of the simplest schemes for summarizing the organization of the nervous system is diagramed in Figure 2.6. As you can see, the term **central nervous system** refers to the spinal cord and the brain.

The Spinal Cord. The **spinal cord** is a long, thin column of neurons that emerges from the bottom of the brain and runs down the back next to the *spinal vertebrae,* the bony structures that protect the spinal cord from injury. There is no precise point at which the spinal cord ends and the brain begins. As we shall see in the next section, the spinal cord widens as it enters the skull and becomes the brain stem.

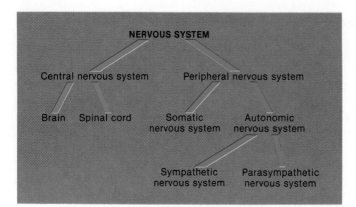

Figure 2.6
The organization of the nervous system is shown in this schematic diagram.

People whose spinal cords are damaged in an accident learn all too clearly how essential this structure is for normal body function. Since the spinal cord transmits sensory information to the brain and motor commands from the brain, a person whose spinal cord is damaged near the top can be completely paralyzed and have no sensation whatever from the neck down. Oddly, however, this person will retain reflexes that do not require the brain. When the tendon of the knee is lightly tapped, a message is transmitted from sensory to motor neurons directly through the spinal cord, and the knee jerks automatically. Thus, in the normal person, the spinal cord has two major roles: to regulate certain reflex movements and to transmit messages to and from the brain.

All these messages to muscles and organs and from sensory receptors involve the **peripheral nervous system,** which includes all the nerve fibers in the body except for those of the brain and the spinal cord. As Figure 2.6 illustrates, this is further subdivided into the somatic nervous system and the autonomic nervous system.

The Somatic Nervous System. The **somatic nervous system** connects the brain and spinal cord with sensory receptors and voluntary muscles. The neurons are divided again into two major categories according to their function: afferent and efferent. **Afferent neurons** (also known as **sensory neurons**) convey information from sensory receptors to the spinal cord and brain. For example, receptor cells in the skin translate feelings of pressure or cold into the electrochemical code of the nervous system. Afferent neurons then convey these messages to the spinal cord, and from there the information passes to the brain. Some details of how the receptor cells code physical stimuli are presented in Chapter 4 in the discussion of sensation. The **efferent neurons** (also known as **motor neurons**) of the somatic nervous system transmit the commands of the spinal cord and the brain to the muscles. Efferent neurons cause our fists to clench, our eyes to blink, and our fingers to do the walking through the Yellow Pages.

Thus, when your lover touches your hand, afferent neurons transmit the feeling of pressure to the brain, and efferent neurons allow you to move your own hand in reply. In contrast, we are rarely so aware of the activities of the autonomic nervous system.

The Autonomic Nervous System. The **autonomic nervous system** regulates the activity of smooth muscles and controls internal bodily processes (such as heart rate and contraction of the bladder). The primary task of the autonomic nervous system is to regulate the internal organs of the body. Ordinarily, this goes on without our awareness or conscious involvement. We do not have to decide whether to inhibit secretion of the pancreas, constrict the bronchial tubes of the lungs, or discharge stored blood from the spleen. If we had to spend our days consciously controlling all these bodily processes, we would never find time to read *War and Peace*, to watch "The Price Is Right," or to ponder the meaning of existence.

Referring again to Figure 2.6, you can see that the autonomic nervous system consists of two branches, the sympathetic and the parasympathetic. The **sympathetic nervous system** activates the glands and smooth muscles of the body in periods of emotional excitement; its nerve fibers originate in the two middle portions (thoracic and lumbar regions) of the spinal cord. The **parasympathetic nervous system** maintains appropriate internal states in times of relaxation; its nerve fibers originate at either end of the spinal cord (the cranial and sacral regions).

Figure 2.7 illustrates the sympathetic and parasympathetic branches of the autonomic nervous system and some of their effects on the body's major organs. Note that many organs are connected to both these branches. For example, activation of the sympathetic nervous system increases heart rate, while activation of the parasympathetic nervous system lowers it; the sympathetic nervous system dilates the pupil of the eye, and the parasympathetic nervous system constricts it. In short, these two branches work together to regulate the state of the internal organs.

Walter Cannon (1927) argued that the major function of the sympathetic nervous system is to mobilize the body for an emergency, which he called the fight-or-flight reaction. When you suddenly notice a mysterious figure lurking in the shadows as you walk through a deserted neighborhood at 2 a.m., your body secretes adrenaline, your heart beats faster, and blood flows to your muscles and away from your skin, stomach, and intestines. All these physiological changes are designed to prepare you to deal with an emergency. For example, if you are forced to fight or to flee, you will need additional blood flowing to your muscles to supply them with oxygen and nutrients during their exertion.

When you get a little closer to the mysterious figure and identify him as an 83-year-old retired postman with insomnia, you will relax. In this case, your parasympathetic nervous system will become more active and work to restore your bodily processes to normal. The parasympathetic nervous system also dominates when you watch a dull TV program or take a nap.

Because the sympathetic and parasympathetic branches often work together to maintain the equilibrium of the internal organs, they are called antagonistic. However, there are exceptions to this rule. Crying, for example, is controlled strictly by the parasympathetic nervous system, and sweating is controlled by the sym-

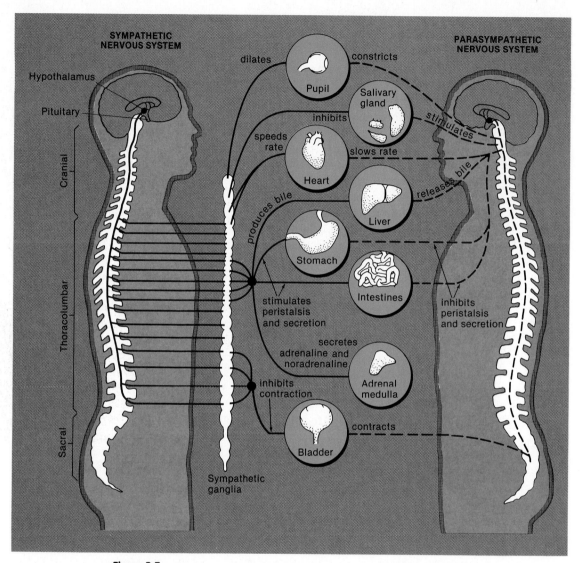

Figure 2.7

The two branches of the autonomic nervous system. The sympathetic nervous system arouses bodily processes, some of which are shown here. The parasympathetic nervous system counteracts many of these processes.

pathetic nervous system. For our purposes, it is sufficient to emphasize that the sympathetic nervous system is involved with the fight-or-flight reaction and the parasympathetic nervous system with more restful activities.

The Endocrine System. Closely related to the autonomic nervous system, although technically not a part of the nervous system at all, are the **endocrine glands,** which secrete special chemical messengers (called *hormones*) directly into the bloodstream.

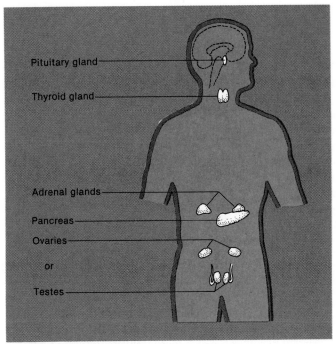

Pituitary gland

Thyroid gland

Adrenal glands

Pancreas

Ovaries

or

Testes

Figure 2.8
Major glands of the endocrine system secrete hormones that help regulate growth and behavior.

Figure 2.9
Robert Wadlow was a victim of giantism, caused by oversecretion of the growth hormone of the pituitary gland. At the time of his death in 1940 at the age of 22, he was 8 feet 11 inches tall, weighed 439 pounds, and wore a size 37AA shoe (18½ inches long).

The most important glands of the endocrine system are the pituitary, the adrenal glands, and the gonads.

The **pituitary gland** is located deep inside the brain, just below the hypothalamus (see Figure 2.8). It is sometimes called the master gland because it controls the secretion of other endocrine glands. But it is not an independent master; it comes under the control of the hypothalamus. Among the many chemicals secreted by the pituitary are hormones that regulate such internal functions as the reabsorption of water by the kidneys, the constriction of the arteries, and the stimulation of the thyroid, the adrenal glands, and the gonads. Still another pituitary hormone controls the growth process. If too much of this growth hormone is secreted during development, it produces a condition called giantism (see Figure 2.9); too little can produce a dwarf.

The **adrenal glands** are two small endocrine glands that lie just above the kidneys. The two most important adrenal hormones, at least to psychologists, are adrenaline (also known as epinephrine) and noradrenaline (also known as norepinephrine). Both hormones are involved in the mobilization of the body's resources for fight or flight. Adrenaline is particularly involved in the action of the sympathetic nervous system; its effects include increased heartbeat and sweating.

Finally, the **gonads** are the sexual glands: *testes* in men and *ovaries* in women. The secretion of these glands controls the development of the reproductive organs, secondary sexual characteristics such as the distribution of body hair, and some aspects of sexual behavior. In Chapter 9, we discuss the many physical changes triggered at puberty by the secretion of sex hormones.

The endrocrine glands interact with each other and with portions of the nervous system in a series of complex circuits that ultimately regulate much of our development and behavior.

THE BRAIN

The earliest recorded observation of the relationship between the brain and behavior appears in a surgical guide written about 30 centuries before Christ (Breasted, 1930). An Egyptian physician described a patient who fractured his skull and later walked with a shuffle. Thus, nearly 5,000 years ago it was noted that damage to the brain may lead to partial paralysis. But despite the astute observations of some early physicians, little or nothing was known about precisely how the brain was involved in simple motor reactions or complex thoughts about itself.

We have probably learned more about the brain in the last 100 years than in the preceding 49 centuries. We are learning more each day. And new research findings generally make the brain seem more complicated rather than simpler. So, as you read this section, remember that complex behaviors involve many different areas of the brain. The fact that the hypothalamus is involved with eating and the hippocampus with memory does not imply that eating and memory have nothing to do with the rest of the brain or that the hypothalamus and hippocampus are not involved in other complex behaviors as well.

The Brain Stem and the Cerebellum.   The **medulla** is the first brain structure that emerges from the spinal cord as it widens upon entering the skull; it contains all the nerve fibers that connect the spinal cord to the brain. Interestingly, most of these fibers cross over in the medulla so that in general the left side of the brain is connected to the right side of the body, and vice versa. As a result of this contralateral design, a person who has a stroke, say, on the right side of the brain may become paralyzed on the left side of the body. The medulla is also connected to the autonomic nervous system and helps regulate such vital functions as heart rate, breathing, and digestion. Overdoses of opiates and barbiturates can depress the vital actions of the medulla and lead to death.

Next in line is the **pons,** a structure that continues out of the medulla and also contains fibers connecting the brain and spinal cord. (The name presumably came from an early anatomist who was reminded of a bridge—*pons* in Latin—by its humpbacked shape.) Passing through the pons are nerve fibers involved in breathing, muscular coordination, hearing, and facial expression, among many others.

The **reticular formation** is not a separate structure that can easily be isolated; it is a complex network of neurons and fibers that passes through the medulla, pons, and other structures. It is sometimes called the *reticular activating system* because research has shown that the reticular formation is particularly involved in sleep, waking, alertness, and attention. Thus, if an inconsiderate roommate or some charming relative insists on turning the radio up while you are trying to study for a psychology exam, your ability—or inability—to concentrate on the definition of the reticular formation and ignore the "top forty" may depend on physiological processes in the reticular formation. Drugs that increase alertness, such as amphetamines, are believed to stimulate the reticular formation; drugs that decrease alertness, such as barbiturates, are believed to inhibit the reticular formation.

The **midbrain** contains structures that relay information from the eye and ear to higher centers for visual and auditory processing. Fibers from the pons also continue through the midbrain.

Taken together, the medulla, pons, reticular formation, midbrain, and closely related structures are referred to as the **brain stem.** Brain-stem structures are quite primitive in evolutionary terms. While only the highest mammals (including monkeys and humans) have a well-developed *cerebral cortex* (the thick layer of nerve cells covering the brain), even lowly snakes and fish have developed brain stems to control basic life processes such as breathing and digestion. Although a human with extensive brain damage to the cerebral cortex may be surprisingly normal, brain-stem damage often leads to death.

Closely related to the brain stem but anatomically somewhat separate is the

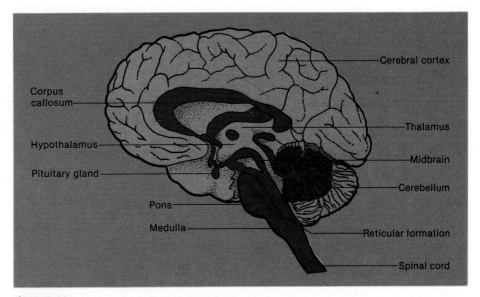

Figure 2.10
Major structures of the brain are shown in this diagram. The limbic system surrounds the area of the hypothalamus but is difficult to depict in a two-dimensional drawing like this.

cerebellum, the structure removed in Flouren's classic studies in the 1820s. In appearance, it is one of the most distinctive structures in the brain. Like two very small fists, the lobes of the **cerebellum** extend out toward the back of the skull from either side of the pons; its primary known role is the coordination of muscle movements. The classic signs of drunkenness—loss of coordination and balance, staggering, and speech problems—seem to be largely due to an alcohol-induced depression of the cerebellum. Although the cerebellum does not initiate movement, its healthy functioning is essential for smooth, coordinated motion. It functions in much the same way to help fish swim, birds fly, and bank executives play golf.

The Thalamus, Hypothalamus, and Limbic System.   The **thalamus** looks a bit like two eggs lying on their sides on top of the brain stem; it is often referred to as a way-station because so many nerve fibers meet there. Information from the eye, the ear, and the skin (pressure, warmth, cold, and pain—see Chapter 4) passes through the thalamus on its way to be analyzed by higher processing centers in the cerebral cortex. Some analysis of sensory information also probably occurs here.

The **hypothalamus** is a much smaller structure that lies between the thalamus and the midbrain. It seems to be involved in a wide variety of complex behaviors, including eating, drinking, temperature regulation, sexual behavior, and aggressive behavior. The hypothalamus also helps to regulate the sympathetic nervous system and the pituitary gland. It is an extremely important structure; we discuss its role in eating in Chapter 10.

Some anatomists consider the hypothalamus to be part of the **limbic system,** a series of structures located near the border between the cerebral hemispheres and the brain stem (the name comes from the Latin word *limbicus,* meaning "bordering"). The limbic system is involved in the regulation of such "animal instincts" as fighting, fleeing, feeding, and reproduction.

The limbic system is sometimes called the *old cortex* because it appeared in evolution before the *new cortex,* or cerebral cortex. Lower animals like fish and reptiles do not have any cortex at all—their brains are limited to the brain stem and related structures. In mammals, the portion of the brain devoted to the cortex increases in more advanced animals. The more developed the cortex of a species, the more complex and flexible is its behavior. Thus, humans have a proportionally larger cortex than monkeys, and monkeys have a larger cortex than rabbits. Conversely, as one ascends the evolutionary scale, the proportion of limbic system (old cortex) declines. Thus, humans have a relatively smaller limbic system than monkeys, and the monkey's limbic system is proportionally smaller than the rabbit's. To some researchers, this suggests an anatomical basis for the fact that humans do not seem to be tied to instinctual drives in the same way that lower animals are—the larger new cortex dominates the primitive drives of the old cortex.

The Cerebral Cortex.   The **cerebral cortex** is the thick layer of nerve cells that covers the brain. In humans, the cerebral cortex contains at least 70% of the neurons in the central nervous system (Nauta & Feirtag, 1979), and it is here that we must search for the physiological basis of human nature.

Earlier, we compared the brain to a 3-pound walnut to emphasize the fact that the **cerebral hemispheres**—the two symmetrical sides of the brain—are mirror images of each other. We will have much to say about the similarities and differences in function of these two hemispheres in the next section of this chapter. In this anatomical overview, let us only note that the **corpus callosum** is a large band of nerve fibers that connects the two hemispheres of the brain.

The surface of each hemisphere of the human brain appears to be very wrinkled because it is covered with fissures, which have been described as the kinds of folds that would appear if you were to press the skin of an orange inward with a ruler (Thompson, 1975). In contrast, lower mammals such as the rat have a smoother and smaller cortex. This further supports the generalization that the more complex and flexible an animal's possible range of behavior, the greater the proportion of brain devoted to cerebral cortex. As the cortex of the brain grows and folds back on itself, fissures appear on the surface.

As you can see in Figure 2.11, two major fissures serve as landmarks that divide the cerebral cortex into four major lobes. The central fissure separates the **frontal lobe,** at the front of the brain, from the **parietal lobe,** at the top rear. Just over the ears, underneath the parietal lobe and separated from it by the lateral fissure, is the **temporal lobe.** Finally, the **occipital lobe** is a relatively small area of the cerebral cortex at the back of the head.

As mentioned earlier, some basic psychological functions seem to be precisely localized in specific areas of the cortex. **Primary projection areas** receive input from the sense organs or control the movement of particular muscle groups. Figure 2.11 lists the known primary projection areas of the cerebral cortex. Lesions in these

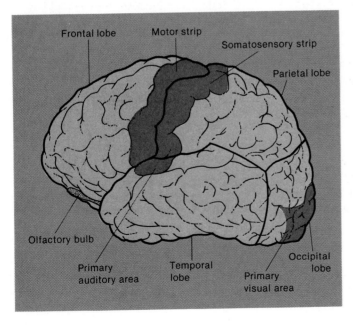

Figure 2.11

The lobes of the cerebral cortex and primary sensory and motor areas. Damage to the primary areas produces specific deficits. For example, damage to a specific portion of the primary visual area leads to blindness in one part of the visual field.

areas produce specific sensory and/or motor deficits. For example, damage to a small area in the occipital cortex would lead to blindness in only one part of the visual field; a comparable lesion in the temporal lobe would lead to a specific type of partial hearing loss.

Another primary projection area, called the **motor strip,** lies inside the frontal lobe, in front of the central fissure. Because electrical stimulation of the motor strip of one cerebral hemisphere produces muscular movements on the opposite side of the body, it is possible to draw a detailed map of how these cortical areas are involved in movement (see Figure 2.12). Stimulation of the top end of the motor strip of the right hemisphere causes you to move your left toe; stimulation a few millimeters down provokes left ankle movement; the next spot controls the left knee; and so on.

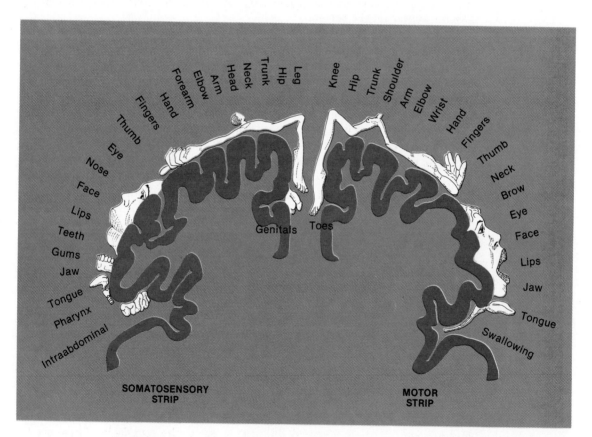

Figure 2.12

This illustration of the somatosensory and motor strips shows body parts drawn in proportion to the brain areas to which they are connected. For example, the lips and tongue are exaggerated on the motor strip because considerable brain tissue regulates the movement of muscles in these areas.

At the front of the parietal lobe and across the central fissure from the motor strip is the **somatosensory strip.** Here, electrical stimulation produces the sensations you would feel if someone touched various parts of the opposite side of your body. Consequently, it has also been possible to map the connections to the somatosensory strip (see Figure 2.12).

Interestingly, the amount of brain tissue devoted to an area of the body is proportional to that area's sensitivity, not to its size. For example, a greater area of the cerebral cortex is connected to the lips than to the shoulders, although most people have shoulders that are larger than their lips. The difference in brain area reflects the fact that the lips are extremely sensitive to touch and the shoulders are not. Similarly, the amount of tissue in the motor strip is related to the degree and delicacy of control we have over the movements of specific muscles. Large areas of the brain are devoted to the fingers, lips, and tongue; relatively small areas govern the shoulders, neck, and trunk.

Perhaps the most striking fact about the primary projection areas is that they account for a relatively small proportion of the human brain. What does the rest of the cerebral cortex do? One hint comes from an analysis of the brains of other species. The proportion of the brain devoted to nonprimary cortex is higher for humans than for any other species.

The term **association areas** refers to all cortical areas that are not specifically involved with simple sensory or motor reactions. This name is based on the belief that these brain areas are involved in higher mental processes, such as forming associations. Some researchers prefer the term *silent cortex*, which makes no assumptions about the overall function of these areas but stresses the fact that electrical stimulation here does not produce obvious motor or sensory responses (the areas are silent).

The areas immediately adjoining primary sensory areas seem generally to be involved with the higher-level analysis of sensory information. For example, a person with brain damage to certain portions of the right occipital lobe sometimes has trouble recognizing faces. This patient is able to see and respond normally to simple visual stimuli but is not able to integrate the information into a complete perception of someone's face. Damage to portions of the temporal lobe adjoining the primary hearing areas produces a comparable auditory deficit—the person may be able to hear normally but fails to recognize the sound of running water or a ringing telephone.

Damage in the frontal lobe immediately next to primary motor areas produces an analogous deficit in the organization of movement. One example is Broca's aphasia, which involves the disorganization of speech (see Figure 2.1).

Another type of association area is involved in the integration of more complex information, often from several different senses at the same time. These are the brain areas that are believed to be involved with our most complex thoughts and actions, from deciding whether to cut class and go to the beach to trying to remember the difference between the German words *Gemeinschaft* and *Gesellschaft*.

Of all the aspects of brain organization that distinguish man from the beasts, the most important is the development of the frontal lobes. It is therefore distressing—though perhaps not surprising—that the frontal lobes have proved to be the most difficult area of the brain to study.

Although much controversy remains, the frontal lobes have been implicated in the planning and organization of actions. Patients with damage to the frontal lobes have special difficulty with abstract problems that require them to remain intellectually flexible, shifting from one solution stategy to another.

Personality changes have also been observed after frontal damage. This was first noted more than a century ago in the classic case of Phineas Gage, a man whose frontal lobes were severely damaged in a construction accident (see "How Do They Know?"). Later observations that frontal-lobe damage seemed to produce a calming effect led for a time to the use of frontal lobotomy (in which connections from the frontal lobes to the rest of the brain were destroyed) in the treatment of mental illness, as described in the next section.

Ultimately, it is in the frontal lobes that many brain researchers expect to find the solutions to some of the mysteries of what makes us human.

How Much Do Scientists Really Know About the Brain?

The more you learn about brain research, the more impressed you will be by how much scientists must learn. To provide a more concrete feeling for our current state of knowledge, this section will concentrate on one area of applied brain research, psychosurgery, and on one topic of more theoretical interest, cerebral asymmetry.

APPLIED PSYCHOLOGY

Psychosurgery

Psychosurgery is brain surgery aimed at changing a person's thought patterns or behavior patterns. Removal of a brain tumor or treatment of some other organic problem may have unintended side effects on a person's behavior, but this is not psychosurgery. Only when a surgeon sets out to alter a patient's psychological function do we use this term.

In 1935, Egas Moniz performed the first human **frontal lobotomy**—cutting the connections between the frontal lobes and other brain structures. The effect was equivalent to physically removing part of the frontal lobe. Animal research had suggested that this operation might calm extreme anxiety; and of the first 20 mental patients Moniz operated on, 7 were considered recovered and another 7 had improved. Other surgeons quickly became interested in the operation and began performing brain surgery to treat mental disorders on a large scale. There are no precise figures available, but the best estimate suggests that by the late 1950s over 25,000 frontal lobotomies had been performed in the United States alone (Valenstein, 1980).

One reason why so many frontal lobotomies were performed during this period is that the operation offered hope where before there had been none. The psychiatry and psychology of the 1930s and 1940s had no effective treatment for the seriously disturbed mental patient; frontal lobotomy seemed to offer a chance at improvement.

Several large-scale studies found that after fronal lobotomies, most patients were less anxious, less depressed, and generally better adjusted. But there were other, more subtle personality and intellectual changes as well. One group of psychosurgeons characterized these changes as follows:

> Patients after lobotomy always show some lack of personality depth. They are cheerful and complacent and are indifferent to the opinions and feelings of others. . . . Their goals are immediate—not remote. They can recall the past as well as ever, but it has diminished interpretive value for them, and they are not more interested in their own past emotional crises than if they had happened to someone else. They seem incapable of feeling guilt now for past misdeeds. (Robinson, Freeman, & Watts, 1951, p. 159).

When Moniz won the Nobel Prize in medicine in 1949, a *New York Times* (October 30, 1949, p. 8E) editorial provided the following glowing picture of frontal lobotomy: "The sensational operation justified itself. Hypochondriacs no longer thought they were going to die, would-be suicides found life acceptable, sufferers from persecution complexes forgot the machinations of imaginary conspirators."

But even in 1949, some critics were less enthusiastic. They noted that faulty operations sometimes led to physical problems such as huge weight gain, partial paralysis, epileptic seizures, and even death. Popular beliefs about frontal lobotomy (as portrayed in the 1975 Oscar-winning film *One Flew Over the Cuckoo's Nest*) seem to have been influenced greatly by this negative view. There is no question that some frontal lobotomies had tragic consequences. But while critics can cite individual cases of people whose lives were ruined by the operation, proponents of the operation can answer with individual cases of extremely successful lobotomies. One psychosurgeon described a physician who was discharged from two internships for his aggressive behavior and his delusions of being persecuted. After a frontal lobotomy, the doctor got married, established a 10-person medical clinic, and learned to fly his own plane (Valenstein, 1973).

For a more balanced picture of the effects of frontal lobotomy, we must turn not to individual cases but rather to large-scale studies. Valenstein (1973, p. 315) summarized the research on frontal lobotomies as follows: "There is certainly no grounds for either the position that all psychosurgery necessarily reduces people to a 'vegetable status' or that it has a high probability of producing miraculous cures. The truth, even if somewhat wishy-washy, lies in between these extreme positions."

In the mid-1950s, drugs became available that relieved some of the more severe symptoms of mental disorders. In the proper hands, lobotomy had always been seen as a treatment of last resort. The new, less drastic drug therapies (see Chapter 14) were a major factor in reducing the number of frontal lobotomies.

From the mid-1950s through 1980, approximately 500 psychosurgical operations were performed in the United States each year (Valenstein, 1980). During this period, many neurosurgeons turned away from frontal lobotomy and instead investigated the effects of more limited operations on structures deep inside the brain. Among the most promising of the new procedures was **cingulotomy,** an operation in which certain fibers connecting the frontal lobes to the limbic system were cut. One study of its effects (Teuber, Corkin, & Twitchell, 1976) followed 11 patients who suffered from chronic pain and depression; they had been under medical treatment for years, and all other therapies had failed. Cingulotomies cured 9 of these 11. The same operation also helped 5 people out of a group of 7 who were suffering from depression alone. Results for another 15 patients with other types of problems were more variable.

The need to understand more about psychosurgery is clear. A later report by the same research group on the effects of 85 cingulotomies continued to support the idea that many patients were helped. But, the report also noted, "It is not understood why cingulotomy is effective in some cases and not in others, or what brain mechanisms or other factors are responsible for the improvement when it does occur" (Corkin, 1980, p. 204).

A careful reading of this conclusion reveals that this researcher is not even willing to assert that cingulotomies are effective due to physical changes in the brain; other factors may be responsible for its success. For example, some researchers believe that these operations may succeed as a result of the **placebo effect**—medical treatments of no value in themselves sometimes seem to cure patients by the power of suggestion. Whether this is so, or whether cingulotomy works by altering specific aspects of brain function, can only be learned by further research.

CEREBRAL ASYMMETRY

The term **cerebral asymmetry** refers to differences between the two sides, or hemispheres, of the brain. Although physically they look very much alike, it is now clear that the left and right hemispheres play different roles in our behavior and mental life. The earliest evidence of this split came from studies of patients with brain damage. When Paul Broca presented his famous cases of aphasia patients with left-hemisphere damage in 1861, he helped establish the idea that language abilities are localized on the left side of the brain. Partly because damage to the right hemisphere produces more subtle deficits, widespread recognition of its role in such areas as depth perception and spatial relationships began only around the 1930s.

It is now clear that the classical distinction between a verbal left hemisphere and a nonverbal right hemisphere applies primarily to right-handed people. The picture for the 10% of the population that is left-handed is more complex. Most of our discussion will therefore be limited to the right-handed majority; we shall conclude with a section on the special status of lefties.

Split-Brain Surgery.   **Split-brain surgery** involves cutting the corpus callosum, the fibers that connect the left and right hemispheres. This operation was first tried in humans as an experimental treatment for certain epileptics whose seizures could not be effectively controlled in other ways. This extreme procedure was a success: Severing the connection between the hemispheres of the brain did indeed reduce the incidence and severity of epileptic attacks. But Roger Sperry, Michael Gazzaniga, and their associates at the California Institute of Technology were more interested in the psychological side effects of these radical operations. How would these people fare when they literally had two separate brains in one head?

One of the first patients awoke from surgery and quipped that he had a "splitting headache." However, there is no evidence that his jokes had been funnier before the operation. All in all, split-brain patients seemed surprisingly normal. But subtle tests gradually revealed that these people now had a number of intriguing problems.

As mentioned earlier, each hemisphere is primarily connected to the opposite side of the body. For example, the right hand is connected to the left hemisphere, and the left hand is connected to the right hemisphere. The connections of the visual system are more complicated (see Figure 2.13). Both eyes are connected to both

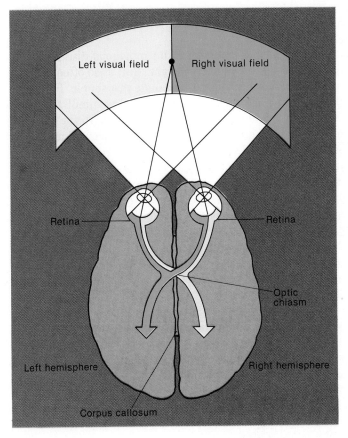

Figure 2.13

When a person fixates the eyes by staring at a point, information from the left visual field goes to the right hemisphere and information from the right visual field goes to the left hemisphere. In a normal person, information is quickly transferred to the opposite side via the corpus callosum. But in split-brain patients, these fibers are cut and the information is received by only one hemisphere.

sides of the brain. But information from the left visual field (that is, the left portion of the area that each of your eyes sees) goes to the right hemisphere; information from the right visual field goes to the left hemisphere. Under ordinary conditions, the eyes are constantly moving, so the split-brain person would get a complete picture of the world on each side of the brain.

But Gazzaniga (1967) devised a special test so that he could send visual messages to one brain hemisphere at a time. A split-brain person stared at a dot on a screen, and a visual stimulus was flashed briefly on one side of the dot or the other. If the stimulus appeared in the left visual field, the information would go to the right hemisphere; if the stimulus was flashed to the right visual field, only the left hemisphere would see it.

When a picture of a spoon was flashed at the left hemisphere, a split-brain person could easily say that she saw a spoon. But when the same picture was flashed to the right hemisphere, the split-brain patient often denied seeing anything. Yet when this person used her left hand to feel a group of objects hidden behind the screen, she was easily able to pick out the object she had seen—a spoon.

In an even more dramatic demonstration, a picture of a cigarette was flashed to the right hemisphere, and a split-brain patient picked out an ashtray with his left hand as the most closely related article in a group of 10 objects. But the "speaking" left hemisphere of the brain was no longer connected to the left hand, and so the patient could not *say* what he had picked.

These early experiments seemed to support an unambiguous distinction between the verbal left hemisphere and the nonverbal right. But, as so often happens in psychology, further research revealed that it was not quite that simple. For example, Eran Zaidel (1978) developed a new technique for presenting stimuli to the left and right visual fields through a special contact lens that moved with the eye. The earlier method of staring at a dot had allowed each hemisphere to see a stimulus only for fractions of a second. When Zaidel's new system made it possible for either hemisphere to see stimuli for much longer periods, more subtle linguistic abilities in the right hemisphere began to emerge. In one test, split-brain patients were given vocabulary questions that required choosing a picture that corresponded to a spoken word. When the pictures were presented only to the right hemisphere, people did not do as well as they did with the left. But they were able to perform at roughly the level of a 10-year-old child. On the basis of this study and others, psychologists now agree that verbal abilities are primarily—but not exclusively—located in the left hemisphere. Further research will be required to specify precisely the limits of the linguistic abilities of the right hemisphere.

Asymmetries in the Normal Brain.   Dramatic as the discoveries on split-brain patients were, some skeptics wondered how relevant they were to the normal person whose corpus callosum was intact. Many different methods were then devised to study cerebral asymmetry in the normal human brain.

The most direct evidence comes from the Wada test, which is used to localize language in patients who are about to undergo brain surgery. (This is necessary to ensure that removal of diseased brain tissue does not unintentionally interfere with language.) The Wada test involves anesthetizing one hemisphere of the brain. A small tube is inserted into the carotid artery on one side of a person's neck; when the drug sodium amytal (a barbiturate) is injected into the tube, it circulates primarily through the hemisphere on the same side of the brain.

The results of this chemical ablation are quite dramatic to see. The patient is generally asked to keep both arms raised in the air and count backward from 100. Within seconds of an injection, the arm on the opposite side of the body falls limp, indicating that one side of the brain is now "asleep." If the drug has been injected into the nonspeaking hemisphere, the patient quickly resumes counting and can answer simple questions. But if the drug has reached the speaking hemisphere, the patient is not able to talk for two to five minutes. Later, the person returns to normal.

Of course, this serious surgical procedure is not used in routine research on cerebral asymmetry. Other, more indirect tests are used for routine assessment of the function of the hemispheres. EEG measurements have revealed that the electrical activity on the two sides of the brain systematically changes as a person performs different sorts of tasks. Verbal tasks, such as writing a letter or thinking of words that begin with certain letters, have been found to result in relative signs of EEG activation on the left side of the brain. Spatial tasks, such as memorizing geometric designs or pictures of people's faces, generally led to relative EEG activation on the right side of the brain.

Sensory asymmetries have also been observed. Even normal individuals have been found to respond more quickly and accurately to words and letters presented to the right visual field (left hemisphere). There is also evidence that the left visual field (right hemisphere) is superior on such tests as facial recognition and identifying the spatial position of certain figures. Under some conditions, the right ear has also proved superior at recognizing verbal stimuli and the left ear at recognizing musical chords and melodies.

Encouraged by the consistency of these results, some theorists began to speculate about the more general implications of the "logical left brain" and the "intuitive right brain." At times, these speculations have gotten out of hand, as when Marshall McLuhan argued that excessive television watching caused the children of the 1960s to become the first generation in centuries whose thinking was dominated by the right brain and that the social upheavals of the sixties could be blamed on the conflicts between left-brained parents and right-brained children (Goleman, 1977). Statements like this, which are based on no evidence whatsoever, are not taken seriously by brain scientists.

Nevertheless, the idea of the logical left brain and the intuitive right brain has been publicized widely. A best-seller entitled *Drawing on the Right Side of the Brain* promised to "unlock the door to the neglected right half [of the brain] and integrate both halves, so that everyone . . . can realize full artistic and creative potential" (Edwards, 1980). In perhaps the ultimate tribute, the notion of cerebral asymmetry served as the basis for an automobile advertisement that would appeal to both sides of the brain (see Figure 2.14).

Researchers in this field have generally been more cautious about characterizing

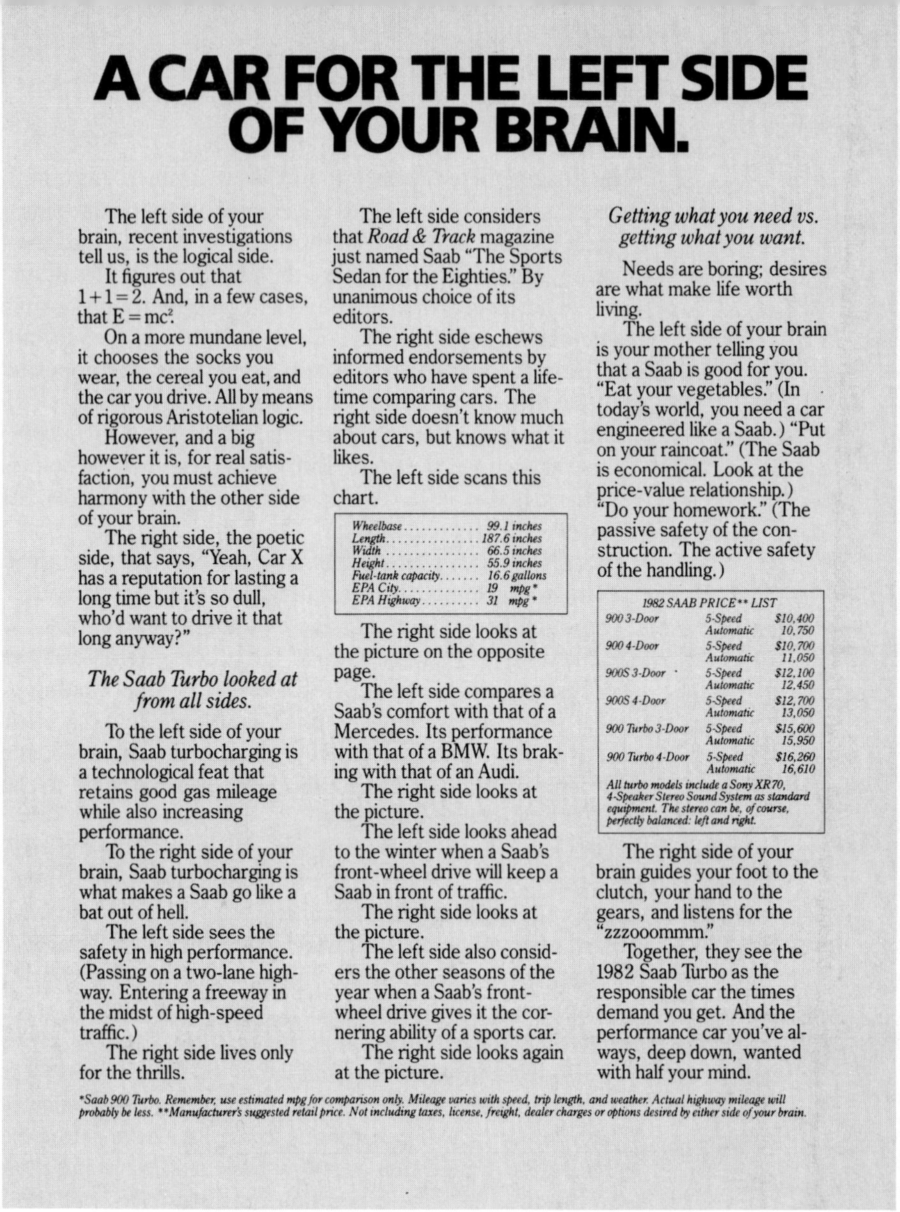

A CAR FOR THE LEFT SIDE OF YOUR BRAIN.

The left side of your brain, recent investigations tell us, is the logical side.

It figures out that $1+1=2$. And, in a few cases, that $E=mc^2$.

On a more mundane level, it chooses the socks you wear, the cereal you eat, and the car you drive. All by means of rigorous Aristotelian logic.

However, and a big however it is, for real satisfaction, you must achieve harmony with the other side of your brain.

The right side, the poetic side, that says, "Yeah, Car X has a reputation for lasting a long time but it's so dull, who'd want to drive it that long anyway?"

The Saab Turbo looked at from all sides.

To the left side of your brain, Saab turbocharging is a technological feat that retains good gas mileage while also increasing performance.

To the right side of your brain, Saab turbocharging is what makes a Saab go like a bat out of hell.

The left side sees the safety in high performance. (Passing on a two-lane highway. Entering a freeway in the midst of high-speed traffic.)

The right side lives only for the thrills.

The left side considers that *Road & Track* magazine just named Saab "The Sports Sedan for the Eighties." By unanimous choice of its editors.

The right side eschews informed endorsements by editors who have spent a lifetime comparing cars. The right side doesn't know much about cars, but knows what it likes.

The left side scans this chart.

Wheelbase	*99.1 inches*
Length	*187.6 inches*
Width	*66.5 inches*
Height	*55.9 inches*
Fuel-tank capacity	*16.6 gallons*
EPA City	*19 mpg**
EPA Highway	*31 mpg**

The right side looks at the picture on the opposite page.

The left side compares a Saab's comfort with that of a Mercedes. Its performance with that of a BMW. Its braking with that of an Audi.

The right side looks at the picture.

The left side looks ahead to the winter when a Saab's front-wheel drive will keep a Saab in front of traffic.

The right side looks at the picture.

The left side also considers the other seasons of the year when a Saab's front-wheel drive gives it the cornering ability of a sports car.

The right side looks again at the picture.

Getting what you need vs. getting what you want.

Needs are boring; desires are what make life worth living.

The left side of your brain is your mother telling you that a Saab is good for you. "Eat your vegetables." (In today's world, you need a car engineered like a Saab.) "Put on your raincoat." (The Saab is economical. Look at the price-value relationship.) "Do your homework." (The passive safety of the construction. The active safety of the handling.)

*1982 SAAB PRICE** LIST*

900 3-Door	*5-Speed*	*$10,400*
	Automatic	*10,750*
900 4-Door	*5-Speed*	*$10,700*
	Automatic	*11,050*
900S 3-Door	*5-Speed*	*$12,100*
	Automatic	*12,450*
900S 4-Door	*5-Speed*	*$12,700*
	Automatic	*13,050*
900 Turbo 3-Door	*5-Speed*	*$15,600*
	Automatic	*15,950*
900 Turbo 4-Door	*5-Speed*	*$16,260*
	Automatic	*16,610*

All turbo models include a Sony XR70, 4-Speaker Stereo Sound System as standard equipment. The stereo can be, of course, perfectly balanced: left and right.

The right side of your brain guides your foot to the clutch, your hand to the gears, and listens for the "zzzooommm."

Together, they see the 1982 Saab Turbo as the responsible car the times demand you get. And the performance car you've always, deep down, wanted with half your mind.

**Saab 900 Turbo. Remember, use estimated mpg for comparison only. Mileage varies with speed, trip length, and weather. Actual highway mileage will probably be less. **Manufacturer's suggested retail price. Not including taxes, license, freight, dealer charges or options desired by either side of your brain.*

Figure 2.14
Popular accounts of the functions of the two sides of the brain are often vastly oversimplified, as in this advertisement.

the functions of the two hemispheres. While the verbal left hemisphere and nonverbal right are good first approximations, a closer look at the data inevitably yields many ambiguities.

For example, consider the case of music. In support of the idea that this nonverbal stimulus would primarily involve the right hemisphere, several researchers at first reported that melodies are more easily recognized by the left ear (which is connected primarily to the right hemisphere). But later research revealed that this relationship held only for nonmusicians; trained musicians recognized melodies better through the right ear, suggesting that *they* were using the left hemisphere to

A CAR FOR THE RIGHT SIDE OF YOUR BRAIN.

SAAB
The most intelligent car ever built.

process music (Bever & Chiarello, 1974). Following this, still further research showed that the kind of musical task also made a difference. For example, in one study the left hemisphere proved superior in recognizing excerpts from unfamiliar melodies, while the right hemisphere was better at recognizing excerpts from familiar melodies (Gates & Bradshaw, 1977).

Taking these observations and many others into account, Bradshaw and Nettleton (1981) argue that the fundamental difference between the two sides of the brain involves a continuum rather than a simple dichotomy. They believe that the left hemisphere is especially involved in the sequential analysis of stimuli presented one after another, as in listening to the words of a sentence. The right hemisphere is more involved in the global, holistic response to complex stimuli, as in recognizing a face.

Whether this distinction will ultimately be accepted as the best possible characterization of the left-right difference remains to be seen. But on one point all scientists can agree: The brain is a tremendously complex organ that cannot be described adequately by simplistic dichotomies between left and right.

Handedness.   About 9 out of 10 people are right-handed, and the traditional distinction between a verbal left hemisphere and a nonverbal right hemisphere was based primarily on studies of righties. Apparently, the high frequency of right-handedness goes back many thousands of years: Even the people pictured in ancient Egyptian tomb paintings were predominantly right-handed.

Sodium amytal (Wada) tests of lefties have found that 70% have language primarily in the left hemisphere (versus 95% of all right-handers). Another 15% of the lefties had language in the right hemisphere, while the final 15% had some speech on each side of the brain. This range of possibilities would be confusing enough, but other techniques to assess the localization of language—including studies of visual-field differences, auditory asymmetry, and brain damage in left-handers—all yield slightly different estimates of the percentages (Springer & Deutsch, 1981).

Many people have speculated about the significance this more complex pattern of brain organization might have for personality and intellect. For example, one author (Fincher, 1977) cites the fact that Leonardo da Vinci, Charles Chaplin, and Harpo Marx were all lefties to support his contention that left-handers have a greater cognitive capacity for surprise and are thus able to see relations that escape more conventional brains. To put it kindly, these speculations have no scientific basis.

One thing we do know about left-handedness is that it runs in families. According to one classic study (Rife, 1940), when both parents are lefties, about 45% of their children are also left-handed; the figure drops to 30% if only one parent is a lefty and to 8% if both parents are right-handed. But there is still controversy about whether left-handedness is strongly influenced by genetic factors or is predominantly a function of learning.

Large-scale research on left-handedness began only in the last decade. One of the most interesting discoveries is that brain organization may be revealed by writing posture. While right-handers usually hold the hand below the line on which they write, many left-handers have adopted an inverted posture in which the hand is held above the writing line and the pencil or pen points toward the bottom of the page. Levy and Reid (1976) found that these inverters generally had language on the same side of the brain as the writing hand (as measured by a test of visual fields). Thus, left-handed inverters generally had language on the left side of the brain, whereas left-handed noninverters had language on the right side of the brain. (The same sorts of relationships applied for right-handers.) Although there is still some question about this conclusion (Herron, 1980), the notion that one could learn something about a person's brain organization by watching the way that person writes is a fascinating idea, one that will surely spark more research.

PROBLEMS AND PROSPECTS

As our review of brain research draws to a close, it may leave you with somewhat mixed feelings. While the last few decades have seen an incredible explosion of knowledge in the brain sciences, it is almost impossible to avoid the frustration of thinking about how much we have yet to learn.

The way researchers describe the crudity of current methods often reflects this frustration. After reviewing numerous conclusions based on ablation studies, for example, Thompson (1975, p. 106) notes that trying to understand brain function by destroying specific structures "is like trying to determine the function of one part of a TV circuit by smashing it with a hammer and noting how the TV set misbehaves." In a similar vein, others (Margerison, St. John-Loe, & Binnie, 1967, p. 353) have described EEG interpretation of the simultaneous electrical activity of thousands of brain cells as follows: "We are like blind men trying to understand the workings of a factory by listening outside its walls."

An introductory textbook chapter, by its very nature, is likely to make current knowledge seem more definitive than it really is. Virtually every introductory psychology text, for example, gives an estimate of the number of nerve cells in the brain. Some say 10 billion, some say 13 billion, some say 15 billion. In a special *Scientific American* 1979 issue on the brain, one article (Nauta & Feirtag) accepted the estimate of 10 billion, while another (Hubel) put the number at 100 billion. Both articles explained carefully that their estimate could be off by many billions.

We must never forget how far our understanding of the brain has advanced in the three centuries or so since Gall suggested that a woman's character could be read in the pattern of bumps on her skull. But neither must we forget how far we still have to go.

The epileptic who was freed by surgery from seizures and the parkinsonian patient whose tremors are controlled by drugs will personally testify to the value of all that researchers have learned thus far. But these accomplishments are nothing compared to what brain scientists hope someday to be able to do.

Summary

1. There are five major methods of studying the brain. **Neuroanatomical studies** focus on the structure of the nervous system. **Ablation studies** involve surgically removing or destroying brain tissue and observing the effects on behavior. In **electrical stimulation studies**, brain tissue is stimulated by an electric current while the effects on behavior are observed. **Electrical recording studies** involve measuring the normal electrical activity of the brain. And, **chemical studies** of the brain involve introducing a chemical into brain tissue to determine its behavioral and/or physiological effects.
2. According to the theory of **cerebral localization**, different areas of the brain are responsible for different psychological functions. In contrast, the theory of **holism** contends that psychological functions are controlled by a wide variety of cells throughout the brain.

3. **Neurons** are the individual nerve cells that are the fundamental building blocks of the nervous system. They consist of three major parts: **dendrites** receive electrical and chemical messages from other cells; the **cell body** is usually shaped like a sphere or pyramid; **axons** transmit electrical impulses away from the cell body to other neurons. The point at which an axon is connected to the dendrite or cell body of another neuron is called a **synapse.** A **neurotransmitter** is a chemical released at the synapse by the electrical activity of one neuron that influences the electrical activity of another.

4. The **central nervous system** includes the spinal cord and the brain. The **spinal cord** is a long thin column of neurons that emerges from the base of the brain and runs down the back; it connects sensory and motor organs to the brain and mediates simple reflexes.

5. The **peripheral nervous system** includes all nerve fibers outside the brain and spinal cord. It consists of two major divisions, the somatic and autonomic nervous systems. The **somatic nervous system** connects the brain and spinal cord with sensory receptors and voluntary muscles. The **autonomic nervous system** regulates the activity of smooth muscles and controls internal bodily processes. It consists of two major divisions: the **sympathetic nervous system** activates the glands and smooth muscles in periods of emotional excitement; the **para-sympathetic nervous system** maintains appropriate internal states in times of relaxation. The **endocrine glands** secrete special chemical messengers (called **hormones**) directly into the bloodstream. They include the adrenal glands, the pituitary, the ovaries, and the testes.

6. The **brain stem** includes a variety of structures at the base of the brain that relay information from the spinal cord to the cortex and regulate basic bodily processes such as breathing, heart rate, digestion, and sleep and waking. The two lobes of the **cerebellum** extend outward toward the back of the skull from either side of the pons; it is involved in the coordination of muscular movements. The **thalamus** passes along information from the eye, ear, and skin senses to the cortex. The **hypothalamus** is a smaller structure lying between the thalamus and the midbrain that is involved in complex behaviors like eating, drinking, temperature regulation, sex, and aggression.

7. The **limbic system** is a series of structures located near the border between the cerebral hemispheres and the brain stem. It is primarily involved in the regulation of such basic animal instincts as fighting, fleeing, feeding, and reproduction.

8. The **cerebral cortex** is the thick layer of cells that covers the brain and is well developed only in humans and the higher mammals such as apes. It consists of two **cerebral hemispheres**—the symmetrical sides of the brain—which are connected by a band of fibers called the **corpus callosum.** Each hemisphere is divided into four major lobes: frontal, parietal, temporal, and occipital. **Primary projection areas** receive input from the sense organs or control the movement of particular muscle groups; damage here produces very specific deficits, suggesting that functions are highly localized in these areas. All other areas of the

cortex are called **association areas** and are believed to be involved in higher mental processes.

9. **Psychosurgery** is brain surgery intended to change a person's thought patterns or behavior patterns. For example, in **frontal lobotomies** the connections between the frontal lobes and other brain structures were destroyed as a treatment for mental illness. Other psychosurgical operations are still performed and seem to help some patients.

10. **Cerebral asymmetry** refers to differences between the two hemispheres of the brain. In **split-brain surgery** the corpus callosum is cut, surgically isolating the right and left hemispheres. Traditionally, the left hemisphere has been described as verbal, the right as nonverbal. Some scientists now believe that the left hemisphere is especially involved in the sequential analysis of stimuli that are presented one after another, while the right hemisphere is more involved in global holistic responses to complex stimuli.

Discussion of "Becoming a Critical Consumer"

Most brain scientists would argue that this passage seriously overestimates the power of brain surgery to alter behavior. This author accepts Dr. Delgado's conclusion that electrical stimulation directly inhibits aggression. Other brain scientists disagree, arguing that Dr. Delgado's bull was actually responding with a sterotyped muscle movement. One of the most difficult problems for the critical consumer is dealing with the fact that scientists themselves often disagree. The safest policy involves caution and skepticism.

In any case, it is interesting to note this 1971 prediction that "the next few years will bring a frightening array of refined techniques for making human beings act according to the will of the psychotechnologist." More than a decade later, it is clear that this was wrong. More recent articles on brain research often contain similar predictions, which will probably also prove to be wrong. The progress of science is rarely dramatic or sudden enough for headline writers.

To Learn More

Valenstein, E. *Brain Control*. New York: Wiley, 1973. The best single introduction to the human brain. Although it focuses on psychosurgery, the book provides an excellent perspective on what current science knows and what it does not.

Springer, S. P., & Deutsch, G. *Left Brain, Right Brain*. San Francisco: W. H. Freeman, 1981. A balanced discussion of cerebral asymmetry.

Scientific American, September 1979, consists of 11 articles summarizing current research on the brain. These were reprinted as a book titled *The Brain*. San Francisco: W. H. Freeman, 1979.

3

Biology and Human Behavior

Most people would probably be willing to agree that biology influences behavior, particularly after reading Chapter 2 or another account of the human brain. But it is one thing to admit that brain damage can change personality and quite another to admit that our own personalities may be partly based on our brains.

Nevertheless, the evidence that we are biological beings is everywhere. If you go out after work and have a few drinks, your personality will change. You may loosen up a little, feel friendlier, and begin to laugh loudly at mediocre jokes. These changes are not accidental; they are based on biochemical reactions in your brain.

The drug alcohol affects the transmission of electrical impulses in the nervous system. The way these physiological changes affect behavior depends on both biological and psychological factors. For example, one relevant biological factor is the amount of food in your stomach. If you skip lunch the day you go out drinking, the changes in your personality will be quicker and more dramatic. This phenomenon is based on the way alcohol is distributed in the human body. When you drink a glass of California Chardonnay wine, for example, alcohol passes through the walls of your stomach into your bloodstream and from there to your brain. If your stomach is full, some molecules of alcohol will become chemically bound to the proteins in the food. But if your stomach is empty, alcohol passes more quickly into the bloodstream, and you may soon find yourself standing on the table singing a medley of Irish folk songs.

Psychological factors also affect your reaction to alcohol. If you are drinking at a stylish bar with an attractive co-worker, a few glasses of wine may produce a warm glow of well-being. But if you are drinking at home alone watching the paint peel off the walls of your tacky studio apartment, the same amount of alcohol may make you feel lonely and sorry for yourself.

As this example suggests, biological and psychological factors may be so closely interrelated that it is difficult to separate them. Behavior and experience are based on an intricate interplay of factors involving brain, body, and external stimuli. In their search for simple answers, people often find it hard to accept the fact that both psychology and biology can influence the same behavior at the same time. A person who knows little about psychology may ask whether intelligence is inherited or learned, as if these were the only two possibilities. As we shall see, the complex truth is that intelligence is both inherited and learned; both psychological and biological factors have an impact.

This is a subtle conclusion that psychologists have only recently come to. Just a few decades ago, many researchers thought in terms of a simple dichotomy between behaviors that were based on physiology (the biological paradigm) and those based on external stimuli (the behavioral paradigm). For example, diseases were divided into two categories—physical diseases (such as cancer or the common cold), which were caused by biological problems, and psychosomatic diseases (such as ulcers or high blood pressure), which were usually caused by psychological factors such as stress. But as we shall see, several lines of evidence have challenged this distinction. Researchers have found that people are more susceptible to "physical" diseases when they are subjected to psychological stress and that "psychosomatic" diseases are often linked to biological problems and genetic predispositions.

In 1980, psychologists and psychiatrists adopted a new classification scheme for diagnosing mental disorders (called DSM-III; see Chapter 13). One of the changes in this system is a new diagnostic category called "Psychological Factors Affecting Physical Condition," which recognizes that psychology and biology are so closely interrelated that one cannot draw a firm line between psychosomatic and physical disease.

Some of the research discussed in this chapter is not based only on the biological paradigm or the behavioral paradigm, but rather on a kind of marriage of the two. We will illustrate the complexity of the relationships between biology and behavior by describing research on four topics that may at first seem to have little in common: behavioral genetics, biological rhythms, drugs, and stress. Indeed, other psychology texts rarely group these topics together.

A brief overview of behavioral genetics provides some insight into the role of internal inherited predispositions in a wide range of individual differences in behavior, including the reactions to drugs and stress. Next, we consider the nature of biological rhythms—how our body's internal clocks regulate sleep, physiology, and performance. Then we turn to an external biological factor—the drug alcohol—to describe its effects on behavior. Finally, we consider how an external psychological variable—stress—influences biology and is influenced by it.

At times, this chapter may seem to tell four separate and independent stories, but there are some links. Drugs may be used to induce sleep or control reactions to stress, for example, and the response to a particular drug may be partly based on genetics. Overall, however, research on each of the four topics has been developed independently of the others. Nevertheless, the study of behavioral genetics, biological rhythms, drugs, and stress provide four different views of the same underlying theme. Behavior is best understood by considering how psychological and biological factors work together rather than trying artificially to isolate them.

Behavioral Genetics

The idea that human characteristics can be passed by heredity from parent to child can be traced back at least to ancient Greece. Four centuries before the birth of Christ, Plato wrote in *The Republic* that in an ideal society, young men who distinguished themselves in war or other pursuits should be rewarded with "the most ample liberty of lying with women" so that they could have many children and thus pass on their desirable characteristics to the largest possible number.

Similarly, for many centuries farmers have systematically mated male and female animals and plants to try to produce desirable offspring. However, until recently the rules that breeders relied on to form these unions were a confusing mass of contradictions. As one commentator put it, the first rule of breeding was "like produces like" and the second was "like does not always produce like" (Lush, 1951, p. 496). This confusion began to clear up after a monk named Gregor Johann Mendel published his theory of heredity in 1867, based on his experiments with pea plants.

Mendel's work became widely recognized around the turn of the century, and the science of **genetics**—the study of the transmission of inherited characteristics—has developed rapidly ever since. However, human beings are difficult organisms for geneticists to study. Humans may pause 20 or 30 years between generations, they do not have many children, they cannot be raised in controlled environments, and they cannot be forced to mate with specific people to see what happens.

Psychologists are particularly interested in the field of **behavioral genetics**—the study of the inheritance of behavioral characteristics. Research with lower animals has revealed the importance of genetic factors in helping to determine such general behavior patterns as activity level, emotionality, aggressiveness, and eating habits (Fuller & Thompson, 1978).

This chapter concentrates on the basic principles of human behavioral genetics. Later, we shall see how these principles have been applied to the study of the roles of heredity and environment in intelligence (Chapter 12) and in mental disorders such as schizophrenia (Chapter 13).

GENES AND CHROMOSOMES

Genes are the physical structures that transmit characteristics from parent to child. If you have your father's short nose and your mother's short temper, this resemblance may be partially based on the fact that from the moment of conception you developed according to a blueprint provided by your parents' genes.

Genes are composed of complex molecules of a substance called DNA (deoxyribonucleic acid). Through a complicated code involving the precise order of four chemicals (the organic bases adenine, guanine, cytosine, and thymine), DNA determines the production of proteins and enzymes in the cells of the body. The precise way in which this genetic blueprint influences physical and behavioral development is just beginning to be understood.

Genes are so small that, given the limits of present technology, they cannot be seen. However, we can see **chromosomes,** long thin structures in the nucleus of every cell that contain hundreds or thousands of genes. Almost every cell in the human body ordinarily has 46 chromosomes arranged in 23 pairs (see Figure 3.1). In contrast, frogs have 26 chromosomes; chimpanzees, 48; and chickens, 78. But human reproductive cells—the mother's egg and the father's sperm—have only 23 chromosomes. When egg and sperm combine in conception, the fertilized egg begins life with the requisite 23 pairs—half of each pair contributed by Mom and half by Dad.

The specific chromosomes a child receives from each parent are chosen at random. As a result, according to the laws of probability, two children with the same mother and father will have about half of their genes in common. More complex calculations can reveal the genetic similarity between any two relatives, from stepsisters to second cousins. In general, the more closely related two people are biologically, the more closely they resemble each other genetically.

The average person may conclude that height is inherited if he notices that very few jockeys have children who are tall enough to play professional basketball. The

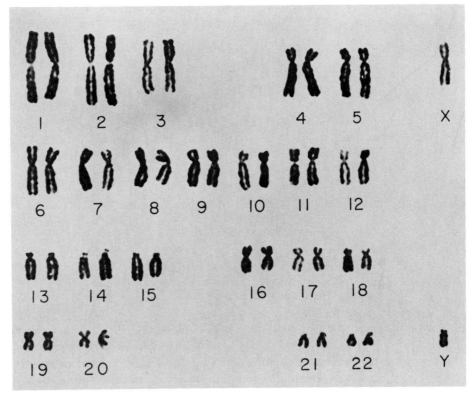

Figure 3.1
Except for the reproductive cells, every cell in the human body contains 46 chromosomes. Chromosomes were first observed in 1951 when a laboratory technician accidentally washed some slides in the wrong cleanser and the chromosomes became swollen enough to be seen through a microscope. This photograph shows them neatly arranged in pairs; the twenty-third pair determines an individual's sex, in this case male.

behavioral geneticist goes beyond this to analyze systematically the resemblances between large numbers of people who are related in a variety of different ways.

METHODS IN HUMAN GENETICS

The first scientist to study human behavioral genetics systematically was Francis Galton, an English cousin of Charles Darwin's. In 1869, Galton published *Hereditary Genius*, which summarized his study of nearly 1,000 eminent judges, politicians, military commanders, scientists, artists, religious leaders, and scholars. Because there were at that time no objective measures of intelligence or achievement, Galton (p. 37) developed his own scale of reputation as "a leader of opinion, of an originator, or a man to whom the world deliberately acknowledges itself largely indebted." A careful statistical analysis of the relatives of eminent men found that they were

Few people have made such a variety of contributions to science as Sir Francis Galton (1822–1911). A cousin of Charles Darwin, Galton was independently wealthy; for his entire adult life, he simply followed his curiosity wherever it led. As a meteorologist, Galton developed several techniques now used in weather forecasting. As a criminologist, he pioneered the study of fingerprints for criminal investigations. As a statistician, Galton helped lay the mathematical groundwork that led to the development of the correlation coefficient. As a social scientist, Galton invented the questionnaire— in 1874, he sent 200 British scientists a long list of questions covering everything from their religious beliefs to their hat sizes. But Galton is best remembered by psychologists for his pioneering studies of behavioral genetics and individual differences in intelligence.

much more likely than the average person to achieve eminence themselves. Indeed, the closer the blood relationship to an eminent man, the more one was likely to achieve.

Galton was aware that people in the same family not only share similar genes but are also ordinarily raised in similar environments. The resemblances he found could have been caused by heredity, by environment, or by both. Galton cited several arguments to support his idea that eminence resulted from "hereditary genius." For example, he noted that many men had risen to achievement from humble families. Further, he found that the biological sons of eminent men were more successful than the adopted relatives of Roman Catholic popes, despite the fact that these adopted children were given many advantages.

Since Galton, the measurement of human abilities has advanced considerably and mathematical tools of analysis have also become far more sophisticated. By today's standards, Galton's studies prove little or nothing about the inheritance of genius. But his pioneer research did help to establish two of the most important techniques in human behavioral genetics—the study of twins and the study of adopted children.

The rationale of adoptive studies is quite straightforward. If a characteristic is primarily based on heredity, children should resemble their biological parents even if they never knew them. However, if environment is the key to a particular trait, children should come to resemble the adoptive parents who raised them.

More common than adoptive studies are comparisons of the behavioral characteristics of twins. About 1 out of every 87 white births in North America is a twin birth. Thus, 2 out of every 88 babies, or about 2.3% of the white population, are twins. (Interestingly, North American blacks have a somewhat higher proportion of twin births—1 in every 73).

Identical twins are called **monozygotic** because they develop from the division of a single fertilized egg (zygote) and thus have precisely the same genes. Fraternal twins are called **dizygotic** because they develop from two different eggs that happen to be fertilized by two different sperm at the same time. They are often male and female, whereas monozygotic twins, being identical, must always be of the same sex. Dizygotic twins are no more similar genetically than any other two siblings; that is, they share about half their genes.

To geneticists, the most interesting cases are those rare individuals who were separated from an identical twin at birth. Although few in number, these people are great in significance; they represent a kind of natural experiment in which heredity is held constant while the environment is varied.

Figure 3.2
Behavioral genetics can estimate the heritability of a trait by studying resemblances between identical and fraternal twins.

A review of all the published cases of monozygotic twins raised apart found only 95 pairs that were adequately reported. The results were quite striking: "There are remarkable—sometimes unnerving—similarities in many dimensions, including physical characteristics as disparate as height and the pattern of tooth decay; temperament and personality; mannerisms, such as a firm or limp handshake; smoking and drinking habits; tastes in food; and special aptitudes and interests, especially in the arts or in athletics" (Farber, 1981, p. 59). Other similarities included weight, blood pressure, EEG, voice characteristics, and even symptoms of anxiety such as nail biting and headaches.

Fascinating as these results are, they must be considered provocative rather than conclusive. Many of the twins had met before they were studied, and some were even raised in different branches of the same family. Thus, in some cases they shared the same environment, and their resemblances may not depend on heredity alone.

A much larger body of research compares the degree of resemblance between identical and fraternal twins. Typically, these studies assume that pairs of twins who grow up in the same family are exposed to similar environments whether they are monozygotic or dizygotic. Thus, if identical twins generally resemble each other more in terms of some characteristic, it seems reasonable to conclude that heredity played a part.

One typical study of this sort (Loehlin & Nichols, 1976) studied 850 sets of same-sex twins who took the National Merit Scholarship Test in 1962. In addition to taking this standard test of academic ability, each set of twins and their parents filled out several questionnaires regarding their personalities and interests. Table 3.1 shows some of the basic results.

Note that in each category, the correlation between identical twins was greater than the correlation between fraternal twins (see "How Do They Know?" for more details on correlations). Since each pair of twins was raised in a similar environment, it seems reasonable to conclude that the greater resemblance of identical twins was based on their genes.

However, also note that even the identical twins are never precisely the same; if every pair of scores were a perfect match, those correlations would be 1.0—but they are not. Since two people with identical genes never end up precisely the same, it is obvious that the environment shapes their differences. These data suggest the rea-

TABLE 3.1
Resemblance Between Twins

	Correlation Between Identical Twins	*Correlation Between Fraternal Twins*
General ability	.86	.62
Personality scales	.50	.28
Self-concepts	.34	.10
Ideals, goals, and vocational interests	.37	.20

Based on Loehlin and Nichols, 1976, p. 87.

sonable conclusion that complex human abilities are determined by *both* heredity and environment. In this particular case, the researchers (p. 90) concluded that "genes and environment carry roughly equal weight" in accounting for these traits. This conclusion was based on a series of calculations that yielded a mathematical estimate of the relative importance of genetics and environment called heritability.

THE CONCEPT OF HERITABILITY

Heritability is a mathematical estimate of the relative importance of genetics and environment in determining a particular trait for a specific population. For our purposes, the technical details of how it is computed are not important. However, it is important to understand what it means to say that intelligence or extraversion or schizophrenia has a high heritability for a particular group. There are two points to remember: heritability estimates are always limited to a particular group; and a trait that is highly heritable is not necessarily fixed at birth and impossible to change.

Genes provide a biochemical blueprint for development. But many other factors affect development, and the way genes are expressed always depends to some extent on the environment. Suppose, for the sake of argument, that a tendency toward obesity is partially inherited. A person with the obesity genes could gain weight just by sitting near chocolate, while another individual with another set of genes could stay thin even if she lives entirely on potato chips and pecan pie. These genetic predispositions will be expressed only if these two people are raised in an environment in which fattening food is freely available. If both are unfortunate enough to be born in a time of famine, the genetic differences might never be expressed, and both children could be extremely thin.

The fact that the environment affects the way genes are expressed implies that one can never totally isolate nature from nurture. This is the reason psychologists think it is naive and misleading to ask such a question as, is intelligence inherited? The answer is that it depends on the group you study and the environment in which they were raised.

Imagine two different studies of our obesity example, both using the same technique of comparing adopted children's weight with that of their biological and adoptive parents. A study of middle-class American children would probably find that adopted children were more likely to resemble their biological parents and conclude that obesity was influenced by genetics. But suppose the study was replicated precisely in a society in which lower-class children suffered from poor nutrition and inadequate food but upper-class children overate. For this group, children would probably resemble their adoptive parents' weight, since this population had such a wide variety of eating habits. These studies would come up with two different estimates for the heritability of the same trait, and each would be correct for a different group.

Human characteristics are always determined by a mixture of heredity and environment. The relative importance of nature and nurture varies from one group to another. Further, even when a trait is largely inherited in a given group, that does not mean it can never be changed. Quite the contrary. Understanding the genetic basis of a phenomenon may make it easier to control.

Correlation Coefficients: How Similar Are Twins?

Psychologists are often concerned with the problem of estimating the strength of a relationship between two variables. As noted in Chapter 1, they can compute a figure called a *correlation coefficient*, which is a precise statistical expression of the relationship between two variables.

Consider the question of how closely twins resemble each other. It is easy to say in general terms that most twins seem pretty much alike, but it is much more difficult to specify how much is "pretty much." Quantification is essential for psychology to advance as a science.

The absolute value of a correlation coefficient is always between 0 and 1. If a correlation coefficient is 0, the two variables are unrelated; if it is 1, one variable predicts another perfectly, with no exceptions. Such perfect relationships are hard to find in this imperfect world; most correlation coefficients are somewhere between 0 and 1. The closer they are to 1, the stronger the relationship between two variables.

As an additional complication, every correlation coefficient is preceded by a + or − sign. The sign of a correlation coefficient indicates the direction of the relationship. In *positive correlations*, high values on one variable (for example twin *A*'s score) are associated with high values on another variable (twin *B*'s score). In some cases, high values on one variable are associated with low values on another; these are *negative correlations*.

Imagine computing the correlation coefficient between the average temperature of each week in winter and the amount paid for fuel oil that week. Low temperatures mean high heat bills; high temperatures mean low heat bills. Thus, the correlation would be negative. Similarly, there is often a negative correlation between psychological variables, such as when high levels of math anxiety are associated with

low scores on math tests. The important thing to remember is that the sign only indicates the direction of the relationship, not its magnitude. Correlation coefficients of +.47 and −.47 represent relationships of equal strength. The difference is that +.47 means that high scores for one variable are associated with high scores for another, while −.47 implies that high scores for one are associated with low scores for the other.

Earlier in this chapter, we explained why geneticists are interested in comparing the resemblances between identical and fraternal twins. The simplest way to do this often involves computing correlation coefficients. For example, Loehlin and Nichols (1976) studied 850 pairs of twins who took the National Merit Scholarship Test as high school juniors in 1962. Several of their major findings were summarized in Table 3.1; here, our question is, what do these numbers mean?

Consider a graph summarizing the scores on a math test in which each dot on the graph represents the scores of one pair of twins. Suppose we had four pairs of twins with these scores: *A* 5, 5; *B* 6, 6; *C* 9, 9; *D* 6, 7. The graph

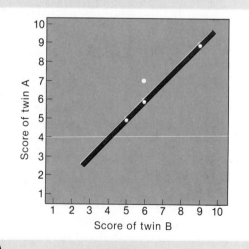

A

would look like the one in Figure A. Note that the dots fall more or less on a straight line. If you knew one twin's score, you could use this straight line to predict the score of the other. High correlations imply more accurate predictions.

Loehlin and Nichols compared the mathematics scores of 216 pairs of identical male twins on the National Merit Test. If they had summarized all this data on a graph, it would have looked something like the graph in Figure B. Even a casual glance makes it clear that the twins' scores were correlated; when one twin did well in math, the other also tended to get a high score. Loehlin and Nichols went on to compute a correlation coefficient of +.74, indicating a strong relationship.

The math scores from the 135 pairs of fraternal male twins in this study looked something like the graph in Figure C. These scores still seem to be related, but not as strongly as those of the identical twins. The lower correlation coefficient of +.41 between fraternal male twins' math scores implies that the prediction from one twin's score to the other is less accurate; thus, they are spread out more. The actual correlation coefficients provide a precise estimate of the relative accuracy of the predictions from one identical twin to the other or

from one fraternal twin to the other. (As explained on page 84, the difference observed here implies that genetic factors influenced performance on this test.)

Of course, psychologists are interested in the relationships between many pairs of variables aside from twins' scores on a particular test. Correlation coefficients have been computed to study the relationships between income and education, frustration and aggression, extraversion and sexual activity, anxiety and test performance, and countless other pairs of variables. In each case, the basic interpretation of the correlation coefficient is the same: absolute values close to 0 imply little or no relationship; absolute values close to 1 imply a very strong relationship.

Even when this is clear, people often misinterpret correlations. Later, we explain why strong correlations do not necessarily imply that one variable causes another. For example, the simple fact that people who are anxious about taking tests do more poorly does not mean that anxiety necessarily interferes with performance. It could imply that people who begin to do poorly worry more. See "How Do They Know?" in Chapter 12, p. 453, for a discussion of how correlations should be interpreted.

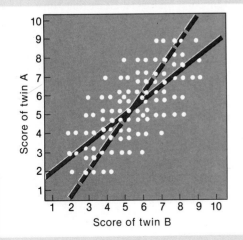

B

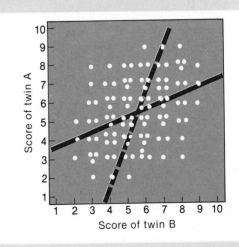

C

The best example of this comes from research on a rare disease called phenylke-tonuria—PKU, for short. Children with PKU seem normal at birth, but their intellectual and motor development soon slows down. One-third never learn to walk and two-thirds never learn to talk. Doctors now know that PKU is caused by a genetic disorder that results in the lack of a liver enzyme involved in the digestion of a specific protein (phenylalanine) found in milk and other foods. The undigested protein becomes toxic and attacks nerve cells, causing progressive mental retardation. Once PKU children are identified, they can be put on a diet that includes very little of the culprit protein, and they will then develop normally. Since the mid-1960s, routine blood tests on newborn babies have identified over 1,000 American infants who had this disease, and dietary treatment has saved them from becoming mentally retarded. In this case, knowledge of genetic factors actually made it possible to change the course of a very serious disease.

This brief introduction to behavioral genetics should serve as a warning that biological effects on behavior are neither separate nor independent from psychological factors. This point will become even clearer as we go on to consider biological rhythms, drugs, and stress.

Biological Rhythms

Since the dawn of history, observers have noted rhythmic patterns in the ebb and flow of life. The daily human cycle of activity and sleep is the most obvious example. But there are many others, including the daily openings and closings of the leaves of plants, the sexual cycles of lower animals, and the human menstrual cycle.

In 1729, a French scientist named Jean de Marain reported that a plant would continue to close its leaves at night and open them during the day even in the continuous darkness and near constant temperature of a cave. Thus the plant's leaves were not simply responding to sunlight, as earlier observers had believed. Instead, the plant seemed to have some internal biological clock that timed the leaf movements.

More than a century later, Ogle (1866) reported that humans too appeared to have an internal biological clock. Body temperature rises each morning and falls at night, apparently without regard to external cues or the time of sleep. Although these discoveries go back several centuries, widespread research on the nature and sources of biological rhythms only began in the 1950s. We are just beginning to understand how the body measures and reacts to the passage of time.

TYPES OF BIOLOGICAL RHYTHMS

Biological rhythms are generally divided into three major classes—those that are shorter than a day (ultradian), those around 24 hours long (circadian), and those longer than a day (infradian). The most important category involves **circadian rhythms,** cyclical changes in behavior or physiology that repeat themselves once every 24 hours or so. The word *circadian* comes from the Latin *circa,* "about," and *dies,* "a day." Under normal conditions, most of these rhythms last almost precisely 24 hours. But when a person or animal is removed from all external cues of day and night, circadian rhythms vary from about 22 to 28 hours in length.

The most obvious human circadian rhythm is the sleep-waking cycle. One of the most convincing demonstrations that sleep will follow roughly a 24-hour cycle even without external cues was provided by a French geologist named Michael Siffre (1964). In 1962, he spent two months in the French Alps, in a damp, chilly cave where no light or sound could reach him. He went to sleep and arose when he felt like it, with no clocks or other clues to tell him the time. Under these isolated conditions, Siffre slept once every $24\frac{1}{2}$ hours, and other bodily rhythms conformed to similar cycles.

Because of its importance, the sleep-waking cycle will be described in detail. Circadian rhythms have also been identified in a wide variety of behavioral and physiological variables, including body temperature, hormone secretion, and performance.

Body temperature ordinarily reaches its lowest point between 4 and 6 a.m. and begins rising before a person wakes up. It continues to go up until it peaks in midafternoon, typically between 5 and 7 p.m. Under normal conditions, people tend to work most efficiently and feel best when their body temperature hits its peak (Wilkinson, 1982). This is particularly interesting in light of the fact that those who describe themselves as "morning people" show an earlier temperature peak than evening people (Ostberg, 1973).

Most of the hormones secreted by the endocrine glands also follow a circadian rhythm. The time of day associated with maximum concentration varies from one hormone to the next. For example, the female hormone prolactin peaks in the middle of the night; this helps explain why twice as many pregnant women go into labor at midnight as at noon.

Like hormones, behavioral rhythms each have a cycle of their own. Studies of people who work shifts have consistently found that job performance is less efficient at night than during the day, and it declines markedly from around 2 to 5 a.m. Laboratory studies have revealed that efficiency on short and simple tasks (such as adding columns of numbers) is best in the afternoon, while tasks involving memory are generally performed more efficiently in the morning (Naitoh, 1982).

Infradian rhythms involve cyclical changes in behavior or physiology that repeat themselves at intervals of more than a day. In humans, the most obvious infradian rhythm is the menstrual cycle, the changes in the female reproductive system that typically occur once a month. There is no doubt that some women experience cyclical changes in mood and behavior that are related to hormonal changes, although the actual mechanisms are still unclear. There is also evidence that men have cyclical changes in mood (Parlee, 1978), although the cycles vary far more widely in length and have not been related to hormonal changes.

Finally, **ultradian rhythms** refer to cyclical changes in behavior or physiology that repeat themselves more often than once a day. Little is known about cycles of this sort. There is still controversy over the existence of a basic rest-activity cycle, which may lead people to become more alert every few hours (Kripke, 1982). However, we shall see in the next section that there are regular ultradian rhythms during sleep that are associated with dreams.

None of these categories should be confused with the pseudoscientific theory of "biorhythms," which claims that human behavior is determined by three separate cycles—physical, emotional, and intellectual—that begin at the moment of birth. Despite the fact that this theory has been proved incorrect in many studies, the use of calculators and computer programs to chart an individual's "biorhythms" remains popular.

Let there be no confusion. There is considerable scientific evidence that "biorhythm" calculations based on the date of birth do not work (Brown, 1982). But there is no doubt that human behavior and physiology are affected by a large number of legitimate infradian, circadian, and ultradian rhythms. The actual biological mechanisms and the locations of internal "clocks" are still being identified. As this research continues, it seems likely that psychological effects on biological rhythms—such as the way in which stress can interfere with sleep patterns or lengthen the menstrual cycle—will become increasingly apparent.

SLEEP AND DREAMS

If you sleep 8 hours every night and live for 70 years, you will be asleep for a total of 23 years and 4 months of your life. More of your time is likely to be devoted to sleep than to working, playing, or even worrying about your weight.

The modern era of sleep research began around 1950 with an accidental discovery. Eugene Aserinsky, a graduate student at the University of Chicago, was studying infant sleep patterns, carefully watching their cycles of thrashing around the crib hour after hour. During these tedious observations, he noticed that behind their closed lids, the infants' eyes were often flicking rapidly back and forth. Several similar observations were buried in the archives of sleep researchers, but Aserinsky wisely decided to pursue this phenomenon.

In 1953, Aserinsky and his mentor, Nathaniel Kleitman, reported the results in an article in *Science*. They had attached electrodes to 20 normal adults to measure the movements of their eyes as they slept. Like the infants, the adults passed through several periods of rapid eye movement (or **REM**) during each night's sleep. More important, when Aserinsky and Kleitman awakened people during this REM sleep, 20 of 27 times the sleepers reported that they had been dreaming. In contrast, when the same people were awakened during the longer periods in which their eyes were not darting back and forth (non-REM-sleep), they reported dreams on only 2 of 23 occasions.

Stages of Sleep. REMs provided one of the first objective physiological indicators of the inner world of thought, and many scientists rushed to confirm these findings. Their EEG recordings revealed that the activity of the brain does not remain constant as a person sleeps; rather, there are five distinct stages of sleep. These are called, cleverly enough, stage 1, stage 2, stage 3, stage 4 (all non-REM), and REM sleep. All four non-REM stages have been called quiet sleep because this period is

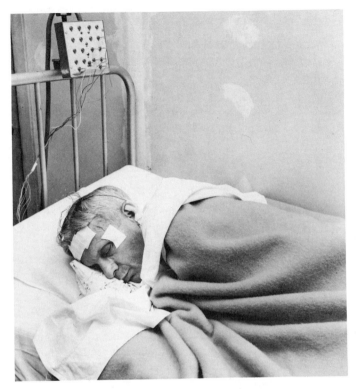

In the sleep laboratory, electrodes attached to a polygraph measure a person's eye movements, EEG, and other physiological systems. Posing as the subject for this photograph is pioneer sleep researcher Nathaniel Kleitman, shown here wearing his best pajamas.

characterized by slow, regular breathing and brain activity and a general lack of body movement (Dement, 1974).

In contrast, the fifth stage, REM sleep, is a relatively active period. Although the sleeper does not move, the face and fingertips start to twitch. If the sleeper has been snoring, this stops. Breathing becomes irregular. The eyes dart back and forth; because the cornea of the eye bulges slightly behind the eyelid, anyone who happens to be nearby can see this REM activity. Blood flow in the brain increases, while the arms, legs, and trunk are temporarily paralyzed. All males—from newborn infants to retired bank presidents—have erections during REM sleep.

In terms of brain-wave activity, REM sleep is almost identical to stage-1 sleep. Despite these EEG signs of brain activation, REM sleep is the deepest of the night. People are most difficult to awaken during this time. This stage is sometimes called paradoxical sleep because of the contrast between the apparent alertness of the brain (in terms of the EEG) and the difficulty of awakening.

The sleeper passes through these five stages in a cyclical progression each night. As shown in Figure 3.3, the sleeper moves up and down through the stages several times during a normal night. Most of the deep sleep of stage 4 occurs relatively early. But the periods of time that a person spends in REM sleep, dreaming, get longer as the night progresses. The first dream appears a little more than an hour after sleep begins and lasts only 10 minutes or so. Typically, another three or four REM periods follow at intervals of about 90 minutes, getting longer as the night goes on. Most people dream for a total of about 90 minutes each night.

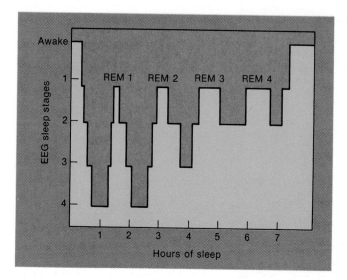

Figure 3.3
The progression through sleep stages over the course of a typical night's sleep. Note that stage-4 sleep occurs only during the first few hours and that REM-stage length increases as the night goes on. This record shows awakening in the middle of a REM period, which would probably lead the sleeper to remember this dream.

Although a few individuals have been reported to sleep as little as 45 minutes per night (Meddis, Pearson, & Langford, 1973), the average adult requires about 7½ hours and dreams 20% of the time. Interestingly, newborn infants sleep about 16 to 18 hours out of every 24 and spend half this time in REM sleep. These sleep needs decline rapidly in the first year of life; by his first birthday, the average child sleeps 11 or 12 hours and dreams perhaps one-third of the time. Both the total amount of sleep and the proportion spent in REM continue a much more gradual decline throughout life. According to one theory (Dewan, 1970), REM sleep helps consolidate new information in memory; newborns devote more sleep to REM because most of their experience is new.

REM Sleep and Dreams. Up to this point, we have been using the terms *REM sleep* and *dreaming* interchangeably. But the data we cited from Aserinsky and Kleitman's original experiment suggest that occasionally people wake up from a non-REM period and report a dream and that sometimes they fail to report a dream after awakening from REM sleep. In a review of 16 studies of this topic, Snyder and Scott (1972) found that dreaming was always reported more frequently after REM than after non-REM sleep. But precise estimates of the relationship varied. Typically, dreams were reported about 74% of the time after awakening from REM, and 12% of the time after awakening from non-REM sleep.

Many of the differences in experimental opinion about the exact relationship can be attributed to the difficulty of deciding just what qualified as a dream. Almost everybody will mumble something if you suddenly wake him up and ask what he was dreaming about. Most researchers specify some sort of coherent narrative as the critical characteristic of a dream, but differences in the application of this criterion have led to differences of opinion about the precise relationship. In any case, it is clear that there is a strong but not perfect relationship between REM sleep and dreaming.

Although some people claim that they never dream, no one who has been tested in a sleep laboratory has failed to have periods of REM sleep. When one group of researchers (Goodenough, Shapiro, Holden, & Steinschriber, 1959) compared the sleep of eight people who said that they dreamed often with another eight who claimed to dream rarely or never, they found that the second group reported dreams less frequently upon being awakened from both REM and non-REM sleep. Even so, the "nondreaming" group reported dreams 46% of the times they were awakened from REM sleep. Thus, it is also clear that all people dream, whether they remember dreaming or not.

However, the question of what the thousands of dreams each person has every year actually mean is quite controversial. There have been many attempts to decode the mysteries of dreams, from Babylonian records 5,000 years before Christ to the countless popular guides now available. In psychology, different theoretical paradigms have led to different conclusions. At one extreme, many psychoanalysts argue that dreams hold the key to our unconscious desires (see Chapter 11). At the other extreme, some biological researchers hold that dreams construct arbitrary stories to "explain" physiological events that occur during REM sleep. For example, people often dream about being paralyzed or running in slow motion because muscle movement is inhibited during REM sleep, and dreams of floating can be traced to electrical stimulation of the inner ear (McCarley, 1978).

Philosophers may wonder whether it is sensible to ask what a particular dream "really means." Scientists are not likely to shed much light on this question, but they can and will continue to study how particular types of dreams are related to both biological and psychological variables.

DISTURBANCES IN CIRCADIAN RHYTHMS

There are wide variations in the individual need for sleep; a few individuals seem to be able to function on less than 1 hour a night, while others may need 10 hours. Perhaps even more impressive are individual differences in adapting to disturbances in circadian rhythms caused by traveling across time zones or working night shifts.

Jet Lag. At the dawn of the jet age in the 1950s, U.S. Secretary of State John Foster Dulles flew to Egypt to conduct sensitive negotiations over the Aswan Dam. When the project was lost to the Soviet Union, Dulles attributed this diplomatic failure to his own travel exhaustion. Later, he warned his employees against negotiating soon after travel (Moore-Ede, Sulzman, & Fuller, 1982).

Jet lag may be defined as discomfort or decreased efficiency caused by traveling across time zones. Its symptoms may include gastrointestinal distress, insomnia, headaches, irritability, and general malaise. Some individuals are more susceptible to jet lag than others, but almost everyone feels some distress after crossing three or more time zones.

Interestingly, flying from west to east (for instance, from California to New

York) takes longer to adjust to than flying in the opposite direction. In one study (Klein & Wegmann, 1979), some individuals took as much as 18 days to adjust totally to an eastbound flight that crossed six time zones. The maximum readjustment time for a westbound flight of equal duration was 8 days.

Greater jet lag after eastbound flights has been replicated in many studies. It now seems that this is just one example of a more fundamental phenomenon—humans find it easier to delay going to sleep than to go to sleep early. When you fly westward, you gain several hours of clock time. For example, if you take a 5 p.m. flight from Washington, D.C., and arrive in San Francisco at 10 p.m. Eastern Standard Time, the local (Pacific) time will be 7 p.m. To maximize adjustment to California time, you should go to sleep near your ordinary bedtime according to the local clock. Given the time difference, this implies that you will be awake about three hours longer than usual. Most people find this delay relatively easy.

However, if you fly from San Francisco to Washington, going to bed at your regular time according to the local clock means trying to sleep three hours earlier than usual. Most people find this a more difficult adjustment, and it takes longer for all of their circadian rhythms to synchronize to the local clock.

There is some evidence that people who have larger daily variations in body temperature and certain hormones have more problems with jet lag than those with less pronounced circadian rhythms (Klein & Wegmann, 1979). In the future, it may be possible to predict travelers' distress in advance.

Shift Work. Similarly, some people adapt to night-shift schedules far more easily than others. Before the industrial use of artificial illumination in the nineteenth

Workers at the Great Salt Lake Minerals and Chemicals Corporation exchange information during a shift change. Shift rotation schedules for this company were changed when studies revealed that a new type of schedule improved workers' health and satisfaction.

century, very few people worked through the night. According to some estimates, as many as 60 million people now work late shifts in industrialized countries around the world (Moore-Ede, Sulzman, & Fuller, 1982). Some of these people suffer from chronic medical problems, particularly stomach ailments and sleep disturbances. Even people who seem perfectly satisfied and have worked night shifts for long periods of time never seem to adapt their physiological circadian rhythms completely. Further, performance is consistently poorer on night shifts than day shifts, particularly between 2 and 5 a.m. (Naitoh, 1982).

Increased awareness of the nature of circadian rhythms may help to improve working conditions in the future. For example, one study of rotating shift workers at a Utah mineral processing plant found that many had problems with the three-week rotating schedule of one week on the day shift (8 a.m.–4 p.m.), one week on the night shift (midnight–8 a.m.), and one week on the swing shift (4 p.m.–midnight). Researchers compared this traditional schedule with two experimental schedules: a three-week sequence of day, swing, night (versus the old day, night, swing) and a nine-week sequence of three weeks on days, three on the swing shift, and three on nights (Czeisler, Moore-Ede, & Coleman, 1982). Note that the new sequences always required workers to go to bed later, rather than earlier, when they switched shifts. As studies of jet lag have shown, this is an easier transition. Workers on the experimental schedules were healthier and more satisfied than those who worked the traditional hours. They particularly liked the nine-week schedules that called for fewer rhythm shifts. As a result of this experiment, the Great Salt Lake Minerals and Chemicals Corporation adopted the new schedule permanently.

This study is a good example of the way research on the relations between psychology and biology may have practical implications. Other examples may be found as we consider how external chemical stimuli can affect behavior.

Drugs

A **psychoactive drug** is a chemical substance that influences behavior or subjective experience by altering responses in the nervous system. If you drink two cups of coffee to get going in the morning, the psychoactive drug caffeine increases the arousal of your brain. Some psychoactive drugs, such as caffeine and alcohol, are legal and widely used in our society. Others, such as marijuana and cocaine, are illegal and less widely used. A third category includes drugs that are prescribed by physicians, including tranquilizers, barbiturates, and amphetamines. No matter how these drugs are legally regulated, all share the power to alter behavior and emotions by changing the chemistry of the brain.

CLASSES OF PSYCHOACTIVE DRUGS

Thanks to the miracles of modern chemistry, Americans now use and abuse a wide variety of drugs to make themselves feel good. Table 3.2 provides an overview of five major classes of psychoactive drugs and their effects.

Sedatives depress the activity of the central nervous system; they include alco-

TABLE 3.2
An Overview of Psychoactive Drugs

Drug	Effects	Psychological Dependence[1]	Tolerance[2]	Physical Dependence[3]
Sedatives				
Alcohol; Barbiturates (e.g., Seconal, Amytal, Nembutal); Methaqualone (e.g., Quaalude)	CNS depressants: relaxation, drowsiness, sometimes euphoria; impaired judgment, coordination, and emotional control	High	Yes	Yes
Tranquilizers (e.g., Valium, Librium)	Selective CNS depressants: relaxation, relief of anxiety	Moderate?	No	No
Stimulants				
Caffeine	Increased alertness, reduced fatigue	Moderate	Yes	No
Cocaine; Amphetamines (e.g., Dexedrine, Benzedrine)	Increased alertness, reduced fatigue, loss of appetite, often euphoria	High	Yes	No
Narcotics				
Opium; Morphine; Heroin; Methadone; Codeine; Demerol	CNS depressants: sedation, euphoria, pain relief, impaired intellectual function	High	Yes	Yes
Hallucinogens				
LSD; Mescaline; Psilocybin	Production of visual imagery, increased sensory awareness, sometimes anxiety, nausea, impaired coordination, "consciousness expansion"	Minimal	Yes (rare)	No
Cannabis (marijuana, hashish)	Relaxation, euphoria, some alteration of time perception, possible impairment of judgment and coordination	Moderate	Yes	No
Antipsychotics				
Thorazine; Serpasil; Haldol	Calm (in psychotic patients); reduction of anxiety and initiative without excessive sedation	Minimal	No	No

[1]A compulsion to use a drug for its pleasurable effects.
[2]Over time, higher doses are needed to produce similar effects.
[3]Withdrawal syndrome is experienced when drug is stopped.
Based on *A Primer of Drug Action*, by R. M. Julien, copyright © 1975, by W. H. Freeman and Co. All rights reserved.

hol, the barbiturates, and tranquilizers. In large doses, these drugs put people to sleep, sometimes permanently; in smaller doses, they relieve anxiety and reduce inhibitions. **Stimulants** increase the activity of the central nervous system. **Narcotics** are opiates that relieve pain and induce sleep. Opiates include the natural products of the opium plant and other drugs that resemble them chemically and pharmacologically. **Hallucinogenic drugs** cause hallucinations and alter sensory perceptions. Finally, **antipsychotic drugs** are used primarily to decrease the hallucinations and disordered behavior of psychotic individuals (see Chapter 14).

The last three columns of Table 3.2 refer to the potential of each class of drugs to lead to abuse. From a medical point of view, **drug addiction** is defined by physical dependence and tolerance. **Physical dependence** means that a regular user who stops taking a drug will experience a variety of physical problems. For example, a heroin addict who stops taking heroin will experience an extremely unpleasant withdrawal syndrome that includes irritability, insomnia, violent yawning, severe sneezing, nausea, diarrhea, and muscle spasms. **Tolerance** means that if a person takes the same dose of a drug day after day, it will gradually have smaller effects because the person's body becomes accustomed to, or tolerates, that dosage; increasingly larger doses will be required to produce the original effect.

A close look at Table 3.2 makes it clear that by this medical definition, only alcohol, the barbiturates, and the opiates are addicting drugs, for only these produce tolerance and physical dependence. That does not mean that regular users of other drugs will find them generally easy to stop. Frequent use of amphetamines, tranquilizers, or other drugs may be a hard habit to break. This more subtle potential for abuse is called **psychological dependence**, a compulsion to use a drug that is not based on physical addiction. The potential of a particular drug for producing a pattern of psychological dependence, in which people use the drug regularly despite ambivalence or attempts to quit, is hard to measure precisely. As a result, there may be some controversy over specific items in Table 3.2, such as whether Valium and Librium lead to minimal rather than moderate psychological dependence.

To provide a more complete picture of the psychological, social, and biological factors that determine drug effects and physical addiction, we shall describe the drug alcohol in some detail.

THE CASE OF ALCOHOL

Beer and berry wine were known and used at least 6,400 years before Christ. Today, alcohol use is so firmly established in our society that two drunks in a bar might get into an argument about the evils of drug addiction without ever realizing that they themselves are addicted to our society's number one problem drug—alcohol.

Doses and Effects. The effects of alcohol are directly related to its concentration in the blood. Low doses of alcohol may appear to stimulate behavior, but this is generally believed to be an indirect effect. Sedative drugs, including alcohol, depress activity in the central nervous system. One of the first sites affected in the brain is the reticular activating system, which is responsible for alertness, attention, and the regulation of the cerebral cortex. As with other sedatives, alcohol first disrupts complex, abstract, and poorly learned behaviors. The precise mechanism for alcohol's depressive action on the brain is not known, but many investigators now believe that it affects the ability of neurons to produce electrical impulses, rather than acting at the synapse like most other drugs (Ray, 1978).

The specific behavioral effects of low doses of alcohol vary from one individual to the next and, as explained below, depend on psychological as well as biological factors. Higher blood-alcohol levels depress sensory and motor capacity, then lead to a loss of muscular coordination and staggering (as the cerebellum is depressed), then to stupor, anesthesia, and coma, and finally to death. The anesthetic effect of alcohol encouraged early surgeons to use it as a painkiller in primitive amputations and other operations. But alcohol has several disadvantages for the surgical patient; for one thing, the dose that produces anesthesia is very close to the dose that depresses respiratory centers in the brain and causes death. Thus, a minor miscalculation in dose could have tragic consequences.

Several biological factors influence how quickly high blood-alcohol levels are reached. We mentioned earlier that drinking on an empty stomach causes alcohol to move into the bloodstream more quickly. Champagne or sparkling burgundy can also get you drunk quickly, because carbonation moves alcohol more rapidly through the stomach into the small intestine and accelerates its flow into the blood.

The precise effects of a given dose of alcohol also vary from one person to the next but in general depend on sex and body weight. Alcohol is distributed throughout the body fluids, including the blood. Since heavier people have more body fluids, they take longer to reach a given blood-alcohol level. Women have proportionately more fat and less body fluids than men of the same weight and thus reach high blood-alcohol levels more quickly.

Alcohol interacts with other drugs in complex ways. A person who is taking tranquilizers or barbiturates will get drunk much more quickly than usual. Sudden and unexpected reactions between alcohol and other drugs can cause coma or death.

Psychological Factors. At relatively low doses, psychological factors exert a major influence on the response to alcohol. People's expectations that alcohol will make them feel more aggressive, more relaxed, or more sexual can affect their behavior just as much as what they drink.

One study (Lang, Goeckner, Adesso, & Marlatt, 1975) examined the links between alcohol, aggression, and expectations by deceiving some experimental subjects about what they were drinking. The experimenters began by looking for a drink that could fool people; they discovered that a mixture of 1 ounce of 100-proof vodka and 5 ounces of tonic water tasted the same as plain tonic water to most people. They then divided 96 male college students who were defined as heavy social drinkers into four groups. Two groups were told the truth—that one would be drinking plain tonic and the other vodka and tonic. But the other two groups were deceived. One of these groups was told they would be drinking vodka and tonic but were actually given plain tonic; the other group was told they would be drinking plain tonic, but were given vodka and tonic.

The researchers who talked to the subjects did not know which group each one was in; this reduced the chances that the experimenters would unintentionally influence the results (for more details, see "How Do They Know?" in Chapter 14, p. 533, regarding double-blind studies). Subjects who received vodka drank enough to produce a blood-alcohol concentration of 0.10%, which is the legal definition of drunkenness in many states. The actual dose depended on body weight; for example, a 150-pound man in this study drank 6 ounces of vodka in one hour.

To maximize the chances of observing aggression, a research assistant later provoked half of these subjects by sarcastically criticizing their performance on a complex task, asking the subject whether his attempt to solve a problem was really serious and whether he was so dumb that he had to cheat to stay in college. To measure aggression, each subject was then given an opportunity to evaluate the research assistant's performance on another task and penalize him for mistakes by giving electric shocks. (No one was actually shocked.)

The findings were clear-cut. Whether provoked or not, subjects who believed they had drunk alcohol were more aggressive. They gave longer and more intense shocks to the research assistant. The alcohol itself did not affect aggression. Those who thought they had tonic but actually drank vodka were less aggressive than those who thought they had vodka but actually drank tonic. The beliefs had greater effects than the drug.

Other studies have shown similar effects for sexual arousal. Ogden Nash expressed one common belief about alcohol and sex when he wrote

> Candy is dandy
> But liquor is quicker.

But Wilson and Lawson (1976) found that men were more likely to become aroused by erotic films when they thought they were drinking. Whether they actually received alcohol or not was again less important than their beliefs.

Attitudes and expectations have also been shown to help determine the response to other drugs, such as hallucinogens. In one typical study, subjects who said they were apprehensive before taking the drug psilocybin tended to be anxious and experience headaches and nausea after taking it; those who said they felt good about taking psilocybin were more likely to report that it put them in a pleasant mood (Metzner, Litwin, & Weil, 1965).

The point here, and throughout this chapter, is not that psychological factors are more important than biological ones, or vice versa. It is that psychology and biology work together in complex ways to determine the response in any given situation.

Alcoholism. Somewhere between 8 and 12 million Americans are alcoholics (Ray, 1978); the precise number depends on how you define the term. Psychologists today distinguish two types of alcoholism—alcohol dependence and alcohol abuse. The less serious form, **alcohol abuse,** is defined by the presence of three criteria: a pattern of pathological use, for example a need for alcohol every day or an inability to cut down or stop drinking; impairment of social or occupational function, such as

This French postcard series depicts the tragic decline of a worker who fell victim to the evils of alcohol.

absence from work or arguments with family or friends; and duration of the problem for at least one month. The more serious form, **alcohol dependence,** corresponds to the medical definition of drug addiction: a syndrome involving withdrawal symptoms and tolerance (American Psychiatric Association, 1980).

The fact that heavy drinkers develop tolerance, that is, need larger doses of the drug alcohol to produce the same effect, has been well established. It is also clear that a person who is addicted to alcohol will go through a physiological withdrawal syndrome if she does not drink. This process of withdrawal usually involves several of the following: anxiety, depression, insomnia, restlessness, muscle tremors, high blood pressure, and increased body temperature. More serious cases may lead to delirium tremens (or the "DTs"), characterized by hallucinations, delirium, disorientation, and epileptic seizures. This withdrawal syndrome is medically more severe and more likely to cause death than withdrawal from heroin or other narcotic drugs.

Long-term use of large amounts of alcohol is associated with damage to the liver and the brain, as well as other medical problems. Excessive drinking also plays a major role in traffic deaths and has been linked to several forms of criminal activity and violence.

It is hard to quantify all the human unhappiness caused by alcohol abuse. It is easier to estimate how much it costs. According to the most recent estimates of the National Institute on Alcohol Abuse and Alcoholism, in 1975 alcoholism cost the United States $43 billion. This figure includes such factors as the cost of medical care for alcoholics, days lost from work by alcoholics, and expenses incurred in fires and auto accidents in which drinking was involved. (In that same year, other drug-abuse problems cost $10.5 billion, for a total of $53.3 billion—which is 2.5% of the country's gross national product.) Given this grim picture of the social costs of alcoholism and alcohol abuse, the question is obvious: What can be done about it?

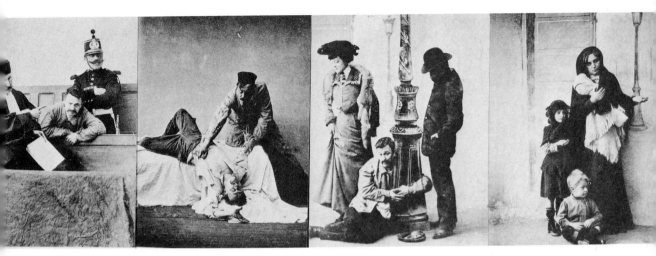

In the late 1950s, the American Medical Association defined alcoholism as a disease and began to try to treat it as a medical problem. At first, doctors believed that the cure for this disease was total abstinence. This position was entirely consistent with the philosophy of Alcoholics Anonymous, a worldwide treatment organization with over 800,000 members. Founded in Akron, Ohio, in 1935 by two reformed alcoholics, Alcoholics Anonymous bases its program on the belief that "for an alcoholic, one drink is too many and a thousand not enough."

On the basis of numerous studies of alcoholics many experts have now accepted the more moderate conclusion that controlled drinking is possible for "some alcoholic subjects for some length of time" (Nathan & Goldman, 1979, p. 261). The problem is that there is still considerable controversy over "two additional crucial questions: How many alcoholics? For how long a time?"

Unfortunately for the individual with a drinking problem, complex questions like this can take quite some time to answer. In the meantime, the best advice for alcoholics is to seek professional help. A review of 384 studies of psychologically oriented alcoholism treatment programs (Emrick, 1975) found few differences in the average success rate of Alcoholics Anonymous, various types of psychotherapy, and other treatments. But this review did show that patients who entered a treatment program were more likely to improve than those who did not. Psychological treatment "increases an alcoholic's chances of reducing his drinking problem" (Emrick, 1975, p. 88), but no approach offers a guaranteed cure.

DRUGS AND THE BRAIN

While drugs differ widely in their effects and potential for abuse, in at least one way all psychoactive drugs are alike. They all act on the brain. But to act on the brain, first a chemical must get there.

Theories of Drug Action.   When a drug is swallowed, it dissolves in the stomach fluids, is carried into the intestine, penetrates the lining, and passes into the blood-stream. Once a drug enters the bloodstream, it circulates quickly through the entire body. It can enter most body tissues by passing through pores in the walls of the capillaries (tiny blood vessels). But nature has devised a way to protect the brain from poisons. There are no pores in capillaries in the brain, and each neuron is surrounded by a protective covering (formed of glial cells); thus, only certain types of small molecules can pass through to brain cells. This structure of the circulatory system of the brain, which makes it difficult for certain types of chemicals to pass from the blood to the neurons, is referred to as the **blood-brain barrier.**

If a drug manages to pass the blood-brain barrier ultimately it will reach specific brain cells that are equipped with the appropriate **drug receptor,** the part of a neuron that responds to a specific type of drug. It is now thought that different types of drugs act on different drug receptors. For example, some brain cells have recep-tors stimulated by amphetamines, others have receptors stimulated by narcotics. After a drug reaches the appropriate receptor, it is believed to affect the transmission of nerve impulses, usually by influencing neurotransmitters.

In Chapter 2, we defined a *neurotransmitter* as a chemical released at the synapse by the electrical activity of one neuron, that influences the electrical activity of another. Several important clues to how drugs can affect neurotransmitters came from the study of patients with Parkinson's disease, who suffer from severe muscu-lar tremors of the limbs, hands, neck, and face. Other physiological and psychologi-cal problems appear in later stages of this progressive disease.

Within the last few decades, neurologists discovered both the cause and cure of this disease, which afflicts 1.5 million Americans. Apparently these problems were caused by a lack of the neurotransmitter dopamine in certain structures of the brain. Dopamine neurons inhibit the action of certain muscle fibers; without this inhibi-tory effect, uncontrollable tremors are produced. At first, researchers gave the drug dopamine to Parkinson's patients, but it had no effect because the molecules were too large to pass through the blood-brain barrier. Currently, many cases of Parkin-son's disease are treated with the drug L-dopa, a closely related chemical that is converted to dopamine in the brain.

Many new neurotransmitters have been identified since the early 1970s, and many more probably remain to be discovered. Some of the most exciting work currently going on in this area involves a class of neurotransmitters called endor-phins.

Endorphins.   **Endorphins** are natural brain chemicals that are structurally similar to opiates such as morphine and heroin. Around 1970, scientists identified drug receptors in the brain that responded specifically to opiates. It seemed unlikely that these receptors had evolved just in case an animal consumed an opium plant or a Percodan tablet. Their existence suggested that some naturally occurring brain chemical was structurally similar to morphine—an endogenous morphine sub-stance, or endorphin. So far, five major endorphins have been identified; all are peptides (the chemical building blocks of proteins), which are produced in the brain, spinal cord, and other tissues of many animals. All mimic the effects of morphine.

Because opiates are such powerful painkillers, early speculations about the endorphins centered on the idea that these neurotransmitters were the body's natural painkillers. Proof of this theory would require that biochemists measure endorphin release in a specific part of the brain and show that pain is reduced when endorphins are released and not reduced when they are blocked. But as Goldstein (1980) noted, "Technology does not yet permit such measurements in the living animal, much less the conscious human."

Scientists were forced to rely on less direct tests. One common procedure involves administering other drugs, called **narcotic antagonists,** that are known to block the effects of opiates. Naloxone, for example, reverses the effects of any narcotic; it is used in emergency rooms to treat patients who have taken an overdose of heroin or morphine. Narcotic antagonists are believed to work by occupying opiate receptor sites so that the narcotic cannot affect neurons. Scientists reasoned that if naloxone blocked some form of nonchemical pain relief, this would suggest that natural opiates—endorphins—were involved in the original process.

Doctors have known for centuries that **placebos,** chemically inactive substances, can relieve pain by the power of suggestion. In 1978, one group of researchers (Levine, Gordon, & Fields) published data suggesting that endorphins might be the mechanism behind this mysterious effect. They studied dental patients a few hours after they had undergone oral surgery. As in many earlier studies, some people who were given a placebo reported that it eased their pain. But these researchers went on to administer naloxone and found that this drug increased the pain of those who had responded to the placebo. They concluded that the placebo worked by somehow causing the brain to release endorphins; when the naloxone reversed the effect of these natural opiates, the pain returned.

The ink was barely dry on this report before other scientists challenged the details (Goldstein & Grevert, 1978). Is is only by this sort of claim and counterclaim that science progresses. But it does take time for a consensus to emerge, and in an active area like this, claims must be examined with more than the usual degree of caution. While some scientists were speculating about the role of endorphins in everything from eating, sleeping, and temperature regulation to drug addiction, schizophrenia, obesity, and depression, others warned that the major lesson of their discovery was to remind scientists "how little we really know about the constituents of the brain" (Pert, Pert, Davis, & Bunney, 1982).

Whatever one's view, it is clear that these studies support the general argument of this chapter that biological and psychological processes work together to determine behavior. If endorphins are the biochemical basis for the placebo effect, it is fascinating that the brain releases these chemicals only when it believes a placebo will work. Similarly, the studies of psychological expectations and responses to low doses of alcohol demonstrate the intricacy of the connections between mind and body. The same complexity is apparent in the relationship between psychological stress and physical disease.

Stress

Stress involves a perception of threat to physical or psychological well-being and the individual's reaction to that threat.

One of the first researchers to explore the consequences of stress was Hans Selye. In 1936, he reported that animals responded to a variety of stressors, ranging from extreme cold to injection of a small amount of poison, with the same physiological pattern. Selye called this physiological response to stress the **general adaptational syndrome** and divided it into three stages: alarm, resistance, and exhaustion.

The *alarm stage* began at the first sign of stress, as the animal's body tried to defend itself by mobilizing the endocrine glands. In particular, the adrenal glands became enlarged and secreted higher levels of the hormone adrenaline into the bloodstream. This in turn led to a variety of physiological changes including a breakdown of some tissue into energy-giving sugars.

After several days of stress, the animal would adapt and its body chemistry would return to normal. This *resistance stage* was only temporary, however. If the stress continued, the adrenal glands again became enlarged and lost their stores of adrenal hormones. In this final stage—*exhaustion*—the endocrine glands, the kidneys, and other internal organs were damaged, and the animal ultimately died.

Inspired by these findings, many researchers went on systematically to expose animals to various types of stressful stimuli and to chart their precise physiological responses. But scientists who chose to study human responses to stress were forced to rely on a clumsier method, letting Mother Nature choose the people who would be subjected to the greatest physical and emotional strain.

STRESS AND ILLNESS

At first, human stress research focused on a group of illnesses known as psychosomatic disorders. In everyday language, the term *psychosomatic* is often used incorrectly to refer to imaginary diseases. If you feel sick to your stomach before your final examination in Zen Accounting, a friend may tell you smugly, "it's only psychosomatic," as though there were nothing really wrong with you, almost as though it were your own fault that you threw up. In fact, however, a **psychosomatic disease** is a real physical illness that is partly caused by psychological factors. The most common psychosomatic disorders are ulcers, high blood pressure, migraine or tension headaches, asthma, and a variety of skin conditions such as eczema, hives, and psoriasis.

Countless studies have shown that people under stress are particularly vulnerable to these problems. For example, when London was bombed by the Germans at the beginning of World War II, the number of people who came to London hospitals with ulcers increased substantially (Stewart & Wisner, 1942). High-stress jobs can also lead to physical problems. In the early 1970s, air traffic controllers were twice as likely to have ulcers and four times as likely to have high blood pressure as comparable groups of pilots (Cobb & Rose, 1973). Psychologists have known for some time that stress can trigger psychosomatic disorders. More recent is the idea that stress can trigger other diseases as well.

Victims of German air raids on London in World War II often suffered from ulcers and other physical diseases precipitated by stress.

One of the most important lines of research that led to this new view began in 1967 when Thomas Holmes and Richard Rahe published the **Social Readjustment Rating Scale** to measure normal life stress. Holmes and Rahe listed 43 events that they believed were particularly likely to cause stress for the average American adult. They then asked 394 people to rate each event according to the amount and intensity of readjustment it required. The death of a spouse was considered the most stressful event and was given an average rating of 100 "life-change units." This event was rated twice as stressful as getting married (rated 50) and about four times as stressful as beginning or ending school (rated 26). Any person could now be assigned a life-stress score simply by adding the point values of all the events that had occurred in a certain period of time, usually the last 6 or 12 months.

Despite the fact that these were only average scores and that any individual might rate specific stressors somewhat differently, many researchers have shown that the higher a person's score on the Social Readjustment Rating Scale, the more likely he is to get sick. For example, Rahe (1972) studied the illnesses of sailors in the U.S. Navy. Before beginning a cruise, each man completed the Social Readjustment Rating Scale, describing how much stress he had been under in the last six

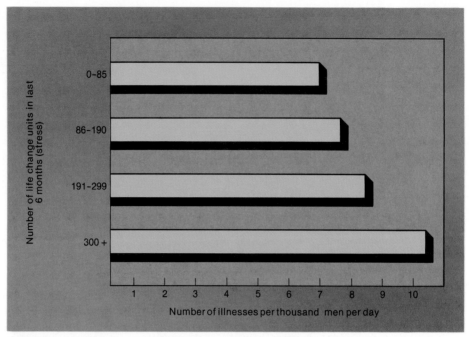

Figure 3.4
During a 6-month U.S. Navy cruise, sailors who had experienced more stress in the previous 6 months were more likely to become ill.

months. When the ship returned to port six to eight months later, Rahe simply counted the number of times each sailor had reported to the sick bay with objective signs of a new illness. He then divided the men into four groups on the basis of their life-stress scores and found an orderly and statistically significant progression in the frequency of illness (see Figure 3.4). Stress seemed to increase the risk not only of psychosomatic problems such as hives and asthma but also of all sorts of physical diseases.

Some researchers went on to develop alternative questionnaires that were specially suited to the life experiences of different groups. Table 3.3 illustrates the College Schedule of Recent Experience, the questionnaire likely to be relevant for most readers of this text. Another group compared the effects of major stressors such as the death of a spouse with more mundane hassles such as worrying about weight, misplacing things, and being too busy. They found that hassles were even more highly correlated with physical and mental health than major life events. They also measured uplifts, such as relating well with family members and friends, eating out, and meeting responsibilities. They had expected to find that these uplifts would counterbalance the effects of stress, but there was little evidence in this study that positive events affected health one way or the other (Lazarus, 1981).

Overall, a large number of studies using a variety of scales have shown that people who have recently experienced a great deal of stress are more likely to develop minor medical complaints as well as heart disease, tuberculosis, leukemia, diabetes,

TABLE 3.3
The College Schedule of Recent Experience

Event	Numerical Value
(1) Entered college	50
(2) Married	77
(3) Trouble with your boss	38
(4) Held a job while attending school	43
(5) Experienced the death of a spouse	87
(6) Major change in sleeping habits	34
(7) Experienced the death of a close family member	77
(8) Major change in eating habits	30
(9) Change in or choice of major field of study	41
(10) Revision of personal habits	45
(11) Experienced the death of a close friend	68
(12) Found guilty of minor violations of the law	22
(13) Had an outstanding personal achievement	40
(14) Experienced pregnancy or fathered a pregnancy	68
(15) Major change in health or behavior of family member	56
(16) Had sexual difficulties	58
(17) Had trouble with in-laws	42
(18) Major change in number of family get-togethers	26
(19) Major change in financial state	53
(20) Gained a new family member	50
(21) Change in residence or living conditions	42
(22) Major conflict or change in values	50
(23) Major change in church activities	36
(24) Marital reconciliation with your mate	58
(25) Fired from work	62
(26) Were divorced	76
(27) Changed to a different line of work	50
(28) Major change in number of arguments with spouse	50
(29) Major change in responsibilities at work	47
(30) Had your spouse begin or cease work outside the home	41
(31) Major change in working hours or conditions	42
(32) Marital separation from mate	74
(33) Major change in type and/or amount of recreation	37
(34) Major change in use of drugs	52
(35) Took on a mortage or loan of less than $10,000	52
(36) Major personal injury or illness	65
(37) Major change in use of alcohol	46
(38) Major change in social activities	43
(39) Major change in amount of participation in school activities	38
(40) Major change in amount of independence and responsibility	49
(41) Took a trip or a vacation	33
(42) Engaged to be married	54
(43) Changed to a new school	50
(44) Changed dating habits	41
(45) Trouble with school administration	44
(46) Broke or had broken a marital engagement or a steady relationship	60
(47) Major change in self-concept or self-awareness	57

To quantify the stress you have been subjected to lately, multiply the value for each event by the number of times it occurred in the past year (up to a maximum of 4) and add all values. In the original study, scores below 347 were considered to fall in the low-stress category, and scores above 1,435 were classified as high stress (Marx, Garrity, & Bowers, 1975, p. 97).

and multiple sclerosis. They are also more likely to have accidents or to injure themselves in athletic competition (Rabkin & Struening, 1976).

Critics have been quick to point out that the fact that life stress *correlates* with physical disease does not necessarily mean that life stress *causes* physical disease. It is possible that people under stress smoke more, drink more, sleep less, eat poorly, or act in other ways that increase the risk of medical problems. In other words, it remains to be seen whether stress causes disease directly or if the link is more subtle.

Further, it is important to emphasize that while the relationship between stress and illness is quite consistent, it is rather modest in size. (The typical correlation is about .30; see "How Do They Know" for an explanation.) Stress is one of a large number of factors involved in physical disease; many people who are not particularly stressed get sick, and many others go through very stressful periods and remain healthy.

This leads directly to a fascinating question of individual differences: Why do some people get sick when they are stressed while others do not? One group of researchers (Nuckolls, Cassel, & Kaplan, 1972) wondered whether social supports such as strong relationships with family and friends and positive feelings about oneself could reduce the harmful effects of stress. In a study of pregnant women, they found that 91% of those who had high-stress scores, poor opinions of themselves, and little help from relatives and friends had complications in later pregnancy or childbirth. Only 33% of those who were equally stressed but in a better sociopsychological position had similar complications. Life stress by itself did not predict medical problems; neither did lack of sociopsychological supports. But when the two factors came together, health problems were likely to result. Research of this sort will continue to build a more sophisticated picture of the complex relationships between stress and disease.

REDUCING STRESS

Once it became clear that stress can be harmful to health, psychologists became interested in the question of reducing and controlling stress. Two promising techniques now under study are biofeedback (see also Chapter 5) and meditation.

Biofeedback. The basic principle of biofeedback is simple—feedback makes certain types of learning possible. Imagine trying to learn to play the electric guitar if you always wore earplugs when you practiced. Without the feedback of hearing your mistakes, you would never be able to learn to play a recognizable version of "The Star-Spangled Banner." Or imagine trying to learn to throw darts while blindfolded. If you never knew whether you had hit the bull's-eye or an innocent bystander, how could you ever improve your aim?

Our bodies are not designed to allow us to be consciously aware of subtle feedback about internal physiological states. At this moment, you do not know precisely how fast your heart is beating, what your blood pressure is, or how tense the muscles in your forehead are. If you were given this information, you could learn to control these physiological processes to some extent.

Biofeedback involves learning to control physiological states on the basis of precise physiological information (feedback). For example, suppose your heart beats about 80 times per minute (or once every three-fourths of a second) and you want to learn to slow it down. You could be connected to a machine that measures precisely the time interval between the beats of your heart. Whenever two beats were more than three-fourths of a second apart, a light would go on, telling you that your average heart rate was now lower than 80 beats per minute. If you sat quietly watching the machine and concentrating on whatever thoughts seemed to make the light go on more frequently, you could gradually learn to keep the light on and thus make your heart rate go down. Precisely how would you do this? It's hard to say. When researcher David Shapiro (1973) asked a person in one of his experiments how he had lowered his heart rate, the subject asked in return, "How do you move your arm?"

However people do it, subjects in biofeedback experiments have learned to control a wide variety of physiological processes. They have raised and lowered their heart rates and their blood pressures and precisely regulated the level of tension in many different muscles. They have changed the rhythms of their brain waves (as measured by EEG; see Chapter 2) and changed the diameter of their blood vessels.

Such remarkable feats have led many researchers to investigate whether biofeedback can be used to help patients suffering from various diseases (Olton & Noonberg, 1980). Some epileptics, for example, have been able to learn to control a specific type of EEG rhythm that is associated with seizures (a 12- to 14-cycle-per-second wave that appears over the motor cortex) and have had fewer seizures as a

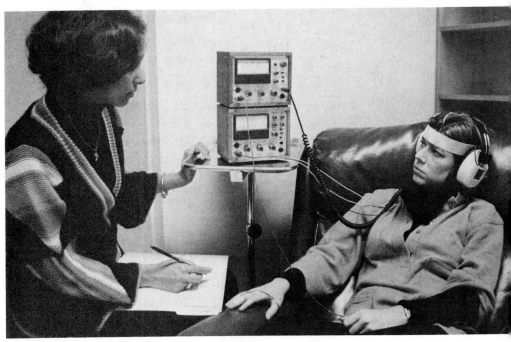

A biofeedback patient learns to control physiological responses with the help of precise information (feedback) regarding physiological states.

result. Biofeedback has also been successfully used in some cases to help people regain use of muscles that were damaged by accident or disease.

When you feel anxious or under stress, you may tense many muscles in the body, including the frontalis muscle in your forehead. Biofeedback training to reduce this muscle tension has been used to treat many types of disorders, including insomnia, chronic anxiety, certain types of headaches, asthma, and high blood pressure.

At this point, it is clear that biofeedback therapy has helped some people learn to relax and overcome some of the effects of stress. What is not so clear is what makes biofeedback therapy work. Some skeptics believe that the biofeedback may be less important than factors such as the patient's commitment to getting better and active involvement with the therapist. Some of these issues will become clearer later, when we discuss the biofeedback treatment of high blood pressure. But first, let us consider an alternative form of relaxation training—meditation.

Meditation. Biofeedback is a twentieth-century American approach to stress reduction, involving expensive and sophisticated technology. In contrast, **meditation** involves techniques of internal reflection whose roots are found in religious practices that are thousands of years old.

Keith Wallace (1970) was one of the first scientists to study meditation. He himself practiced transcendental meditation, a technique that Maharishi Mahesh Yogi introduced in the United States in the 1960s. For his PhD thesis at the University of California at Los Angeles, Wallace compared the physiological states of people while they were relaxing and while they were meditating. He found that meditation produced a uniquely relaxed physiological state characterized by decreased heart rate and oxygen consumption and specific EEG changes.

Later investigations verified and extended these basic findings. The findings are all the more impressive when you consider how uncomfortable it can be to participate in physiological experiments of this sort. One early study (Wallace, Benson, & Wilson, 1971) required meditators to wear a tight-fitting mask (to measure respiration), have a needle stuck in their arm (to measure blood chemistry), and sit on a rectal thermometer (to measure body temperature). Despite the discomfort one might expect, these meditators gave evidence of a deep state of relaxation.

Herbert Benson (1975) went on to demystify meditation and develop a simple meditative technique of his own. Benson argues that many forms of meditation elicit a specific physiological reaction, which he called the **relaxation response.** The opposite of Walter Cannon's fight-or-flight response (see Chapter 2, p. 55) the relaxation response was said to be physiologically distinct from more casual states of relaxation or sleep. Four basic elements are required to elicit the relaxation response: a quiet environment, a comfortable position, a mental device (such as a word repeated over and over again or a physical object that the meditator concentrates on), and a passive attitude. Benson particularly emphasized this last element; the person should not try too hard to relax, should not be disturbed by thoughts that intrude on his reverie.

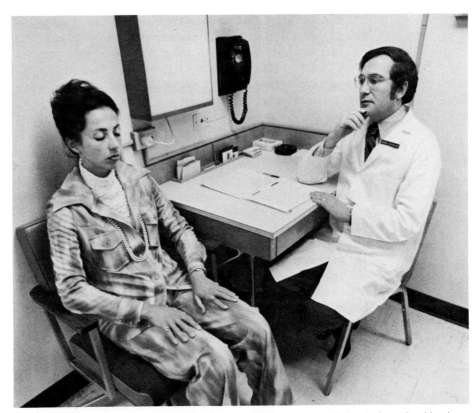

Physician Herbert Benson is shown with a patient who practices meditation to lower her blood pressure. Benson's procedure for eliciting the relaxation response is summarized in the following instructions (quoted in Hassett, 1978, p. 35):

Sit quietly in a comfortable position. Close your eyes. Deeply relax all your muscles, beginning at your feet and progressing up to your face. Keep them deeply relaxed.

Breathe through your nose. Become aware of your breathing. As you breathe out, say the word "one" silently to yourself. Continue for 20 minutes. You may open your eyes to check the time but do not use an alarm. When you have finished, sit quietly for several minutes, at first with closed eyes and later with opened eyes.

Do not worry about whether or not you are successful in achieving a deep level of relaxation. Maintain a passive attitude and permit relaxation to occur at its own pace. Expect distracting thoughts. When these distracting thoughts occur, ignore them and keep repeating "one."

Practice the technique once or twice daily, but not within two hours after a meal, since the digestive processes seem to interfere with elicitation of anticipated changes.

Throughout history, Benson said, men and women have used the relaxation response. He cited as examples the contemplative practices of St. Augustine and Martin Luther's instructions for prayer. But not all researchers agree that the relaxation response is physiologically unique; some feel it is quite closely related to sleep (Pagano, Rose, Stivers, & Warrenburg, 1976). In any case, it is clear that meditation reduces stress for some people and can be beneficial to health (Orme-Johnson & Farrow, 1977).

The fact that biofeedback, relaxation, and other psychological techniques have proved useful in the treatment of many physical diseases helped lead to the formation of a new medical specialty called behavioral medicine.

Behavioral Medicine

Behavioral medicine is concerned with understanding the role of psychological factors and behavior patterns in physical illness. Researchers in this area often emphasize the practical aspect of changing behavior to cure or prevent disease. Although psychologists have studied health-related problems for many years, it was only in the late 1970s that behavioral medicine was formally defined as a separate field (Schwartz & Weiss, 1977).

The success of twentieth-century medicine has actually changed the major causes of death in this country as well as the problems doctors face (Sexton, 1979). In 1900, more people in the United States died of influenza, pneumonia, and tuberculosis than of any other illnesses. In 1973, the three leading causes of death in the United States were heart disease, cancer, and stroke. While doctors at the turn of the century struggled primarily with contagious diseases, today's major medical problems have more subtle causes. To provide a concrete picture of what behavioral medicine can contribute, we focus here on its approach to a single medical problem, high blood pressure.

Blood pressure is the force exerted as blood moves away from the heart, pushing against the artery walls. One factor that can raise blood pressure is psychological stress; visiting the dentist, taking an examination, thinking about how much money you had to borrow to go to college, even drinking a cup of coffee (a mild stimulant) will increase blood pressure temporarily. When blood pressure goes up and stays above normal levels, this medical condition is called **high blood pressure** or **hypertension.**

About 1 out of every 3 American adults has high blood pressure. It is particularly common among blacks, older people, and those with a family history of hypertension. Hypertension is called "the silent killer" because it usually produces neither pain nor any other symptoms or warnings before causing severe damage to the cardiovascular system or other organs. But a killer it is. It is a primary cause of stroke (blood-vessel damage in the brain) and, like smoking and high cholesterol levels, increases the risk of heart attack and coronary artery disease.

Most serious cases of hypertension require drug therapy to return blood pressure to safer levels. However, there is no drug that can cure hypertension permanently; if a patient stops taking his pills, his blood pressure will rise again.

This is where behavioral medicine comes into the picture. The patient with definite hypertension must take drugs every day for the rest of his life. But 50% or more of all hypertensives fail to take their pills. There are many possible reasons: they may not understand the treatment, they may find it too expensive or too much trouble, or they may be bothered by side effects.

One study of an inner-city hypertension clinic found a dropout rate of 42%. Researchers discovered that part of the problem was the inefficient way the clinic was run. The average waiting time to see a doctor was $2\frac{1}{2}$ hours, and the patient was likely to see a different physician at each visit. Simply by cutting down the waiting time and assigning each patient to a specific doctor, the clinic cut its dropout rate to 4% (Wingerson, 1977). Future improvements in twentieth-century medicine may have more to do with restoring the personal touch than with inventing ever more sophisticated machines and treatments.

Behavioral medicine has also proposed alternate techniques for treating high blood pressure without pills. These include blood pressure biofeedback, electromyographic (EMG) biofeedback for reducing tension in the frontalis muscle in the forehead, relaxation training, and meditation. Because all these techniques produce similar effects (Agras & Jacob, 1979) and biofeedback requires physiological measurement devices whereas the other techniques do not, it seems likely that meditation and relaxation will be more widely practiced.

How do biofeedback and meditation compare with more traditional medical treatments? According to one review (Jacob, Kraemer, & Agras, 1977), relaxation reduces blood pressure far more than placebos do (indicating that relaxation involves more than the power of suggestion) and even compares favorably with some drugs. This report also notes that regular practice is necessary for the development and maintenance of the treatment effect, which builds up gradually over a period of several months.

This idea of regular practice over an extended period of time is the one great weakness of biofeedback treatment. Even in the very first study of blood pressure biofeedback, there were hints that the effects did not always last after the subjects left the laboratory. Psychologist Gary Schwartz noticed that one man had a puzzling pattern of successes and failures. Five days a week, this hypertensive gentleman faithfully attended training sessions, collecting $35 from the researcher every Friday as a reward for his success in lowering his systolic pressure. When he returned each Monday morning, however, he again had a high blood pressure reading. After several weeks of this, Schwartz took the patient aside and asked for an explanation. It seemed that on Saturday nights the man took his biofeedback earnings to the racetrack, gambled, and lost both his money and his controlled level of blood pressure. Over the long term, then, the clinical usefulness of relaxation treatments and other forms of treatment depends not just on the biological issue of its immediate effects but also on the psychological question of whether people will continue to use it.

Whether we try to understand behavioral genetics, biological rhythms, drugs, stress, or other topics not mentioned here, the lesson remains the same. It is not productive to try to separate biology from psychology or to ask what is caused by nature and what by nurture. Human behavior does not recognize this simplistic dichotomy. Instead, scientists are now focusing on the way these factors work together to try to understand the intricate connections among body, brain, behavior, and experience.

Summary

1. Behavior is best understood by considering how psychological and biological factors work together rather than trying to isolate one from the other.

2. **Behavioral genetics** studies the inheritance of behavioral characteristics. **Genes** are the physical structures that transmit characteristics from parent to child. Hundreds or thousands of genes are grouped together on **chromosomes**—long, thin structures found in the nucleus of every cell.

3. Studies of human behavioral genetics often compare the behavior of relatives with various degrees of blood relationship or other ties (such as adopted children). One of the most powerful methods compares the similarity of **monozygotic** (identical) and **dizygotic** (fraternal) twins. Analyses like these allow geneticists to compute the **heritability** of a trait, a mathematical estimate of the relative importance of heredity and environment in determining a particular characteristic for a specific population. The heritability of the same trait can vary for different groups of people and in different environments.

4. There are three major types of biological rhythms. **Circadian rhythms** are cyclical changes in behavior or physiology that repeat themselves once every 24 hours or so. **Infradian rhythms** last longer than 24 hours, and **ultradian rhythms** last less than 24 hours.

5. The most basic circadian rhythm is the sleep-activity cycle. Sleep is divided into several physiologically distinct stages. During **REM** (rapid eye movement) sleep, the sleeper's eyes dart back and forth and there are many signs of physiological activity. People are more likely to report dreams when awakened during REM sleep than when awakened from one of the four non-REM stages. About 20% of the average adult's sleep is devoted to REM; it seems that all people dream, whether they remember it or not.

6. **Jet lag** involves discomfort or decreased efficiency caused by travel across time zones. Shift work may also alter circadian rhythms, producing stomach ailments, sleep disturbances, and other problems. Some people adapt more readily than others, but all find it easier to adapt to later schedules (as in westward travel) than earlier schedules.

7. A **psychoactive drug** is any chemical substance that influences feelings and actions by changing the chemistry of the brain. One classification scheme divides psychoactive drugs into five major classes: sedatives, stimulants, narcotics, hallucinogens, and antipsychotics. **Psychological dependence** refers to a compulsion to use a drug that is not based on physical factors. In contrast, **drug addiction** is a medically defined syndrome that includes **physical dependence,** in which withdrawal from the drug produces physical symptoms such as nausea and muscle spasms, and **tolerance,** in which increasingly large doses are required to produce the same effects.

8. At low blood concentrations, alcohol appears to stimulate behavior by depressing certain areas of the brain. These effects may be strongly influenced by psychological factors such as expectations. Higher doses lead to loss of coordination and judgment, anesthesia, coma, and death. In the United States, there are

8 to 12 million alcoholics, depending on how one defines the term. Professional help seems to increase an alcoholic's chances of bringing drinking under control, but there is some controversy about whether total abstinence is necessary for a cure.

9. To affect the brain, a drug must reach the bloodstream and pass through the **blood-brain barrier,** the structure in the circulatory system that prevents certain large molecules from reaching brain cells. After a drug reaches appropriate receptors, it usually influences neurotransmitter chemistry. **Endorphins** are natural brain chemicals that are structurally similar to opiates such as morphine. They are believed to be involved in the regulation of pain and may play a role in the placebo effect.

10. **Stress** is a perception of threat to physical or psychological well-being and the individual's reaction to that threat. Hans Selye described the body's physiological response to stress as a **general adaptational syndrome** divided into three stages: alarm, resistance, and exhaustion.

11. A **psychosomatic disease** is a physical illness caused by psychological factors; examples are ulcers, high blood pressure, migraine and tension headaches, asthma, and such skin conditions as hives and eczema. People who are subjected to important life changes are also likely to develop physical illnesses ranging from colds and influenza to heart disease, tuberculosis, and leukemia.

12. **Biofeedback** involves learning to control physiological states as a result of precise physiological information (feedback). It has been used to lower stress, primarily through training to reduce muscle tension. According to Herbert Benson, **meditation** requires four basic elements to elicit a distinct physiological **relaxation response**: a quiet environment, a comfortable position, a mental device, and a passive attitude.

13. **Behavioral medicine** studies the role of psychological factors and behavior patterns in physical disease. One example of how it is applied concerns **high blood pressure (hypertension)**—abnormally high levels of the force of the blood moving away from the heart, pushing against the artery walls. Behavioral treatments of this disorder include promoting compliance with medical orders, biofeedback, and relaxation exercises.

To Learn More

Ray, O. *Drugs, Society, and Human Behavior,* 2d ed. St. Louis: C. V. Mosby, 1978. Fun to read and extremely informative.

Fuller, J. L., & Thompson, W. R. *Foundations of Behavior Genetics.* St. Louis: C. V. Mosby, 1978. An excellent reference, but not a book for reading at the beach.

Brown, F. M., & Graeber, R. C., eds. *Rhythmic Aspects of Behavior.* Hillsdale, N.J.: Lawrence Erlbaum, 1982. Twelve scholarly chapters written by different experts on aspects of biological rhythms.

4
Sensation and Perception

About 300 years ago, philosopher John Locke described an imaginary experiment that might shed light on the question of how we perceive the world. Suppose a man who had been blind from birth was suddenly able to see. Would he immediately perceive the world as we do, as though a blindfold had simply been removed? More specifically, suppose that while he was blind, the man had learned to distinguish between a cube and a globe by touch. If these objects were placed on a table before him, could he say which was which? Locke thought not. He believed that direct experience was required for learning and that the tactile sensations produced by feeling a shape would not help to interpret the visual sensations produced by looking at it.

In fact, Mother Nature has actually performed this rather macabre experiment; there are about 100 documented cases of adults who have suddenly gained sight, usually as a result of surgery. One of the most intensively studied was a man known to science as S. B. (Gregory & Wallace, 1963).

S. B. lost his sight at the age of 10 months. He adjusted well to his blindness and lived a full and active life. Sometimes he even went for bicycle rides by holding the shoulder of a friend who rode alongside on another bike. But S. B. always longed to see the world in which he lived—the flowers in his garden, the tools in his shed, and the rich colors of the morning sky. Finally, at the age of 52, he underwent an operation to restore his sight.

When the bandages were first removed from S. B.'s eyes, he turned toward the voice of his surgeon and saw only a blur. During the next few days, the images gradually sharpened. At first, S. B. was thrilled and would sit by his hospital window for hours, just watching the world go by.

S. B.'s process of recovery suggested that Locke's guess was wrong; he did learn to recognize objects more quickly if they were already known by touch. He soon learned to read a clock on the wall, apparently as a result of the fact that he had learned to tell time by feeling the hands of a pocket watch. Even more convincing, S. B. rapidly learned to recognize capital letters he had previously learned by touch. Recognition of small letters came more slowly; S. B. lacked any experience with these shapes.

In some ways S. B.'s vision was never entirely normal. Like other patients whose sight has been restored, S. B. had trouble perceiving distance and depth. Although his hospital room was several stories up, he thought the ground was only a few feet away.

Similarly, S. B. did not perceive visual illusions the way most people do. For example, if you look at the two lines in the Mueller-Lyer illusion in Figure 4.1, one line will seem longer than the other even though they are physically equal. S. B. was not fooled by this or other common illusions (see Figure 4.22); to him, the two lines looked equal.

Sadly, like many others whose sight was restored in adulthood, S. B. became rather withdrawn and depressed after the operation. He loved bright colors but found much of the world drab. He brooded over all that he had missed, and he often sat in the dark at night, not bothering to turn on the lights. The difficulty he had trusting his new sense was most obvious when he had to cross a street:

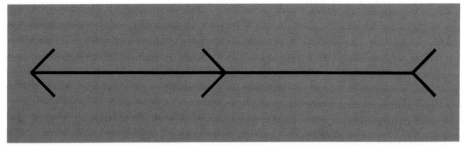

Figure 4.1
Do the two sections of this line look equally long? In fact, the center arrow is drawn precisely at the midpoint of the line. This is called the Mueller-Lyer illusion; like many other perceptual phenomena, it suggests that physical stimuli are actively interpreted by the human observer, sometimes incorrectly.

Before the operation, he would cross alone, holding his arm or stick before him, when the traffic would subside as the waters before Christ. But after the operation it took two of us on either side to force him across a road: he was terrified as never before in his life (Gregory, 1978, p. 197).

S. B. died a few years after the operation and never regained the contentment he had felt when he was blind.

For our discussion, one of the most interesting features of this case is the difficulty S. B. had with depth perception and other complex visual processes. Traditionally, psychologists have distinguished between two types of sensory processes. **Sensation** is the process of responding to a simple physical stimulus such as a spot of light or a musical note. **Perception** is a more complex process of actively interpreting a pattern of stimuli as an organized mental image. The fact that S. B. had trouble mastering perception underlines the complexity of organizing sensations into a complete picture of the world.

Although it is often hard to say where sensation ends and perception begins, the two have been studied in somewhat different ways. The biological paradigm has dominated studies of sensation; most focus on the way the physical structures of sensory organs are related to experience. While there have been many studies of the biology of perception, more commonly this research proceeds from a cognitive perspective, trying to understand the active mental processes involved in interpreting patterns of stimulation. In this chapter, we shall draw on these two theoretical perspectives and others as we explore the relationships between physical stimuli and the psychological sensations and perceptions they produce.

These relationships are not always as straightforward as you might expect. For example, if an electric shock doubles in physical intensity, it will feel more than 11 times stronger. This estimate comes from a precise mathematical formula that relates the psychological sensation to the actual electrical charge. Other formulas describe the relationships between the intensity of light and the sensation of brightness, between sound waves and loudness, and dozens of other sensory dimensions to the corresponding physical stimuli.

While you probably do not lie awake nights wondering what these formulas are, they have many practical uses. Electrical engineers who design stereo systems must understand how the physical characteristics of sound waves are related to loudness, pitch, and other sensory dimensions; and the lighting director for a play must understand the physical stimuli that are required to produce a certain psychological effect. Even food companies use these formulas in the never-ending search for the perfectly crispy cracker and the ideally spicy tomato sauce (Rice, 1978). The research area that explores these questions is called *psychophysics*.

Psychological Sensations and Physical Stimuli

Psychophysics examines the relationships between the physical attributes of stimuli *(physics)* and the psychological sensations they produce *(psycho)*. The science of psychophysics may be the oldest specialty in psychology; formal experiments in this field were published several decades before Wilhelm Wundt established the first psychology laboratory in 1879. One of the most important issues in psychophysical research involves establishing the limits of each of the senses.

ABSOLUTE THRESHOLDS

If you are sitting in the stands at a football game, you probably will not be able to hear what the players say to one another in the huddle. Some stimuli are simply too weak to be noticed. Early psychophysicists developed the concept of the **absolute threshold,** the minimum physical energy that causes a given sensory system to respond. Under ideal conditions, the human senses are extremely responsive. Table 4.1 provides one psychophysicist's everyday examples of the limits of the five major senses. These vivid analogies involve a certain amount of poetic license; in the real world, absolute thresholds are neither quite this straightforward nor quite this precise.

At first, researchers thought that these thresholds would prove to be absolute. Just as your TV set will go on only if you press the power switch with a certain amount of force, so it was thought that sensory receptors went on only when they were stimulated by a particular level of physical energy.

If things were really this simple, we might expect that whenever the minimum physical energy needed to create a sensation of light in the eye was flashed, people would say they saw it. Further, a physical stimulus below the absolute threshold would never be seen. In fact, the transition is not that abrupt. When you try to spot a very dim light in the distance on a dark night, you will often find yourself unsure about whether you have seen a light or not. Similarly, when visual stimuli near the eye's lower limits of sensitivity are presented in an experiment, sometimes a subject says she sees something and sometimes she does not.

There are several ways to measure absolute thresholds, and each is affected by this uncertainty in slightly different ways. In the **method of constant stimuli,** a number of stimuli of different physical intensities are presented in random order.

TABLE 4.1
Some Approximate Absolute Threshold Values

Sense Modality	Absolute Threshold
Light	A candle flame seen at 30 miles on a dark, clear night
Sound	The tick of a watch under quiet conditions at 20 feet
Taste	One teaspoon of sugar in two gallons of water
Smell	One drop of perfume diffused into a three-room apartment
Touch	The wing of a bee falling on the cheek from a distance of 1 cm

Note: In this table, precise psychophysical findings have been imaginatively translated into everyday terms (Galanter, 1962, p. 96). As the text explains, these are rough approximations.

After each trial, the subject indicates whether or not she has sensed anything. For example, in a hearing test using the method of constant stimuli, a person might listen to a series of tones of different physical intensities, such as 10 decibels, 6 decibels, 12 decibels, 14 decibels, 8 decibels, and so on; after each, she would indicate whether she had heard anything. (As explained in the section on hearing, the physical characteristic of a sound wave that is most closely related to loudness is called *sound pressure level* and is measured in decibels.)

Figure 4.2 illustrates the results of one such hypothetical test; not surprisingly, the subject's likelihood of reporting the tone gradually increases as the tone becomes louder. The S-shaped graph shown here (technically called an *ogive*) is characteristic of threshold measurements for every sensory system. For the method of constant stimuli, the absolute threshold is defined as the point at which a person senses a stimulus 50% of the time. This definition is based on convention rather than firm theoretical requirements; psychophysicists have simply agreed that this is the most sensible cutoff point. The subject in our imaginary experiment in Figure 4.2 has an auditory threshold of about 10.5 decibels for a tone of this frequency.

Other methods of measuring thresholds produce slightly different results, emphasizing the fact that these thresholds are not really absolute, and they do not reflect a fixed physical characteristic of the sensory system. Even such a simple task as saying whether a tone is present or absent involves a psychological decision that can be complicated by expectations, motivation, and other factors. The attempt to deal with these complications led to the development of signal-detection theory.

SIGNAL-DETECTION THEORY

Signal-detection theory attempts to account for both psychological and sensory factors that influence psychophysical judgments; indeed, precise mathematical pro-

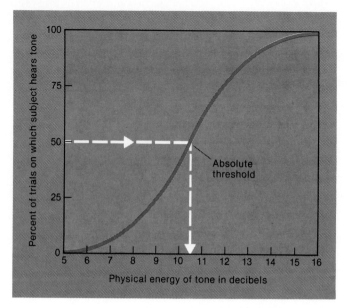

Figure 4.2
Data from an imaginary test of the absolute threshold of hearing. This subject sometimes hears the tone at many different physical intensities; the absolute threshold is the point at which the subject senses it 50% of the time.

cedures have been proposed to separate true sensory limits from more psychological factors.

Signal-detection theory grew out of engineers' studies of how people distinguished sensory signals from a background of random noise. (In this context, *noise* means any random disturbance of a particular process.) For example, in World War II, radar operators worked with relatively crude equipment that made it difficult to distinguish between a visual signal on a screen indicating that enemy aircraft were approaching and the random visual signals (called *noise*) caused by weather conditions or birds.

Suppose a radar operator aboard an aircraft carrier in the Pacific saw a speck on his screen. It might have meant that a kamikaze pilot in an airplane filled with explosives was heading for his ship, planning to crash into it. Even if the operator were not entirely certain what the radar signal meant, he would pass on the information so that his own fighter planes could take off and have a closer look. In this case the price to be paid for missing the signal was extremely high; the cost of a false alarm was less serious.

But as long as we are creating a fictional problem, let's make it a bit more difficult. Suppose that the American airplanes were low on fuel. If they took off to intercept a kamikaze and found a flock of seagulls, they might not have enough fuel to stop enemy planes later. In this case, the radar operator would be more conservative. As the cost of sounding a false alarm went up, his criteria would have to change.

In less melodramatic terms, the observer in a psychophysical laboratory is faced with a similar problem. Consider a typical psychophysical experiment. On some trials a tone is sounded; on others, it is not. The subject's task is to say whether or not he heard a tone. He can make two different types of errors. False alarms occur when he says he heard a tone when in fact there was none; misses occur when he says there was no tone when in fact there was one. Signal-detection theorists have shown

TABLE 4.2
Two Experiments in Signal Detection

| | | Experiment 1. | Faint tone is present on 9 out of every 10 trials; subject must say whether she hears a tone. Note high proportion of false alarms when signal is presented at this frequency. |

		Signal Present	
		Yes	*No*
Subject Says Signal Present	*Yes*	97% correct	62% false alarms
	No	3% misses	38% correct

Experiment 2.   Faint tone is present on 1 out of every 10 trials; subject must say whether she hears a tone. Note high proportion of misses under these conditions. The different error rates in experiments 1 and 2 show that expectations influence performance.

		Signal Present	
		Yes	*No*
Subject Says Signal Present	*Yes*	28% correct	4% false alarms
	No	72% misses	96% correct

Source: Galanter, 1962, p. 102.

how the proportion of different types of errors is affected by factors such as motivation and expectations.

Table 4.2 illustrates the results from actual experiments in which subjects' expectations were manipulated by changing the likelihood of a tone's occurring on each trial. The first example in Table 4.2 shows the proportion and types of errors for a study in which a near-threshold signal was presented in 9 out of every 10 trials. In that experiment, the subject got into the habit of hearing the tone and correctly noticed its occurrence 97% of the time. However, this expectation was so strong that she often heard a tone even when there was none; the false alarm rate was a distressing 62%. The second example in Table 4.2 shows that exactly the opposite occurred when a signal was presented in only 1 of every 10 trials. In that case, our psychophysical observer was nearly always right (96% of the time) when she said she heard nothing. But this mind-set was so strong that her miss rate—saying she heard nothing when the tone was really there—jumped to 72%.

Thus, expectations clearly influence the kinds of mistakes a person makes. The effects of motivation can be seen in similar experiments in which people are paid for each correct response and penalized for each error. If the penalty for false positives is high, the observer will tailor her performance to minimize them. If the penalty for false negatives is set even higher, she will work to minimize them instead. Signal-detection experiments have made it clear that you cannot eliminate error, but you can stack the deck so that one type of error is more likely to occur than another. Signal-detection theory also provides sophisticated mathematical tools for separating an observer's *sensitivity*, a true measure of the response of sense organs, from his *criterion*, the rules and guidelines he uses to decide how to label a given sensory event.

With the development of signal-detection theory, psychophysicists have put the human being back into the equation, to take account of the cognitive processes involved in even the simplest decisions. As we go on to consider the nature of vision, hearing, and the other senses, we begin with a simpler approach by concentrating on the physical characteristics of sensory receptors. But in the final sections of this chapter, we return to the more complex world of perceptual processes influenced by motivation, expectations, and thought.

Vision

What would the world be like if the human species did not have the sense of vision? Other animals are stronger, faster, and perhaps even meaner; the success of the human species has been largely a result of its intelligence. But one can only wonder how this intelligence would have been expressed if all humans lacked the detailed knowledge of the external world provided by the visual system. Could a species without eyes build the pyramids, sail across the sea, or invent sunglasses? Of all the senses, none has been studied more intensively than sight.

LIGHT

Each sense organ is designed to respond to a different type of physical energy. The eye, of course, responds to visible light, a particular type of electromagnetic radiation. Although physicists are still learning about the nature of light, we do know that only a few of the many types of electromagnetic radiation can be seen by the human eye.

One important physical characteristic of light is the **wavelength**—the distance from the crest of one wave to the crest of the next. Visible light varies from about 380 nanometers (millionths of a meter) to 760 nanometers. In contrast, X-rays are billionths of a meter long. Most of the energy that reaches the surface of the earth from the sun, however, falls within the visible spectrum.

Our understanding of the visible spectrum of light dates back at least to the seventeenth century. In the summer of 1666, Sir Isaac Newton went to Cambridge, England, to avoid an outbreak of the plague in London. He passed the next few months performing a series of elegant experiments that laid the foundation for modern theories of color vision. Newton cut a hole in a window shutter and directed a beam of sunlight through a triangular piece of glass called a *prism*, which separates white light into a spectrum of colors based on their wavelengths. A similar phenome-

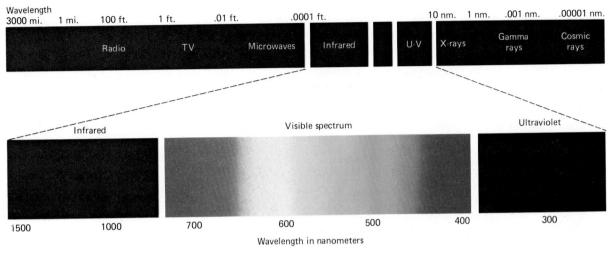

Figure 4.3
The human eye is sensitive to a small portion of the spectrum of electromagnetic radiation. Color perception is partly dependent on the wavelength of light within this range.

non occurs naturally when sunlight is bent by the atmosphere to produce a rainbow. Most of the time, however, psychological sensations of color are produced by more complex processes, as described later in this chapter.

THE STRUCTURE OF THE EYE

Figure 4.4 illustrates the structure of the human eye. The outer covering of the eye is called the **sclera,** a tough covering that protects the delicate structures within. Near the front of the eye, this protective layer forms the **cornea,** the curved transparent window that helps focus light as it enters the eye. The most frequently noticed physical structure in the eye is the **iris,** a circular arrangement of muscular cells that controls the diameter of the opening that admits light. The **pupil** is simply a hole in the center of the iris, which appears black. In dim light, the iris muscles contract and increase the diameter of this hole (to about 8 millimeters) to let in more light; in bright light, the iris can decrease the diameter (to about 2 millimeters) so that less light enters. Thus, the area of the opening that admits light is about 16 times greater at the maximum opening than at the minimum.

The diameter of the pupil also changes in response to emotional arousal. It is said that Turkish rug merchants have taken advantage of this fact for centuries. When a customer's pupils dilate as he looks at a rug, the merchant reads this as a covert sign of interest and bargains accordingly. Experienced rug buyers may wear sunglasses to hide the testimony of what researcher Eckhard Hess (1975) calls "the telltale eye." This shows that our sensory systems are influenced by other factors in addition to physical stimuli.

After light passes through the cornea and the pupil, it is filtered through a structure called the **lens,** a body of tissue that changes its shape to focus light on the

125

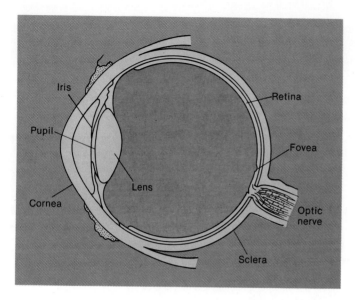

Figure 4.4
Major structures of the human eye are
illustrated in this diagram.

retina at the back of the eye. Normally the lens is slightly flattened and is thus ideally shaped for looking at objects at a distance. But when a person looks at a stimulus near the eye, the lens assumes a more rounded shape, which brings light rays from the object into sharper focus on the retina.

If the lens does not respond properly, visual defects result. As people grow older, the lens often becomes less flexible, thus less able to focus properly. Some people become nearsighted; they can see objects nearby but may need corrective lenses to watch TV or drive, activities that require focusing on faraway objects. Others develop the opposite problem of farsightedness; they may need glasses to read or sew, because of focusing difficulties with stimuli close to the eyes. These visual problems may also result from an eyeball that is too long or too short for proper focusing.

The Retina. The **retina** is a light-sensitive surface at the back of the eye. It includes two types of receptor cells that respond to light energy by firing electrical impulses in the nervous system. These receptor cells are named on the basis of their shape. **Rods** are rod-shaped with cylindrical tips, and **cones** have cone-shaped tips. Rods and cones are connected to bipolar cells, the next level of the nervous system that processes visual information (see Figure 4.6). Since several rods or cones are connected to a single bipolar cell in some parts of the retina, visual information is transformed at each step of its journey to visual centers in the occipital lobe of the brain.

The 6.5 million cones in the eye are responsible for color vision. The 125 million rods in the eye are more responsive than cones in dim light, but they can only distinguish black, white, and various shades of gray. This accounts for the black and white appearance of visual images seen in the dim light of night.

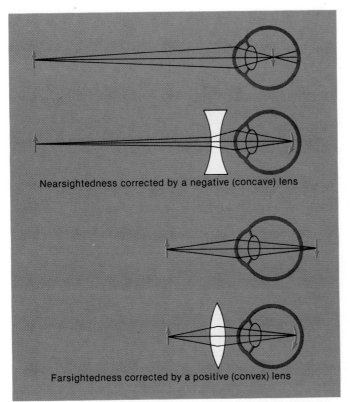

Figure 4.5
When objects are not focused properly on the lens, nearsightedness or farsightedness results. Either can be corrected with lenses that refocus the image.

Nearsightedness corrected by a negative (concave) lens

Farsightedness corrected by a positive (convex) lens

When you want to see an object clearly in good light, you look directly at it. This causes an image of the object to be projected on the **fovea,** a slight depression at the center of the retina. The fovea contains only cones and is more sensitive to fine visual detail than any other part of the retina. The cones are packed so tightly at the fovea that their conical tips are flattened to look like rods. But other sources of physiological evidence make it clear that not a single rod is to be found in this central portion of the retina.

The extreme visual acuity of the fovea is based on several factors, including the density of the cones and the fact that the blood vessels and nerve cells that cover the rest of the retina are absent here. A visual image is projected more directly on the receptor cells of the fovea than on other portions of the retina. Also, each of the cones in the fovea is connected to a separate bipolar cell, allowing highly detailed information to be passed on for further processing. Outside the fovea, several rods or cones may connect to one bipolar cell, and the messages passed on represent a summary of their activity.

Not too far from the fovea is an area of the retina called the **blind spot.** The blind spot has no receptor cells because nerve fibers are gathered here to form the *optic nerve,* which transmits information from the retina. Under normal conditions, you do not notice the blind spot because the brain fills in this missing information,

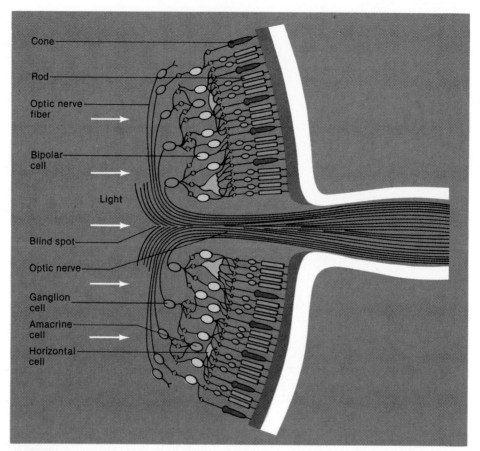

Figure 4.6
The layers of the retina. When light stimulates the rods and cones in the retina, signals travel through the bipolar cells to the ganglion cells, whose axons form the optic nerve. Integration is accomplished by horizontal cells, which connect rods and cones, and amacrine cells, which connect ganglion cells.

based on what is seen by both eyes as they constantly scan the visual field. But Figure 4.7 shows how easy it is to demonstrate that each of us does indeed have a blind spot.

Dark Adaptation. The fact that there are only cones in the fovea makes it more sensitive under normal lighting conditions but insensitive at night. Astronomers and navigators know that if you look directly at a faint pinpoint of light at night, it seems to disappear. Thus to see a tiny star in the distance, it is best to look slightly off to the side so that its image will be registered on the rods on the outside of the fovea.

The sensitivity of the retina gradually increases after a period in the dark, a

Figure 4.7
To demonstrate the blind spot, close the right eye, stare at the upper X, and move the book back and forth about 12 inches from your eye until the circle disappears. Now repeat with the lower X; at the same distance, the break in the bottom line will fall in the blind spot, and the line will appear continuous. This shows how the brain fills in information missing as a result of the blind spot.

phenomenon called **dark adaptation.** If you walk into a darkened movie theater from a well-lit lobby, your eyes will be so insensitive that you will have trouble seeing an empty seat. But if you wait a few minutes in the back of the theater, your eyes will adapt to the dark and you will be able to see quite well.

The change in sensitivity is dramatic; after 30 minutes in the dark, the retina may become 100,000 times more sensitive to light. In general, for the first 5 to 10 minutes in the dark, the cones become somewhat more sensitive. The rods adapt to the dark more slowly, reaching peak function only after 30 minutes or so. After the process of dark adaptation is complete, a weak stimulus in a dark environment may be detected only by the rods and therefore seems black and white.

Interestingly, the rods are less sensitive than the cones to certain extremes of red light. As a result, one can speed up the process of dark adaptation by limiting general illumination to long wavelengths. For example, during World War II, pilots often prepared for night missions by wearing red goggles that allowed only long-wave light to reach the retina. The fact that the rods were relatively insensitive to this red light allowed them to begin the process of dark adaptation. When the pilot took off, he removed the goggles, and the rods more quickly reached their maximum sensitivity for night vision.

COLOR VISION

Few people would choose to watch a TV program in black and white if a color version were just as cheap and convenient. A world without green grass, blue skies, and lavender tuxedos would seem harsh, drab, and, well, colorless.

Attempts to count the number of different colors that can be distinguished by the human eye have proved to be surprisingly complex. Psychophysicists have iden-

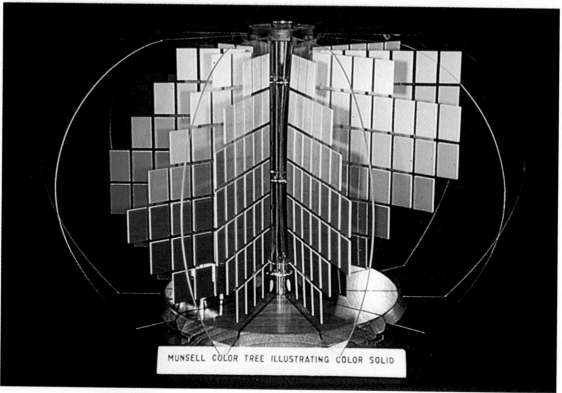

MUNSELL COLOR TREE ILLUSTRATING COLOR SOLID

Figure 4.8
The color solid displays three separate dimensions involved in the perception of color: hue varies along the circumference; saturation, along the radius; and brightness, along the vertical axis. Thus, a single vertical slice shows several possible saturations and brightnesses for a single hue.

tified three separate dimensions that contribute to the psychological sensation of color: *hue,* which corresponds roughly to color names, such as blue or red; *saturation,* the apparent purity of the color, as in fire-engine red versus a duller grayish red; and *brightness,* how dark or light a color is. Various three-dimensional color solids have been formed to provide a concrete feeling for the way hue, saturation, and brightness define color (see Figure 4.8). The human eye can probably distinguish about 7.5 million different colors (Nickerson & Newhall, 1943), but much remains to be learned about the precise way in which the visual system accomplishes this remarkable feat.

Theories of Color Vision. Soon after Sir Isaac Newton discovered that a prism would separate a beam of sunlight into several bands of color, he used a second prism to recombine this artificial rainbow back into a single beam of white light. Newton went on to explore the basic laws of color mixture by blocking part of the spectrum before recombining the beam and seeing how various combinations produced different colors.

In 1802, Thomas Young showed that he could produce any color from the spectrum by mixing only three different colors of light: red, blue, and green. (It is important to note that Young's laws of color mixture apply only to light. The complications introduced by mixing paints or pigments are described in Figure 4.9.) Young concluded that there were three basic receptors in the retina, one for each of these primary colors. According to this theory, a sensation of yellow would be produced by simultaneously stimulating the red and the green receptors, for example, and white would result from the simultaneous stimulation of the red, the green, and the blue receptors. This view has come to be known as the **trichromatic theory** of color vision, from the Greek word for "three colors."

In the 180 years since, Young's conclusions have been challenged many times but never completely rejected. The major theoretical alternative to the trichromatic theory was proposed by Edward Hering in 1870; **opponent-processes theory** holds that each of the three separate systems in the retina responds not to one color but to two. This theory was proposed partly to explain certain types of color blindness, such as the fact that some people have trouble perceiving red and green but can see

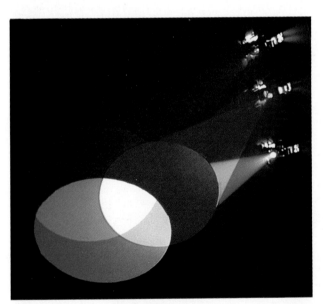

Figure 4.9
The effects of color mixture differ for lights and pigments. The term *additive color mixture* refers to the colors produced by mixing lights (shown on the left). Mixture of two colors produces the complement of the third, as shown in the triangular sections where the lights overlap. The term *subtractive color mixture* refers to the colors produced by mixing pigments or to light that passes through overlapping filters (shown on the right). While additive mixtures always produce the same colors, subtractive mixtures are less predictable and may vary for different filters.

yellow. Since the trichromatic theory claims that yellow is a mixture of red and green, it cannot easily explain this deficit.

Also, the trichromatic theory does not provide an explanation for certain **afterimages**—sensory impressions that remain after a stimulus is taken away. One example appears in Figure 4.10; if you stare at this yellow, green, and black version of the American flag for about 30 seconds in good light and then look at a piece of white paper, you should see the old familiar red, white, and blue version. A green image produces a red afterimage; a yellow stimulus produces a blue afterimage. The opponent-processes theory of color vision claims that there are three different visual systems, which respond to red-green, blue-yellow, and black-white. The afterimages are then said to result from a kind of rebound effect—when a green stimulus stimulates the red-green system and is then withdrawn, the red portion of the system reacts.

Recent physiological recordings have shown that both the trichromatic and the opponent-processes theory are true for different portions of the visual system. Three different types of light-sensitive pigments have been identified in the cones of the human eye; the first responds primarily to blue light, the second to green, and the third to yellowish and red light. This supports the trichromatic theory. But electrical recordings from the retinal ganglion cells and other visual cells deep in the brain

Figure 4.10
Stare at the center of this oddly colored flag for about a minute and then look quickly at a white surface. You should see a negative afterimage of the familiar red, white, and blue American flag.

support the opponent-processes theory. These cells seem to code opposing colors, for example, firing rapidly when stimulated by long-wave (red) light and not firing when stimulated by short-wave (green) light. Thus, color vision consists of at least two stages. The cones respond to three different colors, and this information is transmitted to brain cells that fire more or less frequently based on pairs of opponent colors. However, even this account is not the entire story.

Another phenomenon that emphasizes the complexity of color vision was accidentally discovered by Edwin Land (1959) when he tried to produce a high-quality instant color film for his invention, the Polaroid camera. In one experiment, Land superimposed the images of three color slides of the same scene, one taken through a red filter, one through a blue filter, and one through a green filter. When these three slides were simultaneously projected on the same screen, the colors of the original scene were reasonably well produced, as expected. But one day, the light from the blue projector was accidentally eliminated; at first neither Land, nor his assistant was aware that the colors had changed, although in fact they had.

Land went on to show that the color of many natural scenes can be reproduced when photographed through only two filters (red and green) instead of the three required by the trichromatic theory of color vision. If a bowl of fruit is photographed through red and green filters, bananas will look reasonably yellow, apples, red, and oranges, orange. But images of a color test chart (like the one you might get in a paint store) photographed in the same way will not look like the original. According to Land, this experiment suggests that color perception is influenced by memory and expectations; the banana in the unusual two-filter photograph looked yellow partly because everyone knows that bananas are yellow. If this explanation holds up, it will prove that an experience of color depends not just on the physical intensity and wavelengths of light nor just on photochemical changes in the retina but on a complex series of events in the brain.

Color Blindness. The fact that some people have trouble telling the difference between colors was not widely known until the late eighteenth century. Around that time, an English chemist named John Dalton reported that he had trouble recognizing certain substances by their color. (The French word for color blindness is *daltonisme*.)

The fact that color blindness was not widely noticed in ancient times suggests that the visual defect is usually rather subtle—few people are actually blind to all color differences. The most common problem involves an inability to distinguish between red and green. Like other forms of color blindness, this deficiency has been found far more frequently among men than women.

There are a few people who are truly color-blind and see the entire world in blacks, whites, and grays. Several sources of evidence suggest that these people have few functional cones in the retina; their vision is based almost entirely on rods. People who suffer from this rare affliction are often forced to wear dark glasses because the rods are overstimulated by normal daylight.

There are at least nine different types of color blindness, ranging from these severe deficits to various forms of color weakness, borderline problems in distin-

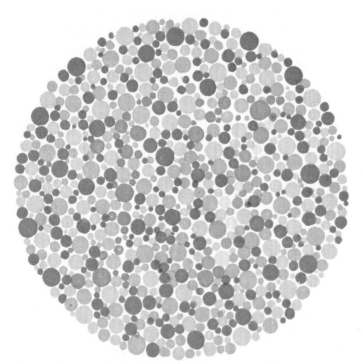

Figure 4.11
Two items from a test for red-green color blindness. The numerals in each plate can be distinguished from the background only by their colors. Red-green color blindness would be diagnosed if a person failed to distinguish 5 of the 14 items in the test. (The correct answers are 15 and 89.)

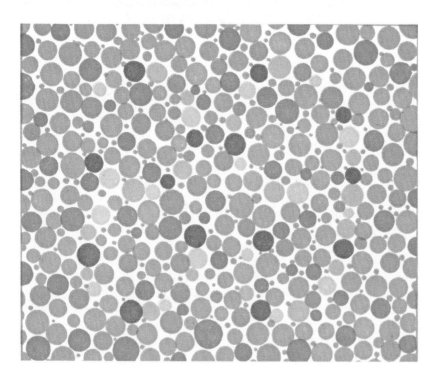

guishing reds from greens or yellows from blues. A person who is color-blind may be unaware of this visual defect without taking special tests that force him to make fine distinctions between specific colors. One such test appears in Figure 4.11.

Hearing

Superficially, Beethoven's Fifth Symphony may appear to have little in common with the sound of an automobile screeching to a halt or the loud whine of a 3-year-old who wants another chocolate peanut butter cup. But our ability to sense each of these stimuli depends on the physiological responses of the auditory system to the mechanical energy of sound waves.

SOUND WAVES

Perhaps the simplest way to think of a sound wave is to imagine what happens when one strikes a tuning fork (see Figure 4.12). As the fork vibrates, it creates waves of sound as air molecules are compressed by each vibration. In general terms, the frequency of the vibration (measured in *hertz*, abbreviated Hz—the number of times per second that it vibrates) determines the **pitch** of the sound, the psychological sensation that a sound is high (for example, a note played on a piccolo) or low. Although there are some exceptions and complicating factors, high-frequency sounds are generally perceived as high in pitch. Similarly, **loudness,** the psychological dimension corresponding to the intensity of a sound, is most highly related to the amplitude or physical height of a sound but also depends on other factors.

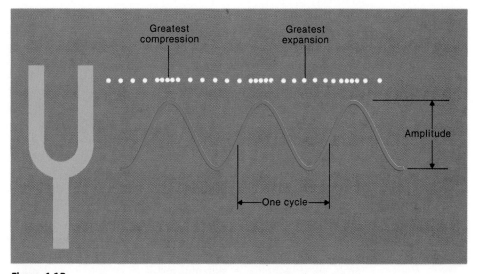

Figure 4.12
If you strike a tuning fork, its vibrations will alternately compress and expand the surrounding air, creating a sound wave.

More formally, we may define **sound** as a wave motion through a material medium (such as air) that is generated by physical vibrations. The speed of sound varies with air temperature; it is about 1,100 feet per second at 15°C. The speed of sound is about four times greater underwater and even faster through solid materials.

Frequency and Pitch. In general terms, humans can hear sounds in the range from 20 Hz to 20,000 Hz. Animals such as cats, dogs, and rats sometimes seem terrified by police sirens because these animals are sensitive to much higher frequencies.

One of the first to demonstrate the wider range of animal hearing was Sir Francis Galton, the English researcher who was involved in the development of IQ tests and genetic research (see Chapter 3). He developed a special whistle that produced sounds ranging from about 6,500 Hz to 84,000 Hz and carried it around wherever he went. Although Galton (1883) later admitted, "My experiments on insect hearing have been failures," he also reported that his impromptu studies of animals had greater success: "I have walked through the streets, and made nearly all the little dogs turn around" (p. 40).

Sound waves with higher frequencies are generally perceived as being higher in pitch. However, slight changes in the intensity of a pure tone of a single frequency may be perceived as changes in pitch rather than loudness. (A similar phenomenon is also found for other senses; increasing the brightness of a visual stimulus may change its perceived color slightly, even when wavelength is held constant.) In the real world of clashes, bangs, and country and western music, pure tones of only one frequency rarely occur. Even one key on a piano produces a complex tone characterized by one dominant frequency combined with many other sound-wave components.

Amplitude and Loudness. The physical intensity of sound waves is usually expressed in terms of *decibels*, a unit of measurement developed by telephone researchers and named after Alexander Graham Bell. According to one widely used decibel scale, 0 decibels is the threshold of hearing for the average young adult. (The human ear is more sensitive to some frequencies than others, so the actual physical intensity of the zero point varies according to frequency.) Figure 4.13 shows the physical intensity of some common sounds as measured on this scale. Obviously, sounds get louder as the number of decibels increases.

Under ideal conditions, the ear, like the eye, is about as sensitive as it possibly could be. If the eardrum were any more sensitive, we might sometimes hear the sound of blood passing though vessels in the ear (Green, 1976).

THE STRUCTURE OF THE EAR

When most of us think of the auditory system (see Figure 4.14), we picture the external structures on either side of the head that hold up eyeglasses. In functional terms, these two folds of skin and cartilage are among the least interesting elements of the auditory system. About the only useful thing that you can do with this structure is point it in a certain direction to make a sound louder; the external ear is

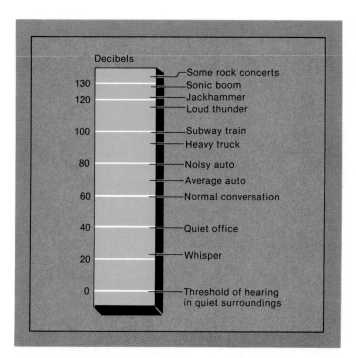

Figure 4.13
The decibel scale showing approximate values for familiar sounds.

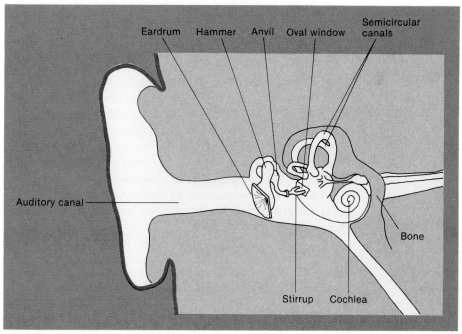

Figure 4.14
Major structures of the human ear are illustrated in this diagram.

merely a funnel that transmits the vibrations of sound waves to the auditory canal. Sound waves travel from the external ear to the eardrum (also known as the tympanic membrane) via the **auditory canal,** a tube about 7 millimeters in diameter and 24 millimeters long. If the auditory canal is blocked by wax accumulations or bony growths, hearing deficits result.

The **eardrum** is comparable in function to the diaphragm of a microphone; it vibrates in response to sound waves. The vibrations of the eardrum are transmitted through three tiny bones in the middle ear to another membrane called the **oval window.** The names of these three bones roughly describe their appearance: the *hammer* is connected to the eardrum and vibrates with it; sound waves are then conducted to the *anvil*, which transmits these vibrations to the *stirrup* and then to the oval window. (These bones are also referred to by their original Latin names, *malleus, incus,* and *stapes*.) These bones form a system of mechanical rods and levers that alters the vibrations somewhat but accurately transmits the original message and forms the basis of normal hearing.

This route of direct mechanical transmission from the eardrum to the inner ear is not the only way we hear. Even if the auditory canal is completely blocked, sound waves vibrate the entire skull and are thus transmitted to the fluids of the inner ear. This is a very inefficient route, but it does contribute to normal hearing.

If you have ever heard a tape recording of your own voice, you were probably disappointed enough to ask, "Do I really sound like that?" That is because the vibrations of the voice box are transmitted not just through air to the eardrum but also through the jawbone to the inner ear. This bone-conduction route adds another dimension to the sound of the voice; low-frequency components that make the voice sound fuller are especially prominent. As a result, your own voice sounds richer to you than to anyone else.

Hearing tests also take advantage of this alternative kind of hearing to diagnose certain auditory problems. In bone-conduction hearing tests, a vibrator is placed directly against a person's skull. Some people's auditory thresholds are normal when measured in this way, but they have trouble hearing through headphones. This implies that their auditory canal is blocked.

Several other ear structures are not primarily concerned with hearing. The **semicircular canals** help regulate the sense of balance and will be described later in this chapter. The **eustachian tube** runs from the middle ear cavity to the throat and is designed to equalize pressure on both sides of the eardrum. When the eustachian tube is blocked during a head cold, the eardrum may bulge or retract painfully as atmospheric pressure changes.

As Figure 4.14 suggests, the cochlea is the major auditory portion of the inner ear. The **cochlea** is a tube 35 millimeters long, coiled about $2\frac{1}{2}$ times like a snail shell. The walls of this tube are made of the hardest bone in the body. Sound waves are usually transmitted to the **oval window** of the cochlea through the stirrup bone. These vibrations move the fluid in the cochlea; this displaces the **basilar membrane,** which then translates these physical vibrations into a pattern of electrical activity in the nervous system. A number of different theories have been proposed to explain the precise details of this and other processes involved in hearing.

THEORIES OF HEARING

The nineteenth-century German physiologist Herman von Helmholtz was the first to suggest that vibrations of the basilar membrane are responsible for sensations of sound, and he also proposed the first explanation of how this occurs. Helmholtz believed that the basilar membrane contained fibers that were activated much like the strings of a piano. In the simplest terms, high sounds cause the short fibers to vibrate and low sounds affect the longer ones. This became known as the **place theory of hearing** because it suggests that different sounds activate different places on the basilar membrane. Other theorists later proposed an alternative. According to the **frequency theory of hearing,** the basilar membrane acts like the diaphragm of a microphone or a telephone; it vibrates as a whole in response to sound stimulation. According to this view, differences in the frequency of sound waves are directly coded by changes in the frequency of electrical firing in the auditory nerve.

Much of what we now know about the relative merits of these two theories is based on the work of Georg von Békésy. In one series of studies, Békésy drilled tiny holes in the cochleas of animals and human cadavers. He filled each cavity with a salt solution containing aluminum and coal particles so that he could use a microscope to observe movements of the basilar membrane. Békésy found that at very low frequencies (roughly, under 150 Hz) all portions of the basilar membrane respond at once, supporting the frequency theory. Higher frequencies, however, seemed to produce characteristic waves of basilar-membrane motion that affected some areas more than others, supporting the place theory.

Thus, just as physiological studies of color vision revealed that several processes were involved, studies of hearing have revealed that different aspects of sound are coded in different ways. Much remains to be learned about these and other processes involved in hearing the sound of a heartbeat or the voice of Barry Manilow.

APPLIED PSYCHOLOGY

Noise

On July 27, 1968, Biovanni Gatto just couldn't take it anymore. According to a report from United Press International in Palermo, Italy, the 44-year-old man "attempted suicide with an overdose of drugs . . . because his eleven children made too much noise while he was watching the Olympic Games on television" (Berland, 1971, p. 49). Few people react this melodramatically to the stresses of everyday life. But society seems increasingly aware of noise pollution, and researchers are trying to determine just how harmful chronic noise really is.

The most obvious effect of prolonged exposure to loud noise is deafness. This phenomenon was noted as early as the nineteenth century, when doctors reported that many weavers in noisy textile mills gradually lost their hearing. According to one conservative estimate, people who are exposed to noise levels over 80 decibels for eight hours each day will have some permanent loss of hearing. The time course of the loss depends on both the individual and the type of noise (Green, 1976).

The Occupational Safety and Health Administration (OSHA, 1971) has set standards for acceptable levels of noise in American industry. Depending on the dominant frequency of the noise, the maximum levels range from 85 to 100 decibels.

Interestingly, sound levels at rock concerts and nightclubs often exceed these recommendations. In one study of rock musicians (Kryter, 1970), temporary partial losses of hearing were found immediately after a performance. When these same musicians were tested at other times, the hearing loss was less serious but still noticeable.

While the extreme noise levels that can cause deafness are now reasonably well understood, there is still a great deal of controversy about more subtle effects of somewhat lower noise levels. Laboratory studies have revealed that the effects of noise on performance vary from one situation to the next. Even very loud noises often do not affect performance on simple tasks (like pressing a button as quickly as possible after a light comes on). In fact, performance on very boring tasks may actually improve in a noisy environment, possibly because the racket keeps subjects awake and alert. Performances on more complex tasks (such as multiplying long strings of numbers) and those that require a high degree of attention (such as watching carefully for a specific light) are more likely to suffer under noisy conditions. Unexpected noises over which the subject has no control are particularly likely to disrupt performance (Glass & Singer, 1972).

Early psychological studies of noise were primarily concerned with its effects on industrial and military performance and concentrated on the kinds of simple tasks described above. But in recent years, many psychologists have begun to study the long-term effects of living in noisy cities and have turned to more complex behaviors. For example, several social psychologists have found that people are less friendly and helpful in noisy environments. In one field study (Mathews & Canon, 1975), a student wearing a cast on his arm dropped a pile of books and papers. Under low-noise conditions (about 50 decibels), 80% of those who passed by offered to help. But when a noisy lawn mower was running nearby (increasing the background noise to 87 decibels), only 15% of those who passed by were this helpful.

One of the most disturbing studies of chronic urban noise (Cohen, Glass & Singer, 1973) considered its effects on elementary school children who lived in the Bridge Apartments in New York, four high rises that were built directly over the Cross Bronx Expressway, a heavily traveled road that leads to the George Washington Bridge (see Figure 4.15). The design of these apartment towers unintentionally produced an echo-chamber effect that magnified sounds from the highway underneath and made them very noisy places in which to live. In this study, average readings taken outside the buildings at ground level were about 84 decibels, near the border of sound levels that OSHA would consider unacceptable if they occurred in a factory.

This experiment analyzed the abilities of elementary school children who lived in these noisy apartments. Fifty-four children were given a special test of auditory discrimination. Each child listened to 40 tape-recorded pairs of words and was asked whether the two words were the same or different. Ten of the word pairs were identical; the other 30 were only slightly different, such as *gear/beer* and *cope/coke.*

Figure 4.15
The Bridge Apartments in New York City are the four high-rise buildings in the center of this photo. The Cross-Bronx Expressway passes directly under these buildings and leads to the George Washington Bridge. Sound levels from traffic noise averaged 66 decibels behind closed windows on the eighth floor. Children who grew up on the lower (and noisier) floors scored lower on certain auditory-discrimination tests conducted in a quiet environment.

For the 34 children who had lived in the Bridge Apartments for at least four years, there was a significant correlation ($r = .48$) between the floor they lived on and their score on the discrimination test. Even though the children took this test in school under identical conditions, those who lived in the noisier apartments on the lower floors made more mistakes.

Interestingly, the 20 children who had lived there three years or less did not show this relationship. A separate series of statistical tests verified that the longer the children had lived in the Bridge Apartments, the more trouble they had making these auditory discriminations. After ruling out a number of other explanations (such as the possibility of mild carbon monoxide poisoning from automobile fumes on the lower floors), these researchers suggested that children in the noisier apartments learned to pay less attention to auditory cues. This helped them to adapt to their apartments, but it also gave them less practice distinguishing speech sounds.

Another study tested the abilities of third- and fourth-graders from "the four noisiest elementary schools in the air corridor of Los Angeles International Airport" (Cohen, Evans, Krantz, & Stokols, 1980, p. 232). Even in quiet surroundings, these children had higher blood pressures than a control group and were more likely to give up when they were given a difficult puzzle to solve. Thus, urban noise is more than just an annoyance; it can lead to learning deficits and physiological symptoms of stress.

The Other Senses

At least since Aristotle, many people have spoken of five major senses: vision, hearing, taste, smell, and touch. Psychologists accept the first four but substitute four separate skin senses (pressure, warmth, cold, and pain) for touch and add two internal senses, balance and muscle movement.

TASTE

A gourmet's delight in savoring veal piccata or an anchovy pizza is only partly based on the sense of taste. As anyone who has ever had a cold knows, the sense of smell is essential for appreciating a fine meal. Further, the temperature of food, its texture, and its physical appearance all contribute to the joy of eating. The actual sense of taste is rather limited, consisting of only four basic sensations: sweet, salty, sour, and bitter.

Taste buds contain the receptor cells responsible for taste sensation. As Figure 4.16 indicates, different areas of the tongue are particularly sensitive to different

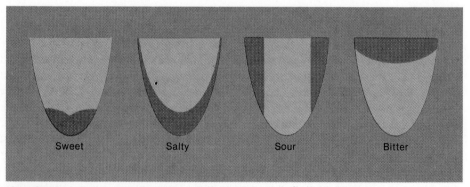

Sweet	Salty	Sour	Bitter

Figure 4.16
This map depicts the tongue's areas of maximum sensitivity to four basic tastes.

tastes. The tip of the tongue is most sensitive to salty tastes, for example, and the rear, to bitter. Other taste buds are located on the cheeks, lips, tonsils, and elsewhere throughout the mouth, but these areas are far less sensitive than the surface of the tongue.

Taste sensations can also be produced by some rather odd stimuli. Electrical stimulation of certain taste buds can produce either sour or soapy tastes, depending on the direction in which the current flows. Injections of certain drugs can produce sweet or bitter tastes. These demonstrations remind us that the inner world of experience does not necessarily mirror external stimulation; sensations result from electrical and chemical events in the nervous system.

There are wide variations in taste sensitivity; some of us may be "taste-blind" for specific substances. This phenomenon was discovered in 1931 when two chemists in the duPont laboratories accidentally spilled a substance called PTC (phenyl thiocarbamide). One chemist noted that it gave the air a bitter taste, while another noticed nothing. Further investigation revealed that thresholds to PTC vary widely; everyone can taste it sooner or later, but some people only notice high concentrations. The fact that most people do not know whether or not they are taste-blind again calls attention to the modest role of taste sensations in human affairs.

SMELL

For many animals, smell plays a crucial role in locating food, enemies, and mates. Dogs, rats, and other animals have long snouts to help them follow scents on the ground. Their sense of smell is far more developed than ours; it is said that a bloodhound can track a man's scent for days, or even weeks, after he has walked along a certain path. As primates evolved to swing from trees, vision became more important for survival, and smell less so. In lower animals who still rely heavily on the sense of smell, the olfactory structures occupy a large proportion of the brain. In monkeys, apes, and humans, these structures are relatively reduced in size.

In insects, the smell of chemicals called **pheromones** can elicit sexual and other behavior patterns. These patterns are primitive and irresistible; if something smells like a female silkworm moth, a male silkworm will try to mate with it, even if it's only a piece of paper doused with a female silkworm pheromone called bombykol.

This kind of automatic and unthinking reaction does not occur in higher animals, but they too may respond to the odor of species-specific pheromones. A female dog in heat secretes a pheromone that powerfully attracts any male dog that smells it. Monkeys have also been found to secrete substances that seem to play a role in sexual attraction. Some studies have even raised the possibility that humans too secrete sexual pheromones, although the evidence to date is not conclusive (Hassett, 1978).

There are many less esoteric examples of human reliance on this forgotten sense. Many blind people, including Helen Keller, have claimed that they were able to identify friends and acquaintances by their odors. Recent experiments have shown that people who are married can identify their spouses' clothes by their odors, and parents can similarly identify the clothes of their children (Porter & Moore, 1982). Interestingly, nineteenth-century doctors sometimes diagnosed disease by the odor of their patients; yellow fever produced a butcher-shop smell, the plague produced a smell like apples, and typhoid patients smelled like freshly baked bread (Winter, 1976).

Olfactory receptor cells are located inside the top of each nasal cavity. They are stimulated by substances that are suspended in gases. Although there are many theories about how smells are sensed by the nervous system, little is certain. Attempts to categorize odors into nine basic groups (including categories of smells such as coffee, garlic, vanilla, and bed bugs), six basic groups (flowery, fruity, foul, burnt, spicy, and resinous), or four basic groups (fragrant, acid, burnt, and "goaty") all have problems accounting for some olfactory phenomena.

THE SKIN SENSES

The actual number of different types of sensations the skin can respond to has been a matter of controversy for centuries. The best evidence now available suggests that there are four separate skin senses: pressure, warmth, cold, and pain.

Although we usually think of the skin as one type of body tissue, in fact its appearance and structure vary widely. The sole of the foot may be tough and hardened, while the skin on the inside of the arm is soft and sensitive; the skin on the elbow is stretched tight, while around some stomachs it is considerably looser; the back of the hand is covered with hair, while the palm is usually hairless. Similarly, the sensitivity of the skin to pressure—a sensation usually caused by pushing on the skin—varies from one site to another. Areas like the lips and tips of the fingers are extremely sensitive to pressure, while the kneecap, abdomen, and chest are relatively unresponsive.

When the sensitivity of the skin is mapped by applying a small stimulus to one point after another, some points are found to be responsive to cold stimuli, while others are sensitive to warmth and not to cold. This is the major source of evidence for the claim that cold and warmth are separate sensations.

Paradoxically, when both warmth and cold receptors are stimulated at the same time, people experience a stinging sensation of intense heat. This can be demonstrated with a heat grill consisting of two sets of parallel pipes (see Figure 4.17). If cold water is run through both pipes, they feel cold. If warm water runs through both, they feel warm. But if cold water runs through one pipe and warm water through the other, a vivid sensation of heat is produced. A person who places his arm firmly against the grill may have a hard time holding it there, even if he is intellectually aware that the intense heat is only an illusion.

The most complex of the skin senses is pain. Although masochists and other connoisseurs of pain can distinguish many different types—including burning pain, cutting pain, stabbing pain, and throbbing pain—all these sensations are generally considered to be variations on a single sense.

In a delightful book titled *The Puzzle of Pain*, Ronald Melzack (1973) argues that "pain perception . . . cannot be defined simply in terms of particular kinds of stimuli. Rather, it is a highly personal experience, depending on cultural learning, the meaning of the situation, and other factors that are unique to each individual" (p. 22). As one example, Melzack cites a religious ceremony practiced in remote parts of India in which a man blesses the crops while hanging on a rope from strong

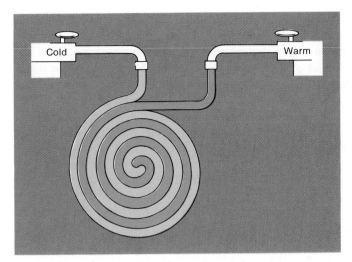

Figure 4.17
Cold water is run through one tube of this coil, and warm water through the other; if a person firmly places a broad area of skin—such as the forearm—against the coil, it will produce a feeling of intense heat. This demonstration of paradoxical heat suggests that the sensation of heat is produced by the simultaneous stimulation of skin receptors for warmth and cold.

steel hooks embedded in his back. The exhilarated participant seems to feel no pain. Closer to home, a football player who hurts his arm in a big game is likely to experience far less discomfort than a person who gets a comparable bruise by walking into a door.

One laboratory study explored social influences on pain perception by comparing the pain thresholds of Boston housewives from several different ethnic backgrounds (Sternbach & Tursky, 1965). These women were asked to rate the pain of electric shocks that gradually increased in intensity until they were unwilling to tolerate any more. In keeping with the attitudes from similar groups in earlier studies, the Italian-American housewives had significantly lower pain thresholds than the others. Physiological responses differentiated the groups in other ways. For example, Yankee and Irish-American housewives tolerated the same amount of pain, but the Yankee women were less reactive physiologically (measured by sweat-gland responses), reflecting their "phlegmatic, matter-of-fact" attitude toward pain. Like other studies, this experiment shows that learning and expectations play an important role in sensations of pain.

INTERNAL BODILY SENSATIONS

The familiar senses reviewed to this point translate physical stimuli in the external world into psychological sensations. But there are several other classes of sensation that originate within the body.

The **kinesthetic sense** is a sense of body movement and position based on feedback from the muscles, joints, and tendons. Proper function of the kinesthetic sense is required to walk up a flight of stairs or lift a hammer. It is ironic that the first psychophysical research—Ernst Weber's experiments in 1834 on the difference thresholds for holding weights—concentrated on this minor sense.

The **visceral sense** provides feedback from internal organs and is responsible for such delights as gas pains, cramps, and pressure in the bladder.

The **vestibular sense** provides information about the pull of gravity and helps maintain balance. Major organs involved in balance are the **semicircular canals** and the **vestibular sacs** of the inner ear. Fluids within these structures move when the body rotates or the head is tilted. These fluids stimulate hair cells within the inner ear that can cause dizziness.

An understanding of the workings of the vestibular sense is particularly important in aviation, where unusual feedback in the inner ear may deceive the normal observer. For example, blindfolded airplane passengers typically report that a plane feels like it is tilting forward when it slows down (Clark & Graybeil, 1949). Under conditions of poor visibility, pilots must be aware of how these vestibular illusions work so that they know when the sense of balance can be trusted and when it cannot.

Principles of Perception

Perception is the process of interpreting a pattern of stimuli as an organized whole. When you look at a photograph of your mother's face, the retina of your eye responds to a large number of spots of light and contours. But you are not aware of these elementary sensations; you simply see dear old Mom.

Some researchers have attempted to explore the biological basis of the complex process, particularly regarding visual perception. As noted earlier, stimulation by a spot of light causes an electrochemical response in a rod or a cone. This in turn stimulates a bipolar cell, which stimulates a ganglion cell in the retina, which stimulates other cells deeper in the brain. At each stage in this chain, visual information from earlier stages is summarized and transformed.

Beginning in the late 1950s, David Hubel and Thorsten Wiesel charted the pathways from eye to brain by recording the electrical activity of individual cells in the visual system. In a typical experiment, an anesthetized cat or monkey would stare at various patterns of light on a screen while Hubel and Wiesel (1979) recorded the electrical activity of a particular neuron, observing how it responded to different types of stimuli.

Painstaking experiments over several decades gradually revealed several different categories of cells arranged in a hierarchy of complexity; cells farther from the retina responded to increasingly complex classes of stimuli. In the retina and the first few neurons in the chain, a particular cell would fire when stimulated by a spot of light that fell on a specific area of the retina. Farther along in the chain, they identified three different types of cells: *simple cells*, which respond to a bar of light with a particular orientation—such as vertical or horizontal—in a particular location; *complex cells*, which respond to a bar of light with a particular orientation regardless of its location; and *hypercomplex cells*, which respond to a bar of light with a particular orientation only if it has a particular length and width.

For our purposes, the major conclusion from Hubel and Weisel's research is that visual processing in the brain proceeds hierarchically, cells later in the chain responding to increasingly complex stimuli. Thus, the eye does not transmit a miniature replica of a stimulus for the brain to "look at." Instead, cells in receptor organs and throughout the nervous system transform information into codes of their own. Science knows more about the simpler transformations early in this chain than about the complex processes in the cerebral cortex that finally determine our perceptions. While our review of sensation emphasized the biological paradigm, the discussion of perception will focus on a more cognitive perspective, analyzing the nature of perceptual experience. Many of the laws that govern human perception were first discovered by a group of German researchers known as the Gestalt psychologists.

GESTALT PRINCIPLES

When Wilhelm Wundt founded the first psychology laboratory in 1879 (see Chapter 1), he hoped to discover the principles of the mental chemistry of conscious experience. Just as water is composed of hydrogen and oxygen, Wundt believed that the perception of a tree or a sausage could be broken down into basic psychological elements.

But in 1890, the German philosopher Ehrenfels argued against this kind of search for the molecules of the mind. He believed that a perception was more than just the sum of its sensory parts. For example, if you hear a song in two different keys, every note—and thus every single elementary sensation—will be different for the two versions. Yet you hear the same melody because the relationship among the notes remains the same. What is important, then, is not the elementary constituents but the overall relationship among them. To describe this phenomenon, Ehrenfels used the German term *Gestaltqualität*, which can be roughly translated as "form quality." A number of German psychologists pursued the implications of Ehrenfels's analysis, and by the 1920s they had developed a series of observations and theories now known as Gestalt psychology.

Grouping. In 1925, Gestalt psychologist Max Wertheimer described several major principles by which the human mind grouped stimuli into patterns (see Figure 4.18). One major principle involved **proximity**—stimuli that are physically close

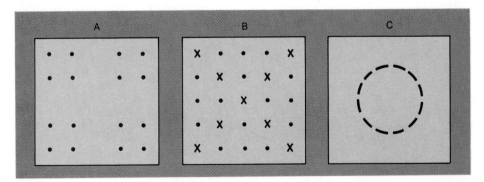

Figure 4.18
Gestalt principles. According to the principle of proximity, *A* should be perceived as four squares. According to the principle of similarity, the diagonals formed by the *X*s should be prominent in *B*. According to the principle of closure, *C* should be perceived as a circle.

together tend to be perceived as belonging together and forming a group. Another principle involved **similarity**—stimuli that resemble one another also tend to be perceived as belonging together and forming a group. According to the principle of **closure,** an incomplete pattern is often perceived as a complete whole. In these and other ways the human mind structures the sensory world according to its own internal laws.

Since vision is our primary sense, most psychologists have emphasized the importance of Gestalt principles of grouping for visual perception. But they can be applied to other senses as well. Imagine tapping a pencil with different patterns of pauses between beats: *tap/tap . . . tap/tap . . . tap/tap* versus *tap/tap/tap . . . tap/tap/tap.* Although the physical stimuli are the same, perception is based on their grouping. According to the principle of proximity, the taps that come close together tend to be perceived as parts of the same group.

Figure-Ground Relationships.   In the normal course of perception, some objects seem to stand out from the background. For visual perception, the object of attention, or **figure,** is usually seen as a distinct shape in front of the ground; it may even seem more solid and substantial. Again, these relationships show how the human mind imposes structure on physical stimuli and perceives them in terms of patterns.

In 1915, E. Rubin emphasized this distinction by publishing perhaps the first reversible figure, in which figure and ground can be easily reversed. As you stare at Figure 4.19, notice that whether you see the faces or the vase, the figure (that is, whichever object you see) seems to have well-defined boundaries and the ground does not. You may also see the figure as nearer and more substantial. These same phenomena can be seen in the more elaborate reversible figure painted by Salvador Dali (see page 116).

Figure 4.19
Rubin's reversible figure can be seen as a vase or as two faces, depending on which color is perceived as figure and which as ground.

As with the grouping principles, research and theory regarding figure-ground relationships have focused on vision, but the idea can also be applied to the other senses. When a restaurant critic tries to identify the herbs and spices in an unfamiliar chicken dish, her attention may shift from the hint of tarragon to the subtle aroma of basil, leaving the taste and odor of the chicken itself in the background. Or when a jazz fan concentrates on the classic album *Kind of Blue,* his attention may shift from Miles Davis's trumpet to John Coltrane's tenor sax to Bill Evans's piano; each instrument sometimes serves as figure and sometimes as part of the ground.

PERCEPTUAL CONSTANCIES

Other phenomena were also analyzed by Gestalt psychologists to show that the perceptual whole is different from the sum of its simple sensory parts; it is determined by the nature of the human mind. One important class of phenomena involves **perceptual constancy,** the tendency of observers to perceive an object as stable even when its sensory image changes. Here we shall concentrate on three of the most important ways in which changing objects appear the same: size, shape, and color.

Size Constancy. Suppose you are driving along a highway carefully observing the 55-mile-per-hour speed limit when a Toyota passes you doing 90. As this car speeds off to a fatal accident, its image on your retina will change dramatically. The Toyota image on your retina is largest when the car is right in front of you; the farther ahead it goes, the smaller the retinal image. Despite this obvious reduction in the retinal image, you do not perceive the Toyota as shrinking as it pulls away. This is an example of **size constancy,** the tendency to see objects as constant in size even when a visual image changes.

Size constancy is not perfect, as you can see by closing one eye and staring at your hand at arm's length and then bringing it toward your face. If you concentrate on this sensation, your hand may seem to get slightly larger as you move it in. But the relative increase in the retinal image will be greater than the slight change you perceive.

Several factors influence size constancy, including previous experience, attention to other cues, and physiological feedback from the lens of the eye. Previous experience and knowledge of objects is probably the most important factor. We know that baseballs are not 6 feet across no matter how big an incoming pitch looks as it approaches home plate. And we know that rock singers are not 2 inches tall, no matter how small they may look from the cheap seats in the balcony. Other cues promoting size constancy in this situation would include the view of the rest of the theater and the stage in the distance as well as physiological feedback from the lens as it changed its shape to focus on the pop star in the distance. Size constancy is always based on a compromise between retinal size and other clues about the actual dimensions of an object.

Shape Constancy. The speeding Toyota from our original example also illustrates the principle of **shape constancy,** a tendency to perceive objects as maintaining the same shape regardless of the view from different angles. If you watch the front of a car approaching in your rear-view mirror, then look at the side as it passes you, and finally watch the rear of the car recede into the distance, you will see at least three different views of the same object. Nevertheless, you continue to perceive the Toyota as having a single shape rather than a constantly changing appearance.

Similarly, if you flip a silver dollar and watch it carefully, your retinal image will change from a circle to an ellipse as it flips in the air. Yet your brain will not be confused by this ever-changing image, and you will see the coin as a simple object with a constant shape. Like size constancy, shape constancy involves the brain's judgment about an object based not just on the sensory image but on all available information, including previous experience.

Color Constancy.   To most of us, lemons look yellow whether we see them in bright sunlight, in the artificial fluorescent light of a supermarket, or through colored sunglasses. **Color constancy** refers to the tendency to see objects as retaining the same color under a variety of lighting conditions. In fact, the physical stimulus does change when lighting changes. If you looked at a piece of a lemon through a long, thin tube under the three conditions described above, and you did not know what it was, you would see three different colors. Like other perceptual constancies, color constancy is based partially on learning and memory and partially on other sensory clues (in this case, knowledge of the light source and the colors of other visible objects).

DEPTH PERCEPTION

The images projected on the retina are two-dimensional, like pictures printed on a page. But we live in a three-dimensional world of cube-shaped desks, cylindrical jars, and well-rounded opera stars. How are two-dimensional images transformed into a three-dimensional picture?

One of the most important factors in depth perception is **binocular disparity,** the difference between the retinal images of the two eyes. Since the pupils of the eyes are 2 or 3 inches apart, each eye registers a slightly different view of the same object.

One simple demonstration of binocular disparity involves looking at an object with one eye at a time. For example, if you hold a finger 6 inches from your face and close first the right eye and then the left, the finger seems to move. The closer your finger is to the eyes, the more it seems to move. When you open both eyes, the brain integrates these sensations into a single image. The disparity between the two retinal images helps the brain estimate distance; the closer an object, the more different it appears to the two eyes. This principle of binocular disparity has been used since the early days of photography to create three-dimensional pictures, known as stereographs (see Figure 4.20).

Figure 4.20
Around the turn of the century, stereoscopes, which produced three-dimensional images by means of binocular disparity, were quite popular. These advertisements appeared in the 1906 Sears, Roebuck catalog.

Figure 4.21

Interposition as a cue to distance. In the figure on the left, the king of clubs seems closest because it appears to block out the other two cards. On the right, one way to create an illusion: the king of spades is actually much closer, as suggested by its larger size. But the cards have been notched to make it seem that the king of clubs overlaps.

There are also a number of cues to depth that can be perceived by one eye alone and are thus called monocular. Several physiological factors, including **accommodation,** involve changes in the shape of the lens of the eye. To produce the sharpest possible image on the retina, the lens changes shape—it bulges to focus on objects close to the eye and flattens to focus on objects farther away. These changes are produced by the action of tiny muscles attached to the lens; when the muscles contract for near vision, kinesthetic receptors provide feedback to the brain. Accommodation of the lens provides information about distance only for objects that are relatively close, within 3 or 4 feet of the eyes.

For objects farther away, monocular cues depend not on physiological feedback but on the physical arrangement of objects. Four of the most important monocular cues to depth are linear perspective, aerial perspective, relative size, and interposition.

Linear perspective refers to the fact that distant objects seem closer together than nearby objects. If you look down a long road or a pair of railroad tracks, the two sides seem to get closer together in the distance. **Aerial perspective** refers to a slight blurring and tinge of blue in distant objects. If you look at the Rocky Mountains from downtown Denver, the mountains that are farthest away seem least clear and look somewhat blue.

The **relative size** of objects is also a monocular cue to depth; all other things being equal, larger objects are generally perceived as closer. If you see a large mountain and a small mountain in the distance, the large mountain probably seems closer. However, relative size may be overruled by other cues such as **interposition**—if one object blocks our view of another, the partially obscured object seems more distant. Therefore, if you see all of one mountain from downtown Denver and only parts of a larger mountain peeking out behind it, the smaller mountain is perceived as closer. A clever demonstration of how interposition can lead the brain to the wrong conclusion is shown in Figure 4.21. The visual system was designed to produce an accurate picture of the world, but it can be fooled.

VISUAL ILLUSIONS

The eyes are the windows through which we see the world, and the picture they provide is generally quite accurate. But the eyes and brain are quite consistently fooled by certain stimuli, occasionally with disastrous results.

One of the most dramatic examples was an aircraft collision that occurred over New York City in 1965, in which 4 people were killed and 49 injured. An investigation by the Civil Aeronautics Board concluded that this crash was caused by the pilot's misjudgment of altitude based on a well-known visual illusion. Figure 4.22 illustrates one version of the **Poggendorf illusion**—a continuous line seems to be misplaced when it is partially obscured. In the aircraft accident, two planes emerged from a sloping cloud bank. Although the aircraft were holding steadily at altitudes of 10,000 and 11,000 feet, each pilot saw the other plane emerge from the clouds on an angle and thought they were headed for a crash. As both maneuvered to avoid an accident, they did crash. The passengers and crews were thus the victims of a complex version of the Poggendorf illusion, a phenomenon discovered more than a century before (Coren & Girgus, 1978).

Psychologists have discovered many phenomena that consistently fool the eye and brain and have studied what each has to tell us about the nature of perception.

Figure 4.22
The Poggendorf illusion was discovered in 1860; the line is straight, although its ends seem displaced.

For example, some researchers have asked whether the Mueller-Lyer illusion (see Figure 4.1, p. 119) is caused by basic sensory processes in the eye or higher thought processes in the brain. One line of evidence for the role of brain processes is based on the fact that if people stare at the Mueller-Lyer lines for several minutes, the difference between them gradually seems to shrink. Porac and Coren (1977) asked people to look at the figure with just one eye until the illusion decreased. Immediately afterward, these people judged the difference between the lines through their other eye. If the original adaptation took place in the eye, the other eye should not have been affected and the illusion should have seemed as large as it had at first. But this was not the case. The subjects' second eye also judged the illusion as smaller, suggesting that some adaptation had taken place in their brain. However, other sources of evidence suggest that when defects in the lens of the eye cause images to blur slightly, the magnitude of the illusion increases (Coren & Girgus, 1978). Like many other sensory and perceptual phenomena, visual illusions seem to depend on a number of different processes at various levels of the nervous system.

THE EFFECTS OF EXPERIENCE

While some researchers have investigated the physiological basis of perception, others have focused on a more general question about the role of experience: Must we learn how to see or are we born with the ability to perceive the world? Several lines of evidence approach this problem in different ways.

Perhaps the most direct approach involves testing the perceptual capabilities of newborn infants. One researcher found that as early as four days after birth, infants spend more time looking at a simple picture of a face than at a similar picture with the mouth, eyes, and nose randomly scattered about (Fantz, 1961). This may mean that infants are born with a predisposition to attend to certain types of stimuli (see Chapter 8).

Anthropologists have investigated the role of experience in perception by studying people who have been raised in different cultures with perceptual histories far different from ours. Colin Turnbull (1961) described the reactions of a BaMbuti Pygmy on his first trip out of the dense tropical rain forest of the Congo. For his entire life, this man had never seen anything farther than a few hundred feet away, because of the dense foliage in his jungle world. When Turnbull drove this man to a plain, he pointed to a herd of buffalo grazing several miles away. From that distance, the Pygmy insisted they must be insects. When the buffalo appeared to get larger, as they drove toward them, the Pygmy muttered that it was witchcraft. Like S. B., the blind man whose sight was restored (see page 118), the Pygmy had never learned some of the perceptual constancies so familiar in our world.

Still another approach to understanding the role of learning in perception began in 1897 when psychologist George Stratton published the results of a rather odd experiment. Stratton had devised a system of lenses and mirrors that reversed the visual world—objects near the top of his visual field were now seen at the bottom, and objects actually on his right appeared on his left. For eight days, he walked around with this device over his right eye and with his left eye blindfolded.

As you might expect, the effect was quite disorienting. At first, even the simplest acts were extremely difficult. For example, when Stratton tried to pick up a pitcher that seemed to be on his left side, he actually had to reach to his right. Pouring a glass of milk became a major production, because the glass seemed to be upside down. On his first day, Stratton reported that he quickly became tired, depressed, and tense and that he avoided activity as much as he could.

By his third day of looking at this topsy-turvy world, Stratton began to adapt. He was able to write notes, despite their strange appearance, and he could walk around without bumping into every piece of furniture. By the fifth day, he had gained some confidence in his new perceptions—for the first time, he sat down in a chair without feeling it first to make sure it was really behind him. He mastered the art of putting the right shoe on the right foot by matching the shape of each foot to the appropriate shoe.

Although this adaptation was dramatic, it was never complete. For example, on the eighth and last day of the experiment, Stratton (1897) reported "I often hesitated which hand was the appropriate one for grasping some object in view, began the movement with the wrong hand and then corrected the mistake" (p. 466).

When he removed the reversing lens, Stratton was once again disoriented. The location of objects seemed "surprising" and "bewildering"—but not upside down. Thus, the aftereffects of this unusual experiment, like the original effects, were dramatic but incomplete. Stratton learned to function in the reversed perceptual world, but he never experienced it as completely normal.

In later research with devices that altered the visual world in a variety of ways, for longer periods than Stratton's eight days, some people were able to function surprisingly well. After wearing goggles that reversed right and left for several weeks, one show-off subject rode a motorcycle through the streets of Innsbruck, Austria, while wearing his goggles (Kohler, 1962). But this dramatic demonstration did not involve total reversal; it was probably a case of learning to function in a world where the rules were changed rather than totally restructuring perception.

One of the most important factors in perceptual adaptation is the opportunity for activity. In one study (Held & Bossom, 1961), people who wore prisms that displaced the world to one side were divided into two groups—half walked freely about, while the other half were taken over the same routes in wheelchairs. Subjects who walked around gave evidence of the usual aftereffects—their world had been slightly displaced. But the passive subjects who had been wheeled about gave no signs of adaptation.

These studies of visual distortion show that even for an adult, adaptation is possible—experience can have an effect on the perceptual world. Some types of experience—involving active movement—are also likely to be particularly influential. Overall, studies of infant perception, cross-cultural comparisons of perceptual abilities, and studies of restored vision have contributed to our understanding of the way innate abilities are molded by experience. Like all complex forms of human behavior, perception is not based on nature *or* nurture but rather on the complex interplay of the two.

Extrasensory Perception

Several researchers have argued that another important category of awareness exists well outside the mainstream of accepted scientific knowledge. **Extrasensory perception** provides awareness of external events without the use of known sensory receptor organs. The abbreviation *ESP* is now familiar, but few realize that the term *extrasensory perception* was invented (by J. B. Rhine) only about 50 years ago.

In the 1920s, *Scientific American* offered a $5,000 prize to anyone who could convincingly demonstrate psychic abilities. A distinguished committee appointed by the magazine was particularly impressed by the abilities of Margery Crandon, the wife of a Boston surgeon. During séances held in a dark room, the spirit of Margery's dead brother Walter took over her body. Even as a dead man, Walter was the life of the party—his spirit hurled objects around the room, impressed his fingerprints on a piece of wax, and told dirty jokes.

After observing nearly 80 séances, the committee was prepared to award Margery the prize. But when the magician Harry Houdini sat in on a séance, he declared that Margery was using tricks and the prize was never awarded. The controversy over Margery continued for nearly 10 years, until one investigator discovered the trick behind her most impressive demonstration—Walter's mysterious wax fingerprints matched those of Margery's dentist, a frequent participant in her séances. Many researchers had staked their reputations on Margery's authenticity, and psychic research nearly came to an end right then.

The lessons of this scandal led a young researcher named J. B. Rhine to take a different approach. Rhine hoped to win scientific acceptance for this controversial field by demonstrating psychic phenomena in the laboratory, following accepted scientific procedures and standards. In most of his early experiments, Rhine asked people to guess the symbols on a special deck of cards. Sometimes, another experimenter looked at each card first; this was a test of **telepathy,** thought transmission from one person to another. On other occasions, the subject tried to guess the order of the cards immediately after they had been shuffled; these were tests of **clairvoyance,** in which physical stimuli are identified without using the known senses or telepathy. Rhine also was one of the first to use the term **parapsychology** (literally, "beyond psychology") to refer to research on occult or psychic phenomena.

In a 1934 book titled *Extrasensory Perception*, Rhine reported that some subjects in his laboratory had remarkable abilities to identify the hidden cards. The decks he used consisted of 25 cards—5 copies of each of 5 different symbols. According to the statistical laws of probability, subjects who guessed at random should be right about 5 times out of every 25. But several did far better. The most successful, a ministry student named Hubert Pearce, averaged 8 correct guesses out of every 25 trials over a total of 690 times through the deck. The odds against a performance like this occurring by chance are very large. Indeed, when Rhine combined the data from his eight best subjects, the odds were $10^{1,000}$ to 1 that the results did not occur by chance. It might seem that the controversy over the existence of ESP should have ended there; in a way, it was only beginning.

Psychologists at Princeton, Brown, Colgate, Johns Hopkins, and Southern

Methodist universities soon reported that they had tried to replicate Rhine's experiments but failed to locate anyone with ESP. Further confusion followed when Rhine himself tested more people; he was never again able to find such an intense concentration of psychic talent. Skeptics suggested that the early successes resulted from a lack of adequate scientific controls in the first tests. For example, some of the early decks of cards had been printed poorly, and subjects might have unconsciously noticed marks on the backs that gave hints about their identity. Rhine had another explanation. He believed that the tremendous excitement surrounding the first studies created ideal conditions for observing ESP.

In the half-century since Rhine's classic studies were published, many parapsychologists have followed in his footsteps. They now use computers and electronic devices rather than decks of cards, but subjects are still asked to predict hundreds or thousands of random events. Occasionally, some individual achieves a dramatic success. But whenever successful subjects have been retested, their ESP has disappeared.

This discouraging pattern has occurred even when researchers have tried to go beyond the narrow limits of card- or number-guessing tasks. In one study of dreaming (Ullman, Krippner, & Vaughan, 1973), a researcher tried to use ESP to communicate an image of a famous painting to a person who slept in another room in the same laboratory. Whenever the sleeper showed signs of rapid eye movements (a physiological indicator of dreaming; see Chapter 3), he was awakened and asked to describe his dream. Later, another experimenter studied the transcripts of the dreams and a series of eight paintings that included the one that had been "sent by ESP." This observer was asked to rank the paintings in terms of the appearance of their images in the dreams—number 1 for the painting that most resembled the dream content, number 8 for the painting with the least resemblance. For one particular subject, the correct painting was ranked in the top four for eight successive nights. The odds against this occurring by chance are 256 to 1. But when the same subject tried to repeat the performance on another occasion, there was no evidence whatsoever of ESP (Belvedere & Foulkes, 1971).

Thus, there are a number of reasons why most psychologists remain skeptical about ESP. Among the most important are the failure of attempts to replicate any single instance of ESP and the possibility of experimental fraud of the sort so common in early psychic research. Even the strongest supporters of ESP research agree that it had not yet been accepted into the scientific mainstream. One former president of the Parapsychological Association summed it up this way (Beloff, 1977): "As an academic discipline [parapsychology] remains precarious and peripheral" (p. 20).

Summary

1. **Sensation** is the process of responding to a simple physical stimulus, such as a spot of light. **Perception** is the process of actively interpreting a particular pattern of stimuli as an organized mental image.
2. **Psychophysics** studies the systematic relationship between the physical attributes of stimuli and the psychological sensations they produce. An **absolute**

threshold is the minimum physical energy that causes a given sensory system to respond. Different techniques for measuring absolute thresholds produce slightly different results.

3. **Signal-detection theory** proposes mathematical techniques to estimate separately two factors that influence sensory measures—*sensitivity*, the physical response of sense organs, and *criterion*, the guidelines an observer uses in labeling or classifying sensory events.

4. The major structures of the eye include the **cornea,** the curved transparent window that helps focus light as it enters the eye, and the **iris,** a circular arrangement of muscle cells that changes the diameter of the **pupil.** This allows light to pass through the **lens,** tissue that changes its shape to focus the light on the **retina,** the light-sensitive surface at the back of the eye.

5. Receptor cells in the eye are divided into two types. **Rods** are primarily responsible for night vision, and **cones** are primarily responsible for color vision. The **fovea,** a slight depression precisely in the center of the retina, consists entirely of cones and is very sensitive to fine visual detail.

6. According to the **trichromatic theory** of color vision, there are three types of color receptors in the eye—for red, green, and blue. The **opponent-processes theory** also holds that there are three systems for color vision, but each is thought to respond to two colors: red and green, blue and yellow, and black and white. Physiological recordings suggest that the trichromatic theory applies to the cones and the opponent-processes theory to brain cells.

7. Two important psychological dimensions of sound sensations are **loudness,** primarily determined by the amplitude of sound waves, and **pitch,** primarily determined by the frequency of vibration, measured in *hertz*—the number of vibrations per second.

8. The major structures of the ear include the **auditory canal,** a tube that carries sound waves from the external ear to the **eardrum,** tissue that vibrates in response to these waves. The vibrations are transmitted by the three bones of the middle ear—the *hammer, anvil,* and *stirrup*—to the **cochlea** in the inner ear. There are several major theories describing how the cochlea translates physical vibrations into sound.

9. Long-term exposure to loud noises can lead to deafness. Studies of children who live near noisy highways and airports have also revealed other deficits, including problems in hearing subtle differences between words and high blood pressure.

10. **Taste buds** contain receptor cells responsible for the four major taste sensations: sweet, salty, sour, and bitter. There are four separate skin senses: pressure, warmth, cold, and pain. Other senses include the **kinesthetic sense,** feedback from muscles, joints, and tendons regarding body movement and position; the **visceral sense,** from internal organs; and the **vestibular sense,** involved in balance.

11. Gestalt psychologists have described many principles by which stimuli are grouped together to form perceptions. For example, according to the principle of **proximity,** stimuli that are physically close to each other tend to be perceived as belonging together. Further, the object of attention—or **figure**—is usually seen as a distinct shape in front of the ground.

12. **Perceptual constancy** refers to the fact that people tend to perceive an object as stable even when its sensory image changes. Three of the most important examples are *size constancy, shape constancy,* and *color constancy.*

13. Several factors contribute to the perception of depth, including **binocular disparity,** the difference between the retinal images of the two eyes; **linear perspective; aerial perspective;** the **relative size** of objects; and **interposition.**

14. Subjects who have worn goggles that distort the location of physical objects— making everything seem upside down or reversed, for example—report that they are able to adapt to some extent. Active movement seems to provide an important source of feedback that aids in this type of perceptual learning.

15. Many scientists doubt the existence of **extrasensory perception** (ESP), which is said to provide awareness of external events without the use of known sensory receptor organs. Two major reasons for this skepticism are the failure to replicate positive results and the possibility of fraud.

To Learn More

Gregory, R. L. *Eye and Brain: The Psychology of Seeing* (3d ed.). New York: McGraw-Hill, 1978. If this book doesn't convince you that the study of vision can be absolutely fascinating, nothing will.

Geldard, F. A. *The Human Senses* (2d ed.). New York: Wiley, 1972. More than you ever wanted to know about psychophysics. A great book for looking things up.

Hansel, C. E. M. *ESP and Parapsychology: A Critical Re-Evaluation.* Buffalo, N. Y.: Prometheus Books, 1980. Skeptics will love this powerful attack on the very idea that ESP exists. Believers should be aware of its arguments.

5
Learning

Very few 3-year-olds know how to play the tuba. A musician may take many years to learn all the complex skills involved in playing this instrument. Similarly, people have to *learn* how to barbecue spareribs, read James Joyce, and cheat on their income tax.

Learning may be defined as a relatively permanent change in behavior that occurs through experience. The words of this formal definition have been chosen carefully to distinguish learning from other processes. For example, *relatively permanent* excludes temporary changes in behavior that could be caused by other factors, such as fatigue. *Experience* excludes behavioral changes caused by drugs, maturation, or other external processes. Learning is a fundamental process underlying human language, culture, and values. It is not surprising, then, that the study of learning had been one of psychology's major concerns.

What is surprising to many people is the way that psychologists have chosen to study learning. One might expect them to focus on human learning in the familiar world of the classroom or nursery. Instead, the most influential researchers established animal laboratories in which they studied the learning of pigeons, rats, monkeys, and dogs. Few people choose a career in psychology because of their interest in pigeons, yet some of the best minds in social science have devoted their lives to the study of simple learning processes in lower animals. Why?

Part of the reason can be found in the early history of psychology. When Wilhelm Wundt established the first psychology laboratory in 1879, he hoped to establish psychology as the science of mental life, which would discover the laws of consciousness and the mind (see Chapter 1). To John Watson and others, these terms were vague and imprecise; their dissatisfaction led to the rise of the behavioral paradigm, which focused on observable physical stimuli and responses (thus the name, S-R psychology). Many of the pioneers in the behaviorist movement were trained in physiology, a discipline that had long used animals in laboratory research.

The practical advantages of studying lower animals are obvious. An experimenter can precisely control the environment of large numbers of animals from birth to death in a way that would never be possible with humans. Further, Charles Darwin's theory of evolution held that all animals are descended from common ancestors. Many behaviorists therefore argued that the laws of learning would be fundamentally the same throughout the animal kingdom and that these laws could be most efficiently identified in the pure and simple world of the animal laboratory.

Many of the early behaviorists also believed that virtually all behavior was shaped by the environment and that the study of learning was therefore the most important topic in psychology. Some were confident that their studies would quickly reveal general laws that could be applied to the complex world of human behavior. In 1930, John Watson boasted:

> Give me a dozen healthy infants, well-formed, and my own specified world to bring them up in and I will guarantee to take any one at random and train him to become any type of specialist I might select—doctor, lawyer, artist, merchant-chief, and yes, even beggar-man and thief—regardless of his talents, penchants, tendencies, abilities, vocations, and race of his ancestors. I am going beyond my facts and I

John B. Watson (1878–1958) is sometimes referred to as the father of behaviorism. He was the youngest person ever to complete the PhD degree at the University of Chicago and was appointed a full professor at Johns Hopkins at the age of 29. His academic career was cut short in 1920 when his romantic involvement with graduate assistant Rosalie Rayner (with whom he studied Little Albert) led to a scandalous divorce. After he married Rayner and was forced to resign, he went to work for the J. Walter Thompson advertising agency, conducting door-to-door surveys on rubber boots. Although Watson continued to write popular articles and books on psychology, he advanced rapidly in the business world and devoted the rest of his career to advertising.

admit it, but so have the advocates of the contrary and they have been doing it for many thousands of years (p. 82).

Today, after half a century of intensive research, it would be hard to find a psychologist who would support such an arrogant claim. Genetics has more influence than Watson believed, and complex behavior patterns are not nearly so easy to manipulate. In this chapter, we shall see that psychologists have developed many sophisticated techniques for changing behavior. But success has been a humbling experience; each answer that psychologists have discovered has led to at least two new questions.

Attempts to understand human learning through studies of memory, language, thought, and children's reasoning are described in the next three chapters. Here, we focus on the behavioral paradigm to show how studies that began in animal laboratories have contributed to understanding the real-world behavior of humans and other species.

Classical Conditioning

Traditionally, psychologists have distinguished between two types of learning, classical conditioning and operant conditioning. Classical conditioning was so called because it was discovered first and was thus considered the classical form. It provides a model of the processes involved in many human learning situations, such as

Ivan Petrovich Pavlov (1849–1936) won the Nobel Prize in 1904 for his studies of the physiology of digestion. In one of these experiments, he accidentally noticed that animals sometimes salivated in response to "psychic" stimuli such as hearing a caretaker approach with food. For the next 30 years, Pavlov studied this learning process, now known as classical conditioning. Ironically, Pavlov characterized the infant science of psychology as "completely hopeless." He insisted that his co-workers take a physiological approach; any assistant in his laboratory who used psychological terminology to describe his research was required to pay a small fine.

developing a fear of flying or dentists or mailmen. As we shall see, it also explains why my friend Bob salivates whenever he drives past the golden arches of McDonald's.

PAVLOV'S DISCOVERY

Like many other scientific advances, classical conditioning was discovered by accident. Near the turn of the century, a Russian physiologist named Ivan Petrovich Pavlov spent many years studying the digestive processes in dogs, quantifying the relationships between eating various amounts of food and the secretions of the digestive glands. But Pavlov noticed that the precise mathematical relationships he discovered occasionally broke down. Sometimes, secretions of saliva began unexpectedly when a dog saw the pan containing its food or the person bringing it or even when it heard his footsteps. Pavlov set out to study these mysterious "psychic secretions" with the same meticulous precision that had won him the Nobel Prize for his earlier physiological studies (Pavlov, 1927; Gantt, 1973).

The basic experiment began with a delicate surgical operation. A small cut was made through a dog's cheek and the duct of its salivary gland was diverted. Now the dog's saliva could be measured precisely—it flowed into a glass funnel cemented to its cheek. The dog stood in a harness while the experimenter watched through a small window in a soundproof room.

In one typical study, G. V. Anrep, a researcher in Pavlov's laboratory, struck a tuning fork about eight seconds before giving a dog "a measured dose of biscuit powder" (1920, p. 373). Not surprisingly, at first the animal salivated only when it got the food. Anrep repeated this pairing three times a day. Finally, after 10 joint presentations, Anrep tried a test—He just struck the tuning fork. Even though no food was presented, the dog secreted a few drops of saliva 18 seconds after it heard the sound. After another 20 presentations of food and sound together, the test was tried again. This time, the dog began to salivate just a few seconds after hearing the tuning fork and secreted 60 drops even though no food was presented. The animal had learned that the tuning fork and the food were associated.

Several technical terms are used to describe this learning situation. An **unconditional stimulus (US)** is a stimulus that automatically elicits a natural reflex response called the **unconditional response (UR)**. In Anrep's study, food was the unconditional stimulus and salivation the unconditional response. The word *uncon-ditional* emphasizes that this is a natural, inborn reflex that did not depend on learning. (The Russian word was originally mistranslated as *unconditioned*, and many psychologists still use that term; Miller & Buckhout, 1973, p. 234.)

A **conditional stimulus (CS)** is a neutral stimulus that is repeatedly presented with the unconditional stimulus and gradually comes to elicit the **conditional response (CR),** a learned response that resembles the original unconditional response.

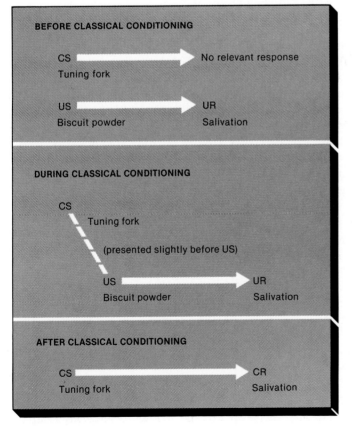

Figure 5.1

This diagram reflects the events in one pioneer study of classical conditioning (Anrep, 1920). CS = conditional stimulus; CR = conditional response; US = unconditional stimulus; UR = unconditional response.

For Anrep, striking the tuning fork was the conditional stimulus; after learning, it came to elicit the conditional response of salivation.

This type of learning, which later became known as **classical conditioning,** involved repeated pairing of a stimulus that naturally elicited a reflex response with a second stimulus; in time, the neutral stimulus came to elicit a response similar to the original reflex. Pavlov and his colleagues went on to investigate all the precise details of this simple learning process. They found, for example, that almost anything could become a conditional stimulus. The sound of a metronome, the sight of a circle, the feel of a vibration on the thigh—all could easily be substituted for the tuning fork.

One important variable that affected the ease of conditioning was the time relationship between the unconditional stimulus and the conditional stimulus. If the unconditional stimulus was presented before the conditional stimulus, little or no conditioning occurred. Learning is most efficient when the conditional stimulus begins before the unconditional stimulus; the precise optimal timing depends on the reflex that is being conditioned.

Many American psychologists first learned of Pavlov's work through John Watson's presidential address to the American Psychological Association in 1914. Pavlov's careful experimental techniques soon caught the imagination of an entire generation of researchers, who saw an opportunity to establish psychology as a systematic scientific discipline. They proceeded to investigate a wide range of natural reflexes. Conditional stimuli were paired with puffs of air (US) to elicit reflex closing of the eye (UR); with sudden lights (US) to elicit contraction of the pupil of the eye (UR); with blows to the patellar bone (US) to elicit knee jerks (UR); and with electrical shocks (US) to elicit changes in breathing patterns (UR).

Other researchers turned to different animals. They conditioned the responses of guinea pigs, chickens, flatworms, monkeys, rabbits, sheep, college students, and even a human fetus. In 1938, Spelt found that a loud noise—the US—caused a $6\frac{1}{2}$-month-old fetus to move suddenly—the UR. A vibrating stimulus—the CS—attached to a pregnant woman's stomach was repeatedly paired with the noise until it too came to elicit movement by the fetus—the CR.

Taken together, these studies strongly supported the idea that classical conditioning was a fundamental type of learning that applied to many natural reflexes throughout the animal kingdom. For example, when my friend Bob salivates as he passes McDonald's, it is probably a conditional response based on a previous pairing of the golden arches (CS) with the sights and smells of a Big Mac or french fries (US). Scientific analysis of the principles of classical conditioning observed in the laboratory can provide insights into many examples of learning in the everyday world.

EXTINCTION AND SPONTANEOUS RECOVERY

Pavlov and his co-workers went on to investigate the basic principles that governed classical conditioning. One early series of experiments studied how conditional responses can be eliminated. A dog that had been trained to salivate for a bell heard the bell over and over but did not get any more food. Gradually, the dog took longer and longer to salivate less and less, until it finally seemed to stop. Pavlov used the term

extinction to refer to the gradual disappearance of a learned response, in this case salivation. Classically conditional responses are extinguished by repeatedly presenting the conditional stimulus without the unconditional stimulus.

But Pavlov soon found that extinction was not just a matter of simple erasure. If the dog in the original extinction experiment was returned to the laboratory the next day, it began to salivate again when it first heard the bell. This phenomenon is called **spontaneous recovery,** the reappearance, after a rest period, of a response that has been extinguished. However, it returns in a weaker form; the response may be smaller or less rapid when it reappears after extinction, and fewer trials are required to extinguish it again.

GENERALIZATION AND DISCRIMINATION

In real life, stimuli often vary from one occasion to the next. Most learning would be of little value if it were linked to only one type of stimulus. If a child who was burned on a white Kenmore electric stove had to relearn this lesson on yellow stoves, gas stoves, and Hotpoint stoves, the original experience would have little significance. Pavlov studied this phenomenon by investigating the way slight changes in stimuli affect behavior. Two important concepts emerged. **Generalization** involves responding in a similar way to stimuli that resemble each other; the greater the similarity, the closer the response. The other side of the coin is **discrimination,** learning to respond only to a specific kind of stimulus. This, too, is necessary in real life. If the child was burned because there was something wrong with that particular stove, it is important that the lesson be limited to that stove alone.

G. V. Anrep (1923) began one important study of generalization by teaching a dog to salivate when a vibrator (CS) was applied to the dog's thigh. The dog later salivated when the vibrator was placed on his trunk, shoulder, or front paw. The farther the vibrator moved from the thigh (the original spot), the less the dog salivated. The learning had become generalized from the original conditional stimulus to others that resembled it.

Pavlov then purposely tried to develop techniques to teach dogs to discriminate and respond only to one specific stimulus. In these experiments, two different stimuli were presented; one was always paired with the unconditional stimulus, and the other was always presented alone. For example, a dog might be given meat every time a vibrator was placed against its thigh but never after the device was held against its shoulder. This procedure sharpened distinctions, and the dog learned to salivate only when the vibrator touched its thigh. In this way, discrimination was demonstrated in the laboratory for the first time.

Studies of generalization and discrimination can provide a unique method for asking animals questions. If Pavlov wanted to know whether dogs are color-blind, he could randomly alternate a green conditional stimulus that was always paired with food (US) with a red conditional stimulus that was never paired with food. If the dog learned to discriminate, that implied that it saw a difference between red and green. As we shall see, studies like this have since provided great insights into the perceptual world of lower animals and preverbal infants.

In later studies, Pavlov (1927) and his students made the discrimination problem more difficult by training dogs to distinguish between a circle and an ellipse and then presenting them with ellipses that looked more and more like circles. Finally, one poor dog couldn't stand it anymore. It began to squeal and wiggle in its harness, then bit through the tubes in the apparatus, and finally began to bark violently. These disturbed behaviors were very unusual for the docile dog, and Pavlov concluded that he had discovered the animal equivalent of human neurosis.

Pavlov was so impressed with this "experimental neurosis" that he devoted the remainder of his career to applying the principles of conditioning to psychiatry. Most of his theories were more influential in Russia than in the United States or Europe. But the idea that abnormal behavior can be caused by classical conditioning (and other types of learning) is now widely accepted (see Chapters 13 and 14).

LITTLE ALBERT

In the United States, the most important demonstration that learning could be involved in abnormal behavior was performed by John Watson and his colleague Rosalie Rayner. Watson and Rayner (1920) wanted to show that human fears could be learned by classical conditioning. Their subject was Albert B., a "stolid and unemotional" 9-month-old child who "practically never cried." They began by confronting Little Albert (as the child later became known) with a standard series of stimuli including a rat, a rabbit, a mask, and a burning newspaper. True to his unemotional reputation, Albert showed no fear. But when Watson made a loud noise by striking a

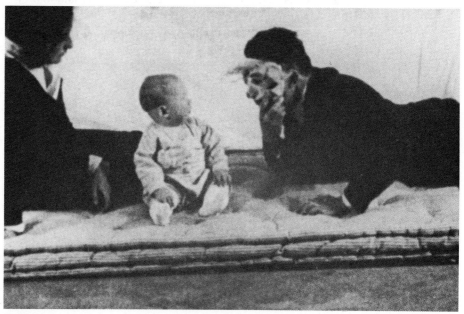

Figure 5.2
Little Albert himself in the famous experiment on how human fears may be learned.

hammer against a steel bar behind Little Albert's head, the child "started violently." After two more loud sounds, Albert "broke into a sudden crying fit."

About two months later, they began the actual conditioning. They planned to use the loud sound as an unconditional stimulus that evoked an unconditional response of fear (behaviorally defined by withdrawal and other responses). The conditional stimulus was a rat, and fear was to be the conditional response. Here are their laboratory notes from the first conditioning session:

1. White rat suddenly taken from the basket and presented to Albert. He began to reach for rat with left hand. Just as his hand touched the animal the bar was struck immediately behind his head. The infant jumped violently and fell forward, burying his face in the mattress. He did not cry, however.

2. Just as the right hand touched the rat the bar was again struck. Again the infant jumped violently, fell forward and began to whimper. In order not to disturb the child too seriously, no further tests were given for one week (Watson & Rayner, 1920, p. 4).

Later, they continued the test with five more pairings of the rat and the sound and three presentations of the rat alone. Their description of the last trial for the day notes:

8. Rat alone. The instant the rat was shown the baby began to cry. Almost instantly, he turned sharply to the left, fell over on left side, raised himself on all fours and began to crawl away so rapidly that he was caught with difficulty before reaching the edge of the table. (Watson & Rayner, 1920, p. 5).

Five days later, when Albert returned to the laboratory, he whimpered and withdrew from the rat. He also drew back in fear from a rabbit, a dog, a seal coat, and a Santa Claus mask, all stimuli that had not bothered the boy before. Albert's fear had generalized to a specific set of similar furry stimuli. He was still quite content to play in the experimental setting with stimuli that did not resemble the rat, such as a set of blocks.

This experiment seems unethical by today's standards. It is extremely unlikely that a study of this sort would or could be repeated in the 1980s. But in fairness to Watson and Rayner, it can be misleading to view actions taken over half a century ago by today's ethics and attitudes toward science. Watson and Rayner believed that many people would benefit from their demonstration that fears were learned and "felt that we could do [Albert] relatively little harm" (p. 2). (See "How Do They Know?" in Chapter 15 for a discussion of ethical issues in psychological research.)

They went on to propose seven techniques to help cure Little Albert's fear. Unfortunately, Albert's mother moved away with him before they had a chance to try them out. (About 50 years later, one psychologist—Murray, 1973—tried to locate Albert to see if he had any unusual fears as an adult, but he was unable to find him.)

A few years after the original experiment, Mary Cover Jones (1924) tried Watson's proposed therapies on several other young children. Some of his suggestions, such as telling the child pleasant stories about the feared object, did not work at all. Others, such as watching other children play with the feared object, were more promising. Behavior therapists have since developed a variety of related techniques to treat people with phobias or irrational fears (see Chapter 14).

Watson and Rayner believed they had demonstrated that human fears could be learned by classical conditioning. In the next section, we see that technically their experiment involved elements of operant as well as classical conditioning. Despite these and other flaws (Samelson, 1980), the experiment with Little Albert influenced many psychologists to study classical conditioning as a model of human fears and other everyday behaviors.

Operant Conditioning

At about the same time that Pavlov's dogs were salivating in St. Petersburg, a New York psychologist named Edward L. Thorndike was trying to debunk popular myths about the incredible mental abilities of animals. "Dogs get lost hundreds of times and no one ever notices it . . . " he wrote. "But let one find his way from Brooklyn to Yonkers and the fact immediately becomes a circulating anecdote" (Thorndike, 1898, p. 4). In his book *Animal Intelligence*, Thorndike described a series of experiments involving a different kind of conditioning.

OPERANT VERSUS CLASSICAL CONDITIONING: THE ORIGINAL DISTINCTION

In his most famous studies, Thorndike put hungry cats in puzzle boxes with tasty morsels of fish just out of reach. Sometimes the cat had to pull a string to get out of the box and reach the fish; other times the cat had to slide a bolt or press a lever. The animals typically thrashed around for a while before discovering the solution, apparently by accident. Once they escaped and were placed back in the box, they went through this groping trial-and-error process again. Only gradually did they seem to learn the trick.

Thorndike proposed several laws that governed the learning of his fumbling cats. The most important of these, the law of effect, emphasized the critical importance of the reward the cat got for escaping from the box (a piece of fish). The **law of effect** stated that rewards "stamp in" learned connections between actions and their consequences.

In 1938, Burrhus Frederic Skinner called attention to some of the differences between Pavlov's salivating dogs and Thorndike's puzzled cats. Salivation was **elicited**—it was a response to a specific stimulus (food). But pulling a string and manipulating a latch were not reflexes; they were **emitted** behavior, spontaneous acts that were not responses to any known stimuli. The first type of relatively passive learning became known as respondent conditioning (the animal passively responds) or classical conditioning (as in Pavlov's first, classical experiment). Such conditioning always involves new connections ultimately based on involuntary reflexes, such as salivation to a piece of food or withdrawal from pain.

In contrast, the second kind of conditioning involved more active, voluntary behavior. This more complex type of learning in which the animal actually had to do

B. F. Skinner (1904–   ) is probably the most famous behaviorist. Skinner hoped to be a writer and was encouraged to pursue this path when the poet Robert Frost praised some of his college essays. In his three-volume autobiography, Skinner described the "dark year" after college graduation in which he tried to write full-time and discovered that he "had nothing to say." After reading Watson's book *Behaviorism*, Skinner went to study psychology at Harvard. His fame is based not just on his research on animal learning but also on his extensive writings on the implications of a behavioral approach.

something to gain a reward was called operant conditioning (the animal operates on the environment) or instrumental conditioning (the act is instrumental in obtaining a reward). In **operant conditioning,** the probability of a response changes when reinforcement is presented following that response. Less formally, when a response is rewarded, it will be repeated more frequently; when punished, it will be repeated less frequently.

Both types of learning are found in the everyday world. Classical conditioning is involved in human fears and emotional reactions, for example, when you cringe (CR) at the sight of a hypodermic needle (CS) as a result of learning from earlier shots. Operant conditioning may occur when a child tells Grandma his latest joke; the likelihood of repeating the joke again increases if Grandma rewards it with a smile and decreases if she punishes it by frowning and saying, "You shouldn't tell jokes like that, dear." In similar ways, rewards and punishments influence all our voluntary behavior.

The fact that people and other animals will work for rewards is not an earth-shattering insight; it is at least as old as barter and bribery. What was new and important about the work of the early learning researchers was the development of a technology and a systematic approach to the study of how rewards and punishments shape behavior. Ultimately, this led to the formulation of precise empirical laws of learning. The single most important concept behind these laws is the idea that behavior is shaped by its consequences.

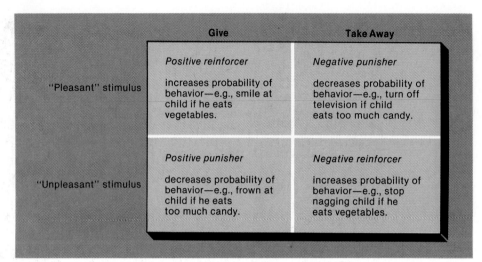

Figure 5.3
A general summary of the relationships between reinforcement and punishment. The words *pleasant* and *unpleasant* appear in quotes because these terms are used here only for purposes of simplification. See the text for more formal definitions.

REINFORCEMENT AND PUNISHMENT

There are two major classes of consequences that shape behavior: reinforcement and punishment. A **reinforcer** is any stimulus that, when paired with a particular behavior, increases the probability of that behavior. A **punisher** is any stimulus that when paired with a particular behavior, decreases the probability of that behavior.

Reinforcers are further subdivided into positive and negative groups. A **positive reinforcer** is any stimulus that increases the probability of a behavior when it is presented after the behavior. In everyday language, positive reinforcers are called rewards. If you give your poor dog a bone when he barks and then he barks again, the bone probably serves as a positive reinforcer. But a closely related concept is a bit more confusing. A **negative reinforcer** is any stimulus that increases the probability of a behavior when it is removed after the behavior. Getting your hair cut to stop your parents' nagging is an example of a negative reinforcer.

These relationships are summarized in Figure 5.3. The most difficult idea for most people to understand is the concept of a negative reinforcer. To repeat, then, a negative reinforcer *increases* the likelihood of a certain act by ending unpleasantness; anything that *decreases* the likelihood of behavior is called a punisher.

Note that in Figure 5.3, the words *pleasant* and *unpleasant* are in quotation marks. The reason is that everyday words like these invite intuitive assumptions that can be misleading. For example, many young children would probably classify a plate of creamed spinach as an unpleasant stimulus. But for Popeye the sailor man or a vegetarian on a macrobiotic diet creamed spinach could be a reinforcer.

Skinner was one of the first to argue that psychologists should make no assumptions about pleasantness and unpleasantness and instead let the facts speak for themselves. One empirical procedure for identifying reinforcers is called the **Premack principle,** which states that a more preferred behavior reinforces a less preferred behavior.

For example, in one study, kindergarten children were allowed to choose between several activities, including watching a movie cartoon and playing a pinball machine. Some children spent more time watching the cartoon; for them, the cartoon was a preferred activity that could serve as a reinforcer. These children learned to increase the frequency of pinball playing when segments of the cartoon were presented as a reinforcer for playing pinball. Other children, however, spent more time playing pinball when given free choice. For them, the opportunity to play pinball could be used as a reinforcer to increase the frequency of watching the cartoon. Studies like this of children, monkeys, and rats have generally verified the Premack principle (Premack, 1965).

The fact that these relationships can get confusing and that different organisms respond to different reinforcers should serve as a reminder that intuitive terms such as *reward* and *unpleasant* can be misleading. The Premack principle and its revisions (Timberlake, 1980) are important because they enable researchers to identify reinforcers without making any assumptions about what an organism likes or dislikes.

Of course, most studies of animal learning rely on simple and standard reinforcers such as food and water. Although cartoons routinely portray psychologists hovering over rats in mazes, the most common device in the animal laboratory these days is the Skinner box. In its simplest form, a *Skinner box* is a soundproof box with a lever for a rat to push or a key (a button) for a pigeon to peck and a device to deliver food (see Figure 5.4). A deluxe model may include options such as an electrified floor to deliver shocks and a series of colored lights to serve as stimuli.

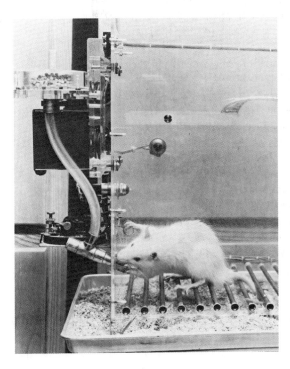

Figure 5.4
This device for studying operant conditioning is often called a *Skinner box.* When the rat presses a bar, a food pellet is delivered through an automatic feeder.

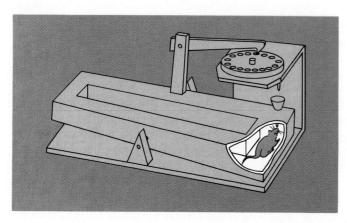

Figure 5.5

An early version of the Skinner box. In the late 1920s, Skinner performed a study in which rats were reinforced for running down an 8-foot alley. To save himself the trouble of replacing the food after each trial and physically lifting the rat back to the starting point, Skinner devised this long rectangular box with two parallel alleys so the rat could simply walk back to the starting point. The whole device was balanced on a fulcrum like a miniature seesaw. When the rat ran to the end, the box tipped and a mechanical device dropped a homemade food pellet. Running back to the start tipped the device again and reset it.

As Skinner (1956) explained in his delightful article "A Case History in Scientific Method," this apparatus grew out of his attempts to develop an efficient system to deliver rewards automatically and chart the progress of animal learning (see Figure 5.5). But the efficiency of Skinner's invention created new problems. Skinner was working with eight rats at once, and each had learned how to earn about 100 reinforcements a day. Soon he was spending his weekends stamping out food pellets with a primitive pill machine. So what did Skinner do? He decided to save pellets by not reinforcing every lever press. The result, he was astonished to find, was that the rats sometimes worked even harder for fewer rewards. Thus the study of schedules of reinforcement was born.

SCHEDULES OF REINFORCEMENT

In the real world, you are usually not rewarded every time you act in a certain way. You do not receive a paycheck every time you go to work, and you do not have a wonderful time every time you ask someone new to dinner. Instead of experiencing what psychologists call **continuous reinforcement,** in which every act is reinforced, you experience **partial reinforcement** (sometimes called intermittent reinforcement), in which some acts are reinforced and others are not. You will probably not be surprised by the fact that learning is acquired more quickly with continuous reinforcement. However, you may be surprised to learn that partial reinforcement can establish behavior patterns that are more stable and resistant to extinction than those produced by continuous reinforcement.

Pet owners often learn the power of partial reinforcement the hard way; in effect, they may unintentionally train animals to be annoying. Consider the typical actions of a pet owner whose dog hangs around the dinner table waiting for scraps. When the animal first starts rubbing dinner guests' knees and whining, it will probably be ignored or told to go away. But sooner or later, the owner may get so frustrated that he gives in and feeds the dog. What has the animal learned in this case? It has learned that if it makes itself a big enough pain in the knees, sooner or later it will earn a table scrap.

This behavior is difficult to extinguish. If an animal is trained to be annoying with continuous reinforcement (a reward for every annoying act), discontinuing the reward soon ends the behavior. But partial reinforcement teaches an animal to perform many irritating acts to gain a single reward. It can be difficult to get across the message that no more rewards are coming. Thus, partial reinforcement often produces persistent behavior patterns that are hard to change.

Many psychologists have studied how different patterns of reinforcement and punishment, or **schedules of reinforcement,** influence learning. There are four basic types. Two—fixed-ratio and variable-ratio—demand a certain number of responses before a reward is offered; and two—fixed-interval and variable-interval—are based on the passage of time.

Fixed-ratio (FR) schedules are probably the easiest to understand. An organism is rewarded for making a specific number of responses. For example, a rat on an FR25 schedule receives a pellet of food after every 25 bar presses; a pigeon on an FR12 gets a piece of grain after every 12 key pecks. Animals on fixed-ratio schedules tend to respond rapidly so that they can get more rewards, pausing briefly after each reinforcement. Interestingly, the length of this pause is systematically related to the number of responses required—larger ratios yield longer pauses. In a natural example of a fixed-ratio scale, garment workers in turn-of-the-century sweatshops were often paid for what they accomplished—perhaps 1 or 2 cents for every 100 buttons

Figure 5.6
Around 1900, entire immigrant families sometimes worked in "sweatshops" in which they were paid low wages based on the number of garments completed. In operant terms, this would be considered a fixed-ratio schedule of reinforcement.

sewn. As labor unions grew in power, workers rejected this arrangement, perhaps because it tends to produce an unpleasantly fast pace.

Variable-ratio (VR) schedules vary the number of responses required for each reward. A pigeon on a VR10 schedule might have time to peck 8 times for the first piece of grain, 14 times for the next, then 12 times, 10 times, and 6 times. (Note that the average ratio here is 10). Variable-ratio schedules also produce high and stable rates of response but without the pauses characteristic of fixed-ratio schedules. Las Vegas gamblers who feed Dixie cups full of quarters into slot machines as fast as they can are painfully familiar with the high response rates generated by variable-ratio schedules. After all, they are reinforced with the jackpot after some average number of responses. (The average, of course, is carefully chosen to make slot-machine owners rich at the players' expense.)

Fixed-interval (FI) schedules reinforce the first response emitted after a certain amount of time elapses. A pigeon on an FI30-second schedule is reinforced for the first key peck it makes after 30 seconds is up. A lazy pigeon might simply wait 30 seconds and then peck the key once to get its dinner. Although most animals are not quite this efficient, well-trained animals on fixed-interval schedules do take a long break after each reinforcer and then gradually increase their response rate until the interval is over and they get their reinforcer. A person who gets mail every day at precisely 11 a.m. is also on a fixed-interval schedule. Somewhere around 10:30 she may start checking her mailbox for that acceptance to medical school. As 11:00 approaches, she may check more and more frequently until the first response after 11:00 is rewarded. Then there will be no more mailbox checking until the next day.

Finally, **variable-interval (VI) schedules** vary the time that must elapse before a response is reinforced. A VI40-second schedule might reward a rat for the first bar press after 50 seconds, then 60 seconds, 20 seconds, and 30 seconds. (The average here is 40 seconds.) Animals respond steadily without pausing on variable intervals, much as they do with variable ratios. More frequent rewards increase the rate of response. When you dial a busy number, you are on a variable-interval schedule. Sooner or later, your dialing will be reinforced by the welcome sound of a ring at the other end. If you are calling American Airlines and past experience has taught you that the lines are only busy for a few seconds at a time, you will probably dial again immediately. But if you are trying to reach your Uncle Tony, a notorious gabber, you may wait several minutes or hours before trying again.

These days, most animal research focuses on far more complex schedules of reinforcement. For example, **concurrent schedules** involve two or more different responses that are reinforced simultaneously according to independent schedules. A pigeon trained on a concurrent schedule might be faced with two keys; pecks on the right key could be reinforced on a VI30-second schedule, while pecks on the left key are simultaneously rewarded according to a VI45-second schedule. In another case, pecking the right key could produce food, while pecking the left key produces water. Complex schedules of this sort can provide subtle information about an animal's choices. Studies have shown that animals on concurrent schedules respond to each alternative in proportion to the frequency and type of reward (Herrnstein, 1970). By giving an animal a choice between two rewards, concurrent schedules permit quantitative estimates of which reward an animal prefers and by how much. Concurrent schedules could reveal, for example, whether an animal would prefer a small reinforcer offered immediately or a large reinforcer offered after some delay. The possibilities are endless. Such subtle information is useful not only for understanding animal behavior; it has also been applied to therapeutic work with humans (McDowell, 1982).

SHAPING

Studying schedules of reinforcement is fine once you have a rat who has learned to press a bar, but how do you get it to press the bar for food in the first place? One way is patience. Put a hungry rat in a Skinner box and wait for it to press the bar. Once the bar press is rewarded by food a few times, the rat will press it more frequently. But you may have a long wait. A more efficient way is to use a technique called **shaping**—teaching a complex behavior by reinforcing *successive approximations* of the desired activity. If the goal is to teach a rat to press a bar for its dinner, one first reinforces any movement whatever toward the lever. Once this movement has been firmly established, the experimenter might reinforce only closer movements or actually touching the bar. Gradually, the animal could be trained to touch the bar and finally to press it firmly. Thus, in shaping, a complex desired behavior is broken down into a series of simpler responses, which are taught one at a time.

Extremely sophisticated response patterns can be taught in this manner. For example, two of Skinner's students used the method of successive approximations to train animal acts (Breland & Breland, 1951) such as Priscilla the Fastidious Pig. Priscilla's behavior was gradually shaped into a complex chain that included turning on a radio, eating breakfast at a table, picking up dirty clothes and dropping them in a hamper, vacuuming the floor, and answering questions from the audience by lighting up a sign that said "yes" or "no." The biggest problem with this act was that Priscilla, being a pig, tended to eat too much and had to be replaced every four months or so for ease of shipping. Other acts developed by the Brelands included chickens that tap-danced and played tug-of-war and a calf that acted the part of a bull in a china shop.

Shaping is important because it involves a practical way of quickly teaching novel complex behaviors. For example, behavior therapists have used the method of successive approximations to teach nonverbal and retarded children to speak. They begin by reinforcing any verbal response, then reinforcing any responses that match simple words spoken by the teacher, and finally reinforcing only functional speech (Harris, 1975). The process may be long and difficult and the end results are limited by the mental abilities of the child, but it can provide hope and help where before there was none.

EXTINCTION AND SPONTANEOUS RECOVERY

Many of the concepts that apply to classical conditioning also apply to operant conditioning. Among the most important are extinction, the gradual disappearance of a response, and spontaneous recovery, the reappearance, after a rest period, of a response that has been extinguished.

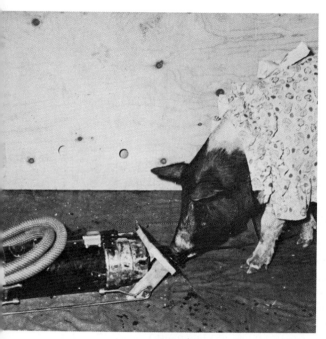

Figure 5.7
Two animal acts based on the shaping of operant responses. Priscilla the Fastidious Pig turns on a vacuum, and a nameless raccoon imitates Doctor J dunking a basketball.

Skinner first observed the extinction of an operant response by accident, when his food pellet dispenser jammed on a Friday afternoon. When the food reward was discontinued, the animal gradually stopped pressing the bar. Skinner later wrote (1979, p. 95) that he was so excited by the discovery of this parallel between classical and operant conditioning that "All that weekend I crossed streets with care . . . to protect my discovery from loss through my death." He later observed that rats also show spontaneous recovery after extinction, suddenly trying a few bar presses as if for old time's sake.

There are a number of interesting parallels between human and animal behavior during extinction. For example, one classic finding is that the form of a response becomes more variable during extinction. In one study (Notterman, 1959), rats in a Skinner box usually developed a stereotyped way of pressing the bar—a soft, efficient push. But when rewards were discontinued, they varied the response, pushing both harder and softer. In much the same way, you may develop a stereotyped way of striking your cigarette lighter. If you suddenly find that your lighter doesn't work, you'll probably experiment—hit it sharply, strike it softly, turn it upside down, and shake it.

Another phenomenon often observed in the animal laboratory during extinction is aggression. During extinction, a rat may attack and bite the bar (Mowrer & Jones,

1943). When a pigeon's pecks are no longer rewarded, it may attack another pigeon who is just an innocent bystander (Azrin, Hutchinson, & Hake, 1966). Anyone who has ever kicked a Coke machine when it fails to deliver has experienced a similar phenomenon. Here, aggression (kicking) is elicited when the response (putting coins in the machine) is no longer reinforced (delivery of a Coke). Similarly, when all else fails with your cigarette lighter, you may angrily hurl it into the garbage. If your phone happens to ring at that moment, the unsuspecting caller may become the target of your rage.

GENERALIZATION AND DISCRIMINATION

Just as the concept of extinction applies to operant as well as classical conditioning, so the phenomena of generalization and discrimination have parallels in both types of learning. (As noted earlier, generalization involves responding in a similar way to stimuli that resemble one another; discrimination involves learning to respond to a specific kind of stimulus.)

Much of our everyday operant learning involves generalizing from one situation to the next. If you try out a joke on a friend and she rewards you with laughter, you will be encouraged to tell it again. At first, you may generalize the response of telling this joke in other situations and try it out wherever you go. When you discover that it goes over much better at the corner bar than at a church supper, you will probably learn to discriminate the types of situations in which this type of humor is appreciated. Similarly, a 3-year-old may learn that his cute trick of jumping on the sofa as if it were a trampoline is rewarded with laughter by Grandma, but not by Mom, Dad, or Uncle Tony. In this case, Grandma could technically be called a **discriminative stimulus** that signals that a particular response will be reinforced. When the discriminative stimulus (Grandma) is not present, the response (jumping on the couch) is not rewarded.

In the laboratory, a discriminative stimulus can be identified by testing an organism with a wide variety of similar stimuli to see which control the response. For example, if a pigeon is trained to peck at a yellow key, the extent to which this response generalizes to other colors can by tested by gradually changing the color of the key (by increasing or decreasing the wavelength of the light; see Chapter 4). As you can see in Figure 5.8, a pigeon trained in this way does indeed generalize and peck at other colored keys; the closer the wavelength of light to the original discriminative stimulus, the more it pecks (Guttman & Kalish, 1956).

To sharpen this pigeon's distinction between yellow keys and others, a researcher can use **discrimination training**—reinforcing a particular response and extinguishing all others. In this case, the color of the key would be changed during training. Whenever it was yellow, the bird would be rewarded with a piece of grain; when the key was green, pecks would not be reinforced. The results of discrimination training are also shown in Figure 5.8; the pigeon pecks at a much higher rate for yellow lights than for other wavelengths.

Obviously, this training procedure can provide subtle information about an animal's sensory capabilities. We know that pigeons can distinguish yellow from

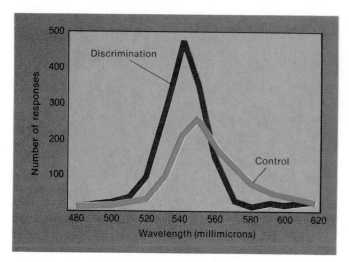

Figure 5.8
Diagram of generalization and discrimination in learning. Pigeons in the control group were reinforced for pecking at a yellow key (550 millimicrons); this response later generalized to similar colors. In discrimination training, pecks were reinforced for 550 millimicrons but not for 570 millimicrons. These pigeons later had a much higher response rate for colors near the reinforced color.

green because they have learned to discriminate between stimuli of these colors. If they had failed to learn this discrimination—as other species have—that would suggest they were color-blind.

One particularly ingenious experiment on animals' sensory capacities (Blackwell & Schlosberg, 1943) tested rats' responses to various tones. As explained in Chapter 4, for humans the frequency of a tone (measured in hertz) is related to its pitch. Similarly, researchers have found that when a particular tone is used as a discriminative stimulus, animals generalize the response to other tones; the closer the frequency of the test tone, the greater the response.

One interesting exception involves two tones that differ from each other by a muscial interval of one octave. To the human ear, tones of 5,000 Hz and 10,000 Hz sound more similar than tones of 8,000 Hz and 10,000 Hz, even though the latter pair is closer in frequency. Similarly, rats trained to respond to a 10,000-Hz tone generalized more to a 5,000-Hz tone than to an intermediate tone of 8,000 Hz. Like humans, rats seem to perceive tones an octave apart as more similar than other tones closer in frequency. This fact about their sensory world would never have been known without studies of stimulus generalization and discrimination.

PUNISHMENT

Being punished by paying a large fine, getting 40 lashes, or hearing your best friend tell you that you are a disgrace to the human race are probably not a few of your favorite things. But punishment is not susposed to be fun; it is supposed to change the way you behave. Simply defined, **punishment** reduces the likelihood that a response will be repeated. In this way, it is the mirror image of reinforcement, which increases the likelihood of behavior.

For many years, little research was done in this area, probably because the topic is "unaesthetic and unattractive . . . tainted by association with brutality" (Walters & Grusec, 1977, p. 2). The pioneer researchers who did venture into this taboo area

Punishment in *Walden Two*

B. F. Skinner's novel *Walden Two* (1948) described a utopian community whose laws and regulations were derived from behavioral principles discovered in the learning laboratory. In the excerpt printed here, two characters in the novel discuss this community's attitude toward punishment. In what way does this disagree with our account of the effects of punishment? Can you explain the contradiction? (A short discussion of these issues appears after the "Summary" at the end of this chapter.)

"The old school made the amazing mistake of supposing that by removing a situation a person likes or setting up one he doesn't like—in other words by punishing him—it was possible to reduce the probability that he would behave in a given way again. That simply doesn't hold. It has been established beyond question. What is emerging at this critical stage in the evolution of society is a behavioral and cultural technology based on positive reinforcement alone. We are gradually discovering—at an untold cost in human suffering—that *in the long run punishment doesn't reduce the probability that an act will occur.* We have been so preoccupied with the contrary that we always take 'force' to mean punishment. We don't say we're using force when we send shiploads of food into a starving country, though we're displaying quite as much power as if we were sending troops and guns." . . .

"It's *temporarily effective*, that's the worst of it. That explains several thousand years of bloodshed. Even nature has been fooled. We 'instinctively' punish a person who doesn't behave as we like—we spank him if he's a child or strike him if he's a man. A nice distinction! The immediate effect of the blow teaches us to strike again. Retribution and revenge are the most natural things on earth. But in the long run the man we strike is no less likely to repeat his act."

"But he won't repeat it if we hit him hard enough," said Castle.

"He'll still tend to repeat it. He'll want to repeat it. We haven't really altered his potential behavior at all. That's the pity of it. If he doesn't repeat it in our presence, he will in the presence of someone else. Or it will be repeated in the disguise of a neurotic symptom" (p. 244).

generally came to the conclusion that many of us would like to believe—punishment is not an effective way to change behavior and therefore should be avoided.

In 1932, Edward Thorndike announced that punishment was not very effective in weakening learned connections. But the punishers Thorndike experimented with were quite mild. College students who failed to match a Spanish word with its English equivalent were simply told they were wrong; chicks that chose the wrong arm of a maze were confined there for 30 seconds. Despite the obvious limitations of these studies, they were widely publicized (see, for example, "Becoming a Critical Consumer") and helped lead to a period of permissive education and child rearing that is ending only now, half a century later (Walters & Grusec, 1977).

It was not until the 1950s that animal researchers seriously investigated the

Experiments with a Single Subject: The Effect of Punishment on Self-Destructive Behavior

In scientific research, most psychologists study the average responses of large groups. In contrast, many learning researchers concentrate on controlling the behavior of one individual organism at a time. In the simplest case, they measure the frequency of a particular behavior during a *baseline* period of observation, then experimentally manipulate a particular variable while continuing their observations. If the frequency of behavior increases or decreases substantially during the manipulation, behavior is said to be controlled by that variable. Typically, baseline periods are alternated with experimental periods to test repeatedly the power of the manipulation. Behavior therapists use this approach to alter the frequency of troublesome behaviors.

Therapists use punishment rarely and only in extreme cases. But John, the 8-year-old subject of the experiment we discuss here (Lovaas & Simmons, 1969), had some extreme prob-

lems. Besides being severely mentally retarded, John was self-destructive. He hit himself so often that his face and head were covered with scars. Hospital staff members sometimes had to tie John's arms and legs to a bed to keep him from hurting himself. At the time this study began, John had been restrained in this way for six months.

Two behavior therapists began by trying to extinguish John's self-destructive behavior. They reasoned that busy staff members had unintentionally reinforced this bizarre behavior by paying more attention to the child when he tried to hurt himself. To extinguish this activity, they removed John's restraints and left him alone in a small hospital bedroom for 90 minutes while they watched through a one-way mirror. The results were quantified by counting the number of times John hit himself: 2,750 times during those 90 minutes. This first measurement could be considered a baseline

effects of punishment. When they did, they found that Thorndike had been wrong. Punishment clearly does decrease the frequency of behavior. These scientists then set out to analyze the precise effects of punishment, just as earlier investigators had studied the nature of reward.

One typical experiment (Camp, Raymond, & Church, 1967) examined the effects of delaying punishment. Some rats were shocked immediately after a critical lever press; others were shocked 30 seconds later. Earlier studies had made it clear that the sooner reward comes, the more effective it is (Kimble, 1961). This experiment proved that when punishment is delayed, it too loses some of its power. Rats who were shocked immediately after each bar press responded less frequently than those who got a shock 30 seconds later.

estimate of the frequency of self-destructive behavior. Each day, John hit himself less and less frequently in his hour-and-a-half alone. By the tenth day, he had stopped completely.

Thus, the experimenters demonstrated that self-destructive behavior was subject to the laws of operant conditioning; if it was not reinforced, it would gradually disappear. But the price of extinction in this case was high. "John hit himself almost 9,000 times before he quit" (p. 146). And other self-destructive children might do themselves far more serious injury.

John's extinction did not generalize to other situations. Although he no longer hit himself in the experimental room, his behavior elsewhere in the ward was as self-destructive as ever. Extinction was clearly not the answer.

The behavior therapists reluctantly turned to punishment to see if that could control John's bizarre behavior. He got an electric shock, which felt "like a dentist drilling on an unanesthetized tooth," on his leg whenever he hit himself. This was extremely effective. After only 12 shocks, John's self-destructive behavior virtually disappeared.

But again, careful observation revealed that the effect was limited. John had stopped hitting himself when he was in the vicinity of the experimental room or when one of the experimenters was nearby, but this did not generalize to other situations. After John was shocked five more times in other settings, however, his self-destructive behavior disappeared altogether. Interestingly, once the self-destructive behavior was gone, John improved in other ways as well. For example, he spent less time whining and avoiding adults.

A careful application of the scientific method to John had made it clear that self-destructive behavior could be controlled like any other learned response; its frequency was decreased by either extinction or punishment. This finding was then replicated with several other self-destructive children.

Note that this type of experimentation with a single subject provides practical information. If Lovaas and Simmons had studied a large group of children and found that punishment significantly reduced the frequency of self-destructive behavior on the average, the results might have been less applicable to therapy. What works on the average does not necessarily work for every individual. Experiments with a single subject are particularly useful for identifying variables that can be used to predict and control individual behavior.

Why, you might ask, did the rats continue to press the bar at all? Why didn't they just stretch out on the floor of the Skinner box and relax? If all that pressing the bar ever got them was a shock, they would have stopped. But as in most natural situations, the same response was sometimes rewarded and sometimes punished; some of the bar presses produced food for the hungry rats while others led to shock.

When does punishment work best? Among the suggestions offered in one classic review by Azrin & Holz (1966), punishment should be immediate, intense, and unavoidable. It is best to decide in advance the maximum punishment that is appropriate for a particular situation and then apply this maximum immediately. Starting with a mild punisher and gradually increasing the penalty for repeated offenses may seem more humane and it is certainly easier for the average parent, but it does not work. In the short run, mild punishers have mild effects. And in the long run, organisms adapt to punishment if its intensity is gradually increased and it loses its power to change behavior. Therefore when Junior is caught stealing hubcaps, Dad should immediately cut off his allowance (or whatever).

While research has shown quite clearly that punishment reduces the frequency of behavior, it has also shown that harmful side effects may occur, including increased aggression and long-term emotional damage. These harmful effects are particularly likely when the punishment is severe and unpredictable and thus not clearly related to particular behaviors or when it is administered by a hostile caretaker (Walters & Grusec, 1977).

Much remains to be learned about the effects of different types of punishment in various situations. For example, there is some research that suggests that physical punishment, such as spanking a child, may lead to imitation, so that the child becomes more aggressive toward his peers. However, nonphysical punishment, such as a verbal scolding or requiring the child to mow the lawn or stay in his room, probably does not increase aggression. More research is required to establish this point definitively and to explore the role of other factors such as the relationship between the child and the person who administers the punishment.

Unfortunately, in the past, some psychologists made far-reaching conclusions that were not supported by research evidence; they argued that punishment should not be used on the basis of "ethical as well as scientific judgment" (Catania, 1979, p. 97). Researchers are now trying to maintain a more objective position on this emotional issue, to provide information on both the short- and long-term effects of various types of punishment.

Ultimately, practical decisions about whether society should punish a heroin addict or whether a parent should punish a misbehaving child will be based on value judgments. But psychologists must be careful not to let such value judgments cloud their research. Whether punishment works is one question; whether it should be used is quite another.

AVOIDANCE

People do not always sit still and wait for punishment. A man may learn to leave the room when his wife loudly complains about how much he spent on a new pair of jeans; after a while, he may learn to read the early warning signs and leave the room before her tirade begins. The first situation—in which some response (leaving the room) ends an aversive stimulus that is already under way (the tirade)—is called **escape.** The second situation—in which a response prevents or avoids an unpleasant stimulus before it begins—is called **avoidance.**

In one of the most important laboratory studies of avoidance, Richard Solomon, Leon Kamin, and Lyman Wynne (1953) placed dogs in a shuttle box with two compartments separated by a tall barrier (see Figure 5.9). When a dog received a shock in one compartment, it could jump over the barrier to the other side and escape the shock. In a pilot study, Solomon turned on a buzzer 10 seconds before each shock began. Two dogs quickly learned to jump when they heard the buzzer and thus avoid the shock altogether. Then Solomon turned off the shock and waited to see how long extinction would take. And waited some more. The psychologists

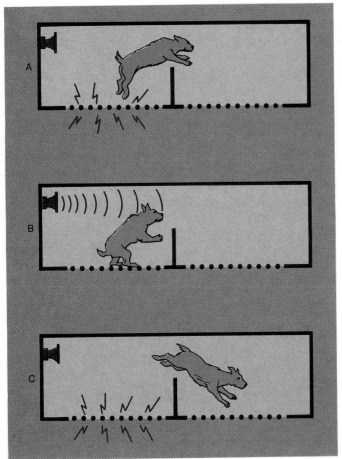

Figure 5.9
Escape conditioning: (A) The dog quickly learns to jump over a barrier to escape an electric shock on the floor of one compartment in a shuttle box. Avoidance conditioning: The dog hears a tone (B) that has previously signaled that a shock will soon begin. It jumps over the barrier (C) before the electricity is actually turned on and thus avoids being shocked.

gave up before the dogs did. One dog jumped 190 times, the other 490 times. Neither dog gave any indication that it would ever stop jumping; in fact, they seemed to be getting better at it.

Solomon and his colleagues proceeded to do more systematic studies with more dogs. Still no sign of extinction. Intuitively, we might say that the avoidance response continues because the dog never waits around long enough to find out that the shock is gone. But even that is not the whole story. Some dogs were forced to stay in the original compartment by a glass barrier that prevented their jump. Although they now heard the buzzer, stayed in the compartment, and were not shocked 40 times, only 2 of 9 dogs stopped jumping over the barrier after the glass was removed. The most effective procedure the experimenters found for extinguishing the dogs' response combined two different strategies. On some extinction trials, a glass barrier was present; the dog was forced to stay in the compartment and was not shocked. On other trials, the dogs were allowed to jump into the safe compartment, but they were shocked on that side.

The analogy to human fears is obvious and somewhat disturbing. Once you learn to avoid something, you may never try it again. Suppose, for example, that the electricity goes off and you're trapped in a small elevator with 17 strangers who've just come from a garlic festival. The combination of close quarters, no lights, and no idea when you'll get out could make for a sickening or even frightening experience. In the future, you may choose to walk up 12 flights of stairs rather than take a chance on being trapped again. But as long as you keep avoiding elevators, you'll never have a chance to unlearn your fear. And even if you do go for an occasional elevator ride, that might not be enough.

Laboratory studies of animal escape and avoidance have also provided insights into possible causes of depression. In 1967, Martin Seligman accidentally discovered that under some conditions, dogs have severe problems learning to avoid shocks. If the animals were first given a series of unavoidable shocks while they were physically restrained and then placed in a shuttle box that provided an opportunity to escape from electrical shock (as in Figure 5.9), these dogs never learned to jump to the other compartment. Instead, Seligman (1975) noted, when the dog first received the shock:

> It ran frantically around for about thirty seconds. But then it stopped moving; to our surprise, it lay down and quietly whined . . . On the next trial, the dog did it again; at first it struggled a bit, and then after a few seconds, it seemed to give up and to accept the shock passively (p. 22).

Seligman called this bizarre behavior pattern *learned helplessness*, because the dogs seemed to have learned that they were helpless; they had no control over the shocks in the earlier part of the study, and they generalized this to a later situation when it was no longer so. Other experimenters later showed comparable phenomena in a wide variety of species, including mice, rats, cats, fish, chickens, and humans.

In general terms, **learned helplessness** refers to an organism's belief, based on prior experience, that it is helpless or lacks control over a particular situation. Interestingly, there are many parallels between the behavior of humans who are depressed and animals who have learned to become helpless. For example, both groups appear passive in the face of stress, do not cope appropriately with the demands of the environment, develop eating problems, and show systematic changes in the chemistry of the brain (specifically, lower levels of the neurotransmitter norepinephrine). Many researchers now believe that human depression may be caused by learned helplessness (see Chapter 13).

Theoretical Issues in Conditioning

OPERANT VERSUS CLASSICAL CONDITIONING: A MODERN VIEW

Throughout this chapter, we have carefully distinguished between two different learning processes, classical conditioning and operant conditioning. Classical conditioning was said to involve involuntary reflexes such as salivation elicited by a food stimulus. In physiological terms, this learning is often linked to the autonomic nervous system (which regulates internal bodily processes—see Chapter 2). In contrast, operant conditioning was a more active form of learning in which voluntary responses were shaped by reinforcement and punishment. Physiologically, it is linked to the central nervous system (the brain and spinal cord).

However, complex forms of learning are not always easy to classify in one category or the other. Even the case of Little Albert, which is often cited as an illustration of classical conditioning, involves elements of both types of learning. After all, Watson struck the bar only when Albert reached out to touch the rat (see page 169); this is a voluntary response controlled by the brain, which might be regarded as operant conditioning.

Complicating the picture further, operant and classical conditioning seem to be governed by some of the same laws. The principles of generalization, discrimination, and extinction, for example, apply equally to both. Although the distinction between classical conditioning and operant conditioning has had a major impact on the study of learning, many researchers have come to believe that they are not fundamentally different processes. Several lines of research have contributed to this view, particularly studies of biofeedback and autoshaping.

Biofeedback. As described in Chapter 3, biofeedback uses reinforcement to teach organisms to control internal physiological states. Earlier, we described some of the practical uses of biofeedback to treat hypertension and other disorders. But most of the first studies of biofeedback grew out of the theoretical controversy over differences between operant and classical conditioning.

Traditionally, researchers believed that involuntary responses controlled by the autonomic nervous system—such as heart rate and blood pressure—could be altered only by classical conditioning. This idea was challenged by Neal Miller (1969) and his colleagues when they claimed that "involuntary" responses could be shaped by rewards.

It is difficult to demonstrate this directly. When a rat is given food pellets as a reward for raising its heart rate, for example, the animal might learn to tense its muscles or run around the cage. Although either of these activities do indeed raise the heart rate, neither provides proof that involuntary responses are being directly controlled; rather, the rat is making a voluntary response (running) that influences an involuntary response (heart rate). To eliminate these voluntary skeletal responses, Miller used the drug curare to paralyze temporarily a group of rats. When reinforced by electrical stimulation of certain brain areas, these rats learned to raise and lower their heart rates, blood pressure, and other physiological functions to obtain this reinforcement.

There was tremendous scientific excitement over this discovery that involuntary responses could be shaped by rewards and thus really were not involuntary after all. As described in Chapter 3, this work had many practical applications, and biofeedback is now widely used in the treatment of certain diseases. But the theoretical impact of the original animal research was blunted when Miller tried to replicate some of his earlier studies and found that he could not. Several years of intensive research failed to reveal the reason (Dworkin & Miller, 1977). Like a murder mystery that has never been solved, the case of the disappearing biofeedback effects continues to puzzle scientific researchers.

Autoshaping.   Biofeedback got all the headlines, but a relatively obscure phenomenon called autoshaping (short for *automatic shaping*) was probably more important in motivating scientists to rethink the relationships between operant and classical conditioning, when some psychologists suggested that key-pecking was an involuntary reflex.

In one experiment (Brown & Jenkins, 1968), "naive" pigeons (birds that had never before spent time in a Skinner box) were first trained to peck grain from an illuminated food tray. Then, a circular key on the wall of the Skinner box was lighted for 8 seconds before each presentation of food. However, the birds received grain whether they pecked or not. After a while, the birds began to peck at the key. This procedure was called **autoshaping;** it eliminated the need for step-by-step shaping of the first key-pecking response.

Since the key-pecking had started without being rewarded, this learning looked suspiciously like an example of classical conditioning. According to this interpretation, food (the unconditional stimulus) led to pecking (the unconditional response); when the lighted key-pecking (conditioned stimulus) was repeatedly paired with food, the key came to elicit pecking (the conditional response).

Further support for the idea that autoshaping involved classical rather than operant conditioning came from an experiment (Williams & Williams, 1969) that showed that the pigeons would continue to peck the key even if this response deprived them of food. If key-pecking were an arbitrary, voluntary, operant response, then the law of effect would hold. When pecking was rewarded, it would increase, and if a pigeon was rewarded for not pecking a key, it would learn to do that too. But pigeons continued to peck even when they would have earned more food by not pecking.

Thus, pecking seems to be an inborn, involuntary reflex. This biological interpretation was strengthened by a study of the way pigeons peck (Moore, 1973). When the reward is food, they peck briefly and forcefully, as they do in eating; but when the reward is water, the pecks are soft and prolonged as they are in drinking (see Figure 5.10).

As a result of these and other studies, most researchers no longer see classical and operant conditioning as two fundamentally different types of learning. At the same time, studies of autoshaping have helped lead to a greater emphasis on trying to understand the natural biological factors that constrain animal learning.

BIOLOGICAL FACTORS

One night when psychologist Martin Seligman was in graduate school, he got sick several hours after a fancy meal of filet mignon with sauce Béarnaise. After that ill-fated evening, he found that his love of this sauce was gone (Seligman & Hager, 1972); in fact, Seligman now thought that sauce Béarnaise was a rather disgusting thing to put over a piece of meat.

A   B

Figure 5.10
When a pigeon pecks a key to obtain water (A), its beak movements resemble those for drinking. When the same pigeon pecks a key to obtain food (B), its beak movements resemble those for eating. This suggests that key-pecking is not simply learned arbitrarily, it may have an inborn biological basis.

At first glance, this looks like a straightforward example of classical conditioning. Illness (the unconditional stimulus) elicits vomiting (the unconditional response) and, through learning, sauce Béarnaise (the conditional stimulus) comes to elicit nausea (the conditional response). But in reality, Seligman's experience violates several widely accepted laws of learning. Long delays between the conditional stimulus and the unconditional stimulus usually lead to little or no learning. But here a sickness six hours later had yielded a strong association. And the problem was limited to sauce Béarnaise. Seligman was not nauseated by filet mignon, the white plates he ate from, or the company of his wife, as traditional learning theory might predict.

That same week, an article by John Garcia and Robert Koelling (1966) provided part of the answer. When animals get sick, they instinctively seem to conclude, "It must have been something I ate." In their experiment, Garcia and Koelling had artificially made two groups of rats sick by exposing them to X-rays after they drank saccharine-sweetened water or "bright, noisy" water (lights flashed and relays clicked while the rats drank). After a single illness, rats avoided the sweet water but drank just as freely of the bright, noisy water. Another two groups of rats were given an electric shock after drinking sweetened or bright, noisy water; they showed the opposite pattern, avoiding bright, noisy water but continuing to drink sweet water. These rats seemed biologically prepared to associate illness with taste and shock with other sorts of stimuli. Later studies (Garcia, McGowan, & Green, 1972) demonstrated that animal taste aversions could be established with long delays and that novel foods were particularly likely to be singled out. Human taste aversions seem to follow similar patterns (Logue, Ophir, & Straus, 1981).

Taste aversions are only one example of the way biology may limit learning. Traditional learning researchers found to their surprise that it is difficult to teach a pigeon to peck a key to avoid a shock, although a rat in the same situation quickly learns to press a bar. Bolles (1970) argues that this is because pigeons naturally respond to a threat by flying away, not by standing there thinking about it. Animal trainers too have found that some behaviors—such as getting a cow to kick or a chicken to stand still—are almost impossible to shape. Breland and Breland (1961) concluded that instincts are sometimes stronger than rewards.

All these findings came as a shock to traditional learning researchers. When behaviorists first began to study animal behavior, some assumed that the fundamental laws of learning were the same for all responses and all animals. In its more extreme version, this led a few researchers to act as though "a white rat is a simple version of a human being" (Lockard, 1971, p. 169). These days, no reputable psychologist accepts such a simplistic view. The result has been a growing interest in such topics as **species-specific behavior,** behavior patterns that are characteristic of a particular species; examples are the unique courting patterns of ring doves and aggressive behavior in the stickleback fish. Much of this research has been conducted by **ethologists,** who study the behavior patterns of a particular species in its natural environment. They have been particularly interested in the influence of inborn biological instincts in determining complex behavior (see Chapter 10).

As in other areas in which researchers are active, there is still considerable controversy regarding these findings. For example, Logue (1979) argued that most taste-aversion phenomena can be explained within the context of general laws of learning that apply across species and across situations.

At the moment, there are no final answers regarding the relative importance of species-specific behavior and general laws of learning. But it is clear that several decades of research have made psychologists far more sophisticated about the questions they ask. Even seemingly simple animal behavior patterns have, on closer inspection, proved to be quite complex.

Cognitive Approaches to Learning

When John Watson announced the birth of behaviorism in 1913, he helped found a school of thought that was to dominate American psychology for nearly half a century. According to many behaviorists, virtually all behavior resulted from classical and operant conditioning. To understand these forms of learning, behaviorists focused on the stimuli that affected an organism and the responses they produced. However, strict behaviorists were unwilling to speculate about the internal processes within an organism (such as memory or thought) that linked stimulus to response. This is sometimes referred to as the black-box approach. Behaviorists study what goes into the box (stimuli) and what comes out (responses) but not the nature of the box itself.

The traditional behavioral view, with its strong emphasis on the study of animal learning, began to be challenged in the 1960s as increasing numbers of psychologists turned to **cognitive psychology,** the study of higher mental processes involved in such areas as attention, perception, memory, language, imagery, and reason. The next two chapters are devoted to cognitive research on human memory (Chapter 6) and language and thought (Chapter 7). Here, we discuss how the cognitive approach has influenced research on animal learning as some researchers have begun to consider the internal mental processes involved even in simple forms of learning.

COGNITIVE FACTORS IN CONDITIONING

A few pioneers in animal learning did resist the behaviorist majority and stressed the importance of internal processes. Wolfgang Köhler, for example, rejected Thorndike's conclusion that animals solve problems through a random process of trial and error. In one of Köhler's classic studies (1925), a chimpanzee named Sultan was placed in a cage with a basket of fruit dangling from the ceiling out of reach. After several vain attempts to jump up and grab the fruit, Sultan solved the problem by dragging over a crate, climbing on top, and jumping from there.

Sultan and his cagemates solved one problem after another. When one box was not enough, they piled two or three; when the box was placed at the side of the cage and filled with heavy stones, they took out the stones before moving the box to a more convenient spot. They used sticks, lengths of wire, and rope to pull objects within reach of their cages; when one stick was not enough, they jammed two together; when no stick was available, they tore a branch off a tree (see Figure 5.11). In fact, the chimps' ingenuity sometimes went further than planned. One chimp

Figure 5.11
Chica the chimp uses a pole to reach for food. According to Wolfgang Köhler, this chimp and others faced with similar problems had sudden insights that produced the solutions.

learned to tease innocent bystanders—including dogs, chickens, and presumably Dr. Köhler—by suddenly stabbing them with a stick whenever they passed within reach of the cage.

Köhler argued that the chimps had solved the problems by **insight,** a sudden understanding of the basic nature of the solution. He cited several sources of evidence, including the fact that chimps often discovered the solutions quite suddenly, sometimes after pausing to examine the materials. These animals were not blindly learning to associate stimuli and responses, Köhler said; they used internal thought processes to comprehend the world around them.

Edward C. Tolman, the most influential American learning theorist to stress cognitive factors, tried to bring such commonsense notions as planning, knowledge, and purpose back into learning theory. Tolman believed that stimuli did not simply become associated with responses (S-R psychology) but rather with each other (S-S, stimulus-stimulus, psychology). According to one traditional S-R view, a rat learned to find the food in a maze by practicing a particular set of muscle movements that must always follow one another in the same sequence. Tolman believed that the rat learned more than a particular chain of stimuli and responses; it learned where the food was.

He was one of the first psychologists to distinguish clearly between *learning* (in this context defined as what the organism knew) and *performance* (what the animal did). Thus, learning is an internal representation of knowledge, which may or may not be expressed in a particular behavioral performance.

To demonstrate the importance of this distinction, Tolman and his colleagues performed a series of experiments to show that a rat's knowledge of the maze was only expressed under certain conditions. According to many black-box behaviorists, a rat learns a path through a maze only when it receives some reward. Tolman and Honzik (1930) placed rats in a maze for 10 consecutive days, allowing them to explore it but providing no food reward. When they put food at the end of the maze on the eleventh day, the rats went straight to the goal. In fact, they made no more errors than a control group that had been rewarded with food from the beginning. Judging by their performance during the first 10 days, the unrewarded rats did not seem to have learned anything about the maze. But when provided with the proper motivation (food), the rats' performance made it clear that they had indeed learned something about the maze. Ingenious experiments like this helped move psychology away from Watson's hard-line behaviorism to include the role of the internal processes involved in thought.

A more recent series of elegant experiments by Robert Rescorla has brought the notion of cognitive expectancy firmly into the mainstream of animal psychology. Rescorla (1968) showed that rats' learning abilities are much more sophisticated than traditional models suggest. Rats seem quite capable of making complex judgments and weighing probabilities.

Rescorla based his research on earlier studies of the classical conditioning of fear. Of course, it is always risky to describe rats' reactions in terms of human emotions. But consider the following procedure. A hungry animal is first trained to press a lever at a high, steady rate to get food. Then, while the rat is pressing the bar, a tone is sounded and the rat is given an electric shock. The shock is not controlled by the bar-pressing, and no matter what the rat does, it continues to hear occasional tones and get shocks for the rest of the experiment. The rat's typical reaction to this situation is called *conditioned suppression*—an animal slows down or stops responding whenever it hears a tone that signals an oncoming shock. Note that this conditioned suppression of responses costs the hungry rat food; when it presses the bar less often, it earns fewer rewards. Speaking loosely, we might say that this irrational reaction to the tone is a sign of fear.

In Rescorla's 1968 study of the cognitive capabilities of rats, the conditional stimulus was a tone that was presented for two minutes. One group of rats was shocked 10% of the time when the tone was on and never when it was off. A second group was shocked 40% of the time whether the tone was on or off. According to traditional theory, the second group should have been more afraid of the tone because they had been shocked four times more often while it was on. In fact, however, the first group was more afraid of the tone (as measured by conditioned suppression). Intuitively, we might say that the fearful rats knew that the tone meant "maybe there will be a shock," whereas the tone provided no information for the other group. Rescorla and Wagner (1972) went on to develop complex mathematical models that successfully predicted how animals respond under various degrees of uncertainty. These results seem to imply that even the lowly rat makes internal judgments about the likelihood of various events and concludes that some stimuli mean more than others.

Traditional studies of the conditioning process in humans have also proved the need to consider complex cognitive factors. For example, classical conditioning of the human eye blink seems to be affected by such factors as anxiety, hostility, and the power of positive thinking (Kimble, 1967, p. 658), precisely the kinds of complex human variables that conditioning experiments had hoped to banish from the laboratory.

Not surprisingly, cognitive factors seem to be even more important for people than for animals. For example, many animal experiments have shown that immediate punishment is more effective than punishment that comes long after a response (Azrin & Holz, 1966). But people are smarter than rats, and immediacy is probably not as important for the average child (Walters & Grusec, 1977). The difference is that you can explain to a 7-year-old that she has to go to bed early tonight because she called Mommy something unpleasant this morning. To understand a child's response we must explore her expectations and interpretations—in short, what she thinks. The next three chapters describe some relevant cognitive processes. Here, our discussion of cognition concludes by introducing a new form of learning, one that is based on imitation.

OBSERVATIONAL LEARNING

People do not always behave in certain ways simply because they were rewarded or punished in the past; sometimes they seem to imitate the actions of others. When your new boss takes you out for dinner at an expensive restaurant, you may not know what you're supposed to do with the third fork from the left. To learn by operant conditioning, you would have to try the fork on each new dish and watch the boss carefully to see if she frowned, indicating an incorrect guess. A more efficient and less embarrassing strategy involves learning by observation. Watch the boss carefully and use your fork when she uses hers. Anyone who has ever watched a child mimic the actions of a favorite cartoon superhero has seen a similar process at work. **Observational learning** involves modeling or copying the behavior of another.

In one of the first and most famous experiments on observational learning, Bandura, Ross, and Ross (1963) studied preschool children's reactions to observing aggression. Ninety-six 3- to 5-year-olds from the Stanford University Nursery School were divided into four groups. Three groups observed different types of aggressive models; the fourth was a control group with no special training. Each child in the first group was left in a room to play with some papers, while a stranger played with more elaborate toys at the other end of the room. After a few minutes, the adult model began to attack a 5-foot-tall inflated "Bobo doll" using "highly novel responses which are unlikely to be performed by children independently." For example, the adult model sat on the doll and repeatedly punched it in the nose, hit it on the head with a mallet, then tossed it in the air and kicked it around the room.

Throughout this aggressive act, the model said things like "Sock him in the nose," "Hit him down," "Kick him," and "Pow."

In the second experimental condition, children watched an identical performance on film. The third group saw a cartoon in which Herman the Cat beat up a Bobo doll. The children in the control group did not participate in this stage of the experiment.

A few minutes later, each child (including those in the control group) was led into another room. At first, he was given a set of attractive toys, but as soon as he got involved in playing with them, the experimenter took the child into still another room. This mild frustration was designed to increase the likelihood of aggression. The toys in the next room fell into two categories. "Aggressive toys" included a child-sized (3-foot-tall) Bobo doll, a mallet, a peg board, two dart guns, and a tether ball with a face painted on it hanging from the ceiling. "Nonaggressive toys" included a tea set, crayons, dolls, and plastic farm animals.

For the next 20 minutes, each child's behavior was carefully observed through a one-way mirror. Sure enough, the children who had watched aggressive models were more likely to engage in aggressive play. Some of them displayed virtual "carbon copies of the model's behavior" (see Figure 5.12). Although there were some signifi-

Figure 5.12
The top row shows the aggressive behaviors displayed by an adult model. Looking down each column, note how closely children later imitated these actions.

cant differences among the groups, in general it did not seem to matter whether a child had seen a live model, a film, or a cartoon; the children in all three experimental groups were more aggressive than the children in the control group. Simply watching the actions of a model had led the children to imitate those actions.

Some of the subtleties of imitation learning began to emerge in later studies. One follow-up study (Bandura, 1965) looked at the effects of rewarding or punishing a model's act. In this experiment, nursery school children watched an adult abuse a Bobo doll on television. This time, the experimenter paired each aggressive act with a distinctive phrase, to see just how closely the child mimicked the behavior. While the model sat on the doll and punched it, he said, "Pow, right in the nose, boom, boom"; when he beat it over the head with a mallet, he said, "Sockeroo . . . stay down," and so on.

For children in the "model-rewarded" condition, the film went on to show a second adult congratulating the model for being a "strong champion" and rewarding him with popcorn, candy, Cracker Jacks, and a large glass of Seven-Up. In the "model-punished" condition, other children saw the second adult come on the scene shaking his finger and saying, "Hey there, you big bully. You quit picking on that clown" (p. 591). When the model backed up and tripped, the other adult sat on him and spanked him with a rolled-up magazine. The control group of children saw only the first part of the film.

Not surprisingly, when the children were later given their own chance to beat up a Bobo doll, the group who had seen the model punished were least likely to be aggressive themselves. (The group who saw the model rewarded were about as aggressive as the control group.) Every child was later able to repeat the distinctive phrases and tell the experimenter what the model had done in the movie. But children who had seen the model punished did not repeat this behavior themselves; in Tolman's terms, their learning was not reflected in their performance.

We shall return to some of the implications of these studies for understanding human personality in Chapter 11. In this context, observational learning is important primarily because it is a far more subtle form of learning than classical or operant conditioning. Both types of conditioning depend on direct experience with external stimuli and reinforcers. In observational learning, the organism learns through a more cognitive process that involves interpreting one's observations.

As psychologists have become increasingly sophisticated about the complexity of learning, many of their theoretical advances have been applied in practical attempts to change people's behavior.

APPLIED PSYCHOLOGY

Behavior Modification

Behavior modification (or behavior therapy) is a type of psychotherapy based on principles derived from studies of learning. The idea of applying behavioral principles to problems in human behavior first became popular around 1960 and has been growing in influence ever since.

Just as behavioral research focuses on observable actions and the variables that control them, behavior modification is primarily concerned with changing specific behaviors. Wanting to "be a better person" may be a fine statement for a high school yearbook, but a behavior therapist demands more specific goals. Suppose you want to have more friends. The behavior therapist might begin by translating this general desire into a more specific behavioral goal such as going out one night a week with a new friend.

Just as researchers gradually shape the behavior of laboratory animals by rewarding one small segment of a complex behavior at a time, so a behavior therapist's program probably involves a step-by-step approach. In this case, you could start by forcing yourself to make one pleasant remark every day to a co-worker or schoolmates.

The confirmed behavior therapist does not believe in analyzing where a problem comes from or how deep it runs. She would probably not suggest that the reason you have trouble forming friendships is that your family moved every few years when you were a child. Beyond being skeptical about the possibility of proving this type of speculation, the behaviorist frankly does not care why you have few friends. And neither, she believes, should you. The important thing is to develop new friendships—now.

Behavior modification also emphasizes the careful measurement of behavioral change. For example, one study of first-graders (Ward & Baker, 1968) began by asking teachers to identify problem students. But the researchers did not simply accept the teachers' classifications. Observers carefully watched these and other children in the class, 15 minutes a day, 4 days a week. After 5 weeks, they totaled the number of times each child had behaved appropriately (for example, paying attention or raising his hand before speaking) and inappropriately (such as hitting other children or blurting out comments in class).

This preliminary stage established a baseline of just how bad the troublemakers really were. The teachers were then instructed to reward the problem children with attention and praise whenever they acted appropriately and simply to ignore them when they misbehaved. Observers continued to rate classroom behavior in the same way as before. This operant conditioning was quite effective; appropriate behavior increased among the troublemakers and inappropriate behavior decreased.

Learning principles like these have been applied in many different settings; here we focus on one of the most straightforward applications. In a **token economy,** behavior is changed by rewarding specific actions with tokens that can be exchanged for reinforcers. The first token economy was established in a special ward in Anna State Hospital in Illinois (Ayllon & Azrin, 1968). Forty-four severely disturbed female patients were chosen for this experiment. The typical patient was about 50 years old, had been diagnosed as schizophrenic (see Chapter 13), and had spent the last 16 years confined in mental institutions. Most were severely withdrawn; some had never been heard to utter a single intelligible word.

Setting up a token economy involved three stages: identifying specific behaviors to be changed, identifying effective reinforcers for the particular population, and establishing a set of rules for rewarding behavior with tokens (such as poker chips or coins) and exchanging them for rewards.

Given the extreme pathology of this group, the behaviors chosen for reinforcement were quite basic; for example, patients could earn one token by either dressing themselves, brushing their teeth, making their beds, or participating in an exercise class. Helping with work around the ward—emptying the trash, washing pots and pans, cleaning the tables and trays after a meal—earned each patient additional tokens. These could be exchanged for a wide variety of reinforcers, such as cigarettes and candy, a pass to walk around the hospital grounds, permission to attend a movie, or a more desirable dormitory assignment.

The effects on behavior were quite dramatic. Patients who had been withdrawn for years began to help around the ward to earn tokens. The average patient earned almost 500 tokens in the first 20 days of the experiment, and every person earned and spent some tokens. However, the behavior was maintained only for as long as the reinforcement was contingent on specific actions. In the second 20 days of the experiment, patients were given a "vacation with pay" in which they were told, "We

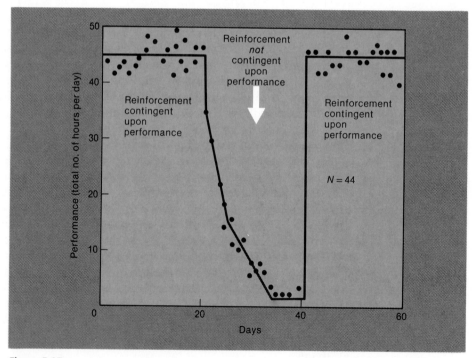

Figure 5.13

Results of a study of a token economy at Anna State Hospital in Illinois. Mental patients were reinforced (with tokens later exchanged for rewards) whenever they performed specific acts, such as dressing themselves. When reinforcement was suspended, performance declined.

are very pleased with your work and would like you to continue working, [but] there will be no extra tokens for work" (Ayllon & Azrin, 1968, p. 243). As Figure 5.13 shows, during this period, work on the ward gradually fell off. But when tokens were once more given only after the performance of tasks, behavior improved rapidly.

Later studies revealed that token economies can dramatically alter the behavior of the mentally retarded, alcoholics, drug addicts, autistic children, and preschoolers. Research continues on the question of producing more general changes in patterns of behavior that can be transferred to other situations.

This is just one example of the way behavioral principles have been applied to the real world of human problems; others are described in Chapter 14.

Summary

1. **Learning** may be defined as a relatively permanent change in behavior that occurs through experience.
2. Ivan Pavlov discovered a basic learning process called **classical conditioning.** This involved repeatedly pairing a stimulus (called the **unconditional stimulus,** or **US**) that elicited a reflex response (the **unconditional response,** or **UR**) with a previously neutral stimulus (the **conditional stimulus,** or **CS**). In time, this came to elicit a similar response (the **conditional response,** or **CR**).
3. The gradual disappearance of a learned response is called **extinction.** In classical conditioning, CRs are extinguished by repeatedly presenting the CS without the US. **Spontaneous recovery** refers to the reappearance of an extinguished response after a rest period.
4. **Generalization** involves responding in a similar way to stimuli that resemble each other; the greater the similarity, the closer the response. **Discrimination** involves learning to respond only to a specific kind of stimulus.
5. In **operant conditioning,** the probability of a response increases when reinforcement is presented or decreases when punishment is presented following that response. Traditionally, operant conditioning has been said to apply to active, voluntary processes, and classical conditioning applies to passive, involuntary reflexes.
6. A **reinforcer** is any stimulus that, when paired with a particular behavior, increases the probability of that behavior. There are two different types. **Positive reinforcers** present a stimulus and **negative reinforcers** remove a stimulus; both increase the probability of behavior. In contrast, a **punisher** is any stimulus that, when paired with a particular behavior, decreases the probability of that behavior.
7. Reinforcers and punishers can be presented according to many patterns or **schedules of reinforcement. Continuous schedules** involve reinforcing every single response. The four most common schedules of **partial reinforcement** are

fixed-ratio schedules, variable-ratio schedules, fixed-interval schedules, and **variable-interval schedules.**

8. **Shaping** involves teaching a complex behavior by reinforcing *successive approximations* of the desired activity; it is important because it is a practical and quick way to teach novel and complex behaviors.

9. Most psychologists now agree that if a response is punished, it is less likely to be repeated in the future. However, under some conditions, punishment has negative side effects.

10. **Avoidance** refers to a response that avoids or prevents an unpleasant stimulus. Avoidance responses are difficult to extinguish and seem to be involved in many human fears. Certain types of avoidance learning produce **learned helplessness,** an organism's belief that it is helpless or lacks control over a particular situation. Learned helplessness may be one cause of human depression.

11. Many researchers now believe that operant and classical conditioning are not fundamentally different processes. Studies of **autoshaping** (automatic shaping) suggested that the key-pecking of pigeons—previously believed to be a voluntary, operant response—may in fact be an involuntary reflex.

12. Studies of taste aversions have helped reveal how biological factors can limit learning. Animals seem to be biologically prepared to associate illness with novel tastes, even if the illness occurs several hours after eating. This research has helped stimulate interest in **species-specific behavior,** behavior patterns that are characteristic of a particular species.

13. **Cognitive psychology** studies the higher mental processes involved in such areas as attention, perception, memory, language, imagery, and reason. For example, Köhler studied chimpanzee **insight**—the sudden understanding of the basic nature of a problem solution. **Observational learning** involves modeling or copying the behavior of another.

14. **Behavior modification,** or behavior therapy, is a type of psychotherapy that is based on principles derived from studies of learning.

Discussion of "Becoming a Critical Consumer"

Skinner's opinion that punishment does not work directly contradicts the research described in the text. The explanation is simple. The novel was written in 1948, and research cited in the text was conducted after that date. When Skinner wrote his novel, most psychologists agreed that punishment was ineffective. Today, there is still a great deal of controversy about the negative effects of punishment, particularly under certain conditions described in the text. But virtually all agree that punishment does reduce the frequency of behavior.

The critical consumer should never blindly accept the opinion of an expert, no matter how famous he or she may be. It is always useful to examine the evidence behind a claim and to see whether new discoveries have challenged old beliefs.

To Learn More

Skinner, B. F. *Walden Two.* New York: Macmillan, 1948. A novel that describes a utopian community based on behavioral principles and research. Outdated in some ways, but still a classic.

Bower, G. H., & Hilgard, E. R. *Theories of Learning* (5th ed.). Englewood Cliffs, N.J.: Prentice-Hall, 1981. An overview of the history of psychological theories of learning.

Schwartz, B. *Psychology of Learning and Behavior*. New York: Norton, 1978. A textbook emphasizing current research on animal learning.

6

Remembering and Forgetting

H. M. had his first epileptic seizure at the age of 10. By early adulthood, the disease was so severe that he could not work or lead a normal life. Despite the fact that he took a variety of anticonvulsant medicines, H. M. had a grand mal seizure in which he lost consciousness and fell into convulsions at least once a week. Less severe petit mal seizures occurred about once an hour, leaving H. M. in an almost continuous state of confusion.

Finally, in desperation, H. M. agreed to experimental surgery to destroy apparently diseased tissue in the temporal lobe of the brain, including a structure called the hippocampus. Although the operation virtually eliminated H. M.'s seizures, this success was overshadowed by an unexpected and tragic side effect—H. M. lost the ability to learn anything new.

When psychologist Brenda Milner (1959, p. 49) met H. M. for the first time nearly two years later, he was quite confused and kept repeating, "It is as though I am just waking up from a dream; it seems as though it has just happened."

When his family moved to a new home after the operation, for several years H. M. was unable to learn the new address or to find his way home alone. He did not recognize his neighbors even after he had met them many times and could never remember where common household objects such as the lawn mower or frying pans were kept. H. M. was able to read newspapers and magazines, but he totally forgot their contents within 15 minutes. As a result, he often read the same material over and over again without ever realizing that he had seen it before.

Almost as amazing as the things H. M. could not do were the things he still could. IQ tests indicated that his intelligence had actually improved somewhat after the operation, probably because the frequent epileptic attacks had left him too confused and disoriented to do well on tests. In general, H. M. had a normal memory of everything that happened before the operation, although he was a bit hazy about the two years immediately before the surgery. He could briefly remember a string of digits, respond appropriately to everyday events, and reason normally; H. M. simply could not remember anything new for more than a few minutes.

To a limited extent, H. M.'s ability to remember increased as time went by. After eight years of living in the same house, he was able to draw a diagram showing how the rooms were laid out. He gradually became familiar with the two or three blocks around his home. In systematic tests, he was able to recognize the faces of some people who became famous after his operation, including Elvis Presley, Nikita Khrushchev, and John Glenn (Marslen-Wilson & Tueber, 1975).

At this writing, H. M. is nearly 60 years old and is still being tested by psychologists at regular intervals. To a certain extent, he has learned to cope with his disability; he apologizes frequently for not being able to remember the names of people to whom he has been introduced and uses the weather to deduce the time of the year. But his ability to learn new information remains severely limited. Even after six months of employment at a rehabilitation center for the retarded, H. M. could not describe where he worked, what he did there, or the route along which he was driven every day (Milner, Corkin, & Teuber, 1968).

H. M.'s disability has had a major impact on the practice of medicine; neurosurgeons are now reluctant to perform any operation that might involve damage to the hippocampus. But this tragic case has also led to greater understanding of the nature of human memory. For example, as we describe in detail later, H. M.'s deficits suggest that there may be at least two separate memory systems, one for storing old information (which was not damaged by the operation) and another for learning new information (which seems to involve the hippocampus).

Despite this promising beginning, the results of biological research on memory have been rather discouraging. There have been many attempts to localize memory precisely in the brain but no clear successes. As explained in Chapter 2, complex psychological functions such as memory seem to involve a bewildering array of changes in the central nervous system.

Instead, studies of memory have been dominated by other theoretical paradigms. Like research on animal learning, the early history of memory research was dominated by behaviorism, and recent developments owe more to a cognitive perspective. To see how this theoretical progression applies to theories of why we forget, we must begin by describing the techniques psychologists have developed to measure precisely how much people remember under various conditions and how much they forget.

Measuring Memory

THE ORIGINS OF MEMORY RESEARCH

In 1885, Hermann Ebbinghaus published a slim volume titled *On Memory*. It was his first and last book on the topic, but it had an enormous impact on the development of psychology.

Earlier scholars had been content to speculate about human memory, but Ebbinghaus was determined to measure it objectively. His first problem was choosing appropriate materials to memorize. Ebbinghaus (1885) believed that poetry or prose involved too many complicating factors:

> The content is now narrative in style, now descriptive, now reflective; it contains now a phrase that is pathetic, now one that is humorous; its metaphors are sometimes beautiful, sometimes harsh; its rhythm is sometimes smooth and sometimes rough (p. 23).

So he invented new materials of his own, designed to be meaningless, simple, and varied: three-letter nonsense syllables like ZOK, LAR, and BEF, each consisting of a vowel between two consonants.

To discover the laws of human memory, Ebbinghaus experimented on himself. Hour after hour, day after day, year after year, Ebbinghaus memorized thousands upon thousands of lists of nonsense syllables. He compared the number of repetitions it took to learn short lists and long lists. He learned other lists, waited various periods of time, and plotted the mathematical curves of forgetting. He compared repeated learning of the same list in one day with the same amount of practice spaced over several days. Then he memorized more lists to study still other variables that might affect memory.

Hermann Ebbinghaus (1850–1909) was one of the first to study human memory systematically, and the techniques he developed shaped the course of the next 70 years of research. After receiving a PhD in philosophy at the University of Bonn, he went on to a period of private study. While supporting himself by tutoring in France and England, Ebbinghaus devoted several hours each day to studying lists of standard stimuli and later testing how well he remembered them. This lonely research led to the publication of his book *On Memory* and helped him to gain a faculty appointment in Berlin.

The care and precision of these one-man experiments is still admired by scientists today. For example, because Ebbinghaus suspected that memory might vary at different times of day, throughout 1883 and 1884 he always tested himself between 1 and 3 p.m. Recent research on biological rhythms (see Chapter 3) supports the wisdom of this course.

In one typical series of experiments, Ebbinghaus quantified how memories fade with the passage of time. In 1879 and 1880, he memorized 1,228 lists of 13 nonsense syllables. He began by reading each list aloud, at a regular pace timed by the loud ticking of a watch. After Ebbinghaus had repeated the list often enough to feel that he had learned it, he looked at the first nonsense syllable and tried to repeat the others from memory. When he was able to do this twice without pausing or making a mistake, he recorded the time it had taken to learn and went on to memorize five to seven more lists.

Then, Ebbinghaus would pause for a precise period of time—19 minutes, 63 minutes, 525 minutes, 1 day, 2 days, 6 days, or 31 days. When the interval was up, he would take out the original lists and memorize them again. Almost invariably, the second learning went more quickly. The actual amount of time he saved on this relearning provided a precise measure of how much he had remembered.

Figure 6.1 shows the average results of Ebbinghaus's tedious memorization of the 15,964 nonsense syllables in this experiment. As you can see, Ebbinghaus forgot more in the first hour than he did in the next month! In the 100 years since this report, many researchers have verified this systematic time course; memory drops off sharply at first, then much more slowly.

Important as this discovery was, it was probably not Ebbinghaus's greatest contribution. The first step for scientific pioneers often involves developing new methods for measuring old phenomena. Above all, Ebbinghaus showed that higher thought processes could be studied scientifically. His emphasis on carefully controlled experimental conditions and rigorous analysis of the results laid the foundation for a new science of human memory.

RELEARNING, RECOGNITION, AND RECALL

Contemporary psychologists now distinguish between three major ways of measuring memory: recognition, recall, and relearning. Ebbinghaus relied primarily on the last of these techniques.

Relearning studies involve a comparison between learning material once (perhaps measured by time or the number of repetitions required) and relearning the same material on a second occasion. For example, Ebbinghaus's "savings scores" in Figure 6.1 were computed by measuring the time saved on the second occasion and dividing this by the original learning time.

Relearning is a sensitive procedure for measuring memory and often reveals that we know more than we realize. One of the most dramatic examples of this sensitivity appeared in a study that psychologist Harold Burtt began in the 1920s with his own son. When the boy was 15 months old, his father started reading him three short sections from Sophocles' play *Oedipus Tyrannus* in the original Greek. Burtt read each passage of 20 lines or so aloud once a day for three months. By the time the child was 3 years old, he had listened to 21 different ancient Greek selections 90 times each.

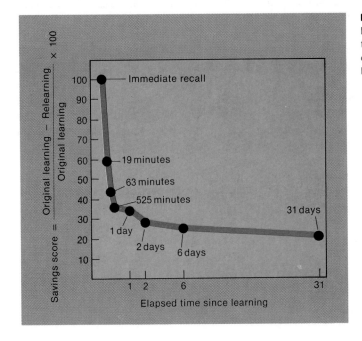

Figure 6.1

Ebbinghaus's forgetting curve. Note that the time saved relearning nonsense syllables declined very rapidly in the first day, then leveled off.

Years later, the psychologist father tested his son to see whether all that Greek had made any impression. Using the method of relearning, he was able to show that it had. At the age of $8\frac{1}{2}$, the son was able to memorize the passages he had heard as an infant 30% more quickly than control passages (which he had not heard before) from the same play. Subsequent tests of different passages revealed that this dim memory continued to fade with time. At the age of 14, he relearned passages only 8% faster, and by age 18 there were no savings whatever (Burtt, 1941). In short, the relearning tests indicated that the mind of an infant records its surroundings even when it cannot make sense of them.

Most of the time, psychologists measure memory in terms of more familiar tasks. **Recognition** involves deciding whether we have encountered information before (that is, whether we recognize it). **Recall** involves remembering information spontaneously or on the basis of certain clues. Multiple-choice examinations test recognition; fill-in-the-blank examinations test recall.

You would probably find it harder to recall the year that the Magna Charta was signed than to recognize whether it was 1066, 1215, or 1492. And in general, psychologists have indeed found that recognition is easier than recall. For example, one group of researchers (Bahrick, Bahrick, & Wittlinger, 1975) investigated how well people remembered the names and faces of high school classmates anywhere from 2 weeks to 57 years after they graduated.

This particular experiment is a good example of the way many researchers are now trying to study human memory in the "real world." But leaving the laboratory has its price, and this study had to overcome a variety of complications. Some people came from larger graduating classes than others; some never opened their yearbooks and others had read them often; some people saw their old classmates frequently and others almost never did. The researchers collected data on all these factors and used a complex series of statistical corrections to minimize their effects.

They used several different tests of memory. The first was free recall; people were simply asked to write down the names of as many classmates as they could remember. Two other tests involved the recognition of names and faces. People were shown five yearbook portraits or five names at a time and asked to pick the one from their class.

A few months after graduation the average subject could remember the names of only about one-sixth of his classmates. This free recall dropped slowly but surely with the passing years; nearly a half century after graduation, only 1 out of every 15 classmates came easily to mind.

On the other hand, the average subject could recognize the faces of 9 out of 10 of his classmates a full 35 years after graduation; it made no difference whether the subjects came from large or small graduating classes. The recognition of names was almost as impressive. Up to 15 years after graduation, 90% of their classmates' names still rang a bell.

These findings provide an impressive testimonial to the staying power of human memory. The fact that people could remember the names and faces of several hundred classmates while spontaneously recalling only a few dozen supports the idea that there is a great deal more information hidden away in our minds than we may

Before reading on, try to name the actors in this classic scene from the film *Casablanca*. Since recognition is easier than recall, the task would be far simpler if you were told the actors' names and asked merely to match the names of the people in the photograph. (Ingrid Bergman, Claude Raines, Paul Henreid, and Humphrey Bogart are the actors pictured; the male actors are listed from left to right.)

realize. Later in this chapter, we stress the distinction between storing information and retrieving it. The fact that you cannot find a book in the library does not mean that it is not there, and the fact that you cannot recall a classmate's name does not mean that this information has disappeared entirely from your mind.

Psychologists have measured relearning, recognition, and recall in many different contexts in a continuing search for the laws of human memory. In the next section we outline briefly how progress has been made over the last century on one of the most fundamental problems in this field—why people forget.

Forgetting

In Chapter 5, we saw how early behaviorists took a black-box approach to animal learning by focusing on external stimuli and the responses they produced while ignoring what went on inside the organism. The pioneers in memory research followed a similar path.

For several decades, most of their studies were based on the notion of **associationism,** the belief that even the most complex memories are ultimately based on associations between simple ideas. From this perspective, Ebbinghaus's decision to develop a simple and pure measure of memory makes perfect sense. He assumed that once psychology understood how associative bonds were formed between simple nonsense syllables, the same laws could be applied to more complex stimuli like words, images, and ideas.

Through the 1950s, most researchers focused on the variables that influenced the formation of associative bonds. The experimental subject who happened to memorize a particular list was seen as a passive participant; memory was shaped by external forces. For example, many studies revealed that short lists were learned more easily than long lists. The assumption was that this external variable (the length of a list) directly influenced the strength of the bonds between stimuli, and there was little interest in how this process occurred within the human mind or whether the feelings and expectations of the memorizer made any difference.

AN ASSOCIATIVE APPROACH: DECAY VERSUS INTERFERENCE

Given this orientation, the problem of forgetting could be restated in another way: How is the association between two verbal stimuli broken? Traditionally, researchers accepted one of two conflicting theories. Either we forget simply because the passage of time weakens the associative bond (decay theory) or forgetting results when the formation of one bond interferes with another (interference theory).

At first glance, this might seem to be an easy question to resolve. Simply ask people to memorize a list, do nothing for a while, and then see whether time alone makes the memory fade. The problem is that even Zen masters find it impossible to do absolutely nothing. And anything they do in that critical waiting period between the original learning and the subsequent test may interfere with memory. This problem of logic fueled the theoretical controversy between interference and decay for several decades.

More formally, the **decay theory** holds that a physical memory trace gradually fades as time passes. Like a message drawn in sand at the beach, a physical memory first fades and then disappears altogether. In some ways, this is the simplest possible explanation of Ebbinghaus's famous forgetting curve (Figure 6.1).

The **interference theory** holds that people forget information because one memory prevents another from being recovered. For example, you may make the unfortunate mistake of calling your new boyfriend Howard when that is actually an old boyfriend's name; the old memory interferes with the new one.

In one early experiment contrasting the effects of interference and decay, Jenkins and Dallenbach (1924) asked people to memorize lists of nonsense syllables just before they went to sleep. When subjects were awakened one, two, four, or eight hours later, those who had slept longer had forgotten more. People who memorized the same lists in the morning and were tested after equal periods of staying awake had forgotten more than the sleepers at every interval. The simplest interpretation is that the passage of time does indeed cause some forgetting (by decay), but the interference of other intervening activity causes even more. However, studies of electrical activity in the brain during sleep (see Chapter 3) suggest that this period is more than just an empty period of time.

Despite continuing difficulties with performing a pure test of interference theory versus decay theory, these results and others made it clear that interference played some role in forgetting. There are two major types of interference: old learning can interfere with new learning (proactive inhibition) or new learning can interfere with old learning (retroactive inhibition). More formally, **proactive inhibition** occurs when information is forgotten as a result of interference from material that was presented before the learning task. **Retroactive inhibition** occurs when information is forgotten as a result of information that was presented after the learning task. Although this may seem confusing at first, Figure 6.2 illustrates that the difference simply depends on whether the interference comes before or after the task in question.

Before the 1950s, memory researchers focused on the workings of retroactive inhibition. In one typical study (Melton & Irwin, 1940), subjects learned a list of nonsense syllables and then relearned it 30 minutes later. During the half-hour delay, some subjects simply rested; others were exposed to a second list of nonsense syllables from 5 to 40 times. This intervening task interfered with the memory of the first list. In fact, the relationship was quite systematic; the more times people had heard the second list, the more trouble they had remembering the first. This study demonstrates that if you memorize a list of seventeenth-century English poets and then another of eighteenth-century English poets, the second list will retroactively interfere with your memory of the first.

But in 1957, Benton Underwood emphasized that interference could also work in the other direction. In a classic piece of scientific detective work, Underwood demonstrated that the more nonsense syllables a person has learned in the past, the more trouble he will have mastering new ones. To prove this, Underwood directly compared the performance of old pros like Ebbinghaus (who memorized literally thousands of nonsense syllables) with volunteers who were encountering stimuli like

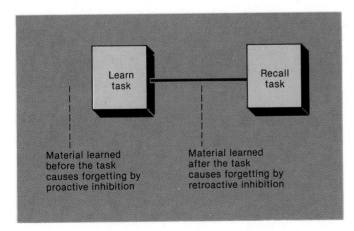

Figure 6.2

According to the interference theory, one memory prevents another from being recalled. The interfering information may come before or after the task in question.

Learn task

Recall task

Material learned before the task causes forgetting by proactive inhibition

Material learned after the task causes forgetting by retroactive inhibition

ZED, CIK, and JOP for the first time. The naive volunteers consistently performed better. In fact, on the average, people recalled their first list best, the second list they learned second best, and so on. The more nonsense one had encountered in the past, the greater the proactive inhibition and the more forgetting. In this case, the more you know, the more likely you are to forget.

Just two years after Underwood broadened the theory of interference, Lloyd and Margaret Peterson (1959) published an influential study that rekindled interest in the possibility of memory decay. These experimenters simply read three-letter nonsense syllables aloud, waited a few seconds, and asked subjects to repeat the syllables. This sounds like an absurdly easy task. The average person could remember any syllable for seconds, minutes, or even years simply by repeating it silently while waiting. However, the Petersons prevented this type of covert rehearsal by requiring subjects to perform a distracting task while they waited. When the subject heard the nonsense syllable, he also heard a three-digit number. He was required to count backward by 3s from the number (e.g., 308, 305, 302, 299 . . .) until a light flashed on, signaling that it was time to report the original syllable.

Under these conditions, the Petersons were amazed to see how quickly memories faded. As you can see in Figure 6.3, after 3 seconds of counting backward, people correctly repeated about 80% of the syllables, after 9 seconds only 30%, and after 18 seconds less than 10%.

Since memory declined so rapidly, it seemed likely that the neglected physical trace had simply faded away. But proponents of interference theory soon came up with another explanation. According to Keppel and Underwood (1962), these memories did not fade quickly as a result of decay; rather, the Petersons' subjects confused later syllables with what had come before. To test their alternative explanation, Kepple and Underwood looked more closely at the first few trials. Using a large

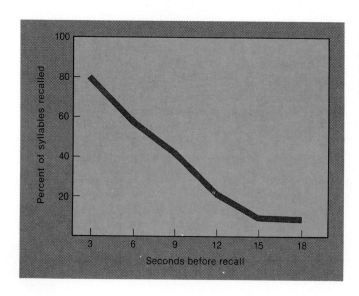

Figure 6.3

When rehearsal is prevented by engaging in a distracting task, memory for nonsense syllables declines rapidly. This suggests that short-term memory maintains storage for seconds rather than minutes.

number of subjects, they found that the first time people were asked to remember three letters, almost everyone did so perfectly, even after counting backward for 18 seconds. On the second trial, more than 1 out of every 5 subjects forgot the letters, and by the third trial 2 out of every 5 could not remember. Proactive inhibition mounted quickly, and early learning interfered with later memory even in this simple task.

This study, like many others, shows how interference is clearly one factor in forgetting. It is also a reminder of how difficult it can be to demonstrate that the passage of time, by itself, causes memories to decay.

A COGNITIVE APPROACH: CUE-DEPENDENT FORGETTING

Virtually all the research comparing the interference and decay theories arose from Ebbinghaus's associative tradition of verbal learning—trying to understand the way individual stimuli (usually words or nonsense syllables) were linked to responses. In the last few decades, this black-box approach has been rejected by animal-learning researchers (see Chapter 5) and by those who study human memory. It has been replaced by a more **cognitive approach** that explores the inner structure and organization of the mind and the active processes used by a learner. More specifically, many take an **information-processing approach,** which attempts to analyze thought processes as a series of separate steps. Just as a computer reads information, transforms it, and produces output, so the human mind is seen as a device for processing information.

Cognitive psychologists distinguish between three major processes in remembering: encoding, storage, and retrieval. **Encoding** is the transformation of a physical stimulus into a form that human memory accepts. **Storage** is the retention of this memory, and **retrieval** involves recovering information from storage. Current views of forgetting stress the role of these active internal processes.

Thus, instead of focusing on whether forgetting is caused by interference or decay, many researchers are now concerned with what happens to information that is forgotten. Is it entirely lost from memory (dropped from storage) like a computer tape that has been erased? Or is it still locked away in storage but difficult to retrieve because it has been "misplaced?" This latter possibility, the failure of retrieval, is the focus of the theory of cue-dependent forgetting.

Some theorists believe that little information is ever lost from storage in long-term memory. (This will be distinguished from short-term memory in the next section.) What we lose is the ability to find, or retrieve, the information. The mind is like a giant reference library with books that never leave the shelves. The problem is, we often do not know where to look for a specific volume. According to Endel Tulving's (1974) theory of **cue-dependent forgetting,** forgetting is caused by a failure to retrieve information from storage due to inadequate memory cues.

Intuitively, this theory seems appealing. Every time we give someone a hint to prod memory, we acknowledge the importance of retrieval cues. Many experiments have systematically shown the difference such cues can make. In one of the simplest (Tulving & Thompson, 1971), people were asked to memorize lists of 28 words.

They were generally able to remember only about 20% of the words under the specific testing conditions. But when the first three letters of "forgotten" words were offered as a hint (for example, *gra* as a retrieval cue for *grape*), these same people remembered more than 50% of the list. Therefore, they had not lost the words from memory storage; they were just temporarily unable to retrieve them.

According to Tulving's **encoding-specificity principle,** recall improves if the same cues are present during recall as during the original learning. For example, you may have had the experience of failing to recognize a person in an unfamiliar context. This happened to a friend of mine when she saw her new gynecologist in a singles bar. She knew the man seemed familiar, but she just couldn't place him. Tulving's explanation is that this "stranger's" identity was encoded into memory in terms of particular cues. If he had worn his white lab coat—one of the cues present when she first met him—to the bar, she would have recognized him more easily. Memories are sometimes like a locked file cabinet that can only be opened with the right key.

Tulving (1974) and his colleagues have performed a series of studies demonstrating that recall can indeed be improved by providing appropriate cues. Other aspects of his theory have been questioned. For example, later in this chapter we shall question the idea that all information remains permanently stored in long-term memory. But on one point virtually all researchers now agree: forgetting is a complex process that can only be understood by exploring the active internal workings of the mind. The next section describes the most influential model of these internal processes.

The Atkinson-Shiffrin Model of Memory

In 1968, Richard Atkinson and R. M. Shiffrin proposed that human memory is organized into three stages (see Figure 6.4). Our sensory impressions of the world are first held for a moment in sensory storage. As we shall see in the next section, this memory system holds a great deal of information but loses it within seconds. Information that is lost from sensory storage is forgotten forever, but a small amount of information is transferred to short-term memory.

Short-term memory has a limited capacity. New information displaces the old; and when an item is displaced, it too is forgotten. But information can be held in short-term memory by repeating it (this is called *rehearsal*). The longer an item is held in short-term memory, the more likely it is to be transferred into long-term memory.

Long-term memory is seen here as a storage system that can hold information almost indefinitely. However, conscious awareness of this knowledge involves transferring a memory back into short-term memory, and such factors as interference can make it difficult to retrieve some information.

To make this model more concrete, consider what happens when you flip through the Yellow Pages fo find a pizzeria that will deliver at 3 a.m. Each time you read a phone number, a literal picture of what you see is held for a fraction of a second in the portion of memory called *sensory storage*. If you choose to dial a certain number, it is passed to a second level, called *short-term memory*, which will hold that information a limited period, perhaps as long as 30 seconds. But once you dial an unfamiliar phone number, it is usually forgotten. In fact, if the line is busy, you will probably have to look up the number again to redial it a few seconds later. Thus, short-term memory quickly fades away unless you rehearse the number or make some effort to retain it. If, however, you are forced to dial Guido's Pizza City 18 times before you get through, you will probably begin to remember the number. At this point the telephone number has passed into *long-term memory*, the major memory system, which contains everything you know about the past.

The original Atkinson-Shiffrin model was actually far more complex than this short explanation suggests. Each of the three major stages was further subdivided. For example, sensory storage included separate auditory, visual, and other components. Less common routes for memory transfer were also outlined. For example, Atkinson and Shiffrin believed that it was sometimes possible for information to bypass short-term memory, proceeding directly from sensory storage to long-term memory. For our purposes, however, it is best to concentrate on the broad outlines of the model as portrayed in Figure 6.4.

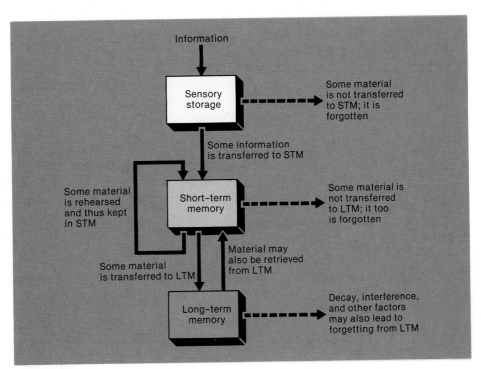

Figure 6.4
A simplified diagram of the Atkinson-Shiffrin model, showing the relationships between three memory systems.

EVIDENCE FOR SEPARATE MEMORY SYSTEMS: AMNESIA

The idea that short-term memory for immediate events is somehow separate from and different from long-term, more permanent memories can be traced back to the 1890s in the writings of William James. But it was only in the 1960s that several lines of evidence convinced the scientific community of the importance of this distinction.

Some of this evidence came from laboratory studies of verbal learning. Other evidence came from clinical studies of people with **amnesia**—a loss of memory usually caused by damage to the brain. **Anterograde amnesia** involves a lack of ability to remember new information for more than a few seconds. This was the problem faced by H. M., the epileptic whose hippocampus was removed. In the final stages of chronic alcoholism, patients often suffer from a similarly confused state called Korsakoff's syndrome. For both H. M. and Korsakoff's patients, short-term memory seems intact; they can remember material for up to 30 seconds. And older information that had been stored in long-term memory before the onset of disease can still be remembered. Thus, these disorders seem to involve a permanent loss of the ability to transfer information from short-term memory to long-term memory.

Another type of memory disorder is called **retrograde amnesia.** This involves an inability to recall events that occurred before some trauma to the brain. The most common causes of retrograde amnesia are head injury, electroconvulsive shock (see Chapter 14), and carbon monoxide poisoning. Although amnesia victims who appear in soap operas often cannot even remember their names, in most cases in real life the material forgotten is quite limited. When Russell and Nathan (1946) reviewed the records of 200 people who were hospitalized for head injuries, over half of those who experienced retrograde amnesia had forgotten only the 60 seconds or so immediately preceding their accidents. This too seems easy to explain in terms of the distinction between short-term and long-term memory. Brain trauma temporarily interferes with the ability to transfer information, and the events immediately before an accident never enter long-term storage and are thus lost forever.

One particularly clever study of retrograde amnesia was made possible by the violent nature of American sports. Lynch and Yarnell (1973, p. 644) succinctly described their approach: "We waited on the football field until a player was injured, and then examined him neurologically and tested his memory status." Although they did not mention how many days they spent on the sidelines, they were able to test 6 players with concussions and compare them to a control group of 12 football players with other injuries, such as torn knee ligaments and broken noses.

The opportunity to question players within 30 seconds of their injuries revealed that retrograde amnesia was not immediately apparent in any of the six players with concussions, but it did show up later. As Lynch and Yarnell put it:

> The delayed forgetting was quite striking. One concussed player, immediately after injury, told the interviewer that he had been hit "from the front while I was blocking on the punt." Questioned 5 minutes later he said, "I don't remember what happened. I don't remember what play it was or what I was doing. It was something about a punt" (p. 644).

This finding suggests that brain trauma does not immediately erase the contents of short-term memory but interferes with their transfer to long-term memory at some later time.

Taken together, the findings from clinical studies of amnesia and laboratory studies of verbal learning were sufficient to convince many psychologists that the Atkinson-Shiffrin model was basically sound. In the final part of this section, we consider some challenges to this view. But first we shall use this model to describe some basic facts about sensory storage, short-term memory, and long-term memory.

SENSORY STORAGE

Sensory storage maintains a vivid and complete image of sensory impressions for about 0.25 to 2 seconds. The exact duration of this image depends on the type of stimulus and the context in which it is presented.

Some people think of human memory as the equivalent of a videotape recorder, which permanently stores a literal reproduction of every event. Psychologists know that this analogy is misleading. Memory is an efficient system that does not burden itself with every insignificant detail of every stimulus we have been exposed to in our lives. Rather, the mind actively picks and chooses what we need to know by paying attention to the most relevent details. Sensory storage briefly holds a literal picture of a stimulus while this information processing takes place, giving us the time to read a sentence or hear a melody in context.

Researchers in perception have long known that a visual image remains behind for a fraction of a second after the stimulus disappears. When a lighted cigarette is moved in a dark room, for example, you see a streak of light rather than a series of points (Woodworth, 1938). But it was not until 1960 that George Sperling provided an ingenious demonstration of just how complete this immediate image can be.

Sperling flashed visual displays briefly—for about 0.05 second—so that subjects would barely have time to see them. Typically, the stimulus was a group of 12 letters arranged in 3 rows like this:

Z	Q	B	R
M	C	A	W
T	K	N	F

When people wrote down the letters they had seen, they could typically remember only 4 or 5 of them. Other researchers had reported similar results before and concluded that people simply could not read more than 4 or 5 letters in such a short period of time.

Sperling had another idea. He believed that the viewer registered all 12 letters but that this photograph-type image faded away quickly, before the viewer had a chance to report all 12 letters.

This is where Sperling's ingenuity came in. He told his subjects that he would ask them to remember only one of the three rows—but they would not know which row until *after* the visual stimulus was turned off. Immediately after the 12 letters disappeared, each person heard one of three tones. A high-pitched tone meant repeat the top line, a low tone signaled the bottom line, and the intermediate tone asked for the middle line. Under these conditions, people could report any line with almost complete accuracy. Sperling had asked his subjects to report only part of what they had seen, and the accuracy of these partial reports implied that all the original information was briefly held in memory. In effect, the subjects seemed to be reading the relevant letters back from a rapidly fading mental photograph.

Sperling was able to estimate the duration of this image by varying how long he waited after the visual stimulus to sound the tone. He found that if he waited only about half a second, people could no longer report the relevant row. Apparently, the image had already faded in that time.

Sperling's experiment and many subsequent replications left little doubt that we retain a literal image of a visual stimulus for a fraction of a second after it is presented. This visual image is sometimes referred to as **iconic memory.**

Echoic memory refers to an analogous phenomenon for the auditory system. Just as we can see a picture of a stimulus for a moment after it disappears, so we can hear a sound for a moment after it stops (Moray, Bates, & Barnett, 1965). Echoic memory seems to last a bit longer than iconic memory; auditory replicas of a stimulus may last for several seconds. This difference might be explained in terms of the function of sensory storage—to maintain a literal impression of the world long enough for us to make sense of it. It seems reasonable to suppose that auditory information such as music and speech takes longer to put into context.

Many researchers believe that other senses such as touch, taste, and smell may have separate sensory-storage systems of their own. But only time and future research will tell.

SHORT-TERM MEMORY

Information disappears rapidly from sensory storage. Some is forgotten and some is passed along to the next stage. **Short-term memory (STM)** stores a limited amount of information for no more than about 30 seconds. The exact duration is somewhat controversial and may depend on the type of material. To hold information in STM, we often rehearse it, as in the case of silently repeating a phone number. According to Atkinson and Shiffrin (1968), without this type of repetition, information seems to fade away from STM and is forgotten forever.

One of the most important facts about STM is that it has a limited capacity; it can hold only a small amount of information at any given time. This idea can be traced back to a memory researcher named Joseph Jacobs, who wrote in 1887:

> It is obvious that there is a limit to the power of reproducing sound accurately. Anyone can say Bo after once hearing it; few could catch the name of the Greek statesman M. Papamichalopoulos without the need of a repetition (p. 75).

And so Jacobs set out to determine the precise limits of people's ability to reproduce strings of letters and numbers without mentally rehearsing them first. When he tested students at the North London Collegiate School for Girls, he found that 8-year-olds could repeat lists of about 6.6 numbers; 13-year-olds, about 7.3 numbers; and 18-year-olds, 8.6 numbers without error. Children with higher grades in each class seemed able to remember more numbers.

The obvious implication that such a test might be useful in measuring intelligence was further supported by Sir Francis Galton (1887) when he showed that inmates at the Earlewood Asylum for Idiots (*idiot* was the nineteenth-century term for the mentally retarded) performed poorly on this task. When IQ tests were developed several decades later (see Chapter 12), most included a test of digit memory. People were asked to repeat four numbers, then five, then six, and so on, until they made an error. We now know that most adults can successfully remember about six words, seven letters, or eight digits (Clark & Clark, 1977).

In 1956, George Miller reviewed these observations and many others in a classic paper titled "The Magical Number Seven, Plus or Minus Two: Some Limits on Our Capacity for Processing Information." He concluded that STM can hold about seven "chunks" of information.

Miller used the word *chunk* to refer to any discrete unit of information. When you try to remember a string of letters, you usually remember each letter separately, and each thus constitutes one chunk of information. For example, if you read the following letters once, you will probably remember about seven of them:

B T R D E R R O E D R O F

But if you regrouped these same letters to spell

R O B E R T   R E D F O R D

they would be much easier to remember. In this context, we could say that *Robert Redford* is a chunk. The name represents a single piece of information and we remember it as one unit, not as 13 separate letters. Similarly, it is quite difficult to remember the number

1 4 9 1 6 2 5 3 6 4 9 6 4 8 1 1 0 0

as a string of digits. But if you know that this number was formed by stringing together the squares of every integer from 1 to 10 ($1^2 = 1$; $2^2 = 4$; $3^2 = 9$; $4^2 = 16$, etc.), you are faced with only one piece of information, and the 18 digits become quite easy to commit to memory (at least if you can remember how to square the numbers from 1 to 10).

In everyday life, we often break information into chunks to make it easier to remember. You probably remember your Social Security number not as a string of nine digits (098388412) but as a series of three chunks (098-38-8412). Again, according to Miller, the capacity of short-term memory is about five-to-nine (that is, seven-plus-or-minus-two) chunks of information.

What happens when we try to exceed this natural limit? Our short-term memories become overloaded, and we forget. In an oversimplified way, you might think of short-term memory as a cabinet with about seven shelves; once all the shelves are filled, the only way to put something new in is to take something old out (Waugh & Norman, 1965). To remember larger amounts of information, some must be transferred to long-term memory.

LONG-TERM MEMORY

Can you remember what you had for dinner last Tuesday? The capital of Argentina? Your teacher in the first grade? Your mother's birthday? The number of ounces in a pound? Who played Captain Kirk in "Star Trek"? The difference between stimulus generalization and stimulus discrimination?

Long-term memory (LTM) is the memory system that stores large amounts of information for long periods of time. The storage capacity of LTM is absolutely astounding; if you tried to take an inventory of its contents, you might spend weeks simply listing all the important information and trivia stored in it. How does all that information ever fit between your ears? And what sort of incredible filing system allows you to sort through this clutter in a fraction of a second and effortlessly recover the words to the Pledge of Allegiance or the ingredients in your favorite meat loaf?

The question of how LTM is organized is far from settled, but it is currently the subject of a great deal of intensive research. One of the most influential theories is based on Endel Tulving's (1972) distinction between episodic and semantic memory.

Episodic versus Semantic Memory. According to Tulving, there are two types of information stored in LTM. **Episodic memory** is a record of an individual's past experiences, the episodes of daily life. For example, if I remember the first time I noticed that my Aunt Emily has a faint mustache, that event would be stored in episodic memory. So would my recollection of a television talk show I saw yesterday morning regarding fashion trends in men's socks. Episodic memory is both specific and autobiographical.

In contrast, **semantic memory** involves more abstract knowledge of words, symbols, ideas, and the rules for relating them. For example, I know that if the Boston Red Sox are in first place on September 1, they will probably have a losing streak and fail to win the pennant. Similarly, my long-term memory stores the information that if the weather is cold and wet, there is a good chance my car will stall when I make a left turn. These facts are not specific memories of particular events; rather, they are more general conclusions drawn from a variety of experiences.

So, if you remember waiting in line for $2\frac{1}{2}$ hours at the registrar's office to change a class and that when you finally got your turn the clerk told you that you had filled out the wrong form, the details would be stored in episodic memory. But the more general knowledge that the university registrar's office is inefficient and its employees are rude would be stored in semantic memory.

The rule-governed nature of semantic memory makes it possible to retrieve information to which you have never been exposed. If someone asks you what month comes after June in alphabetical order, you will probably be able to "remember" that it is March even if you have never seen a list of the twelve months arranged in this way.

Traditional research on verbal learning, in which people memorize lists of words or nonsense syllables, involves episodic memory; each list is remembered as a specific event in a subject's life. It was only in the 1960s that cognitive psychologists became concerned with exploring the workings of the more general system of semantic memory, which is directly involved in such ordinary activities as reading, writing, and most types of learning. Indeed, according to Tulving (1972), the term *semantic memory* was first used in a 1966 doctoral dissertation by Ross Quillian. Three years later, Quillian and Allen Collins published one of the first and most famous models of how semantic memory is organized.

One of the most amazing aspects of human memory is the ability to recover so many different types of information so quickly. Imagine how difficult it would be to find a book in the main branch of Chicago's public library if the books were not arranged according to the Dewey decimal system or some other systematic procedure. Similarly, there must be some Dewey decimal system of the mind that tells us where to look for seldom-used memories of African countries, Greek philosophers, and kinds of tropical fruits.

Collins and Quillian (1969) proposed that semantic knowledge is arranged in a network of associations. Figure 6.5 illustrates one of their most famous examples of how the meaning of different words and concepts may be arranged in the human mind. In the interest of efficiency, they argued, semantic memory is organized in a hierarchy of concepts. In this example, *canary* is stored under *bird*, and *bird* is stored under *animal*, because each is a member of that larger class.

The mind stores certain key properties along with each class. For example,

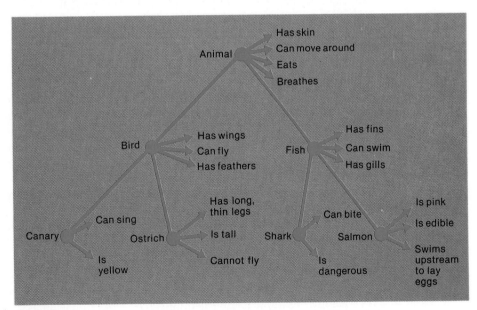

Figure 6.5
According to one model, information is organized in semantic memory in a hierarchy. In this example, to retrieve the fact that a canary has skin and can move around, the person who remembers must search through two levels of the hierarchy to find this information "filed under" the larger category of *animal*.

birds have wings and can fly. Although a canary also has wings and can fly, this information is not repeated at the lower level; these properties are implied by the fact that a canary is a bird.

This theory is a good example of the way an information-processing approach tries to analyze the internal steps involved in thought. Such models are often tested by measuring whether people take more time to perform tasks that the model sees as more complex or involving more steps. Here, Collins and Quillian reasoned that if their model was correct, it should take longer to answer the question "Does a canary eat?" than to answer "Is a canary yellow?" The reason is that the property *yellow* is stored at the same semantic level as *canary,* and one does not have to waste time searching the memory network for it. But the concept of *eating* is stored two levels away with the more general category *animal.* Therefore, answering a question about a canary's eating requires searching through two levels of the memory network, and this should take more time.

To test this prediction, Collins and Quillian (1969) flashed various statements about canaries on a TV screen. Subjects were asked to press one button if they thought a statement was true and to press another button if they thought it was false. In general, these reaction times supported the researchers' views. For example, it took about 1.3 seconds to press a button verifying the statement "A canary can sing," in which information was stored at the same level. In the same experiment, people took about 1.35 seconds to verify the statement "A canary can fly," in which information was stored one semantic level away, with the concept *bird* (see Figure 6.5). Agreement took 1.4 seconds for "A canary has skin," information stored two semantic levels away, with the concept *animal.* Although these differences were small, they were statistically significant and supported the idea that information was organized along these general lines.

Many memory researchers later questioned this view and proposed alternative models of their own. This is an active area of research, and in the near future our understanding of semantic memory should become far more complete than it is today. The work of Collins and Quillian is important not because it provides the final word but because they proposed one of the first testable models of how semantic information is organized in the mind.

Storage Capacity. Aside from the question of how information is organized in LTM, many psychologists have conducted research to try to determine its storage capacity. This issue is complicated by the distinction between storage and retrieval. When an item is stored in STM, it can usually be easily retrieved and brought into awareness. In contrast, we often have trouble retrieving information from the vast storehouse of LTM. We saw one example in the people who could recognize the names and faces of their high school classmates but not recall them.

Another example is the frustrating experience of having a name or fact "on the tip of your tongue" and just not being able to recover it. One psychologist became interested in this phenomenon when he had trouble remembering the street on which a relative lived. After guessing Congress, Corinth, and Concord, he looked it up and discovered that the street was named Cornish. The fact that his guesses were so close to the correct answer suggested that he was not just guessing; in the tip-of-the-tongue state, he seemed to have a dim picture of the forgotten name. So he set out with another psychologist (Brown & McNeil, 1966) to see what happens when people can remember some, but not all, of stored memory.

They began by developing a list of vocabulary words that college students might know but were likely to have trouble recalling, such as *apse, nepotism, cloaca, ambergris,* and *sampan.* An experimenter read a definition of each word to a group of Harvard and Radcliffe undergraduates and asked them whether they could name the correct word. Whenever a student experienced that tip-of-the-tongue feeling of knowing but not quite remembering the correct word, he was asked to describe what he could of the elusive word—its first letter, how many syllables it had, words that sounded like it, and so on.

Analysis of the resulting 233 cases of the tip-of-the-tongue feeling revealed that people could sometimes describe the first letter or other characteristics of the correct word, suggesting that there was only a partial failure of memory. Interestingly, when these subjects reported the wrong words, they made two different kinds of errors. People who were given the definition of the word *sextant,* for example, sometimes guessed words that sounded about the same (like *sexton* and *secant*) and sometimes offered words that were closer to meaning (like *compass* and *astrolabe*). Sound and meaning, then, seem to be two different features we can use to retrieve information from storage.

Since information may be stored in LTM even when it appears to have been forgotten, it is difficult to determine exactly what information—or even how much information—is held in long-term storage. This fact has helped lead some to wonder whether every piece of information that enters LTM might be held in storage. Tulving's notion of cue-dependent forgetting is in this tradition.

One study suggesting a more limited form of LTM storage examined people's ability to remember an object they had seen probably thousands of times—a United States penny (Nickerson & Adams, 1979). Figure 6.6 illustrates one part of this experiment. Before reading on, see if you can identify which of these versions is a correct illustration of a penny.

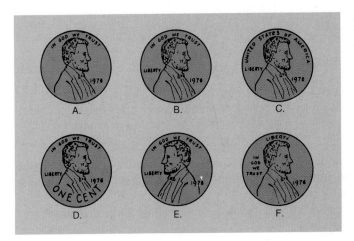

Figure 6.6
Which of these is an accurate illustration of a U.S. penny?

When introductory psychology students at Brown University looked at these and other choices, only about half of those who were shown an accurate drawing (*B* in Figure 6.6) believed that it was correct. Each of the other choices was considered correct by at least some students. In a series of related studies, other U.S. citizens were unable to draw a penny, accurately describe its appearance, or tell what was wrong with a series of incorrect drawings. The authors concluded that even familiar objects may be stored in LTM in an abbreviated code.

In an informal survey, Loftus and Loftus, (1980) found that most people agreed with this statement:

> Everything we learn is permanently stored in the mind, although sometimes particular details are not accessible. With hypnosis, or other special techniques, these inaccessible details could eventually be recovered (p. 410).

Acceptance of this statement was even greater among psychologists (84%) than nonpsychologists (69%). But when they reviewed all the studies that attempted to recover long-forgotten material—such as hypnotizing witnesses to a crime or electrically stimulating the brain to elicit particular experiences—they came to a different conclusion. Observers often think they can remember long-forgotten details, but there is evidence that sometimes they reconstruct past events from partial memories, filling in the blanks with imagination and educated guesswork.

Constructive Memory. Much of the early research on verbal learning treated memory as a passive process of learning to associate stimuli and responses. One version of this approach led to the false conclusion that the human mind is like a videotape machine that stores a complete record of every event in our lives.

A different view of the mind was proposed in 1932 by Frederick C. Bartlett. At a time when most researchers were compiling lists of nonsense syllables, Bartlett used more natural stimuli. People simply read a story and then tried to recall it hours, days, or months later. One stimulus was an old Indian tale called "The War of the Ghosts," which ended with these words:

> He told it all, and then he became quiet. When the sun rose he fell down. Something black came out his mouth. His face became contorted. The people jumped up and cried.
> He was dead.

Eight days after reading the original story, one typical subject recalled the event this way:

> The next morning at dawn he was describing his adventures to his friends, who had gathered round him. Suddenly something black issued from his mouth, and he fell down uttering a cry. His friends closed around him, but found that he was dead.

Note how the original story was subtly altered and embroidered. For example, in the new version, his friends gathered around and it is the dead man, rather than those around him, who cried.

Six months later, another subject recalled a much more garbled account:

A voice said: "The black man is dead." And he was brought to the place where they were, and laid on the ground. And he foamed at the mouth.

These reports, and many others, led Bartlett to propose the term **constructive memory** to refer to an observer's tendency to rebuild pictures of past events from the few details remembered by filling in the details that have been forgotten. He also described the concept of a **schema,** or active organization of past experience, a kind of general impression created by the original material. The new stories were constructed around these schemas. People also altered the details in predictable ways; they omitted specific details, for example, and added details to explain incongruous passages.

Bartlett's work was largely ignored by his contemporaries. But when cognitive psychology began to take hold several decades later, Bartlett's view of the active learner who expands a limited amount of information into a complete story became influential.

A particularly vivid example of constructive memory and the way people may come to believe the details they have manufactured was provided by developmental psychologist Jean Piaget (1962) in an account of his own childhood:

One of my first memories would date, if it were true, from my second year. I can still see, most clearly, the following scene, in which I believed until I was about 15. I was sitting in my pram which my nurse was pushing in the Champs Elysées, when a man tried to kidnap me. I was held in by the strap fastened around me while my nurse bravely tried to stand between me and the thief. She received various scratches, and I can still see vaguely those on her face. Then the crowd gathered, a policeman with a short cloak and a white baton came, and the man took to his heels. I can still see the whole scene, and can even place it near the tube station. When I was about 15, my parents received a letter from my former nurse saying that she had been converted to the Salvation Army. She wanted to confess her past faults, and in particular to return the watch she had been given as a reward on this occasion. She made up the whole story, faking the scratches. I, therefore, must have heard, as a child, the account of this story, which my parents believed, and projected into the past in the form of a visual memory (pp. 187–188).

The idea that humans sometimes construct memories around schemas is now widely accepted. One of the most practical lines of research encouraged by this view concerns the way the legal system evaluates eyewitness accounts of a crime.

APPLIED PSYCHOLOGY

Eyewitness Testimony

In 1975, Lonnie and Sandy Sawyer were convicted of kidnapping the assistant manager of a North Carolina department store. Despite their repeated claims of innocence, the brothers were given sentences of 28 to 40 years in prison, largely on the basis of the testimony of Robert Hinson, the man who had been kidnapped. Although Hinson had only a glimpse of his kidnappers before they put on stocking

Figure 6.7
Mistaken eyewitnesses' identifications led to the arrest of Lawrence Berson (left) for several rapes and George Morales (right) for robbery. It later became clear that both men were innocent; Richard Carbone (center) was later convicted of the rapes and confessed to the robbery.

masks, his identification of the Sawyers was enough to convince a jury. Private detectives pursued the case and later found the man who had actually committed the crime. In January 1977, the Sawyer brothers were pardoned and released after nearly two years in jail (Loftus, 1979).

What could be more impressive than having the victim of a crime point to a woman in a courtroom and say, "She's the one. I saw her do it?" When a British government commission studied all the legal cases in England and Wales that involved a police lineup (or "identification parade," as the British call it) in 1973, they found an 82% conviction rate for people who were prosecuted after being picked from a lineup. Even more impressive were the 347 cases in which people were prosecuted when the only evidence against them was the word of one or more eyewitnesses; 74% of these people were found guilty (Devlin, 1976).

In one experiment (Loftus, 1974), college students were asked to judge guilt or innocence in a fictitious case of a man accused of robbing a grocery store and murdering the owner and his 5-year-old granddaughter. On the basis of the evidence they read, only 9 of 50 jurors considered the man guilty. A second group of 50 jurors were given precisely the same case with one twist—a clerk in the store who saw the crime testified that the accused was guilty. Under these conditions, 36 of 50 people voted for conviction, proving once again that eyewitness reports are given a great deal of weight.

But the results for a third group of 50 college students were far more surprising and disturbing. These people read the original evidence and the eyewitness testimony, but they also learned that the eyewitness had been discredited. The defense attorney had proved that the eyewitness had very poor vision, had not been wearing his glasses that day, and could not possibly have seen the face of the robber from where he stood. If the jurors were totally rational and fair, they should have voted for conviction at about the same rate as the first group (9 out of 50). In fact, however, 34 of these 50 jurors voted "guilty." It was almost as if they believed that a mistaken eyewitness was better than no eyewitness at all.

This is particularly distressing in light of the fact that other studies have consistently shown that eyewitnesses often do make mistakes. For example, on December 19, 1974, viewers of the local NBC news on Channel 4 in New York saw a short film of a staged purse snatching; the young man who committed the crime was seen running directly toward the camera for a second or so. Viewers were then shown a lineup and asked which of the six men pictured, if any, had committed the crime televised only a moment before. Over 2,000 people called a special telephone number to identify the culprit. There were seven possibilities—the purse snatcher could have been one of the six men or he might not have been in the lineup at all. If people guessed randomly, they should have been right about 1 out of 7 times, or 14.2% of the time. The results were that 14.1% picked the right man. Thus, these 2,145 eyewitnesses could have performed just as well without ever seeing the crime; the identification seemed completely random (Buckhout, 1975).

Even more disturbing than eyewitnesses' sheer inaccuracy is the fact that later information can change people's schemas and thus the memories they construct. Of particular interest to unethical lawyers is the fact that the wording of a question can influence what a witness remembers.

In one study (Loftus & Palmer, 1974), students saw various films of car crashes. Some of these eyewitnesses were asked, "About how fast were the cars going when they *smashed* each other?" They estimated the speed at an average of 40.8 miles per hour. When other eyewitnesses who saw the film were asked, "About how fast were the cars going when they *contacted* each other?" the estimate dropped to an average of 31.8 miles per hour. Other verbs produced intermediate results: *collided* produced an average response of 39.3 mph; *bumped* produced 38.1 mph; and *hit* yielded 34.0 mph.

To show that these subjects were really misremembering and not just trying to be cooperative, another group of subjects was brought back to the laboratory a week after seeing the film. This time, the question was whether the witnesses had seen any broken glass lying around after the accident. In fact, there was none in the film. But subjects who had estimated that the cars were traveling at high speeds might be expected to have a schema of a more serious accident and to construct a memory that included more signs of damage. This is precisely what was found; 16 of 50 subjects who had originally been asked about "smashing" cars said they had seen broken glass versus only 7 of the 50 who had been questioned about "hitting" cars.

Results like these suggest that lawyers who ask leading questions can manipulate not just what an eyewitness says but even what that person remembers.

The Levels-of-Processing Model of Memory

Table 6.1 summarizes some of the main differences involved in sensory storage, short-term memory, and long-term memory. Although most psychologists agree that this division into three separate systems is a useful way to think about human memory, this approach has not been without its critics. A vocal minority argues that the whole idea of "boxes in the head"—as illustrated in Figure 6.4—puts too much emphasis on the structure of memory and too little on memory processes.

One of the most serious challenges to the Atkinson-Shiffrin model came from Craik and Lockhart's (1972) notion of **levels of processing**—the theory that information does not pass from one storage system to another but rather is encoded in a particular way during input depending largely on the person's intentions. A young man who intends to remember a woman's phone number for all time will process the information differently from the way he would the phone number of a store that sells used snow tires. The amount of forgetting is thus determined not by the transformations of information from STM to LTM but by the way it was encoded in the first place.

Craik and Lockhart argue that we can process information at many different levels. For example, the stimulus 6/22/47 can be seen at a very shallow level as a configuration of lines and curves or at a slightly deeper level as a series of numbers and lines. Information that is processed only at shallow levels like these will soon be forgotten. But when we attend to information, analyze it, and associate it with meaningful images, we are more likely to remember it. Thus, if I recognize 6/22/47 as a shortened form of June 22, 1947, I am more likely to remember it. And when I recognize this as my date of birth, I will have a hard time forgetting it.

TABLE 6.1
General Characteristics of Three Stages of Memory

	Sensory Storage	*Short-term Memory*	*Long-term Memory*
Information enters by	Sensation	Attention	Rehearsal
Information is maintained by	(not maintained)	Continued attention; rehearsal	Repetition; organization
Storage capacity	Large	About 5 to 9 items	No known limits
Information is lost by	Decay	Displacement; perhaps decay	Little or no loss (?); interference makes information less accessible
Truce duration	0.25 to 2 seconds	Up to 30 seconds	Minutes to years
Retrieval	Immediate readout	Items in consciousness	Involves search process

Based on Craik and Lockhart, 1972

To test this theory, Craik and Tulving (1975) tried to manipulate the level of processing by asking people four types of questions about words flashed briefly on a screen. For example, after seeing the word *crate*, a subject might be asked any of the following questions:

Is the word in capital letters?

Does the word rhyme with *weight?*

Is the word a type of fish?

Would the word fit the following sentence: "The girls placed the _____ on the table?

These questions were chosen to reflect four different levels of processing. At the simplest level, people merely had to notice the physical structure of the word. At successively deeper levels, they had to be aware of its sound, its category, and its meaning in context. Craik and Tulving predicted that when people pressed buttons to answer these questions "yes" or "no," they would take longer to respond to questions involving deeper levels of processing. They were right. The differences were small but consistent; capital letters were noted in about 0.6 second, the sentence took about 1.8 seconds to figure out, and the other categories fell in between.

More important, when people were later given a surprise recognition test of the words, they recognized only about 16% of the words from the most shallow level and 90% of the words they had fit into sentences. Again, results for the two intermediate categories fell in between, just as the theory predicted they would.

Many later studies continued to support the idea that depth of processing is indeed involved with memory. However, it is important to emphasize that this does not mean that the concepts of sensory storage, STM, and LTM were wrong. These theories do not directly conflict. Even in their original paper, Craik and Lockhart (1972) grudgingly noted: "It is perfectly possible to draw a box around early analyses and call it sensory memory and a box around intermediate analyses called short-term memory, but that procedure both oversimplifies matters and evades the more significant issues" (p. 675). Only further research can reveal which emphasis—process or structure—will provide the more significant breakthroughs. In the meantime, the conflicts between different models should continue to advance psychology's understanding of the complexities of human memory.

How to Remember

In ancient Greece and Rome, before the invention of cheap notebooks, ballpoint pens, and TelePrompTers, politicians were often forced to commit their speeches to memory. Some of the memory aids they devised are still used today. However, what the Roman orator Marcus Tullius Cicero described as the "art of memory" has begun to evolve into a science, as contemporary psychologists have developed new strategies and improved old ones.

MNEMONIC DEVICES

Mnemonic devices are techniques for organizing information so that it can be remembered more easily. One of the simplest mnemonic devices involves rhyming, as in "*I* before *e* except after *c*" and "Thirty days hath September, April, June, and November." Because these rhymes place information in a context and give it structure, they help many people remember what would otherwise be isolated facts.

Similarly, acronyms provide structure by taking the first letter of a series of words and forming a single item. The acronym ROY G. BIV, for example, has helped generations of students remember the order of the color spectrum: red, orange, yellow, green, blue, indigo, violet. This strategy can be seen as an example of converting several chunks of information into a single chunk, thus reducing the load on memory.

Less familiar to most people is a mnemonic device invented by the ancient Greek poet Simonedes. According to legend, Simonedes was called outside a banquet one evening moments before the roof of the hall caved in. All the other guests were crushed to death; their bodies were mangled beyond recognition. As the sole survivor, Simonedes had to identify the corpses by remembering where each victim

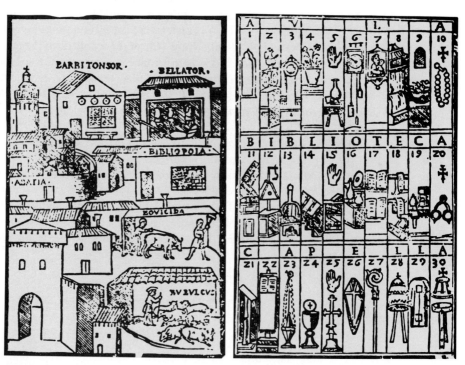

Figure 6.8
These woodcuts come from a sixteenth-century text describing how the method of loci can be used to improve memory. On the left are the sample loci at an abbey; on the right are the objects to be remembered by picturing them at specific locations on the abbey grounds.

had been sitting. This grisly experience gave Simonedes an idea for improving memory. The **method of loci** (*loci* is Latin for "places") involves visualizing images of the things to be memorized in an orderly arrangement of locations.

Suppose you want to remember the following shopping list: pecan pie, potato chips, chocolate fudge cookies, and Diet Pepsi. Using the method of loci, you would begin with a series of familiar places. You might, for example, visualize walking around your living room—from the couch to the rocking chair to the fireplace to the TV. You would then proceed to associate a vivid picture of each item from your shopping list with one of these locations: a pecan pie on the couch, the rocking chair covered with potato chips, a bag of chocolate fudge cookies in the fireplace, and a can of Diet Pepsi on top of your TV. When you get to the store, you could simply take a mental stroll through your living room and look at each image.

In one systematic test of the effectiveness of the method of loci (Ross & Lawrence, 1968), college students memorized a list of 40 nouns by visualizing each at a specific campus location. Immediately after, the students were able to remember an average of 38 items in the correct order; a day later, they still remembered 34. This performance is astounding, especially when compared with the results of experiments in which people tried to master lists without the help of such memory aids.

Other research investigated the effectiveness of various strategies for using the method of loci. Many memory experts claim that the most effective memory images are bizarre ones (see "Becoming a Critical Consumer"). Following this theory, you would be most likely to remember the pie if you imagined some bizarre image, such as a 6-foot pecan pie reading a newspaper while reclining comfortably on the couch. However, several direct tests of this claim have failed to find evidence that it is true (Bower, 1970). One study (Wollen, Weber, & Lowry, 1972) asked students to memorize pairs of easily imagined words such as *elephant, sofa,* and *cigar.* One group saw the stimuli in ordinary drawings; the other group saw the objects pictured in much more bizarre and imaginative drawings. Both groups remembered the objects equally well.

On the other hand, this same study verified another claim of memory experts: Two objects are easier to remember together if their images interact in the mental picture. For example, *elephant* and *sofa* are easier to associate if one pictures an elephant actually sitting on a sofa. Drawings that illustrated two interacting images did indeed lead to better memory for the word pairs. Thus, this systematic study helped reveal which claims of memory experts are accurate and which are myths.

ORGANIZATION AND MEANING

The success of these and other mnemonic devices calls attention to the underlying importance of meaning and organization to effective memory. We have referred to the significance of meaning several times in this chapter, most obviously in the levels-of-processing model, which holds that memory depends in part on how fully we analyze information and associate it with meaningful images. This theory was a formal outgrowth of observations made by the first memory researchers—it is easier to memorize meaningful material such as a story or poem than a meaningless list of digits or nonsense syllables. In fact, some nonsense syllables are easier to remember

A Bizarre Route to a Better Memory

There are many books that promise to help people improve their memories. In one highly respected guide, Harry Lorayne and Jerry Lucas (1974) described some of the strategies they have used to improve their own memories. As you read the following passage, evaluate its recommendations in light of the study of Wollen, Weber, & Lowry (1972) described in the text. Then see the "Discussion" section after the "Summary" at the end of this chapter.

> In Order to Remember Any New Piece of Information, It Must Be Associated to Something You Already Know or Remember in Some Ridiculous Way. . . . [This] will force the Original Awareness that's necessary to remember anything, it will force you to concentrate and use your imagination as you never have before, and it will force you to form associations consciously.
>
> Assume you wanted to memorize [an

association between the words *airplane* and *tree*] . . . All you need to do is to form a ridiculous picture, or image, in your mind's eye—an association between those two things.

There are two steps involved. First you need a ridiculous—impossible, crazy, illogical, absurd—picture or image to associate the two items. What you don't want is a logical or sensible picture.

An example of a logical picture might be: an airplane parked near a tree. Though unlikely, that is not ridiculous, it is possible—therefore, it probably won't work. A ridiculous or impossible picture might be: A gigantic tree is flying instead of an airplane, or an airplane is growing instead of a tree, or airplanes are growing on trees, or millions of trees (as passengers) are boarding airplanes. These are crazy, impossible pictures. Now, select one of these pictures, or one you thought of yourself, and see it in your mind's eye (pp. 25–26).

than others simply because they seem more meaningful. DOZ, LIF, and RUF remind us of English words and are generally remembered better than less familiar-sounding syllables such as GIW, ZOJ, and JYQ (McGeoch, 1930).

It took longer for memory researchers to recognize explicitly the importance of organization. In one classic experiment (Bousfield, 1953), people memorized lists of 60 words from 4 categories of 15 words each. For example, the category *animals* included *baboon, zebra, camel,* and *giraffe;* the category *professions* included *milkman, florist, dentist,* and *waiter.* Although the words were presented in random order, people recalled them in distinct clusters based on the categories. Memory imposed organization on the unstructured material.

Later investigations were able to show that knowledge of categories or an underlying organization actually helped memory. One of the more elaborate tests (Bower, Clark, Lesgold, & Winzenz, 1969) involved memorizing lists of apparently unrelated words such as *cookie, germ, tiger, cheese, yellow, bear, tan, hot, moth, wheat, cat, net, cow, cage, cool, mouse, bread, butterfly, milk, field, sun, trap.* Not surprisingly, high school students who were given this type of list had trouble memorizing all the words. But others from the same classes learned these words in the more organized form illustrated in Figure 6.9. Although their performance was not perfect, the group exposed to the organized list did remember significantly more words.

Most books on how to study emphasize the practical importance of understanding the overall meaning and content of materials. For example, when you study a chapter in this book, it might be helpful to begin by leafing through, noting the headings and major topics. Reading the chapter summaries before the actual text should also help.

Bransford and Johnson (1973) demonstrated how much an overview can help in understanding and remembering information. They presented several ambiguous selections and found that people had considerable difficulty remembering them without a meaningful introduction. As you read the following paragraph from their study, try to determine what activity "the procedure" refers to.

> The procedure actually is quite simple. First you arrange things into different groups. Of course, one pile may be sufficient, depending on how much there is to do. If you have to go somewhere else due to lack of facilities, that's the next step.

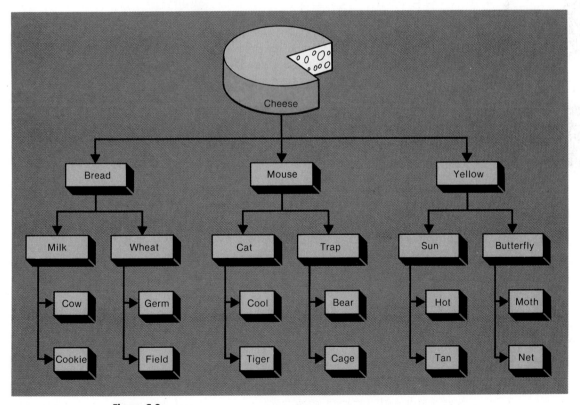

Figure 6.9
Organization aids memory. In one study, people who saw these words organized in this way later remembered them far better than others who saw the same words in an unorganized list.

Otherwise, you're pretty well set. It is important not to overdo things. That is, it is better to do too few things at once than too many. In the short run, this may not seem important, but complications can easily arise. A mistake can be expensive as well. At first, the whole procedure will seem complicated. Soon, however, it will become just another fact of life. It is difficult to foresee an end to the necessity of this task in the immediate future, but then one can never tell. After the procedure is completed, one arranges the materials into different groups again, and then they can be put in their appropriate places. Eventually, they will be used once more, and the whole cycle will have to be repeated; however, that is a part of life (p. 400).

People who were not given hints about the underlying meaning found this passage quite difficult to remember. But others, who were told that this referred to washing clothes, had far less trouble. If you reread the paragraph with this organizing principle in mind, you too will probably find it much easier to understand and remember.

PRACTICE

No matter how effective one's study techniques, in the final analysis memorization and understanding always require the effort of practice—and the more practice, the better. Memory researchers use the word **overlearning** to refer to practice beyond the point of mastery. In terms of traditional memory experiments, a person who reads and rehearses a list beyond the point where she can repeat it without error has overlearned the material. Many experiments have shown that overlearned material is remembered longer and better than information that is barely mastered. It is particularly helpful when one wants to remember material for days or weeks rather than minutes or hours.

Of course, overlearning eventually reaches a point of diminishing returns. You

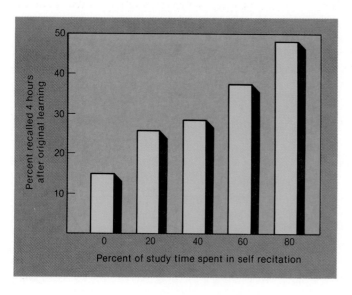

Figure 6.10
Reciting material aloud improves recall. In this experiment, subjects who spent a larger proportion of study time reciting aloud remembered material better four hours later.

probably would not gain much by rehearsing the spelling of your last name; this material is already firmly established in your memory. Deciding just how much practice is enough can sometimes be difficult. But it is probably safe to assume that most students who do poorly in school have studied too little rather than too much.

The type of practice also makes a difference. About 70 years ago, A. I. Gates (1917) demonstrated the advantages of active recitation. Figure 6.10 compares the performance of several groups of students who spent the same amount of time studying but devoted different proportions of their time to reciting material aloud. As you can see, the more they recited aloud, the more they remembered. On the basis of this study and others, many experts provide the following advice: If you have three hours to study a chapter that takes one hour to read carefully, you should probably read it once and use the remaining time to ask yourself questions and rehearse the answers.

The more actively you participate in this process, the more effective it is likely to be. Relating new ideas to known information, organizing material in personally relevant ways, and forming images can all be useful strategies. Asking yourself questions also provides immediate feedback that can help you identify the material that needs the most work. It also encourages deeper levels of processing in which you try to understand the material instead of just repeating it by rote. Last but not least, active study techniques make it difficult to fall asleep.

Summary

1. There are three major ways to measure memory. **Relearning** compares the time or effort it takes to learn material the first time with a second, later time. **Recognition** involves deciding whether specific information has been seen or heard before. **Recall** involves remembering information spontaneously or on the basis of certain clues.
2. According to the **decay theory** of forgetting, physical memory traces gradually fade with the passage of time. More evidence supports the **interference theory,** which holds that people forget information because one memory prevents another from being recovered. This can result from **proactive inhibition,** when interference comes from material presented before the learning task, or from **retroactive inhibition,** when interference comes from material presented after the learning task.
3. Many researchers now take an **information-processing approach,** which analyzes thought processes, including memory, as a series of separate steps. These researchers also distinguished between three major processes in remembering. **Encoding** involves transforming a physical stimulus into the kind of code that memory accepts. **Storage** involves retaining a memory, and **retrieval** means recovering information from storage.
4. One information-processing theory, called **cue-dependent forgetting,** argues that forgetting is caused by a failure to retrieve information from storage because of inadequate memory cues. This is closely related to the **encoding-**

specificity principle, which states that forgetting is minimized if the same cues are present during learning and recall.

5. According to the Atkinson-Shiffrin model there are three major stages of memory. **Sensory storage** maintains a vivid and complete sensory image for about 0.25 second to 2 seconds. **Short-term memory** stores a limited amount of information for no more than about 30 seconds. **Long-term memory** is a relatively permanent system that can store large amounts of information.

6. Studies of **amnesia**—loss of memory usually caused by damage to the brain—support the distinction between short-term and long-term memory. **Anterograde amnesia** involves an inability to remember new information for more than a few seconds; in this disorder, the ability to transfer information from short-term memory to long-term memory is permanently lost. **Retrograde amnesia** involves an inability to remember events that occurred before some damage to the brain, perhaps because trauma temporarily interferes with the transfer of information from short-term memory to long-term memory.

7. Sensory storage holds a precise image of a stimulus for no more than 2 seconds while information processing takes place. **Iconic memory** briefly retains a visual image; **echoic memory** briefly retains an auditory image. Other systems may operate for taste, touch, and smell.

8. The capacity of short-term memory is limited to about five to nine discrete units (or chunks) of information.

9. According to one theory, long-term memory can be further subdivided into **episodic memory,** which records personal experience or episodes, and **semantic memory,** a more abstract record of words, ideas, and rules for relating them.

10. The tip-of-the-tongue phenomenon reveals that in some cases information held in LTM storage is difficult to retrieve. There is some controversy about how much material is actually stored in LTM and how it is organized.

11. **Constructive memory** refers to an observer's tendency to rebuild complete pictures of past events around the incomplete details that are remembered. Particularly important in this process are **schemas,** active organizations of past experience that form a kind of general impression. Partly as a result of this, eyewitness memories of a crime or other event are often extremely inaccurate.

12. Some psychologists are skeptical about the distinctions among sensory storage, short-term memory, and long-term memory. One alternative is the theory of **levels of processing,** which holds that memory depends on how information is encoded during input.

13. **Mnemonic devices** are techniques for organizing information so that it can be remembered more easily. One such technique, the **method of loci,** involves visualizing images of a list of things to be memorized and mentally placing them in an orderly arrangement of locations. Other common mnemonic devices include rhyming and acronyms.

14. Other techniques for improving memory include focusing explicitly on meaning, reciting material actively, and **overlearning**—practicing material beyond the point of mastery.

Discussion of "Becoming a Critical Consumer"

This strategy probably sounds convincing; many memory experts agree that bizarre interacting images improve memory. But when Wollen and his colleagues tested this idea, they found that bizarre images did not *improve memory. Although an expert may know that a particular strategy seems to work for him, it takes systematic research to learn which elements of the strategy are truly vital to success and which are based on habit or superstition.*

To Learn More

Loftus, E. R. *Eyewitness Testimony*. Cambridge, Mass.: Harvard University Press, 1979. Should be required reading for every prospective lawyer and criminal. Also recommended for the rest of us.

Lorayne, H., & Lucas, J. *The Memory Book*. New York: Ballantine Books, 1974. All right, so it makes a few mistakes (see "Becoming a Critical Consumer"). Still a fascinating guide to practical strategies for improving memory.

Klatzky, R. L. *Human Memory: Structures and Processes* (2d ed.). San Francisco: Freeman, 1980. A textbook overview of research.

7

Thought and Language

Thought
The origins of cognitive psychology
Problem solving
Artificial intelligence
Concepts
Language and thought

Language
Competence versus performance
Linguistics and grammar
The problem of comprehension
Language development
Teaching apes to "speak"

Summary

BECOMING A CRITICAL CONSUMER
What would a chimpanzee say?

Slips of the tongue in which sounds are misplaced are called *spoonerisms*, after the Reverend William Spooner, an Oxford dean who was famous for errors of this sort. On one notorious occasion, Spooner meant to refer to "the dear old queen" and instead mentioned "the queer old dean." On another, he wanted to say to a student, "You have missed all my history lectures . . . in fact, you have wasted the whole term." What Spooner actually said was, "You have hissed all my mystery lectures . . . in fact, you have tasted the whole worm."

Although there is some question whether Spooner himself made these errors intentionally, there is no doubt that people sometimes transform words and phrases by accident. Recordings of radio and television bloopers often include spoonerisms, such as an announcer's introduction of President Herbert Hoover as Hoobert Heever. Psychologists and linguists see errors of this sort as more than a chance for a cheap laugh; slips of the tongue may provide valuable clues about the way we use language and thus about the workings of the human mind. (In Chapter 11, we review another approach—Sigmund Freud's contention that these errors may also reveal powerful unconscious forces that shape our behavior.)

Slips of the tongue seem to follow certain rules. For example, when new words are formed by an English-speaking person, they always conform to characteristics of English. When a nervous bridegroom says, "With this wing, I thee red," his statement almost sounds as though it makes sense; the error produces other English words.

Even when people form nonwords, they follow certain rules. You may say "stips of the lung" by accident, but you will not say "tlips of the sung." Although you could repeat this phrase easily enough, speakers of English know that words do not begin with *tl*. Other languages do begin words with this sound; some Indian tribes in America's Northwest, for example, speak a language called Tlingit, which allows this combination. Along the same lines, you will never hear an English-speaking person accidentally create the word *nga*. English words do not begin with *ng*, although, as Fromkin (1973) notes, "'nga' . . . is a perfectly good word in the Twi language of the Ashanti in western Africa" (p. 111). In short, when people make errors speaking a certain language, they continue to follow its specific rules.

More complex errors also provide insights into the general question of the organization of human speech. Consider the gentleman who meant to say, "On the verge of a nervous breakdown," and instead said, "On the nerve of a vergeous breakdown." Note that this error involves two words that are separated by *of a*. According to one simplistic model of human language, a speaker associates each individual word with the next rather than thinking through a phrase or sentence in advance. But this slip of the tongue involves a reversal of the sounds in two words that are not next to each other but are separated by others. Therefore, it seems reasonable to assume that the phrase *verge of a nervous breakdown* had been held in memory before it was uttered, and the confusion entered at that point.

In general, researchers have found that slips of the tongue resemble the intended word or phrase in either sound or meaning. This suggests that our "mental dictionaries" may be organized along these lines and that the speaker who makes a mistake has retrieved a word that is stored nearby in the network of words that sound alike or share similar meanings.

This analysis may remind you of the information-processing approach described in Chapter 6. While some psychologists have studied the active internal processes involved in the storage and retrieval of memory, others have used similar concepts to explore such topics as problem solving, concept formation, and language. Thus, even an apparently trivial phenomenon like a slip of the tongue can provide insight into the rules that govern speech. In this chapter, we provide an overview of what is known about these rules and the active internal processes involved in thought and language.

Thought

THE ORIGINS OF COGNITIVE PSYCHOLOGY

The same historical forces that shaped psychology's approach to learning and memory also affected studies of language and thought. One of the most influential approaches was John Watson's attempt to remove all reference to internal processes from the science of behavior. Common sense tells us that people can perform internal thought processes, such as multiplying 4 by 30, without emitting an observable response. In his extreme version of behaviorism, Watson (1930) was not willing to grant even this simple point. Thinking, he said, was simply a case of subvocal speech in which an external stimulus (such as the command "multiply 4 times 30") produced an overt behavioral response (here, activating the muscles of the speech apparatus slightly for the answer—120).

Philosopher Herbert Feigl mocked this radical proposal when he said that Watson "made up his windpipe that he had no mind." But many psychologists took it seriously; one even allowed himself to be temporarily paralyzed by curare to see if that would affect his thought processes (Smith, Brown, Toman, & Goodman, 1947). The behaviorist theory was not supported. Despite the fact that this brave soul could not move a single muscle (or even breathe without the help of a respirator), he was able to observe, understand, and think about the events that went on around him.

This study was just one small piece of a much larger puzzle. Over the last few decades, the interests of American psychology have shifted from a behavioral emphasis on the isolation of stimuli and responses to a more cognitive approach that analyzes the nature of thought. This change in the dominant scientific paradigm (see Chapter 1) resulted from the joint effect of many lines of research described throughout this text, such as Köhler's and Tolman's studies of animal learning (see Chapter 5), Atkinson and Shiffrin's model of human memory (see Chapter 6), Chomsky's analysis of human language (described here in Chapter 7), and Jean Piaget's observations of children's intelligence (see Chapter 8). In these cases and others, scientists have focused on the active internal process involved in thinking.

Another important force in the shift to a cognitive approach was far less theoretical. In the 1940s, psychologists were called out of their laboratories to help solve some of the practical problems involved in waging World War II. Sophisticated new devices like radar and aircraft made heavy demands on their operators, and human

Figure 7.1
Before World War II, the printing inside the holes of a telephone dial was difficult to see from certain angles. A 1947 experimental model with the numbers outside the holes led to slower dialing by about 1 second per call; with 500 million calls per day, that adds up to over 139,000 hours extra hookup time and considerable money. Human engineers proposed a simple solution for the 1949 model. They placed a white dot in the center of each hole. People could aim at these dots while the dial spun, and this reduced dialing to the original time.

errors often had disastrous consequences. Many psychologists therefore turned away from the "pure" problems faced by rats negotiating a maze and focused instead on how skilled radar operators and pilots could avoid mistakes in moments of stress. These new questions inevitably led psychologists to reconsider issues, like attention and decision making, that had been ignored by strict behaviorists.

This work led to the emergence of the field of **human engineering,** which applies scientific principles to the design of equipment and machines to maximize human efficiency. Earlier, we described one example—an airplane with a history of crashes caused by the design of the cockpit controls (see page 12). Figure 7.1 provides another example; human engineers in Bell Laboratories helped develop telephone dials that human callers could use most efficiently. These practical examples underline the value of a cognitive approach that analyzes how quickly people can process and respond to different forms of information.

In general, we can define **cognitive psychology** as the study of the way observers gain knowledge about the world and how that knowledge is represented, stored, retrieved, transformed, and related to overt behavior. Cognitive psychologists therefore focus on such higher mental processes as attention, perception, memory, language, imagery, and reasoning. Several of these topics are discussed elsewhere; in this chapter we concentrate on the cognitive processes involved in language and thought.

PROBLEM SOLVING

The Gestalt Approach. The first social scientists to examine systematically the processes involved in solving a problem were a group of German researchers now known as Gestalt psychologists. In Chapter 4, we described the Gestalt approach to perception—the human mind imposes order and structure by grouping stimuli according to such principles as proximity, similarity, and closure. In like manner, Gestalt studies of thought focused on how the human mind imposes structure on a problem by understanding how its elements are related to one another.

One of the problems Gestalt psychologists asked their subjects to solve has since become a classic brainteaser. Take six matchsticks or toothpicks of equal length and try to arrange them into four equilateral triangles with each side equal to one stick. If you try to find the answer by pushing six matches around the table top, you are likely to come to the conclusion that there must be some mistake; any idiot can see that six sticks can only form two equilateral triangles.

Figure 7.2 illustrates another classic Gestalt problem. This, too, is likely to confuse and frustrate the average puzzle solver; repeated attempts may make it seem that there is no solution.

If you are the type who would rather turn ahead to the answers than work up a sweat trying to solve these problems yourself, go directly to the solutions (in Figure 7.4). There you will see two examples of what Gestalt psychologists called the principle of **reorganization**—solving a problem by perceiving new relationships among its elements.

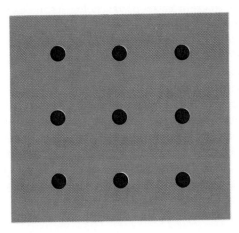

Figure 7.2
One of the classic Gestalt problems: Connect all nine dots using only four lines and without lifting your pencil. Solution appears in Figure 7.4.

Figure 7.3

Elias Howe's invention of the sewing machine is an example of the Gestalt principle of problem solving by reorganization.

On the other hand, if you are a good sport who will valiantly push matchsticks around for 15 minutes before turning to the answer, your first reaction to the solution in Figure 7.4 may be to grumble about psychologists and cheap tricks. But you will have the last laugh if your experience helps you remember that "simple" assumptions (such as the idea that the matches must be arranged in two dimensions) can stand in the way of creative thinking.

Many great inventions can be traced to the Gestalt principle of reorganization. For example, in the nineteenth century, many attempts to design a sewing machine failed because people accepted the simple assumption that a needle has a point at one end and an eye at the other. Sewing machines that tried to pass a needle completely through the fabric for each stitch were very cumbersome and hard to design. But in 1846, Elias Howe invented the sewing machine by placing the eye of the needle in its point; in Gestalt terms, he had reorganized the elements of the problem.

Gestalt psychologists distinguished between two major types of thinking—productive and reproductive. **Productive thinking** solves problems by producing a new organization, as in the preceding examples. It is similar to what Wolfgang Köhler called *insight* in his studies of chimpanzees who reached fruit by standing on a crate or reaching with a stick (see Chapter 5). In contrast, **reproductive thinking** applies past solutions to new problems; it reproduces habits that worked in the past. Many researchers emphasized the value of productive thinking and demonstrated how old habits can interfere with solutions.

For example, Abraham Luchins (1942) studied how people solved a series of water-jug problems such as the following: A person is given three jugs of different sizes. Jug *A* holds 5 quarts, jug *B* holds 40 quarts, and jug *C* holds 18 quarts. Measure out 28 quarts by filling the jugs completely as often as you like and pouring the water from one jug to another. The solution is quite straightforward. Fill jug *A* twice and pour it into jug *B;* then fill jug *C* and pour it into jug *B*. This gives $5 + 5 + 18 = 28$ quarts. After you understand this example, try to solve the problems in Table 7.1. Complete as many as you can before you read on.

If you are like Luchins's subjects, you will probably discover that most of these problems can be solved with the formula $B - 2C - A$. That is, fill jug *B*, pour it into jug *C* twice, and pour it into jug *A* once. This leaves the desired quantity in jug *B;* for example, in problem 1, $127 - 3 - 3 - 21 = 100$. However, you may have trouble with problem 8 because $B - 2C - A$ does not work in this one case; 64% of Luchins's subjects fell into this trap and failed to solve problem 8 even though it involved a simpler approach ($A - C$: fill jug *A* and pour it into jug *C;* the amount remaining in jug *A* is the desired quantity).

Further, some of the problems in Table 7.1 can be solved in more than one way. For example, for problems 7 and 9, simply adding the contents of jugs *A* and *C* is the simplest solution. However, problems 7 and 9 can also be solved with the more complex formula used for problems 1 through 5: $B - 2C - A$. Luchins found that the majority of his subjects (81%) used this familiar formula on problems 6, 7, 9, and 10, even though there were simpler solutions.

TABLE 7.1
Luchins's Water-Jug Problems

Problem number	Given containers of these sizes			Measure out this much water
	A	*B*	*C*	
1	21	127	3	100
2	14	163	25	99
3	18	43	10	5
4	9	42	6	21
5	20	59	4	31
6	23	49	3	20
7	15	39	3	18
8	28	76	3	25
9	18	48	4	22
10	14	36	8	6

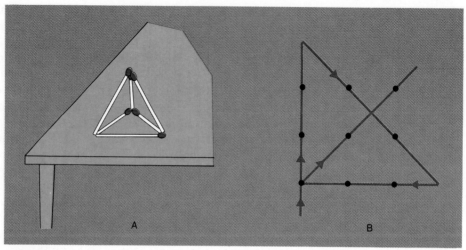

Figure 7.4
Solutions to the six-matchstick problem *(A)* and the nine-dot problem *(B)*. Both are examples of productive thinking and require a reorganization of the elements—considering the possibility of a three-dimensional solution *(A)* or going beyond the boundaries *(B)*.

Psychologists use the term **set effect** to describe this tendency to solve problems in terms of old habits and assumptions, even when they no longer apply. In Gestalt terms, the set effect produces reproductive thinking when a problem demands productive thinking.

Luchins's study and others like it provided fascinating insights into the processes involved in solving certain types of problems. But this knowledge was like a small island in a vast sea of ignorance. The Gestalt psychologists were not able to develop a complete scientific theory that applied to all human problems—from how to start the car on a cold, rainy morning to how to avoid nuclear war. Many psychologists have been discouraged by the complexity of these issues; and there has been far less research on problem solving than on related issues, such as memory and language. However, the rise of a new theoretical approach has helped to revive psychology's interest in this important topic.

The Information-Processing Approach.   As noted in Chapter 6, the *information-processing approach* attempts to analyze thought processes as a series of separate steps. Partly as a result of the computer revolution, this theoretical approach to memory, thought, and language has become so common and so influential that students sometimes mistakenly equate it with the more general area of cognitive psychology. The two are not the same. Cognitive psychology consists of a series of general questions concerning the way observers gain knowledge and use it; the information-processing approach provides one particular set of answers to these questions.

Probably the best-known information-processing model of problem solving is summarized in a series of computer programs called the General Problem Solver originally developed by Allen Newell and Herbert Simon (1972).

The model began by noting that any problem can be seen as the difference between some initial state *(A)* and a desired goal *(B)*. For example, in Luchins's water-jug problem, the initial state *A* involves three jugs with fixed capacities and an unlimited amount of water, while the goal *B* is some particular amount of water. Solving the problem, then, consists of a series of steps, operations, and transformations to get from *A* to *B*.

To discover the actual steps that human problem solvers take, Newell and Simon first used themselves as subjects. They tried to trace the sequence of their own thoughts as they played chess, cracked a code, or solved other problems. Then they asked other subjects to do the same—to think out loud, giving a running commentary as they worked through problems. The systematic steps these people consciously reported were used to develop a computer program that would solve the same problem in the same way. This is called *computer simulation*, imitating some behavior or process (here, problem solving) on a computer.

This computer model of problem solving can be tested in a fairly straightforward manner: Give another problem to the person and the computer and see whether they go through basically the same steps and reach the same conclusion. If so, it seems reasonable to conclude that the person and the computer have used similar strategies.

One of Newell and Simon's conclusions after reviewing how people thought aloud was that problem solvers systematically pursue one line of thought at a time. Ordinarily, this is not a process of trial and error; rather it is guided by general rules called algorithms and heuristics. An **algorithm** is a procedure or formula that guarantees the solution to a given problem. For example, to find the area of a rectangle, multiply the length by the width; this formula invariably provides the area. A **heuristic** is a more general solution strategy usually derived from experience; it is a kind of rule of thumb.

For example, one important heuristic, called **means-end analysis,** tries to solve problems by repeatedly comparing the current state of affairs with the final goal state and taking steps to reduce the difference between the two. Suppose you have a job interview tomorrow and want to be sure you will create a good impression. If you try to solve this problem by means-end analysis, the process might go something like this. What is one way to create a good impression? Be well groomed. What do you need to be well groomed? Nice clothes. Where do you find clothes? In the bureau drawer. But it's empty. Where else can you find clothes? In a tangled heap on the floor of the closet. But they are filthy and smell like something other than lemon-fresh Fab. How can you make them clean? Wash them at a laundromat. But that would take hours. Where else can you find clean clothes? In your roommate's drawer. But your roommate would rather pour Jell-o on your record collection than lend you a shirt. How can you convince your roommate to let you borrow nice clothes? . . . And so on through a step-by-step process that gradually brings you closer to the final goal.

To see whether human beings really do solve problems with this type of means-end analysis, Atwood and Polson (1976) programmed a computer to solve a Luchins-type water-jug problem using this strategy. They then asked 250 college students to solve the same problem.

The performance of the computer was found to be similar to that of the humans. They started with the same steps, took about the same number of moves to solve the problem, and made the same types of errors. Thus, computer simulation supported this information-processing model of thought. Note, however, that its scope was limited; another type of problem would require a new computer program and, possibly, a different heuristic or algorithm.

Researchers have written programs to solve a wide variety of problems; computers now play chess and backgammon, crack codes, prove logical theorems, even diagnose medical diseases and write poetry. Each new advance in the technology of computer sciences opens new possibilities for researchers in this field. But in recent years, many have become less interested in using the computer to imitate human thought processes and more interested in seeing what it can accomplish on its own terms—a field called artificial intelligence.

ARTIFICIAL INTELLIGENCE

Newell and Simon's attempt to simulate human cognitive processes on a computer is one example of the larger field of **artificial intelligence**—the ability of machines to perform tasks that require intelligence, such as recognizing a pattern, responding to a sentence, or solving a problem.

These days, many researchers in this area are not concerned with computer simulation or creating models of the human mind; they simply want to program a computer to play chess or translate a language in the most efficient way. Just as aerospace engineers do not necessarily design planes to imitate the flight of birds, so computer engineers may program machines to solve intellectual problems using different strategies from humans.

Consider the problem of programming a computer to play chess. Suppose a player opens a game by moving his queen's pawn. One thing a chess-playing computer might do is consider each possible legal response and every possible succeeding move and then determine which early move has the highest likelihood of winning. This would be an algorithmic solution; if the computer took the time to consider every possible combination of moves, ultimately the solution would be found. However, the number of possible combinations quickly becomes huge. In a typical game, looking ahead just five moves would require between 20 million and 50 million calculations.

When the first chess-playing programs were written in the 1950s, the details required to consider every possibility took far too long to be practical. Therefore, researchers attempted to imitate human strategy and employ certain rules of thumb—or heuristics. One of Newell and Simon's chess-playing programs looked for moves that achieved various subgoals such as controlling the center of the board and exchanging minor pieces for major ones (for example, giving up a pawn to capture a queen).

The competition at a World Computer Chess Championship in Stockholm, Sweden. The man in the striped jacket is David Slate, from the Northwestern University team.

But none of these heuristic programs was able to beat high-level chess experts. Recent advances in technology have so dramatically increased the speed of computers that it is now practical to perform millions of calculations within the time of a game, so programmers went back to the algorithmic approach of having a computer try everything. The result, according to Hunt (1982), is that "in the past five years chess programs have become dumber, faster, and much harder to beat" (p. 327). A program called Chess 4.7, developed at Northwestern University, can beat about 99.5% of all competition-level chess players. By the time you read this sentence, other programs may be even better.

However, despite rapid technical advances in some areas, it is unlikely that a computer will soon be elected to the U.S. Senate or appointed movie critic of the *Los Angeles Times*. And the limits of artificial intelligence tell us a great deal about the capabilities of the human mind.

One of the most conspicuous failures in artificial intelligence involves computers' understanding of language. At the dawn of the computer age, many scientists were optimistic about the prospect of using computers to translate from one language to another. Early experiments on machine translation, however, often produced bizarre results. According to one famous story, when the Biblical passage "The spirit is willing, but the flesh is weak" was translated into Russian and then back into English, the final version read "The wine was agreeable, but the meat was spoiled."

As we explain in the following section on language, part of the problem lies in the fact that understanding even simple sentences frequently requires a vast storehouse of related knowledge. For example, consider the following story (Abelson, 1981):

> John was feeling very hungry as he entered the restaurant. He settled himself at a table and noticed that the waiter was nearby. Suddenly, however, he realized that he'd forgotten his reading glasses (p. 715).

The average reader will know why John might be disturbed; he needs his glasses to read the menu. Notice, however, that a menu was never mentioned in this passage. For a computer to be able to respond sensibly to simple questions about this story, it needs to be told more than just the meaning of individual words; the computer must be told about restaurants.

In Chapter 6, we introduced Bartlett's notion of a schema as an organization of past experience that could influence constructive memory. This has become an important concept in both cognitive psychology and artificial intelligence. Here, we might define a **schema** as an area in the memory network that contains information and expectations about familiar events. In these terms, the human reader has a schema about restaurants and the computer does not. The solution then is obvious. To understand narratives, a computer must be provided with relevant schemas of its own.

Schank and Abelson (1977) used the term **script** to refer to a schema that summarizes general knowledge about particular situations. They then programmed specific scripts into a computer to understand the restaurant scenario and other simple situations. For example, one artificial-intelligence program along these lines was capable of reading items from the United Press International news wire and writing short summaries. It accomplished this by programming more than 30 separate scripts for such categories as earthquakes, military invasions, and diplomatic actions.

The large number of scripts that might be required to enable a computer to write a book report on *Crime and Punishment* or to engage in a written form of cocktail-party chitchat fills programmers with awe for the complexity of the human information-processing system.

Interpretation becomes even more complicated when a message is spoken rather than typed into the computer. In principle, programming a computer to transcribe the written word sounds like a time-consuming task but not a conceptually difficult one. After all, words are composed of a limited number of distinctive sounds. If you could find some electronic whiz to build a circuit that could recognize these several dozen sounds, a typewriter could easily be hooked up to spell out each word. Of course, the computer might have trouble transcribing unusual spellings or telling the difference between words like *wait* and *weight*, but all in all this sounds like a task that the massive resources of a major corporation like IBM or Digital could solve without a great deal of fuss.

However, as we shall see, human speech is an imperfect signal filled with ambiguity. Listeners actively perceive speech on the basis of a large number of implicit grammatical rules, expectations, and pieces of knowledge stored in memory. Although some computers have been programmed to understand a limited vocabulary, none can even begin to approach the comprehension level of a 4-year-old child. At this writing, perhaps the most advanced program for understanding spoken English is on an experimental IBM computer that has a vocabulary about one-fiftieth that of the average adult, is limited to a narrow range of topics, and takes about three hours to comprehend one minute of speech (Hunt, 1982).

Predictions about the future achievements or limits of technology are a risky business. For example, in 1957 Herbert Simon predicted that within 10 years, a chess program would be written that could beat any expert. He was wrong. Others now predict one will exist by 1990. They may be wrong, too.

But of one fact we can be sure. Future studies of artificial intelligence and computer simulation will stimulate research not just on microchips and software packages but also on the workings of the most amazing device of all—the human mind.

CONCEPTS

In studying the organization of the human mind, one of the most important concepts is the concept of a concept. In other words, concepts are important; they summarize past knowledge and help us deal efficiently with the world.

A **concept** is a mental category of objects or events, grouped on the basis of certain common features. A person who was unable to form concepts would be forced to deal with every unfamiliar object or event as if it were entirely new and never encountered before.

Suppose, for example, that as you enter a friend's home for the first time, a large, brown, four-legged animal jumps up on you and tries to lick your face. If you lacked the concept *dog*, you might be quite alarmed and try to defend yourself by kicking the animal in the head. But in fact your previous experience allows you to categorize the animal under the concept *pet dog* and respond appropriately by playfully wrestling with the animal or by telling your friend please to prevent this disgusting creature from licking your face.

Concepts not only help to predict future events; they also summarize past knowledge. For example, we noted in Chapter 4 that the human eye can distinguish between as many as 7.5 million different colors. Imagine how confusing it would be if these many gradations were not summarized under a few basic concepts such as *red, yellow,* and *blue.*

The first major studies of human concepts focused on the rules people use to identify concepts. Bruner, Goodnow, and Austin (1956) presented a series of problems like those listed in Figure 7.5 to see whether people found some types of concepts more difficult to identify than others. For instance, to be an example of a **conjunctive concept,** an item must possess two attributes at the same time. The concept *red square* is conjunctive; to belong, an item must be both red and square. In contrast, to belong to a **disjunctive concept,** an item may possess one or both of two attributes, such as red or square. Disjunctive concepts are more difficult to learn;

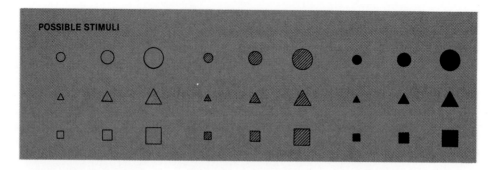

Try to deduce the concept by studying which items belong and which do not

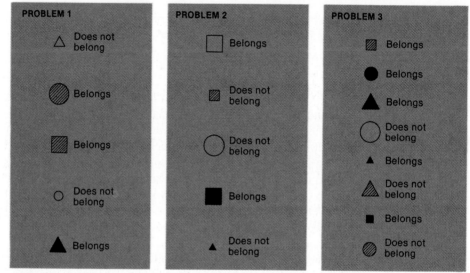

Figure 7.5
Simplified version of a concept-identification experiment. For each problem, try to identify the concept that is based on a particular value for one or more of the three dimensions: size (small, medium, large), color (blank, striped, solid), and shape (circle, triangle, square). See footnote on page 254 for answers.

this example would include red squares, green squares, and red circles, but not green triangles. The examples become even more complex if a judgment is made on more than two dimensions (such as big, red, or square).

Studies of the rules people use to identify such concepts in the laboratory provided many insights into the nature of logical reasoning processes. However, in the 1970s, several researchers argued that in the real world, concepts are rarely as well defined as these laboratory examples. Eleanor Rosch (1975) noted that some items are more *typical*, or better examples of a concept, than others. For example, the concept *furniture* includes some items that are typical and easily agreed upon, such as chairs, beds, and tables. But the boundaries of this concept can get rather fuzzy. Is an ashtray furniture? Or a vase? Or drapes?

Rosch found that there is a clear consensus on which members of a category are typical and which are not. When a group of subjects independently rated how typical certain examples were, the agreement was quite high. For example, a robin is a typical bird, a chicken is not; murder is a typical crime, vagrancy is not; and an apple is a typical fruit, but a fig is not.

These differences in typicality may determine how information is stored in long-term memory. For example, people take longer to answer the question "Is a chicken a bird?" than to answer "Is a robin a bird?" Experiments that require people to identify diagrams, stick figures, and dot patterns lead to the same conclusion. More typical instances are easier to recognize as belonging to a concept.

Figure 7.6
Which is the best example of a bird? For most people, a robin is a more "typical" example of the concept *bird* than a chicken or an ostrich. This difference seems to be related to the way information is stored in long-term memory.

This suggests that similar chunks of information may be stored together in the network of semantic memory (see Chapter 6), overlapping each other according to their similarity. At the center of this network is the "pure concept"; a bird, for example, is defined by certain characteristics such as wings and feathers. All the many kinds of birds are stored in the same network, with atypical birds like chickens, penguins, and ostriches at the outer fringes.

This new emphasis on the fuzzy boundaries of natural categories is also a reminder that concepts can be subjective. To take an extreme example of an abstract category, to one person "roughing it on vacation" may mean hiking through a virginal forest, eating only wild berries, and sleeping on pine cones. Another may feel that he is roughing it if the motel he stops at has no room service and the TV is black and white.

Clearly, abstract concepts like this can depend on a whole lifetime of learning. According to some theorists, classifications and concepts of reality may therefore vary from one culture to the next, particularly as a result of language differences.

LANGUAGE AND THOUGHT

From the time anthropologists first began to study other cultures, they noted that the languages these people spoke often had little in common with the familiar European languages descended from Latin and Greek. A linguist named Benjamin Lee Whorf argued that these differences were so fundamental that they could actually change the way a person perceived the world. This idea became known as the **linguistic-relativity hypothesis**—that language determines the content of thought or the way a person perceives the world.

Whorf (1956) cites the example of an Eskimo language that has three different words for referring to snow—one for falling snow, another for slushy snow, and a third for snow packed hard as ice. These extra categories, Whorf argued, lead the Eskimo actually to perceive a snowy world in a different way from a resident of South Dakota who has only a single basic word. And both an Eskimo and a South Dakotan would perceive the scene differently from an Aztec, for Aztecs have only one word stem to refer to snow, ice, and cold.

This is a provocative idea, but one that is difficult to test. After all, the way we learn another individual's thoughts is by asking a question. We already know that an Eskimo will use several different words for snow in the answer. But how can we go beyond that to see whether the Eskimo actually thinks in a different way?

No one would be surprised to learn that Eskimos know more about snow than Aztecs; after all, how many Aztecs live in igloos? The Eskimos' greater experience with snow is bound to give them more knowledge about it. And greater knowledge is often expressed in a more discriminating vocabulary. For example, English-speaking skiers also have several words for snow—such as *powder* and *corn*—because these distinctions are important to them. There is a bit of a chicken-and-egg problem here; which comes first, the difference in language or the difference in perception?

*Answers to Figure 7.5:   1. A simple concept—large size.   2. A conjunctive concept—large size and square shape.   3. A disjunctive concept—dark color or square shape.

One Eskimo language has three different words for the English concept *snow*. Does this difference imply that speakers of the two languages perceive snow differently?

The most intensive tests of this idea have considered the question of color perception. Do languages that divide the color spectrum differently actually lead to differences in color perception? In one study, Heider and Olivier (1972) compared the ability to remember colors for English speakers and for members of a primitive tribe from Indonesian New Guinea named the Dani. The Dani language has only two words for identifying colors; one refers roughly to light colors, the other to dark colors. In this study, each person was shown a colored chip for 5 seconds; 30 seconds later, the subjects were asked to pick out the chip they had seen from among 40 different colored chips. Both the English speakers and the Dani made many mistakes on this task, but the pattern of errors suggested that they perceived the color spectrum in the same way. If the linguistic-relativity hypothesis were correct, one might predict that people would be most likely to confuse two similar colors that they called by the same name; if similar colors had different names, they could be linguistically coded into two different categories. But this was not the case; labeling did not seem to affect the confusion among colors.

Despite the fact that the strong claim that language *determines* thought is not supported by the most careful research to date, there is evidence for a weaker version of the linguistic-relativity hypothesis: The words a person uses can certainly have some influence on thought processes.

One typical study of this phenomenon examined the use of pronouns like *he* and *his* as neutral terms that may refer to either men or women (Moulton, Robinson, &

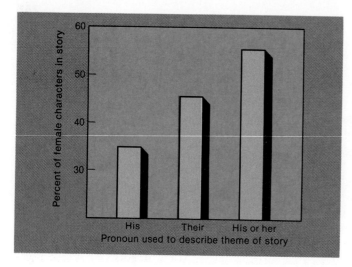

Figure 7.7

Sexist pronouns produced sexist stories. When the pronoun *his* was used to describe the theme of a composition, fewer people wrote about female characters than when the more neutral terms *their* or *his or her* were employed.

Elias, 1978). When feminists proposed substituting expressions like *he or she* in neutral contexts, some writers argued that they were being overly sensitive, as if English speakers automatically assume that in some contexts *he* can refer to males or females.

In one study of the implications of using masculine pronouns, men and women were asked to make up stories about themes like this: "In a large coeducational institution, the average student will feel isolated in _____ introductory courses." The blank was filled with *his, their,* and *his or her* for three different groups. The researchers then noted whether the students wrote about male or female characters. The results appear in Figure 7.7; the actual pronoun used had a pronounced effect on the sex of the fictional characters. There is no question that language and thought are linked; the challenge for future research will be to specify the precise nature of these interrelationships.

Language

Most of the time, we take our astounding language abilities for granted. Yet it is hard to imagine what human society would be like without language. Communicating simple thoughts such as "pass the salt" and "I love blue eyes" could become major undertakings. Although we would all save money on our telephone bills, a world without language would almost certainly be far more primitive. Without language, how could one generation tell the next how to build a bridge, treat a broken leg, or bake moist and tender Toll House cookies?

COMPETENCE VERSUS PERFORMANCE

Orators and philosophers have studied the nature of language at least since the ancient Greeks. But in the last few decades, two separate disciplines have arisen to study language from somewhat different perspectives.

Linguistics is the study of the fundamental nature and structure of human language. It is concerned with language in the abstract, such as the way words may be combined in English to form an acceptable sentence.

Psycholinguistics is the study of how people actually speak and use language. For example, a psycholinguist might study the way children learn to speak for the first time in the hope of discovering fundamental principles of language use. A linguist would be less concerned with the question of language acquisition; for her, the key issue would involve the nature of linguistic rules rather than the way children learn them or violate them.

The differences between these two specialties can be understood in terms of a fundamental distinction, drawn by linguist Noam Chomsky, between competence and performance. **Linguistic competence** is abstract knowledge of a language; **linguistic performance** involves applying this knowledge to speaking and listening. Psycholinguists tend to concentrate on performance, while linguists focus on competence. It is a bit like choosing to understand the game of Monopoly by concentrating on its formal rules, as a linguist might, or by observing how people play the game, as a psycholinguist might—noting which rules they follow religiously and which seem less important. (Note that this is also similar to Tolman's distinction between a rat's learning a cognitive map of a maze versus the animal's performance; see Chapter 5.)

Each type of research provides valuable clues about the nature of human language; this is just one more example of how complex human behavior is best understood by viewing it from several perspectives.

LINGUISTICS AND GRAMMAR

One of the most amazing features of human language is the fact that each of us is capable of creating an infinite number of sentences. Similarly, there is no limit on the combinations of words that we can understand. It is relatively easy to produce a sentence that is unique. Consider the following statement: "Richard Nixon's political beliefs inspired three teenagers in Seattle, Washington, to form Citizens for Integrity, a political action group that now has over 16 million members." Although there is no way to be entirely certain, it seems likely that no one on the face of the earth has ever before strung these specific words together in precisely this way. Yet I had no trouble writing this sentence, and you have no trouble understanding it. (You will probably also have no trouble concluding that the statement is false.)

Given our ability to use language in infinitely novel ways, linguists have come to the conclusion that each of us must master some fundamental principles that we use to generate sentences. Taken together, all these rules form the grammar of a language. When most of us think of the word *grammar*, we picture an English teacher sternly reminding students that nice girls don't say "ain't." But for a linguist, **grammar** is the complete system of rules that relates sounds to meanings for a specific language. In this section, we consider the three main branches of grammar—*phonology*, the study of sounds; *syntax*, the way words combine to form sentences; and *semantics*, the meaning of words and sentences.

Phonology. **Phonology** refers to the rules that govern the use of sounds in a specific language. Every language contains a limited number of **phonemes,** the distinct sounds that make a difference in meaning in a particular language. By one count, English contains 41 phonemes, or distinct perceptual units. While there are only 26 letters in English, the same letter may stand for several different sounds. For example, if you place your fingers over your Adam's apple and say the word *sounds,* you will notice that the *s* at the end of the word vibrates the vocal cords and therefore is called a voiced consonant, while the *s* at the beginning produces no vocal-cord vibration and is called voiceless.

The human vocal apparatus is capable of producing many more sounds than the limited set English speakers use—perhaps several hundred of them. Other languages use roughly 20 to 60 phonemes, often making distinctions that English speakers do not or failing to make distinctions that English speakers consider important.

For example, the two words *keep cool* may seem to begin with the same sound. But there is a subtle difference between those two hard sounds. For the *k* in *keep,* the tongue touches the roof of the mouth farther toward the back of the oral cavity than it does for the *c* in *cool.* You may have difficulty specifying the precise placement of the tongue in the mouth for these two sounds, but if you listen closely enough you should be able to tell them apart.

While English treats these sounds as interchangeable versions of the same phoneme, Arabic does not. In Arabic, the word *kalb,* meaning "dog," begins with the sound of *k* in *keep.* The spoken word *qalb,* meaning "heart," sounds different only because it begins with the sound of *c* in *cool.*

Such differences between the basic phonemes of various languages are one of the major obstacles faced by those who want to perfect their pronunciation of a foreign

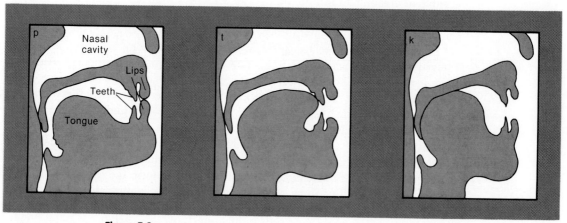

Figure 7.8
When we talk, air from the lungs is forced through the larynx, mouth, teeth, lips, and sometimes the nose. Different speech sounds are produced by varying the shape of this system. This illustration shows the position of major vocal-tract structures for the English consonants *p, t,* and *k.*

tongue. Native Japanese speakers may say *read* instead of *lead* because in Japanese *r* and *l* are interchangeable versions of the same phoneme.

Phonology is concerned not just with a list of acceptable sounds but also with the rules by which they are combined. For example, you intuitively know that *kpax* and *gdoller* are not English words; each violates certain phonological rules in our language by requiring an unfamiliar pattern of lip and tongue movements. These letter combinations, however, would be perfectly acceptable words in Russian or Czechoslovakian, languages that have different phonological rules.

Syntax. **Syntax** (from Greek roots meaning "arranging together") refers to the rules that specify the way words can be combined to form sentences.

On the simplest level, the rules of syntax specify which strings of words form acceptable sentences and which do not. Intuitively, we know that the statement "Bob Barker was my favorite game-show host" is grammatically correct. In contrast, there is clearly something wrong with the statement "Bob Barker was favorite game-show host my." We may have difficulty stating the precise grammatical rule this violates, but a native speaker of English has no problem recognizing that this string of words is not a well-formed sentence.

Beginning in the 1950s, Noam Chomsky developed an influential theory that attempted to make intuitive rules like this explicit. He hoped to lay the groundwork for a detailed grammar that would be capable of generating every string of words that a person who spoke English would recognize as a well-formed sentence. At the same time, this grammar should never generate a string of words that would not be an acceptable sentence. Thus, Chomsky proposed a model of linguistic competence, the abstract nature of language—the word strings that form acceptable sentences. He did not claim that this model would apply to linguistic performance—that is, that people would actually rely on these particular processes when they spoke or listened.

At the simplest level, Chomsky's (1965) theory analyzed the **surface structure** of sentences, the actual words in a sentence and the relations among them. In some ways, Chomsky's analysis of the surface structure is similar to the exercises school children perform in grammar classes. The basic idea involves breaking a sentence down into its component parts. For example, the sentence

The dachshund bit the bus driver.

might be broken down into

(The dachshund) (bit) (the bus driver).

Analyses of the surface structure of a sentence are often summarized as tree diagrams, as in Figure 7.9. This figure suggests one important element of Chomsky's system. He saw language as organized into a hierarchy, from the highest level—a sentence—to the lowest level—an individual noun, verb, or adjective. It is important to note that the parts of the surface structure of a sentence are not interchangeable. If we were to reverse the two noun phrases, it becomes

The bus driver bit the dachshund.

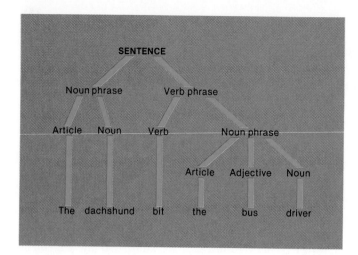

Figure 7.9
A tree diagram of the surface structure of a simple sentence. (The name comes from the many branches.)

Reporters everywhere would recognize this sentence as far more newsworthy than the original version.

Chomsky tried to specify the actual rules that were capable of generating the surface structure of the original sentence. One rule is that a sentence can be rewritten as a noun phrase followed by a verb phrase. Another is that a noun phrase consists of an article, sometimes an adjective, and then a noun or another noun phrase. Sentences with more complex structures than our example require additional rules. For our purposes, it is not necessary to remember the details of the many possible rules. What is important is Chomsky's goal—to develop a complete, logical system capable of generating every sentence that is grammatically correct.

However, Chomsky also noted that the surface structure of a sentence was only part of the story. For example, consider the following two sentences:

The dachshund bit the bus driver.
The bus driver was bitten by the dachshund.

These sentences are obviously similar; grammar fans will recognize the first as the active voice and the second as the passive voice. The surface structures of these two sentences—the order of the words and the relationships among them—are quite different, yet at the level of meaning they are practically the same.

Chomsky (1957) therefore introduced the notion of **deep structure**—the underlying organization and intent of sentences. In the case of a simple sentence in the active voice, such as

The dachshund bit the bus driver.

the surface and deep structure are exactly the same. But for the passive voice, the surface structure is

The bus driver was bitten by the dachshund.

and the deep structure is the simpler

The dachshund bit the bus driver.

Two sentences with different surface structures (active and passive voice) can have the same deep structure (here, the active voice).

The theoretical importance of deep structures can be seen more clearly in the analysis of this ambiguous sentence:

Visiting relatives can be boring.

The sentence can mean that going to Uncle Harry's house is a sure cure for insomnia, or it can mean that when Uncle Harry stays for a while in your guest room, you begin to wonder whether life has any meaning. As Figure 7.10 suggests, an analysis of surface structure does not distinguish between relatives being visited and relatives doing the visiting. However, Chomsky's system posits two separate deep structures, each distinctly referring to only one of these possibilities:

It can be boring to visit relatives.
Relatives who visit can be boring.

Again, Chomsky's ultimate goal was to develop a complete set of rules that would make it possible to transform the surface structure of every sentence in the English language into the underlying deep structure. He believed that linguists should concentrate on the analysis of syntax to understand the nature of language. Others, however, have put more emphasis on the study of meaning.

Semantics. **Semantics** refers to the rules governing the meaning of sentences, words, or morphemes. A **morpheme** is the smallest unit of speech that has meaning; it may be a word or a part of a word. For example, the word *slip, sense,* and *squeal* are all morphemes. Many prefixes and suffixes that change the meaning of a word are also morphemes. The word *slips* contains two morphemes: *slip* is one, and the *s* that makes it a plural is the other. Similarly, the words *nonsense* and *squealed* each contain two morphemes (*non-sense* and *squeal-ed*).

The meaning of morphemes and words in a given language are generally based on arbitrary symbols. There is no particular reason why the word *green* refers to a color midway between blue and yellow. This color could have just as easily been

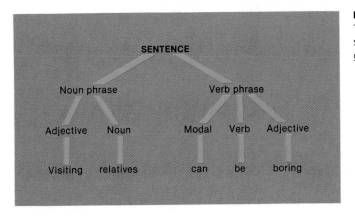

Figure 7.10
The surface structure of this ambiguous sentence can be transformed by Chomsky's grammar into two different deep structures:

It can be boring to visit relatives.
Relatives who visit can be boring.

named *orange* or *justice* or *Harold*. However, centuries of usage by English speakers have given the word *green* a certain meaning.

But semantics involves far more than just a mental dictionary that specifies the meaning of every morpheme in the English language. A word like *dictator* or *house-wife* may conjure up emotional associations that go far beyond its literal dictionary definition.

Further, the interpretation of a statement may involve knowledge that goes far beyond the words themselves. The sentence "That doesn't sound right" may mean different things to a musician playing a tune for the first time, a doctor listening to a patient breathe, and an auditor reviewing your income tax returns. As a result of the fact that so many factors can affect meaning, semantics is probably the most complex area in linguistics. Some of these complications will become apparent in the next section, as we focus on the processes involved in understanding language.

THE PROBLEM OF COMPREHENSION

Noam Chomsky's influential views of language were developed as a model of linguistic competence—the abstract nature of language. But psycholinguists wondered whether it might also apply to linguistic performance—the actual processes people use in speaking and listening. Thus, Chomsky's model stimulated serious research on the problem of language comprehension; that is, what are the processes you use to understand this text or to comprehend Joe Garagiola's description of the World Series?

Testing Chomsky's Model.   One of the first studies inspired by Chomsky's theory examined whether the structure of syntax helped people understand and remember linguistic stimuli; in other words, did normal listeners seem to use surface structure in some way? To avoid the complications produced by word meaning, Epstein (1961) developed a series of nonsense stimuli. Some, like Lewis Carroll's poem "Jabberwocky," were made to appear to conform to English syntax. For example, one of Epstein's stimuli read

> A haky deebs reciled the dison tofently um flutest pav.
> The glers un cligs wur seping un vasing a rad moovly.

Although few of the words make sense, this seems to read like an English sentence in which *haky* is an adjective, *deebs* a noun, *recile* a verb, and so on. Other nonsense strings removed the punctuation, capitals, and grammatical endings:

> haky deeb um flut recile pav tofent dison
> clig sep wur rad un moov gler un vas

People were able to learn the first set of stimuli far more easily than the second, despite the fact that the first list is somewhat longer. Syntax provided a structure that helped people remember, even when it was arbitrarily applied to meaningless syllables and words. This finding seemed consistent with Chomsky's strong emphasis on the importance of syntax.

Other early studies also supported the idea that Chomsky's model of linguistic competence might describe linguistic performance as well. For example, in Chomsky's system, a simple statement in the active voice requires no transformation to uncover its deep structure. A statement in the passive voice, however, must be transformed. Thus, if people actually use deep structures to understand a sentence, the active voice should be comprehended more quickly than the passive, because it does not require this time-consuming transformation.

In one test of this prediction, Gough (1965) asked people to read a sentence and then look at a picture. Sometimes the sentence accurately described the picture and sometimes it did not. The subjects in this experiment were asked to decide as quickly as possible whether the sentence and picture were consistent. Gough found that people responded more quickly when the statements were in the active, rather than the passive, voice, supporting the idea that people might actually analyze deep structures in order to comprehend a sentence.

Not surprisingly, however, later researchers found that things were not always this straightforward. To cite just one example, Olson and Filby (1972) found that in some cases the passive voice is easier to understand than the active voice. When people were told a story about a truck and then shown a picture of a car hitting it, they were able to verify the passive sentence:

The truck was hit by the car.

more quickly than the active one:

The car hit the truck.

This finding suggests that context (in this case, hearing a story) also plays a large role in human speech comprehension. This was one of many studies that made psycholinguists reconsider their optimism about Chomsky's model and think more seriously about the role of factors other than syntax.

Context and Schemas.   In the last few years, many psycholinguists have focused on the role of context, schemas, and outside knowledge in comprehension. To paraphrase a sentence properly, we often need to understand a great deal about the context in which it was uttered. If an employee says to his boss, "I am not paid enough," he probably means, "Please give me a raise." But if the same man tells his teenaged daughter, "I am not paid enough," when she asks for a new car, he means, "I can't afford it." In this case, comprehending a statement properly depends on far more than the syntax of the sentence or even the literal meanings of the individual words. If you did not know that bosses decide how much to pay their employees or that cars are expensive, you might interpret these sentences differently.

In part of one study, Rummelhart read subjects a story that began

Mary heard the ice-cream truck coming down the street. She remembered her birthday money, and ran into the house (Hunt, 1982, p. 117).

When he questioned the listeners, they explained easily that Mary is a little girl who wants ice cream and that she went into the house to get money to buy some. These facts are obvious, but they are not stated in the story. Comprehension is based not just on words and their meanings but on schemas that fill in the gaps of what is mutually understood.

Both the study and the conclusion may sound familiar because of their resemblance to Roger Schank's work on scripts and artificial intelligence. In the late 1970s, several cognitive psychologists—including Rummelhart, Schank, and others—proposed ambitious models of the way knowledge is stored in long-term memory and how it is involved in the everyday comprehension of language. The details are controversial, as psycholinguists are just beginning to test their specific predictions. For our purposes, however, the similarities are more important than the differences between these models. All portray the listener as an active participant in the comprehension process who brings to the situation knowledge that allows him to understand not just the specific words in a statement but also the larger message it was intended to convey.

Speech Perception.   The notion of an active listener becomes even more critical when one considers the further problems posed by the spoken word. Your ear probably does not distinguish differences in the sound of the letter *b* in the words *bill, ball, bull, able,* and *rob.* Yet careful acoustic analysis would reveal that each of these *b*s has a slightly different sound. Add to this the complications of different speakers with different accents, some talking with their mouths full of roast beef and others whispering sweet nothings, and you may begin to wonder how we ever understand another human being.

Further, listeners sometimes make distinctions that speakers do not. In the normal course of conversation, the statements "'Why choose,' she said" and "'White shoes,' she said" are pronounced in precisely the same way. Although you as a listener will have little trouble knowing which phrase was meant in a certain context, if you had nothing to go on but the physical sounds of speech, you would never be able to tell these phrases apart.

In normal conversation, the quality of pronunciation is very low. This was most vividly demonstrated in a study (Pollack & Pickett, 1964) in which people were simply asked to repeat isolated words that were spliced from tape-recorded conversations. Astoundingly, fewer than half of these individual words were intelligible; listeners correctly identified single words only 47% of the time. The researchers went on to show that this result was not limited to conversational English. When people tried to identify single words from a tape of a person reading, they were correct 55% of the time. When the passages were read quickly, only 41% of the words were correctly identified.

Note that there was nothing unusual about the readings or conversations used in this study. When people listened to the entire tapes under normal conditions, they had no trouble understanding what was said with almost 100% accuracy. The researchers also asked people to identify two words in a row, three words, four words, and so on. The longer the stretch of speech, the more accurately listeners were able to identify the words. These findings again suggest that when a person listens to speech, he does not passively respond to a series of sounds. Rather, he actively uses clues from the context to fill in the gaps in an imperfect auditory stimulus.

Additional support for this active picture of the listener comes from a study of the kinds of errors people make when they misunderstand what others say (Garnes & Bond, 1975). In virtually every case, mistakes involved substituting a similar word that served the same grammatical function: "Wrapping service" was heard as "wrecking service," for example, and "get some sealing tape" was heard as "get some ceiling paint." It is almost as though the listener has an implicit idea of what should come next; after hearing "get some," he expects a noun and possibly an adjective. Ambiguous sounds are then perceived as conforming to this pattern.

Normal speech is at best an imperfect signal filled with ambiguity. Yet despite sloppy pronunciation, we usually hear it properly and make few mistakes. The listener starts out with certain implicit syntactic and semantic rules and actively perceives speech in terms of these expectations.

LANGUAGE DEVELOPMENT

The more you learn about the complexity of the processes involved in adult language comprehension and production, the more amazed you will be by the fact that children are able to learn to speak so quickly. Indeed, in one expert's opinion (Moskowitz, 1978), in the first few years of life, the average child is able to accomplish more than "ten linguists working full time for 10 years to analyze the structure of the English language" (p. 92).

This rapid and efficient learning is tied to the child's growing cognitive abilities. English children, French children, Russian children, and others all seem to learn their native tongues in similar ways, moving through comparable stages at roughly the same pace. Understanding the process of language development can lead to fundamental insights into the nature of human linguistic abilities.

From Sounds to Words. The sounds a baby makes in the first weeks after birth seem to be reflexive. A father may read a message into his child's shrill cry—"It's time for a fresh diaper" or "I wish Tommy would stop pushing in my face"—but most of the communication seems to be in the eye or the ear of the beholder.

By the third or fourth month, the vocal tract has matured to become capable of speech sounds, and the infant begins to **babble**—to produce speechlike sounds, usually alternating consonant and vowel sounds such as *babababa* or *googoogoogoo*. Proud parents often claim that their child is desperately trying to communicate some profound message through this string of syllables. Most psychologists disagree.

Interestingly, babbling infants seem to produce phonemes (speech sounds) from all the world's languages. Adult speakers of English may find it difficult to form some of the harsh consonants of German, the changing pitch of Vietnamese, or the hard clicks found in certain African languages. The babbling infant in any culture, having not yet learned these limitations, seems to make all these sounds and more. The American infant who babbles an African-type click that she has almost certainly never heard thus seems to be responding to some biological program for exercising the speech apparatus. Further evidence that babbling is a built-in stage of language development comes from the observation that deaf children—who cannot hear their own sounds—began babbling around the normal age (Lenneberg, Rebelsky, & Nichols, 1965).

Sooner or later, a child's meaningless babble shades over into his long-awaited

Studies of the precise words children use as they learn to speak and read can reveal underlying rules of language organization.

first word. This historic moment may be difficult to pinpoint. Before the child correctly uses adult words, he may begin to communicate with more primitive sounds. For example, six of the first seven "words" used by one intensively studied American child bore little resemblance to English (McNeill, 1970). At the age of 6 months, the child began to say *uh* whenever he tried to address people, distant objects, or "escaped" toys. A month later, his vocabulary doubled; the new word, *dididi*, seemed to reflect disapproval when he said it loudly and contentment when he repeated it softly. During the tenth month, he added five new sounds: *Nenene* involved scolding; *tt!* was used to call squirrels; *piti* seemed to mean "interesting"; *deh* was an interjection something like *uh;* and *mama* seemed to refer not to his mother but rather to food.

The first words that seem clearly based on adult models tend to appear between the ages of 10 and 13 months (deVilliers & deVilliers, 1978). Most often, they are simple sounds that alternate consonants and vowels. Countless mothers have been thrilled when Junior's first word was *mama* and his second was *papa*. Beyond the selective perception that may be involved, this choice probably has at least as much to do with the child's vocal capabilities as with his fondness for Mom and Dad. There is not a single documented case of an infant whose first three words were *iambic, pentameter,* and *onomatopoeia*. That is not because children lack interest in poetry but rather because these words are complex and hard to pronounce.

Consonant sounds like *m, p,* and *d* are easily produced by closing the front of the mouth. The sound of the vowel *a* is produced at the rear of the mouth by opening the oral cavity completely. This contrast makes words like *mama, papa,* and *dada* easy to pronounce. It is probably no accident that words like these have come to refer to parents in many of the world's languages.

By the age of 18 months, most children have a vocabulary of dozens of words. In one study of 18 children, Nelson (1973) found that some children had a vocabulary of 50 words as early as 15 months, while others did not have this large a vocabulary until they were 2 years old. The words these toddlers actually used suggested that children actively chose to talk about things that interested them rather than passively imitate the words used most by the adults around them. Nelson did not observe a single child who could say *diaper*, *mittens*, or *pants*, despite the fact that they had almost certainly heard these words repeated many times. Instead, they talked about such fascinating categories as foods (juice, milk, and cookies were the most common), animals (such as dog, cat, and duck), and toys (including ball and block).

From Words to Sentences. It is easy enough to list the things that children say; it is much harder to decide what they mean. When a child points at the household pet and says, "doggie," does she really mean, "This is a dog"? When she reaches out to her mother after dinner and cutely says "cookie, cookie," does she really mean, "Mother, I certainly would appreciate it if you would bring me another one of those tasty Oreos"? A **holophrase** is a single word a young child seems to use to express an entire message. Some question remains about just what messages young children intend to send and how much is inferred by the listener.

One line of research has examined this question by trying to determine whether young children use different intonations—as adults do—for statements, questions, and emphasis. For example, Menyuk and Bernholtz (1969) tape-recorded several different versions of the same word uttered in different contexts by one child between the ages of 18 and 20 months. They found that questions and statements could be identified with 80% accuracy by adults who simply listened to the tapes without any information about the situation in which the child used the words. This study suggests that there are real differences in intonation and supports the idea that children who utter holophrases do have some larger message in mind. This study is not the final word, but it suggests that further research may be able to provide some insights into the abilities and intentions of even very young children.

Around the age of 2, children begin to put words together into two-word sentences like "see doggie," "book there," and "my candy." Like holophrastic speech, the two-word message seems to be a stage of speech development that appears at roughly the same time in many different cultures. American children may say "more milk," while Germans say "mehr milch" and Russians say "yeshche moloko," but in each culture toddlers begin expressing their thoughts in two-word sentences somewhere around the age of 2 (Slobin, 1971).

During this period, children use a shortened style called **telegraphic speech,** avoiding "unnecessary" words such as articles, prepositions, and adjectives and using only words that communicate the essence of their message. The term *telegraphic speech* calls attention to the fact that young children usually simplify their messages as much as possible. Since long messages cost more than short ones, few telegrams begin with idle chat: "As I was walking past the grocery store today, I thought of you. . . . " Instead, the message in a telegram is likely to be stripped to the bare essentials: "Lost all money. Send cash" or "Met another man. Goodbye." Similarly, a young child will not say, "May I please have a piece of Duncan Hines double fudge layer cake?" but rather, "Have cake?" or "I have cake?" Again, telegraphic speech has been observed not only in studies of English but also in studies of other languages.

Throughout the preschool years, children make certain systematic errors that reveal a great deal about their language use. In English, most verbs form the past tense by adding *ed* to the present tense, as in *walked, talked,* and *asked.* But a number of irregular verbs do not follow this rule; the past tense is not related to the present in any obvious way in *go/went* or *break/broke.* Interestingly, some children learn the irregular form early in development and may form such telegraphic sentences as "Daddy went" and "It broke."

Their parents may be alarmed when these children later discover the *ed* rule and start saying things like "Daddy goed" and "It breaked." However, this is a normal phenomenon in language development called **overregularization,** in which children force every utterance to conform to the regular rules of grammar, even when it means making an error. Similarly, children often overregularize the formation of English plurals, and say things like *foots, mans,* and *mouses.* After children have firmly mastered these rules, they are able to go back and learn the exceptions.

The phenomenon of overregularization is strong evidence that language acquisition involves more than a simple process of imitation learning. Four-year-olds do not talk about *foots* and *mouses* because they are repeating words they have heard elsewhere; rather, they seem to be applying a general rule that they have deduced regarding the English language. Such rules resist gentle efforts at correction, as shown in the following conversation recorded by Jean Berko Gleason (1967):

Child: My teacher holded the baby rabbits and we patted them.

Mother: Did you say your teacher held the baby rabbits?

Child: Yes.

Mother: What did you say she did?

Child: She holded the baby rabbits and we patted them.

Mother: Did you say she held them tightly?

Child: No, she holded them loosely.

Despite Mom's efforts to prod the child to say *held,* he continued to repeat the incorrect form *holded.* The appeal of the overregularized rule seems to be stronger than any desire to imitate.

In general, studies of children in many cultures suggest that learning to speak is strongly influenced by a biological process of maturation and that toddlers master a set of underlying grammatical principles that they use actively to construct a world of language.

Viki the chimp was raised by Cathy and Keith Hays as if she were a normal child. She never learned to "speak" more than a few words, but she did learn to light cigarettes.

TEACHING APES TO "SPEAK"

At least since the time when Clever Hans tapped his foot to answer Herr von Osten's questions (see Chapter 1), psychologists have been fascinated by the idea of teaching animals to "talk." Several early researchers took this goal quite literally. In her delightful book *The Ape in Our House*, Cathy Hayes (1951) described how she and her husband valiantly tried to teach a chimpanzee to hold a reasonable conversation.

They treated Viki the chimp like their own child. Viki wore diapers, followed her "mother" around the house, and for several years was generally treated as though she were merely an ugly person. In some ways, Viki behaved like any mischievous child. She could open windows, turn on lights, wash her face, listen to the radio, and scribble on walls. On the other hand, she never did master toilet training, she had an unsettling habit of biting the Hayes' visitors, and she was a whiz at swinging from trees. More to the point, after six years of intensive psychological training and motherly love, poor, slow-learning Viki could only mutter a few simple words like *mama*, *papa*, and *cup*.

The First Success: Washoe. In 1969, Allen and Beatrice Gardner published a groundbreaking report. They had actually taught a chimp to communicate with humans! In retrospect, the insight that made this achievement possible seems quite simple. Chimpanzees have trouble talking because their mouths and vocal apparatus are not designed to speak. Like some people, however, monkeys frequently gesture with their hands. The Gardners therefore decided to teach a chimpanzee American Sign Language, a linguistic system used by the deaf. While some deaf people use hand signals to spell out words, letter by letter, American Sign Language uses signs to represent entire words. To say *always*, for example, a person rotates the arm at the elbow while holding his hand in a fist with the index finger pointed forward. The sign for *flower* intuitively seems closer to its source—all five fingertips are held together and touched first to one nostril and then to the other, as if sniffing a flower.

The female chimpanzee the Gardners chose to study was born in the wild. When Washoe moved to her new family at the University of Nevada in June 1966, she was about a year old. Reasoning that Washoe would be most likely to speak if she were raised in a pleasant environment with lots of things to talk about, the Gardners built a home for Washoe in a trailer in their backyard. She was constantly surrounded by friendly humans who chattered away in sign language with her and with one another.

For the first few months, Washoe lived the lazy life of the typical infant. Most of her time was devoted to sleeping, crawling, and having her diaper changed. But as she grew, she gradually began to imitate the signs of her human friends and to respond to their encouragement and guidance.

About a year after the project began, the Gardners established a firm criterion for deciding when Washoe was using a sign properly. Three different people had to notice an appropriate use of a sign, and Washoe had to use the sign appropriately without prompting at least once a day for 15 consecutive days. By this criterion, Washoe had mastered 30 signs at the time of the initial report, 22 months into her training (Gardner & Gardner, 1969).

Some of the signs Washoe used were quite concrete, including *flower, brush, hat,* and *toothbrush*. Others represented more abstract concepts, such as *hurry, more, sorry,* and *funny*.

Her use of some signs seemed to be based on imitation. For example, Washoe was one of the few chimpanzees in the world who was required to brush her teeth after every meal. Whenever she brushed, the adults around her frequently repeated the sign for *toothbrush*. In the tenth month of her training, Washoe wandered into the bathroom on a visit to the Gardner home. To their infinite delight, she climbed up on the counter, saw a mug full of toothbrushes, and, for the first time, spontaneously signed *toothbrush*.

Washoe's acquisition of the sign for *funny* was somewhat less direct; the Gardners saw it as the chimpanzee equivalent of an infant's babbling. One day while Washoe was fooling around with her psychologist playmates, she happened to press the tip of her index finger to her nose and snort. The American Sign Language symbol for *funny* involves pressing the index and second fingers to the tip of the nose, without the simian snort. But, amid much giggling, the trainer imitated Washoe's action. Washoe repeated the sign, then her trainer did, then Washoe did, and so on. Later, Washoe's trainers repeated the sign whenever they began to laugh and smile. "Eventually," the Gardners reported, "Washoe came to use the 'funny' sign spontaneously in roughly appropriate situations" (p. 667). There were, however, occasional disagreements about what was appropriate. On at least one occasion, Washoe giggled and signed *funny* after urinating on one of her trainers (Linden, 1974). The trainer did not agree.

After a while, Washoe began to combine signs into strings such as "gimme tickle" (*gimme* was a single sign for "give me"), "gimme drink, please," and "please

What Would a Chimpanzee Say?

Newsweek magazine (December 20, 1971) described the abilities of Washoe, the talking chimp. Can you find any errors? (A short discussion appears after the "Summary" at the end of this chapter.)

The Gardners raised Washoe almost as if she were their own child. . . . Within one year, Washoe had begun to associate gestures with specific activities. . . . Then, by early 1967, she had begun to link things together in a series—to form whole, if admittedly simple, expressions. If thirsty, for example, Washoe made the symbol for "give me" and then added the one for "drink." Soon she was able to differentiate between similar objects. If all she wanted was a drink of water, for example, she gave only the gesture for "drink"—thumb in the mouth, fingers drawn into a fist. But if she craved soda pop, she prefaced the "drink" signal with that for "sweet"—a quick touching of the tongue with her fingertips . . . (p. 101).

open, hurry." Later reports placed Washoe's vocabulary at 160 signs (Fleming, 1974).

The Gardners and others saw these phrases as evidence that Washoe was mastering basic rules of syntax. But, as we shall see, others were far more skeptical about precisely what Washoe had learned.

A More Systematic Approach: Lana. Soon after the Gardners published their report, other accounts of communicating chimps began to appear. David Premack (1971) trained a chimpanzee named Sarah to communicate by manipulating plastic symbols on a magnetic board. Later, Roger Fouts and others taught several other apes to use American Sign Language. One of the most impressive demonstrations to date involves the Lana Project (Rumbaugh, 1977), which developed an automatic system that made it possible to study language learning more efficiently and more objectively. Twenty-four hours a day, seven days a week, Lana the chimp was able to type messages on a special keyboard. A computer recorded every message and automatically responded to appropriate requests.

On Lana's special typewriter, each key represented a geometric symbol that corresponded to a word in Yerkish (a special language invented for the experiment and named after pioneer ape researcher Robert Yerkes). When Lana pressed a key, a copy of the appropriate symbol was projected on a small screen above the keyboard; permitting Lana to read as she wrote.

At first, Lana was simply taught that when she pressed the key with the Yerkish symbol for *banana* on it, she got a piece of banana. If she felt that things went better with Coke, a press on the Coke key gave her a taste of cola. Then the task was made slightly more difficult—Lana had to precede each request by touching the *please* key and follow it with a period for proper punctuation. Lana learned quickly. Within two weeks, she was able to produce correctly three types of grammatical requests: "Please machine give _____." for liquids such as juice or coffee; "Please machine give piece of _____." for foods such as apples or bread; and "Please machine make _____." for music, slides, or movies—30-second segments from the film *A Gorilla's First Year.*

New words were gradually added as the computer kept track of every success and failure. Some of Lana's communications were truly amazing. For example, one evening after about a year of training, a research assistant named Beverley was closing up for the night and had just filled all of Lana's vending machines. Several times, Lana correctly typed, "Please machine give piece of bread," but nothing happened. As if realizing that the equipment did not work, Lana dashed off a series of messages including, "Please Shelley," "Please Tim," and then "Please Beverley move behind room."

Addressing the research assistants by name was nothing new; Lana had learned to make personal requests early in the project. But the command "move behind room" had been learned as part of a game in which a researcher walked behind Lana's cage and tapped on the wall. Perhaps coincidentally, much of the automatic equipment for the experiment was located behind the same wall. On this particular evening, Beverley responded to Lana's request, walked behind the room, noticed that the bread machine was jammed, and fixed it. Lana contentedly went back to her earlier request, "Please machine give piece of bread." Whether her direction of Beverley was intentional or not, whenever a machine broke again, Lana would type, "Please _____ move behind room," filling in the blank with the name of any familiar person who happened to be handy.

In a related study conducted by the same research group, two chimpanzees named Sherman and Austin actually learned to talk to each other through a similar system (Savage-Rumbaugh, Rumbaugh, & Boysen, 1978). First, the chimps were taught to name and use several tools: a stick that enabled them to push food out of a long hollow tube, a straw to drink from cups that they could see but not reach, and a wrench to unscrew bolts. Sherman and Austin learned to ask their trainers for the tools they needed to get food in various situations. Then the chimps were placed in adjoining rooms, connected by a plastic window and a small opening. One chimp was given the tools; the other got access to the food. Under these conditions, the chimps "talked!" For example, in one experiment Austin asked Sherman for a wrench, used it to open a box containing banana chips, then rewarded Sherman with some of the food.

The Critics. Despite the drama of these demonstrations, many scientists remained skeptical about whether these apes had learned *language* or just a complex chain of conditioned responses. Interestingly, the Lana Project researchers were among the skeptics. They argued that there was no evidence that any of the communicating apes, including Sherman and Austin, actually used signs or symbols to represent objects or events that were not physically present (Savage-Rumbaugh, Rumbaugh, & Boysen, 1980).

Another vocal critic is Herbert Terrace, who studied an animal of his own, whimsically named Nim Chimpsky. Like Washoe, Nim was raised somewhat as a human child would be. (There were some slight cultural differences. Since he was raised in the Bronx, in New York City, Nim slept in a loft bed and commuted to classes at Columbia University.) But there was at least one important respect in which Nim differed from Washoe; Terrace and his colleagues attempted to record literally every statement Nim ever made. Within two years, they noted over 20,000 statements of two or more signs.

As Terrace tells the story in his book *Nim* (1979), at first he and his co-workers were amazed by the chimp's linguistic abilities. But when they later reviewed video-tapes of Nim's learning sessions, they began to suspect that the chimp was just imitating his teachers and responding to their prompting. He was not forming novel utterances the way young children do when they learn language.

For example, Nim tended to form long "sentences" by almost randomly stringing together symbols that roughly applied to a given context, such as "You me sweet drink give me." When children speak in sentences this long, they seem to choose and arrange words far more carefully to convey meaning, such as "Johnny's mother poured me some Kool-Aid."

Terrace's charges led to more countercharges. In a review of the book *Nim*, Beatrix Gardner (1981) charged that Nim's upbringing was not comparable to Wash-oe's; Nim was largely restricted to a "windowless cell," for example, and trained by over 60 different teachers, many of whom lacked sign language competence them-selves.

While the debate has gotten rather heated at times, several conclusions are quite clear. Chimpanzees are capable of far more elaborate forms of communication than most scientists previously believed. Nevertheless, compared to humans, their lin-guistic abilities are quite limited; no chimpanzee has been able to reproduce the achievements of the average 3-year-old child.

The issue for future research, then, is not whether apes are different from people or what the "correct" definition of language is. The more interesting ques-tions involve specifying *exactly how* apes are different from people and how each species can use words and symbols to communicate.

Summary

1. Slips of the tongue follow implicit grammatical rules regarding sound (phonol-ogy) and syntax. This suggests the importance of internal mental processes that organize thought and language.
2. **Cognitive psychology** is the study of the way observers gain knowledge of the world and how that knowledge is represented, stored, retrieved, transformed, and related to overt behavior. Cognitive psychologists focus on higher mental processes such as attention, perception, memory, language, imagery, and rea-soning. Several historical forces, including the failures of strict behaviorism, the rise of computer sciences, and advances in linguistics and human engineering, led to the rise of this approach in the 1960s.

3. Gestalt studies emphasized the importance of **reorganization**—solving a problem by perceiving new relationships among its elements. In general, **productive thinking** solves a problem by reorganizing its elements; **reproductive thinking** applies solutions that worked in the past to new problems. The **set effect** produces a tendency to use reproductive thinking for a problem that could better be solved by productive thinking.

4. The *information-processing approach* attempts to analyze thought processes as a series of separate steps. For example, the General Problem Solver simulates human problem-solving strategies on a computer. Some problems can be solved by **algorithms** (formulas that guarantee a solution), others demand **heuristics** (rules of thumb). One heuristic used by human problem solvers, called **means-end analysis,** repeatedly compares the current state of affairs with some final goal and tries to reduce the difference between the two.

5. **Artificial intelligence** is the ability of machines to perform intelligent tasks such as recognizing patterns and solving problems. Attempts to program computers to understand language have helped lead to the conclusion that human comprehension relies on **schemas,** areas in the memory network that contain information and expectations about familiar events. Language-comprehension programs include **scripts,** schemas that summarize general knowledge about particular situations.

6. A **concept** is a mental category of objects or events, grouped on the basis of certain common features. For many natural concepts, some items are more *typical,* or better examples of the concept, than others.

7. According to Benjamin Whorf's **linguistic-relativity hypothesis,** language determines the content of thought or the way a person perceives the world. Studies of people whose languages have different systems for describing colors has not supported the strict version of this hypothesis. However, studies of the use of the pronoun *he* to refer in a general context to both males and females do support the idea that the words we use have some effect on assumptions and thought processes.

8. **Linguistics** is the study of the fundamental nature and structure of human language; it is primarily concerned with the problem of **linguistic competence**—the abstract nature of language. In contrast, **psycholinguistics** is the study of how people actually speak and use language; it focuses on **linguistic performance,** the way people apply knowledge when they produce and comprehend language.

9. **Grammar** is the complete system of rules that relates sounds to meanings for a specific language. It consists of three major parts: phonology, syntax, and semantics.

10. **Phonology** refers to the rules that govern the use of sounds in a language. **Phonemes** are the distinct sounds that make a difference in meaning in a particular language; they vary somewhat from one language to another.

11. **Syntax** refers to the rules that specify the way words can be combined to form sentences. Noam Chomsky developed an influential theory to make intuitive syntactical rules explicit. He distinguished between **surface structure**—the ac-

tual words in a sentence and the relationship among them—and **deep structure**—the underlying organization and intent of sentences.

12. **Semantics** refers to the rules governing the meaning of sentences, words, and morphemes. A **morpheme** is the smallest unit of speech that has meaning.

13. Chomsky's model stimulated research in psycholinguistics. Studies of language comprehension now emphasize the importance of outside knowledge, context, and schemas. Even the perception of spoken sounds involves an active listener who reconstructs messages from partial information.

14. Children from different cultures seem to learn language in a series of comparable stages. Around the age of 4 months, an infant begins to **babble**, alternating consonant and vowel sounds. The first real words generally appear between the ages of 10 and 13 months. At first children may express entire ideas in a single-word statement called a **holophrase.**

15. Two-word sentences appear around the age of 2. Throughout early childhood, children use **telegraphic speech,** shortened sentences that drop "unnecessary" words such as articles, prepositions, and adjectives. In later childhood, language acquisition involves **overregularization**—children force every utterance to conform to grammatical rules, even when they are inappropriate.

16. The chimpanzee Washoe learned to communicate about 160 signs in American Sign Language. Later experiments with other primates supported the idea that they could learn complex communication systems of various sorts and on occasion even "speak" to one another. Critics such as Herbert Terrace, however, charged that these animals were not learning an abstract linguistic system but merely to imitate certain combinations of signs.

Discussion of "Becoming a Critical Consumer"

If you found errors, I fooled you; there are no errors. While all the previous critical consumer boxes criticized journalistic errors, that does not mean that newspaper and magazine articles are always wrong. Becoming a critical consumer does not mean automatically rejecting everything you read; it means learning to evaluate material fairly and carefully weighting its merits.

To Learn More

Hunt, M. *The Universe Within.* New York: Simon & Schuster, 1982. By far the most interesting book describing cognitive research for the general reader. A prime example of effective science writing.

Lachman, R., Lachman, J. L., & Butterfield, E. C. *Cognitive Psychology and Information Processing: An Introduction.* Hillsdale, N.J.: Lawrence Erlbaum, 1979. Heavy going at times, but there is no better overview of the historical development of cognitive psychology.

Solso, R. L. *Cognitive Psychology.* New York: Harcourt Brace Jovanovich, 1979. An excellent textbook summary of the field.

8
Childhood

Physical development
Prenatal development
From infancy to childhood
Motor development

Perceptual development
Testing infant perception
Depth perception
Perceptual abilities of the newborn

Cognitive development
Piaget's theory
Evaluating Piaget's contribution
Social cognition
Applied psychology: Learning disabilities

Personality and social development
Temperament
Monkeys and motherly love
Human attachment

Child rearing
Historical trends
Effects of day care
A new perspective on early experience?

Summary

BECOMING A CRITICAL CONSUMER
Ask Doctor Spock

HOW DO THEY KNOW?
Longitudinal research: Studies that can last a lifetime

Why does a stork stand on one leg?
If he lifted up the other one, he would fall down.

Somewhere around the age of 7, I devoted several months of my life to this joke. I told it to my mother, my father, my sister, my brother, my aunts, and my uncles. I told it to my friends, my relatives' friends, my friends' relatives, the mailman, the butcher. And then I told them all again. And again.

At this very moment, third-graders all over America are driving their families crazy with similar riddles:

Why did the moron throw butter out the window?
To see the butterfly.

What's big and green and has a trunk?
An unripe elephant.

How do you catch a rabbit?
Hide in the bushes and make noises like a carrot.

In response to this onslaught of riddles, patient parents everywhere reassure themselves that "it's only a stage" and hope that the next stage won't be worse.

The commonsense notion that a certain pattern of behavior is only a stage calls attention to an obvious fact—people change as they grow older. But exactly how do they change? And how do they remain the same? Do all children pass through similar stages at more or less the same rate? What causes a specific change?

These are just a few of the questions asked by the field of **developmental psychology**—the study of how and why people change physically, intellectually, and emotionally as they grow from infancy to old age. Developmental psychologists have investigated all the traditional topics in psychology—from learning and memory to personality and motivation. Their many diverse studies have one thing in common—an emphasis on the process of development, on change and continuity throughout the life span.

Consider, for example, the development of humor. While humor is not one of the central issues of the field and relatively few psychologists have studied it, a brief review of the development of humor can provide insights into the way researchers compare the abilities of children at different ages.

As you might expect, it is difficult to pinpoint the precise age at which humor begins. In one thorough study of infant laughter, Sroufe and Wunsch (1972) asked mothers to try to amuse their 4- to 12-month-old infants in 33 different ways. The least funny stimuli involved sounds like Mom's falsetto imitation of Mickey Mouse saying, "Hi, baby, how are you?" and parental horse sounds. The 4-month-olds laughed most for coochie-coochie-coo games, like four quick kisses on a bare stomach. The 1-year-olds preferred more complex social interactions, such as a silent version of peek-a-boo. Overall, children laughed more as they grew, and they increasingly came to appreciate more complex stimuli.

But this appreciation comes slowly. A 4-year-old's idea of a comedy routine may simply be to point to his nose and say, "Here's my ears." If an adult smiles cooperatively, he is likely to follow that by pointing to his cute little behind and saying "Here's my eyes." And so on.

In a study designed to trace the gradual development of sophistication in humor, Schultz and Horibe (1974, p. 14) told jokes like this to elementary school children:

Doctor, doctor, come at once! Our baby swallowed a fountain pen!
I will be right over. What are you doing in the meantime?
Using a pencil.

Most children thought this was reasonably funny. To see just what was funny about it, the researchers created another "joke," which was just as silly but lacked a sensible punchline:

Doctor, doctor, come at once! Our baby swallowed a rubber band!
I will be right over. What are you doing in the meantime?
Using a pencil.

You might be reluctant to classify this new anecdote as a joke. Children from the third, fifth, and seventh grades agreed; it simply was not funny. But first-graders did not seem to care what the baby had swallowed; to them, both versions of the joke were funny.

To rule out the possibility that first-graders will chuckle at absolutely anything, Schultz and Horibe developed a third version, which they told to still another group:

Doctor, doctor, come at once! Our baby swallowed a fountain pen!
I will be right over. What are you doing in the meantime?
We don't know what to do.

Even first-graders knew this was not funny. Their definition of humor seemed to demand incongruity; if it's silly, it's funny. For older children, humor required something more. Silliness must have a point to be amusing and a joke has to "make sense," as it did in the original form.

Patterns of change like this are quite common throughout development. As children grow, they increasingly come to see the world as adults do. This is no surprise. But one of the things that makes developmental psychology such a fascinating field is the way it charts these step-by-step changes, to reveal what people feel, think, and do at different ages.

Many students find development more interesting than any other topic in psychology and are amazed to learn that it was only in the nineteenth century that scientists began to record and analyze the changes that occur in childhood. In 1877, Charles Darwin published one of the first systematic accounts of human development, a diary detailing the growth of his son William—his reflexes, his sensory abilities, and the gradual appearance of more complex traits. From this baby biography we may learn, for example, that William Darwin first laughed at the age of 53 days, a sound proudly recorded by the father of evolutionary theory as "a little bleating noise."

In 1878, one year after Darwin published these observations, Harvard University granted the first American PhD in psychology to G. Stanley Hall. Hall is often referred to as the first developmental psychologist; he conducted nearly 200 surveys of children's behavior, attitudes, and beliefs. But despite Hall's tremendous energy and enthusiasm, few of his contemporaries studied children, and developmental psychology remained outside the mainstream of psychological research. In 1907, Wilhelm Wundt wrote that experimental studies of children were doomed to be "wholly untrustworthy on account of the great number of sources of error" (p. 336).

For the first few decades of this century, developmental psychology was an isolated field studied by just a few scattered experts like Jean Piaget. The dominant figures of the time—including Sigmund Freud and John Watson—had some strong opinions about childhood, but little data. Among social scientists, only those who studied intelligence and IQ directly observed large numbers of children.

The entire field of psychology grew rapidly after World War II (see Chapters 14 and 15), and for the first time large numbers of researchers began to explore the dramatic changes that occur in the first few years of life. Much of this research focused on the way heredity and environment interact in determining behavioral development and physical growth.

Physical Development

Developmental psychologists use the word **maturation** to refer to sequences of growth and internal bodily changes that are primarily determined by biological timing. Environmental factors such as health and nutrition can affect the rate of maturation, but the limits are set by biology. No matter how well a 3-month-old child is fed and taken care of, she will not weigh 60 pounds or walk across a room. This biological pacing of an orderly process of physical growth begins the moment a human being is conceived.

PRENATAL DEVELOPMENT

During sexual intercourse, the male releases approximately 400 million sperm cells into the female reproductive tract. If this occurs during the ovulatory phase of the menstrual cycle, a sperm cell may unite with a female's egg, or ovum, causing pregnancy. The fertilized egg, called a **zygote,** begins to develop immediately. This tiny cell is only about $\frac{1}{175}$ of an inch in diameter at conception; over the next months, it will divide, and divide, and divide again until a human being is formed. About one week after the egg is fertilized, it becomes firmly attached to the wall of the uterus.

The developing organism is called an **embryo** during the next stage of rapid development, which lasts roughly from the second to the eighth week of pregnancy. By the fourth week of pregnancy, the embryo is $\frac{1}{5}$ of an inch long and has begun to develop a heart, a brain, a gastrointestinal tract, and other primitive organs. By the eighth or ninth week, the embryo is about 1 inch long and has developed human features; face, mouth, arms, and legs are clearly recognizable.

From the time bone cells begin to develop, about eight weeks after conception, the developing organism is called a **fetus.** Dramatic development continues throughout the fetal period. Around 16 to 18 weeks, the mother is likely to feel the first fetal movements. A fetus born prematurely at the age of 24 weeks can open and close its eyes, cry, and hiccup. Normal development, however, takes about 40 weeks from conception to birth.

The timing of these changes throughout the prenatal period is partly determined by the organism's genes (see Chapter 3) and partly by the mother's condition. If the mother contracts certain diseases during pregnancy, the illness may interfere with development, particularly if the problem occurs during the weeks immediately following conception. In one study of mothers who had German measles (Michaels & Mellin, 1960), maternal illness during the first month of pregnancy produced abnormalities in 47% of the offspring, versus 7% for mothers who had the same illness in the third month of pregnancy.

Many drugs are also known to increase the risk of birth defects. Pregnant mothers who use narcotics, barbiturates, or even some prescription drugs, such as certain antibiotics, are more likely to have abnormal infants. There is even evidence that smoking cigarettes or drinking moderate amounts of alcohol during pregnancy may interfere with fetal growth. For obvious reasons, many researchers are now trying to learn the precise effects of these and other, more subtle prenatal influences.

FROM INFANCY TO CHILDHOOD

A newborn baby enters the world covered with a white lubricating liquid that helps ease its passage through the birth canal. The skull consists of somewhat flexible cartilage, which may be somewhat misshapen by compression, and the rest of the body may look somewhat the worse for wear. In 1891, G. Stanley Hall described his overall impression of the newborn in terms of its "monotonous and dismal cry, with its red, shriveled, parboiled skin . . . squinting, cross-eyed, pot-bellied, and bow-legged . . . " Fortunately, most parents find, as I did, that their own children are gorgeous exceptions to this unattractive rule.

Within a few weeks, infants begin to fill out; even neutral observers see them as roly-poly bundles of joy. Physical growth is not a simple matter of increasing size; as Figure 8.1 shows, body proportions change dramatically during development. Before birth, the head grows faster than any other part of the body. In the first year of

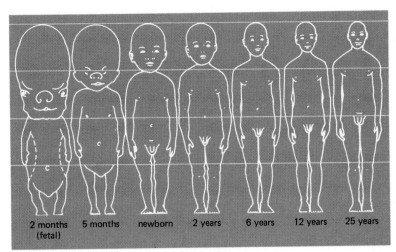

2 months (fetal)   5 months   newborn   2 years   6 years   12 years   25 years

Figure 8.1

As the human body grows, it changes in size and proportion. The decrease in the relative size of the head is particularly dramatic during the prenatal period and infancy.

life, the trunk of the body grows fastest. From then until adolescence, the legs grow fastest.

Interestingly, big babies do not necessarily grow up to be oversized adults; the correlation between infant size and adult size is quite low. The fast pattern of infant growth begins to slow down around the age of 3 into a slower, more predictable course. Height at age 3 is a good predictor of how tall the child will grow up to be. The next sudden increase in physical growth occurs in adolescence, a period that will be described in Chapter 9. These processes of physical growth and maturation help provide the infant and child with ever-increasing abilities to deal with the external world. Perhaps the most obvious changes in ability involve motor activities.

MOTOR DEVELOPMENT

The newborn baby enters the world with a number of **reflexes,** involuntary acts automatically elicited by certain stimuli. For example, newborn babies close their eyes when stimulated by bright light and move their limbs away from sources of pain. Some of these reflexes are clearly linked to survival, as is the case with breast-feeding's being aided by the *rooting reflex*—a newborn baby turns toward any object, such as a finger or a nipple, that gently stimulates the corner of its mouth (see Figure 8.2). Like many other reflexes, this reaction tends to disappear as a child grows older.

At birth, the child's behavior is largely controlled by subcortical structures deep within the brain (see Chapter 2). As the child grows, the cortex develops and voluntary control of behavior becomes possible. Doctors monitor the changes in these and other reflexes as one clue to patterns of development in the brain.

To chart the course of motor development, some researchers have followed the progress of large groups of children to establish **norms,** standard figures that describe the performance of the average person. Pediatricians and psychologists use such norms to help locate problems in development for specific children.

The widely used Denver Developmental Screening Test (Frankenburg & Dodds, 1967) was developed from tests in Denver, Colorado, of 1,036 normal children between the ages of 2 weeks and 6½ years. One section of the test measures gross motor movements, while another section is concerned with finer muscle control. Figure 8.3 lists the age ranges for the first appearance of several typical abilities in each category. It is important to remember that norms like this simply reflect the average performance of large numbers of babies. Although the average baby begins walking around 12 months, 25% of all babies start before 11.3 months and 10% start after 14.3 months. And despite the hopes and fears of parents, the actual date does not predict later development. The child who first walks at 10 months will not necessarily grow up to win the Boston Marathon, and the one who begins walking at 14 months will not necessarily be slow to develop in other ways.

Of course, at some point extreme slowness in development does suggest that there may be a problem. In the Denver Developmental Screening Test, a child who lags behind 90% of the children of the same age on two different motor skills will generally be referred for further tests to see whether there is some underlying prob-

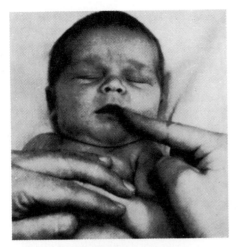

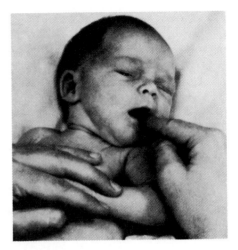

Figure 8.2
The rooting reflex. When a finger touches the side of an infant's mouth, the child turns toward the finger and tries to suck it.

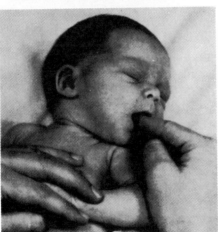

lem. But the range of ages in Figure 8.3 demonstrates that normal development is far more variable than some anxious parents suspect.

These sequences of behavior are primarily determined by maturation. A child's nervous system and muscles must develop to a certain point before complex behavior becomes possible. No matter how well they are raised, 2-week-old infants will not sit up by themselves, 3-month-old babies will not walk, and 2-year-old children will not discuss the state of the economy. However, throughout this text we have emphasized that behavior is determined by the interaction between heredity and environment. In the case of motor development, for example, one group of researchers has shown how specific training can speed the process of maturation (Zelazo, Zelazo, & Kolb, 1972).

Week-old babies have two simple reflexes that resemble walking. The *placing*

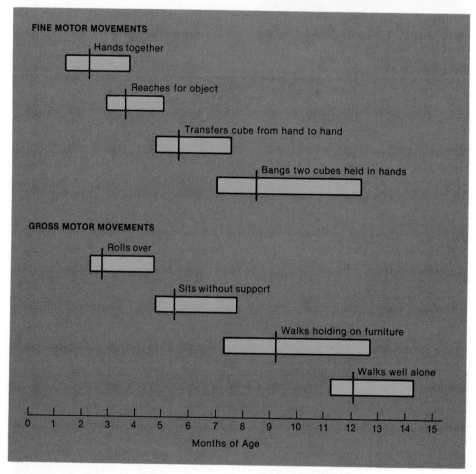

FINE MOTOR MOVEMENTS

Hands together

Reaches for object

Transfers cube from hand to hand

Bangs two cubes held in hands

GROSS MOTOR MOVEMENTS

Rolls over

Sits without support

Walks holding on furniture

Walks well alone

0 1 2 3 4 5 6 7 8 9 10 11 12 13 14 15

Months of Age

Figure 8.3

Infants develop motor control at different rates. This chart illustrates norms for typical motor movements from the Denver Developmental Screening Test. Of all infants, 25% have mastered the particular movement by the age at the left side of the bar; 50% by the age at the mark on the bar; and 90% have mastered the movement by the age indicated by the right end of the bar. Note that many different patterns of development fall within the normal range.

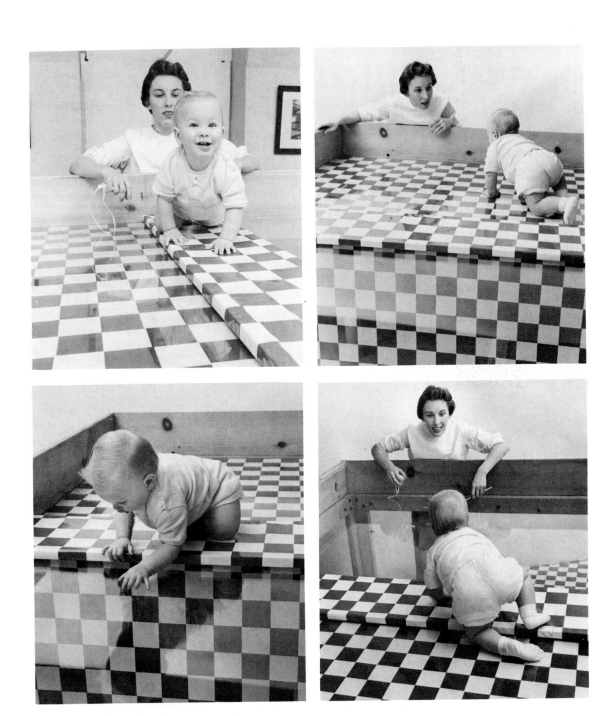

Figure 8.5
In these photos of Gibson's original study of the "visual cliff," a young child crawls toward his mother on a piece of glass laid directly over a checked cloth (top). But when the glass is suspended over a "cliff," with the cloth several feet below (bottom), the child refuses to cross over to his mother despite patting the glass to assure himself that it is a solid surface.

month-old babies were placed on the deep side of the visual cliff, their hearts beat faster, suggesting that they were afraid. In contrast, 2-month-old infants in the same situation had slower heart rates. In other studies, slow heart rates have been shown to be a sign of attention. This suggests that younger babies may have focused on the fact that the deep side was different without being aware of its apparent danger.

PERCEPTUAL ABILITIES OF THE NEWBORN

Since the pioneer studies of Fantz and Gibson, many different techniques have been invented to ask babies sophisticated questions about how they perceive the world. Some of the most exciting work has involved the development of techniques for testing the abilities present immediately after birth, before the child has had much opportunity to learn.

In 1969 two researchers at Brown University (Siqueland & DeLuca) reported that young infants can learn to suck a pacifier harder to produce a reward. Just as a rat will press a bar or a pigeon will peck a key to produce food, an infant can learn to suck harder to produce a reinforcer such as an auditory stimulus.

In one study, researchers used this technique to test the ability of 3-day-old babies to recognize their mothers' voices (DeCasper & Fifer, 1980). Each mother tape-recorded a lengthy selection from Dr. Seuss's *To Think That I Saw It on Mulberry Street*. Later, the 10 babies wore tiny headphones while they sucked on a pacifier that held a pressure-sensitive electronic device. After the infants adapted to this rather odd situation, their normal sucking pattern was recorded for 5 minutes. Then for 20 minutes, 5 of the infants heard their own mother's voice when they sucked faster than normal and heard another woman's voice when they sucked more slowly. This relationship was reversed for the other 5 infant subjects. Slow sucking produced their own mother's voice and fast sucking produced the stranger's voice.

Sure enough, 8 of the 10 infants changed their sucking pattern so that it produced their own mother's voice. These particular newborn infants had spent their first three days of life in a hospital nursery, and none had had more than 12 hours of contact after birth with their mothers. How much was learned during that 12 hours and how much was based on prenatal experiences can only be determined by further research.

Even younger infants were tested in a study of responses to crying (Martin & Clark, 1982). Forty newborn infants were tested at an average age of 18 hours; each sometimes heard a tape recording of another newborn crying and sometimes heard a tape recording of himself or herself crying. Astoundingly, these produced different reactions. In response to the cry of another newborn child, infants cried along. But when each heard a recording of his or her own cries, the child actually stopped crying.

Of course, there is no way of knowing what went through these little minds— whether the children were fascinated by hearing their own voices, for example, and stopped their crying to listen. But we do know that they responded differently; it is clear that they could distinguish between the two cries just 18 hours after birth.

Similar studies of vision and the other senses increasingly seem to support the notion that some perceptual abilities are present at birth and do not depend on learning.

These perceptual abilities are some of the building blocks from which a child gradually constructs a cognitive view of the world. Other researchers have focused on this larger problem of cognitive development—how children's thought processes change as they grow.

Cognitive Development

Some of the major issues of cognitive development have already been encountered in our discussion of language acquisition (see Chapter 7). Here we concentrate on the theories of Jean Piaget, one of the most influential figures in the history of psychology.

These days, developmental psychologists usually study statistical patterns of behavior in large groups of subjects, sometimes with the help of elaborate tests and

Jean Piaget (1896–1980) was one of the most influential figures in the history of developmental psychology. Born in Switzerland, he published his first article—a description of an albino sparrow for a natural history magazine—at the age of 10. After completing a PhD in biology, he accepted a position at the Binet Laboratory in Paris developing items for IQ tests. While most IQ researchers were interested in developing standardized items for assessing intelligence, Piaget became fascinated by the errors children made and discovered that children of the same age frequently made the same kinds of mistakes. Piaget gradually came to the conclusion that young children are not just "dumber" than adults—rather, they actually think in different ways. He rejected the idea of using rigid test questions and began to experiment instead with flexible and free-flowing interviews, following the natural thought processes of his young subjects. Piaget hoped to establish a biological basis for *epistemology*, the philosophical study of the nature of knowledge—that is, how we come to know about the world.

procedures. Piaget preferred a different approach. He observed children's behavior in naturalistic situations, taking detailed notes hour after hour. Sometimes he asked the children questions, and sometimes he developed special tests of their abilities. But above all, he never stopped observing. Indeed, many of Piaget's books and articles describe his detailed observations of his own three children, Jacqueline, Lucienne, and Lauren.

These unorthodox methods gradually led Piaget to develop a highly influential theory of cognitive development that focused on the organization of intelligence and how it changes as the child grows. For Piaget, an 8-year-old boy is not a miniature adult, a shorter and dumber version of his father. Rather, the child perceives the world in a fundamentally different way from his parents because of the very nature of his thought processes. By studying the growth of intelligence, Piaget hoped to establish a biological basis for **epistemology**—the philosophical study of the nature of knowledge, that is, how we come to know about the world.

PIAGET'S THEORY

Jean Piaget focused on the active processes a child uses to learn about the world. The young infant must experiment to learn basic lessons, such as the fact that his arms and legs are attached to him and under his direct control and his mother's breast is not. The process of discovery continues through adolescence, when the child learns how to deal with the realm of hypothetical possibilities. Along this path from infancy to adolescence, there are several important shifts in the way children think. For Piaget, intellectual growth was not just a matter of adding one skill to another; it was far more complex and far more interesting, involving several different ways of understanding the world.

These cognitive differences were summarized in four major stages of development, as outlined in Table 8.1. It is important to emphasize that the ages given to identify the stages throughout this section are only approximations. Each child develops at a slightly different rate. While psychologists who study IQ are concerned with such differences among individuals, Piaget focused on the underlying processes that are common to all. The exact timing for a given individual depends on the interaction of maturation and experience. Further, moving from one stage to the next is a gradual process—a child does not suddenly enter what Piaget called the concrete operational stage on her seventh birthday. However, Piaget did believe that these stages must always occur in the same order.

The Sensorimotor Stage.   In the **sensorimotor stage,** which lasts roughly for the first two years of life, infants gradually discover the relationships between sensations and their motor acts. During this period, the child develops a primitive sense of identity, differentiating herself from the rest of the world, and begins to understand cause and effect.

Piaget's choice of the term *sensorimotor* emphasizes his belief that in this stage the child learns directly from sensations and motor actions. More abstract types of thought do not appear until later.

A newborn baby's behavior is largely a matter of reflex. Her eye closes when you touch it; her knee flexes when you prick her foot; and if you put a nipple in her mouth, she begins to suck. But almost immediately after birth, the child begins to adapt her behavior to the demands of the environment. She will begin to adjust her sucking, for example, to make her mother's milk flow at the ideal rate. As the infant becomes capable of more complex behavior, this active process of experimenting on the world grows more elaborate.

Perhaps the most important development in the sensorimotor stage is the achievement of **object permanence**—the awareness that objects continue to exist even when they are not present to be seen, touched, or sensed. This is such a basic level of intellectual achievement that it is often hard for adults to comprehend it fully. Unless you have ingested large quantities of drugs or become enchanted by the paradoxes of Zen Buddhism, you probably take it for granted that objects continue to exist in your absence. If you put a pen in a drawer, you do not doubt that there is now a pen in a drawer, even though you can no longer see or touch it. Similarly, you are willing to accept the fact that the Statue of Liberty sits on an island in New York Harbor even if it's been years since you've been there and seen it. But, for a 6-month-old infant, out of sight is quite literally out of mind.

In early infancy, a child responds only to what he can sense directly. He will stare at his mother's face as she looks down into the crib, but if Mom suddenly moves away, the child will casually look in another direction as if she had never been there. Piaget studied this phenomenon by manipulating objects in front of his own

TABLE 8.1
Piaget's Stages of Cognitive Development

Stage	Approximate Age	Characteristics
Sensorimotor	Birth to 2 years	Child learns to distinguish self from external objects; lacks symbolic thought—lives entirely in the present; gradually develops a sense of cause and effect and object permanence (objects continue to exist even when they are not physically present).
Preoperational	2 to 7 years	Child begins to develop symbolic thought—words, play, gestures, and mental images begin to represent external objects; remains *egocentric*—unable to take the viewpoint of another.
Concrete-Operational	7 to 11 years	Child becomes capable of logical thought but only about concrete, observable objects; is gradually able to *conserve*, that is, recognize that certain basic properties of objects remain constant even when appearances change.
Formal-Operational	Begins at 11 years or later	Child can solve abstract problems; logically takes different factors into account and can systematically test hypotheses; is concerned with the future and hypothetical possibilities.

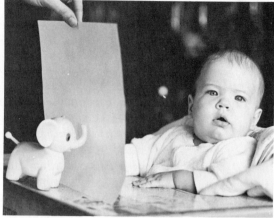

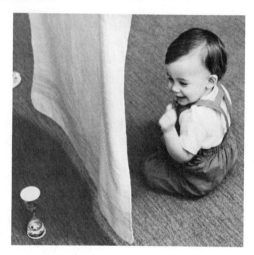

Figure 8.6

Piaget's concept of object permanence. The younger infant in the top pictures stares intently at the toy elephant when it is present but seems unaware of its existence when it is blocked from view. In contrast, the older child in the bottom panel searches for an object after it is placed behind a towel.

children and observing their reactions. When Piaget dropped a paper ball into his son's crib, at first the infant did not react at all. But at the age of 6 months, he began to look for the ball after it dropped. The infant had become more aware of the existence of the object. Still, he looked only in front of him, where the ball had originally been. When Piaget's daughter was $10\frac{1}{2}$ months old, he played a game in which he took a toy from Jacqueline's hands and placed it under the left side of her mattress. Each time he did this, the child watched his movements and retrieved the toy. But when Piaget slowly moved the toy to the right until Jacqueline could no longer see it, she immediately looked again under the mattress on the left. Piaget concluded that his 10½-month-old daughter had not yet developed a full understanding of object permanence.

In a test of Jacqueline's abilities at 18 months, Piaget put a coin in his hand, placed the hand under a blanket, and then withdrew it. Jacqueline showed how far she had advanced by first opening her father's hand and then, when she found that the coin was not there, looking under the blanket until she found it. Around the age of 12 months, most children master the concept of object permanence; they understand that objects continue to exist even after they have disappeared from their view.

One of the continuing themes in cognitive development that Piaget identified is called egocentrism. Although in normal English usage this word implies selfishness, Piaget defined it in a different way. *Egocentrism* involves the child's failure to take the perspective of another person into account. At first, the child is intellectually centered around herself (or her ego) and fails to realize that other people may perceive the same events in a different way. Intellectual growth involves gradually becoming less egocentric. The first milestone in this process comes near the end of the sensorimotor stage, when the child becomes fully aware of the distinction between her own body and external physical objects. Egocentrism continues to decline throughout the next period of Piaget's scheme of development, the preoperational stage.

The Preoperational Stage. Symbolic thought first appears in the **preoperational stage** of development, as the 2- to 7-year-old child gradually learns to use speech, play, gestures, and mental images to represent the world. The infant in the sensorimotor stage can deal only with objects that are physically present; the toddler in the preoperational stage is able to manipulate mental symbols and therefore deal with the world on a somewhat more abstract level.

But the young child's ability to deal with abstract information is quite limited; he is called *preoperational* because of his inability to perform the mental transformations that Piaget called *operations*. The term is borrowed from mathematics, which recognizes certain operations such as addition and subtraction for specifying the relationship between numbers. For Piaget, **operations** were mental actions that reorganize one's views of the world. For example, an adult who has put a hat on can mentally reverse this action and imagine never having done it. A child in the preoperational stage is not capable of mentally performing this logical operation.

The preoperational child remains egocentric, unable adequately to take others' perspectives into account. These limitations can be seen in the way children use language. In one of his first psychological investigations, Piaget (1926) observed two 6-year-old schoolchildren in Geneva. For about a month, he followed them around in a progressive school and wrote down everything each said. While adults use language primarily to communicate with one another, Piaget found that about 35% to 40% of these children's statements did not involve the transmission of information.

For example, when one child sat down alone at a table, he said to himself aloud, "I want to do that drawing there . . . . I want to draw something, I do. I shall need a big piece of paper to do that" (Piaget, 1926, p. 37). Monologues of this sort sometimes went on at great length, despite the fact that from the child's point of view no one was there to listen to him.

A similar type of egocentric ongoing commentary often occurred when several children played together. In fact, Piaget noted, the children often became so absorbed in their own idiosyncratic conversations with themselves that they paid little attention to the comments of their playmates. The proportion of a child's speech that conforms to this egocentric pattern declines over the course of the preoperational stage.

In a more systematic study of how youngsters use language to communicate, Piaget asked children to repeat a story he had told them. Again, the younger children often failed to communicate. They reported events in the wrong order, left out key details, referred to characters without naming them, and often confused cause-and-effect relationships. For example, in repeating a story about a fairy who turned children into swans, one young subject said, "There was a fairy, wicked fairy. They turned themselves into swans" (Piaget, 1926, pp. 126–127). In this example, the child clearly fails to take the perspective of his audience into account. Although he may know who "they" were, he does not fill in the gaps in the story for the listener. As a result, the imprecise use of the pronoun *they* muddles the whole story and makes it almost impossible to understand.

This type of egocentrism is familiar to anyone who has ever tried to get a straight story from a 5-year-old. An amusing anecdote about life at the playground may make little sense unless the listener repeatedly asks for more details about who, what, when, where, and why. Only as children grow older do they begin to take another person's knowledge and perspective into account and thus communicate more effectively. This sort of egocentric speech points to the most fundamental characteristic of the preoperational period—the lack of logical operations and symbolic thought.

The Concrete-Operational Stage.   During the **concrete-operational stage** (roughly ages 7 to 11), the child becomes capable of logical thought but only regarding concrete, observable objects. In Piaget's terms, the child becomes capable of performing operations, mental actions that reorganize the world. Later, during the formal-operational stage, the adolescent is able to perform mental operations on more abstract stimuli, such as words and mathematical symbols.

The best-known landmark between the preoperational thought of the young child and the concrete-operational ability of the school-aged youngster involves mastery of **conservation**—the recognition that certain basic properties of objects (such as volume and number) remain constant even when appearances change.

For example, in a typical test of the conservation of liquid, young children are shown two identical containers filled with the same amount of water. After the child agrees that the two containers hold the same amount, the liquid from one container is poured into another that is taller and thinner than the original. Of course, the water rises to a higher level in this thinner container.

Figure 8.7
In this test of Piaget's concept of conservation, a child points to the container he believes contains more liquid.

Typically, 4-year-olds think that the simple act of pouring has changed the amount of liquid. They may argue that there is more water because it rose higher or less water because the container is thinner, but clearly they feel there has been a change. In contrast, 5- and 6-year-olds often have mixed reactions. They may have trouble deciding, or they may think that the amount of liquid is changed only if the difference between containers is great. By the age of 7 or 8, most children have learned the principle of conservation—the amount of liquid remains constant even when its appearance has changed.

Closely related to conservation is the mental operation of **reversibility,** in which a person can think of a transformation that would restore the original condition. For example, addition and subtraction are logical opposites; the operation of adding $3 + 4 = 7$ can be reversed and the original situation can be restored by subtracting: $7 - 4 = 3$. In the conservation-of-liquid task, older children understand that pouring has not changed the amount of liquid in part because the action is reversible. You can always pour the liquid back to restore the original situation. Nonconservers are fooled by appearances, by irrelevant transformations that make things look or feel different.

Earlier, we referred to the ability to conserve as one landmark that separates the preoperational from the concrete-operational child. However, the picture is complicated by the fact that there are several types of conservation, and they do not all appear at the same time. For example, to test conservation of weight, a child might be shown on a scale that two balls of clay balance each other perfectly and weigh the same amount. After the child watches the experimenter roll one ball of clay into the shape of a long, fat sausage, he is asked whether the sausage and ball still weigh the same. Interestingly, many children who have mastered the conservation of liquid are not able to conserve in this situation; they believe that the change in shape yielded a change in weight. Conservation of weight seems to be a more subtle concept than conservation of liquid, and it typically appears a year or two later in development.

The fact that a young child may be able to conserve in one situation but not in another emphasizes the concreteness of thought between the ages of 7 and 11. Reasoning seems closely tied to specific situations and objects.

The Formal-Operational Stage. The highest stage of intellectual achievement discussed by Piaget appears in early adolescence. (It might easily be described in Chapter 9, which discusses postchildhood development, but for continuity, we shall consider it here.) In the **formal-operational stage,** which can begin as early as the age of 11, the child is capable of solving abstract problems and dealing with hypothetical possibilities. The formal-operational thinker tests hypotheses as a scientist might, considering all the alternatives and efficiently looking for a way to choose among them.

Many of the experiments Piaget devised to test formal-operational thinking involved problems from the chemistry or physics laboratory. In one typical study, adolescents were given five containers filled with clear liquid, four "test chemicals" and one "indicator." When the proper combination of one or more test chemicals was added to the indicator, it turned yellow. The adolescents were faced with the problem of finding the proper combination of test chemicals.

Preoperational children given this problem simply mix chemicals randomly; concrete-operational children are more systematic but generally fail to consider all the possible combinations. Only children in the formal-operational stage consider all the alternatives and systematically vary one factor at a time in their search for the correct combination. They often write down all the results and draw general conclusions about each chemical.

While Piaget's earlier stages of intellectual development have been accepted by most developmental psychologists, the formal-operational stage has proved far more controversial. Some people seem to arrive at these strategies only at the age of 15 or 17, and some never master them at all. As a result of this limitation and others, Piaget (1972) withdrew his earlier claims that the formal-operational stage naturally occurs in every culture without any special training.

EVALUATING PIAGET'S CONTRIBUTION

Among psychologists, there is a vast range of opinion about the ultimate value of Piaget's complex views. But on one point there can be no argument—Jean Piaget has had a tremendous impact on the ways developmental psychologists have tried to understand children's thought processes.

Some of this influence has been quite direct. For example, literally hundreds of studies have explored the appearance of conservation. This is considered an important landmark in cognitive development because the conserving child can, for the first time, reverse a physical action in his head (mentally pouring the liquid back into the original container). On a broader scale, the concrete-operational child has mastered the ability to imagine future actions and their consequences.

Some of the most interesting research on conservation has focused on the possibility of teaching preoperational children to conserve. According to a strict interpretation of Piaget's theory, this should not be possible. Ordinarily, a 5-year-old lacks both the mental capacity and sufficient active experience to conserve; ordinarily the 4-year-old simply does not have the mental capacity to conserve.

In one early study (Smedslund, 1961), 5- to 7-year-old children were first tested to see whether they conserved weight. Nonconservers were children who claimed that the weight of a ball of clay had changed after it was rolled or flattened. These children were then given specific instructions to conserve. They were repeatedly shown that changing the shape of the clay ball did not change its weight on a scale. After sufficient training, these children began to conserve; when the ball was flattened, they now said that its weight had not changed.

But Smedslund was not content with this demonstration; he devised several clever tests to see whether the children really understood. In one subsequent test, when he flattened a clay ball, he secretly removed a piece of it. Now the flat piece of clay really *did* weigh less. Children who had been trained to conserve were not surprised or upset when the scale proved that the two pieces of clay were now different. In contrast, many of the children who were true conservers on the initial test suspected foul play. One suggested diplomatically, "We must have lost some clay on the floor," and a more direct child said, "I think you have taken away some of the clay."

Smedslund concluded that although preoperational children could be trained to imitate conservation responses, they did not really understand what they were doing. Other researchers took this as a challenge and developed increasingly sophisticated techniques for teaching even 3- and 4-year-old children to conserve (Brainerd, 1974). This led to still further controversy over the precise criteria for defining a child as a conserver or nonconserver. Researchers scurried back to their bookshelves to find out *exactly* what Piaget had said about the matter. They found that Piaget's own proposals contained a certain amount of ambiguity.

Similar events occurred when large numbers of experimenters tested other aspects of Piaget's theory. This led at first to disillusionment and later to an attempt to find something better. John Flavell (1982), one of the most influential researchers in this field, summarized Piaget's current status in this way:

> Piaget's stage theory has made an enormous—indeed unmatched—contribution to the field of cognitive development . . . . Like all theories of great reach and significance, however, it has problems that gradually come to light as years and years of thinking and research get done on it. Thus, some of us now think that the theory may in varying degrees be unclear, incorrect, and incomplete (p. 2).

In the 1980s, researchers will continue to study this theory and develop "neo-Piagetian" alternatives to try to develop a more complete and accurate picture of children's cognitive growth. One of the more interesting trends in this new research involves the relationship between a child's cognitive abilities and her larger understanding of the social world.

SOCIAL COGNITION

Traditionally, studies of cognitive development have focused on how children understand physical objects and the relations among them. Recently, many developmental researchers have turned to the study of **social cognition**—the understanding of the social world, including other people's behavior, thoughts, and feelings.

For example, Berndt (1981) studied children's ideas of what friends are and how they should treat one another. In several studies comparing kindergarten children with third- and sixth-graders, he asked questions like, "How do you know that someone is your friend?" and "What would make you decide not to be friends with someone anymore?" The children's answers revealed systematic changes in the way children define friendship.

Some social scientists believe that intimacy and trust are two of the more important characteristics of adult friendship. Sixth-grade children often mentioned this

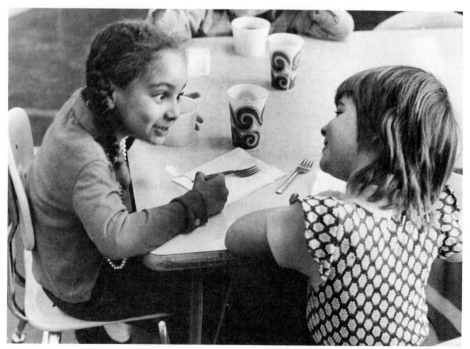

Studies of children's concept of friendship can reveal the relationships between cognitive and social development.

factor, saying such things as, "We can talk freely to one another," "I can tell secrets to her," or simply, "I can trust him." In contrast, younger children rarely mentioned intimacy or trust. Other defining features of friendship showed less change. Children of all ages, for example, often mentioned physical association, such as, "I sleep over at his house sometimes" or "She calls me all the time."

Developmental trends of this sort seem to be related to the child's growing cognitive capabilities. The younger child defines friendship in terms of obvious surface characteristics like association, just as his understanding of physical objects is based on superficial appearances. In the concrete-operational stage, the child begins to understand that an object—like water poured from one glass to another—can remain the same despite changes in appearance. At roughly the same age, his definition of friendship begins to reflect a deeper level of understanding; it is based not just on obvious features like physical association but also more subtle notions such as trust and intimacy.

Studies of social cognition are almost inevitably more complicated by cultural differences than studies of nonsocial cognition. In some cultures, for example, intimacy is not considered a vital part of adult friendship. Children raised in these cultures would therefore be expected to have a different pattern of social cognitive development regarding intimacy issues. In contrast, the way children perceive glasses of liquid would be far less likely to vary from one culture to the next. Despite such difficulties, many researchers are now beginning to study social cognition in the hope that it will provide new information about the child's changing world.

APPLIED PSYCHOLOGY

Learning Disabilities

While Piaget tried to identify stages of cognitive development that applied to all children, other developmental psychologists have focused on the more immediate question of diagnosing the cognitive problems of individual children and working to overcome them. The term **learning disabilities** refers to children who do poorly in school despite the fact that they have no apparent physical, intellectual, or emotional defects. Although problems in school are probably as old as the first educational system, the term *learning disability* was first used only about 20 years ago.

Children with learning disabilities are sometimes said to be suffering from minimal brain damage or minimal brain dysfunction, but many psychologists strongly object to the use of these terms. The use of the term *minimal brain damage* became common almost by accident. Several early researchers on learning disabilities began by studying the severely retarded and children with diseases like cerebral palsy. When they proceeded to investigate children with less serious and less obvious problems, they continued to assume that brain damage was an important factor. After all, they reasoned, learning occurs in the brain; if a child has trouble learning, there must be something wrong with his brain.

This rather loose logic had some unfortunate consequences. In our society, *brain damage* sounds much more serious than *learning disability*. Parents are likely to assume that a brain-damaged child requires the latest medical technology. If they realized that this term is just another way of saying that the child is having trouble with school, they might be more inclined to look for cures in the classroom.

The most common form of learning disability is called **hyperactivity** (or hyperkinesis) in which extreme restlessness and a short attention span are associated with impulsive and disorganized behavior. Technically, this problem is now diagnosed as "attention deficit disorder with hyperactivity."

There is a great deal of controversy over exactly how many children are hyperactive, in part because many questions have been raised about the precise definition of the syndrome. A 1971 report from the Department of Health, Education, and Welfare estimated that 3% of all schoolchildren suffer from moderate or severe hyperactivity. Other estimates have ranged as high as 40% (Schrag & Divoky, 1975). All experts agree, however, that most hyperactive children are boys—they outnumber girls by at least 3 to 1.

In many cases, the child's teacher is the first to notice a problem. The inability to focus attention and complete tasks can often be tolerated by parents on a one-to-one basis. But in a classroom with 25 or more youngsters, the child often becomes disruptive. When the child has trouble in school, the parents may be asked to take him to a doctor. After examining the problem student, a doctor may prescribe a trial period on one of several stimulant drugs, most often an amphetamine-like drug with the trade name Ritalin. If the child becomes more attentive in class while taking this drug, he will probably continue to take it for several years. The initial diagnosis is usually made between the ages of 6 and 10; drug use is discontinued before puberty.

The idea that drugs can help hyperactive children can be traced back to the 1930s, when a Rhode Island researcher accidentally discovered that benzedrine (a form of amphetamine, or "speed") improved school performance for some institutionalized children (Bradley, 1937). Intuitively, it may seem surprising that amphetamines would improve the behavior of a child who was already hyperactive. But for many children, the major symptom of hyperactivity is a short attention span. Amphetamines increase the attention span not just for hyperactive children but also for normal children and adults. Drug treatment of hyperactivity became popular in the 1960s and peaked in the mid-1970s.

The manufacturers of Ritalin estimate that 150,000 American schoolchildren were taking this drug in 1970; 250,000, in 1972; and 265,000, in 1976. But around this time several experts charged that these drugs were prescribed too freely and might have harmful effects over the long run. Partly as a result, the number of hyperactive children taking drugs started to decline. By 1978, the figure was only 120,000. (Many other drugs are sometimes prescribed for hyperactivity, and the total number of hyperactive children taking drugs in 1978 was probably over 200,000.)

There is little doubt that drug treatment helps some children function in school. Indeed, one group of experts called it "the best documented . . . [therapy] in child psychiatry" (Gittelman, Abikoff, Pollack, Klein, Katz, & Mattes, 1980, p. 221). But when people became concerned about possible side effects of long-term use of the drugs, many researchers started looking for nondrug alternatives. The major candidate thus far has been behavior modification (see Chapters 5 and 14).

After several researchers showed that behavior modification can help hyperactive children, one group set out to compare the effects of Ritalin, behavior therapy, and the combination of the two (Gittelman et al., 1980). The behavior therapy tested here involved both teachers' and parents' rewarding certain instances of good behavior and ignoring or punishing bad behavior. Sixty-one hyperactive elementary schoolchildren were divided into three groups. The first received behavior therapy plus Ritalin, the second received behavior therapy plus a placebo (an ineffective pill that works by the power of suggestion; see Chapter 14), and the third received just Ritalin.

Evaluations of the children's later behavior included standard assessments by parents and teachers, as well as objective observations of classroom behavior by researchers who did not know which group each child was in. The results from many different measures were quite consistent. The children who received behavior therapy and Ritalin improved the most, followed by those who just took Ritalin. Behavior therapy plus a placebo produced the least improvement.

In conclusion, these researchers noted that they had defined hyperactivity quite strictly and that their results might not apply to children with milder problems. This caution illustrates one major trend in the treatment of hyperactivity in the 1980s. There is greater awareness of the many complexities that may be involved with an individual child and an expectation that different children—even those with the same diagnosis—often require different forms of treatment.

Personality and Social Development

While some researchers have concentrated on the growth of intellectual and perceptual abilities, others have been more concerned with the formation of personality. As we shall see in Chapter 11, **personality** can be defined as an individual's characteristic pattern of thought, behavior, and emotions. From the pioneer theories of Sigmund Freud to the present day, many personality psychologists have argued that lifelong patterns of behavior may be established in childhood. Here, we focus on several lines of research that specifically examined the effects of early experience and predisposition.

TEMPERAMENT

From the moment of birth, each child gives signs of individuality. One infant sleeps peacefully while another tosses and turns. One child quickly and easily accepts an irregular feeding schedule; another will eat only when he is good and ready. One child fusses the second her diaper is wet; another barely seems to notice.

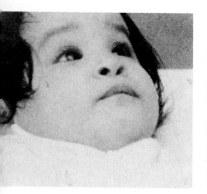 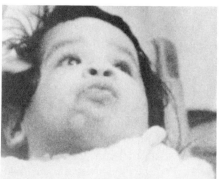 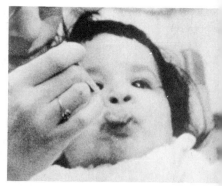

Figure 8.8
Individual differences in the temperament of 3-month-olds. The "easy" child in the first three photos accepts a new type of cereal easily; the "difficult" child in the next three photos rejects the cereal.

Temperament refers to an underlying energy level or other factor that helps produce a consistent style of responding in many different situations.

Mothers have observed such differences for centuries. However, some psychologists questioned the idea that individual differences were present at birth. In Chapter 5, for example, we quoted John Watson's famous claim that he could train any child to become a doctor, lawyer, or thief. Many behaviorists argued that mothers' perceptions of consistency were exaggerated (see Chapter 11) and that real individual differences appear only after the infant had an opportunity to learn certain behavior patterns.

Many researchers have therefore tried to see whether temperament differences are present at birth or only appear later in development. One such study compared the behavior of 24 Chinese and 24 Caucasian infants immediately after they were born (Freedman, 1979). Caucasian babies cried longer and harder and had more trouble adapting to changes in position. When their noses were pressed briefly with a cloth, the Caucasian babies turned away or swiped at the cloth with their hands; the Chinese infants simply lay still and calmly breathed through their mouths. This researcher hesitantly summarized these and other observations by saying: "It was as if the old stereotypes of the calm, inscrutable Chinese and the excitable, emotionally changeable Caucasian were appearing spontaneously in the first 48 hours of life" (p. 38). This finding seems to support the biological paradigm that emphasizes the effects of innate predispositions.

The New York Longitudinal Study is an ongoing attempt to determine whether early differences like this have long-term implications for personality development. Alexander Thomas, Stella Chess, and Herbert Birch (1970) and their colleagues began by studying 141 newborn infants from middle-class families in New York. At first, they interviewed the parents at regular intervals concerning factual details about how the children behaved in specific situations (see "How Do They Know?" for details).

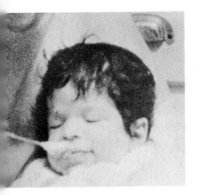 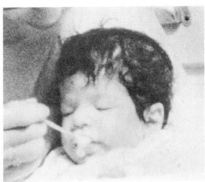 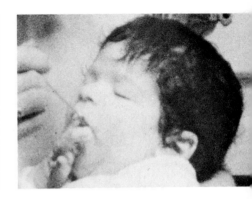

Gradually they found that some personality traits tended to go together to form three more general personality types, which they called *easy*, *difficult*, and *slow to warm up*. For example, infants who had a generally positive mood also tended to be rhythmic (have regular patterns of sleeping and eating), to approach new situations, and to adapt to changes in the environment. About 40% of the children fell into this category; they were easy because their good moods, regular schedules, and easy adaptability made them a pleasure to raise.

Another 10% of the children were difficult because they acted in almost exactly the opposite way. They were generally in a bad mood, had irregular eating and sleeping habits, adapted to new situations slowly, withdrew from new people, and generally reacted intensely. The 15% in the slow-to-warm-up group were generally inactive, adapted slowly, withdrew at first from new people or objects, and were usually in slightly negative moods. (The remaining 35% of the children had a mixture of traits and did not fall easily into any of these three basic personality types.)

Interpretation of the consistency of these traits through childhood is quite complicated, in part because each child interacts in a different family. The relationship between mother and father influences the way a particular type of child is treated. In addition, developmental psychologists have become increasingly aware that influence is not a one-way street— a child also shapes her parents' behavior. And there may be individual differences in parental response. One mother of a difficult child may try to become more understanding, while another could be affected by the same personality pattern in the opposite way and become a harsher disciplinarian.

After taking these and other complications into account, Thomas and Chess (1977) concluded that the personality differences found in infancy did indeed influence the behavior patterns of later years. As the New York Longitudinal Study continues to follow these subjects into the twenty-first century, we shall learn a great deal more about the tortuous path from smiling in infancy to contentment in old age.

Of course, the fact that infant temperament influences personality development does not imply that the environment in which a child is raised makes little difference. Adult character is shaped by a complex interaction between early predispositions and a lifetime of experience. In the remainder of this section, we review two classic lines of research on the effects of infant experience on personality development.

MONKEYS AND MOTHERLY LOVE

One of the first studies of the effects of infant experience on later development focused on the nature of motherly love. Because it would be unethical to deprive human infants of their mothers for the purposes of an experiment, Harry Harlow decided to begin by studying motherhood among Rhesus monkeys.

Before Harlow's research, many psychologists had speculated that an infant's love for his mother could be learned by associating her physical characteristics with the reduction of biological tensions such as hunger and thirst. Psychoanalytic follow-

HOW DO THEY KNOW?

Longitudinal Research: Studies That Can Last a Lifetime

Longitudinal studies involve the repeated observation of the same individual over a long period of time, sometimes through his entire life. Such cradle-to-grave observation provides valuable information about development that cannot be gained in any other way. But it also means that a study can take 80, 90, or even 100 years to complete.

The New York Longitudinal Study began in 1956. The major focus of this study was to trace the evolution of temperament. Can adult personality be predicted from the behavior of a newborn infant? Thomas, Chess, and Birch (1970) began with 141 infants; most of the original subjects, now in their twenties, still participate at regular intervals. In the early stages, most of the data came from regular interviews with the parents—every three months for the first year and a half, then every six months until the age of 5, then once a year.

The results of these interviews led the researchers to focus on nine basic dimensions of personality: activity level, rhythmicity, distractability, approach-withdrawal, adaptability, attention span and persistence, intensity of reaction, threshold of responsiveness, and quality of mood.

Later, these characteristics were assessed by Thomas and Chess (1977) through standard questionnaires. For example, mothers were asked which of the following three statements best applied to their infants:

> With interruptions of milk or solid feedings, as for burping, is:
>
> (a) Generally happy, smiles;
>
> (b) Variable responses; or
>
> (c) Generally cries with these interruptions (p. 213)

Choice *a* was classified as a sign of a positive mood; choice *c* reflected a negative mood. The overall response to a number of similar items provided a general score for the infant's quality of mood.

ers of Sigmund Freud particularly emphasized the importance of breast feeding—the child's first form of gratification—in forming an attachment between mother and child. Harlow (1959) decided to test this idea by comparing monkeys raised by two artificial, or surrogate, mothers. One was a wire cylinder with a crude face and a single nipple supplying milk; the other was an identical cylinder wrapped in terry cloth to make it softer and more comfortable.

In the first experiment, eight newborn Rhesus monkeys were placed in cages with two surrogate mothers. Half received milk through the wire mother, and half through the terry-cloth–covered parent. All eight monkeys drank about the same amount of milk and gained weight normally. If the parental bond was based on this feeding, each monkey should have become attached to the mother that fed it. How-

Another questionnaire assessed the same characteristics for the 3- to 7-year-old child. Parents were asked to rate a series of statements, for example, "When playing with other children, my child argues with them," on a 7-point scale (Thomas & Chess, 1977, p. 242). If a parent said this was hardly ever true of his child, that indicated a generally positive mood. But if this was almost always true, the child was at the negative end of the scale. Again, the average response to a number of items gave an overall rating of positive or negative mood.

By computing correlation coefficients (see "How Do They Know?" in Chapter 3) between each child's scores at different ages, Thomas and Chess (1977) were able to prove that some personality characteristics were reasonably stable. For example, the correlations between mood quality at age 1 and age 2 ($r = .45$) and age 1 and age 3 ($r = .25$) were statistically significant; the predictions from age 1 to age 4 ($r = .10$) or from age 1 to age 5 ($r = .08$) were less reliable. The clearest evidence of personality stability was found over relatively short periods of time. This finding is consistent with other longitudinal studies of personality development.

An inherent problem for all developmental research on the stability of character traits becomes particularly obvious in longitudinal studies. How does one equate the different behavioral patterns observed at different ages? In the example given here, is it really legitimate to consider an infant's fussiness during feeding as somehow parallel to a 7-year-old's argumentativeness? This gradually became a problem for the New York Longitudinal Study; as the children entered adolescence and adulthood, it became increasingly difficult to analyze their personalities in terms of standard reactions to a limited number of situations.

This is only one of the conceptual and practical hurdles that longitudinal researchers face. These studies are expensive and time-consuming; it takes a special kind of commitment for a psychologist to begin a study that she can't possibly live to complete. Still, despite the difficulties, several major longitudinal studies that plan to follow people for their entire lives are now in progress (see Chapter 9). It is a measure of psychology's youth that no large-scale study of this sort has ever followed a complete group from birth to death.

Figure 8.9
When a monkey in Harlow's study is frightened by a toy teddy bear, he retreats to the warm and cuddly terry-cloth–covered "mother" rather than the uncomfortable wire "mother."

ever, the monkeys given milk through the wire cylinder left as soon as they finished eating and went over to cling to the terry-cloth parent. All eight infant monkeys clung to the terry-cloth mother 12 to 18 hours each day. Bodily contact and comfort seemed to be more important factors than feeding in establishing a bond of affection.

Later tests provided an impressive demonstration of the security these infant monkeys felt when they clung to the terry-cloth mother. Into the peaceful world of the monkey cage Harlow introduced a windup teddy bear beating a drum. The poor infants were obviously scared silly. Each monkey rushed over to the cloth mother and hung on for dear life. After a period of rubbing against "Mom" for reassurance, the infant monkeys seemed much calmer; they turned to look at the toy and sometimes even climbed down to approach it (see Figure 8.9).

Less stressful circumstances elicited a similar response. When a motherless monkey was placed in a large cage filled with unfamiliar objects, it ran over to the cloth mother, climbed up, and rubbed against it reassuringly. Again, a few moments of this physical contact seemed to calm the infant. The monkey would climb down after a while and begin to explore the cage, returning frequently to the cloth mother to give it a brief, assuring hug.

Although the surrogate mothers were quite satisfactory in some ways, their monkey children did not grow up to be completely normal. Many of these primates were abusive or indifferent to other monkeys, and virtually all of them grew up to have sexual problems (Harlow & Harlow, 1969).

Even more disturbed behavior was seen in control groups of monkeys who were raised in total social isolation, without monkey playmates or artificial mothers. They spent many hours clutching themselves and rocking back and forth aimlessly, acting in a way that reminded Harlow of some emotionally disturbed children. Their interactions with other monkeys ranged from inappropriate to bizarre. Sometimes they simply ignored other animals, and sometimes they behaved very aggressively. On some disturbing occasions, the isolated monkeys even self-destructively bit their own hands, arms, and legs.

After many attempts to rehabilitate these isolated monkeys had failed, Harlow (1971) concluded that contact comfort between mother and child was an essential ingredient for normal primate development. Further, he believed that this bond had to be formed in the first few months of life. Borrowing a concept from ethological studies of animal behavior, Harlow spoke of a **critical period** for motherly love, a fixed interval during which key events had to occur if normal development was to follow.

During the 1950s and 1960s, many psychologists were influenced by this idea. However, several lines of research later questioned the importance of such critical periods in the development of higher primates. Harlow himself later discovered that the problems of isolated monkeys could be reversed by "monkey therapists"— playful young infants who interacted with the older monkeys without threatening them (Suomi & Harlow, 1972). Other researchers have discovered that closely related species of monkeys were not as dramatically affected as the Rhesus monkeys used in Harlow's studies (Sackett, Ruppenthal, Fahrenbuch, & Holm, 1981).

More to the point for those who are primarily interested in human development, studies of human children who have unfortunately been raised in isolation indicated that even severe problems may be reversed with proper attention in later childhood. (See "A New Perspective on Early Experience?" later in this chapter.)

HUMAN ATTACHMENT

Another influential theory involving the possible role of critical periods in human development was developed by psychiatrist John Bowlby. In his 1969 book *Attachment and Loss*, Bowlby argued that the basis for motherly love has been built into the human species by millions of years of evolution. Unlike newborn animals of some species, the human infant is entirely helpless; to ensure the survival of the species, human infants must be cared for by adults. According to Bowlby, babies are genetically programmed to cling to an adult, usually the mother; and the mother, in turn, is programmed to respond to the child's needs. An emotional bond of love between mother and child is the natural result.

While evolutionary explanations of this sort are difficult to test scientifically, other aspects of Bowlby's work did generate a great deal of research. For example, he argued that at first an infant's grasping, clinging, and crying are not directed at a specific individual; only by the age of 6 months has the infant clearly learned to recognize the primary caretaker. This can often be seen in the differences in the responses of 6-month-old infants to their mother and to other adults.

Stranger anxiety refers to a phase in which infants seem anxious when strangers are nearby. They may cry, fret, or try to move away. Such behavior is likely to increase if a stranger comes too close or the mother moves away. Stranger anxiety typically appears around the age of 6 months, peaks at 8 or 9 months, and disappears around 15 months.

A closely related phenomenon is **separation anxiety**—a more profound distress whenever a child is separated from its mother or primary caretaker. This occurs slightly later in development, beginning around 8 to 12 months and ending between the ages of 2 and $2\frac{1}{2}$.

Many researchers have brought Bowlby's concepts into the laboratory to quantify stranger anxiety and separation anxiety. One typical series of studies (Ainsworth & Bell, 1970) observed the response of 1-year-old babies when they were left in a room with various adults. When mother and child were in a room together, the infant seemed quite content; there was very little crying and a great deal of exploratory behavior—crawling around and looking at and handling everything in the room. When a stranger replaced Mom or when the baby was left alone, the child spent much less time exploring and much more time crying. When both mother and a stranger were in the room together, the response was intermediate—the child cried more than when only the mother was present but less than when only the stranger was present.

In addition to these average differences in response to various situations, there are important and consistent individual differences in children's overall anxieties. Children who are *securely attached* explore confidently when mother is present, become distressed when she leaves, but calm down quickly when she returns. *Insecurely attached* children are usually fussy even with mother present and, when she returns, show ambivalence, such as asking to be picked up and then struggling to get down. In a less common type of insecure attachment, some infants pay little attention to their mothers and are not particularly upset when they leave (Sroufe & Waters, 1977).

Secure attachment is most likely to occur when mothers are sensitive, accepting, cooperative, sociable, accessible, and positive during the child's first year. There is also some evidence that the child can influence parental responsiveness and thus influence the form of attachment. It seems likely that insecurely attached infants will have more problems later in development, but research on this subject is just beginning so it is too early to determine whether this intuition will prove to be correct.

Laboratory studies of stranger anxiety and separation anxiety have now been performed on infants who were raised in a number of different cultures, ranging

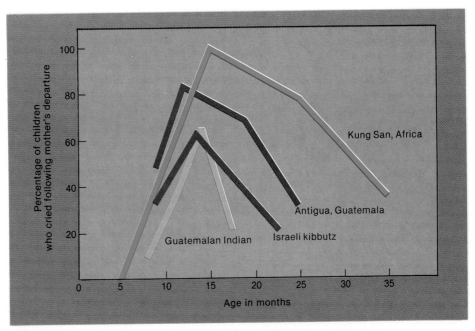

Figure 8.10
Separation anxiety peaked at roughly the same age in studies of four very different cultures.

from an Israeli kibbutz to an African tribe. As Figure 8.10 indicates, the appearance of stranger anxiety was surprisingly regular.

The fact that separation anxiety peaks around the age of 1 year in so many cultural settings led Jerome Kagan and his colleagues (Kagan, Kearsely, & Zelazo, 1978) to argue that this fear is based on the natural emergence of certain cognitive skills. It is only around the age of about 8 months that most infants become cognitively mature enough to understand that Mama may be somewhere else. This separation confuses and upsets the child, who is not yet old enough to test his hypotheses about where she went. One factor involved in the disappearance of separation anxiety is the 18-month-old child's ability to crawl or walk around and, under some circumstances, actually find his mother.

Bowlby's original theory singled out the mother as the primary figure in these early dramas. He believed that the mother is naturally disposed to behave in certain ways (cuddling an infant during feeding, for example) and that motherly love cannot be replaced by the father or any other adult. You might guess that this would be a controversial assertion in a society in which more and more mothers of young children are working outside the home. Many researchers have investigated Bowlby's claim, and most have rejected his exclusive reliance on the mother. In the next section, we examine recent research regarding day-care centers and whether or not they affect the attachment bond between mother and child.

Child Rearing

According to one estimate, nearly 5 million how-to-parent books are sold every year in the United States. Surveys suggest that nearly all American parents read some of these books and articles. People are particularly likely to rely on this type of advice when they are from small families (and thus have little experience with other children) and are isolated from their own parents. The fact that American families are becoming smaller and more mobile suggests that expert advice will become more popular in the future (Clark-Stewart, 1978).

HISTORICAL TRENDS

Many practices that would now be classified as criminal child abuse were commonplace throughout most of recorded history. In the civilizations of ancient Greece and Rome, parents simply abandoned unwanted children—usually girls—and allowed them to die. Until the eighteenth century, nearly every Western society practiced swaddling—tightly wrapping young infants so they could not move and would be

---

BECOMING A CRITICAL CONSUMER

Ask Doctor Spock

The most famous guidebook for parents is Dr. Benjamin Spock's *Baby and Child Care,* which has sold over 28 million copies since it was first published in 1946. Along with medical advice on measles and mumps and practical hints on diapers and diet, this book has much to say about personality and emotional development. As you read the following short selection, consider how much evidence is cited and whether it supports or contradicts the material presented in this chapter. (A short discussion of these issues appears after the "Summary" at the end of this chapter.)

> Whether children will grow up to be lifelong optimists or pessimists, whether warmly loving or cool, whether trustful or suspicious, will depend to a considerable extent on the attitudes of the individuals who have taken responsibility for a major portion of their care in the first two years. Therefore, the personalities of parents and caregivers are of great importance.
>
> One person acts toward children as if they were basically bad, always doubting them, always scolding them. Such children grow up doubting themselves, full of guilt. A person with more than average hostility finds a dozen excuses every hour for venting it on a child; and the child acquires a corresponding hostility. Other people have the itch to dominate children and unfortunately they can succeed.
>
> In the first year, a baby has to depend mainly on the attentiveness, intuition, and helpfulness of adults to get her the things that she needs and craves. If the adults are too insensitive or indifferent to serve (within sensible limits—they shouldn't be submissive slaves) she will become somewhat apathetic or depressed (pp. 38–39).

less likely to bother adults. According to Lloyd de Mause (1974), beatings, sexual abuse, and even the murder of children were frequent occurrences at least through the Middle Ages.

Beginning around the sixteenth century, families became smaller and more mobile, and children began to contribute economically to their success. This led to a new concern with effective child-rearing practices. The dominant educational philosophy of this period held that children were weak, impulsive creatures; only strict discipline could transform them into moral adults.

The dramatic difference from current attitudes can also be seen in the large numbers of parents who sent their children away to be raised by servants. Breast-feeding was considered a vulgar annoyance, and because Nestlé did not yet sell

Figure 8.11
A fifteenth-century illustration of family life. Note that the children are shown performing adult tasks and that the infant is tightly swaddled in its crib.

bottled formula, infants were often sent away to wet nurses who breast-fed the children. In 1780, the police chief of Paris estimated that 17,000 of the 21,000 infants born in that city each year were sent away to live with wet nurses in the countryside (Maccoby, 1980).

In the nineteenth century, the emphasis on beating the bad impulses out of children decreased, and parents began to try to learn the most effective ways to socialize their children. With the advent of scientific psychology, a large number of experts began to offer advice.

One of the first guidebooks for parents was written by none other than behaviorist John Watson. His 1928 book, *Psychological Care of Infant and Child,* was an odd mix of scientific fact and unscientific speculation. Watson believed that too much love can make a child "totally unable to cope with the world it must live in" (p. 44). He therefore offered the following unsentimental advice:

> Treat [children] as though they were young adults. Dress them, bathe them with care and circumspection. Let your behavior always be objective and kindly firm. Never hug and kiss them, never let them sit on your lap. If you must, kiss them once on the forehead when they say good night" (pp. 81–82).

A more permissive approach became popular in the 1930s. In its more extreme versions, this philosophy held that the child is naturally able to choose the best course and that the parent's job is to help the child achieve its full potential by providing love and support. Discipline should be avoided for fear of producing emotional problems or other harmful effects. Consider, for example, one mother's description of the schools her 6-year-old daughter attended in the 1970s: "LuAnn liked the school in California best—the only rules were no chemical additives in the food and no [sex] in the hallways" (quoted in Kessen, 1979, p. 815). Recent evidence suggests that the pendulum is now swinging back from liberalism and that today's parents are less likely to be permissive, believing that a moderate use of punishment is sometimes appropriate (Walters & Grusec, 1977).

These historical changes in expert opinion may leave parents wondering just how useful current advice books are. To some extent, it is probably unreasonable to ask for an entirely objective approach to child rearing; expert advice will always reflect the ethics and goals of a specific culture. Despite such reservations, social scientists continue to believe that knowledge is better than ignorance and that studying the effects of different ways of rearing children can help to reveal how early experiences shape later development.

At least since Freud, many psychologists have believed that childhood experiences can establish lifelong behavior patterns. Freud himself argued that the first five years of life determined the general outlines of adult personality. Taken to its logical extreme, this theory implied that adults had to be extremely careful how they dealt with children in those first critical years. Fortunately, recent research seems to be reducing this burden. The effects of early experience may not be so overwhelming after all. Some of the most interesting research supporting this more moderate position concerns the effects of day care.

EFFECTS OF DAY CARE

As more and more American women have entered the labor force to pursue careers, day-care centers to take care of young children have become increasingly common. In one of the most thorough studies of this subject (Kagan, Kearseley, & Zelazo, 1978), researchers actually set up an elaborate day care center for 33 infants. Beginning at the age of $3\frac{1}{2}$ to $5\frac{1}{2}$ months, each child lived at this day-care center from 8 a.m. to 5 p.m., five days a week, until they were $2\frac{1}{2}$ years old. Standard laboratory tests of emotional and intellectual development were used to compare the progress of these children with a control group raised at home.

In one standard test of emotional development, experimenters observed each child's reaction to being separated from his mother. Once the child began to play happily with his toys in the laboratory, the mother simply left the room for 2 minutes while an observer reported any incidents of fretting or crying. There were no significant differences between day-care children and those raised at home. The developmental course of separation anxiety in both groups of children was nearly identical to that observed in other cultures.

Day-care and home-raised children were compared on a variety of tests of intellectual development. For example, at the age of 20 months they were given a simple vocabulary test in which they had to pair pictures with words. Each child was asked to pick out the fork from the pictures of a knife, a fork, and a spoon and to choose

Figure 8.12
Studies that have compared children raised in day care centers to others raised at home have found no important differences in development.

the apple from pictures of an apple, an orange, and a banana. Here, too, there were no differences between the two groups of children.

In fact, 19 standard tests of attentiveness, sensitivity to discrepancy, fearfulness, language, memory, social behavior, and attachment to the mother failed to reveal any major differences between children raised by mothers at home and those reared in a day-care center. Informal observations and discussions with parents also failed to reveal any differences. Of course, critics could always charge that other tests of other behaviors, or more sensitive measures, might show differences. Thus, it is logically impossible to prove conclusively that day care is just as good as home care.

We shall have to wait for these children to grow up to study possible long-term effects. Further, it is worth noting that this particular day-care center, and most others that have been studied intensively, was well funded and well staffed and probably had a high-quality program. No one knows whether ordinary day-care centers, limited by a lack of money or other problems, are equally successful.

After reviewing all the studies done so far, one researcher (Etaugh, 1980) conservatively concluded that the available evidence "does not warrant the sweeping conclusion that nonmaternal care is not harmful to young children. The evidence does permit the more cautious conclusion that high-quality nonmaternal care has not been found to have negative effects on the development of preschool children" (p. 316).

A NEW PERSPECTIVE ON EARLY EXPERIENCE?

If day-care children do grow up to be just as happy and emotionally well adjusted as children reared at home by their mothers, this might suggest that Bowlby overemphasized the importance of the mother-infant bond. It might even suggest that the first few years of life could be no more critical than any other period of development.

This idea goes against traditional wisdom. At least since Freud, developmental psychologists have emphasized the importance of childhood experiences in determining adult personality. The traditional view may place a heavy burden on anxious parents. For example, Burton White (1975) wrote: "Sometimes when I present my views about the importance of the first three years of life I notice sad looks coming over the faces of parents . . . followed by the questions, 'Is it all over after three? Is there nothing further I can do to be useful?'" (p. 257) Although he mentions several qualifications, White goes on to say that "Answering these questions is rather difficult for me because *to some extent* I really believe that it *is* too late after age three." Fortunately, White's view is rather extreme and in recent years many researchers have moved away from this pessimistic emphasis on early experiences.

One source of evidence that children may be more adaptable than previously believed comes from the victims of neglect in infancy. One classic case study (Davis, 1947) followed the later progress of a child who had been isolated with her deaf-mute mother until the age of 6 and deprived of any other human contact. The girl was later able to learn to speak and interact with other people surprisingly well.

Similarly, a study of adopted children who were refugees from war-torn areas of Greece and Korea found that they developed normally. Despite their having many emotional problems when they arrived in the United States and stress due to the need to adapt to a new language and a new culture, most of these children were emotionally and physically healthy when they were reexamined six years later (Rathbun, McLaughlin, Bennett, & Garland, 1965).

Other systematic studies of neglected children who were removed from their homes by court order, of children who were raised in poverty in rural Guatemala, and of other infants deprived in various ways (Clarke & Clarke, 1976) all point in the same direction. Children seem quite resilient. The first few years of life may prove to be no more important—or less important—than any other period of development.

According to this optimistic view, if a child is deprived during the first few years of life, the resulting problems can be corrected by later improving the quality of care. Most developmental psychologists now believe that human beings are surprisingly flexible and that each of us can continue to change and to grow for as long as we live.

Summary

1. **Developmental psychology** studies how and why people change physically, intellectually, and emotionally as they grow from infancy to old age.
2. **Maturation** refers to sequences of growth and internal bodily changes that are primarily determined by biological timing. Environmental factors such as health and nutrition can influence the rate of physical growth and motor development, but the limits are set by biology.
3. In the course of pregnancy, the developing organism passes through several distinct stages, from a **zygote** (roughly the first two weeks) to an **embryo** (approximately from the second to eighth weeks) to a **fetus** (until birth).
4. Many **reflexes**—involuntary reactions elicited automatically by certain stimuli—present at birth gradually disappear as the cortex of the brain develops and the child gains voluntary control. A number of **norms**, standard figures describing average performance, have been established for the course of motor development.
5. One of the first systematic techniques for testing infant perception involved presenting an infant with two visual stimuli and measuring how long he looked at each. Even very young infants look longer at certain types of patterned surfaces than plain ones, suggesting that they can distinguish these patterns. Other techniques have shown that several perceptual abilities are established within hours of birth.
6. According to Jean Piaget, cognitive development can be divided into several distinct stages, in which children think in qualitatively different ways. The **sensorimotor stage** lasts roughly from birth to age 2; during this stage, infants directly discover the relationship between their own sensations and motor acts. Perhaps the most important achievement of this stage is the development of **object permanence**, the awareness that objects continue to exist even when they

are not present to be seen, touched, or sensed. In the **preoperational stage,** the 2- to 7-year-old gradually learns to use speech, play, gestures, and mental images to represent the world, but the child is unable to perform **operations,** mental actions that reorganize one's view of the world.

7. During the **concrete-operational stage** (roughly ages 7 to 11), the child becomes capable of performing operations on concrete objects and thus able to deal with certain types of logical problems. For example, children become able to **conserve,** that is, to recognize that certain basic properties of objects (such as volume and number) remain constant even when appearances change. Finally, in the **formal-operational stage** (which can begin at 11 or later), the adolescent becomes capable of solving abstract problems and dealing with hypothetical possibilities.

8. Many researchers are now studying the development of **social cognition**—the understanding of the social world, including other people's behavior, thoughts, and feelings. For example, kindergarten children often define friendship in terms of superficial characteristics like physical association; sixth-grade children more often mention deeper features such as intimacy and trust.

9. School-age children with **learning disabilities** have problems in learning that are not caused by known physical, intellectual, or emotional deficits. The most common type is **hyperactivity,** in which restlessness and a short attention span are associated with impulsive and disorganized behavior.

10. One factor that influences the development of individual differences and personality is **temperament,** an underlying energy level or other factor that helps produce a consistent style of responding in many different situations. Some temperament differences observed at birth have been shown to predict behavior later in childhood.

11. Studies in which monkeys were breast-fed by surrogate mothers made of wire cylinders or terry-cloth–covered cylinders suggested that contact comfort was more important than feeding for establishing a bond between mother and child. These studies supported the idea of a **critical period** for establishing motherly love—a fixed interval during which key events had to occur for normal development to follow. Later research, however, questioned the relevance of this idea to humans.

12. Human infants between the age of 6 and 15 months often pass through a stage of **stranger anxiety** in which they often cry, fret, or try to move away when strangers are nearby. Between the ages of 1 and 2½ years, **separation anxiety** is a more profound distress whenever a child is separated from its mother or primary caretaker. The developmental course of these phenomena is surprisingly constant in many different cultures, suggesting that the phases are based on cognitive and emotional changes that occur during the normal process of maturation.

13. Studies have found no important differences between infants raised in well-equipped day-care centers and infants raised at home. Further studies following development over longer time periods and in a wider range of types of day-care centers are needed to provide a final verdict on the effects of day care.

14. Many developmental psychologists now argue that the critical role of early experience in later development may have been overrated. For example, children who have been neglected in infancy show dramatic improvement when placed in a more favorable environment. Development may be a lifelong process in which no one stage can be singled out as the most important.

Discussion of "Becoming a Critical Consumer"

If you read this material closely, you noticed that Dr. Spock did not cite any evidence to support these conclusions. To a developmental psychologist, the idea that all children who are frequently scolded will grow up to be guilty seems far too simplistic. Similarly, the notion that hostile caretakers produce hostile children would only be totally accepted if it were backed up by systematic research. While this popular guidebook on child care may provide accurate advice on medical matters, many of its psychological claims seem to be based on commonsense or casual observations. Unfortunately, as we have stressed throughout this text, common sense often leads to incorrect conclusions.

To Learn More

Mussen, P. H., Conger, J. J., & Kagan, J. *Child Development and Personality* (6th ed.). New York: Harper & Row, 1984. A classic textbook overview of physical and psychological development, from birth to adolescence.

Flavell, J. H. *Cognitive Development*. Englewood Cliffs, N.J.: Prentice-Hall, 1977. Particularly useful for a clear summary of Piaget's complex theories.

Maccoby, E. E. *Social Development: Psychological Growth and the Parent-Child Relationship*. New York: Harcourt Brace Jovanovich, 1980. Summarizes research on attachment, sex differences, moral development, child rearing, and related topics.

9

Adolescence and Adulthood

Erikson's "Eight ages of man"

Adolescence
Physical development
Personality development: Identity
Moral development
Male-female differences

Adulthood
Stages of adult personality development
Successful adjustment
Sexual activity and the life cycle

Old age
A period of cognitive decline?
Improving the quality of life
Death and dying

Summary

BECOMING A CRITICAL CONSUMER
Passages

HOW DO THEY KNOW?
Surveys of sexual behavior

In our society, it is difficult to understand truly the problems and feelings of people in a different age group. The 18-year-old who is just beginning college will probably find it impossible to explain the hopes and fears of this new world to her 12-year-old brother. But the same college student, in turn, may find it very difficult to imagine herself as a 35-year-old mother of two children, forced to stay at a job she doesn't like in order to support her family. Similarly, the 63-year-old man who fears retirement may get little real sympathy and understanding from his co-workers, even if they are only a few years younger.

In the preface to his book *The Seasons of a Man's Life,* researcher Daniel Levinson (1978) eloquently described one implication of this ignorance about other age groups:

> The most distressing fear in early childhood is that there is no life after youth. Young adults often feel that to pass 30 is to be "over the hill," and they are given little beyond hollow clichés to provide a fuller sense of the actual problems and possibilities of adult life at different ages. The middle years, they imagine, will bring triviality and meaningless comfort at best, stagnation and hopelessness at worst . . .

> Adults hope that life begins at 40—but the great anxiety is that it ends there. The result of this pervasive dread about middle age is almost complete silence about the experiences of being adult. The concrete character of adult life is one of the best-kept secrets of our society (p. IX).

Until quite recently, social scientists have offered little to help us understand the way people in our society change as they grow older. Most developmental psychologists have concentrated on the dramatic changes that occur in the first few years of life. Relatively few have focused on adolescence or old age, and fewer still have studied the changes that occur through your adulthood and middle age. If you had taken an introductory psychology course in 1960 or 1970, your textbook probably would not have included a chapter like this one, describing development in adolescence and adulthood. Only recently have large numbers of researchers begun to study development as a lifelong process extending from the cradle to the grave.

Many developmental psychologists are currently exploring these new frontiers to discover how we change and how we remain the same over the full life cycle. Since wide-scale research is just beginning, there are many gaps in our knowledge. As a result, it is difficult to provide an overview of the physical, perceptual, cognitive, and personality changes associated with each phase of later development, as we did for childhood in Chapter 8. Instead, this chapter focuses on some of the most influential topics and lines of research in this rapidly growing area.

Most studies of adolescence and adulthood are also limited in another way. While researchers in such areas as learning, memory, sensation, and perception try to find general laws that apply to all human beings, the developmental changes described in this chapter probably apply only to certain types of technologically sophisticated twentieth-century Western societies. In prehistoric times, for example, few people lived to the age of 40; those who managed to survive into their thirties were therefore perceived as wise old men (Lerner, 1976). Thirty-five-year old Americans are rarely viewed in this way today. Developmental processes found in our culture do not necessarily apply to other times and other places.

Erik Erikson (1902—   ) is best known for his psychoanalytic theory of the "eight ages of man." In early adulthood, he wandered through Europe trying to earn a living as an artist. He took a job teaching art at a school founded by Anna Freud, a famous analyst in her own right and also the daughter of Sigmund Freud. She was impressed by Erikson's ability to work with children and invited him to enter the Vienna Psychoanalytic Institute. When Hitler's forces threatened to overrun Europe, Erikson fled to the United States to work as a therapist and continue his education. In a long and distinguished career, Erikson published records of his investigations ranging from psychoanalytic biographies of Martin Luther and Mahatma Gandhi to anthropological studies of the Sioux and Yurok Indians.

Erikson's "Eight Ages of Man"

Erik Erikson was one of the first and most influential theorists to chart the course of development over the entire life span. Erikson took a psychoanalytic approach, building on the foundations laid by Sigmund Freud's theory of four psychosexual stages of development (see Chapter 11). Erikson stressed the importance of cultural influences on development and outlined eight **psychosocial stages,** periods during which all individuals must confront a common crisis, caused in part by the new demands posed by different phases of life. The individual who resolves such a crisis improperly will, according to Erikson, have later problems as a result. The first four are similar to Freud's oral, anal, phallic, and genital stages; the last four were added by Erikson to provide a fuller account of the entire life cycle. Here is an outline of what Erikson called the "Eight Ages of Man."

1. *Trust versus mistrust.* In the first year of life, the infant must gradually learn to trust his mother or other caretakers to satisfy his basic needs. This can help lead to a more general sense of trust in society and in himself.
2. *Autonomy versus shame and doubt.* The second year brings a new source of conflict between the child's growing independence and his need to depend on adults. As he becomes capable of walking and talking, the child is faced for the first time with important distinctions between good and bad and yes and no. Parental firmness and consistency can lead to a sense of autonomy, but too much criticism can burden the child with a lifelong sense of shame and self-doubt.
3. *Initiative versus guilt.* In the third or fourth year, the toddler begins to play at

being an adult. He can initiate his own activities to a greater extent than before. Conscience begins to develop, as the child measures himself against external standards. If parents are overly harsh and restrictive, the child may lose the desire to initiate new activities and instead be overwhelmed by guilt.

4. *Industry versus inferiority.* From the age of 6 or 7 to puberty, schoolchildren are faced with the task of learning what their culture expects of them and how to achieve it. One danger of this stage is that the child may conclude that his own skills or status are inadequate; this can sometimes establish a lifelong pattern of feeling of inferiority. More often, the child learns to become an industrious and productive member of society.

5. *Identity versus identity confusion.* Around puberty, dramatic physical and emotional changes lead the adolescent to question her own identity, to wonder who she really is. Failure to integrate all the different roles each person must fill can lead to identity confusion, with no firm sense of self.

6. *Intimacy versus isolation.* The major challenge of young adulthood involves commitment to relationships and to a career. The person who is secure in her own identity can make the compromises necessary for an intimate partnership with another person. The alternative is to remain isolated from others. The isolated person may have many affairs, or even a single long-term relationship, but always avoids true emotional closeness.

7. *Generativity versus stagnation.* In middle age, the major crisis involves a sense of making a contribution to society; *generativity* is a concern for establishing and guiding the next generation. It may be expressed in a variety of ways of giving to others, whether it be to children of our own or of careers and activities designed to help younger people find their place in society. The generative person leads a productive life that can serve as a model for the next generation. The other side of the coin is *stagnation*—a selfish concern with one's own goals that can lead middle-aged people to become insensitive to the needs of others or to live in the past.

8. *Integrity versus despair.* Finally, in old age, some people achieve integration; they look back over life with a true long-term perspective and a sense of satisfaction, accepting the bad as well as the good. For those with a sense of integrity, death loses some of its final sting. Others despair that there is no time left to pursue new paths; they face death with bitterness and regrets.

Like many other psychoanalytic theories, Erikson's conclusions were based on his clinical experience rather than on empirical data from a series of systematic tests. Nevertheless, many professionals who deal with problems of adult adjustment have found this scheme very useful. To this day, it remains one of the most complete accounts of the entire life cycle; most developmental psychologists have focused on one specific aspect or period of development rather then trying to develop a coherent view of the life span.

Critics wonder whether these 8 stages are really the best way of subdividing the life cycle. Might there really be 6 ages of man, or 7, or 23? Only future research can tell. Erikson is important to psychology not because he provided the final answers

In middle age, many people become concerned with guiding the next generation, an issue Erikson calls generativity.

but because he was one of the first to ask the question. And, as you will see in this chapter's description of the identity crisis in adolescence, some of Erikson's ideas have stimulated research that has begun to help us specify more precisely how individuals change as they grow older.

Adolescence

Scientific studies of the teenage years are usually traced back to G. Stanley Hall's 1905 text *Adolescence*, which described "a period of storm and stress" in which "every step of the upward way is strewn with the wreckage of the body, mind, and morals" (p. xiii). This notion of *Sturm und Drang* (German for "storm and stress") is quite consistent with many popular stereotypes. American teenagers are often portrayed by the mass media as moody, rebellious, alternately energetic and lazy, and overly influenced by peer groups that bring them into conflict with parental values.

However, systematic research has provided a far more ambiguous picture. One study of the families of middle-class American adolescents (Bandura & Walters, 1959) suggested that adolescence is no more stressful than childhood or adulthood. This research found that the average adolescent accepted most parental values quite fully and associated with other adolescents who also shared these beliefs.

Historical, economic, and social forces can also influence the course of teenage development. Michael Katz (1975) studied how industrialization changed life patterns in Hamilton, Ontario, in the middle of the nineteenth century. In 1851, more than half of all 13- to 16-year-old boys in Hamilton did not work or attend school. Presumably, this large group of idle youth spent much of their time roaming the streets and giving teenagers a bad name. By 1871, as a result of increased opportunities for education and employment, less than 30% of the same group fell in this category. During the same 20-year period, the median age for leaving home rose from 17 to 22 for males. Clearly, these shifting social patterns influenced the activities of adolescents and the way they were perceived by society.

Studies of cultures that are quite different from ours and studies of subtle changes within a culture caused by historical forces suggest that the precise details of adolescent development do not remain constant. It seems likely that some individuals in any society will experience adolescence as a period of storm and stress. The exact proportion, and thus the accuracy of the general description of adolescence as a particularly stressful period, will vary from time to time and place to place.

However, there are some constant themes that influence the development of adolescents in every culture. The most obvious ones involve the physical changes that occur during this period.

PHYSICAL DEVELOPMENT

The most obvious physical changes in adolescence are associated with **puberty**—the period when sexual maturation begins. Technically, puberty begins with the enlargement of the prostate gland and seminal vesicles in males and enlargement of the ovaries in females. The actual age at which these changes occur is determined by the action of many different hormones—substances secreted into the bloodstream by the pituitary and other endocrine glands (see Chapter 2). For example, at puberty

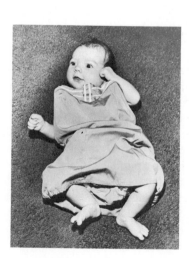

Figure 9.1
One child's development. Photographer Bob Williams photographed his daughter wearing the same bathing suit at different times during 16 years. (It is not known how Kristin felt about publishing these pictures.)

the adrenal cortex, ovaries, and testes dramatically increase the secretion of the sex hormones known collectively as *androgens* (male hormones) and *estrogens* (female hormones). Both males and females have androgens and estrogens in the blood-stream; the sexes are distinguished by their relative proportions. Androgens domi-nate male biochemistry, estrogens are particularly plentiful in females.

The first sign of sexual development in girls is usually a slight increase in breast size and the appearance of pubic hair. This is followed by a **growth spurt,** a sudden increase in the rate of growth for both height and weight, and by the first menstrual period. Further breast growth, increases in the amount of pubic hair, and changes in the female sex organs go on for the next few years.

On the average, puberty begins about two years later for boys than for girls. The first sign of male puberty is an increase in the rate of growth of the testes and the scrotum. For males too, this early development is followed by a growth spurt in height and weight. Pubic hair usually begins to appear at the onset of puberty, while facial and body hair grow about two years later. The larynx, or Adam's apple, becomes much larger late in puberty, and the vocal cords inside the larynx double in length. When this change occurs abruptly, boys may have trouble controlling the vocal cords, and their voices "crack."

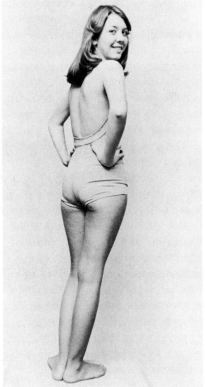

The precise timing of these events varies widely. Testicular growth in boys may begin as early as $9\frac{1}{2}$ or as late as $13\frac{1}{2}$ and still be in the normal range. For girls, the age at onset of menstruation can range from 10 to $16\frac{1}{2}$. Thus, normal adolescents can mature sexually at many different ages. The growth spurt usually occurs at the age of about 11 for girls and 13 for boys, although it, too, can occur over a wide range. This sudden growth can be a source of awkwardness and embarrassment. The head, hands, and feet tend to grow first, producing gawky adolescents whose bodies seem out of proportion by adult standards. The dramatic physical changes of adolescence often confuse the teenager and help lead to what Erik Erikson called an identity crisis.

PERSONALITY DEVELOPMENT: IDENTITY

Identity crisis is now a familiar expression, but it entered the language only a few decades ago. Psychoanalyst Erik Erikson and his co-workers invented the term during World War II to describe the psychiatric disturbance of some soldiers who seemed to lose their sense of personal identity as a result of the stress of combat. Later, Erikson extended the expression **identity crisis** to include "severely conflicted young people whose sense of confusion is due . . . to a war within themselves" (Erikson, 1963, p. 17).

Many psychologists believe that the most fundamental problem of adolescents in our society is to answer the question "Who am I?" Erikson included this as one of his eight basic stages of development, the crisis of establishing a strong sense of personal identity. The alternative is identity confusion—a failure to integrate perceptions of oneself into a coherent whole.

As noted, one factor that makes it difficult for adolescents to feel a sense of continuity is the suddenness of the physical changes of puberty. At the same time, the adolescent becomes sophisticated enough intellectually to question an abstract concept like her own identity. (See Chapter 8 for a description of Piaget's formal operational stage, which begins around puberty.)

Thus, according to Erikson, the adolescent is particularly concerned with finding her own personal spot in adult society and must begin a long and painful process of assessing personal strengths and weaknesses to help set realistic goals. Every person wants to meet her potential and carve out the best possible life for herself. At the same time, the adolescent is concerned with remaining true to her ideals.

Our society frees adolescents from most responsibilities so that they have time to experiment—with different types of relationships with people of both sexes, with different ways of acting and talking, even with political ideologies and philosophies of life. According to Erikson, crushes, infatuations, and puppy love are also involved with the identity crisis—adolescents try to gain insights into their own character partly by seeing themselves idealized through the eyes of others. Even the clannishness and coolness of adolescents who form tight social groups and cliques is seen by Erikson as a step in the search for identity—teenagers help one another through this insecure period by providing stereotypes of acceptable behavior that set their group apart from others.

Adolescents are faced with the problem of establishing a sense of personal identity. The way a particular individual deals with the identity crisis is one important factor that helps determine personality.

Researchers who have studied the process of achieving identity have distinguished between four different states in dealing with these issues. Some people are referred to as *identity achievers* because they have completed a period of decision making and have accepted certain occupational and ideological goals. A second group are called *foreclosures;* they too have accepted certain goals, but they seem to have adopted them directly from their parents, without going through a period of crisis or decision making. *Identity diffusions* are those who have no clear goals, whether or not they went through a period of crisis. Finally, people who are actively trying to set their own occupational or ideological goals are called *moratoriums;* they are in an identity crisis.

Many studies have been done contrasting the characteristics of adolescents in each of these groups. For example, moratoriums are the most anxious of the four groups, as might be expected from the fact that they are facing an identity crisis. Further, both identity achievers and moratoriums seem to be more independent and to take more responsibility for their actions than adolescents in the foreclosure or identity-diffusion categories.

Several studies have suggested that the ages 18 to 21 are a very important period for establishing identity, particularly for people who attend college. Interestingly, foreclosures tend to be most satisfied with their college experience, perhaps because it helps them progress toward unambiguous occupational goals. Moratoriums are the least satisfied with their college experiences and tend to change their majors more than any other group (Marcia, 1980).

Other studies of these groups bear more directly on Erikson's idea that people must achieve a sense of identity before they become capable of intimate relationships. One study that graded the depth and mutual basis of adolescents' interpersonal relationships found that identity achievers and moratoriums achieved the most intimacy. Foreclosures were more likely to have "stereotyped relationships" that lacked depth, and identity diffusions were often isolated from other people (Orlofsky, Marcia, & Lesser, 1973). It is particularly interesting that foreclosures, who have a strong sense of identity, lack intimate relationships. The greater intimacy of the moratoriums, who were actually experiencing identity crises, suggests that simply achieving identity is not the only factor in intimacy; other personal characteristics may be more important for deep relationships.

It is worth noting that all the studies of identity described to this point used male subjects. Before 1970, most psychologists simply assumed that female adolescents would experience similar crises. This type of sexist bias was common throughout psychology, as it was throughout our entire society. Most of the early research on moral development, as described in the next section, also focused exclusively on males. However, later in this chapter we describe more recent studies that place equal emphasis on the psychology of women.

MORAL DEVELOPMENT

Adolescence is a period of physical, emotional, and cognitive change. The growing intellectual sophistication of the teenager coupled with the demand that he suddenly make important decisions about such issues as careers, relationships, and sexuality helps lead the adolescent to ask questions not just about his own identity but also about moral standards, to begin to decide for himself what is really right and what is really wrong.

One of the most influential techniques for studying the development of values and morals was developed by Lawrence Kohlberg for his doctoral dissertation in 1958. Building on earlier work by Jean Piaget, Kohlberg showed how the growth of cognitive abilities made it possible for adolescents to reason about moral values in increasingly sophisticated ways. Higher stages of morality could emerge only after thought became more logical, structured, and personalized.

It is important to emphasize Kohlberg's commitment to the cognitive (paradigm); he was primarily concerned with the process of moral reasoning—how people decide what is moral and what is not. We begin with an overview of this influential cognitive approach before turning to the behavioral question of what people actually do.

Kohlberg's Stages of Moral Reasoning. For his PhD thesis Kohlberg asked boys between the ages of 10 and 16 to resolve nine moral dilemmas. Here is the most famous one:

In Europe, a woman was near death from a rare form of cancer. There was one drug that doctors thought might save her, a form of radium that a druggist in the same town had recently discovered. The druggist was charging $2,000, ten times what the drug cost him to make. The sick woman's husband, Heinz, went to everyone he knew to borrow the money, but he could only get together about half of what the drug cost. He told the druggist that his wife was dying and asked him to sell it cheaper or let him pay later. But the druggist said, "No." So Heinz got desperate and broke into the man's store to steal the drug for his wife.

Should the husband have done that? Why?

Kohlberg was not particularly interested in whether each subject thought the husband should steal the drug; he argued that judgment depends too much on a person's religious or ethical upbringing. Instead, he analyzed the way each boy came to a decision—what sorts of factors were involved in actually making a choice.

The results led Kohlberg to distinguish between three levels of moral reasoning, which the boys seemed to progress through as they grew older. Each level consisted of two separate stages, for a total of six stages in the development of moral reasoning (see Table 9.1).

At the lowest level, some boys were said to be at the **preconventional level** of moral reasoning—they accepted parents' or society's commands because they

TABLE 9.1
Kohlberg's Six Stages of Moral Reasoning

Orientation	*Characteristics*
Preconventional Level	
Stage 1	
Punishment and obedience orientation	Obeys rules to avoid punishment
Stage 2	
Marketplace orientation	Seeks rewards, or having favors returned
Conventional Level	
Stage 3	
Good-boy orientation	Conforms to avoid disapproval by others
Stage 4	
Law-and-order orientation	Conforms to avoid blame by legitimate authorities
Postconventional Level	
Stage 5	
Social contract, legalistic orientation	Obeys rules for approval by others concerned with the welfare of the community
Stage 6	
Universal ethical principle orientation	Acts on basis of own abstract ethical principles, freely chosen

wanted to gain rewards and avoid punishments. In other words, they simply responded to external rules. Most of the time, this type of reasoning was characteristic of children in Piaget's concrete-operational stage. For example, Kohlberg (1975) cites the response of one 10-year-old boy to Heinz's dilemma over the drug that could cure his wife:

> "Why shouldn't you steal from a store?"
>
> "It's not good to steal from the store. It's against the law. Someone could see you and call the police" (p. 36).

The preconventional level consisted of two separate stages. In the first, as seen in the quote, children simply try to avoid being punished for doing something bad. In the second, some notion of other people's needs enters the picture, but only at the most fundamental level of making a deal: "You scratch my back and I'll scratch yours." For example, a child might choose not to reveal another person's secret so that later on the other person will not reveal his.

Next comes the **conventional level** of moral reasoning at which a person accepts the standards of the family, society, or some other group. These conventional views are completely adopted as one's own. This type of reasoning can first appear in adolescence, with the emergence of Piaget's formal-operational thought. To illustrate this level, Kohlberg (1975) quoted the more sophisticated response to Heinz's dilemma of the same boy at the age of 17:

> "Why shouldn't you steal from a store?"
>
> "It's a matter of law. It's one of our rules that we are trying to help protect everyone, protect property, not just to protect the store. It's something that's needed in our society. If we didn't have these laws, people would steal, they wouldn't have to work for a living and our whole society would get out of kilter" (p. 36).

The first stage of the conventional level is often called the good-boy orientation, a stage of conformity to what most people expect of a good person. For the first time, judgments are based on people's intentions—whether they meant well. The second stage (reflected in the quote) is called the law-and-order orientation, because it involves an active support of society's laws and rules in the interest of maintaining social stability. Here, good intentions are not enough; rules must be obeyed because they provide the basis for an orderly society.

Finally, the highest level of moral reasoning is called the **postconventional level** because it involves the application of the universal principles of right and wrong, which are more fundamental than the laws of any specific society. At this more abstract level, each person must follow his own conscience, regardless of what society says. This type of reasoning becomes possible only in the advanced stages of formal-operational thought, and many adults never reach the postconventional level. As an example of this type of reasoning, Kohlberg (1975) quotes one more time from the same male subject, this time at the age of 24:

> "Why shouldn't someone steal from a store?"
>
> "It's violating another person's right, in this case to property."

"Does the law enter in?"

"Well, the law in most cases is based on what is morally right, so it's not a separate subject, it's a consideration."

"What does 'morality' or 'morally right' mean to you?"

"Recognizing the right of other individuals, first to life and then to do as he pleases as long as it doesn't interfere with somebody else's rights" (p. 36).

Here, too, there are two stages. In the first, what is right depends on a consensus reached by a society of people who may hold somewhat different values. Laws can change as society's idea of what is good changes. Finally, at the most advanced stage in Kohlberg's original scheme, judgments are based on abstract universal ethical principles such as the golden rule: Do unto others as you would have them do unto you.

Kohlberg argues that as a person grows, these six stages always appear in the same order. Not everyone goes through all six, but Kohlberg says that the stages always appear in the same order, no one will go through the postconventional level before the conventional, or the law-and-order stage before the good-boy stage. Studies of the growth of moral development among adolescents in other cultures, such as Mexico and Taiwan, are often cited to support the idea that this theory is not limited to the United States; the six stages are said to be universal.

Thus, Kohlberg believes that moral reasoning is linked to age; as a person grows, his increasing cognitive capabilities make it possible for him to take increasingly sophisticated moral stands. But the fact that someone is intelligent enough to understand ethical principles does not necessarily mean that he will apply them. It is what logicians call a necessary, but not sufficient, condition.

Kohlberg has found that most children under 9, some adolescents, and many adolescent and adult criminals have preconventional morality. Conventional morality is the most common stage for adolescents and adults; only a few achieve the highest level of postconventional morality.

Evaluating Kohlberg's Theory.   Many psychologists have challenged specific aspects of Kohlberg's theory and methods. Some have criticized Kohlberg's actual test of nine moral dilemmas; others have questioned whether every person really moves through these stages, one after another, in every culture.

On a more fundamental level, psychologists who prefer the behavioral paradigm (see Chapter 1) wonder about the links between moral reasoning and moral action. When Blasi (1980) reviewed studies relating moral reasoning to delinquency, honesty, altruism, resistance to conformity, and other types of moral behavior, he found that the relationships are often rather complex.

As any priest can tell you, the fact that a person knows that something is right does not necessarily mean that he will do it. In one study (Hassett, 1981), adults were asked to predict their behavior in a number of everyday ethical dilemmas, such as whether to return extra change to a grocery clerk. In many cases, people said that keeping the change would be wrong, but they would do it anyway. On a list of eight mundane ethical dilemmas of this sort (including driving away without leaving a note after scratching a parked car and buying a stolen color TV set), 2 out of 3 respondents predicted that in at least one case, they would act in a way that they themselves considered wrong. This finding and others suggest one important question for future studies of moral behavior: Under what conditions is a person most likely to choose a course of action he considers wrong?

Among researchers who prefer Kohlberg's cognitive approach, another question that is attracting increasing attention involves possible differences between male and female conceptions of morality. The original proposal of six stages of moral reasoning was based on a study of males. Later research found that when these criteria were applied to women's responses, most reflected a stage-three concern with approval by others. Carol Gilligan (1982) argues that while men may conceive of morality in terms of abstract ethical principles, women are more concerned with the immediate goal of not hurting the people around them. Women's judgments of morality are thus more closely tied to feelings of empathy and compassion for others than those of men.

Much remains to be learned about possible differences between male and female conceptions of morality. However, the simple fact that psychologists have begun to explore this question is a sign of progress toward more sophisticated theories of human behavior.

MALE-FEMALE DIFFERENCES

Psychologists are people who live and work in a specific society, and their research will almost inevitably reflect some of the current biases of their culture. In the 1960s and 1970s, many Americans became interested in "women's issues." In 1972, a new division of the American Psychological Association devoting itself exclusively to the psychology of women was formed. Many researchers began to examine issues that had long been ignored by this male-dominated profession. One of the most central was the "simple" question of the extent to which men and women differ and the causes of any sex differences.

Sexual Stereotypes. In our society, males and females have traditionally been thought to differ in a number of important ways. In one typical study of sexual stereotyping (Rosenkrantz, Vogel, Bee, Broverman, & Broverman, 1968), the average subject described men as more competent, skillful, assertive, and aggressive than women. As a group, women were seen as warmer and more emotionally expressive than men. One does not have to look far to find additional evidence for the existence of such stereotypes.

When a feminist group from New Jersey called Women on Words and Images analyzed 134 children's readers, they found that most of the fictional characters were male, whether the stories were about children, adults, or even animals. Boys were characterized as curious, clever, and adventurous; girls, as fearful and incompetent. The adult males portrayed in these books held 147 different jobs, ranging from astronauts and cowboys to clowns. The career options for females were more limited—only 26 different occupations, including such impractical choices as circus fat

Traditionally, boys and girls have been socialized to fulfill very different roles, as suggested in this photograph of a turn-of-the-century tea party.

lady and witch. An updated survey of books published after 1972 found some changes, but still an overwhelming male bias (Tavris & Offir, 1977).

Some psychologists claim that all this propaganda takes a heavy toll on female self-esteem. In one often-quoted study (Goldberg, 1968), college women were asked to rate short articles on their persuasive impact, profundity, professional competence, and other criteria. Some of the articles were consistently rated higher when these female students thought they had been written by men. In another study (Pheterson, Kiesler, & Goldberg, 1971), two groups of women judged the quality of several paintings. Some of the paintings were rated more highly when the artist was thought to be a male rather than a female.

The major lesson of these studies—that women often underrate the works of other females—has been widely publicized. Some of the more subtle feelings, however, have often been ignored. For example, paintings by male artists were rated more highly only when they were described as "attempts" or "entries"; paintings described as prize winners were equally valued whether the artist was said to be male or female.

Further, some later studies failed to replicate the original finding. When a group of students from the University of California at Berkeley were given a task similar to Goldberg's original procedure, women did not seem biased against other women (Isaacs, 1981). The author argued that this reflected the effects of women's liberation; in the few years between the two studies, the bias had been reduced. These complications serve as another reminder of the fact that complex beliefs and behav-

Changes in American society's perception of women's roles can be seen in the contrast between these advertisements from 1951 and 1977.

ior patterns are affected by culture, and findings from one time and place may or may not apply to another.

In any case, people's beliefs about differences between the sexes can affect their perceptions and behavior from the moment of birth, when the obstetrician announces "It's a boy" or "It's a girl." In one classic study (Rubin, Provenzano, & Luria, 1974), fathers were asked to describe their first babies almost immediately after they were born; mothers were asked the same questions within 24 hours of birth. Despite the fact that objective hospital records showed that the baby boys and girls in this study were almost identical in terms of color, muscle tone, reflex responses, and even weight and length, the parents described them differently. Baby girls were perceived as softer, finer-featured, smaller, and less attentive. The fathers were particularly susceptible to this type of selective perception and the tendency to describe sons and daughters differently. Other studies have shown that as children grow, fathers pressure their children to behave in "sex-appropriate" ways, such as encouraging boys to play with toy armies and girls to play with dollhouses (Maccoby, 1980).

No one knows whether these pressures will be reduced as society's expectations for little boys and little girls change. However, it is possible to draw some general conclusions about current differences between the sexes.

Maccoby and Jacklin's Summary.   In 1974, Eleanor Maccoby and Carol Jacklin published a careful review of over 2,000 studies of the differences between males and females. Many common sexual stereotypes turned out to be myths. For example, girls are not more sociable than boys, they are not more suggestible, and they do not have lower self-esteem. Maccoby and Jacklin did, however, find evidence that by adolescence clear differences have emerged between the sexes in four main areas— verbal ability, visual-spatial ability, mathematical ability, and aggressiveness.

Girls seem to mature more rapidly in terms of verbal skills. From the preschool years through early adolescence, the sexes seem equal in this respect. But beginning at around age 11 and continuing at least through high school girls become more verbal. They have larger vocabularies, are more fluent, and score higher in reading comprehension and creative writing.

In contrast, adolescent boys do better on visual-spatial tasks such as reading maps, solving mazes, and locating hidden geometric patterns. Similarly, greater male facility with mathematical problems also becomes established in adolescence. But since many mathematical problems involve verbal abilities, the relative standings of the sexes may vary for some types of problems.

Finally, cultural stereotypes about aggression have some basis in fact. Boys are more aggressive than girls, on the average, both physically and verbally. This difference has been observed in many cultures, and it appears much earlier in development than other sex differences. Greater male aggression can be observed in children as young as 2 or 2½. This male-female difference applies to indirect measures of aggression, such as mock fighting and fantasy, as well as direct measures. At least until their early twenties, men remain more aggressive than women; there is little data on older adults.

As you might expect, these conclusions generated a tremendous amount of controversy. One major question was whether such differences were caused by nature or nurture. (See Chapter 3 regarding the interaction of biology and environment and the difficulty of disentangling these factors.)

In the case of aggression, Maccoby and Jacklin (1974) argue that "the sex difference has a biological foundation" (p. 242). They were careful to note that there is clear evidence that aggression is affected by learning; nevertheless, they believed that males inherited a tendency to react more aggressively. They cited four separate lines of evidence for this belief: males are more aggressive than females in all known human societies; sex differences in aggression appear early in life; similar sex differences are found in apes and other primates; and higher levels of male sex hormones can induce aggression.

Each of these assertions was challenged in a review by Todd Tieger (1980) and subsequently defended again by Maccoby and Jacklin (1980). The details of these arguments and counterarguments quickly became rather involved, concerning both the quality of the original research and the various authors' interpretations. For example, Tieger summarized the results of 23 comparisons of male and female children between the ages of 2 and 6 and concluded that there is no consistent difference in the level of aggressiveness at this tender age (although he did concede that after the age of 6, males are more aggressive). Maccoby and Jacklin (1980) countered with a fuller tabulation of 38 experimental comparisons that led to the opposite conclusion—even among preschoolers, males are more aggressive than females.

For now, it seems safe to conclude only that there may be a biological foundation for male aggressiveness. This issue has tremendous theoretical significance, and it is likely to take considerable time and effort to resolve. In the meantime, most people are probably more concerned with a more fundamental question about male-female differences—so what? More concretely, are any differences between the sexes large enough to have an important impact on the way men and women will behave in our complex technological society?

The clearest answer comes from an analysis of the cognitive differences mentioned earlier—girls' greater verbal skills and boys' greater abilities in mathematics and visual-spatial tasks like map reading. When Janet Hyde (1981) reanalyzed 53 of the studies from Maccoby and Jacklin's original 1974 review, she found that while sex differences were quite consistent, they were also rather small. (In technical terms, they ranged from .24 to .52 standard deviations.)

In Chapter 12, we emphasize that the average performance of a particular group (such as women) does *not* apply to every individual. To cite one simple commonsense example, men are taller than women but many women are taller than some men. Similarly, sex differences in aggression and certain cognitive abilities are quite consistent on the average, but there are many individual exceptions.

After noting how small the average sex differences were, Janet Hyde was particularly concerned with the possibility of misinterpretation. For example, a guidance counselor would be very wrong if he concluded that young girls should not try to become engineers or computer programmers because females lack mathematical ability. This fear led Hyde to wonder whether such differences should even be mentioned in introductory textbooks. "At the very least," she cautioned, it is "important to stress how small the differences are and how unwise it would be to apply them in counseling a given individual" (1981, p. 897).

Adulthood

If the self-appointed experts are to be believed, American society worships youth. But it is only in adulthood that most people become fully productive and achieve their career goals. Adulthood can bring a new perspective on life, as a middle-aged woman noted:

> It is as if I'm looking at a three-way mirror. In one mirror I see part of myself in my mother who is growing old, and part of her in me. In the other mirror, I see part of myself in my daughter. I have had some dramatic insights, just from looking in those mirrors. . . . It is a set of revelations that I suppose can only come when you are in the middle of three generations (Neugarten, 1975, p. 383).

Social scientists are just beginning to collect data on the perspective provided by adulthood and the many other issues in adult development, from family life and relationships to work, leisure, and retirement. In this introduction, we focus on three of the most promising lines of research: stages of adult development, personality mechanisms associated with healthy adjustment, and sexuality.

STAGES OF ADULT PERSONALITY DEVELOPMENT

One of the most careful and systematic studies of life changes in adulthood began when Daniel Levinson (1978) and his colleagues at Yale interviewed four groups of men between the ages of 35 and 45, carefully chosen to represent a range of American lifestyles—10 hourly workers in industry, 10 business executives, 10 university biologists, and 10 novelists. For example, to secure a representative group of executives, Levinson first considered all major companies located within a 50-mile radius of New Haven, Connecticut, where the research was conducted. They chose two different companies—one an old and established manufacturer and the other a rapidly growing technology specialist—secured a list of all managers, and chose 10 for maximum diversity. All 10 agreed to take part. (Compare this careful procedure to that for the best-seller *Passages*, as described in "Becoming a Critical Consumer.")

The major data involved 10 to 20 hours of detailed biographical interviews with each man. The interviews were spread out over several months and included stand-

BECOMING A CRITICAL CONSUMER

Passages

In the influential best-seller *Passages*, journalist Gail Sheehey (1976) described a series of "predictable crises" that American adults face as they grow from the "trying twenties" to the "deadline decade." These stages of adult development were identified primarily on the basis of Sheehey's interviews of 115 people between the ages of 18 and 55. As you read the following paragraphs from Sheehey's account of her sample and method, decide whether it seems reasonable to conclude that the general trends she described actually apply to most middle-class Americans. A discussion of this issue of generalizability appears after the chapter summary.

The people I chose to study belong to America's "pacesetter group"—healthy motivated people who either began in or have entered the middle class. . . . The men include lawyers, doctors, chief executives and middle managers, ministers, professors, politicians, and students, as well as men in the arts, the media, the sciences, and those who run their own small business. I sought out top-achieving women as well and also followed the steps of many traditional nurturing women

. . .

Although many of my respondents were raised in small towns, the urban centers to which they have gravitated include New York, Los Angeles, Washington, San Francisco, Chicago, Detroit, Boston, New Haven and Dayton, Ohio (p. 20–21).

ard psychological tests like the Thematic Apperception Test, in which the men were asked to make up stories about ambiguous pictures (see Chapter 10). In addition, whenever possible, researchers interviewed the men's wives, studied the companies for which they worked, and conducted follow-up interviews two years later.

Levinson was surprised to find that all the men seemed to face very similar problems at specific ages. Of course, they did not discover that every man faced precisely the same crisis the day he turned 39. But every man did seem to go through the same stages, in the same order, and within a surprisingly narrow age range.

Figure 9.2 illustrates Levinson's scheme of adult development. Note that he distinguished among four major periods: childhood and adolescence, from birth to age 17; early adulthood, roughly ages 17 to 40; middle adulthood, ages 40 to 60; and late adulthood, beginning at 60. The clear boundaries between the three adult phases were quite a surprise to these researchers. They were also impressed with the orderly progression between reasonably stable periods of life, in which people

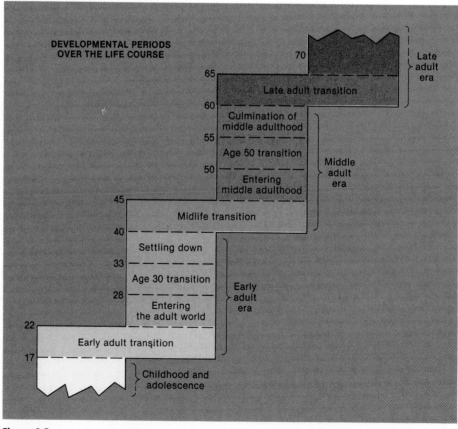

Figure 9.2
Daniel Levinson's model of male development divides the life cycle into four major periods which are separated by stressful periods of transition.

worked toward clear goals, and the emotional turmoil of the period of transition between stages.

The first major period of early adulthood extends roughly from ages 22 to 28, a stage Levinson called "entering the adult world." In this phase, the novice adult must explore all the possibilities open to him and begin to put down roots, establishing a stable life structure. During the "age thirty transition," life decisions seem less tentative and more serious. Suddenly, the person feels that he is playing for keeps. This is a period of fine-tuning to meet the goals of adulthood; it is likely to be far less stressful than the transition at the beginning (age 17) or end (age 40) of early adulthood. In the later thirties, men begin "settling down," working toward the goals they established in early years. They strive to develop competence in their chosen field and work to build a better life. The novice period of adulthood ends as each man begins to find his own place in society.

The relative security of these years is threatened during the midlife transition at ages 40 to 45. For about 80% of the men Levinson studied, the **midlife crisis** was a tumultuous period of severe stress, a time of new doubts and new decisions. For example, before the age of 40, the 10 novelists were simply concerned with establishing themselves as professional authors. In the midlife transition, those who had failed were forced to admit that they probably would never make it. Now, in middle age, they saw themselves as failures who had to begin over again.

But even the larger group who had succeeded felt that they had not accomplished enough; thus, the business executives who got the promotions they had been working for discovered that their success was flawed. They were forced to face realistically a future in which they would never serve as chairman of the board for General Motors or IBM. Successful biologists wondered about a future that did not include a Nobel Prize; and successful laborers realized that they would probably be trapped in their current jobs as long as they worked.

At the end of this period of intense questioning and self-doubt, most men entered middle adulthood around the age of 45 with a new sense of finality. For better or worse, their lives had taken shape. In some cases, this meant they had made peace with their marriages and occupations and were able to enjoy what they had to the fullest. Not everyone was this fortunate, however, and for others, middle adulthood was a period of decline.

Figure 9.2 describes other stages leading through late adulthood, but because Levinson studied men in their thirties and forties, his theory becomes much less detailed and much more speculative at this point. Also, it is important to remember that Levinson studied only men. He explained in his book that he had the resources to study only 40 people and "despite my strong desire to include women, I finally decided against it. A study of 20 men and 20 women would do justice to neither group" (1978, p. 9). Similar studies of female life cycles are now under way and may be published by the time you read this book.

SUCCESSFUL ADJUSTMENT

Other researchers have investigated American adulthood without outlining clearly defined stages of this sort. For example, after noting that medical and psychiatric

Figure 9.3
President John F. Kennedy was probably one of the subjects who was tested over several decades in the Grant Study.

research almost always focused on disease, philanthropist William T. Grant established a fund in 1937 for a "systematic inquiry into the kinds of people who are well and do well". The Grant study began by choosing 268 undergraduates from the Harvard classes of 1939 through 1944 on the basis of their superior physical and mental health. The latest major report on the Grant study, George Vaillant's 1977 book, *Adaptation to Life,* reports how 95 of these men have fared through the years.

Now in their sixties, the subjects included best-selling novelists, recognized scholars, and successful executives, physicians, teachers, and judges. One of the original subjects was described as "a man destined to play a role in every child's history book . . . pointlessly murdered before he reached his prime" (p. 366); at least one reviewer concluded from this remark that one subject in Grant's study was John F. Kennedy, a member of the Harvard class of 1940 (Muson, 1977). This was hardly a representative sample of the American population—but it was never meant to be one. The intent of the Grant study was reflected in the subtitle of Vaillant's book: *How the Best and the Brightest Came of Age.*

While they were still in college, the men took part in about 20 hours of psychiatric interviews, medical examinations, and psychological tests. At this time, one investigator traveled around the country to interview all their parents about family histories and early experiences. After graduation, the men regularly filled out questionnaires, at first every year and later every other year. Around 1950 and again around 1970, many of the men were interviewed once more. All told, the investigators had several hundred pages of information about each man's medical and psychiatric history as it developed over 30 years.

One key set of findings related physical and mental health to the way each man characteristically coped with conflict and stress. The Grant study was strongly influenced by Freud's psychoanalytic perspective, and Vaillant was particularly interested in the long-term effects of using different types of **defense mechanisms** to defend the ego from excessive anxiety by unconsciously denying, distorting, or falsifying reality (see Chapter 11).

Vaillant classified some defense mechanisms as immature. Although they are normal up to about the age of 15, in adults they are a sign of inadequate adjustment. One immature defense mechanism was *passive-aggressive behavior*, expressing anger and hostility indirectly or ineffectively. For example, one man in the Grant study had a chronic history of lateness and procrastination; when something annoyed him, he simply put it off. He was separated from his wife for many years, but he never divorced her and would not admit overt conflict. He dealt with his hostility passively, by not doing anything.

In contrast, suppression was classified as a mature defense mechanism, a healthy way for an adult to deal with stress. *Suppression* involves a conscious decision to postpone attention to sources of conflict. For example, in World War II one subject in the Grant study became so angry at his superior officer that he wanted to hit him. He forced himself to think of other things and later discussed his anger with another officer. In another example, just before getting married, this man was so anxious that he refused to answer a questionnaire item about marriage; later on, at a more relaxed time, he was willing to discuss this anxiety.

Vaillant identified six major defense mechanisms that he classified as mature and another six that were immature. He then collected about 20 short descriptions of key conflicts in each subject's life and how the person dealt with them. In most cases, two mental health workers independently used these descriptions to rate the characteristic defense mechanisms of each subject without any other knowledge of the man. Vaillant then went on to compare 25 men who used mostly mature defense mechanisms with 31 whose responses were characteristically immature. As you can see in Table 9.2, men who characteristically responded to stress in a mature way

TABLE 9.2
Comparisons of Grant Study Subjects Who Used
Mature or Immature Defense Mechanisms

	Percent Mature *(N = 25)*	*Percent Immature* *(N = 31)*
"Happiness" (top third)	68	16
Income over $20,000 per year	88	48
Job meets ambition for self	92	58
Active public service outside job	56	29
Rich friendship pattern	64	6
Marriage in least harmonious quartile or divorced	28	61
Ever diagnosed mentally ill	0	55
Emotional problems in childhood	20	45
Recent health poor by objective exam	0	36
Subjective health consistently judged "excellent" since college	68	48

Source: Vaillant, 1977, p. 87

Alfred Kinsey interviewing one of the subjects of his famous survey of sexual behavior.

were more successful in their careers, had more satisfying friendships and marriages, were physically sick less often, and seemed better adjusted psychologically. Mature defense mechanisms seemed to help people do well in life.

The Grant study went on to dig deeper into these men's histories to find the causes and correlates of adjustment. As these men continue to develop into old age and finally die, this landmark longitudinal study will continue to provide clues to complex processes of being a success in twentieth-century America.

SEXUAL ACTIVITY AND THE LIFE CYCLE

While the Levinson and Vaillant studies focused directly on the adult years, many of the important issues of adult life—such as family, work patterns, and sexuality—involve continuing themes that extend through the entire life cycle. Instead of separating adolescent from adult sexuality, in this section we provide an overview of lifelong patterns of sexual behavior.

Although there have been a number of excellent studies of the physiology of human sexual response and of sexual problems (Masters & Johnson, 1970), at this time there is no fully accurate source of data on sexual behavior. The major surveys to date are discussed in "How Do They Know?". As explained there, although sexual behavior has changed dramatically in the United States in recent decades, some of the most important insights into this subject come from a series of surveys that began nearly half a century ago at the University of Indiana under the direction of Alfred Kinsey.

Perhaps the most important lesson of the Kinsey surveys was the tremendous variability of human sexual response. As we shall see, average figures do show that sexual activity is related to age. But these average figures must always be considered in the perspective of wide individual differences. One of Kinsey's co-workers (Pomeroy, 1972) summarized the problem this way: "The smallest person in our society . . . might be 25 inches high, and the tallest 8 feet, or a variation of one to 10 . . . This is the normal kind of range. But in sex behavior . . . the range can be one to 10,000. People have difficulty understanding this fact. For example, roughly 10% of women never have orgasm, but it is possible for a woman to have 50 to 75 orgasms in 20 minutes. The range is tremendous" (p. 467).

Men, too, show tremendous variability. One middle-aged man in the Kinsey sample claimed to have had only one orgasm in his life; another reported averaging 30 orgasms per week over the last 30 years. Both men were in good physical health and seemed perfectly normal in every respect. Thus, the averages presented here do not apply to every person and should not be seen as standards for normal activity. And if you assume that all other people have sexual needs and desires similar to your own, you are wrong. The sexual differences between people are much more impressive than the similarities.

With those reservations firmly in mind, it is interesting to note that Kinsey found that sex was differentially related to age for males and females. As Figure 9.4 indicates, sexual activity for men peaks in adolescence and early adulthood and then begins a gradual decline. Women show a different pattern of sexual activity, increasing gradually from puberty to about the age of 30, then maintaining this peak for a full decade while male rates are declining. Although sexual activity does decline

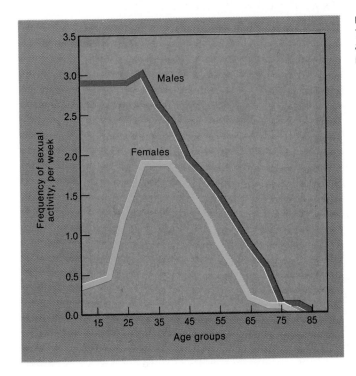

Figure 9.4
The relationship between age and sexual activity. Note that male activity peaks earlier in life, and declines more rapidly.

through later adulthood on the average for both sexes, some individuals maintain vigorous sex lives through old age. In general, people who are sexually active early in life maintain this pattern of activity as they grow older. To gain more insight into the nature and course of human sexuality, let us consider age trends for several specific forms of activity.

HOW DO THEY KNOW?

Surveys of Sexual Behavior

Surveys gather information about the attitudes and behaviors of a specific population by asking people questions. Because it is impractical to ask every person in a large group (such as United States voters) to answer questionnaires, survey results are ordinarily based on a smaller group called a **sample.**

Many people think that larger samples lead to more accurate survey results. That is not necessarily true. For example, in the early days of public opinion polling, *Literary Digest* magazine polled voters about the 1936 presidential election by sending 10 million postcards to people listed in telephone directories and auto registration lists. Over 2 million people replied, and overwhelmingly they picked Alf Landon as the next president of the United States.

They were wrong. In the middle of the Depression, people with phones and cars were far wealthier than the average person and were likely to vote Republican. Their opinions did not reflect those of the majority of American voters—who elected Franklin D. Roosevelt by a landslide.

This outcome was correctly predicted by a novice pollster named George Gallup, who had surveyed a mere 312,551 people. The reason this smaller group provided more accurate results was that Gallup had carefully chosen a

stratified random sample in which subjects were chosen in proportion to their frequency in the general population. (Advances in sampling techniques have substantially reduced the same size required for accurate results; many national surveys now test fewer than 2,000 people.)

Sexual behavior and attitudes may be one of the most difficult topics to do a survey on, because this information is so personal and so private. Ironically, the best information we have comes from a survey that was concluded more than three decades ago.

The Kinsey Report was the popular name for a series of studies published by Alfred C. Kinsey and his associates at Indiana University's Institute for Sexual Research (Kinsey, Pomeroy, & Martin, 1948; Kinsey, Pomeroy, Martin & Gebhard, 1953). Starting in 1938, some 18,000 volunteers were recruited and questioned about their sexual behavior. Each interview lasted several hours and included up to 521 standard questions covering everything from a person's socioeconomic background to his or her sexual experiences alone, with others of both sexes, and even with lower animals.

An elaborate code was used to protect people's confidentiality, and the nine project interviewers were trained never to seem shocked or to express value judgments. For example, they

Masturbation. For many people, the first sexual activity consists of self-stimulation. Ordinarily, deliberate masturbation does not become common until the early teens. Here, Kinsey and his colleagues found some fascinating differences between the sexes. Some 92% of all men and 58% of all women had masturbated to orgasm at some time in their lives. As for other forms of sexual activity, male and female age

did not ask if people had ever engaged in a particular activity; they asked when such activity first began. One measure of their success in establishing the right tone is the fact that fewer than 10 of the 18,000 people who allowed themselves to be interviewed by this group refused to give a complete sexual history (Pomeroy, 1972).

There are a number of obvious problems with the Kinsey data. The sample did not accurately reflect the American population, and ultimately it relied on the reports of volunteers, who might well differ from people who refused to cooperate. But as one text stated, "Unfortunately . . . there is no better information available" (Katchadourian & Lunde, 1975, p. 180).

According to the same text, the next best survey of sexual behavior was one sponsored by the Playboy Foundation in the early 1970s (Hunt, 1974). This survey was based on questionnaires completed in private by a representative sample of 2,026 people who were chosen on the basis of age, education, race, marital status, and other characteristics to match the United States population as a whole. Unfortunately, only 1 out of every 5 people who were originally contacted agreed to participate. This heavy reliance on volunteers and the fact that published reports omitted many important details about procedures makes the quality of this sample a distant second to the Kinsey reports.

More reliable information is available for some more limited questions about sexual behavior. For example, Kanter and Zelnick

(1972) studied a representative sample of 15- to 19-year-old women living in the continental United States; 91% of these respondents (versus 20% in the Playboy survey) agreed to be interviewed. This study provided excellent information, but only on the topic of heterosexual intercourse among adolescent females.

At the other end of the continuum, some widely publicized sex surveys are virtually impossible to generalize to any larger group. For example, for *The Hite Report,* writer Shere Hite (1976) distributed 100,000 questionnaires through such sources as chapters of the National Organization for Women, abortion rights groups, and university women's centers. Advertisements were placed in *The Village Voice* and *Mademoiselle, Brides,* and *Ms.* magazines; *Oui* magazine printed the questionnaire in its entirety. Only 3,019 questionnaires were returned, each with essay answers to 50 questions such as "Do you think sex is in any way political?" and "How do you masturbate? Please give a detailed description. . . . " While the detailed revelations this book contained were entertaining enough to make it a bestseller, you don't need a PhD in methodology to suspect that the Hite survey results do not apply to the United States population as a whole.

A survey's results are only as good as the sample it is based on. Applying the strictest criteria, no adequate survey of human sexual behavior has yet been published.

trends were different. Almost every man who would ever masturbate in his life had done so by the time he reached the age of 20; by this age only 1 out of 3 females had ever masturbated. According to more recent data (Hunt, 1974), both boys and girls now begin masturbating at an earlier age than they did in Kinsey's day.

As with other forms of sexual behavior, the variability of masturbation was far more impressive than any general population of trends. Some men never masturbated or did so only once or twice in their entire lives; others averaged two or three orgasms every day over a period of many years.

Heterosexual Intercourse. One of the most dramatic changes resulting from the "sexual revolution" of the last few decades had been the increase in the frequency of premarital sexual intercourse. However, even in his interviews in the 1930s and 1940s, Kinsey found that half the women in his sample were not virgins when they married. The figures for men were highly dependent on education and social class. Virtually all the men (98%) who quit school before the eighth grade had tried premarital sex; the figure for college-educated men was much lower (68%). Kinsey's data also suggested that even several decades ago America was gradually becoming more permissive about women having sex before marriage.

Some of the most reliable information about more recent rates of premarital sex comes from a series of national surveys of teenage American women (Zelnick & Kanter, 1980). Table 9.3 presents a summary of their findings for the age at which unmarried women first experienced premarital sex in surveys they conducted in 1971, 1976, and 1979. Even over this short period, the changes were obvious—in each survey year, more women were experiencing premarital intercourse at younger ages. The changes are even more dramatic when compared with the data collected by Kinsey in the 1940s. According to Kinsey and his colleagues (1953), 20% of white American females had had premarital sex by the age of 20 (Kinsey collected little information on blacks). In 1979, the comparable figure for unmarried white 19-year-olds was 65%.

Virtually all sex surveys have supported the idea that premarital sex has become more and more common in recent years, particularly for women. However, early experiences with sex are still troublesome for some. More than 1 out of 3 young

TABLE 9.3
Percentage of Unmarried Women in the United States Who Have Had Premarital Sexual Intercourse

By the age of	1971	1976	1979
15	14%	19%	23%
16	21	29	38
17	26	43	49
18	40	51	57
19	46	60	69

Source: Zelnick & Kanter, 1980

The formal pose of this couple suggests the more reserved approach to affection and sexuality that was considered proper a century ago.

males and 2 out of 3 young females in the Hunt survey (1974) felt regret and worry over premarital sex. Problems ranged from sexual inadequacy to fears of venereal disease and pregnancy. There is also evidence that many people feel rushed into sex before they are ready for it and continue to experience moral and emotional conflicts.

Regarding marital sex, it was no surprise that the Kinsey surveys found that virtually every married couple had tried sex at least once. But when husbands and wives were asked independently how often they had sex, women consistently gave higher estimates. Kinsey et al (1953) believed that some women objected to frequent intercourse and therefore overestimated its rate, while many men wanted to have more sex and therefore underestimated its rate (p. 349).

The frequency of intercourse decreases as a married couple gets older. According to Kinsey, the youngest group (16 to 25 years old) had sex about $2\frac{1}{2}$ times each week (median frequency); by the age of 60, this had declined to once every 12 days. More recent data from Hunt's 1974 survey suggest that married people are now having sex more often and are experimenting more. Married couples in the 1970s were more likely to try different sexual positions and more likely to have oral sex than the couples questioned by Kinsey in the 1940s.

Despite such liberating trends, many young adults still have unrealistic ideas about the effects of aging on sexual activity. According to one survey at a midwestern university, most college students believe that their parents have intercourse no more than once a month, never have oral sex, and never had sex before they were married. About 1 out of every 4 students believed that if their parents had sex at all during the last year, it happened only once. In fact, some students were offended by the very idea of a questionnaire on parental sexuality. One wrote, "Whoever thinks about their parents' sexual relations, except perverts?" (Pocs, Godow, Tolone, & Walsh, p. 54). No one knows whether these students would be willing to admit that other people's parents have sex after 40. But even the outdated Kinsey figures make it clear that college students have some quaint ideas about their parents' sexual habits.

These students might be even more upset to learn of their parents' infidelities. According to Kinsey, by the age of 40, half of all husbands and 1 out of 4 wives had had at least one extramarital affair. The Hunt survey of sex in the early 1970s found about the same rate of infidelity for men as Kinsey had but noted that married women were gradually catching up in the infidelity department—their rate, too, now seems to be gradually approaching 50%.

Homosexuality. In 1951, Clellan Ford and Frank Beach conducted a worldwide survey of sexual practices in primitive societies that had been studied by anthropologists. Information on homosexuality was available for 76 studies; in 26 of these, adult homosexuality was "totally absent, rare, or carried on only in secrecy" (p. 129). But in the majority of cases, homosexual activities were socially acceptable for some members of the community. Sometimes, puberty rites included homosexual activity; in other cases, specific males who were believed to have magical powers were raised to live as women. Still other societies considered homosexuality a normal form of activity for unmarried men and young boys. (Anthropological reports provided little information about female homosexuality.)

One of the most sensitive, controversial areas in the original Kinsey survey was homosexuality. Perhaps the most widely disbelieved figure in the Kinsey volumes was the report that 37% of all American males had had at least one homosexual orgasm by the age of 45. But the data showed that not all these men were equally homosexual; some had had exactly one experience with another man and a lifelong pattern of lovemaking with women, while others were exclusively involved with other males.

As with masturbation, premarital sex, and extramarital sex, the proportion of women involved in homosexual activity was much lower. Only 13% had had a homosexual orgasm by age 45 (versus 37% of the men). About three to four times as many men as women were exclusively homosexual; the best guess currently puts these figures at 2% to 4% for American males and 0.5% to 1% for American females. Similar proportions of homosexuals have been found in surveys of other countries such as Germany and Sweden (Katchadourian & Lunde, 1975).

As one might expect, there is considerable controversy over the developmental forces that cause homosexuality. Some of the most recent and best evidence comes from an elaborate study of 979 male and female homosexuals who lived in the San Francisco Bay area in 1969 and 1970 (Bell, Weinberg, & Hammersmith, 1981). While earlier studies of homosexuality often concentrated on individuals who sought psychiatric help, this sample was recruited through the gay community and was carefully chosen to include representative proportions of people according to age, race, education, and so on.

Each person was interviewed about his or her childhood, adolescence, and sexual history for three to five hours. The homosexuals' responses were compared with the answers given by a control group of 477 heterosexuals to the same questions. The results revealed the fallacy of several widely accepted myths.

For example, many people believe that lesbians turn to other women because of disappointing or traumatic early experiences with men. In fact, there were few differences between the early heterosexual histories of lesbians and other women. Similarly, Freud's notion that male homosexuality is caused by a dominating mother and a weak or detached father had little basis in fact.

What they did find was that homosexuals reported a lifelong pattern of gender nonconformity. At least for exclusive homosexuals (as opposed to bisexuals), there were signs of nonconformity long before puberty—little boys who had little interest in masculine activities like baseball and little girls who were tomboys. Of course, many tomboys and males who hate baseball grow up to be heterosexual. But these early signs sometimes indicate an unwillingness or inability to accept traditional sex roles. These authors suspect that the roots of exclusive homosexuality lie in biological factors present as early as birth.

This is sure to be a controversial view, particularly since it is inferred from the reports of adults rather than direct observation of children or actual biological differences. As pointed out in Chapter 6, human memory often reconstructs the past to fit certain beliefs or schemas; whether these subjects were distorting the memories of childhood remains to be seen. But one thing is sure—before the issue is settled there will be many more studies of the way each person comes to choose a sexual path.

Old Age

In 1900, only 4% of the population of the United States was 65 years old or older; currently this proportion is over 10%. One reason that our society seems to be growing older is the dramatic increase in **life expectancy,** the number of years the average person lives. In 1900, life expectancy was about 47 years; by 1971, this figure had increased to 71 years.

However, these average figures are quite deceiving. In 1900, a far larger proportion of the population died in infancy and childhood, thus substantially lowering the average of death. The life expectancy of people who survived into adulthood has not changed very much in this century. In 1900, a 65-year-old could expect, on the average, to live to the age of 77; in 1971, the average 65-year-old would survive to 80. Thus, the life span of adults has been surprisingly constant; what has changed in the last 100 years is the proportion of the population that has survived into old age.

As the proportion of elderly people in our society continues to grow, developmental psychologists are likely to focus increasingly on their special abilities and problems. The scientific study of the elderly is called **gerontology** (from the Greek root *geron,* meaning "old man").

A PERIOD OF COGNITIVE DECLINE?

One problem that has fascinated gerontologists involves the common belief that old age is a time of decreasing physical and mental abilities. Folklore has it that as each of us grows older, we can expect to get gradually dumber. But systematic tests of cognitive decline in adulthood have revealed just how complex the relationships between age and abilities can be.

The first studies of this topic were quite consistent. When large groups of people took the Wechsler Adult Intelligence Scale and other IQ tests (see Chapter 12), older groups almost invariably made more mistakes, on the average. Depending on the precise nature of the specific IQ test this intellectual decline might begin as early as age 35. In any case, pronounced drops in test scores were observed in the sixties and beyond.

Beginning in the 1950s, however, K. Warner Schaie and his colleagues began to question this view. They pointed out that virtually all the studies showing IQ decline used the **cross-sectional method**—they compared groups of different ages at one point in time. Schaie believed that longitudinal studies tracing the progress of specific individuals over many years (see "How Do They Know?" page 306) might reveal a different pattern.

In 1956, Schaie began a major study of IQ change that combined elements of the longitudinal and cross-sectional approaches. He administered an IQ test called the Primary Mental Abilities Test to 500 adults ranging in age from 20 to 70. Analysis of these cross-sectional results yielded the typical pattern of apparent declines of intelligence scores beginning around middle age. But Schaie proceeded to follow these 500 people through adulthood. In 1963, 7 years after his first study, he was able to retest 302 of the original group. In 1970, 14 years after the original test, he measured IQ in 161 of the original subjects. (We shall see later that this gradual reduction in sample size created certain problems for interpretation of the results.)

Analysis of the longitudinal data from the 7-year and 14-year follow-ups yielded a different picture. The individuals who were tested several times showed much smaller and more gradual changes. Many intellectual abilities did not decline at all before the age of 60, and subsequent decreases were quite minor. Figure 9.5 illustrates the results for tests of verbal meaning, the ability to understand ideas expressed in words.

Schaie explains this contradiction by pointing to the importance of differences between **cohorts,** groups of people who were born at roughly the same time. For example, the youngest cohorts were 20 to 25 years old in 1956, when Schaie's study began. They were born during the Great Depression and were children during World War II. The oldest cohorts in Schaie's study were 64 to 70 in 1956, born near the end of the nineteenth century. Compared to the younger subjects, they probably received less education and less adequate medical care in childhood and grew up in larger families and in more rural areas. These social and cultural differences, along with other factors, seemed to affect scores on certain tests. And these differences between cohorts were enough to bias the results of cross-sectional studies.

This does not mean that cross-sectional studies have no place in developmental

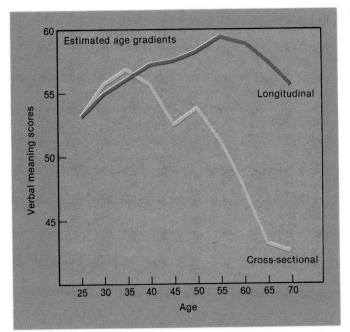

Figure 9.5
The relationship between age and test scores of the ability to understand verbally expressed ideas. Cross-sectional studies seemed to show that this ability declined rapidly beginning as early as age 35. But longitudinal studies which followed individuals through life suggest that the decline is far smaller, and only begins around the age of 55.

psychology. As pointed out earlier, longitudinal studies are costly and take a long time to complete. For other types of behavior, cohort differences may be less dramatic and less likely to bias cross-sectional studies. And longitudinal studies have methodological problems of their own. Botwinick (1979), for example, has called attention to the problem of decreasing sample size in the study by Schaie and Labouvie-Vief (1974). As you may remember, Schaie started out with 500 subjects but 14 years later could find only 161 of them. Several studies have shown that people who do poorly on IQ tests are less likely to be available for follow-up studies. One reason that this is so is a phenomenon called **terminal drop.** IQ tends to decline in the five years or so preceding death, perhaps as a result of a general decline in health and physical abilities. People who are ill thus may show greater IQ decline; when they fail to reappear for follow-up studies, the average for the remaining healthy group may be misleading (Riegel & Riegel, 1972).

The overall conclusion is a familiar one for psychologists. The study of behavior poses many hard questions and few easy answers. The best answers are likely to emerge from converging data from several different sources. In this context, cross-sectional studies probably overestimate declines in cognitive function in old age, while longitudinal studies may underestimate these changes. Botwinick (1979) concludes that for such cognitive skills as verbal abilities, the decline with age is probably small and does not begin before the age of 50 or 60. Other intellectual skills, particularly those that require fast responses on nonverbal problems (such as timed IQ tests in which people are asked to arrange several pictures to form a coherent story) decline earlier in life and more rapidly.

IMPROVING THE QUALITY OF LIFE

Some gerontologists are now becoming less concerned with cataloging the effects of the aging process and more concerned with how our society can best deal with the problems of senior citizens. Some have found evidence that our society may actually be causing some of these problems. Judith Rodin and Ellen Langer (1977) studied 91 residents of nursing homes between the ages of 65 and 90. One group was given special instructions designed to increase personal responsibility for caring for themselves and increasing the quality of life in the nursing home. In short, they were encouraged to take active control of their lives. For example, as part of the study each elderly person in this group was given a present of a plant, which they chose for themselves and which they agreed to take care of. A control group consisted of elderly patients who were allowed to conform to the nursing-home routine in the more traditional, passive way. For example, these patients were told that the staff would take care of their plants.

The experimental group that was encouraged to seize control of their own lives later scored dramatically higher than the passive group on tests of alertness, active participation, and general well-being. These positive effects persisted even 18 months later; nurses rated the experimental group as happier, more vigorous, and more sociable. Amazingly, the experimental group even had a lower death rate than the traditionally passive patients. The authors explained the importance of this sense of personal control in terms of the link between depression and learned helplessness (see Chapter 13).

While some researchers seek new ways to increase the quality of life in old age, others are exploring a much more difficult problem—promoting a realistic acceptance of the inevitability of death.

DEATH AND DYING

In the fall of 1965, four students from the Chicago Theological Seminary approached psychiatrist Elisabeth Kübler-Ross for help on a research project on dying. As Kübler-Ross later described this meeting (1969): "We . . . decided that the best possible way we could study death was by asking terminally ill patients to be our teachers" (p. 22). But when she approached other doctors in the hospitals in which she worked, the reactions varied from stunned disbelief to avoidance. No one wanted to admit that some patients were dying; death was a taboo topic in the world of medicine.

When Kübler-Ross finally found volunteers, however, they were eager to talk about their feelings. In 1969, she published the book *On Death and Dying*, summarizing some of her interviews with over 200 dying patients. Kübler-Ross was not the first to do research on this topic; her own bibliography listed over 180 professional books and articles relevant to this research. But this psychiatrist's sensitive writing on what people felt as they approached death became a best-seller and helped to break down some of the traditional taboos.

Kübler-Ross believed that people who learned that they were dying go through predictable emotional reactions that can be broken down into five stages. The first is *denial*—the patient simply refuses to believe that she is dying. In one extreme case, a 28-year-old woman who "fell apart" when she learned that she was dying from a liver disease began to feel better when a neighbor told her that there was always hope and urged her to visit a local faith healer. The visit was a "success," and the woman proclaimed herself cured. She stopped following the diet that she needed to stay alive, because she insisted that she was well. She soon needed to be hospitalized. She remained a difficult patient, often refusing to eat properly or take her medication. It was only after several weeks of treatment that she began to accept the reality of her condition and to prepare herself for death.

According to Kübler-Ross, most patients pass from denial to a second stage of *anger*, rage, envy, and resentment in which they ask over and over again, "Why me?" At this stage, patients often alienate family, friends, and the hospital staff. Doctors are criticized for the diets and drugs they prescribe. When a nurse straightens the bed, she is criticized for never leaving the patient alone; when she leaves, the patient is likely to call her back to arrange the bed more comfortably. An innocent TV commercial showing healthy young people having a good time can send the patient into a rage because it reminds him how painful even the simplest movements have become. He snaps at his family and sooner or later they snap back, increasing his anger still further.

As the rage begins to wear itself out, the dying person moves into a third stage of trying to *bargain* with God or fate. The question shifts from "Why me?" to "Why now?" Dying patients react like children who believe that they can get whatever they want for Christmas as long as they remain on their best behavior. Some patients promise their organs to science if the doctor can keep them alive just a little longer; others offer God a life of dedication to His work if only He will let them live. But this self-delusion usually does not last long, and the patient soon moves into a fourth stage of *depression*.

At first, the depression may revolve around mundane matters, such as how to take care of one's children or how to pay for a lengthy hospital stay. Relatives and friends usually react to such worries by urging the patients to look at the brighter side—the children have many happy years left, and sooner or later bills will be paid. This is followed by mourning, in which a person prepares for death by letting go of his attachment to life. For example, one man regretted the fact that he was always away from home trying to make a living when his daughter was young. Now it was too late to spend time with her—she was fully grown and had her own friends and her own life. When people go through this stage of grieving for all the dreams that were never fulfilled and all the hopes that will never be met, the best help others can offer may be just to sit silently with the loved one, letting him detach himself from life.

In the fifth and final stage before death, many patients come to *accept* their fate. The patient who does not die suddenly has time to work through the progression of emotions, from denial to anger to hope to depression. Now, as life draws to a close, she seems too tired for further upset. Void of emotion, and withdrawn from those around her, she seems to accept the inevitable withdrawal that death will bring.

Kübler-Ross's scheme is intuitively appealing and seems to correspond to many

Figure 9.6

In this hospice, a woman who is dying spends her final days visiting with family members in a pleasant environment.

people's experiences. But researchers have remained skeptical about this well-known theory. It is difficult to prove or disprove; so many feelings and behaviors are subject to interpretation. Almost everyone who is confined in a hospital will sometimes become angry or depressed. Kübler-Ross never specified precisely how a psychologist can know when this indicated that the patient is in a specific stage. And she did not provide objective evidence that most of her patients went through each of the five stages in precisely this order.

Other researchers who studied the terminally ill have come to rather different conclusions. One study (Kastenbaum & Weisman, 1972) distinguished between two reactions to death. Some patients, like Kübler-Ross's, seemed to accept death and withdrew from most activities. But others continued to live active lives until the very end. They did not seem to fear death and continued to start new activities and new relationships even though they knew they were dying.

Clearly, more research is needed to understand the complex emotional experiences of people who know they are going to die. The contribution of Kübler-Ross and other pioneers, then, is just a beginning that helped to break down the barriers preventing discussion of this taboo topic.

A new public awareness of the inevitability of death may help our society deal more intelligently and humanely with the terminally ill. One sign of such change is the establishment of special institutions called **hospices,** which are specifically designed to meet the needs of the dying. The most famous facility of this sort is St. Christopher's Hospice in London, England. Dealing primarily with cancer patients,

St. Christopher's tries to relieve pain as much as possible and to provide maximum contact with loved ones. Various mixtures of drugs help relieve pain while allowing patients to remain alert. Paid staff and volunteers work to provide a loving and caring atmosphere rather than the sterile and impersonal one so commonly found in hospitals. Visiting hours are extremely liberal, to allow family and friends to spend as much time as possible with their loved ones.

The first American hospice was established in New Haven, Connecticut, in 1974; by 1981, there were more than 800 hospice programs in the United States (Vandenbos, DeLeon, & Pallak, 1982). Psychologists are now working with the 50,000 patients who enter these programs each year to deal with the inevitability of death and make the most of the time left to them. In this way, and in many others, psychology's studies of the lifelong process of growth and development are being applied to promote the most productive lives possible.

Summary

1. According to psychoanalyst Erik Erikson, each of us passes through eight distinct **psychosocial stages,** periods of life in which we must face certain crises: trust versus mistrust in infancy; autonomy versus shame in the second year; initiative versus guilt in the third or fourth year; industry versus inferiority in late childhood; identity versus identity confusion in adolescence; intimacy versus isolation in young adulthood; generativity versus stagnation in middle age; and integrity versus despair in old age.

2. Beginning with G. Stanley Hall, many psychologists characterized adolescence as a period of great storm and stress. Later researchers have shown how the precise character of this period depends on cultural and historical factors.

3. **Puberty** is the time when sexual development begins. In addition to changes in the structure and function of the sex organs, this period is characterized by a **growth spurt,** a sudden increase in the rate of growth for both height and weight. The precise timing of these changes varies over a wide normal range.

4. Erikson's notion of an **identity crisis** in adolescence has led to research comparing four different states. *Identity achievers* are people who have finished choosing their occupational and ideological goals; *foreclosures* are people who have adopted certain goals (usually, directly from their parents) without going through a period of decision; *identity diffusions* are people who failed to achieve a clear identity; and *moratoriums* are people who are actually in an identity crisis. Adolescents in these four different states have been shown to differ in terms of their anxiety, satisfaction, relationships, and other important characteristics.

5. Lawrence Kohlberg focused attention on the way adolescents' growing cognitive capacities enable them to reason about morality in increasingly sophisticated ways. He also distinguished six major stages of moral development, two at each of three levels. At the **preconventional level** of moral reasoning, people accept society's commands primarily to gain rewards and avoid punishments; at the **conventional level,** society's standards are totally adopted as one's own; at

the **postconventional level,** moral reasoning involves applying universal principles of right and wrong that are more fundamental than the laws of any specific society. Kohlberg has been criticized for his cognitive focus on the way people think about morality rather than on what they actually do.

6. Studies of male-female differences have generated a great deal of controversy. The most widely accepted review of all the research to date concluded that during adolescence, there are three major sex differences that emerge—girls develop verbal skills more rapidly, while boys excel on visual-spatial and mathematical tasks. A fourth stable sex difference appears much earlier in development—boys are physically and verbally more aggressive than girls.

7. Less is known about adulthood than any other period of life. Daniel Levinson studied a group of middle-aged men and found several distinct stages. Around the age of 30, a transition occurs as men settle down to pursue adult goals. Between the ages of 40 and 45, many experienced a **midlife crisis,** a stressful period of questioning their goals and progress.

8. The Grant study includes a longitudinal follow-up of 95 men who graduated from Harvard between 1939 and 1944. Men who typically responded to stress with mature **defense mechanisms** such as suppression were more successful in their careers, more satisfied with marriages and friendships, and physically healthier.

9. Studies of human sexual activity have emphasized the tremendous variability of response. On the average, male sexual activity peaks in adolescence and early adulthood; female sexual activity rises more gradually from puberty and peaks in the thirties.

10. The causes of homosexuality are not understood. According to one recent controversial study, adult homosexuals often report a pattern of lifelong gender nonconformity. The researchers interpreted this as a sign of a biological predisposition, but other explanations are also possible.

11. The proportion of the population that is over 65 has been steadily increasing. One key problem in **gerontology,** the scientific study of the elderly, concerns the possibility of cognitive decline in old age. **Cross-sectional studies,** in which groups of different ages are compared at one point in time, have generally found that IQ declines in adulthood, perhaps beginning as early as the age of 35. Longitudinal studies, however, have found much smaller cognitive declines, beginning much later in adulthood. One reason for this discrepancy involves the differences between **cohorts,** groups of people who were born at roughly the same time.

12. According to Kübler-Ross, people typically go through five stages when they learn they are dying: denial, anger, bargaining, depression, and acceptance. While researchers have challenged the idea that every patient moves through all five stages in precisely this order, the scheme was useful in breaking down the taboos against studying dying. One sign of change is the increasing acceptance of **hospices**—institutions specifically designed to meet the needs of patients who are dying.

Discussion of "Becoming a Critical Consumer"

What is not said in this account is far more significant than what is said. How did Sheehey choose the actual people who were interviewed? Journalists often find people to write about simply by "asking around" among friends and acquaintances; was this highly biased technique used here? Further, what was the exact procedure used for interviews? Did each begin with the same core group of questions? And what criteria did Sheehey use to identify the general characteristics of a particular period of life?

These are the kinds of questions that scientists consider when they evaluate the validity of a particular study. A talented journalist like Sheehey can provide insights into individual lives that are far more intense and fascinating than one usually encounters in scientific reports. But general conclusions about all Americans or another specific population are likely to be valid only when they are based on proper methods of scientific research.

To Learn More

Conger, J. J. *Adolescence and Youth: Psychological Development in a Changing World* (3d ed.). New York: Harper & Row, 1983. A textbook that summarizes what psychologists know about this difficult period of life.

Erikson, E. *Childhood and Society* (2d ed.). New York: W. W. Norton, 1963. The psychoanalytic theorist describes his "eight ages of man" and provides case histories ranging from Hitler's childhood to child-rearing practices among the Sioux Indians.

Levinson, D. J. *The Seasons of a Man's Life*. New York: Alfred A. Knopf, 1978. Many case histories are included in this fascinating account of one of the first major research projects on personality development in adulthood.

10
Motivation and Emotion

Why did Sir Thomas More choose to die as a martyr rather than compromise his religious principles? Why did Elvis Presley sometimes give Cadillacs to perfect strangers (*Newsweek*, August 29, 1977, p. 48)? Why did the King of England abdicate in 1936, giving up his throne to marry the woman he loved? Why did Adolf Hitler order the execution of over 6 million Jews? And why did Henry Marshall try to get his 3-year-old son a place in the *Guinness Book of World Records* by having the child do more than 1,000 push-ups in two hours (*Boston Globe*, June 18, 1980, p. 4)?

According to "common sense," the answers to questions like these about human motivation may be quite straightforward—simply ask the people involved. Thomas More and Elvis may not have much to say, but people who are alive, alert, and reasonably verbal can usually explain their own actions. Or can they?

In an influential paper titled "Telling More Than We Can Know," Richard Nisbett and Timothy Wilson (1977) cited dozens of studies showing how little insight people have into the causes of their own behavior. When subjects were questioned in classic studies of how people react to emergencies, how first impressions influence later judgments, how people solve problems, and how drugs affect behavior, they consistently failed to notice or to admit the influence of critical variables. These subjects almost always gave reasons for what they did. But the reasons they offered were often the wrong ones, explanations that were shown by other research to be factually incorrect.

For example, in one simple study, shoppers were asked to evaluate the quality of four pairs of nylon stockings. In fact the stockings were identical, but when people looked at the four pairs side by side, they overwhelmingly chose the pair that was placed on the right end. While effects like this are familiar to psychologists, none of the shoppers said that the position of the articles had anything to do with their choices. Indeed, when the experimenters asked directly whether the placement of the articles might affect preference, "virtually all subjects denied it, usually with a worried glance at the interviewer suggesting that they felt either that they had misunderstood the question or were dealing with a madman" (Nisbett & Wilson, 1977, p. 244).

This research does not imply that we never have any insight into the underlying reasons for our actions. But it does suggest that psychologists must probe beneath the surface to understand the tangled forces that motivate human behavior.

Although speculation about the underlying causes of behavior probably dates back to the first cave woman who wondered why her husband was late for dinner, "systematic investigations of . . . motivational behavior are almost unbelievably recent" (Brown, 1979, p. 231). Scientific theories of motivation began to appear only about a century ago; widespread experimentation in this area began around the 1920s. It should come as no surprise that there is still considerable controversy over many basic issues.

Even the definition of motivation has proven difficult to specify in an abstract form that satisfies every psychologist. For our purposes, **motivation** involves the forces that influence the strength or direction of behavior. *Physiological motives* direct behavior toward such basic goals as food, water, and sex. *Social motives* direct behavior toward more complex goals, such as acceptance from others, independence, or recognition of one's achievements. In either case, studies of motivation explore how and why behavior is directed toward a certain goal.

Closely related to the concept of motives is that of **emotions,** physical reactions that are experienced as strong feelings. Common sense classifies feelings such as anger, fear, and joy as emotions and distinguishes them from such motivational forces as hunger, thirst, and a need for achievement. However, psychologists have found it difficult to pinpoint the formal or theoretical differences between motivation and emotion.

The American Psychological Association has no division devoted to motivation and emotion, and very few psychologists identify themselves exclusively with this area. Rather, these are general problems faced by psychologists working in many different specialties.

As this chapter reviews what is known about motivation and emotion, it will become clear that psychology is not yet in a position to provide final answers to questions like those posed about the motivations of Elvis Presley and Henry Marshall. It is, however, able to provide insights into questions that are more limited in scope but every bit as fascinating and provocative.

Models of Motivation

The idea that motivation involves the forces that influence behavior implies a hidden assumption—the way you act is determined, at least in part, by internal and external forces. In its more extreme versions, philosophers call this idea **determinism,** that every event is the inevitable product of a series of natural forces. A strict determinist would argue that human choice is an illusion. You may think that you have the power to decide whether you should break up with your boyfriend or whether to eat vanilla or chocolate mint chip ice cream. However, a determinist would say you have no choice at all—that every act is determined by what comes before.

While the roots of this deterministic view can be traced back to the ancient Greek philosopher Democritus, the history of human thought has been dominated by the opposite view of **free will,** that people are free to choose what they will do. Free will does not imply that human behavior is totally independent of outside stimuli and internal desires, only that each of us has the power to choose what we will do.

Different psychologists hold a variety of views on this ancient controversy. At one extreme, B. F. Skinner and some behaviorists believe that science can ultimately discover a set of laws that will fully predict every human act. At the other extreme, Abraham Maslow and some humanistic psychologists argue that people do have control over their actions and that a complete scientific account of human behavior will never be possible. The debate over determinism versus free will has gone on for several thousand years, and it would be presumptuous for psychologists to expect to have the final word in this controversy.

However, it is worth noting that if human behavior is totally unpredictable and capricious, the search for systematic relationships must fail. Therefore, every scientific account of human motivation inevitably implies some acceptance of the deterministic view.

GENERAL THEORIES: FROM INSTINCTS TO INCENTIVES

When psychologists first attempted to specify the forces that determined the direction and intensity of behavior, most sought a single general theory that could account for every type of motivation. The first candidate involved the concept of **instincts,** or inborn forces that direct an organism toward a certain goal. Note that this is quite similar to our earlier definition of motivation; the key difference is the notion that instincts are unlearned and present at birth, part of the biological heritage of a species.

For example, in 1890 William James argued that human beings were born with the following instincts: locomotion, vocalization, imitation, rivalry, pugnacity, sympathy, hurting, fear, acquisitiveness, constructiveness, play, curiosity, sociability, secretiveness, cleanliness, modesty, love, jealousy, and parental love. Unfortunately, James cited little systematic evidence that any of these forces were truly inborn; his list was based largely on arguments about the evolutionary advantage of these traits and observations of his own children.

Other psychologists developed lists of their own, and by 1923 one critic of this concept counted several thousand different instincts that social scientists had invoked to explain every imaginable type of behavior (Tolman, 1923).

One major problem with the indiscriminate use of the word *instinct* was the fact that there were no firm criteria for deciding whether a particular instinct was innate, or universal, or anything else. Another problem was the fact that some researchers seemed to feel that they had explained behavior simply by labeling it instinctive. Thus, a woman who spent all day cleaning her gun collection was expressing her cleanliness instinct; a man who read 20 volumes of the *Encyclopaedia Britannica* from cover to cover was expressing his curiosity instinct. Critics noted that these "instincts" did not explain anything, they simply provided a label such as "cleanliness" or "curiosity" for the actual behaviors observed.

As a result of these arguments and others, most psychologists abandoned the idea that all motivation could be explained by a general theory of instincts. Beginning around the 1920s, they substituted the notions of needs and drives. A **need** is a physiological requirement of the organism, such as a need for food, water, or oxygen. This is distinguished from a **drive,** a motivational force that incites an organism to action. Ordinarily, needs and drives are parallel; a physiological need for food is expressed in the behavioral drive that leads an animal to seek it out. In some cases, however, the distinction is an important one. A woman who is starving may have an overwhelming need for food, but she may become so weak that she has little behavioral drive to search for nourishment.

For learning theorists such as Clark Hull, the concept of drive played a central role in explaining all behavior. According to the behavioral paradigm, which dominated American psychology at least until the 1950s, all behavior was based on learning and all learning was motivated by the organism's attempt to satisfy such drives as hunger, thirst, and sex. According to some theorists, even the most complex forms of behavior could ultimately be traced back to the influence of these few basic biological drives. For example, Tolman (1942) argued that when an infant is hungry, he learns to demand food assertively by crying or whining. Depending on which responses actually succeed in reducing hunger, these assertive behaviors can develop into personality patterns that motivate such complex activities as verbal aggression or learning to manipulate others.

Given the perspective provided by several decades of research, this attempt to reduce all human motivation to a few basic drives now seems far too simplistic. Even the simplest forms of animal learning cannot be fully explained by the push of internal needs and drives. To cite just one example, Guttman (1953) found that rats would press a bar more frequently for sugar water than plain water. These animals were influenced not just by internal states but also by external stimuli called incentives. **Incentives** are external stimuli that influence the probability of behavior. Humans too are motivated by external incentives—a hot fudge sundae can be an incentive to eat even when the internal hunger drive is relatively weak.

Other complications for drive theory arose as psychologists became increasingly concerned with the role of cognitive processes and thought in motivation.

Throughout this text, we have seen how in the last few decades researchers have gradually begun to emphasize the active internal cognitive processes involved in such areas as perception, learning, memory, and thought. Here, we shall see how this shift in emphasis has affected the study of motivation and emotion. For example, according to Schachter and Singer's cognitive theory of emotion (described later), the way a person perceives and interprets the situation in which he finds himself determines the actual emotion he feels.

Psychological thinking has evolved significantly in its first century. Around 1900, psychologists saw human behavior as mindlessly driven by inborn instincts. By the 1980s, the picture seems far more complex. Human beings actively interpret the world and react to both internal drives and external incentives.

CURRENT DIRECTIONS

These days, most researchers believe that motivation and emotion are too complex to be explained by any single theory. Most of this chapter focuses on individual motives—such as hunger and the need for achievement—each on its own terms. It is important to note, however, that an influential minority of scientists rejects this fragmented approach. In the next chapter, we consider how Freud's instinct theory and Malsow's notion of a hierarchy of needs suggest general principles that might account for many different motives. Here, we introduce a more recent and more modest theory of motivation, Solomon's notion of opponent processes.

Opponent-Process Theory.   In the fifth century B.C., Plato noted the paradoxical relations between pleasure and pain: "Whenever the one is found, the other follows up behind." Consider the often repeated story about the man who had a habit of hitting his head against a wall because it felt so good when he stopped. Or consider the common report by marathon runners of the incredible high they experience after "passing through the wall" of nearly unbearable physical pain.

According to the opponent-process theory of motivation, a person's first experience in a physically risky sport is likely to be terrifying. But this fear elicits an opponent process in the brain that produces a feeling of euphoria several minutes later. If the behavior is repeated, the fear decreases and the euphoria increases in length and intensity.

Richard Solomon (1980) drew on these observations and others to develop his **opponent-process theory,** which holds that many acquired motives arise from the interplay of two opposing processes in the brain, such as pleasure in response to pain or pain in response to pleasure. Addictions are also explained by this theory, and Solomon believes that such acquired motives as love, social attachments, thrill seeking, and the needs for achievement, power, and affiliation all follow the same empirical laws as addictions.

When a person first takes the addicting drug heroin, a peak of euphoria (the "rush") is followed by a gradual decline and later a minor craving. A second dose of the drug produces a smaller amount of pleasure and a greater unpleasant craving. By the time a person is addicted, the drug is sought to avoid the pain of withdrawal rather than to produce the pleasure of a rush.

Solomon also argues that this sequence of events is based on structures in the brain that are automatically triggered to reduce any intense feeling. Hence, the rush of pleasure from that first dose of heroin triggers an opponent process to reduce its intensity. After several repetitions, the opponent process increases in strength until it provides the motivational force.

Similarly, he argues, love begins with a wave of euphoria. But over time, the euphoria when the loved one is present is replaced by unpleasant feelings when the loved one is absent. The driving force has shifted from pleasure to pain and has created a kind of addiction to another human being.

At this writing, it seems fair to describe the notion of opponent processes of motivation as a provocative theory that has received some experimental support. Only time and future research can tell whether it will prove to be of enduring value in understanding the nature of motivation.

Analysis of Individual Motives.   Again, Solomon's attempt to develop a general theory of motivation goes against the trend; most modern researchers focus on the workings of an individual motive rather than seeking general principles that apply to all drives or all acquired motives.

Even motives that seem to be closely related are often controlled by different mechanisms and respond to different variables. The most obvious example is the fact that hunger is far more complex than thirst, even though the two intuitively seem to be closely linked. Water intake is regulated within very narrow boundaries, whereas food intake is far more variable and sensitive to external conditions. Richard Thompson (1975) wryly noted one implication of this difference: "Many people are too fat but we never hear of someone being too wet" (p. 308). Because water intake is so closely attuned to the body's needs, a person can survive only a few days without liquids. But the same person can live for weeks or months without food, surviving on stored energy. This sort of difference has encouraged many researchers to consider each individual motive separately and on its own terms.

At this time, there is no single list of human motives that is accepted by all psychologists. Most agree, however, that motives can be divided into two major classes, *physiological motives* and *social motives*. Other names are sometimes used (such as basic or inborn versus derived or acquired motives), and there is sometimes disagreement over the precise definitions and boundaries of each concept. Nevertheless, the broad division into physiological and social categories is widely accepted.

Of the physiological motives, the three that have been studied most intensively are hunger, thirst, and sex. Most of this research has been conducted by experimental and physiological psychologists who seek to understand the bodily mechanisms involved, often by performing surgery on lower animals.

In contrast, the social motives seem more distinctly human, such as the need for achievement, for power, or for self-esteem. These have typically been studied by personality psychologists, who analyze the most complex forms of human behavior. The contrast between these two broad classes should become clearer as we describe each type and focus on research for representative examples.

Physiological Motives

AN OVERVIEW

Physiological motives are internal bodily states that direct an organism's behavior toward a goal. Virtually every list of physiological motives begins with hunger, thirst, and sex. While hunger and thirst are intimately involved with personal survival, there is not a single documented case of a person who died from lack of sex. However, sex is required for the survival of the species. (See Chapter 9 for a discussion of research on human sexuality.)

Other motives involved with survival include the need for oxygen and maintenance of a constant body temperature. Needs for sleep, elimination of wastes, and avoidance of pain are also commonly cited as physiological motives.

More controversial is the issue of whether curiosity is a physiological motive. In the 1950s, at a time when drive theory held that all behavior could be traced back to physical tensions such as hunger, several researchers reported that monkeys will manipulate puzzles and latches with no reward except their apparent satisfaction in solving them. Later studies revealed that the same is true of other species, and some argued that this proved that curiosity (or perhaps manipulation or mastery) was a basic inborn drive.

Maternal behavior also seems to be partly inborn, at least for lower animals. (Although liberated authors sometimes prefer the term *parental behavior* so that fathers will not feel left out, among lower animals the female of the species is responsible for nearly all care of the young.) In rats, injections of certain hormones have been shown to increase maternal activity. However, in apes and humans, experience seems to play a far larger role in parental practices than biology. Thus, the higher one proceeds on the evolutionary scale, the less influence hormones have on maternal behavior.

Some researchers argue that aggression is also an inborn physiological motive (Lorenz, 1966), but that claim is extremely controversial. Social learning researchers have repeatedly shown that aggression is modified by learning (see Chapter 5). No one knows whether it could be abolished from the human species under the proper conditions.

To gain more insight into the nature of physiological motivation, we now focus on one motive that has been studied in some detail—hunger.

HUNGER

Large animals that eat low-calorie foods—cows who survive on a diet of grass, for example—must eat almost continuously to gain sufficient nourishment. In contrast, humans eat meals. Much of the research on hunger has focused on the bodily mechanics of eating meals. Why do we start eating, and why do we stop?

At least for most Americans, food is readily available almost all the time. If you are reading this at home, you are probably only steps away from potato chips and wheat germ, Pepsi and milk, Hershey bars and alfalfa sprouts. What internal force makes you suddenly begin thinking about these foods when it's time for lunch? And after you begin eating, how does your body know when it has had enough?

It is easy to demonstrate that visual sensations arise in the eye, but where does hunger begin? Many early studies focused on this question of localizing the origins of hunger. Being no fools, researchers began by looking at the stomach.

Attempts to Localize Hunger.   Near the turn of the century, Harvard Medical School physiologist Walter Cannon attempted to demonstrate that hunger was

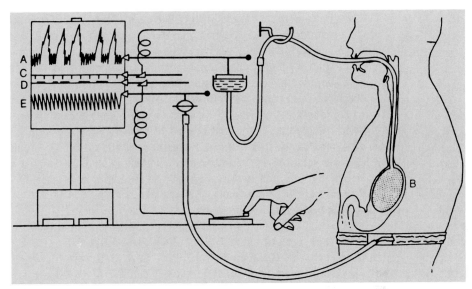

Figure 10.1
In one early study of hunger, a research assistant swallowed a balloon and pressed a telegraph key whenever he felt hungry. Stomach contractions were measured by changes in the pressure on the balloon. Although studies using this unappetizing procedure found that stomach contractions tended to peak with subjective feelings of hunger, this conclusion was later challenged by other types of evidence.

caused by stomach contractions. Unfortunately, at that time the only way to measure stomach contractions involved swallowing a balloon attached to a long air hose. Once the balloon was in the stomach, it could be partially inflated; when the stomach contracted, it would squeeze the balloon, forcing out a certain amount of air, which could be measured on a pressure gauge attached to the hose (see Figure 10.1). The whole experience is rather unpleasant and has a tendency to reduce hunger.

Perhaps demonstrating the wisdom that led to his appointment at Harvard, Cannon decided that he himself would read the pressure gauges while someone else swallowed the balloon. That unappetizing task was left to his research assistant, A.L. Washburn.

It took Washburn several weeks of valiant practice to get used to feeling a tube in his throat and the partially inflated balloon in his stomach; then, the experiment began. Washburn skipped breakfast and lunch each day, came to the laboratory around 2 p.m., swallowed the balloon, and sat quietly while his stomach contractions were measured. Whenever Washburn felt hungry, he pressed a telegraph key, which made a mark on the physiological record. Just as Cannon had predicted, stomach contractions tended to peak right before Washburn felt hungry. These investigators concluded that a psychological sensation of hunger was caused by a definite physiological event, a stomach contraction (Cannon & Washburn, 1912).

Several sources of evidence led later researchers to reject this simplistic theory of hunger. Cutting the nerves that deliver information about stomach contractions to the brain has surprisingly little effect on human or animal hunger. Even humans whose stomachs have been completely removed continue to experience hunger pangs, and animals with no stomachs continue to work for food. Clearly, something other than stomach contractions produces hunger for these individuals.

There is evidence that a full stomach sends to the brain signals that play a role in ending a meal, but they constitute only one factor in the regulation of hunger. Another important part of the story involves the processing of these signals in the brain. According to one theory of brain function, the **ventromedial hypothalamus**—an area in the front and central portions of the hypothalamus (see Chapter 2)—was said to be a "satiety center" that signaled animals when to stop eating. The **lateral hypothalamus**—an area on the sides of this structure—was said to be a "feeding center" that sent signals to start eating.

The evidence for the involvement of these structures in eating goes back to the turn of the century, when a Viennese physician named Alfred Fröhlich observed that people with tumors of the pituitary gland often become obese. Later physicians showed that it was a smaller structure next to the pituitary—the hypothalamus—that actually regulated hunger. Several decades of experimentation followed before researchers agreed on the precise site. Destruction of the ventromedial hypothalamus led to such gross overeating that animals ultimately doubled or even tripled their normal weight (see Figure 10.2). This led to the idea that the ventromedial

Figure 10.2
After surgical destruction of a portion of the brain called the ventromedial hypothalamus, this rat overate until it was about three times its normal weight.

hypothalamus told animals when to stop eating; when it was damaged or destroyed, the animal no longer knew when to stop (Hetherington & Ranson, 1942).

A few years later, researchers discovered that destruction of the lateral hypothalamus produced the opposite effect (Anand & Brobeck, 1951). If the damaged area was large enough, a rat would starve to death even if it was sitting on a mountain of food.

From this evidence arose a relatively simple theory localizing hunger in the brain: the lateral hypothalamus turns hunger on; the ventromedial hypothalamus turns hunger off. Not surprisingly, later researchers found that this model was far too simplistic. For example, rats whose ventromedial hypothalami were destroyed ate more if food were freely available but ate less if they had to work for it by pressing a bar or lifting a heavy lid. When food was mixed with the unpleasant taste of quinine, these rats also ate less than normal ones; but when it was mixed with sugar, they ate far more than usual (Teitelbaum, 1955). Obviously, the ventromedial hypothalamus is involved not just with stopping eating but also with sensitivity to external cues.

Similarly, a rat whose lateral hypothalamus was destroyed would sometimes resume eating. If such rats were forcibly tube-fed for several weeks, they later began to eat again, especially if they were tempted by a treat like eggnog (Teitelbaum & Epstein, 1962).

These findings and others challenged the idea that hunger is a single phenomenon that can be precisely localized in the body and the brain. Eating involves a number of different processes that interact to produce weight gain. For example, one line of research later suggested that rats with ventromedial lesions get fat even when they eat the same amount as a control group of normal rats. Thus, the ventromedial hypothalamus may be involved with food metabolism, particularly the proportion of nutrients that are stored as fat (Friedman & Stricker, 1976).

Continuing studies with increasingly sophisticated methods for destroying precise areas of brain tissue and measuring a range of behavioral effects will provide new information about the many different processes involved in eating and how these processes are regulated by the brain.

Other Variables That Influence Eating. When researchers abandoned the idea of localizing "the hunger drive" in a single spot, they went on to investigate the many factors that influence eating in different situations. Among the physiological factors that have been shown to be involved are body temperature, blood-sugar levels, and fat deposits.

Psychological variables have also been shown to influence human eating. From a social-learning perspective, modeling has proven important: College students ate their lunch faster in the presence of another person who ate quickly and ate more when their companion ate more (Rosenthal & McSweeney, 1979). Another series of studies has shown that the external cues associated with food affect obese individuals more than those of normal weight.

In 1964, psychologist Albert Stunkard found that stomach contractions were more closely related to feelings of hunger for normal-weight individuals than for obese subjects. Specifically, on 71% of the occasions that normal-weight people reported feeling hungry, their stomachs were contracting; the corresponding figure for obese people was 48% (Stunkard & Koch, 1964).

These results suggest that normal-weight people may eat when their bodies tell them to, while obese people eat for other reasons. In a direct test of this notion, Schachter, Goldman, and Gordon (1968) manipulated internal hunger sensations by comparing some subjects who had eaten recently with others who had not. The prediction was that normal-weight people would eat less when their stomachs were full, while obese people would be less affected by these internal signals.

Men in the normal-weight category were about the average weight for people their height; obese subjects were on the average 20% overweight according to the norms published by the Metropolitan Life Insurance Company. The Columbia undergraduates who participated in this study thought they were volunteering for a taste-testing experiment and agreed to skip one meal just before their appointments. Subjects in the full-stomach condition were offered two large roast beef sandwiches and a glass of water when they arrived; those in the empty-stomach condition got only a warm hello. Then both groups were given crackers to eat. Of course, these men had no idea that eating a roast beef sandwich was a key step in the experiment. Figure 10.3 shows that obese subjects ate about the same number of crackers whether their stomachs were relatively empty or full; normal-weight men ate significantly fewer crackers when their stomachs were full.

Schachter concluded that normal-weight people eat when internal bodily sensations signal hunger, while the obese eat in response to external, food-relevant cues. This interpretation was further supported by a long series of creative experiments and natural observations. In a typical follow-up study (Schachter & Gross, 1968),

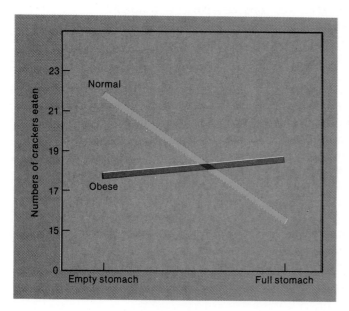

Figure 10.3

In this study, obese subjects ate the same amount whether or not they had eaten recently. In contrast, normal weight subjects ate less when they had just eaten. Along with other evidence, this suggests that normal weight people eat when internal bodily sensations signal hunger, while obese people are more responsive to external cues.

obese and normal-weight subjects filled out questionnaires and sat quietly for an hour of boring physiological tests. The study always began at 5 p.m. and ended at 6 p.m. But a large clock on the wall facing the subjects was altered to run fast for one group and slow for another. When the experimenter brought in a stack of questionnaires near the end of the session, he was casually munching on some Wheat Thins. He left the box behind and invited the subject to eat as much as he liked.

Once again, all the questionnaires and physiological measures were an elaborate ruse. The question was, how many Wheat Thins would obese and normal-weight people eat? As predicted, they found that normal-weight people ate the same amount whether the clock was running fast or slow, whereas obese people ate more when external cues told them that it was dinner time (that is, when the clock ran fast and suggested that it was 6:10 rather than 5:25).

Many investigators have replicated the finding that obese people are, on the average, more responsive to external cues. But this does not mean that every obese person responds to external food cues and every normal-weight person to internal ones. Both internally oriented and externally oriented individuals can be found in any weight category (Rodin, 1981). This distinction is one factor in obesity; but we see in the next section that there are also many others.

HUMAN OBESITY: CAUSES AND CURES

There is no precise border between obesity and normal weight. The tables in every diet book showing the "ideal" weight for men and women of various heights are largely based on the averages found in insurance company records for millions of individuals. **Obesity** is often defined as 15% to 20% over these ideal weights; depending on the precise definition, some 20 million to 40 million Americans are obese.

Many experts believe that charts of ideal weight are misleading (Mayer, 1968). A 5-foot 10-inch, 190-pound linebacker for the Cincinnati Bengals football team could be all muscle, while a dentist of the same height and weight could be all fat. A better definition of obesity, therefore, might rely on the proportion of body fat. A rough estimate of this proportion can be made by measuring the thickness of skin folds, as when you place your hands above your hips on either side and pinch the skin folds known colloquially as "love handles."

It is widely agreed that three major factors determine body weight: the amount and type of food eaten, the amount of energy expended in physical activity, and the storage of fat in cellular tissue. The relations between these factors are complex and probably differ from one person to the next.

Body fat is stored in the form of adipose tissue, or fat cells. Gaining weight can result from an increase in the number of fat cells in the body or an increase in the average size of existing fat cells. Many researchers believe that the number of fat cells is particularly critical. This remains relatively constant over the lifespan. Some research suggests that excessive eating can increase the number of fat cells, particularly during the first few months of life (Knittle, 1975). If this finding is verified, attention to proper diet during this critical period could have lifelong implications.

In the meantime, what are we to do when we start feeling chubby? Nearly 400 years before Christ was born, Socrates warned the overweight: "Beware of those foods that tempt you to eat when you are not hungry and those liquors that tempt you to drink when you are not thirsty."

The wisdom of this common sense has been verified in many studies. In one such study (Sclafani & Springer, 1976), rats who were given unlimited access to the standard boring laboratory menu (Purina Rat Chow and water) maintained relatively constant weights. But another group of rats who were permitted to nibble away at chocolate chip cookies, salami, cheese, marshmallows, milk chocolate, and peanut butter gradually got fatter and fatter. Thus, even rats get chubby when exposed to the external incentives found in any American supermarket.

Unfortunately, there is no simple way to lose weight. To keep the American preoccupation with effortless weight loss in perspective, it is worth noting that fad diets have been with us for more than a century. In the 1860s and 1870s, many Americans went on the Banting Diet, trying to lose weight by eating fewer carbohydrates. This basic principle has been reincarnated in countless form in the last few decades, including the Calories Don't Count Diet, the DuPont Diet, the Air Force Diet, the Mayo Clinic Diet, the Drinking Man's Diet, the Stillman Diet, the Boston Police Diet, and the Atkins Diet Revolution (Goldbeck & Goldbeck, 1975). In the month that you read this, some magazine will almost certainly headline a "new miracle" diet that will make the same basic recommendations.

Low-carbohydrate diets like these do promote in the early stages the sort of rapid weight loss that encourages people to continue. But, like all diets, they are difficult to maintain for long periods. Further, some forms of the diet actually lack adequate nutrition and may be harmful to health.

Almost any weight-loss diet will help people shed pounds, at least temporarily. People who are unsophisticated about social science may be genuinely enthusiastic about a diet they have seen work for specific individuals. Researchers who have conducted carefully controlled outcome studies of the long-term effects of weight-loss programs are far more cautious. New miracle diets are rarely new—and never miracles.

Nevertheless, people do succeed in losing weight. In a study of 40 adults who had been obese at some time and had actively tried to lose weight, Schachter (1982) found that about 2 out of 3 were no longer obese.

Many psychologists now recommend behavior-modification programs for weight control (Stunkard, 1979). Typically, these begin by requiring an individual to keep detailed records of everything he eats and the situation in which it is eaten for several days. Some people are so appalled by the number of potato chips they consume while watching TV that they immediately plan to reform. One possibility is to avoid situations associated with overeating; watching less TV may help our potato chip addict trim down. Another strategy is to replace snacking with another pleasurable activity.

Increasing the frequency of exercise is also an important ingredient in most successful weight-loss programs. However, all behavioral programs demand effort and commitment over an extended period of time.

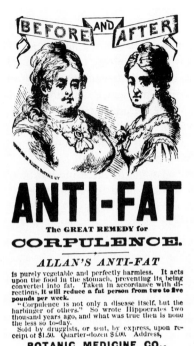

For more than a century, Americans have looked for miraculous weight-loss techniques that would help them shed pounds without expending any effort.

Psychologists now believe that they will never find a single cause for obesity, nor a single cure. Rodin (1981) put it this way: "The plump baby, the chubby adolescent boy, the woman who gets fatter after pregnancy, the overweight business executive—all have fatness in common—but it is doubtful that the cause or natural history of their fatness is the same" (p. 382). Researchers are now searching for ways to tailor weight-loss programs to individual needs, to improve people's chances of maintaining the healthy weight levels they desire.

Social Motives

AN OVERVIEW

Social motives are forces that direct human behavior toward certain patterns of relationships with other people, such as autonomy or affiliation.

Several decades ago, social motives were often referred to as "derived," because many investigators believed that they were learned by association with more basic motives like hunger, as in the case of the child who learns to be assertive to get food and later becomes assertive in other respects. Today, these motives are often referred to more neutrally as "acquired," implying that social motives are learned, but not necessarily derived directly from physiological drives.

There is no universally accepted list of social motives. Perhaps the most influential attempt to catalog social motives grew out of Henry Murray's 1938 book *Explorations in Personality*. After intensively studying a small group of individuals, Murray proposed a list of human needs that included achievement (to accomplish difficult tasks), affiliation (to gain affection from friends), autonomy (independence), exhibition (to make an impression on others), understanding (intellectually asking questions), dominance, order, play, nurturance, deference, and 10 others. He believed that complex human behavior could best be understood by studying the interplay of these social motives within a particular individual.

Later investigators focused on some of these motives more than others. The most intensively studied of all was the need for achievement.

THE NEED FOR ACHIEVEMENT

Because he was influenced by the psychoanalytic paradigm (see Chapter 11), Henry Murray believed that many social motives were unconscious and thus could be measured only indirectly. In the **Thematic Apperception Test (TAT)**, people were asked to use their creative imaginations to make up stories about a series of ambiguous pictures like the one shown in Figure 10.4. There were no right or wrong answers on the TAT. Rather, the fantasies people produced were analyzed to reveal

Figure 10.4
In the Thematic Apperception Test, people are asked to tell a story about ambiguous pictures like this one.

the hidden forces that motivated their behavior. Data from this test helped Murray develop his original list of 20 human needs.

To test the idea that such fantasies really did provide a valid measure (see Chapter 12) of motivation, John Atkinson and David McClelland (1948) began by manipulating the hunger drive to see whether this change in motivation would actually influence people's TAT stories. (They started with hunger, rather than one of the social motives, for a practical reason—it is much easier to increase hunger than to increase the need for autonomy or order.)

In this study, sailors at a U.S. Navy submarine training school were not allowed to eat for 1 hour, 4 hours, or 16 hours. The relative hunger of these three groups was indeed reflected in the stories they told about ambiguous pictures.

Encouraged by this success, McClelland and his co-workers went on to the more difficult task of manipulating social motivation and seeing whether this change influenced the stories people told. Once again, they drew on the work of Henry Murray and chose to study the **need for achievement** (sometimes abbreviated as *nAch*), which involves the attempt to excel and surpass others and to accomplish difficult tasks as rapidly and independently as possible. Again, the choice was partly a practical one; people could be deprived of achievement by creating a situation in which they were almost certain to fail.

In the original study (McClelland, Clark, Roby, & Atkinson, 1949), students at Wesleyan University were given a series of short writing tests that they were told, "directly indicate a person's general level of intelligence . . . [and] demonstrate whether or not the person is suited to be a leader" (p. 244). These men expected success because they were told that Wesleyan students generally did well on this particular test. But when the subjects in this group got their own grades, each person was told that his own score was quite low compared to other Wesleyan students. Several control groups took the same test under less threatening circumstances. A relaxed group, for example, were told that the questions were being perfected for use in a new psychological test; their scores on this pilot version were meaningless.

As in the hunger experiment, this change in motivation was followed by administration of part of the Thematic Apperception Test. The students were asked to write stories about four ambiguous pictures. This time, the stories were scored for the appearance of achievement-related imagery. As the scoring system evolved, three main themes came to be recognized as signs of a need for achievement—competition with a standard of excellence, unique accomplishments, and pursuit of a long-term goal. For example, competition with a standard of excellence could be seen from stories in which a student worried about an exam or a surgeon had to work quickly and accurately. Other stories mentioned unique accomplishments such as inventions and artistic creations. Still other students revealed their needs for achievement by telling stories about a long-term goal, such as becoming a doctor or a successful businessman.

As expected, achievement imagery was far more common among those who thought they had failed. Just as hungry men had fantasized about being deprived of food, so men who were "deprived of achievement" showed an increase in achievement imagery. This experiment supported the basic validity of TAT stories as a measure of this complex social motive.

Later studies revealed that the need for achievement is related to many different behavior patterns. For example, people who are high in the need for achievement work harder at laboratory tasks, learn faster, do their best work when it counts for the record, resist social pressure, are more active in community activities, and get better grades in high school (McClelland, 1958). They also tend to choose moderate risks rather than high-risk or no-risk situations, since this seems to maximize their chances for the greatest success.

In one demonstration of this last phenomenon, McClelland (1958) studied the way 5-year-old children played a game tossing rings onto a peg on the floor. Each child was allowed to stand as close to the peg as he liked. Children who had previously been classified as high in the need for achievement tended to stand at an intermediate distance so that the game was challenging but not impossible. In contrast, children who were low in the need for achievement sometimes stood so close that they virtually could not fail or so far away that they could not succeed. Figure 10.5 illustrates the same pattern of results for a group of college students (Atkinson & Litwin, 1960).

While there have been demonstrations of this sort to show that the need for achievement predicts behavior on a wide variety of laboratory tasks, perhaps the most impressive evidence of the usefulness of this concept comes from studies of its relationship to real-life behavior. One long-term study examined the relationship between 55 college sophomores' scores in the need for achievement between 1947 and 1951 and the jobs these same men held in 1961, some 10 to 14 years later. McClelland (1965) divided the later occupations into two categories: *entrepreneurial* positions, in which the men had more individual responsibility for initiating action and greater risk (such as real estate and insurance sales, or operating one's own company), and *nonentrepreneural* positions, with less responsibility and risk (such as

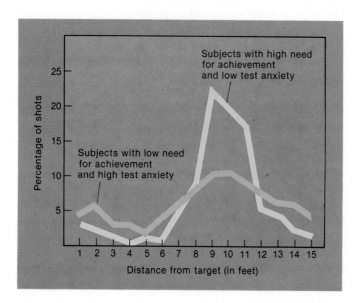

Figure 10.5

In a ring-toss game, subjects who were high in the need for achievement and low in test anxiety were more likely to stand about 8 to 11 feet from the ring, a distance that makes success challenging but not impossible. People who were low in the need for achievement and high in test anxiety were more likely to stand either very close to the ring or very far away.

Dr. Joyce Brothers's Key to Success

In the movie *High Anxiety*, the main ballroom at a national convention of psychiatrists is dominated by huge photographs of four giants in the mental health field: Freud, Jung, Maslow, and Dr. Joyce Brothers. The film was a satire, and may have kiddingly exaggerated the fame of certain figures, such as Jung and Maslow.

Doctor Joyce Brothers first rose to national prominence as a contestant on the popular TV quiz show "The $64,000 Question," on which she won the jackpot in 1955 by answering a series of questions on boxing. She went on to a TV show of her own and national visibility as "the most famous and trusted of psychologists, whose audience . . . numbers in the millions." (Brothers, 1978, cover).

Unfortunately, neither fame nor trust guarantees accuracy. See if you can spot the four errors (which appear after the "Summary" at the end of this chapter) in the following short excerpt from Dr. Brothers's 1978 best-seller *How to Get Whatever You Want Out of Life:*

> Harvard psychologist David McLelland and other scientists have discovered that there is one personality characteristic which seems to be the true key to success. They call it Motive A. And they have developed a test that can disclose immediately whether or not you possess this characteristic (p. 49).
>
> Participants are told that the purpose of the test is to get the ring over the pin. Each one has five tosses. There are no other rules . . .
>
> The player who stands so close to the pin that he can ring it easily has little or no motivation for success. Nor does the player who stands so far away he can't ring the pin more than once. But the player who stands somewhere between these two extremes . . . is the man or woman with the greatest potential for success" (pp. 285–286).

credit managers and appraisers). Those who were high in the need for achievement in college were indeed more likely to end up in entrepreneurial jobs, just as one might predict. Of course, the need for achievement is only one of many factors involved in employment, so the relationship was far from perfect. In business jobs, 67% of the entrepreneurs were high in the need for achievement, versus 35% of the nonentrepreneurs. Nevertheless, it seems astounding that the result of a short test, in which college students simply made up stories describing the ambiguous pictures in the Thematic Apperception Test, could help predict their occupations a decade later.

McClelland went on to try to change people's behavior by increasing their needs for achievement. Four- to six-week training programs were designed to teach people what the need for achievement is and how it is measured. In one study (McClelland & Winter, 1971), 50 businessmen from a small city in India were instructed how to set specific business goals, taught to communicate with other businessmen, and encouraged to try to increase their own need for achievement. Studies of the behavior of these businessmen two years later revealed that they were far more active than a control group of businessmen from a neighboring Indian city. Those who had taken the short course had participated more in community development efforts, started more new businesses, invested more money in expanding their business, and employed more workers.

McClelland (1978) readily admits that "it is difficult to be certain of causation in field studies of this sort" (p. 205). Other economic and social differences between the two locations might have played some role, for example, or the simple act of participating in a special program may have been more important than its focus on the need for achievement. But this study is extremely encouraging for future research on the role of the need for achievement in real-life success.

Since real-life behavior probably most often involves combinations of motives rather than individual motives that work alone, future research is likely to achieve even greater success by concentrating on patterns of motivation. For example, in the study of college students' performance in the ring-toss game (see Figure 10.7), the most accurate predictions were achieved by also considering how anxious each individual felt about tests. Subjects who had high achievement motivation and low test anxiety were the most likely of all to stand at an intermediate distance from the peg, thus making the task somewhat risky. Interestingly, the real-life implications of this pattern have also been documented. College freshmen who score high in the need for achievement and low in test anxiety also tend to choose major subjects of intermediate difficulty rather than majors that are considered very difficult or very easy (Isaacson, 1964). With sufficient information about an individual's pattern of social motives, future researchers may be able to predict behavior years or even decades before they occur.

FEAR OF SUCCESS

Fascinating as the early studies of achievement motivation were, they shared one critical shortcoming: The predominantly male researchers had devoted almost all their attention to men. In 1958, John W. Atkinson edited *Motives in Fantasy, Action and Society*, an 800-page summary of findings, theories, and speculation about achievement motivation; women were mentioned only in one footnote.

In 1965, Matina Horner began to collect the data for her doctoral dissertation of sex differences in achievement motivation. As part of the study, 88 men who were taking introductory psychology at the University of Michigan were asked to write several stories, beginning with sentences like the following: "After first term finals, John finds himself at the top of his medical school class." A typical male subject described John as dedicated and conscientious and concluded: "John continues working hard and eventually graduates at the top of his class" (Horner, 1969, p. 36).

But when 89 women in the same class were asked to tell stories about what "Anne" felt when she was at the top of her medical school class, the answers were far less straightforward. Many involved themes of social rejection, such as "Anne is an acne-faced book worm" and "Everyone hates and envies her." Other responses stressed doubts and guilt about succeeding, such as the story that ended: "Anne will finally have a nervous breakdown and quit medical school and marry a successful

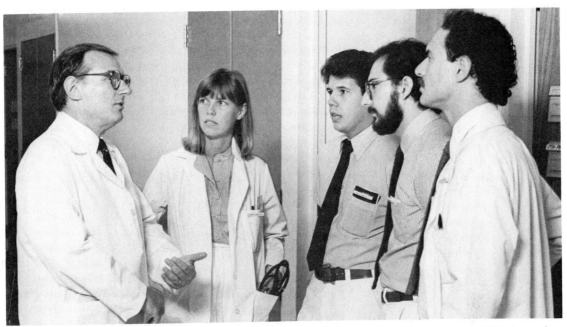

Although the original research on fear of success suggested that many women might do poorly in competitive environments such as medical schools, later studies revealed that fear of success is equally common in men and women.

young doctor." Still other women expressed their conflict by distorting the story: "Anne is a code name for a nonexistent person created by med students. They take turns writing exams for Anne" (Horner, 1969, p. 38).

Horner concluded that some people have a **fear of success**—they are afraid that doing well in competitive situations will have negative consequences, such as unpopularity. Using a standard system to analyze each story, she found that 65% of the women's stories were characterized by fear of success. Only 9% of the men showed this same ambivalence. Horner linked this sex difference to American stereotypes that teach young girls that doing better than men is not ladylike.

She also found that fear of success seemed to affect performance in some situations. Subjects were given a variety of simple verbal tasks, such as seeing how many words they could form from the letters in the word *generation*. Sometimes students worked alone; other times they sat in a large classroom with males and females on opposite sides of the room. Women who were low in fear of success did better in the latter situation, which Horner referred to as "mixed sex competition." But women who scored high on fear of success did better when they worked by themselves. This suggested that fear of success can interfere with doing well in some types of competitive situations.

Horner's research became well known as a result of widespread publicity about its possible significance for the women's movement (*Ms.*, Spring, 1972; *Time*, July 15, 1974). It is not uncommon to hear people talking, even today, about women's career conflicts that are caused by fear of success.

However, psychologists were not willing to accept such sweeping conclusions on the basis of a single study, and many went on to conduct investigations of their own. In 1977, David Tresemer reviewed 42 studies comparing over 6,000 men and women on a variety of measures of fear of success. Most of this research, like Horner's original study, concentrated on white American college students. But there were also surveys of many other groups including high school students, Harvard Law School graduates, and executives of the Atlantic Richfield Company. Taken together, these studies made it quite clear that fear of success is just as common among American men as it is among American women.

Some of the most interesting follow-ups were direct descendants of Horner's thesis. A direct replication of Horner's methods (Hoffman, 1974; see "How Do They Know?") concluded that, at least in 1971, University of Michigan male undergraduates feared success just as much as females did.

HOW DO THEY KNOW?

Replication: Are Women Afraid to Succeed?

In the history of science, one of the most important checks on the accuracy of research has been replication—repeating a study to see if it yields the same result. There are several major types of replication, each with slightly different goals and slightly different procedures (Lykken, 1968). In a **literal replication,** an experimenter tries to repeat a study as precisely as possible. In a **constructive replication,** the experimenter changes the procedure in systematic ways to gain further insight into the result. As we shall see below, a single replication can include both literal and constructive aspects.

As noted in this chapter, Matina Horner, in her doctoral dissertation (1969), found that more women (65%) than men (9%) showed signs of fear of success when they wrote stories about a person of the same sex who had finished first in a medical school class. Because of the tremendous interest in the implications of this study and the controversy generated by it, in 1971 Lois Wladis Hoffman tried to replicate it.

She followed Horner's procedures as closely as possible. Once again, the subjects were students at the University of Michigan who were required to participate in an experiment as part of their introductory psychology course. Even apparently trivial features of the experiment were repeated, for example, "data were collected in two evening sessions; the date was at the same point in the term. . . . The room and the seating arrangements were the same. The male experimenter was chosen because he seemed to several persons who knew both of them to be a 1971 equivalent of the experimenter in the earlier study. The questionnaire books and instructions were identical. . . . The coders were personally trained by Horner to the exact coding procedures that she had used in the earlier study [to quantify fear of success]" (Hoffman, 1974, pp. 354–355).

This slavish attention to duplicating every detail was designed to ensure that any difference in the results could be attributed to the one major factor that *had* changed—the origi-

Interestingly, the same researcher followed up the actual subjects Horner had studied in her doctoral dissertation. In the intervening years, 14 women from the original sample had gotten pregnant at a time when they were on the verge of advancing in their careers or at a time when their achievements threatened to outstrip their husbands'. Of these 14 women, 13 had been diagnosed as fearing success when they were in college. Here again, a short and simple test of social motivation in college seemed to predict important life choices years later.

Continuing research on the fear of success has revealed several layers of complexity. For example, it is often hard to tell whether a person who does not try is afraid of success or failure. Further, being a homemaker might be very satisfying for one woman and a sign of failure for another.

The recognition of such complications is a sign of the maturity of this research

nal study was conducted in 1965, the replication in 1971. If popular stereotypes of women's liberation were correct, the intervening six years had seen dramatic changes in the way American women perceived their roles in society. And any such changes should be especially obvious in a young, highly educated group like college students.

A total of 92 students participated in a literal replication that reproduced every detail of Horner's study. Another 116 subjects took part in several constructive replications in which one key aspect of the original procedure was changed. For example, 24 women were asked to write a story that began, "After first term finals, Anne finds that she is the top child psychology graduate student." Since medicine is traditionally a male-dominated field in the United States and child psychology is not, this cue was designed to see whether the nature of the profession was an important variable.

This minor change and others like it did not make any difference. Some 65% of the women still scored high in fear of success. But Hoffman's figure for 1971 men was 77%. Although the 1971 difference between the sexes did not quite achieve statistical significance,

men actually showed more fear of success than women did. This replication seems to show that the cultural changes in the late 1960s had made men more ambivalent about success rather than making women less so.

But this conclusion was placed in doubt by still more research. It is extremely difficult to reproduce an experiment exactly. When Hoffman (1977) reanalyzed the original stories written for Horner in 1965, she found that her system for measuring fear of success was *not* the same as the original, despite her many attempts to make it the same. In the original study, 8 men out of 71 were classified as having a fear of success; when the same 71 stories were reanalyzed, 39 men showed this fear.

This careful series of replications and reanalyses led to two major conclusions: Fear of success is indeed a common phenomenon, but one that is quite difficult to measure precisely, and American women do not fear success more than men do. These careful follow-ups also make it clear that replication can distinguish between legitimate findings and those based on faulty procedures or random variation. Thus, replication is a critical step in the scientist's search for truth.

and its promise for the future. Like other physiological and social motives, it does not act alone but rather provides another piece in the complex puzzle of human behavior. Fear of success is not a "women's problem"; it is a human problem.

Emotion

The topic of emotion has been a difficult one to study scientifically. Some psychologists have become so frustrated by this subject that they argued—often quite angrily—that "emotion" is not a useful scientific concept at all.

Emotion is the spice of life—indeed, the very stuff of it. The emotion of love inspired Shah Jehan to build the Taj Mahal as a monument to his wife, and hatred and anger lay behind Auschwitz and the atrocities of World War II. If psychology is ever to understand the lustful, spiteful, idealistic world of human behavior, it must explain how we feel the things we do.

According to Webster's dictionary, *emotions* involve "strong feelings (as of love, hate, desire, or fear) . . . manifest in neuromuscular, respiratory, cardiovascular, hormonal, and other bodily changes." Psychologists too have emphasized the role of internal bodily changes in emotion and have attempted to chart its complex interactions between brain and body. The two oldest theories of emotion, the James-Lange and the Cannon-Bard, agree that there is an interaction, but they disagree on whether the fundamental source of emotional feelings lies in the body or the brain.

EARLY THEORIES OF EMOTION

Near the end of the nineteenth century, Harvard psychologist William James and Danish researcher Carl Lange each independently proposed a theory that seems to deny our everyday experience of emotions. According to the mythical woman in the street, we laugh because we are happy and cry because we are sad. What came to be known as the **James-Lange theory** turned this around. According to this theory, an event in the environment automatically stimulates a particular pattern of bodily changes. The brain then recognizes this pattern as belonging to a specific emotion and proceeds to label it. Thus, the feeling and experience of emotion comes second, while a direct physiological response comes first.

Consider the following example: The sight of a stranger in a dark alley may elicit pounding of the heart and sweaty hands. The brain notes these physiological changes and others from the internal organs and realizes, so quickly that we are not aware of any delay, "if my body is reacting this way, I must be afraid!" Implicit in the James-Lange theory is the idea that each emotion is physiologically distinct. If the brain decides when the body is angry and when it is afraid by performing an inventory of physiological changes, these two emotions must be characterized by distinct patterns of physiological activity.

Physiologist Walter Cannon rejected this view. As we noted in Chapter 2, Cannon was the first to discuss the activation of the sympathetic nervous system in "fight or flight." He believed that all strong emotions produced a single pattern of

A self-portrait of William James (1842–1910), one of the founders of the science of psychology. The older brother of the novelist Henry James, William was raised by wealthy parents who provided a rather unorthodox education as the family traveled through England, Switzerland, France, and Germany. After graduating from medical school, William James accepted a position teaching physiology at Harvard. In 1875, he taught the first course in an American university that focused on psychology and founded the first American psychology laboratory. In 1890, he published *Principles of Psychology*, the first textbook in this infant field. Although this book cited no empirical research whatsoever, James's literary insights into psychological phenomena still continue to fascinate contemporary psychologists.

physiological arousal—including increased heart rate, secretion of the hormone adrenaline, reduced blood flow near the surface of the skin, and increased sweating—which prepared the organism to deal with an emergency.

Cannon firmly rejected James's notion of a separate physiological pattern for each emotion. Instead, he saw the key to emotional experience in the brain. For William James, the brain recognized an emotion simply by passively checking which internal organs were on and which were off. For Cannon, the brain played a much more important role. Electrical and chemical changes in the brain (in the area he called the optic thalamus) simultaneously produced bodily changes and emotional experience. Because this view was supported by a series of experiments performed by Philip Bard, this became known as the **Cannon-Bard theory** of emotion.

To support his theory, Cannon (1927) cited evidence that signals from the peripheral organs were not a necessary ingredient in the experience of emotion. Specifically, when internal feedback was cut off by surgically destroying the fibers that connected the sympathetic nervous system to the brain in dogs and cats, the experimental animals still gave behavioral signs of emotion. For example, cats continued to show all the normal signs of feline rage when confronted by a barking dog.

Hohmann (1966) challenged this conclusion in a study of 25 patients with spinal cord injuries. For these unfortunate victims, Mother Nature and human carelessness had performed cruel experiments in which certain nerve fibers were severed accidentally. Some patients had damaged relatively low portions of the spinal cord, so that feedback from internal organs still reached the brain through the higher, undamaged

Figure 10.6
Three theories of
emotion.

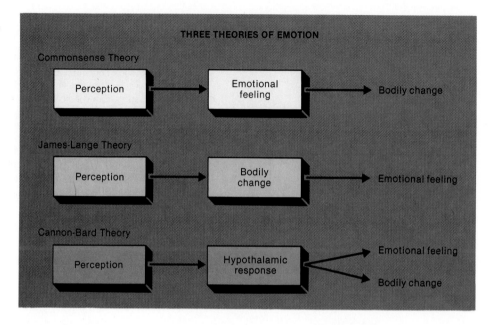

sections. Others, whose damage was closer to the brain, received little or no information from internal organs.

Hohmann (1966) asked these patients to remember an emotional incident that occurred before the injury and to compare it to one that occurred afterward. Interestingly, he found that the loss of internal sensations did indeed reduce emotional feeling. As one subject put it:

> [Now] it's sort of cold anger. Sometimes I act angry when I see some injustice. I yell and cuss and raise hell, because if you don't do it sometimes, I've learned people will take advantage of you, but it just doesn't have the heat to it that it used to. It's a mental kind of anger" (quoted in Schachter, 1971, p. 50).

Even more convincing than such testimonials was Hohmann's evidence that the less feedback patients had from internal organs, the more their emotional experience was reduced.

This evidence suggests that Cannon was wrong when he claimed that bodily responses are only a side effect of emotion and have no role in our feelings. However, some of his other claims were quite influential, particularly the idea that all strong emotions produce a single pattern of physiological arousal.

AROUSAL

As noted earlier, if the James-Lange theory is correct, each emotion must produce a different pattern of physiological activity so that it can be recognized by the brain. While researchers have been able to identify such differences between anger and fear (Ax, 1953), in general most emotions seem to be accompanied by a more general pattern of **arousal** in which several physiological systems are activated at the same time, including higher heart rate, sweat-gland activity, and electrical activity of the brain. Several theories have been proposed to explain the significance of arousal in motivation and emotion.

Low levels of arousal characterize periods of drowsiness or sleep, although a few purists maintain that the *lowest* level of arousal is death. Higher levels of arousal are characterized by high activation or stress (see Chapter 3). Extreme emotions such as panic also produce high arousal. According to one influential theory called the **Yerkes-Dodson law,** there is an *optimal level,* or most desirable amount, of arousal for any activity; too little arousal or too much produces inferior performance. For example, most people would agree that if a student stays up all night to study and comes to a final exam half asleep, this low level of arousal is likely to result in a reduced grade. However, the person who gets a full night of rest and then drinks 16 cups of coffee to increase his concentration is also likely to do poorly, in this case because too much arousal interferes with performance. Figure 10.7 summarizes the Yerkes-Dodson law in a form that is sometimes called the inverted-*U* relationship between arousal and performance (that is, the graph looks like the letter *U* upside down).

The actual ideal amount of arousal may be different for a tennis match and a chess game or may vary from one person to another. But according to this theory, any individual will perform a particular task best at some optimal level of arousal.

While this notion has been influential and has generated a large body of research, it is not without problems. Psychophysiologists have found that different measures of arousal do not always vary together; increases in blood pressure are

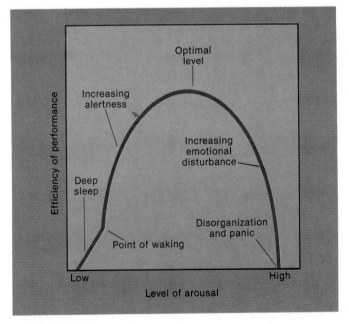

Figure 10.7
The relationship between arousal and performance according to the Yerkes-Dodson law. This theory holds that there is an optimal (or ideal) level of arousal for the most efficient performance of any task. Too little arousal or too much will produce inferior performance.

often associated with decreases in EEG arousal, for example, and some drugs produce behavioral arousal and EEG signs of relaxation (Lacey, 1967). The notion that there is one single variable called arousal is at best only a first approximation. But this notion has proved useful in research in many areas, including the topic of lie detection.

APPLIED PSYCHOLOGY

Lie Detection

Physiological tests to determine whether a person is telling the truth have a long history. In ancient times, the Chinese required a man accused of a crime to chew a mouthful of dried rice; if he could spit it out, he was judged innocent. In retrospect, this test of guilt was crudely based on a physiological fact—when the sympathetic nervous system is activated by stress, salivation decreases. If the man was guilty, he would be anxious and his mouth would be dry; he would find it difficult to swallow or to spit. Unfortunately, the test ignores the fact that the innocent man might also be scared spitless.

The modern era of lie detection began around 1890 when an Italian criminologist named Cesare Lombroso claimed that he could tell when a criminal suspect was lying by measuring his blood pressure while he was being interrogated. About 30 years later, Leonarde Keeler quit his job with the Berkeley, California, police department to manufacture Keeler *polygraphs,* devices that simultaneously recorded breathing, relative blood pressure, and the electrical activity of the skin (an indirect measure of sweat gland activity). Most lie detectors are modern versions of Keeler's primitive machine.

Traditionally, psychologists have had little to do with the lie-detection business. The field of polygraphy—a term most professionals prefer to the popular term *lie detection*—was founded by men with experience in the police and the military. These skilled interrogators often saw academic research as an ivory-tower science that had little to say about a real world full of criminals and liars. Physiological researchers, in turn, saw polygraphers as businessmen who were more interested in selling their own lie-detection tests than in objectively evaluating their accuracy. The relationship between psychology and commercial polygraphy was one of distrust founded on ignorance.

Lie detection is big business. Estimates of the number of polygraph examinations given in the United States each year range from several hundred thousand to several million. Contrary to popular belief, most of these examinations are conducted not for the police but in the world of business. A man who has applied for an executive position in a department store may be tested to see if he has ever been in trouble, or all the employees at the local Burger King may be grilled to see who's been pocketing the money that should have ended up in the cash register.

The legal status of lie detection is somewhat ambiguous. Some states regulate polygraphy; in other states you could become a professional lie detector simply by placing your name in the Yellow Pages. Ordinarily, polygraph examinations are not permitted as evidence in a court of law. But exceptions have been made. And if a suspect confesses as a result of a polygraph test, his statements can usually be held against him.

Typically, a criminal lie-detection test begins with an interview covering the subject's history and background. Before the machine is connected, the interrogator and subject agree on about 10 questions that can be answered simply yes or no. Some questions are emotionally neutral, some are control questions designed to elicit an emotional response (for example, "Have you ever hurt someone?"), and some are relevant to the crime in question. If the questions are designed properly, a person who is innocent should have the largest physiological response to the irrelevant emotional questions; a guilty person's largest physiological response should be to the questions that relate specifically to the crime.

No single physiological response always signals a lie. Rather, the polygrapher looks for signs of general emotional arousal associated with activation of the sympathetic nervous system—irregular breathing, high blood pressure, and electrical signs of increased sweating. The actual decision about whether a particular pattern of responses indicates arousal is based on a complex interaction of the three measures and has not been specified precisely. For this reason, polygraph reading is usually treated as an art rather than a science. Further, most professional polygraphers prefer to base their final verdict on all the evidence available (including the conduct of the suspect during the interview) rather than strictly on physiological responses. Thus, polygraph examination is not a simple and unambiguous physiological test; it is a complex type of police interrogation.

Laboratory tests of lie detection have generally shown that the procedure has some validity. In one of the most realistic experiments (Raskin & Hare, 1978), 24 prison inmates committed a mock crime. They were told to steal $20 from an envelope in a room that was normally off limits. If they could convince the polygrapher that they were innocent, they could keep the money. Another group of 24 prisoners were told to report verbally the details of the mock crime, but they did not steal the money themselves. They, too, denied the crime in the standardized lie-detection tests that followed.

Four of the tests were inconclusive; the polygrapher simply could not say whether these particular prisoners were telling the truth. In 42 of the remaining 44 cases, the prisoners were correctly identified as guilty or innocent of the mock crime. Two prisoners did manage to beat the polygraph—they were judged innocent when in fact they were guilty. The overall success rate was 88% correct, 4% wrong, and 8% inconclusive.

Of course, even a realistic laboratory test like this involves people who have little to lose by being detected. The ideal evaluation of lie detection in the field would involve actual criminal investigations. Unfortunately, studies of this sort are inevitably flawed. When a man is judged innocent by a polygraph, the police often stop investigating him. His innocence is accepted, and there is no independent way of

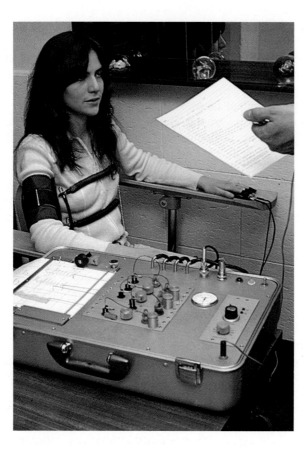

Figure 10.8
As this woman takes a lie detector test, a cuff around her arm measures blood pressure, a tube around her chest measures breathing, and electrodes on her fingertips measure sweat-gland activity.

knowing whether he fooled the polygrapher. Thus, there is an element of self-fulfilling prophesy here.

Reviews of all available literature on the outcome of criminal polygraph examinations have led different experts to different conclusions. One critic (Lykken, 1979) claimed that the polygraph is correct only 64% to 71% of the time when examiners rely on physiological data alone. Others reply that "properly conducted" lie-detection tests are correct 90% of the time (Raskin & Podlesny, 1979).

But all the experts agree on one fact—polygraphy is currently an art rather than a science. As polygraph expert Fred Inbau put it in testimony before the United States House of Representatives: "The technique is no better than the man making the diagnosis" (U.S. Congress, 1965). This is somewhat upsetting, given the lack of legal regulation of the profession. It is also disturbing in the light of evidence that mathematical analyses of polygraph results are less likely to make mistakes than human operators (Szucko & Kleinmuntz, 1981).

Clearly, a properly conducted polygraph examination can help distinguish a liar from someone who tells the truth. Although there is considerable controversy about how often polygraphers are incorrect, there is no argument that even the best do make mistakes. And in the hands of an unskilled operator, the lie detector may be a real menace to civil liberty.

Psychologists must continue to do research to establish the conditions in which lie detection works best and to estimate the reasonable likelihood of its success. Ultimately, however, others will have to decide on the place of lie detection in our society—how good is good enough?

COGNITIVE APPROACHES

Despite the fact that lie detection is closely related to arousal theories of motivation, this work has had little influence on the study of emotion. Within the scientific mainstream, current views have combined the best of past theories with a more cognitive orientation.

Stanley Schachter and Jerome Singer (1962) combined William James's idea that bodily reactions are an important element in emotional experience and Cannon's notion of arousal with a cognitive emphasis on the individual's thoughts and interpretations. According to **Schachter and Singer's cognitive theory,** the specific emotion a person experiences depends on how she perceives and interprets her situation, while its intensity is determined by the degree of physiological arousal. Thus, a woman whose sympathetic nervous system is aroused might feel happy if she is at a party but angry if the same physiological response occurs during an argument.

To test this theory, Schachter and Singer (1962) decided to produce arousal artificially and then place people in situations that might elicit different emotions. Male psychology students at the University of Minnesota were recruited for a study of how the "vitamin compound Suproxin" influenced vision. In fact, no visual tests were planned, and the injection the men received was either a harmless placebo (salt water) or epinephrine, a drug that activates the sympathetic nervous system. The effects of epinephrine (also known as adrenaline) include increases in heart rate and blood pressure, decreased blood flow to the skin, and increases in blood sugar and lactic acid. The injection produced essentially the same physical reaction that you might have if you were frightened suddenly and adrenaline was secreted into your bloodstream by the adrenal glands (see Chapter 2).

One group of subjects—called "epinephrine informed" were warned that Suproxin had certain side effects including shaky hands, a pounding heart, and a flushed face. Another group—called "epinephrine ignorant"—received no such warning. There were several control groups; the most important received placebo injections.

Schachter and Singer then set up situations in which people were likely to label their experience as "happy" or "angry." They predicted that epinephrine-ignorant subjects would experience the strongest emotions because they would attribute their physical reactions to the situations. Epinephrine-informed subjects would have another explanation for their pounding hearts ("it's only a side effect of the drug") and would therefore not experience such intense emotions. Similarly, the placebo group would not experience intense emotions because the salt-water injections would not produce physiological arousal.

To induce happiness, a research assistant posing as another participant joined the first subject while they "waited for the drug to take effect" and proceeded to make a fool of himself according to a prearranged script—flying a paper airplane, using a rubber band as a slingshot, building a tower out of manila folders and knocking it down with the slingshot, and so on.

In the anger-inducing condition, the stooge continually complained about a five-page questionnaire the two subjects were supposed to fill out while they waited. Since the questions were designed to grow increasingly personal and insulting, he had plenty to grumble about. For example, question 25 asked each subject to list one person in his family who "does not wash or bathe regularly," "seems to need psychiatric care," and so on. After saying "I'll be damned if I fill out number 25," the stooge angrily crossed out the item.

The stooge's anger peaked for question 28: "How many times each week do you have sexual intercourse?" At this point he ripped up the questionnaire, threw the pieces on the floor, and stomped out of the room. Had he stayed around, he could have read eight more offensive questions, ending with: "With how many men (other than your father) has your mother had extramarital relationships? Four and under _____; Five–Nine _____; Ten and over _____."

The subjects' emotional reactions were measured in two different ways. Throughout the stooge's act, an observer watched through a one-way mirror and systematically coded how much each subject went along with the stooge. In addition, after the routine was finished, the experimenter returned with a series of questionnaires that included items asking people to rate their anger, happiness, and physical symptoms. Once these were finished, the researcher announced that the experiment was over and explained the deception in detail. (See "How Do They Know?" in Chapter 15 for a discussion of the ethical issues involved in this type of deception.)

After reviewing the results of this experiment and others like it, Schachter and Singer concluded that their cognitive theory of emotion was basically correct. Later researchers (Marshall & Zimbardo, 1979) had difficulty replicating these results, and there is now some question about whether the response to epinephrine injections may produce experiences as easily relabeled as Schachter and Singer argued.

On a more fundamental level, however, their most important conclusion has been supported by further research—cognitive interpretations do affect emotional experience and behavior. One example comes from a series of studies performed by Richard Lazarus and his colleagues in which reactions to a very arousing stimulus are manipulated by providing people with different cognitive attitudes. The stimulus was chosen for its stressfulness: A film showing an Australian aborigine puberty rite—a circumcision performed with a stone knife—in graphic detail and living color.

To influence the way viewers reacted to this film, several sound tracks were developed. One tried to maximize stress by emphasizing the trauma produced by the procedure ("Several men . . . hold the boy so that he cannot escape"); another denied the painfulness ("The words of encouragement offered by the older men have their effect"); a third sound track produced a more detached and intellectual perspective ("The surgical technique, while crude, is very carefully followed"). Physiological measurements of the arousal produced by these and other versions revealed that subjects who heard the denial or intellectualization sound track did indeed respond less than those who heard the more stressful commentary (Speisman, Lazarus, Davidson, & Mordkoff, 1964). Clearly, cognitive factors do affect emotional response.

FACIAL EXPRESSIONS

Even before William James proposed his first theory of emotion, Charles Darwin started a research tradition that continues to the present day. In 1872, he published *The Expression of the Emotions in Man and Animals,* a book that extended his theory of evolution to the study of postures, gestures, and facial expressions. For example, Darwin noted that such widely different species as cats, dogs, monkeys, rats, and humans have been known to defecate and urinate when they are afraid. He wished to show the continuity of emotional expression across species to support his theory that all animals are descended from common ancestors. Darwin believed that some common emotional expressions are innate, that they are biologically wired into the human species.

Of course, the meanings of some nonverbal gestures are simply a matter of convention and vary from one society to the next (see Chapter 15). When Americans disagree, they sometimes wag their heads from side to side to say no; Bulgarians use the same movement to say yes. Tibetans stick out their tongue to say hello, and in parts of Greece the thumbs up gesture Americans use to signify approval has an obscene meaning which we associate with the middle finger (Ekman, 1975). But cross-cultural similarities in facial expressions of emotion do support Darwin's idea that some expressions are innate. In one study (Ekman, Sorenson, & Friesen, 1969), researchers sorted through over 3,000 pictures to choose faces that seemed to represent one of six basic emotions: happiness, sadness, fear, anger, surprise, and disgust. They chose 30 photographs of Caucasian children and adults whose faces seemed to unambiguously communicate one of these six emotions.

In the original study, these photographs were shown to college students in the United States, Brazil, and Japan. Each observer was given the list of six emotions and asked which emotion was expressed by each face. Figure 10.9 lists the results, along with those of later experiments in Argentina and Chile. As you can see, the agreement is not perfect. But what is? This table does show a remarkable degree of consistency; apparently the meaning of an American's happy face would be quite clear in Japan, Argentina, Chile, and Brazil. Similar studies found comparable results from other groups in England, France, Germany, Greece, Hawaii, Sweden, Turkey, and several African nations (Izard, 1971).

Despite this impressive cross-cultural consistency, some critics were still not satisfied. Since the mass media have made our planet a small world, they reasoned that Greeks and Swedes might have learned to read American expressions by watch-

PHOTOGRAPH
JUDGED

JUDGMENT	HAPPINESS	DISGUST	SURPRISE	SADNESS	ANGER	FEAR
Culture			*Percent Who Agreed with Judgment*			
99 Americans	97	92	95	84	67	85
40 Brazilians	95	97	87	59	90	67
119 Chileans	95	92	93	88	94	68
168 Argentinians	98	92	95	78	90	54
29 Japanese	100	90	100	62	90	66

Figure 10.9
This table summarizes data from studies in five countries, showing remarkable consistency among different cultures in interpreting facial expressions.

ing reruns of "Kojak" and the "Mary Tyler Moore Show." To rule out this possibility, Ekman and Friesen (1971) conducted studies of the most isolated group they could find—members of the Fore culture in the southeast highlands of New Guinea.

This primitive group was "discovered by civilization" only 12 years before the study was conducted. The 189 adults and 130 children who participated in the experiment had never seen a movie, spoke neither English nor Pidgin, had not lived in a Western settlement or government town, and had never worked for a Caucasian. They were the most isolated members of an isolated culture. A special task was developed to avoid difficulties in translation. Adults were to pick one of three Caucasian faces that fit the emotion expressed in a particular story. For example, the fear story began: "She is sitting in her house all alone, and there is no one else in the village. There is no knife, axe, or bow and arrow in the house. A wild pig is standing in the door of the house, and the woman is looking at the pig and is very afraid of it." The sadness story said simply: "His child has died, and he feels very sad" (Ekman & Friesen, 1971, p. 126).

Both children and adults in the Fore culture were able to pick out the appropriate Western face. (For example, 92% of the Fore adults picked a smiling face when they heard the happiness story.) There was one interesting exception—these people could not tell the difference between Western faces that represented surprise and fear. One possible explanation is that in the Fore culture, fearful events are almost always also surprising, like the wild pig that suddenly appeared in the empty village.

Interestingly, other studies of facial expression support a modified version of the James-Lange theory. According to Silvan Tomkins (1962), feedback from facial muscles can influence emotional experience. For a do-it-yourself demonstration of this theory, try setting your face in a big, broad, stupid grin and see if it doesn't make you feel just a little happy. In a more systematic test of this notion, people who received mild electric shocks found that they experienced more pain when they allowed the pain to show in their faces than when they maintained more stoic expressions (Colby, Lanzetta, & Kleck, 1977). It is possible that people purposely ignored the shock to achieve stoic expressions and that the direction of attention is the critical factor. Nevertheless, it is a fascinating hypothesis that putting on a happy face really might make you feel better.

Another interesting trend in this research involved physiological recordings of facial muscles to reveal slight changes in expression that cannot be seen by the naked eye. For example, when subjects are instructed to think happy thoughts, changes in the rate of electrical activity in the depressor muscle near the chin can be detected by physiological recording devices even when a person does not seem to be smiling. Similar recordings also revealed that when depressed persons are asked to "imagine a typical day," their facial muscles reveal subtle signs of sadness (Schwartz, Fair, Salt, Mandel, & Klerman, 1976). Although we are far away from a physiological technology that allows us to read people's minds, perhaps we will soon discover new physiological procedures that will help us to read their faces.

Summary

1. **Motivation** involves the forces that influence the strength or direction of behavior. This topic is closely related to the study of **emotions,** physical reactions that are experienced as strong feelings such as happiness, fear, and anger.
2. Early theories of motivation debated the relative merits of **determinism** in which every event is seen as the inevitable product of a series of natural forces, versus **free will,** which assumes that people are free to choose what they will do. Around 1900, psychologists emphasized the importance of **instincts,** inborn forces that direct an organism toward a certain goal. Later, two new theoretical constructs were proposed. **Needs** are physiological requirements of the organism, while **drives** are motivational forces that incite an organism to action. More recently, theories of motivation have recognized the importance of **incentives,** external stimuli that increase the likelihood of behavior.
3. According to **opponent-process theory,** many acquired motives arise from the interplay of two opposing processes in the brain, such as pleasure in response to pain. These days, most researchers have moved away from general theories of this sort and concentrate instead on the analysis of individual motives.
4. **Physiological motives** are internal bodily states that direct an organism's behavior toward a goal such as food, water, or sex. Early studies of hunger tried to localize its origins, first in the stomach, and later in the hypothalamus. Researchers now know that many other processes are involved in hunger, including body temperature, fat deposits, blood-sugar levels, and the responsiveness of obese people to external cues.

5. Body weight is determined by the interactions between three major factors: the amount and type of food eaten, the amount of energy expended in physical activity, and the storage of fat in cellular tissue. The relations among these factors may vary in different individuals.

6. **Social motives** direct human behavior toward certain patterns of relationships with other people, such as autonomy and affiliation.

7. In the **Thematic Apperception Test,** people are asked to make up stories about a series of ambiguous pictures. The results can identify people with a high **need for achievement** who differ from others in a number of ways—they work harder, learn faster, resist social pressure, and are likely to choose moderately risky tasks.

8. In the late 1960s, some studies suggested that women were more likely than men to have a **fear of success.** They are afraid that doing well in competitive situations will have negative consequences such as unpopularity. Later studies revealed that this fear characterized as many men as women.

9. According to the **James-Lange theory** of emotion, an event can automatically trigger a particular bodily response. The feeling of emotion is based on the brain's later identification of the physiological response. In contrast, the **Cannon-Bard theory** held that the brain responded to external events, simultaneously producing both physiological responses and emotional experience.

10. Most emotions are accompanied by a general pattern of **arousal** in which several physiological systems are activated at the same time, including higher heart rate, sweat-gland activity, and electrical activity of the brain. According to the **Yerkes-Dodson law,** there is an *optimal level* (most desirable amount) of arousal for any activity; too little or too much arousal interferes with performance. Tests of lie detection assume that deception will produce a pattern of physiological arousal including irregular breathing, high blood pressure, and increased sweat-gland activity.

11. According to **Schachter and Singer's cognitive theory** of emotions, the intensity of emotional experience is determined by the degree of arousal of the sympathetic nervous system, but the actual emotion is determined by the perception of the situation. Most psychologists now believe that cognitive factors have a major influence on emotional experience.

12. Studies of facial expressions have identified six basic emotions that are expressed the same way in virtually every culture: happiness, sadness, anger, fear, surprise, and disgust.

Discussion of "Becoming a Critical Consumer"

Two of the errors are relatively minor and may have been typographical. The researcher's name is McClelland (not McLelland), and the motive is called the need for achievement (abbreviated nAch, not Motive A).

The other two errors resulted from oversimplification. If it is possible to define success as a single goal, it is surely not possible to predict it from one personality characteristic. And the ring-toss game is definitely not appropriate for diagnosis. As Figure 10.5 suggests, people who are high in the need for achievement get many different scores. Although certain average trends have been demonstrated, they do not apply to every individual in every case.

To Learn More

Arkes, H. R., & Garske, J. P. *Psychological Theories of Motivation.* Monterey, Calif.: Brooks/Cole, 1977. A textbook survey of different theoretical approaches to motivation, from psychoanalysis to attribution theory.

McClelland, D. *The Achieving Society.* New York: Van Nostrand Reinhold, 1961. The dominant researcher on the need for achievement considers some of the larger societal issues raised by this motive.

Ekman, P., & Friesen, W. V. *Unmasking the Face.* Englewood Cliffs, N.J.: Prentice-Hall, 1975. An illustrated guide to the study of facial expression and emotion.

11
Personality

read

The psychoanalytic approach
The case of Anna O.
Instincts
The organization of personality
Psychosexual stages
Defense mechanisms: The example of repression
Evaluating Freud's contribution

The social-learning approach
From radical behaviorism to social learning
Self-efficacy

The humanistic approach

Type and trait approaches
Basic concepts
Allport's research

Current issues in personality research
Of persons and situations
Androgyny

Applied psychology: Type *A* behavior and heart disease

Summary

BECOMING A CRITICAL CONSUMER
Is psychology sexist?

The first ten chapters of this book have focused on the search for general laws of behavior and experience. For example, we described how the memory of the average eyewitness distorts the details of a crime and how the typical infant lacks a sense of object permanence. In each case, researchers have tried to establish principles that apply generally to all people. However, intuitively we believe that people are not all alike—that Uncle Jim is far more extraverted than Uncle Ed and that the fact that the local butcher tells so many meat jokes implies that he has a better-than-average sense of humor.

Consider the cases of two hypothetical students who fail their first psychology exam. One might be so upset that he would cut his next class, skip lunch, and feel sick to his stomach for the next several days. He might even wonder whether he should forget about college and go directly to a $40,000-per-year job selling used cars. Another student could react quite differently; she might glance quickly at the *F* on her way to the cafeteria and then sit down to a lunch of extra-hot curried chicken while telling jokes about balding psychology teachers as if she didn't have a care in the world.

Studies of personality raise two basic questions about these hypothetical cases. Do different reactions in this specific situation give insight into a general pattern of individual behavior? If so, what causes these individual differences? The first question is the more fundamental one. Would the man with the upset stomach react the same way to an *F* in Art History, an inability to repair a broken window, and a bad job evaluation from his boss? For if he reacts to each of these situations in entirely different ways, it would not be legitimate to characterize him as insecure or easily upset on the basis of a single observation.

In general, personality psychologists argue that there are consistent patterns of differences among people. Indeed, **personality** may be defined as an individual's characteristic pattern of thought, behavior, and emotions. Recently, some psychologists have argued that the consistency of these patterns may be an illusion caused by biases in the way people perceive one another (see "Of Persons and Situations" later in this chapter).

But it is the second question we raised, on the causes of the complex behavior patterns of a specific individual, that has historically attracted the most attention. In other words, why do we do the things we do? This is a broad question indeed; it almost seems arrogant for a psychologist to try to answer it. After all, one might argue that the entire history of literature and a good part of philosophy reflect an attempt to solve the puzzle of human character. From Homer's attempt to understand Odysseus to Shakespeare's characterization of Julius Caesar and Carolyn Keene's insights into Nancy Drew, writers have tried to understand and explain specific personalities.

The complexity of the subject matter of personality makes it one of the most fascinating topics in psychology. But it is also one of the most frustrating—because psychologists have not agreed on a single, unified, complete, and coherent view. We have encountered such theoretical conflicts before, as in the clash between behavioral and cognitive views of learning or memory. But in the case of personality, all five major paradigms (see Chapter 1) have had some impact. There are psychoanalytic theories of personality, behavioral theories, humanistic theories, cognitive theories, and even biological theories. To add to the complications, many theorists have drawn upon ideas from more than one paradigm. For example, the social-learning theory combines behavioral and cognitive principles.

This chapter is organized around the four most influential approaches to personality: psychoanalytic, social-learning, humanistic, and trait. Although many different theorists belong to each of these schools, each section here focuses on the thought of one major figure: Sigmund Freud for psychoanalysis, Albert Bandura for social learning, Abraham Maslow for the humanistic school, and Gordon Allport for traits. These are not the only theorists associated with each view and not all psychologists would agree that these four figures are the best representatives of these schools. This approach is designed simply to provide a concrete example of each view in order to lay the groundwork for understanding the broader differences. The chapter ends with a description of current trends in personality research.

It would be more convenient for textbook writers and less confusing for students if one particular approach to personality had triumphed, had been proved right, and the other approaches had been proved wrong. But this is not the case. An accurate introduction to this field must portray several approaches to personality that sometimes contradict one another and sometimes go off in entirely different directions to explore phenomena that others ignore.

The Psychoanalytic Approach

The **psychoanalytic approach** to personality emphasizes the importance of unconscious forces and biological instincts in shaping complex human behavior. This school of thought was founded by Sigmund Freud, one of the most controversial and influential figures in the history of psychology.

After receiving his medical degree from the University of Vienna in 1881, Freud decided to specialize in the treatment of mental disorders. At that time, physicians knew little about the nature of mental illness, and many of Freud's ideas about the normal personality grew out of his pioneering work with disturbed individuals. We begin with an account of a woman known to medical science as Anna O., one of the first and most famous patients whose illness helped shape the thinking of the young Dr. Freud.

THE CASE OF ANNA O.

On the surface, Anna O. seemed to have everything a young woman could ask for. She was intelligent, charming, witty, and beautiful. But at the age of 21, she was referred to a Viennese doctor named Josef Breuer for treatment of a severe chronic cough she had developed while caring for her ailing father. Various specialists had been unable to find anything physically wrong with Anna; Breuer diagnosed her as a victim of hysterical neurosis, a nervous disorder that medical science had many theories about but few techniques for curing.

When Anna's father died in 1881, her symptoms multiplied. Anna refused to eat

Sigmund Freud (1856–1939) is one of the most important figures in the history of psychology and psychiatry. He was born in Frieburg, Moravia (now part of Czechoslovakia). After graduating with a medical degree from the University of Vienna in 1881, Freud began a career in physiological research. However, financial pressures forced him to practice medicine. Freud chose to specialize in the treatment of emotional and nervous disorders and experimented with hypnosis and other cures. His work with Joseph Breuer on Anna O. and other cases helped establish some of the basic principles of psychoanalysis. Freud's first major book describing the foundations of this new system was *The Interpretation of Dreams*, published in 1900. Only 600 copies were printed, and it took eight years to sell them all. But Freud began to gain international recognition after he gave a series of lectures at Clark University in 1909. For the next thirty years, he continued to develop his monumental theories of psychoanalysis. Since his death, scholars have written countless books and articles painstakingly exploring the possible implications of every event in Freud's life—from his bed-wetting at the age of two to the remote possibility that he had an affair with his sister-in-law.

and became physically weak. She lost feeling in her hands and feet, became partially paralyzed, and suffered from visual disturbances. Her speech became bizarre; she sometimes left so many words out of a sentence that she did not make any sense. For a period of two weeks, Anna became totally mute; no matter how hard she tried, she could not speak at all. Anna even showed signs of developing two different personalities—one depressed and anxious, the other excited and given to bizarre outbursts in which she threw things at people and suffered from frightening visual hallucinations.

Breuer found the loss of feeling in Anna's hands and feet particularly interesting from a medical point of view. About that time, physicians had discovered that the symptom of *glove anesthesia*—in which feeling was lost in the entire hand (roughly, the area that might be covered by a glove)—could not possibly have a physical basis (see Figure 11.1). Anatomically, the nerves that are responsible for feeling in the

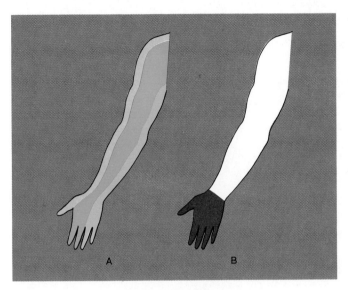

Figure 11.1

Figure *A* shows the areas of the hand and arm connected to three major nerves. Figure *B* shows the area of sensation lost in glove anesthesia. Damage to the nerves that convey sensations from the hand would also eliminate sensation from the arm. Therefore, loss of sensation in the hand alone must have a psychological rather than a physiological cause.

hand also control other areas in the arm; thus, if these nerves were damaged, the loss of feeling could not be limited just to the hand. The obvious conclusion: A patient who reported glove anesthesia suffered from a psychological disorder rather than a purely physical one. This does not imply that Anna O. was faking her disease, only that its causes were buried in her psyche.

Breuer gradually discovered that when Anna O. told him in detail of her hallucinations and fantasies, her condition slowly began to improve. Thus did doctor and patient stumble upon the solution of the "talking cure." The progress of this therapy convinced Breuer that Anna's symptoms were not the random products of an irrational mind. Rather, each symptom had developed as a result of particular events in Anna's life and expressed a hidden emotional logic.

For example, some of Anna's visual problems were traced back to a long and difficult evening by her dying father's bedside. When her father suddenly asked what time it was, Anna found that the tears in her eyes prevented her from seeing the watch clearly. She valiantly tried to keep from crying so that her father would not be upset by her tears. This attempt to strangle such powerful emotions was buried in her unconscious mind and later led to the physical symptoms of visual problems. When Anna consciously remembered this event and described it over the course of many sessions to Breuer, her vision slowly improved.

Aristotle had used the Greek word *katharsis* to describe the emotional release an audience felt during a tragic drama. When Breuer and Freud (1893) described the case of Anna O. in their book *Case Studies in Hysteria*, they used the term **catharsis** to refer to the relief of symptoms of mental illness by bringing unconscious emotional conflicts into conscious awareness.

Perhaps because of his own emotional conflicts regarding the beautiful young Anna O., Breuer did not pursue the study of hysterical neurosis (Pollock, 1968). But

Anna O.—one of the most famous patients analyzed by Freud. "Anna's" real name was Bertha Pappenheim; after her recovery she became famous as a pioneer social worker and militant feminist.

Sigmund Freud went on to work with many other patients to develop new therapeutic techniques for producing catharsis (see Chapter 14). He also explored the workings of unconscious impulses in dreams, in everyday behavior, and even in his own life. In fact, beginning in the summer of 1897, Freud reserved the last half hour of each day for an analysis of his own thoughts and conflicts (Jones, 1953). He continued this practice until he died in 1939.

Over the course of more than half a century of thinking and writing about psychoanalysis, Freud gradually developed an extremely detailed theory about the causes of human behavior. Although we can only hint at its richness and complexity here, the next section of this chapter describes some of Freud's basic concepts.

INSTINCTS

In the nineteenth century, many scientists believed that every action and reaction in the physical world was completely determined by the operation of the forces of nature. If science could uncover these natural laws, they believed, it would be able to predict every event. Freud tried to extend this model by specifying the psychic forces that determined human behavior.

Freud focused on **instincts,** which he defined as the inborn mental representations of physical needs. Ultimately, he traced all human behavior back to the expression of instincts. Freud never compiled a complete list of human instincts, but he did gradually come to the conclusion that they fell into two major classes—life instincts *(eros)* and death instincts *(thanatos).*

The **life instincts** help the individual, and the species, to survive. The most obvious examples are hunger, thirst, and sex. The sexual instinct was the one Freud devoted the most attention to, particularly in his early writings.

For Freud, sex was not a single instinct but involved a number of different types of impulses. He distinguished several **erogenous zones,** areas of the body that are sensitive to feelings of both irritation and pleasure. As we shall see, the major erogenous zones are the mouth, the anus, and the sex organs. Freud's definition of sex was far broader than the everyday meaning of the term.

In opposition to sex and the other life instincts stand another group called **death instincts,** whose workings can be summarized in Freud's (1920) famous statement that "the goal of all life is death" (p. 38). Freud added the notion of an unconscious death wish to his theory partly in an attempt to explain the tragic destruction he saw in World War I. When aggressive drives are directed inward, they can produce depression or even suicide. When these self-destructive forces are blocked, they may be turned outward and produce violence toward other people.

The motivational force of instincts is based on a process of tension reduction; for example, the hunger instinct gradually builds up psychic tension, which is reduced when a person eats. But this tension reduction can sometimes take place in ways that are not at all obvious. The word **displacement** refers to a process by which instinctual energy is rechanneled from one object to another. Displacement is one of the most important concepts in psychoanalysis, because it explains complex forms of adult behavior in terms of basic biological urges.

For example, Freud (1910) argued that Leonardo da Vinci painted Madonnas partly because he had been separated from his mother at an early age. The instinctual energy built up by Da Vinci's unconscious desire for motherly love was rechanneled into painting portraits of the mother of Christ. This particular type of displacement, in which instinctual energy is rechanneled into higher cultural goals, is called *sublimation.*

In some special circumstances, it is possible to glimpse the mysterious workings of unconscious instincts. For example, during sleep the censor of the conscious mind relaxes, and unconscious material may force its way into the content of dreams, sometimes in a disguised form.

In *The Interpretation of Dreams,* Freud (1900) gave many examples of the way instinctual forces can be displaced and otherwise transformed in dreams. For instance, Freud reported a dream he had the night before his father's funeral. It included a scene in a barber shop with a posted sign that said, "You are requested to close an eye." Freud had arranged a simple ceremony for the funeral, in keeping with his father's wishes. He interpreted the barber-shop dream as a reflection of his guilt; the sign asked relatives who would have preferred a more elaborate ceremony to "close an eye"—overlook the inadequacy of the arrangements.

For Freud, things are usually not what they seem. The conscious mind is at best only dimly aware of the workings of instinctual forces. Indeed, our unconscious can purposely deceive our conscious mind to protect us from the knowledge and the consequences of our animal instincts. As a result, even our strongest beliefs about our own actions are often based on error and self-deception.

French author Jean Cocteau's drawing of Sigmund Freud; the second face symbolizes Freud's emphasis on the influence of bodily instincts.

THE ORGANIZATION OF PERSONALITY

According to Freud, the human personality is organized into three interrelated elements: the id, the ego, and the superego. When he described personality in this way, Freud was not referring to physical structures in the brain but to different psychic processes that interact with one another to produce behavior and personality.

The **id** is a primitive force of innate biological instincts. It is the first and most basic aspect of personality, consisting of both life and death instincts which are present at birth. All these instincts chaotically seek one goal—immediate satisfaction. As noted earlier, Freud proposed a tension-reduction model of personality: Instincts automatically build up a state of tension that must be discharged to achieve satisfaction. An infant deprived of food, even for a short time, experiences a buildup of tension from the hunger instinct; an infant who is deprived of oral stimulation experiences increased tension of this "sexual" drive.

The id operates according to what Freud considered the most basic law of life, the **pleasure principle**—the id reduces instinctual tension and returns the organism to a comfortable state. For some primitive responses of the newborn infant, tension can be reduced by reflex. For example, a sneeze reduces irritation of the nose. But most of the infant's instinctual desires cannot be met so quickly and automatically. No matter how much a mother may pamper her infant, there will be times when the child must wait to be fed and instinctual tension will build up. This kind of frustration stimulates the psychological development of the id and activates an unconscious attempt to reduce tension by forming a mental picture of a desired object, in this case perhaps the mother's breast or a Junior Whopper. Obviously, a mental image of food is not enough. A person whose id never developed any further would not be able to survive.

As a result of this frustration, a force begins to develop out of the id that is able to cope with the real world and protect the organism from harm. The **ego** distinguishes between the subjective world of the mind and the objective world of physical reality. It is governed by the **reality principle,** which means it tries to delay the discharge of instinctual energy until an appropriate object is present. Instead of conjuring up an image of food, the ego forces the id to wait for tension reduction until food is actually present. This does not mean that the pleasure principle is forgotten. The ego wants to satisfy instinctual urges just as much as the id does; it simply learns to go about doing so in a productive, realistic way.

The ego is often referred to as the "executive" of personality, because it makes the hard decisions that balance the needs of the id against the demands of reality on the one hand and the demands of the superego on the other. The **superego** is the aspect of personality that represents moral ideals and strives for perfection rather than pleasure. The superego develops from the ego partly as a result of learning. When the Oedipus complex (described in the next section) is resolved, the child internalizes his parents' standards and thus forms a picture of what his society sees as good and bad.

The superego acts to inhibit the impulses of the id, including sexual and aggressive instincts. It strives for perfection and tries to persuade the ego to pursue moralistic goals. Like the id, the superego fails to distinguish between subjective and objective reality. Bad thoughts may be punished as severely as bad actions. The superego controls various rewards and punishments; it can make you feel warm inside when you are good or upset your stomach when you are bad.

PSYCHOSEXUAL STAGES

One of Freud's most influential ideas was the notion that adult personality was shaped by experiences in early childhood (see also Chapter 8). In particular, he proposed several distinct **psychosexual stages**—periods during which sexual instincts associated with different erogenous zones are particularly important. Each stage presents certain developmental challenges that must be resolved to achieve healthy adult adjustments. A poorly adjusted individual sometimes becomes *fixated* when he fails to resolve the problems of a certain psychosexual stage, and as a result, he fails to continue developing normally through later stages. In Freud's view, critical events in any psychosexual stage can determine lifelong patterns of behavior.

The first year of life is called the **oral stage** because infants derive satisfaction primarily through the mouth—sucking, biting, swallowing, and so on. If instinctual tension is not appropriately discharged through oral satisfaction, the child may become fixated. For example, if a child is weaned too early to get enough sucking gratification, she may continue to seek oral gratification later in life by smoking or drinking. Problems with infant biting may be displaced and transformed into adult aggression. More generally, fixation at the oral stage can lead to later problems of dependency and trust, since the young infant depends so totally on others for the satisfaction of instinctual impulses.

When toilet training begins, usually in the second year of life, the child has her first contact with external authority. For the first time she is expected to control her biological urges. This period of development is called the **anal stage,** since the child's major source of irritation and gratification involves processes of elimination. Here too, Freud said, early conflicts may have important long-term consequences. If the parents are too strict about toilet training, the child may resist authority by withholding her feces and becoming constipated. This pattern of response may generalize later to other behaviors, and the adult may be stubborn, stingy, or extremely fastidious—symbolically, always holding back. On the other hand, a child may resist by intentionally soiling herself to get back at her parents. If this person becomes fixated at the anal stage, she may grow up to be messy, irresponsible, wasteful, and extravagant.

The **phallic stage** extends roughly from the ages of 3 to 6, when the child first becomes fully aware of the genital differences between males and females. This knowledge helps produce great affection for the parent of the opposite sex and a sense of jealousy and rivalry with the parent of the same sex.

For boys, this issue is called the **Oedipus complex,** after the ancient Greek king Oedipus of Thebes, who unwittingly killed his father and married his mother. According to Freud, the young boy becomes anxious that his father will discover his rivalry and severely punish him. The Oedipus conflict is successfully resolved when the boy realizes that he can never possess his mother and tries instead to be like, or *identify* with, his father, adopting his values, beliefs, and habits. The superego is sometimes called the "heir to the Oedipus complex" because this process of identification is a crucial step in adopting the parents' moral values. Adult attitudes toward people in authority and the opposite sex are also said to be largely determined by the resolution of the Oedipus conflict. Freud had less to say about female children, who come to adopt their mothers' values through a similar process of identification.

The **latency period** begins around the age of 6. Here, according to Freud, children of both sexes are less concerned with psychosexual conflicts and more involved in refining ego processes for dealing with the environment.

Finally, the **genital stage** begins around puberty, when the physical changes of adolescence reawaken sexual urges. As long as a person has not become fixated in one of the earlier stages of development, mature heterosexual impulses emerge in the genital stage of adolescence and adulthood. Obviously, this is the longest stage, but it is the one least discussed by Freud because he believed that early childhood events were more likely to influence adjustment.

Freud at the age of 16, with his mother.

DEFENSE MECHANISMS: THE EXAMPLE OF REPRESSION

Freud believed that much of our behavior expresses the conflict between the unacceptable sexual and aggressive impulses of the id and the restraining influences of the ego and superego. But the desires of the id are powerful forces that can never be completely denied. When a child learns that society forbids the expression of these instincts, the very existence of these feelings may become a source of great anxiety, even if they are never expressed in action.

One way the ego reduces such anxiety is through **defense mechanisms,** which unconsciously deny, distort, or falsify reality. We have already described two defense mechanisms: *displacement,* in which a threatening motive is rechanneled in another direction, and *fixation,* in which anxiety is reduced by the individual's remaining at a lower psychosexual stage of development. In this section, we discuss a third defense mechanism, **repression,** which reduces anxiety by preventing an anxiety-producing object or feeling from becoming conscious.

Defense mechanisms like repression help to explain many complex forms of adult behavior. For example, Freud (1901) told the story of one man whose memory was blocked by a tip-of-the-tongue phenomenon: While reciting a familiar poem, the man kept getting stuck at the words "with the white sheet," and try as he might, he simply could not remember what came next. His analyst asked him to free-associate to the expression *white sheet.* An abbreviated version of the man's train of thought went something like this: "White sheet—reminds me of a linen sheet over a corpse (pause)—now I think of a friend who died recently of heart disease—he was fat and didn't exercise enough—my grandfather died of heart disease, and I am a little chubby myself—I could die of heart disease." According to Freud, the apparently innocent forgetting of a line of a poem actually involved repression of unconscious conflicts over a fear of death.

In another case, a man had trouble remembering the name of a business associate. His analyst later learned that his business associate had married a woman whom his patient had pursued. The loser in this war of the heart repressed the winner's name because his unconscious was protecting the conscious mind from a painful memory.

Freud provided still another example from his own life—an argument with an acquaintance over how many inns there were in a resort town where the Freud family had spent several summer vacations. Freud later had to admit that he had completely forgotten about the inn named The Hockwartner. Why? This name sounded very much like that of a doctor who competed with Freud for patients. Freud's ego defended his conscious mind from the anxiety-provoking memory of this professional rival. Even the founder of psychoanalysis was subject to repression and was a victim of hidden instinctual conflicts.

EVALUATING FREUD'S CONTRIBUTION

No one in psychology is more controversial than Sigmund Freud. At one extreme, orthodox psychoanalysts read Freud the way biblical scholars read the Old Testament, agonizing over hidden meanings and debating the interpretation of every adverb. At the other extreme, many experimental psychologists dismiss Freud with a wave of the hand. Freud was no scientist, they say; he was merely the creator of a muddled system of untestable ideas.

The roots of this controversy may lie partly in Freud's own ambivalence toward traditional scientific methods. Freud was originally trained as a physiologist and began his career totally committed to nineteenth-century ideals of science. But after years of studying human behavior, he became convinced that the mind was so complex that psychology might never become an exact science. Because small shifts in instinctual energy can have dramatic effects on behavior, Freud (1920) believed that it is often impossible to predict what people will do in advance; thus it became possible to explain behavior only after the fact. This idea is almost a kind of scientific heresy; if a scientist is never willing to make predictions that can be tested against the facts, how can an incorrect theory ever be disproved? Skeptics felt that Freud's approach was a little like that of the racetrack expert who claims to know why every horse won and lost but never tests himself by betting on a race.

Some researchers did go on to test Freud's ideas, but many psychoanalysts were not particularly concerned with the results. In the preface to a book that reviews over 2,000 separate tests of Freud's theory and therapy, Seymour Fisher and Roger Greenberg (1977) told the following story to illustrate how little Freud himself might care about such an attempt:

> One psychologist who wrote to Freud to cheer him with the news that he had been able to find scientific laboratory support for one of his major ideas, was chagrined to receive in return a hostile letter informing him that psychoanalysis did not need outside validation (p. ix).

For Freud, and for many others, the proof of psychoanalysis did not lie in simple-minded lab tests but rather in the internal consistency of the theory and its ability to explain patients' lives.

Indeed, many psychoanalysts would argue that it is impossible to make an informed judgment about this theory on the basis of a brief account like the one provided here. An overview of Freud of 5 or 10 or even 100 pages can acquaint the reader with some of his vocabulary and perhaps provide some feeling for the flavor of psychoanalytic explorations of unconscious motives, but such a short account inevitably misses the rich, detailed observations that provide evidence for the theory's validity.

On the other side of the fence, opponents argue that this type of thinking makes psychoanalysis seem more like a religion than a testable science—either you have the true Freudian faith or you don't. No theory can be exempted from the normal rules of scientific testing, according to these skeptics, not even Sigmund Freud's. So, many researchers have set out to test specific psychoanalytic claims.

For example, one study (Sears, Whiting, Nowlis, & Sears, 1953) asked mothers how severely they had weaned their infants from breastfeeding and examined correlations with character traits observed during the preschool years. They found that children who were weaned more severely were, on the average, somewhat more dependent. After reviewing this study and 30 others like it, Fisher and Greenberg (1977) concluded that the available data do indeed support Freud's idea that dependency in adulthood is linked to early infant oral experiences.

After reviewing over 2,000 studies testing a wide variety of Freudian assertions, Fisher and Greenberg (1977) conclude:

> When we added up the totals resulting from our search, balancing the positive against the negative, we found that Freud has fared rather well. But like all theorists, he has proved in the long run to have far from a perfect score. He seems to have been right about a respectable number of issues, but he was also wrong about some important things (p. 395).

But this brief introduction has told only part of the story of psychoanalysis. Our focus on Freud alone provides an opportunity to explore his views in greater depth than we might have if we reviewed the work of four or five major psychoanalysts. However, it runs the risk of leaving the impression that psychoanalytic theory is synonymous with Freudian theory. Nothing could be further from the truth.

Freud was fascinated by the irrational side of human nature and the immense potential power of unconscious instinctual impulses. It was left to those who came later to develop a more complete picture of the ego as the true executive of personality, able to function on its own and fully capable of dealing with reality.

The most influential developments in psychoanalytic thought after Freud are generally summarized in the term **ego psychology,** which refers to psychoanalytic theories that propose an autonomous ego with its own reality-based processes that can be independent of purely instinctual aims. For example, Robert White (1963) argues that the ego can motivate behavior on the basis of such intellectual processes as exploration, manipulation, and effective competence. Similarly, in Chapter 9 we saw how Erik Erikson revised Freud's psychosexual stages to discuss the motivational significance of ego-based issues such as forming an identity in adolescence and choosing between integrity and despair in old age.

Many other theorists—including Carl Jung, Alfred Adler, Karen Horney, Erich Fromm, and Anna Freud—have enriched psychoanalytic thought and extended its boundaries. Whatever one thinks about the ultimate validity of Sigmund Freud's ideas, there can be no doubt that he founded one of our century's most influential schools of thought about the nature of being human.

The Social-Learning Approach

While the psychoanalytic approach grew out of medical attempts to treat disturbed patients, the roots of social-learning theory lie in behaviorism and the animal-learning laboratory. The **social-learning approach** sees personality as a pattern of learned responses produced in part by a history of rewards and punishments and in part by more cognitive processes such as observational learning.

As we explained in Chapter 5, for the first half of the twentieth century, American psychology was dominated by attempts to provide a scientific account of the learning process. Behaviorists typically assumed that virtually all behavior was learned, including the most complex patterns of human behavior, which we call "personality." They concentrated on the search for fundamental laws of learning that specified the relations between changes in the environment and changes in behavior.

In our review of animal learning, we saw how researchers began with simple models in which external stimuli elicited individual responses (S-R psychology). We also saw how they gradually came to emphasize the importance of internal cognitive processes. Here we consider how theoretical approaches to personality have developed along similar lines.

FROM RADICAL BEHAVIORISM TO SOCIAL LEARNING

While most behaviorists have concentrated on fundamental learning processes in lower species, a few have tried to show how the same principles apply to complex human behavior and personality.

For example, B. F. Skinner (1953) argues that psychologists should concentrate on a **functional analysis** that specifies the external variables that regulate behavior. Behavior is the dependent variable for Skinner, and science is the search for the independent variables that cause it to change. To put it another way, behavior is a function of certain changes in the environment. Thus, scientists should not try to construct elaborate theoretical models (as Freud did) to understand the origins of behavior. Rather, they should focus on a more limited and pragmatic search for external causes that enable them to predict and control behavior.

Skinner particularly objects to attempts to explain behavior in terms of internal traits and conditions. Consider one simple example. When someone asks why your roommate hasn't studied for her courses this semester, you may reply, "Because

Albert Bandura (1925—   ) helped found the social-learning approach, which extended the behavioral analysis of learning to include cognitive factors and observational learning. Bandura's parents were wheat farmers in Alberta, Canada; he was raised in the small town of Mundare and attended a high school that had only 20 students. Bandura received a doctorate in clinical psychology from the University of Iowa in 1952, moved to Stanford University a year later, and has remained there for his entire professional career.

she's lazy." But how do you know she's lazy? The answer is simple—she hasn't studied this semester. Intuitively, laziness may seem to explain her failure to study, but in fact it is nothing more than a label for the behavior you have observed. Skinner would suggest a functional analysis of this behavior, to explore the variables that regulate study activities, including stimuli such as the presence of friends who want to chat and reinforcers such as good grades.

The study of personality, then, would consist of a functional analysis of external events that shape a certain pattern of behavior. The macho behavior of a college football player, for example, might result from certain rewards and punishments. If the middle linebacker opened beer bottles with his teeth and spoke only in four-letter words, he might be rewarded by the approval of his peers. If, however, the same player cut football practice to go see Rudolf Nureyev dance in the ballet *Swan Lake*, he might be punished by his teammates' remarks questioning his virility.

Familiar concepts from the learning laboratory play a large role in such behavioral analyses of personality. For example, when our macho football player went home to visit his mother, he might have a very different pattern of behavior. He would never utter a single four-letter word, because although obscenity may be reinforced in the locker room, it is punished around the family dinner table.

In his later writings, Skinner (1974) describes a position called **radical behaviorism,** which accepts the existence of internal events such as thoughts and ideas but continues to emphasize the relationships between environmental events and observable behavior. While grudgingly admitting that people do have internal sensations of hunger, for example, Skinner continued to maintain that the act of seeking food is usually best understood by focusing on the external conditions that precede it, such as being deprived of food. The feeling of hunger itself, he says, is an unimportant by-product of external conditions.

In contrast, *social-learning theory* holds that internal cognitive processes are an important factor in determining behavior, along with other types of learning. Skinner's accounts of human behavior tended to emphasize learning by doing, in which specific acts were rewarded or punished. In contrast, social-learning theory claims that much of our learning is vicarious; we imitate models and learn symbolically about skilled actions (for example, by reading about them or hearing them explained).

In Chapter 5, we described some of Albert Bandura's classic studies of observational learning in which young children imitated an adult model's aggressive acts (see Figure 5.12). As noted, a large number of factors influence observational learning; for example, imitation is less likely when a model is punished for his acts. To account for the many relationships observed to date, Bandura (1977) proposed a model of observational learning that emphasizes the importance of such internal processes as attention, memory, and motivation. When people learn by observing, they do not form simple bonds between stimuli and responses; rather, they form symbolic images of an act and make judgments about it.

While a radical behaviorist might concentrate on the objective features of a reward or punishment (for example, how big it is in physical terms), a social-learning theorist might focus instead on its subjective characteristics (how big it seems to this learner). Further, radical behaviorism tends to see the individual as a relatively passive responder to a series of external events; social-learning theory sees the learner as a more active agent who can actually change the environment and the way it is perceived. For example, a person who is rude can cause others to act in a hostile manner. Thus, the environment in which we live is partly of our own making.

In summary, social-learning theory stresses the importance of active internal cognitive processes in learning, while radical behaviorism does not. For our purposes, the similarities between these two approaches are greater than the differences—both see personality as a complex pattern of learned behaviors. Thus, an adequate theory of personality must focus on the learning process.

SELF-EFFICACY

One of the most important internal factors studied by social-learning theorists in recent years involves expectations of **self-efficacy**—an individual's belief in her own competence or ability to achieve a goal through certain actions. Albert Bandura (1977) distinguishes self-efficacy expectations about one's own behavior from more general beliefs that certain courses of action have certain consequences for most people, which he calls *outcome expectations*. For example, you might have the outcome expectation that most people need to study at least two hours every day to get an *A* in organic chemistry. However, if you have a low self-efficacy expectation in this regard, you might be convinced that *your* only hope for an *A* in organic chemistry would involve bribery or a clerical error.

Bandura believes that such feelings play a key role in how quickly and how well a person will learn a specific task. His first major study of self-efficacy compared several types of therapy for snake phobias (Bandura, Adams, & Beyer, 1977). (As explained in Chapter 13, *phobias* involve excessive and inappropriate fears of objects

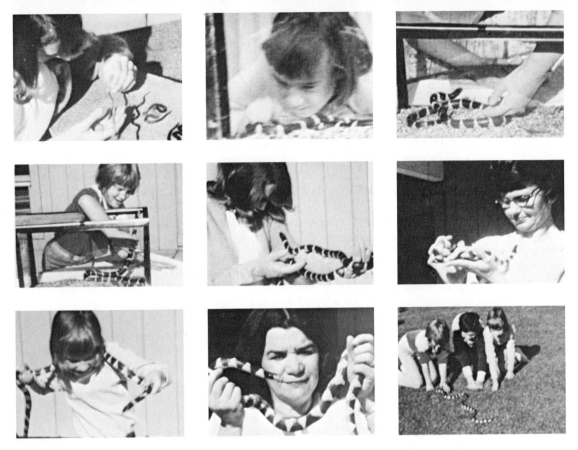

Figure 11.2
Models in a classic study of snake phobia demonstrate their lack of fear of a king snake.

and events.) While many ordinary people may be reluctant to handle the red-tailed boa constrictors used in this study, the 33 subjects in this experiment had such extreme feelings that they were afraid to participate in ordinary activities like gardening for fear they would see a snake.

The subjects participated in a behavioral test of their willingness to approach a snake in a glass cage and also provided self-efficacy ratings—estimates of the probability that they would be willing to touch a snake or approach it in various other specific ways. Since these subjects had been chosen because of their fear of snakes, these preliminary ratings of behavior and self-efficacy were generally rather low.

The subjects were then divided into three groups: participant-modeling, modeling, and control. The subjects in the participant-modeling group were the most active. They were gradually encouraged to watch, and then actually touch, a rosy boa constrictor.

At first, they simply watched through a window while an experimenter handled the snake. Then they came into the room and watched the experimenter and the snake from a distance. Then, they were asked to come closer and put their hands near the snake's head. Those people who just couldn't bring themselves to do it began by wearing gloves and touching the experimenter's hand while she touched the snake. Others worked at first with a smaller baby boa constrictor. In each case, subjects gradually got to the point where they could touch and hold the snake. Indeed, by the end of the therapy session, which typically took about 90 minutes, many subjects were actually able to hold the snake without any help from the therapist and even allow the reptiles to slither over their bodies.

Treatment for the modeling group was more passive. Each subject simply watched the therapist perform a similar set of actions for precisely the same length of time as the participant-modeling subjects. The control group received no treatment at all.

All three groups were tested a week later with another type of snake (a corn snake 90 centimeters long) and asked to provide further ratings of self-efficacy. The major results are summarized in Figure 11.3. As you can see, participant modeling resulted in the largest changes in both self-efficacy and behavior ratings. Modeling produced smaller improvements in both. And the control group apparently still felt that the best place for a snake was far, far away.

All the subjects who had received therapy in this experiment reported that they were now able to participate in activities like picnicking, gardening, and swimming, which they had previously avoided because of their dread of snakes. Some of them also seemed to have gained a more general sense of self-efficacy. As one person put it: "I have a greater self-confidence. When something comes up that is new or unknown to me, I feel, 'Well, I could handle that'" (Bandura, Adams, & Beyer, 1977, p. 136).

Interestingly, the self-efficacy ratings closely paralleled the average behavior changes for the groups and for the individuals within each group. For example, the

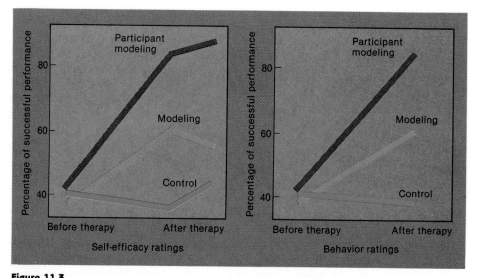

Figure 11.3

In a study of therapies designed to overcome a fear of snakes, participant modeling produced the largest changes in behavior and self-efficacy ratings.

Abraham Maslow (1908–1970) was one of the most influential of the humanistic psychologists. As a student at City College, in New York, the day Maslow first learned of John Watson's work he was so excited by the promise of behaviorism that he danced down Fifth Avenue. But after working for several years on behavioral research, Maslow gradually became disillusioned with this approach. He was profoundly disturbed by the tragedy of World War II and later described how it influenced him to try "to prove that human beings are capable of something grander than war and prejudice and hatred" (Hall, 1968, p. 55).

participant-modeling subjects who actually approached and handled the snake after therapy also had the greatest feelings of self-efficacy. Bandura argues that the participant-modeling procedure was more effective than modeling alone because actual accomplishments are one of the most important sources of efficacy information. While the correlations seen in this particular experiment do not provide conclusive proof that changes in self-efficacy cause changes in behavior, they do provide an excellent example of the kind of processes that social-learning theorists are now investigating in depth.

The Humanistic Approach

The **humanistic approach** to personality emphasizes positive human qualities, such as the freedom to pursue rational and spiritual goals. Humanistic approaches to personality have been called psychology's "third force" because they provide an alternative to psychoanalysis and behaviorism, the two major schools of thought that have long dominated the field. Freud saw human behavior as a product of hidden irrational instinctual forces, and the early behaviorists pictured man as a machine that mindlessly responded to rewards and punishments. But humanistic psychology paints a much more optimistic picture, one that is much closer to the commonsense notion that each of us is mistress of her own fate. As noted in Chapter 10, while other paradigms are largely deterministic, humanism emphasizes the role of free will.

Among the many influential psychologists who are known as humanists, two names stand out—Carl Rogers and Abraham Maslow. Since Rogers is better known for his innovations in psychotherapy than for his theory of personality, we discuss his views in Chapter 14.

Abraham Maslow criticized traditional psychology for taking a negative, pessimistic, and limited view of human behavior. He argued that this lopsided picture was partly a result of the limitations of research methods. "It is tempting, if the only tool you have is a hammer," he wrote, "to treat everything as if it were a nail" (Maslow, 1966, p. 15). This implies that because Freud began by studying people with emotional problems, he ended up with a rather warped view of normal human behavior. Similarly, because behaviorists laid the foundations of their view in the animal-learning laboratory, they failed to consider adequately the qualities that distinguish man from the beasts. As a corrective, Maslow himself turned to the study of healthy, normal individuals.

According to Maslow, normal human behavior is motivated by a **hierarchy of needs,** a series of biological and psychological requirements that must be satisfied in a certain order. As Figure 11.4 suggests, the most basic category includes **physiological needs** such as hunger and thirst. These needs are more urgent than any others and take precedence over everything else. However, in our society, physiological needs are routinely satisfied for most people and are consequently not a major factor in shaping our most important decisions. The next category involves **safety needs** for physical security and freedom from pain or fear. The power of the safety needs may be particularly obvious in high-crime neighborhoods, where people are forced to stay home at night or take other actions to protect their physical security.

Next in importance are the **belongingness and love needs,** to feel accepted and wanted by family, friends, and others. Then come **esteem needs,** to be valued by others and to have respect for ourselves (self-esteem). Some seek esteem by seeking fame or dominance over others; some attempt to find appreciation in more modest ways. It is only after all four of these categories are met that a final set of motives come into play. **Self-actualization needs** involve the attempt to use all of our talents to achieve our potentials.

According to Maslow's conception of the need hierarchy, then, self-actualiza-

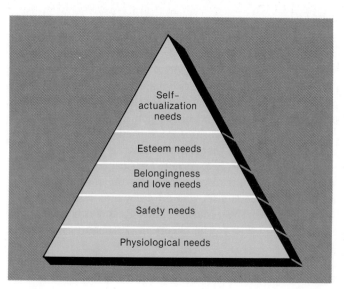

Figure 11.4
Maslow believed that human behavior was motivated by a hierarchy of needs that must be satisfied in a certain order, beginning with physiological needs such as hunger and thirst.

tion needs ordinarily motivate behavior only after all the lower needs are satisfied. If you have not eaten in three days (physiological need), you will probably spend little time worrying about whether your friends really like you (belongingness and love needs). Similarly, if you feel that you are a worthless excuse for a human being (esteem needs), you will not focus your energy on making the best possible use of your talents (self-actualization needs).

Since Maslow was most interested in healthy adjustment and the positive side of human nature, he decided to focus his research on self-actualization. The problems were immense. How could he know, for example, whether a particular pattern of behavior was motivated by self-actualization needs or by a need for esteem or belongingness? The complexity and uncertainty surrounding this issue would have caused many researchers to abandon the subject. In response to this challenge, Maslow (1954) wrote:

> This kind of research is in principle so difficult . . . that if we were to wait for conventionally reliable data, we would have to wait forever. It seems that the only manly thing to do is not to fear mistakes, to plunge in, to do the best that one can, hoping to learn enough from blunders to correct them eventually (p. 199).

He plunged in by studying friends, acquaintances, and historical figures who seemed to use the full range of their abilities and who were free of psychological problems. Ultimately, Maslow (1970) was able to find only 18 fully self-actualized people; half were acquaintances and contemporaries, and the rest were historical figures (Abraham Lincoln, Thomas Jefferson, Albert Einstein, Eleanor Roosevelt,

Two people Maslow classified as self-actualized: Eleanor Roosevelt and Albert Einstein.

Jane Addams, William James, Albert Schweitzer, Aldous Huxley, and Baruch Spinoza).

Maslow's observations of these 18 individuals and others who approached this ideal revealed 15 major characteristics that self-actualized people had in common (see Table 11.1). For one thing, they are accepting—of themselves, of others, and of the world in general. Instead of being crippled by guilt, shame, and anxiety, they have learned to accept the world and human nature as they are. Further, while many of us are obsessed with our own personal problems, the self-actualized person usually takes a larger view and has a mission in life. A somewhat more surprising characteristic of self-actualized people is the fact that they all seem to enjoy a certain amount of solitude and privacy. By being somewhat aloof and reserved at times, they are able to maintain perspective and dignity.

One of the most enviable characteristics of the self-actualized person is the ability to appreciate the everyday pleasures of the world. The smell of a flower or a visit from an old friend can be a source of infinite wonder, amazement, and joy. While most of us easily become rather jaded, the self-actualized person can appreciate the thousandth baby she sees as much as the first.

Maslow also noted that the self-actualized person frequently has **peak experiences,** mystical feelings of happiness, peace, and contentment that are difficult to describe. Many different activities can lead to a peak experience—sex, listening to music, watching a sunset, religious meditation. What all peak experiences have in common is a feeling of ecstasy, peace, and losing oneself in a feeling of oneness with the universe: All is well with the world, and life makes sense. While almost everyone has an occasional peak experience, such occurrences are far more common for self-actualized people.

In his last book, *The Farther Reaches of Human Nature* (1971), Maslow described how people can strive to become self-actualizing. Among his suggestions:

TABLE 11.1
Characteristics of the Self-actualized Person

1. An ability to perceive the world realistically and accurately
2. An acceptance of self and others
3. Spontaneity
4. A focus on problems outside the self
5. A need for privacy
6. A relative independence from the environment
7. Continued freshness of appreciating life
8. Peak experiences of oneness with the universe
9. A genuine identification with and sympathy for the human race
10. Deep personal relationships
11. A democratic belief that all humans are equal
12. A definite sense of right and wrong
13. A sense of humor that is not hostile
14. Creativity
15. A resistance to cultural conformity

We should learn to be completely honest, to take responsibility for our own actions, to become autonomous, and to trust our own instincts and act on them. Although few people ever achieve full self-actualization, those who do are different from the rest of us in degree rather than in kind. Virtually every human being occasionally has a peak experience; the goal is to progress toward self-actualization so that such feelings may come more frequently.

Maslow's emphasis on free will seems more consistent with our everyday experience than the deterministic views of the psychoanalysts or behaviorists. But because his theory grapples so directly with difficult problems of human values, much of Maslow's writing seems to be rather culture-bound. Some of the traits he admires in self-actualizers—honesty, independence, spontaneity—have a distinctly American ring. Indeed, critics argued that the flaw in these studies of self-actualized people is the fact that the ultimate criterion for being included in this category was whether Abraham Maslow thought a given person was admirable. Maslow was fully aware of this difficulty and noted that any study of well-adjusted people will almost inevitably be criticized for its definition of adjustment. He felt that the issue was so important that researchers had no choice but to go ahead and study it as best they could.

Like other global theories of personality, Maslow's notion of the need hierarchy has been difficult to evaluate in traditional scientific terms (Wahba & Bridwell, 1976). It should be seen as a useful first step rather than a firmly established set of facts. But whatever the failings of the details of this theory, Abraham Maslow and other humanistic psychologists have posed an important challenge to social science researchers—to learn more about the positive side of the human experience.

Type and Trait Approaches

BASIC CONCEPTS

The earliest stages of a new science are often concerned with trying to establish a scheme for fitting the world into neat and orderly categories. Some of the first biologists, for example, proposed a taxonomy of the many species of plant and animal life. Similarly, some students of human nature have proposed various **type theories** of personality that sort people into separate personality categories or types.

The first personality theory involved just such an attempt. About 400 years before Christ, the Greek physician Hippocrates tried to classify human temperament into four basic types: choleric (irritable and hot-tempered), melancholic (sad or depressed), sanguine (optimistic or hopeful), and phlegmatic (calm or apathetic). Hippocrates also suggested that these basic differences in character and temperament were related to differences in body chemistry. The sanguine person, for example, had too much blood, while the choleric person had too much bile.

The biochemical details now seem quaint, but the basic typology has weathered 24 centuries rather well. The four temperaments are represented in many famous works of art and serve as the basis for such literary classics as Robert Burton's *Anatomy of Melancholy*, published in 1621. Pioneer psychologist Wilhelm Wundt

Figure 11.5

Medieval woodcuts of the four human temperaments identified by Hippocrates: sanguine, phlegmatic, choleric, and melancholic.

tried to explain the four types in terms of two key underlying personality dimensions—weak versus strong emotions and slow versus quick reactions. In this scheme, choleric people were quick reactors with strong emotions, and melancholic people were slow reactors with weak emotions. When Pavlov found that some dogs were easier to condition than others, he proposed four basic canine personalities that were also closely related to Hippocrates' temperaments.

Theories of character types like these are appealing partly because they seem so simple and straightforward. But as personality psychologist Gordon Allport (1961) put it, "The doctrine is as elastic as the platform of a political party. One may see in it what one wants to see" (p. 39). And in its very simplicity lies the seeds of its downfall, because, Allport went on to note, "Our phlegmatic friends, we know, have choleric moments and our sanguine friends may show threads of melancholy" (p. 39). Thus, a categorization of all the complexity of human behavior into a few basic personality types is likely to have more intuitive appeal than scientific value.

Nevertheless, type theories of personality do have a role to play in a science of human behavior, as is demonstrated in the discussion in this chapter of the relationship between personality patterns and heart disease.

Closely related to the notion of discrete character types is the more modest idea of describing personality in terms of **traits,** predispositions to respond to a variety of situations in similar ways. While personality types are either-or propositions, personality traits are continuous and allow more subtle distinctions (for example, a person may be very aggressive, fairly aggressive, slightly aggressive, or not at all aggressive).

We often use the concept of personality traits in commonsense descriptions of

Gordon Allport (1897–1967) is known not only as one of the most influential proponents of the trait approach to personality but also for his pioneer research on topics ranging from prejudice, attitudes, and values to the psychology of rumor. The son of a country doctor from Montezuma, Indiana, Allport decided to major in psychology in college to follow the example of his older brother. At the age of 23, he managed to arrange a private meeting with Sigmund Freud during a visit to Vienna. When Freud sat silently for several minutes, Allport finally began the meeting by telling about a 4-year-old boy he had seen on the streetcar on the way over who didn't want to sit near any passengers because they were too dirty. Freud hesitated and said kindly, "And was that little boy you?" Allport was amazed that Freud ignored the more obvious explanation that Allport was merely being sociable—relating an anecdote he thought Freud might find interesting. Much of Allport's professional career was devoted to developing theoretical alternatives to Freudian psychoanalysis.

the people around us. When we say that Abraham Lincoln was more straightforward than Richard Nixon or that John Kennedy was more charismatic than Millard Fillmore, we are describing presidential character in terms of personality traits. Because personality can be described as the product of many different traits, this approach allows a much more complex classification than does a simple typology. Thus, you might describe a friend as slightly hostile, quite extraverted, reasonably stable, and totally dependable.

ALLPORT'S RESEARCH

Traits bring order into the chaos of dealing with the complexity of personality by focusing attention on the consistency of behavior. Theorist Gordon Allport saw traits as the best "unit of analysis" for understanding personality. For Allport, traits are the sources of the underlying unity of behavior; they can make a variety of stimuli and responses seem equivalent from a psychological point of view. Figure 11.6 illustrates how this could apply for the trait of introversion. Such widely different situations as waiting in line for the bus, going to a party, sitting in a college class, shopping for groceries, and going to Grandma's house may evoke a similar pattern of behavior. In all these situations, the trait of introversion can be seen in similar responses—remaining quiet with other people, not talking to strangers, doing things alone and avoiding groups whenever possible, and making few friends. Allport emphasized the importance of an underlying personality structure that can be inferred from characteristic patterns of behavior.

He also distinguished between several different kinds of traits that differ in their

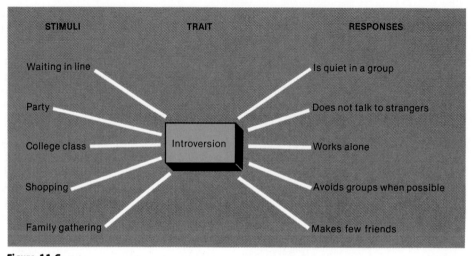

Figure 11.6
Some personality theorists see traits as the source of consistent behavior. This diagram shows how a wide variety of stimuli may evoke similar patterns of behavior through a single underlying trait.

influence on behavior. For example, *central traits* are highly characteristic personality patterns that often influence behavior and are therefore relatively easy to observe. Allport believed that most personalities could be fairly summarized in 5 or 10 central traits. *Secondary traits* are less pervasive patterns of behavior that can be seen only under specific conditions. Other trait theorists use different names for these concepts, but most agree with the fundamental idea that not all traits are created equal; some are more powerful determinants of behavior than others.

Allport also drew a distinction between *common traits*, which characterize most people, and *individual traits* (or personal dispositions), which apply uniquely to a single person. While most personality theorists concentrated on the search for general laws that apply to all people, Allport also emphasized the study of specific individuals as unique human beings. Indeed, he formally defined two distinct approaches to psychological science: The **nomothetic approach** attempts to understand the behavior and experience of people in general or of the average case, while the **idiographic approach** attempts to understand the behavior and experience of a single individual.

One example of Allport's idiographic approach was his detailed study of a woman whom he called Jenny Masterson. The analysis was based on 301 letters Jenny wrote between the ages of 58 and 70 in which the lonely woman described her life to a young couple she had met through her son.

Jenny Masterson was born in 1868. Her parents were Irish Protestants who migrated to Canada when Jenny was 5 years old. When her father died, 18-year-old Jenny left school to work as a telegrapher to support her younger brothers and sisters. At the age of 27, she infuriated her family by marrying a divorced man. He died 2 years later, leaving her estranged from her family and with an infant son to support. For the next 17 years, Jenny devoted every waking moment to caring for her son Ross. She continued to support him through his college years at Princeton. Ross enlisted in the ambulance corps during World War I and returned from the war disillusioned and disoriented. He married secretly and fought constantly with his mother. Many of Jenny's letters describe her continuing arguments with her son and her lonely life in late middle age.

In a systematic analysis of Jenny's personality, Allport (1965) asked 36 people to read the letters and describe her characteristic traits. Although these judges mentioned a total of 198 trait terms, many were synonymous or closely related. Indeed, "nearly all" the judges agreed that Jenny's character revolved around 8 central traits; she was suspicious, self-centered, independent, dramatic-intense, artistic, aggressive, morbid, and sentimental. The judges also identified 13 less important themes that could be considered secondary traits, including intelligence, wittiness, and whimsicality.

Though this was not a particularly flattering portrait, it was quite a consistent one. Indeed, other studies using different techniques to analyze the letters came to surprisingly similar conclusions. Jeffrey Paige, a student of Allport's, used a computer to count the number of repetitions in 56 of Jenny's letters of words falling into 3,000 categories. Elaborate statistical analysis of these word counts revealed 8 underlying character traits that were generally similar to those mentioned by the clinical judges.

Allport's idiographic analysis of individual cases like Jenny's has had a tremendous theoretical impact on the development of trait concepts. However, most researchers now take a nomothetic approach and investigate the average predictive value of particular traits for large groups. One example is described in the next section—the involvement of androgyny in sex-role behavior. First, however, we review recent challenges to the trait approach and to the very idea of studying personality patterns.

Current Issues in Personality Research

Most textbooks in personality are organized around major theorists and schools of thought, just as this chapter is. From this, you might get the impression that if you were an ambitious young psychologist, you would want to develop a personality theory of your own so that your name would go down in history as future generations of psychologists debated the merits of your approach.

In fact, however, personality psychologists are moving in a different direction in the 1980s. We mentioned in Chapter 5 that the global theories of learning that once dominated experimental psychology have now been abandoned. Researchers are instead setting more modest goals and trying to ask one small question at a time. The same thing has happened in personality psychology.

The major theories described up to this point have shaped the direction of the field and have provided the theoretical foundations for many studies. But in recent years personality psychologists have come to believe that we will not be able to explain the infinite complexity of every individual person through one master theory. Instead, researchers are increasingly focusing on more limited and more manageable problems, such as personality differences between women and men or the relation of specific traits to heart disease.

OF PERSONS AND SITUATIONS

Mischel's Challenge. In 1968, Walter Mischel published *Personality and Assessment,* a book that seemed to attack the very essence of personality theory by suggesting that the relationship between personality-trait labels and actual behavior is a weak one at best. To cite just one example, many trait theorists have discussed the way people relate to such diverse authority figures as parents, bosses, and peers. According to this view, some people are rebels and some follow authority meekly. If rebelliousness really is a generalized personality trait, then children who resist their fathers should grow up to resist the boss and give traffic cops a hard time. Burwen and Campbell (1957) studied the relationship among many different measures of the way Air Force men related to authority figures. They found that the correlations were relatively low. This study did not support the idea that people who are rebellious in one situation are also rebellious in another.

In general, Mischel found that correlations between behavior and personality traits rarely exceeded .30. While a correlation coefficient of .30 may be statistically significant and does prove that there is *some* relationship between two variables, it is not strong enough accurately to predict individual behavior. (For a further discussion of correlation coefficients, see "How Do They Know?" in Chapter 3.)

Mischel further argued that social-learning theory could explain why personality traits are such poor predictors of behavior. In essence, he said that a person's behavior in a given situation is shaped by rewards and punishments in that particular situation. One person may seem introverted at parties but quite extraverted with family; another may be introverted at home but extraverted at parties. It all depends on what each individual was reinforced for doing in the past, personal expectations, and the motivating force of particular rewards. From this point of view, it is not surprising that people do not always act consistently from one situation to the next.

Yet common sense tells us that however low psychologists' correlations may be, behavior is reasonably consistent from one situation to the next. We assume this whenever we contrast the characteristics of a social friend with another who is aggressive and a third who is shy. But, according to this point of view, common sense is quite wrong. Consistency may lie in the eye of the beholder.

As explained in Chapter 1, commonsense explanations of behavior are often systematically incorrect because of the limitations of the human observer. The most important of these limitations, at least in this context, has become known as the **fundamental attribution error**—observers consistently underestimate the power of situational forces that influence other people's behavior and overestimate the importance of personal dispositions (Nisbett & Ross, 1980).

In one series of studies of the fundamental attribution error (Jones, 1979), observers read essays and listened to speeches that strongly supported a certain political view—favoring or opposing the legalization of marijuana, for example, or criticizing or supporting Fidel Castro's leadership of Cuba. In each case, the observers were told that the speaker or author had been required to take this particular stand by a debate coach, political science instructor, or psychology experimenter. Nevertheless, observers consistently believed that the speeches and essays expressed the true beliefs of their authors. In other words, they tended to ignore the strong situational constraints of the requirement to take a certain position and to attribute the differences in content to the personal beliefs of the authors.

In our culture, people seem to believe that character is the most important determinant of behavior. Much of our mythology and literature, from Henry Fielding to Horatio Alger, supports the idea that personal traits and abilities can triumph over the accidental circumstances of our birth. It is therefore not surprising that as children grow up in our culture, they increasingly come to believe in the importance of personality traits for explaining behavior (Ross, Turiel, Josephson, & Lepper, 1978). It will be important for future researchers to see whether people in less individually oriented cultures—such as the Republic of China—fall victim to the fundamental attribution error or whether their different world view leads them to perceive their comrades' behavior in an entirely different light.

In any case, Mischel (1968) not only cited evidence for a lack of consistency in personal traits across situations, he also argued that our commonsense impressions of personal consistency may be quite wrong. His book sparked a major controversy that continues to the present time.

The Consistency of Personality.   Researchers were quick to respond to this challenge. Some pointed to problems in the data Mischel himself had cited. For example, the study of attitudes toward authority cited earlier involved 155 Air Force men whose attitudes toward the testing itself left much to be desired. The original authors (Burwen & Campbell, 1957) admitted their subjects showed signs of "perfunctory compliance and occasional humorous sabatoge of the test purpose" (p. 24).

Beyond such point-by-point rebuttals of Mischel's argument, many took his challenge seriously enough to reexamine the direction of personality research. Daryl Bem and Andrea Allen (1974) returned to Allport's idiographic view that some traits may be relevant only to certain individuals. They argued that each of us acts consistently, but only in terms of some traits. They tested this idea by asking 64 undergraduates to rate their own friendliness. Each person was also asked, "How much do you vary from one situation to another in how friendly and outgoing you are?" (p. 512). Later, they found a strong relationship among different measures of friendliness, but only for people who described themselves as consistent on this trait. The correlations between how actively each person participated in a group discussion and how long it took him to strike up a conversation with a stranger was .73 for those who described themselves as consistent on friendliness and .30 for those who did not. Again, a given trait may not be equally relevant for all people.

A different type of response to Mischel's challenge has come from personality psychologists who emphasized the importance of the interaction between traits and situations. According to Norman Endler (1977), two people who get the same score on a psychological test of anxiety may become anxious in very different situations. On the basis of responses to questionnaires, Endler found that some people are frightened by social situations (such as going out on a blind date), while others fear physical danger (such as climbing a mountain). Physiological measurements of anxiety later verified this dichotomy. People who feared physical danger had higher heart rates when they took part in a study that involved a risk of electrical shock; those whose anxiety was related to social factors had higher heart rates before taking a test, presumably because they feared being evaluated. Clearly, it is not enough to say that a person is usually anxious; one must also specify the situations in which this trait is most likely to be seen.

Still another line of research generated by Mischel's book argued that the problem is a methodological one. According to this view, some researchers failed to see the consistency of behavior because they relied too heavily on isolated observations. Many studies compared a person's responses on one questionnaire with a single behavioral test. Seymour Epstein (1979) has shown that when questionnaires are repeated time after time and behavioral observations are made day after day, greater consistency emerges. In one study, college students filled out personality tests before every psychology class for a whole semester. At the same time, the instructor secretly rated them on such behavior as coming to class late, forgetting to bring pencils to fill out computerized forms, and erasing mistakes on the answer sheets.

This averaging technique revealed many substantial correlations. One group showed a strong relationship between feelings of confusion, tension, and powerlessness, and failing to turn in papers, coming late to class, and erasing mistakes. Over the course of a semester, it became clear that at times these students were living in a fog of disorganized carelessness. This would not have been apparent if Epstein had simply measured each student's attitude and behavior on a single day; the pattern emerged only because he averaged his students' daily ratings over several months.

A decade after publishing the work that sparked this controversy, Walter Mischel (1979) wrote: "My intentions in writing that book were not to undo personality, but to defend individuality and the uniqueness of each person" (p. 740). Whatever Mischel's original intentions were, the resulting debate helped psychologists to concentrate on the complex relationships between personal traits and situational determinants of behavior. This continues to be one important theme in current personality research.

ANDROGYNY

Another line of personality research was inspired in the early 1970s by apparent changes in American society's view of the appropriate roles for men and women. According to traditional psychological tests, masculinity involved an instrumental orientation, focusing cognitively on getting a job done; femininity was usually defined as more expressive, involving an emotional concern for other people. When

Sandra Bem (1974) asked college students to rate the "desirability in American society" of 400 personality traits "for a man" and "for a woman," she came up with lists of words that both males and females agreed applied mostly to one sex. The male list included words like *aggressive, ambitious, competitive*, and *independent;* females were characterized as *affectionate, compassionate, loyal*, and *tender*.

In the past, most psychologists had thought of masculinity and femininity as opposite ends of the same continuum; a person could be masculine or feminine, but not both. Bem rejected this idea and added a third category: A person could be classified as masculine, feminine, or androgynous. The word *androgynous* is derived from two Greek roots, *andro*, meaning "man," and *gynē*, meaning "woman." **Androgyny** was defined as a personality pattern that combined traditionally masculine and feminine traits in the same person.

Using precise statistical definitions of all three categories, Bem gave her questionnaire to 723 Stanford University undergraduates in 1973. The results were that 34% of the men and 27% of the women were classified as androgynous. They described themselves by checking off about the same number of masculine and feminine traits.

Right from the start, androgyny was a value-laden concept. Bem (1975) explicitly argued that being androgynous was better than being masculine or feminine: "It is our general hypothesis that a non-androgynous sex role can seriously restrict the range of behaviors available to an individual as he or she moves from situation to situation" (p. 634). She contended that androgynous people are more adaptable to a wide range of situations.

In this study, masculine, feminine, and androgynous people were given an opportunity to play with a kitten (a female task) and to act as a nonconformist (a male task). Both feminine and androgynous males did indeed get more involved with the kitten and enjoyed it more than masculine men did. On the conformity task, masculine and androgynous people were more likely to resist group pressure than those who were classified as feminine. The androgynous people seemed more flexible than those who conformed to traditional sexual stereotypes.

The concept of androgyny became popular among researchers, and many studies appeared attesting to the value of this liberated approach to sex roles. In one of the more extreme examples of the early enthusiasm over this personality trait, Alexandra Kaplan (1976) argued that psychotherapists should encourage women to become androgynous (see "Becoming a Critical Consumer").

Others saw the relation between androgyny and mental health in more complex terms. One study of 20- to 59-year-old women (Hoffman & Fidell, 1979) found that androgynous women were no less neurotic or less likely to visit a doctor than masculine or feminine women. While feminine women had lower self-esteem than androgynous women, they also expressed greater satisfaction with their housework activities. Along with other studies (Lenney, 1979), this suggests that androgynous women may adapt better to some types of situations and feminine women to others.

Although Bem was the first to use the word *androgyny* to describe a personality trait, she was not the only psychologist who studied sex-role changes in the last

Is Psychology Sexist?

In 1906, psychologist Edward L. Thorndike wrote that American education should be designed to deal with "not only the probability and the desirability of marriage and the training of children as an essential feature of a woman's career, but also the restriction of women to the mediocre grades of ability and achievement" (p. 213).

From today's perspective, it is easy to see that this statement was shaped by sexist beliefs. But it is more difficult to identify bias when it agrees with our own beliefs. As you read the following statement, decide whether it is consistent with the evidence cited elsewhere in this text. (A discussion of this issue appears after the "Summary" at the end of this chapter.)

The fact that children are brought up to . . . develop only sex-appropriate personality traits runs directly counter to the idea of androgyny . . . as a model of mental health. [This article] focuses on two traits which, in women's upbringing, tend to be distorted: anger, which in women is rather consistently suppressed, and dependency, which in women tends to be overencouraged. . . . How can psychotherapists help women express their anger effectively and gain control over their dependency? The answer to this has several components. Therapists should attune themselves to recognizing subtle instances of these problem areas, even if the client herself does not raise them as issues of concern" (Kaplan & Bean, 1976, p. 352).

decade. In their studies with the Personal Attributes Questionnaire, Janet Spence and Robert Helmreich (1978) found that masculinity and femininity were separate dimensions. While Bem (1974) believed that American sex roles were best described by three categories (masculine, feminine, and androgynous), Spence and Helmreich added a fourth, *undifferentiated*. They distinguished between people who scored high in both masculinity and femininity (androgynous) and those who scored low in both traits (undifferentiated). And, indeed, when Bem (1977) went back to reanalyze some of her earlier data by dividing her androgynous subjects into these two subgroups, she found that this more sophisticated approach did permit her to improve some of her predictions. People who scored high in both masculinity and femininity, for example, were more likely to play with the kitten than undifferentiated subjects who scored low in both traits.

When a new theoretical concept is suddenly embraced by a large number of other reasearchers, an initial wave of enthusiasm is usually followed by an increasing awareness of the complexity of the underlying issues and of the difficulty of precise measurement. And so it was with the explosion of androgyny research. Personality psychologists have become more sophisticated about measuring androgyny, about what this concept can teach us about how Americans currently define sex roles, and about larger issues such as stereotyping and prejudice in general (Lenney, 1979).

Type A Behavior and Heart Disease

The third and final line of research to be described here built upon the clinical observations of two physicians. When cardiologists Meyer Friedman and Ray Rosenman began treating heart-attack patients, they offered the standard medical advice: Smoke less, exercise more, and eat less red meat, butter, eggs, and other foods high in the chemical cholesterol (which many scientists believe contributes to blockage of the arteries). But as they continued their research and medical practice, they gradually became convinced that they were ignoring one of the most important factors in heart disease—stress.

General observations of their patients suggested to Friedman and Rosenman that many heart-attack victims were very competitive and always in a hurry. They called this personality syndrome **Type A behavior.** In the most general terms, they provided the following list of questions people can ask themselves to see whether they are Type *A:*

> Do you have a habit of explosively accentuating key words in your ordinary speech . . . and finishing your sentences in a burst of speed?

> Do you always move, walk, eat rapidly?

> Do you feel (and openly show) impatience with the rate at which most events take place?

> Do you get unduly irritated at delay—when the car in front of you seems to slow you up, when you have to wait in line, or wait to be seated in a restaurant?

> Does it bother you to watch someone else perform a task you know you can do faster?

> Do you often try to do two things at once (dictate while driving or read business papers while you eat)?

> Do you almost always feel vaguely guilty when you relax and do absolutely nothing for several days (even several hours)? (Friedman & Rosenman, 1974, cover).

For each question, a yes answer is a sign of Type *A* behavior; a no answer suggests the more relaxed Type *B* pattern.

The most thorough study of the Type *A* syndrome began in 1960 (Rosenman, Brand, Jenkins, Friedman, Straus, & Wurm, 1975). The subjects were 3,154 men between the ages of 39 and 59 who had no signs of heart disease at the beginning of the study. On the basis of standardized interviews about their attitudes toward stress and competition, about half the men were classified as Type *A* and half as Type *B*. Researchers also collected data on such variables as medical history, exercise habits, smoking, and blood pressure.

For the next $8\frac{1}{2}$ years, doctors kept track of each man's medical history and gave him an annual physical. None of the physicians who were doing these checkups

As more women enter the high-pressure world of business and the professions, researchers wonder whether the female frequency of Type A behavior and heart disease will increase.

knew which men were Type *A* and which were Type *B*. (This minimized the possibility of experimenter bias.) During the time of the study, 50 men died of cardiovascular disease; 34 of them were Type *A* and 16 were Type *B*. Another 257 men were diagnosed as suffering from heart disease; 178 were Type *A* and 79 were Type *B*. Since the original group consisted of roughly half of each type, statistical analysis of these figures proved that Type *A* men were indeed more likely to develop a heart ailment and to die from it.

Elaborate statistical procedures were used to demonstrate that Type *A* behavior led directly to heart attacks (Rosenman, Brand, Shultz, & Friedman, 1976). Other factors, such as cigarette smoking, high cholesterol levels, and high blood pressure, also increased the likelihood of heart disease. However, a Type *A* man was more likely to have a heart attack than a Type *B* man even if neither of them smoked, had high blood pressure, or had a high cholesterol level.

Thus far, we have discussed only Type *A* men. As you may know, women in our society have traditionally had less heart disease; they are also less likely to have Type *A* personalities. The obvious question is whether women's increasing prominence in the business and professional world will lead to more Type *A* females and more heart disease among women. At this writing, no one knows. But a great deal of research in this area is going on, and by the time you read this a tentative answer may have been reached.

A related question, which is also now a focus of intensive research, involves helping Type *A* people change their behavior in order to improve their health. In one study (Roskies, Spevack, Surkis, Cohen, & Gilman, 1978), 27 executives who seemed to conform to the Type *A* pattern participated in psychotherapy for $1\frac{1}{2}$ hours every Monday night for 14 weeks. Half talked to therapists about how their competitive striving was rooted in their early lives; the others were trained in standard methods of relaxation and learned to avoid the situations that created the most stress for them.

Of the 27 executives, 25 finished the program. The two forms of psychotherapy were almost equally effective. Both groups had lower blood pressure and lower cholesterol levels after treatment. They also reported an increased feeling of emotional satisfaction and less sense of time pressure. These results are promising, but they are not definitive. Large, long-term studies will be needed to demonstrate that such changes last, that they decrease the risk of cardiovascular disease, and that such executives continue to function well in the competitive world of business.

Throughout the 1980s, personality psychologists can be expected to continue this kind of careful, systematic, and modest research. For some time now, most researchers have agreed that it is simply not possible to understand all the richness and complexity of human behavior using one theoretical scheme. And so they have begun the tedious process of chipping away at the problem, one small piece at a time.

Summary

1. **Personality** may be defined as an individual's characteristic pattern of thought, behavior, and emotions. Researchers have focused on two basic questions: How consistent are individual differences in behavior? What causes individual differences?

2. The **psychoanalytic approach** to personality emphasizes the importance of unconscious forces and biological instincts in shaping complex human behavior.

3. Freud traced all behavior back to **instincts,** which he defined as the inborn mental representations of physical needs. These included **life instincts** (such as hunger, thirst, and sex) and **death instincts** (such as aggressive and self-destructive forces). Instinctual energy is often **displaced** or rechanneled from one object to another. The conscious mind is usually unaware of the way instinctual energy is transformed and displaced, though we can glimpse the work of the unconscious mind in dreams and free association.

4. According to Freud, the human personality is organized into three interrelated structures: id, ego, and superego. The **id** is a primitive force of inborn biological urges. The **ego** develops from the id to distinguish between the subjective world of the mind and the objective world of physical reality. The **superego** is developed by restrictions on id impulses that come from parents and authority figures.

5. Freud emphasized the importance of childhood experiences in shaping adult personality. He described four distinct **psychosexual stages** of development—periods emphasizing sexual instincts associated with different erogenous zones, areas of the body that are sensitive to both irritation and pleasurable feelings. **Defense mechanisms** deny, distort, or falsify reality to protect the ego from excessive anxiety. For example, **repression** prevents an anxiety-producing object or feeling from becoming conscious.

6. Even today, many of Freud's assertions remain controversial. While some reject his views entirely, others favor closely related theories called **ego psychology,** which proposes an independent ego with its own reality-based processes.

7. The **social-learning approach** sees personality as a pattern of learned responses produced in part by a history of rewards and punishments and in part by more cognitive processes such as observational learning. It is grounded in behaviorism and the attempt to provide a **functional analysis** of behavior, specifying the external variables that cause an organism to behave in a certain way. Albert Bandura stressed the importance of observational learning, in which people form symbolic images of an act and make judgments about it. For example, he has studied the consequences of an individual's expectation of **self-efficacy,** a belief in one's own competence or ability to achieve certain goals.

8. The **humanistic approach** to personality emphasizes such positive human qualities as the freedom to pursue rational and spiritual goals. According to Abraham Maslow, normal human behavior is motivated by a **hierarchy of needs,** a series of biological requirements that must be satisfied in the following order: physiological needs, safety needs, belongingness and love needs, esteem needs, and self-actualization needs.

9. **Type theories** of personality sort people into separate personality categories or types. Closely related is the idea of describing personality in terms of **traits,** predispositions to respond to a variety of situations in similar ways. Gordon Allport saw traits as the fundamental source of personality unity, but he distinguished between two different approaches to the study of individual differences. The **nomothetic approach** attempts to understand the behavior and experience of people in general or in the average case; the **idiographic approach** attempts to understand the behavior and experience of a single individual.

10. Current personality research tends to avoid global theories and focus instead on more modest problems. For example, Walter Mischel's charge that adult behavior is not particularly consistent from one situation to the next has led to considerable controversy. Bem and Allen have shown that a given trait may be relevant only for people who describe themselves as consistent in that trait.

11. Another line of research investigated the implications of **androgyny,** a personality pattern that combines traditionally masculine and feminine traits in the same person.

12. **Type A behavior** refers to a personality pattern in which certain people are very competitive and always in a rush. Numerous studies have shown that Type *A* individuals are more susceptible to cardiovascular disease and heart attacks.

Discussion of "Becoming a Critical Consumer"

Although this argument may make perfect sense to anyone who shares the authors' feminist views, it is important to remember that the idea that androgyny is a "model of mental health" is a value judgment, just as Thorndike's 1906 statement reflected his values regarding the best possible roles for men and women. Psychologists are people who live and work in a specific society; sometimes their opinions may reflect the current biases of their culture. There have been some empirical attempts to relate androgyny to adjustment (Silvern & Ryan, 1979), but the statement in this excerpt is based primarily on political and social beliefs and must be carefully distinguished from more scientific claims.

To Learn More

Monte, C. F. *Beneath the Mask* (2d ed.). New York: Holt, Rinehart & Winston, 1980. An unusually detailed overview of personality theories. Particularly strong on psychoanalytic theories.

Freud, S. *New Introductory Lectures on Psychoanalysis* (W. J. H. Sproutt, trans.). New York: Norton, 1933. Perhaps the most accessible of Freud's writings describing his theory of personality.

Maslow, A. *Toward a Psychology of Being* (2d ed.). New York: Van Nostrand, 1968. An excellent introduction to humanistic thought.

12
Measuring Intelligence and Personality

Basic concepts of measurement
Reliability
Validity
Human variation and the normal curve
Commonsense errors in evaluating tests

Intelligence tests
Measuring intelligence
The Wechsler adult intelligence scale
Genetics and IQ
Applied psychology: Mental retardation

Personality tests
Personality inventories
Projective tests

Uses and abuses of psychological tests
Interpreting test results
Cultural bias

Summary

HOW DO THEY KNOW?
Correlations and causality: IQ and school grades

BECOMING A CRITICAL CONSUMER
Does this IQ question discriminate against minorities?

More than 2,000 years before the birth of Christ, the emperor of China instituted a system of formal examinations to determine whether particular public officials were capable of continuing in office. Later, the Chinese developed the first "civil service" exams to choose government workers. For example, in 1115 B.C., job candidates had to demonstrate proficiency in music, archery, horsemanship, writing, arithmetic, and the ceremonies of public and private life (Du Bois, 1970). Thus, the first known tests in the history of the human race were designed to choose people for jobs on the basis of their knowledge and abilities rather than on the basis of favoritism or accidents of birth, as practiced in many other societies.

The first psychological tests were designed with similar goals in mind. Alfred Binet developed the first intelligence test in 1905 for the objective identification of mentally retarded schoolchildren who required special schooling. The first personality test was devised by Robert Woodworth for the U.S. Army during World War I to identify draftees who would be unable to function psychologically under the stress of combat.

Today, hundreds of psychological tests are routinely adminstered to millions of Americans every year; indeed, every person who reads this text has almost certainly taken a number of them. Ordinarily, testing starts in grade school with standardized tests of achievement and IQ. The SAT may have helped determine the college you attend, and if you go on to graduate or professional school, your future may depend in part on your scores from an alphabet soup of tests including the GMAT, GRE, LSAT, and MCAT.

The Scholastic Aptitude Test for college admission was developed in 1926 by some of the same psychologists who had developed the first group IQ tests for the U.S. Army in World War I.

If you go to see a counselor or clinical psychologist, you may take the Rorschach, the Thematic Apperception Test, the Bender-Gestalt, or the Minnesota Multiphasic Personality Inventory. If you see a job counselor, you may take the Kuder Occupational Interest Survey or the Strong-Campbell Interest Inventory. If you apply for a job at a large corporation, you may take the Personnel Tests for Industry, and if you go to work for the United States government, you may take the Professional and Administrative Career Examination.

All these tests grew out of attempts to measure people's strengths and weaknesses fairly and objectively. But any type of evaluation is likely to involve problems, and from the beginning tests have been questioned by psychologists and nonpsychologists alike. Some of the questions raised by critics are serious and legitimate; several of these are discussed in the final section of this chapter. But too frequently, attacks on tests have been based on misconceptions and fallacies. Throughout this book, we have seen that trusting common sense can lead to some mistaken conclusions; this is particularly true regarding the interpretation of psychological test scores. Therefore, most of this chapter focuses on the basic principles of testing and measurement so that you, the consumer, can become more sophisticated about how psychological tests are designed to meet specific goals.

Basic Concepts of Measurement

The most important criteria by which psychologists judge any test are two technical characteristics called reliability and validity. In general terms, a **reliable** test is consistent and reproducible. A test is a kind of measuring device, and an unreliable test that gives inconsistent results is of little value.

Suppose, for example, that you bought a new tape measure to check your height. If the first measurement was 5 feet $10\frac{1}{2}$ inches, a second measurement read 5 feet $8\frac{3}{4}$ inches, and a third read 6 feet, this inconsistency (or unreliability) would mean that something was wrong with your new tape measure.

However, even if the tape measure were totally consistent, it could still be wrong. It might give you a reading of 7 feet 2 inches time after time, but if you know you are about 5 feet 4 inches tall, you will be suspicious. Reliability is a necessary, but not a sufficient, condition for good measurement.

If a psychological test is not reliable, there is no need to go any further. But if a test is reliable, we must also ask whether it is **valid**—whether it accurately measures what it is supposed to measure. This is much harder to determine than consistency, so our discussion of specific types of validity is more complex than our discussion of reliability.

RELIABILITY

Measuring the reliability of a psychological test is relatively straightforward. One simply compares two independent scores achieved by the same individual on the test. More specifically, pairs of independent scores are collected for a large number of people, and the researcher simply computes the correlation coefficient (see "How Do They Know?" in Chapter 3) between the two sets of scores.

If the two scores are identical for each individual, the correlation would be 1.0 and the test would be considered totally reliable. Psychologists expect the reliability of most tests to be around .9 or perhaps .8, since there is usually some slight error or variation in scores. This is to be expected even in physical measurements. If you weigh yourself every morning for a week, you will probably find that these measurements are not all precisely the same, because your weight varies slightly from day to day. Your psychological state may also vary from one test administration to another.

To cite just one example, the reliability for the verbal aptitude section of the College Entrance Examination Board's Scholastic Aptitude Test is .89; the reliability of the mathematics section is .88 (Wallace, 1972). These figures suggest that people who take the test a second time often get a slightly different score, but only a small fraction of them score much higher or much lower then they did the first time.

There are different types of reliability, depending on how the two independent scores are collected. For example, **test-retest reliability** is the correlation between pairs of test scores based on repeating precisely the same test on two different occasions. In many cases, however, this technique is not appropriate. For example, once you have taken a particular math test, the answers may come easier the second time around. In this case, a researcher might compute **alternate-form reliability**—the correlation between pairs of test scores achieved by the same person on two different forms (or sets of questions) testing the same material. There are also other forms of reliability; each provides a systematic measurement of consistency or stability over time.

Again, no matter how this characteristic is measured, unreliable test scores are of little scientific value. In some cases, a particular psychological test has been discredited when researchers showed it was unreliable. For example, some early scoring systems for the Rorschach test (a projective test of personality described later in this chapter) were shown to be unreliable and were therefore abandoned.

VALIDITY

The validity of a test is far more difficult to determine or define. Again, there are several types. Let us begin with the most straightforward approach—**criterion validity,** which compares performance on a test with some external and independent measure (or criterion) of what the test is supposed to predict.

For example, a test called the Computer Programmer Aptitude Battery has been designed to identify job applicants who are likely to become effective programmers. One can imagine several external criteria that could be used to evaluate the validity of this test, such as supervisors' ratings of later job performance or the time taken to complete a specific programming assignment. In one study of the validity of this test (Perry, 1967), 114 newly hired computer programmers were given this test before their training began. The external criterion of validity was the grade they received in their job training course. The correlations between the training course grades and scores on two subscales of the Computer Programmer Aptitude Battery were around .6, suggesting that it did indeed have criterion validity. Thus, the test is useful for companies who want to identify the strongest candidates in advance. In contrast, college grades were not highly correlated with performance in the training course and thus were of little predictive value for identifying the potential of applicants.

Note that while correlations of about .9 are expected for reliability, a correlation of .6 is considered adequate evidence of criterion validity. It is extremely difficult, or perhaps even impossible, to measure in advance all the factors that might be related to an external criterion. Performance in the computer training course, for example, was probably affected by a particular applicant's motivation, how much he liked the teacher, how much stress he was under at home, and a wide variety of other factors that the Computer Programmer Aptitude Battery did not even try to measure.

Of course, this analysis assumes that the criterion itself is reliable and relevant. If grades in the computer training course were assigned on the basis of participation in class rather than ability to solve programming problems, or based on how much the teacher liked each student, this criterion would have little value.

If the criterion was adequate, the observed coefficient of .6 implies that this particular company would be wise to use the Computer Programmer Aptitude Battery to screen job candidates. Job decisions based strictly on this test alone will sometimes be wrong; if the test were a perfect predictor of performance, the validity coefficient would have been 1.0. However, wise use of these test scores can increase the likelihood of the best decisions.

As this example suggests, the validity of a test is always evaluated for some specific application. The Computer Programmer Aptitude Battery is a valid predictor of programming performance (at least by this criterion), but it would probably not be able to predict who would be the best Fuller Brush salesman or bus driver.

A test may have criterion validity even if the questions it asks seem to be totally irrelevant. For example, it is theoretically possible that people who say they drink Pepsi for breakfast, are uncomfortable talking to strangers, and wear clothes that do not fit well make better computer programmers than stylish, coffee-drinking extraverts. On a superficial level, these three questions do not seem to have anything to do with performance as a computer programmer. But if they predict later performance, they have criterion validity.

A different approach to defining validity stresses the relevance of the content of a test. **Content validity** involves a systematic analysis of a particular skill followed by the design of test items that directly measure relevant knowledge and abilities. The key term here is *systematic analysis*. A test of French grammar would have high content validity only if one started by compiling a list of specifications of the key points in the field. This could be done by reviewing the content of courses and textbooks in French grammar and consulting experts in the language. The final list of specifications would then serve as the basis for drawing up actual test items.

The third major approach to validity is a bit more more theoretical. A test has **construct validity** if the trait it measures is systematically related to a larger pattern of behavior that makes conceptual sense. For example, suppose a person got high scores on a test of anxiety under three different conditions—when she took a math test she was unprepared for, when she went out on a date with someone new, and when she went skydiving. In this case, the theoretical construct of anxiety seems to explain this pattern of scores. But, as this example suggests, construct validity is a bit more subtle than criterion validity or content validity.

Whether a test approaches the problem of validity in terms of external criteria, test content, or a theoretical construct, it is important to remember that psychologists insist that any test meet certain technical specifications to prove its worth. Intuitive analyses of the superficial characteristics of a test are often misleading.

HUMAN VARIATION AND THE NORMAL CURVE

Reliability and validity are the two most important characteristics of any test. There are a number of other basic principles and concepts, however, that are useful to understand the nature of psychological tests.

Test scores quantify individual differences by assigning numbers to different personal characteristics such as intelligence and extraversion. To understand the rationale of tests, one must learn something about mathematical approaches to human variation.

The nineteenth-century Belgian scientist Adolphe Quetelet was the first to note that many human physical characteristics fell into similar patterns. Figure 12.1 illustrates one example. In 1939, the height of every man in England who was called up for military service was measured. The graph shows that the average height of these 91,163 men was about 5 feet $7\frac{1}{2}$ inches. More important, the distribution of heights was arranged systematically around the average value—that is, the farther one gets from 5 feet $7\frac{1}{2}$ inches, the fewer men there are.

More specifically, height conformed to a **normal distribution,** a particular mathematical distribution in which cases are symmetrically arranged around the average. Figure 12.2 illustrates the form of the normal distribution. As you can see, the normal distribution curve is symmetrical; the left and right sides are mirror images of each other.

The central value of the normal distribution is the **mean,** or arithmetic average. The shape of a particular normal curve is also determined by the **standard deviation,** a mathematical measure of the amount of variability, spread, or dispersion of a particular set of scores. (See "Appendix.")

In Figure 12.1, the mean height is 67.5 inches and the standard deviation is 2.6 inches. Referring to Figure 12.2, the normal distribution implies that about 68% of all men should fall within one standard deviation of the mean. To put it another way, 68% of all English military recruits were between 64.9 inches (67.5 − 2.6) and 70.1 inches (67.5 + 2.6) tall. Again referring to the Figure 12.2 summary of characteristics of the normal curve, note that about 95% of all values fall within two standard deviations of the mean. In this case, that implies that 95 out of every 100 English recruits was between 62.3 inches [67.5 − (2.6 × 2)] and 72.7 inches [67.5 + (2.6 × 2)] tall. Because the normal curve is a particular mathematical distribution that can be specified quite precisely, one can determine exactly how many cases fall within a particular range.

The normal distribution is useful not just for describing such physical characteristics as height, weight, and chest size, but also for psychological characteristics such as intelligence. The first tests of IQ often found that scores were distributed roughly according to a normal distribution.

There is some controversy about whether this distribution tells us something about the nature of intelligence or something about the tests psychologists use to measure it. Whatever the implications, the fact is that IQ scores conform roughly to

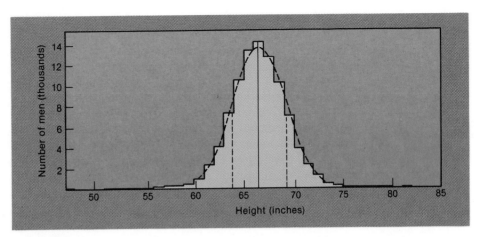

Figure 12.1
The height of 91,163 Englishmen who were called up for military service in 1939. The solid lines show the actual number for each height; the dotted line represents a normal distribution.

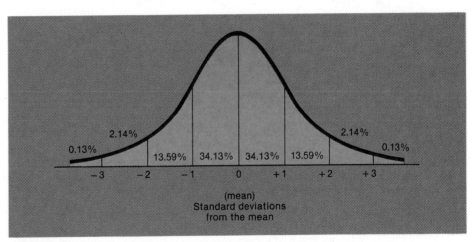

Figure 12.2
The normal distribution. Note that roughly 68% of all cases fall within one standard deviation of the mean; roughly 95% within two standard deviations; and 99.7% within three standard deviations.

a normal distribution and that researchers have found that the normal curve is useful for describing the distribution of many psychological characteristics.

COMMONSENSE ERRORS IN EVALUATING TESTS

Before describing how reliability, validity, and the normal curve apply to tests of human personality and intelligence, it is useful to spell out some of the implications of these concepts in understanding tests. In part because psychological tests are so familiar, people often evaluate them in terms of commonsense criteria. But, as we have seen throughout this text, arguments that are intuitively appealing are sometimes quite wrong. Here, we focus on three common errors of common sense: relying on the appearances of a test, placing too much emphasis on criticisms of individual items, and assuming that population predictions apply to every individual.

Relying on Face Validity.   Psychologists use the term **face validity** to refer to what a test *appears* to measure. Superficial appearances are a weak basis for evaluating a test, and in some cases they can be quite misleading.

Consider an analogy from another field. Many medical examinations have little face validity. If you lived in the fifteenth century, when little was known about the biochemistry of pregnancy, a pregnancy test based on analyzing chemicals in the urine might have seemed magical or even laughable. But that is not the point. If such a test had been available, it could have proved its value by successfully predicting childbirth. This test would have had little face validity but high criterion validity.

Similarly, the items on a personality test may be useful even if they are not related to personality in any obvious way. Art Buchwald poked fun at the superficial appearance of some psychological tests with a satirical personality inventory that included the following true-or-false questions:

Most of the time I go to sleep without saying goodbye.
A wide necktie is a sign of disease.
Frantic screams make me nervous.
When I was a child, I was an imaginary playmate.

If you have ever taken a true-or-false personality test, these items may seem funny. In fact, they are funny. But it would be unfortunate if a satire like this led you to believe that test questions that seem odd—or even silly—are signs of a useless test. For test items, as for used cars and spouses, looks can be deceiving. The question of validity should be tied to performance, not to superficial appearances.

Overemphasis on Individual Items.   Judgments about validity should always be based on the overall performance of an entire test. A second error commonsense critics often make is singling out an individual item for intuitive analysis. For example, journalists are fond of taking one question from the SAT and asking rhetorically whether it is really necessary for a student to be able, say, to define *hirsute* to do well in college.

Aside from the fact that this argument appeals to face validity rather than criterion validity, it makes the additional mistake of assuming that one or two questions would make much difference. Good tests usually consist of many items; they work by the sheer weight of numbers. A person with a large vocabulary might not happen to know the definition of one particular word, but she probably could identify the meanings of most of the other words on the test. The individual skills needed to answer a large number of specific items tend to balance one another out.

In a well-constructed test, a poor item is easy to locate because it is probably not systematically related to the total score. Suppose you constructed a test of 43 vocabulary items and added the irrelevant question, "How many miles is it from Chicago to St. Louis?" You would almost certainly find that, on the average, people who knew that *hirsute* means "hairy" would score higher on other vocabulary items than those who defined it incorrectly. But there probably would not be much difference in vocabulary scores among those who got the Chicago–to–St. Louis item right or wrong. Because it tapped a different type of knowledge, it would be poorly correlated with the total score. To an expert in testing, the results would stick out like a sore thumb.

Even if the mileage question were kept in the vocabulary test, it would not make much difference. It is only one item of many; it would simply decrease the validity of the test slightly.

Individual versus Group Predictions.

A third error that people sometimes make when they evaluate tests is assuming that group predictions apply to every individual. Tests are like the actuarial tables used by life insurance companies to predict the death rate; they are extremely effective in predicting probabilities for large groups but fail in many individual cases.

For example, if your father is a 50-year-old business executive who has high blood pressure and smokes two packs of cigarettes every day, he will have to pay high rates for his life insurance because actuarial tables predict that he is likely to die sooner than a healthy 25-year-old nonsmoker. If he lives to be 100, the life insurance company will not throw away its charts. Some smokers with high blood pressure live to be 100, but they are the exceptions to the rule.

The same is true for test scores. It is possible that a high school senior who gets 300 on his SATs will go on to be the valedictorian of his college class. Anything is possible. But this event is not likely. If you were to collect the SAT scores of 500 valedictorians at major colleges each year, few would have scores as low as 300.

Tests predict probabilities for large groups; they do not determine the future course for every individual. Indeed, test makers can predict just how often they will be wrong by examining validity coefficients. A test with a criterion validity of .8 will be right far more often than a test with a criterion validity of .5; this greater predictive power is exactly what the magnitude of the correlation tells us.

Critics of IQ tests often cite cases of individuals who did far better in school than their IQ scores might seem to predict. These cases come as no surprise to people who understand the nature of tests; the predictions they make are extremely accurate for large groups but less accurate for individuals.

Experienced clinicians assign far less value to a single test score than does the proverbial man in the street. That is one reason that IQ scores and other results are often withheld from the people who take the tests. If one child in a family is told that his IQ is 118 and his older sister's is 123, he may conclude that he is the slow one in the family and start to act the part. A psychologist would know that a difference of 5 points is very likely to result from random variation and is of little or no practical significance. (If the difference were 30 points, however, it probably would have practical implications.)

In summary, people who do not understand the nature of psychological tests often misinterpret them. It is only by learning more about the nature of tests that you can make informed judgments about them.

In 1884, Sir Francis Galton set up this exhibition in a London museum. There were 9,337 visitors who paid to participate in tests of their vision, hearing, reaction time, muscle strength, and other characteristics that Galton believed were related to intelligence. Each participant received a card comparing his performance to the averages for earlier visitors. Later data suggested that the tests devised by Galton were not related to intelligence.

Intelligence Tests

MEASURING INTELLIGENCE

Sir Francis Galton was probably the first scientist to try systematically to measure differences in human intellectual ability. After completing his studies of eminent Englishmen (see Chapter 3), he looked for a more precise index of ability. Galton assumed that people with good eyesight and hearing, fast motor reactions, and other basic abilities would also prove to be superior in reasoning power. It is a testimonial to Galton's own intelligence that he thought of a profitable way to test this hypothesis. He set up an exhibit of tests in a London museum and invited people to see how their mental and physical abilities compared with others'; 9,337 visitors paid 4 pence each for this privilege. Unfortunately, later analysis of these and other studies did not support Galton's idea that reasoning power was associated with sensory and motor skills.

The First IQ Tests. The roots of modern ideas of measuring intelligence can be traced back to a practical problem. After the French government passed a law in 1881 requiring every child to go to school, teachers soon found that some children seemed totally unable to master the curriculum. In 1904, the minister of public instruction appointed a special committee to look into the problem of identifying retarded students who needed special instruction. One of its members, a psychologist named Alfred Binet, devised a special test to screen students so that "no child suspected of retardation would be . . . put in a special school without having taken . . . [an] examination showing that . . . he could not profit, at least moderately, from the teaching in the regular school" (quoted in Du Bois, 1970, p. 34).

In collaboration with Theodore Simon, Binet published this first modern intelligence test in 1905. It consisted of 30 different tests that a trained examiner could quickly administer to an individual child. Virtually all of these tasks had been studied before by Binet and others; what was new was the idea of combining information from a wide variety of tasks to determine a child's mental age. **Mental age** was defined by the average performance of a large number of children who were actually that old.

For example, Figure 12.3 shows one of the items from Binet's 1905 scale. A person with a mental age of at least 3 could point to a simple object in this picture and could also repeat two digits, tell his family name, and perform other specified intellectual tasks. This definition was based on Binet's systematic observation that average 3-year-olds could perform these tasks but younger children generally could not. A person with a mental age of 8 could count backward from 20 to 0 and could repeat five digits. A mental age of 12 or more was indicated by an ability to compose a sentence using three given words (such as *Paris*, *gutter*, and *fortune*) and perform other specific tasks. These are actual examples from the 1911 revision of Binet's scale; similar items are used in present-day tests of children's intelligence.

The idea of computing an **intelligence quotient** (or **IQ**) came from a German psychologist named William Stern. He argued that a 5-year-old with a mental age of 4 was more retarded than a 13-year-old with a mental age of 12. In other words, it is not the difference between mental and chronological age that provides the best index of development but the ratio:

$$\textbf{\textit{Intelligence quotient (IQ)}} = \frac{\textit{Mental age}}{\textit{Chronological age}} \times 100$$

Chronological age is determined by the date of birth; the ratio is multiplied by 100 simply for convenience, so that IQ can be expressed without decimals. Using this formula, the average child's IQ is 100; slower children will have IQs below 100, and brighter-than-average children will have IQs over 100.

Many psychologists around the world tried Binet's test and published revisions

Figure 12.3
An actual item from Binet's 1905 intelligence test. Young children were asked to point out specific objects or persons in the picture, including the window, the broom, the mother, and the big sister.

Alfred Binet (1857–1911) wrote a doctoral dissertation on the nervous system of insects, but later he became interested in the measurement of human intelligence. In 1904 he was appointed to a commission that sought a reliable way to identify retarded children early in their school careers, so that they could receive special instruction. A year later, Binet and Theodore Simon published the first systematic test of intelligence. The scale was an immediate success; revisions in 1908 and 1911 were quickly accepted around the world. At the time of his death, Binet was trying to develop an intelligence test that could be administered to an entire group rather than to one individual at a time.

based on their own data regarding which items successfully distinguished children of different chronological ages. Items shown to be ineffective were replaced with better questions. The most famous revision was published by Lewis Terman at Stanford University in 1916. This scale, now known as the **Stanford-Binet**, underwent further major revisions in 1937 and 1960. Although hundreds of other tests have been published, the Stanford-Binet is still one of the most frequently used tests for assessing the intelligence of an individual child.

When similar tests were later developed for adults, the idea of an intelligence quotient based on mental age no longer applied. There is little or no difference between the reasoning power of 20-year-olds and 40-year-olds. The term IQ was still used, however, and adult scores were standardized in terms of the normal distribution. The IQ of the average adult was defined as 100; once the standard deviation of a particular adult IQ test is specified, it is possible to determine where any other score stands in relation to the total adult population.

After Binet, the next major step in the development of psychological tests involved instruments that could be administered to a large group of people at the same time. Like the notion of IQ, group testing grew out of a practical problem. When millions of men were drafted in World War I, the U.S. Army needed to screen out quickly any retarded individuals who could not function as soldiers. A group of psychologists developed the Army Alpha Test to measure the IQ of soldiers who could read English and the Army Beta Test for those who could not. Alpha was largely composed of verbal and numerical tests, such as vocabulary and arithmetic problems; Beta items focused on such tasks as mazes, counting cubes, and noting missing parts of familiar pictures. Within two years, more than 1.7 million men took these tests in the first mass-testing program in history.

Encouraged by the success of the Army tests, psychologists went on to develop a large number of tests for industry and education after the war ended. Indeed, some historians believe that the success of the Army testing program changed the course of American psychology—an academic discipline focusing on basic research turned into a profession with strong applied interests (Du Bois, 1970).

IQ and Intelligence. As more and more IQ tests were developed, critics became increasingly concerned with a fundamental question. Did IQ tests really measure intelligence? One problem with this question is that people sometimes disagree over the definition of the word *intelligence*. For example, a study of "lay people" such as commuters, supermarket shoppers, and people chosen from the phone book (Sternberg, Conway, Ketron, & Bernstein, 1981) found some specific disagreements. One subject in this study said an intelligent person is "fun to be with"; another said an intelligent person "bores people." Clearly, no measure of intelligence can satisfy such contradictory criteria.

Nevertheless, there was general agreement. The characteristics these lay people listed in definitions of intelligence included the skills measured in IQ tests, such as good vocabulary, verbal fluency, and an ability to see the connections between ideas. But they also included interpersonal characteristics such as "sensitivity to other people's needs and desires" and "gets along well with others." Traditional IQ tests have not attempted to measure this type of "street smarts." Thus, while there is a close relationship between IQ and everyday definitions of intelligence, there may also be some important differences. Intuitively, it is easy to identify individuals with great intellectual abilities who do not relate well to other people. Only future research can tell whether these individuals represent the exceptions or the rule, that is, whether interpersonal skills are independent from more intellectual forms of intelligence.

Most of the research to date on the nature of intelligence has focused on the relationships among performance on various intellectual tasks. For example, if people who score high in verbal ability also generally do well on tests of mathematical ability, it seems reasonable to conclude that both reflect the same underlying dimension of general intelligence. If, on the other hand, the correlation between verbal and mathematical ability is typically low, these intellectual skills are probably independent of each other and represent two different types of intelligence.

Early researchers were impressed by the high correlations between different ways of measuring intelligence. Around the turn of the century, Charles Spearman concluded that IQ tests measure one general intelligence factor (called g). Other researchers later developed new statistical techniques that challenged this view. After analyzing the performance of hundreds of subjects on a variety of mental tests, L. L. Thurstone concluded that there are seven relatively independent primary mental abilities: verbal comprehension, word fluency, number, space, memory, perceptual speed, and reasoning. Thurstone argued that IQ tests that assign a single score of intelligence are too simplistic. One person with an IQ of 120 might have a very good memory, while another person with the same score might have an average memory but above-average word fluency.

The question of whether intelligence is best thought of as one general ability or several separate abilities revolves around sophisticated mathematical analyses of test results; it remains controversial (Carroll & Horn, 1981). For our purposes, however, this theoretical issue may be less important than some of the practical questions considered in the next section: What kinds of performance can be predicted from the results of the most common tests of IQ?

THE WECHSLER ADULT INTELLIGENCE SCALE

At first, tests of adult IQ simply consisted of more difficult versions of items developed for schoolchildren. In 1939, David Wechsler published an IQ test that had been specifically designed with adult interests and abilities in mind. Wechsler's test became the most widely used instrument for assessing the IQ of adults on a one-to-one basis; more than 3,000 articles have been published on its use (Anastasi, 1982).

The scale was revised in 1955 and again in 1981; reliability, validity, and other technical characteristics were improved by replacing items that failed to meet certain statistical criteria. The revisions also updated the test's content so that it could accurately reflect the knowledge and interests of subsequent generations. For example, the 1981 edition (called the **Wechsler Adult Intelligence Scale–Revised,** or **WAIS-R**) eliminated some items that seemed implicitly racist or sexist.

The WAIS-R consists of two major parts, a verbal scale and a performance scale. The verbal scale consists of 6 subtests that ask different types of questions; another 5 subtests make up the performance scale (see Table 12.1). Thus, the WAIS-R includes 11 different categories of questions to test a wide range of intellectual skills and to identify people who don't know—or don't care—about one particular type of question. Under ordinary conditions, the total score an individual receives on the verbal scale is closely related to the total score on the performance scale. For people with little education or verbal facility, however, these two approaches may provide different estimates of IQ.

Actual IQ scores on the WAIS-R are based on the performance of a representative sample of 1,880 Americans tested between 1976 and 1980 (see Figure 12.4). The proportions of subjects were matched to the 1970 census in terms of sex, age, race, geographic region, occupation, education, and urban or rural residence. Tables are provided for the examiner to convert a particular number of correct answers into a normally distributed IQ score, with a mean of 100 and a standard deviation of 15. The actual conversion formula depends on the age of the person taking the test. For example, if a 65-year-old and a 22-year-old got all the same questions right, the 65-year-old would have a higher IQ. The reason is that performance declines somewhat as a person grows older (see Chapter 9), so a 65-year-old would be farther above the average for his age group than a 22-year-old with the same score.

Extensive tests were done to ensure the reliability of the WAIS-R. For example, test-retest reliability was assessed by giving people the WAIS-R on two different occasions (two to seven weeks apart). These correlations were around .95, indicating that the WAIS-R is a highly reliable instrument.

As you might expect, the validity of the WAIS-R is far more difficult to assess. Wechsler (1958) argues for its content validity (as noted earlier, this is based on the systematic analysis of relevant abilities) because the 11 subtests were chosen to sample all the different components of intelligence that have proved important in clinical

TABLE 12.1
Subtests of the Wechsler Adult Intelligence Scale

Subtests	Typical Items
Verbal	
Information	At what temperature does water freeze?
Comprehension	Why are traffic lights needed?
Arithmetic	A car goes 50 miles in one hour. Traveling at the same speed, how far could it go in 15 minutes?
Similarities	In what way are oranges and apples alike?
Digit span	Repeat the following numbers: 7, 4, 3, 6, 2, 6, 5, 1.
Vocabulary	What does *autumn* mean?
Performance	
Digit symbol	Given a key that lists a symbol (such as $\perp$ or $\wedge$) for each digit from 1 to 9, write the symbol for each number that appears on a long list.
Object assembly	A small jigsaw puzzle of a familiar object.
Block design	Arrange a set of blocks (with different designs on each side) so that they reproduce a specified pattern.
Picture completion	What is missing from this picture?

Picture arrangement   Arrange these pictures in the proper order to tell a logical story:

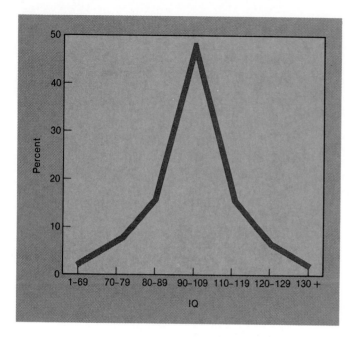

Figure 12.4
The actual distribution of IQs for the most recent standardization sample of the WAIS-R. There were 1,880 adults chosen to represent the United States population in sex, age, race, and other characteristics. Note the similarity to the normal distribution shown in Figure 12.2.

practice. From another perspective, he argues that the fact that the WAIS-R is highly correlated (typically around .8) with other tests of IQ suggests construct validity (based on the test's theoretical relation to other behaviors). Further, the fact that scores on the 11 subtests generally correlate with each other (typically, correlations between pairs of tests range from .3 to .8) supports the idea that they all measure the same underlying construct, intelligence.

The strongest argument for the validity of the WAIS-R probably involves criterion validity (its ability to predict external behavior). Countless studies have shown that a wide variety of IQ tests, including the WAIS-R, predict performance in school (see "How Do They Know?"). Correlations are typically on the order of .5 and tend to be higher for objective achievement tests than for course grades. (Other evidence suggests that course grades reflect more than just intelligence, particularly in elementary school. All other things being equal, teachers tend to give higher grades to socially outgoing students, those who put in extra effort, and girls.) IQ scores also correlate highly (typically .6 to .8) with ratings of intelligence by both teachers and students. People with high IQs also tend to go further in school and work in more demanding occupations with higher income and prestige (Matarazzo, 1972; Jensen, 1980).

Psychologists still do not agree exactly what IQ means in theoretical terms, so there is some controversy over the precise implications of IQ scores. But all three approaches to validity—content, construct, and criterion—suggest that the WAIS-R measures at least one kind of intelligence that is systematically related to a number of behaviors.

GENETICS AND IQ

Of all the human traits studied by behavioral geneticists (see Chapter 3), none has been studied more intensively than IQ and none has provoked more heated debate.

Correlations and Causality: IQ and School Grades

As explained in "How Do They Know" in Chapter 3, a **correlation coefficient** is a mathematical expression of the relationship between two variables. The absolute value of a correlation coefficient varies from 0 (no relationship) to 1 (one variable predicts another perfectly), while the sign of the correlation (plus or minus) indicates the direction of the relationship. But even after a correlation between two variables has been computed, there is still the question of what it means.

When an investigator finds that there is a correlation between education and income, for example, intuitively the implication seems clear: If you stay in school longer, you are likely to make more money. This "obvious" conclusion may be quite wrong, for one simple reason—correlations do not necessarily imply causal relationships.

Statistics teachers are fond of describing correlations where the lack of causality is easy to see. For example, Fuerst (1979) notes that around 1950 someone discovered that there was a correlation of +.90 between the number of babies born in Stockholm, Sweden, each year and the number of storks' nests in the city. Does that mean that storks really do bring babies? Of course not.

However, it is possible to imagine a causal basis of the correlation that most of us could accept. The extra storks in the city may have been noisy as they left their nests early in the morning to find food, leaving the rudely awakened human inhabitants with extra time to make babies. More likely, both more storks and more babies were caused by a third factor—as Stockholm grew during these years, there were more houses for storks to nest on and people to live in.

A significant correlation between A and B can be explained at least three ways—A causes B, B causes A, and changes in both A and B are caused by something else. For example, Vane (1966) found that grammar school IQ scores correlated significantly ($r = .56$) with the average grades of 272 students at a Long Island, New York, high school; dozens of other studies have reported similar correlations between IQ and grades.

The implication seems obvious. Having a high IQ improves your chances of doing well in school. It may seem obvious, but it is not necessarily correct. Perhaps the grades are the more fundamental variable; doing well in courses increases knowledge and helps a person get more items right on an IQ test. Or perhaps it is some third, unmeasured variable that accounts for success on IQ tests and high school grades. Maybe exposure to educational games at the age of 3 is the key to later academic success, and children who watched *Sesame Street* are more likely to do well on IQ tests and school tests. All these explanations—high IQ causes high grades, high grades cause high IQ, and both are caused by something else—are equally plausible explanations of the correlation.

That does not mean that causal relationships can never be uncovered. Experimental studies can prove causality, and sophisticated analyses of some kinds of correlational data can suggest it. In the study described here, the fact that the IQ scores were measured several years before the grades suggests that IQ is the more basic factor.

The most important point for the introductory student is that simple correlations do not prove causal relationships, no matter how obvious the links may seem intuitively.

Individual Differences. In 1963, a classic article summarized all the evidence then available regarding IQ resemblances among biological and adoptive relatives (Erlenmeyer-Kimling & Jarvik, 1963). More than 30,000 pairs of people had participated in 52 studies in eight countries over two generations. Despite the wide range of samples and methods, the overall results proved to be quite consistent. The more closely two people were biologically related, the more similar their IQs. This data suggested that genetic factors strongly influenced individual differences in IQ. But over the next two decades, this conclusion was repeatedly challenged and criticized as other investigators reexamined the original data and conducted investigations of their own.

In the course of this painstaking reanalysis, evidence emerged that one of the most famous investigators, Sir Cyril Burt, had actually falsified data to prove that IQ was inherited (Hearnshaw, 1979). There have been few documented cases of scientific fraud of this sort, and the seriousness of this incident suggests that the debate over the genetics of IQ was no ordinary academic controversy.

On a more positive note, the fact that so much attention has now been devoted to the reanalysis of these data increases scientific confidence in the conclusions that finally emerged. In 1980, Robert Plomin and J. C. De Fries compared results from studies published in the 1970s analyzing 9,300 pairs of relatives with the earlier review of 30,000 pairs. They found that the later studies typically produced somewhat lower estimates of heritability, perhaps as a result of methodological improvements or of differences in the populations studied. However, even these newer, more conservative results "nonetheless implicate genes as the major systematic force influencing the development of individual differences in IQ" (p. 21).

One line of data supporting this conclusion compared IQ resemblance among identical and fraternal twins. According to Plomin and de Fries's summary of the data, identical twins who are raised in the same family are more closely related in IQ (correlation = .86) than fraternal twins of the same sex who are raised together (correlation = .62). Since the major difference between these twin pairs is that identical (monozygotic) twins are genetically identical, while fraternal (dizygotic) twins are no more closely related than any pair of siblings, most psychologists interpret these data to mean that genetic forces are particularly powerful.

The most interesting twins, from a theoretical point of view, are identical twins who are raised in different families, for they represent an experiment in nature in which two individuals with the same genes are exposed to different environments. Such cases are extremely rare, and only three studies have withstood careful scrutiny. Juel-Nielsen (1965) found a correlation of .62 between the IQs of 12 pairs of monozygotic twins raised apart; Newman, Freeman, and Holzinger (1937) reported a correlation of .67 for 19 pairs of twins; and Shields (1962) found a correlation of .77 for 40 pairs of separated identical twins. Although these studies too have been criticized, the fact that these correlations are generally higher than those found for fraternal twins raised together provides further support for the powerful effects of genes on IQ.

Another line of evidence for the genetic hypothesis comes from studies of adopted children. The correlation between IQs of biological parent and child who are separated by adoption is .31, while the correlation between adoptive parent and

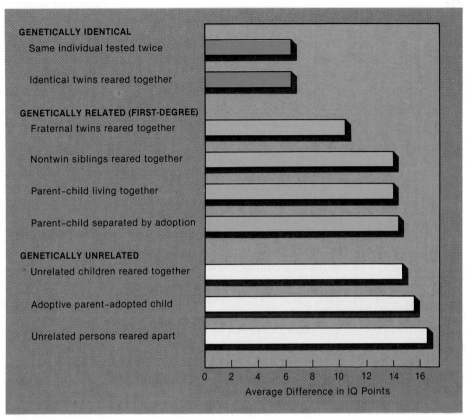

GENETICALLY IDENTICAL
- Same individual tested twice
- Identical twins reared together

GENETICALLY RELATED (FIRST-DEGREE)
- Fraternal twins reared together
- Nontwin siblings reared together
- Parent–child living together
- Parent–child separated by adoption

GENETICALLY UNRELATED
- Unrelated children reared together
- Adoptive parent–adopted child
- Unrelated persons reared apart

Average Difference in IQ Points

Figure 12.5
Summary of data from over 18,000 people regarding similarity between various types of relatives. These data suggest that both genes and environment influence IQ.

child is .15. This is consistent with other evidence that the more closely two people are related biologically, the closer their IQs are likely to be (see Figure 12.5).

Another review of this literature came to the following conclusion: "Within populations of European origin, both the genotype and the environment demonstrably influence IQ, the former tending under present conditions to account for more of the individual variation in IQ than does the latter" (Loehlin, Lindzey, & Spuhler, 1975, p. 233). If the phrasing seems cautious, it is purposely so. Since the vast majority of studies to date have focused on samples of European origin, the authors limit their conclusion to that group "under present conditions." Behavioral geneticists stress such limitations because their findings are so often misunderstood.

Implications of Heritability. In our previous discussion of behavioral genetics (see Chapter 3), we stressed several points about what it means when a particular characteristic has high heritability. The relative importance of nature and nurture is always defined for a specific group. Further, high heritability within a particular group does not imply that a trait cannot be changed, and human characteristics are always determined by both heredity and environment.

The first of these three points caused the greatest confusion. Much of the fuel for the controversy over the genetics of IQ came from a 1969 article by Arthur Jensen. At that time, most psychologists accepted the findings from numerous studies that showed that, on the average, American whites scored somewhat higher on IQ tests than American blacks. However, most believed that these differences reflected the limitations of the test or environmental influences on IQ. Jensen was one of the first to raise the possibility that genetic factors might be involved in this racial difference.

It is important to emphasize that the origin of differences *between* groups is logically separate from the question of whether individual differences in IQ *within* a particular population are strongly influenced by genetics. As noted above, there is a great deal of evidence that IQ is highly heritable within the American white population. But this conclusion may not apply to other groups. According to one school of thought, American blacks have often been raised in educationally disadvantaged environments, so that they are unable to express their genetic potential. If this were so, estimates of the heritability of IQ within the black population would be lower than similar estimates within the white population. There have been direct tests of this idea, but to date the results have been inconsistent and inconclusive (Loehlin, Lindzey, & Spuhler, 1975).

The related question of the origin of differences between groups is even more complex and controversial. To try to get some distance from the emotional issue of race, consider an example of genetics in agriculture. Imagine an Arizona parsley farmer who uses the same seed to plant two different plots of land. One plot is fertilized and watered regularly, the other neglected. Some parsley plants within each field will be taller and sturdier than others, based on the genetic characteristics of individual seeds. But overall, the plants in the plot that was well watered and taken care of will be taller and healthier that those in the neglected field. Thus, the differences *between* these plots of land are the result of environmental variation while, at the same time, the differences *within* each plot are determined largely by genetics.

Analogously, the fact that IQ is strongly influenced by genes for American whites does *not* imply that any differences in IQ between blacks and whites are also based on genetics. There are scientific methods that can reveal the source of group differences, but the convictions of those who debate this topic have often exceeded the quality of their evidence. The details of this controversy are extremely complex and confusing, but the most reasonable conclusion is extremely simple: At this point, no one knows the cause of black-white IQ differences.

In any case, we must remember that a genetic trait is not fixed for life at the moment of birth. In Chapter 3, we described the example of PKU, a genetic disorder that leads to mental retardation when untreated but the effects of which are relatively minor when treated properly. In that example, understanding the genetic basis of a characteristic actually made it easier to change.

And there is no doubt whatever that the environment plays an important role in determining IQ. The simple fact that monozygotic twins have different IQs proves that the environment has an impact. Studies of adopted children have shown that higher socioeconomic status can raise IQ. For example, Scarr and Weinberg (1976) studied 130 black and interracial children who were adopted by economically advantaged white families in Minnesota. If genetics were the only factor in determining intelligence, these children would have been expected to have IQs somewhat below average, around 90. In fact, the mean IQ of this group was 106, testifying to the importance of the conditions under which children are raised. Children who had been adopted within the first year of life had even higher IQs.

It is unfortunate that the high heritability of IQ is so often misunderstood. It does not imply that differences between groups are genetic nor that IQ can never be changed. However, it may imply that the best way to deal with human diversity is to try to understand it fully in order to help each individual achieve as much as possible.

Mental Retardation

As noted earlier, the first IQ tests were designed in part to identify children whose limited intellectual ability would create special problems in their schooling. From the start, however, those who invented IQ measurements worried that a diagnosis of retardation could not be made on the basis of an IQ score alone. Binet and Simon wrote that IQ diagnosis "is not automatic, like a scale in a railroad station, on which it is necessary only to step for the machine to emit a ticket with our weight printed on it. . . . The results of our examination have no value if separated from all comment; they must be interpreted" (quoted in Du Bois, 1970, p. 39).

Similarly, the current guidelines for the diagnosis of mental retardation (American Psychiatric Association, 1980) stress that this label should be based not just on an IQ score but also on a clinical judgment that a person is intellectually unable to function in society without some special help. Unfortunately, human judgment is sometimes wrong and some individuals have been falsely diagnosed as mentally retarded. In the past, diagnosis has been particularly troublesome for blind, deaf, and verbally limited children who may lack the physical skills to respond appropriately on many intelligence tests.

A critical consumer of psychology will remain somewhat skeptical of a diagnosis of mental retardation, for fear that the label itself may become self-fulfilling prophecy, with a child developing low expectations for herself because she believes she is retarded. However, this caution about an individual's diagnosis is not meant to imply that all mental retardaton is in the eye of the beholder; the vast majority of people who are diagnosed as mentally retarded suffer from a serious intellectual deficit that interferes with their ability to function adequately in our society.

The current diagnostic system distinguishes four levels of retardation: mild—IQ 50 to 70; moderate—IQ 35 to 49; severe—IQ 20 to 34; and profound—IQ below 20. Most researchers believe that cases of moderate, severe, and profound retardation are usually caused by identifiable biological problems, while the much more common diagnosis of mild retardation is usually a result of environmental factors summarized by the label *cultural-familial retardation*.

Cultural-familial retardation involves a family pattern of mild mental retardation with no evidence of organic brain damage. About 4 out of 5 mentally retarded people fall into the mild category, and the overwhelming majority of these cases fall into the cultural-familial group. This pattern is rarely found in middle-class or upper-class children; it is limited to people who grow up in homes that are socially, economically, and culturally disadvantaged.

People in this group are often called "educable" because they can develop adequate social and communication skills with special training. Mild retardation often is diagnosed only in late childhood, when problems with reading, writing, and arithmetic become prominent. In nonindustrialized societies that do not emphasize these skills, mild retardation might go unnoticed.

In contrast, the more severe categories of mental retardation are equally common among all social classes and ordinarily seem to be caused by biological and organic problems. People who fall into the moderate group (about 12% of the retarded population) are considered "trainable." Although they are unlikely to pass the second-grade level in academic subjects, they can learn to care for themselves with some supervision. Severe mental retardation (about 7% of the retarded) interferes with motor development and speech. People in this category can learn simple work tasks if they are closely supervised. Profound mental retardation (less than 1% of the retarded) is so severe that people must live in a highly structured environment with aid and supervision.

Among the biological causes of the more severe forms of retardation, the most common and best understood is **Down's syndrome,** first described by British physician Langdon Down in 1866. Down used the term *mongolism* to refer to the physical abnormalities that accompany this condition, including slanting eyes; a flat face and nose; a large, protruding tongue; stubby fingers; and sparse, straight hair. About 1 out of every 660 births produces a Down's syndrome child; the IQ of such a child rarely exceeds 50.

In 1959, physicians discovered that Down's syndrome is caused by a chromosomal abnormality. As noted in Chapter 3, every cell in the human body ordinarily contains 46 chromosomes (structures composed of genes). The Down's syndrome child has an extra, forty-seventh chromosome because of an abnormality in the mother's egg. The risk of this problem increases dramatically as a woman gets older. For mothers under the age of 30, only about 1 in 1,500 births produces a Down's syndrome child; for mothers over 45, the risk is 1 in 65. The possible importance of the father's age is not fully understood.

In recent years, a new diagnostic procedure has been developed that can diagnose Down's syndrome—and many other conditions—before birth. In **amniocentesis,** fluid is withdrawn from the amnion, the sac surrounding the fetus. If chromosomal abnormalities are detected, the mother then has the option of terminating the pregnancy with an abortion.

Moderate, severe, and profound retardation can also be caused by a variety of other biological problems. Along with genetic disorders, these include infectious diseases such as syphilis, traumatic events before birth such as malnutrition or certain types of poisoning, and traumatic events during or following birth such as head injury or deprivation of oxygen.

Figure 12.6
Down's syndrome was originally called Mongolism because physician Langdon Down, who identified the syndrome in 1866, mistakenly believed that this form of mental retardation was somehow linked to the Mongol race.

Society's attitudes toward mental retardation have undergone many changes since the problem was identified by the French physician Edouard Sequin in the nineteenth century. Sequin optimistically believed that special training of the muscles and senses could overcome the limitations of the retarded. Unfortunately, this was not the case. Institutions that started out as training centers gradually evolved into warehouses in which the unfortunate victims of retardation were segregated from society.

It was only in the 1960s and 1970s that the American public became aware of the dismal and dehumanizing condition of these underfinanced and understaffed institutions. The lack of intellectual stimulation often limited the development of retarded individuals. A number of recent laws and court cases have begun to protect the human rights of retarded citizens. It remains to be seen whether our society is willing to make a serious commitment of money and resources to ensure that every victim of retardation is given an opportunity to live up to his or her full potential.

Personality Tests

Like tests of intelligence, the first systematic instruments for measuring personality grew out of practical concerns. During World War I, Robert Woodworth attempted to develop a questionnaire to help locate individuals who might develop a psychiatric condition then known as "shell shock," emotional problems that would interfere with their ability to function as soldiers. Woodworth began with a questionnaire listing symptoms commonly reported by psychiatric patients and tested this survey on groups of normal and disturbed individuals.

In Chapter 11, we discussed the difficulty of defining personality and the controversy over the significance of particular personality traits. It should come as no surprise that there are a number of approaches to assessing personality, each with its own strengths and weaknesses. Here, we focus on two major types of tests—personality inventories and projective tests.

PERSONALITY INVENTORIES

Basic Concepts. A **personality inventory** is a standard list of questions about an individual's behavior and feelings that assesses personality traits. Personality inventories are sometimes called paper-and-pencil tests because they can be administered simply by giving a person a piece of paper with the printed list of standard questions, which are answered in pencil.

The first personality inventory was Woodworth's list of 116 yes-or-no questions, including:

Do you usually sleep well?
As a child, did you like to play alone better than to play with other children?
Has your family always treated you right?
Do you get tired of people quickly?

The war ended before Woodworth had a chance to collect sufficient data to evaluate the test's validity. But this pioneer effort did encourage other psychologists to try to develop systematic and objective devices for assessing both normal and abnormal personality traits.

Some personality inventories were designed to measure a single trait, such as anxiety or extraversion. Others, like the MMPI (described here) measure several traits at the same time. Further, some personality inventories follow Woodworth's lead in trying to assess abnormal traits that may be associated with mental illness (see Chapter 13). Others focus on normal personality traits and types, such as androgyny and Type *A* behavior (see Chapter 11).

Since personality inventories consist of lists of multiple-choice questions, they are easy to administer and score. The objective scores a person achieves can then be related to other criteria to establish the test's reliability and validity. Literally hundreds of personality inventories have been developed to measure normal and abnormal personality traits. To provide more insight into the actual workings of such a test, let us concentrate on the personality inventory that has generated the largest body of research. According to one count (Buros, 1978), over 5,000 different research reports have been published regarding the uses and characteristics of a test called the MMPI.

The Minnesota Multiphasic Personality Inventory. The name *Minnesota Multiphasic Personality Inventory* is such a mouthful that even jargon-loving psychologists refer to it by the abbreviation MMPI. But each of the words in this fearsome title says something about this popular test, which was published in 1942.

The original authors of the MMPI, S. R. Hathaway and J. C. McKinley, began their research at the University of Minnesota in the 1930s. The word *Minnesota* in the title reminds us that the original scoring system—which is still widely used— was based on a sample of about 1,500 normal subjects and 800 psychiatric patients from a single geographical location in and around Minneapolis, Minnesota.

The word *multiphasic* was chosen to emphasize the authors' attempt to include a large and varied group of items that could give insight into many different patterns of behavior. Before that time, most scales were constructed with a single purpose in mind, like Woodworth's test to predict shell shock. But Hathaway and McKinley proposed a single questionnaire that would assess many different personality traits at the same time, and thus be multiphasic.

Finally, of course, the test was a *personality inventory*—a standard list of questions that any individual could answer. The authors began with over 1,000 items chosen from clinical experience, psychiatry textbooks, and previously published scales. After several revisions, they agreed on a list of 550 short, simple, clear statements to which individuals were asked to respond "true," "false," or "cannot say." Here are four examples:

> I get angry sometimes.
> I think most people would lie to get ahead.
> Once in a while I put off until tomorrow what I ought to do today.
> Someone has been trying to poison me.

Since the MMPI was multiphasic, each test taker was assigned separate scores on 13 subscales that measured different aspects of personality. For example, there were separate measures of depression, hypochondriasis, paranoia, and masculinity-femininity. Instead of describing one personality trait with a single number, the MMPI yields a profile of interrelated scores.

The items that composed each scale were chosen strictly in terms of their criterion validity—their actual ability to distinguish between particular groups. For example, responses on the MMPI by a group of paranoid psychiatric patients (who had delusions of being persecuted) in the University of Minnesota hospitals were compared with responses from a "normal" group including hospital visitors and medical patients. Only when there was a statistically significant difference between these groups was an item included on the paranoid scale.

Sometimes, the results of this empirical procedure were quite close to common sense. For example, two of the four sample statements given earlier actually appear on the paranoid scale. Take a moment to review these four, see whether you can pick the two statements that identified paranoids, and predict how these patients would answer each item. If you guessed that paranoids are more likely to say "true" to "someone has been trying to poison me," you are quite right.

The answer to the other question, however, may not be so obvious. If you are like most people, you probably guessed that a paranoid person would say it's true that most people would lie to get ahead. Indeed, this item on the MMPI was borrowed from an earlier psychological test that had graded "true" as a paranoid response on the basis of its face validity—this looked like something a paranoid person would say. In fact, however, researchers who studied the actual responses of a group of paranoid patients found exactly the opposite. Paranoids were more likely to say this statement was false (Meehl & Hathaway, 1946). This provides still another example of the way commonsense or intuitive analyses of test items can be misleading. The original MMPI scores were always empirically defined by the actual responses of a particular group of people.

As a further guarantee that MMPI scores would provide useful information, the authors included several subscales to check for unusual response patterns. For example, the lie scale included 15 items that involved admitting faults that probably apply to almost everyone. Two of the four sample statements come from the lie scale: "I get angry sometimes" and "Once in a while I put off until tomorrow what I ought to do today." If you answered false to both of these questions and to 13 other items like them, you are either Saint Theresa of Avila or a liar. The authors of the MMPI were willing to bet on the latter, that people who admitted few minor faults were probably lying to make themselves look good. When a person gets a high score on the lie scale, all results from that particular MMPI are viewed skeptically.

Perhaps the greatest strength of the MMPI is the fact that it has been used by so many different investigators in such a wide variety of settings. About 300 new scales have been formed from MMPI items, and information on criterion validity is available for many of them. The shortcomings of the original standardization sample have been corrected in some later versions.

In clinical practice, the MMPI is often administered to individuals who seek psychological therapy or counseling. Interpretation of a particular profile of 13 scores is more difficult than their names suggest. For example, a person with a high score on the schizophrenia scale is not necessarily schizophrenic; it is the overall pattern of scores that provides insight, and subscales cannot be isolated from one another.

Figure 12.7 illustrates the MMPI profile of one 34-year-old man who sought psychiatric help. The first four scales (?LFK) refer to response style (for example, L is the lie-scale score); the numbers 1 to 9 refer to the nine major clinical scales. All scores have been standardized (in terms of the original normal sample of about 700 persons), with a mean of 50 and a standard deviation of 10. For example, this individual's score of 88 on scale 2 (depression) is nearly 4 standard deviations above the mean and thus extremely high (see the normal curve in Figure 12.2).

Again, interpretation of this profile depends on the interrelationships of the scores on all 13 scales. Many books have been published to help clinicians interpret MMPI results. For example, in 1951 Hathaway and Meehl published *An Atlas for the Clinical Use of the MMPI*, which included MMPI profiles and case histories of 968 patients with a wide variety of problems.

A number of computerized scoring systems for the MMPI have also been developed in recent years. These systems vary widely in the detail and kind of information they provide. Figure 12.7 also provides a computer-generated interpretation of this particular profile. Even a thorough report like this one, however, should not be considered as a final basis for making decisions about this individual. The MMPI is a tool that a clinician often finds useful, but only she can decide exactly how to use it in a particular case.

PROJECTIVE TESTS

Basic Concepts. While personality inventories like the MMPI were designed to be objective and easy to administer and score, an entirely different type of test was published in 1921 by a Swiss psychiatrist named Hermann Rorschach. Rorschach had been trained in Freudian psychoanalysis and sought a test that could help reveal

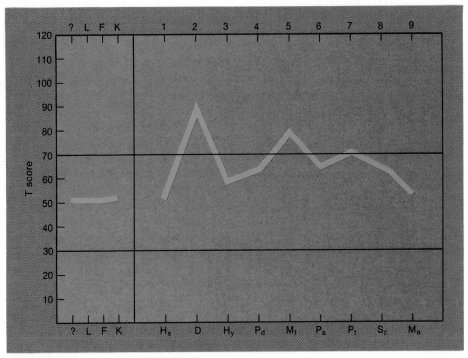

Figure 12.7

The MMPI profile of a 34-year-old male psychiatric patient. ?,L,F,K scores reflect response style and are all within the normal range (50 = mean, 10 = standard deviation of normal standardization sample). Scales 1 to 9 are clinical scales; the most elevated score appears on scale 2, depression. Excerpts from a computer analysis of this profile follow:

> This patient shows a personality pattern which occurs frequently among persons who seek psychiatric treatment. Feelings of inadequacy, sexual conflict and rigidity are accompanied by a loss of efficiency, initiative and self-confidence. Insomnia is likely to occur along with chronic anxiety, fatigue, and tension. He may have suicidal thoughts. In the clinical picture, depression is a dominant feature. Psychiatric patients with this pattern are likely to be diagnosed as depressives or anxiety reactions. The basic characteristics are resistant to change and will tend to remain stable with time. Among medical patients with this pattern, a large number are seriously depressed, and others show some depression, along with fatigue and exhaustion. There are few spontaneous recoveries, although the intensity of the symptoms may be cyclic. . . .
>
> This person may be hesitant to become involved in social relationships. He is sensitive, reserved, and somewhat uneasy, especially in new and unfamiliar situations. He may compensate by unusual conscientiousness in his work and other responsibilities.
>
> Some aspects of this patient's test pattern are somewhat similar to those of psychiatric patients. Appropriate professional evaluation is recommended (Dahlstrom, et. al., 1972, pp. 295, 314).

Although not a substitute for the clinician's professional judgment and skill, the MMPI can be a useful adjunct in the diagnosis and management of emotional disorders. The report is for professional use only and should not be shown or released to the patient.

unconscious impulses by forcing the test taker to use his imagination. He developed a set of ambiguous inkblots and asked people what each blot represented or reminded them of. There were no "right" answers; the ambiguous stimulus was designed as a sort of screen onto which a person could project inner conflicts, fears, and desires. One of the more optimistic accounts of this technique (Frank, 1939) referred to the projective approach as an "X-ray of the personality" because it provided a glimpse of the inner workings of the mind.

Rorschach's inkblots were among the first **projective tests** in which a person projects inner feelings and conflicts by responding to an ambiguous stimulus such as a picture or an inkblot. Another example was mentioned in Chapter 10: the Thematic Apperception Test (TAT), in which people were asked to make up stories about ambiguous pictures. The stories were then analyzed for themes of a need for achievement and other normal personality traits.

The ambiguous stimulus need not be a picture or an inkblot. In the Draw-a-Person Test, people are asked to do just that, and the features of the individuals they draw are systematically analyzed. Other projective tests asks individuals to say the first thing that comes to mind in response to certain words or to complete sentences such as "What worries me . . . " or "My mother always. . . . "

As with personality inventories, a large number of projective tests have been developed to measure both normal and abnormal personality traits. Again let us focus on the test that has generated the largest body of research, Hermann Rorschach's original inkblots.

The Rorschach Test.   The stimuli of the most famous projective test consist of 10 symmetrical inkblots, half of them black and white and half colored. One inkblot is presented at a time and the ten are always shown in the same order. The person is asked what each blot could represent or "what it reminds you of." The examiner records these responses verbatim, as well as other factors such as the time a person takes to respond and any emotional expressions. After all 10 cards have been reviewed in this manner, the examiner asks further questions about the details of each response.

There are a number of different scoring systems for interpreting subjects' responses. Traditionally, most clinicians did not focus on the content of a response—it did not matter whether a particular inkblot was seen as a bat, a butterfly, or two fat clowns dancing the Hucklebuck. Perceptual characteristics of the response were generally considered more important. For example, Rorschach thought that the mention of movement (as in the dancing clowns) suggested imaginative and creative impulses, while reference to color reflected an active emotional life. Other scoring systems consider not just the characteristics of individual responses but also their interrelationships. Graduate students in clinical psychology may study techniques of Rorschach interpretation for several years.

The first research published in the United States on the Rorschach test appeared in 1930. The test gradually gained in popularity, particularly during World War II. At one time, studies of this test completely dominated the field of psychological testing. Many of the reports were unfavorable. Aspects of many scoring systems were so subjective that results did not meet acceptable standards of reliability; two clinicians might interpret the same test in entirely different ways. When reliable scoring systems were used, the results often proved invalid; research often failed to verify theoretical claims that certain types of responses were linked to particular personality traits (Zubin, Eron, & Schumer, 1965).

Hermann Rorschach's (1884–1922) father was an art teacher in Zurich, Switzerland; in his childhood, the younger Rorschach's nickname was *Klex*, meaning "painter" or "inkblot". After studying psychiatry with Eugen Bleuler, Rorschach began to experiment with mental patients' perceptions of inkblots. Encouraged by the test's apparent ability to distinguish among different types of patients, he published a book in 1921 describing his research. Because of space limitations, the printer would include only 10 of the 15 cards Rorschach had studied; the printer also changed their size and color. The Rorschach test consists of the 10 altered cards. Rorschach died a year after his book was published, long before his technique became widely known.

Figure 12.8
One of the cards from the Rorschach test.

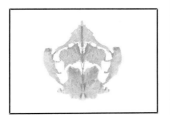

One reason that the Rorschach had gained such popularity despite its shortcomings was the fact that in actual clinical practice, interpretations were often based not just on the inkblot responses but also on other sources of information, such as case histories. Some clinicians used inkblot responses to "verify" their own biases and stereotypes, proving that even the experts are subject to observational errors.

In one study, two researchers interpreted Rorschach tests administered before the Nuremberg trials to 16 Nazi war criminals, including Adolf Eichmann and Hermann Göring. They knew who the test takers were and concluded that these infamous men were quite different from normal people; among other things, that they were depressed, violent, and preoccupied with status (Miale & Selzer, 1976). However, another researcher provided the same Rorschach responses to experts who did not know their origin. One thought that the responses came from a cross section of middle-class Americans; another thought they might be from clergymen (Harrower, 1976). The judgment of disturbance in the Rorschach records of Nazis seemed to be based on external opinions that had little to do with the actual test responses. Similarly, a clinical psychologist who had interviewed a client for many hours might find it difficult to interpret Rorschach responses in a vacuum, as if no other information were available regarding this individual.

Despite such criticisms and problems, the Rorschach test continues to be widely used. In 1970, long after research that attacked the Rorschach had peaked, a survey of 251 clinical settings found that although its popularity had declined somewhat, 91% of the clinics still used the Rorschach in some cases (Lubin, Wallis, & Paine, 1971).

Although efforts are still under way to establish reliable and valid scoring systems of the type originally outlined by Rorschach, many clinicians now see the

Rorschach as a type of standardized interview. People who are reluctant to reveal their inner feelings may be somewhat more open when responding to these ambiguous stimuli. Here, the content of responses—what people actually say—is seen as more important than the perception of movement, color, or other traditional aspects.

To see the potential value of this clinical approach, consider the following brief excerpt from the Rorschach test of a 25-year-old woman who had been hospitalized after a suicide attempt:

> Psychologist: What do you see in this card?
> Client: Two monkeys—warming their hands over a fire.
> Psychologist: What does that remind you of?
> Client: My parents.
> Psychologist: In what way?
> Client: Just the word *monkeys*. The stupidest thing they ever did was to get married. . . . [The] fire they're warming their hands over is their children burning"
> (Aronow & Reznikoff, 1976, p. 286).

This powerful response was buried among a large number of unemotional mundane responses. But as long as people continue to respond to the ambiguous inkblots of the Rorschach test with statements that seem to be so revealing, it is likely that projective tests will continue to play an important role in clinical practice and personality research.

Uses and Abuses of Psychological Tests

The results of psychological tests may help determine the classes a schoolchild takes, the colleges to which a student is admitted, or the job a person is offered. In the ideal world, psychological test results would provide objective information to help make fair and rational decisions. But in case you haven't noticed, we do not live in an ideal world. Before the ink was dry on the first psychological tests, controversies began over their use. Let us examine two of these continuing debates, to show how these problems often defy simple solutions.

INTERPRETING TEST RESULTS

Because of concern over the complexity of the ethical issues involved in the appropriate interpretation of psychological tests, the American Psychological Association has developed several sets of ethical standards for the profession, which are revised at regular intervals (London & Bray, 1980).

Trained psychologists are familiar with the extent to which a single test score can be influenced by such external factors as fatigue, illness, or motivation; they would be very reluctant to use a test score as the sole basis for any important decision. In fact, in some cases, a clinician who administers an IQ test may be less interested in the IQ score itself than in the way a person takes the test. Self-confidence, persistence, concentration, and other personality characteristics may be assessed in this situation, albeit somewhat intuitively.

Because of their keen awareness of the limitations of test scores, psychologists have traditionally taken the position that in many situations, scores should not be revealed, even to the person who took the test. However, others consider this position paternalistic and feel that every individual has the right to know his own scores.

One of the more extreme instances of this concern led the New York state legislature to enact a truth-in-testing law in 1980, which permitted students to obtain a copy of their answers on the Scholastic Aptitude Test. In 1981, the test's publishers voluntarily extended this practice to the entire country.

One positive effect occurred almost immediately, when one student successfully argued that one of his geometry answers, which had been marked wrong, was actually correct. His alternate interpretation led to changes in thousands of scores on a particular version of the PSAT, a preliminary version of the SAT. Since the National Merit Scholarship committee screened applicants on the basis of PSAT scores, 200 additional individuals became National Merit semifinalists after their scores were changed on this one question. As a result of this error and one other, the publishers of the SAT developed new procedures for checking their own answers on solid geometry questions.

On the other hand, this same truth-in-testing law led to certain problems. In the past, test companies have determined individual items that correlate best with later performance. As a result, they could increase the predictive value of a test by reusing only the most efficient items. However, once a particular question is published, it is no longer a fair test of general knowledge, since some individuals may study the actual item. Since it costs companies money to develop larger pools of new items, one unintended result of truth-in-testing laws is that "students might expect to pay a higher fee to take a less valid test" (Kaplan, 1982, p. 22). The new truth-in-testing laws obviously have both positive and negative effects, and the controversy over their value is likely to continue for some time.

CULTURAL BIAS

One of the most controversial issues in psychological testing involves the possible effects of cultural bias, particularly on tests of intelligence. From the outset, it is important to distinguish between the technical characteristics of a test and its political uses. Test bias can be defined in a number of ways; here, we shall use the term **cultural bias** to refer to a statistical difference in the validity of a test for different cultural groups. For example, if white children's scores on a particular IQ test predicted their high school grades but black children's scores did not, that test would be culturally biased in that situation. Note that this definition is based strictly on the actual performance of the test, not on the political or social consequences of using the same criterion for blacks and whites.

This technical issue of cultural bias must be kept separate from the moral and political issue of **fairness,** the justice (or injustice) of using a particular test to select individuals. In a diverse society like the United States, there may be sharp disagreements about what is fair. Psychologists have no special insights or competence regarding fairness, and in a democracy these value judgments must ultimately be made not by social scientists but by all concerned citizens.

A surprisingly large number of psychologists have proved that they are fallible humans by blurring the distinction between fairness and cultural bias, and sometimes even bending the facts, to try to provide scientific support for their political beliefs. For example, IQ data collected by the U.S. Army in World War I provided some information on differences between ethnic groups. This was later cited to support laws setting immigration quotas. It is embarrassing to read technical reports written by some of the leading researchers in the 1920s about the "menace of race deterioration" and the "genuine intellectual superiority of the Nordic [Northern European] group" (quoted in Kamin, 1974, pp. 20–21). In today's political climate, it is easy to see the error of these arguments for racial superiority; clearly, some of these IQ pioneers failed to remain scientific and objective. But it is more difficult to criticize researchers who cite faulty evidence that could be used to support policies that most Americans now believe to be totally just (see "Becoming a Critical Consumer").

To sharpen the distinction between cultural bias and fairness, consider the results of a study comparing the performance of schoolchildren from different ethnic groups in one Arizona county (Reschly & Sabers, 1979). The Wechsler Intelligence Scale for Children–Revised (WISC-R) was used to predict scores on standardized tests of scholastic achievement in math and reading for 910 first- to ninth-graders from four ethnic groups. Table 12.2 shows that the correlations between IQ and achievement were similar for Anglo, black, and Mexican-American children. But the criterion validity was significantly lower for Indian schoolchildren from the Papago tribe. The WISC-R was culturally biased in its predictions of achievement because it was not equally valid for all four groups.

Does that mean that its predictions were unfair? It all depends on your point of view. A closer analysis of the original data from all schoolchildren revealed that the validity coefficient was lower for the Indian group because high-IQ Indian pupils did not do as well in achievement as the WISC-R predicted they should. Suppose, then, that WISC-R IQ scores were used to select children for scholarship classes in these Arizona schools. This application of the test would be culturally biased in favor of Indian pupils, selecting more of them on the basis of IQ than it would on the basis of achievement. Is that fair? One person might argue that given the long history of oppression of American Indians, justice is served by using the test and increasing their chances of getting a better education. Another might reply that the past is the

TABLE 12.2
IQ and Achievement in Four Cultural Groups

		Correlation between WISC-R IQ and	
Cultural Group	*Number of Children*	*Reading Achievement*	*Math Achievement*
Anglo	250	.59	.55
Black	222	.64	.52
Mexican-American	215	.55	.52
Papago Indian[a]	223	.45	.41

[a] The smaller correlations for Papago Indians imply that the test is culturally biased regarding this group (Reschly & Sabers, 1979). See text for a discussion of the implications for policy.

Does This IQ Question Discriminate Against Minorities?

There has been a tremendous amount of controversy over the question of discrimination in IQ tests. This issue involves some complex technical questions as well as value judgments. Popular attempts to analyze the bias in IQ tests have sometimes led to conclusions that may seem convincing but are in fact based on faulty arguments. The following statements were made in the CBS-TV documentary "The IQ Myth." See if you can spot the error in this argument. (A short discussion appears after the "Summary" at the end of this chapter.)

> Dan Rather: Questions [on IQ tests] are based on the experience of the average American child—in school and outside. *Average* meaning "middle-class." And it's economic class that marks the main dividing line on IQ scores. Middle-class children tend to do well

in general, whatever their ethnic or racial background. They are the group the tests are geared to. Lower-class children—blacks, Chicanos, and whites—all tend to do poorly. The tests are slanted against their social and cultural background.

One of the psychologists who has been calling public attention to this built-in cultural bias is Dr. Robert Williams of Washington University in St. Louis. He cites an example from the Wechsler individual IQ test:

> Dr. Williams: "What is the thing you do if a boy or girl much smaller than yourself starts to fight with you?" [The child is graded "correct" only if he says he will not fight back; but] in . . . black communities, a child is told that if another child hits him, hit him back.

past, and tests must be found that choose children with equal predictive power without regard to race, religion, or creed.

A policy decision regarding the fairness of a test is entirely separate from the technical question of cultural bias. In this case, we have a test that has been proved to be culturally biased. But some people could argue that it is still a fair basis for selection. People might argue that in this case, a test that is not culturally biased is unfair.

It is impossible to provide a complete understanding of cultural bias and related issues without going into many complex statistical details regarding the assessment of reliability and validity. Further, different definitions of test bias lead to different conclusions. The issues are so complex that one must be skeptical of any simple solution.

Obviously, our conclusion here cannot provide a complete resolution of this controversial set of issues. But it can emphasize the most important point of all: Psychologists must collect the facts about exactly what a particular test can and cannot do, and society as a whole can then decide how and when the test should be used. There are no simple answers that apply to every case. But there are scientific procedures we can follow to collect the best possible information to make rational policy decisions. As Cronbach (1975) put it, "Sound policy is not for tests or against tests; what matters is how tests are used" (p. 1).

Summary

1. Most psychological tests grew out of attempts to measure objectively people's strengths and weaknesses. Despite the fact that millions of psychological tests are administered every year, many people have misconceptions about the goals and design of tests.

2. A **reliable** test is consistent and reproducible. There are several different ways of measuring reliability, including **test-retest reliability**—the correlation between two different scores achieved by the same individual on the same test on different occasions—and **alternate-form reliability**—the correlation between two different scores achieved by the same individual on two different forms of the test.

3. A **valid** test actually measures what it is supposed to measure. Validity is much more difficult to assess than reliability; there are three major approaches. **Criterion validity** compares performance on the test with some external and independent measure, or criterion, of what the test is supposed to predict. **Content validity** involves a systematic analysis of a particular skill and the design of test items that measure all relevant knowledge. **Construct validity** involves a larger pattern of conceptually meaningful relationships.

4. Many physical and psychological characteristics conform to a **normal distribution,** a particular mathematical apportionment in which individual cases are systematically arranged around the average. The **standard deviation** is a mathematical measure of the amount of variability, spread, or dispersion of a particular set of scores.

5. Several commonsense errors must be avoided when one interprets test scores. Observers should not rely on the **face validity** (superficial appearance) of a test, place too much emphasis on criticisms of individual items, or assume that population predictions will apply to every single individual.

6. Early scales of intelligence defined the **intelligence quotient (IQ)** as **mental age,** the average performance level for a particular group, divided by chronological age times 100. Later, adult IQ scores were defined in terms of a normal distribution with a mean of 100 and a standard deviation of about 15 (depending on the specific test). Although there is some theoretical controversy over the precise nature of intelligence, strong arguments can be made for criterion, content, and construct validity of the most common IQ tests.

7. The **Wechsler Adult Intelligence Scale** includes six verbal and five performance scales. A large body of evidence supports the idea that it is a reliable and valid test of IQ.

8. There is strong evidence that genetic factors account for a larger proportion of individual variation in IQ than environmental factors within populations of Eu-

ropean origin. At this time, differences in IQ between groups cannot be attributed to genetic factors. In any case, the fact that genes account for a high proportion of the variation in IQ does not imply that IQ is fixed at birth; many studies have shown that improved environments can raise IQ.

9. Mild retardation, IQ between 50 and 70, usually originates from a family pattern called **cultural-familial retardation,** with no evidence of brain damage. More severe deficits, such as **Down's syndrome,** are usually biological in origin. These are usually subdivided into three levels, based partly on the ability to function independently: moderate, IQ 35 to 49, severe, IQ 20 to 34, and profound, IQ below 20.

10. A **personality inventory** is a standard list of questions about an individual's behavior and feelings, designed to assess personality traits. The most widely researched test of this sort is the *Minnesota Multiphasic Personality Inventory (MMPI),* a test with 13 personality scales originally based on the performance of criterion groups.

11. In a **projective test,** a person projects inner feelings and conflicts by responding to an ambiguous stimulus such as a picture or an inkblot. The most famous is the *Rorschach test,* a series of 10 inkblots to which a patient reacts.

12. The term **cultural bias** can be defined as a statistical difference in the validity of a test for different cultural groups. This technical term must be kept separate from the moral and political issue of **fairness,** the justice of using a particular test to select individuals. Arguments over these and related issues often become extremely emotional and confuse political desires with technical facts.

Discussion of "Becoming a Critical Consumer"

Intuitively, it may seem that this IQ question discriminates against American blacks who are taught to fight back. But throughout this chapter we have emphasized the fact that intuition can be misleading. In a study that directly compared WISC results for 163 white and 111 black Georgia schoolchildren, there was no evidence that this item discriminated against blacks (Miele, 1979). In fact, the black children found this question relatively easier than the white children. On IQ tests, cultural bias has a precise technical definition (see text) and can only be demonstrated by a systematic comparison of actual test scores from different ethnic groups.

To Learn More

Anastasi, A. *Psychological Testing* (5th ed.). New York: Macmillan, 1982. A textbook overview of basic principles and the major tests currently in use.

Loehlin, J. C., Lindzey, G., & Spuhler, J. N. *Race Differences in Intelligence.* San Francisco: W. H. Freeman, 1975. There are other books on this complex topic that are easier to read or more up to date, but there is no book that provides a more balanced review of the scientific literature.

Buros, O. K. (ed.). *The Eighth Mental Measurements Yearbook.* Lincoln, Nebr.: University of Nebraska, Buros Institute of Mental Measurements, 1978. The ultimate reference for detailed information on any psychological test. Not designed for casual readers; but if you need information on a specific scale, this is the place to find it.

13
Diagnosing Abnormal Behavior

Understanding abnormal behavior
What is abnormal?
From witch hunts to the medical model

The controversy over classification
Criticisms of diagnostic labels
The rationale of DSM-III

Personality disorders
An overview
A case history: Narcissistic personality disorder
Causes of narcissism

Anxiety disorders
An overview
A case history: Agoraphobia
Causes of phobias

Affective disorders
An overview
A case history: Bipolar disorder
Causes of depression and mania

Schizophrenic disorders
An overview
The symptoms of schizophrenia
Causes of schizophrenia

Summary

HOW DO THEY KNOW?
Cross-cultural studies: Abnormal behavior among the Eskimos
and the Yoruba

In a lecture at the Heidelberg Medical School around 1890, Professor Emil Kraepelin described the case of a 35-year-old woman who had started to develop problems in her mid-twenties, soon after her husband died. The young widow became nervous, slept badly, and began to hear voices of people talking loudly in her bedroom at night. She became convinced that people from Frankfurt, the German town in which she had formerly lived, were trying to steal her money and persecute her.

Gradually, her condition got worse until she was committed to a mental asylum. There, the widow decided that the other patients were the people from Frankfurt who were out to get her. She also "noticed poison in the food, heard voices, and felt influences" (Kraepelin, 1912, p. 160). When she was released from the asylum after a year, she accused her former doctors of having mutilated her and abused government officials for failing to protect her. Finally, she was admitted to another hospital.

When Kraepelin brought the woman before his medical school class, she seemed normal at first. She was able to answer questions about her background and knew the date, the year, and where she was. But the professor pointed out that from the start, there was something odd about the woman's manner: "She does not look at her questioner, and speaks in a low and peculiar, sugary, affected tone."

When the physician first asked how she felt, she said that she was quite well. On further probing, however, the widow began to discuss bizarre ideas of persecution: "For many years she has heard voices, which insult her and cast suspicion on her chastity. They mention a number of names she knows, and tell her that she will be stripped and abused. The voices are very distinct, and, in her opinion, they must be carried by a telescope or a machine from her home. Her thoughts are dictated to her; she is obliged to think them, and hears them repeated after her." In her own words, she was also "persecuted by a secret insect from the District Office."

The woman also reported a variety of physical complaints: "Her 'mother parts' are turned inside out, and people send a pain through her back, lay ice-water on her heart, squeeze her neck, injure her spine, and violate her." On cross questioning, she cannot say exactly who is subjecting her to this abuse. Sometimes, it is the doctors who mutilated her at the previous hospital; at other times, it is the people from her hometown.

Perhaps even odder than the woman's complaints was the way she reported them: "without showing much emotion," a manner clinicians call *flattened affect,* meaning with little variation in affective (emotional) response. At other times, her affect seems inappropriate, as when the patient "describes her morbid experiences again with secret satisfaction and even with an erotic bias."

At times, her speech became totally irrational, as the patient referred to herself as "a picture of misery in angel's form" and a "defrauded mamma and housewife of sense of order." She sometimes invented words, such as "flail-wise, utterance-wise, and terror-wise."

After being admitted to the hospital, she was generally apathetic and socially withdrawn. She spent her days sitting idly around and would have little to do with other patients or the staff. Her only occupations were to repeat her complaints day

Emil Kraepelin (1855–1926) proposed the first widely used system for classifying mental disorders into separate diseases. He was trained as a physician in Germany and early in his career worked with Wilhelm Wundt at Leipzig. Kraepelin collected literally thousands of case histories of patients in mental asylums. He examined their early life experiences and their current symptoms to look for similar patterns and a few basic disease processes. Kraepelin's general approach to psychiatry was strongly influenced by nineteenth-century biology and the medical model. He was rather fatalistic about mental illness, believing that many diseases were caused by inherent constitutional factors and could never be cured.

after day "without showing much excitement" and to write "long-winded letters full of senseless and unvarying abuse about the persecution from which she suffered."

In Professor Kraepelin's opinion, this poor woman had little chance of ever recovering. He used the Latin term *dementia praecox* to refer to her condition because this label emphasized the symptoms he considered most fundamental—a progressive intellectual deterioration *(dementia)* that began early in life *(praecox)*. Kraepelin is generally considered the father of the first coherent system for diagnosing abnormal behavior, and the term *dementia praecox* was used until the 1940s (Arieti, 1974).

To a mental-health worker in the 1980s, one of the most remarkable facts about this case is how familiar it seems. While the woman's prospects for improvement would be far better today than they were a century ago, anyone who has ever worked in a mental hospital has met many patients with similar symptoms. Today, the widow's illness would be diagnosed as "schizophrenia, paranoid type, chronic" (Spitzer, Skodol, Gibbon, & Williams, 1981).

Schizophrenia is one of the most dramatic categories of abnormal behavior, but it is not the most common one. Table 13.1 lists the most recent estimates for the frequency of a wide range of abnormal behavior patterns in the United States. The four largest categories (crime, alcohol abuse, anxiety, and depression) are far more ordinary and mundane than the bizarre problems of Kraepelin's patient. And the large number of people involved leaves no doubt that abnormal behavior represents a problem of staggering proportions for our society. In this chapter, we focus on defining abnormality and diagnosing its many forms. In the next chapter, we consider the problem of treatment—what can be done for those among us who suffer from these problems.

TABLE 13.1
Estimates of the Incidence of Abnormal
Behavior in the United States, 1978.

200,000	reported cases of child abuse.
200,000	or more individuals attempt suicide★ (26,000 or more individuals die from suicide).
1,000,000	individuals are actively schizophrenic.
1,000,000	or more students withdraw from college each year as a result of emotional problems.
2,000,000	individuals suffer from profound depression.
6,000,000	or more children and teenagers are considered emotionally disturbed.
7,000,000	individuals are considered mentally retarded.
10,000,000	or more juveniles and adults are arrested in connection with serious crimes★ (190,000 or more individuals are sent to prison, and 500,000 individuals are in prison).
10,000,000	Americans report alcohol-related problems (1,000,000 individuals are being treated for such).
20,000,000	or more individuals suffer from anxiety-related disturbances.
53,500,000	individuals suffer from mild to moderate depression.

★The incidence of suicide attempts and serious crimes may be much higher due to the large number that are not reported.

Source: Coleman, J. C., Butcher, J. N., & Carson, R. C. *Abnormal Psychology and Modern Life.* Glenview, Ill.: Scott, Foresman, 1980.

Understanding Abnormal Behavior

It may be relatively easy to see the difference between the abnormal behavior of a severely disturbed individual like Kraepelin's widowed patient and the normal behavior patterns of most of your friends and relatives. But, as some of the categories in Table 13.1 suggest, clearly distinguishing the normal from the abnormal is not always this straightforward.

WHAT IS ABNORMAL?

Suppose a housewife drinks half a bottle of gin every day to help her through the tedium of her daily chores. Is that normal? What about a man who refuses to drive a car because he's afraid of having an accident? What about a homosexual man who is afraid to tell his parents that he never intends to get married? Is he normal?

There are no easy answers or simple criteria that can be applied to these specific cases. But we can discuss four general approaches to defining abnormality, each of which sheds light on these issues from a different angle: statistical definitions, violations of cultural norms, deviations from ideal mental health, and failure to function adequately.

Statistical Definition: By definition, the word *abnormal* means "deviating from the norm or the average." When we say that Kareem Abdul Jabbar is abnormally tall, this is based on the observation that the average height for adult males is far below 7 feet.

The same logic could be applied to any human characteristic that can be quantified. We simply compute the average value for a particular trait—such as intelligence or personal ratings of satisfaction with life—and define abnormality as a substantial deviation from this average. For example, in Chapter 12 we discussed how IQ tests have been developed that assign the value 100 to average intelligence. On this scale, a mentally retarded child who had an IQ of 50 would be considered abnormal.

However, if we use nothing but the simplest statistical criteria, an intelligent child with an IQ of 150 would be considered equally abnormal. Without some system for distinguishing between desirable and undesirable deviations, the statistical model seems to imply that being just like everyone else is always best. If the statistical definition were taken to its logical extreme, it would suggest that people who are unusually satisfied with their lives, for example, or people whose ethical standards are higher than the rest of ours would be considered abnormal. Perhaps these model citizens would even be considered candidates for treatment that would make them less satisfied and less moral.

The question of deciding which deviations from the norm are desirable and which are undesirable is not the only problem with a strictly statistical approach. In Table 13.1, we cited estimates of the numbers of Americans involved in a wide variety of socially undesirable behavior patterns ranging from mild depression to child abuse. If you add up all the numbers, it will become clear that as many as 1 out of every 2 Americans falls into at least one of these categories. Behavior patterns that characterize half the population cannot be considered abnormal on statistical grounds alone.

Violation of Cultural Norms. A second approach defines abnormality in terms of violations of *cultural norms*, the rules of a culture for what is right and what is wrong. If the newly elected mayor of Billings, Montana, worked in his office from precisely 2:37 a.m. to 10:37 a.m. every day, his work habits would be considered odd. If the mayor always wore the same pink linen suit and bright blue tie, and lunched every day on a thermos full of Raisin Bran cereal mixed with white wine, he would probably be considered downright abnormal. This mayor might have trouble getting reelected even if he ran the town quite effectively, simply because he violated cultural norms.

One problem with using cultural norms to define abnormality is that they vary so much from time to time and place to place. Several decades ago, among natives of the Trobriand Islands in the Pacific, when a man died his sons were expected to clean his bones and distribute them to relatives to wear as ornaments. A Trobriand widow who wore her former husband's jawbone on a necklace would be considered perfectly normal (Malinowski, 1929). In Twin Falls, Idaho, that same behavior would seem more than a little bizarre.

Defining abnormality as any violation of cultural norms ultimately implies that only conformists are normal. A woman who pursued a career as a business executive

Cross-cultural Studies: Abnormal Behavior among the Eskimos and the Yoruba

In a **cross-cultural study,** patterns of behavior and experience from different cultural settings are compared. Few psychologists use this method extensively; such comparisons are usually performed by anthropologists. Nevertheless, cross-cultural studies can provide important insights into the way a particular environment shapes behavior.

Evidence of this sort is particularly relevant to attempts to define abnormal behavior in terms of the violation of cultural norms. Some researchers believe that the line between mental illness and normality is arbitrarily drawn by each society to enforce its own beliefs. This notion is closely related to several theories discussed in this chapter, notably Thomas Szasz's book *The Myth of Mental Illness.* An even more extreme version of this view claims that behavior that our society condemns as mentally ill is actually rewarded by other societies. For example, shamans (holy men or witch doctors) in primitive cultures often hear voices and behave in ways that we might label schizophrenic, yet they are valued members of society who play an important role in their culture (Silverman, 1967).

To evaluate such claims, anthropologist Jane Murphy analyzed mental-health data from two field studies she carried out in non-Western cultures. She spent one year living among Yupik-speaking Eskimos on an island in the Bering Sea and another year living with the Yoruba tribe in Nigeria. Her actual data came from interviews with key informants and healers and from her observations of daily life in these dramatically different settings.

The major question Murphy asked was whether these cultures had a word or a category that corresponded roughly to Western notions of madness or abnormal behavior. Both cultures did. The Eskimo word *nuthkavihak* referred to a complex pattern of behavior that included talking to oneself, believing that one was an animal, refusing to eat or talk, making strange gestures, and threatening others. Similarly, the Yoruba word *were* referred to hearing voices, laughing inappropriately, talking all the time or not at all, and so on. Interestingly, both patterns of behavior were treated by village healers; they were perceived as a kind of illness.

Murphy also questioned the claim that shamans, or witch doctors, would be labeled mad in their own culture. She found that both cultures distinguished the state of madness (hearing voices and so on) that is part of a shaman's religious or healing ceremony from the chronic state of madness that characterizes the *nuthkavihak* or *were.* The shaman can consciously control the state, according to the Eskimos, while the *nuthkavihak* cannot. Indeed, of the 18 Eskimos who had played the shaman's role at some time in their lives, none was considered *nuthkavihak* by other tribe members.

Murphy also noted that percentages for the

in 1937 refused to accept the 1930s cultural norms that a woman's place was in the home. Does this mean that she should have received psychological therapy to restore her normality?

Like the statistical definition of normality, the notion of violating cultural norms has relevance to many cases of labeling behavior as abnormal, but it cannot serve as a complete and acceptable definition by itself.

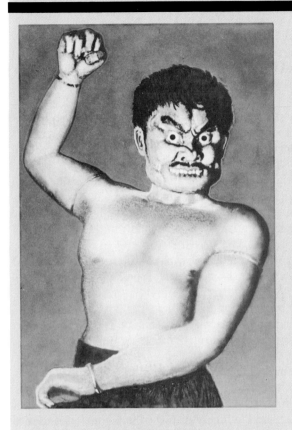

Shamans (roughly, medicine men) in primitive cultures sometimes act in ways that may seem mad or insane to a Western observer (left). But in these same cultures, a shaman's transient mental state is distinguished from a chronic state of mental illness, like that of the unfortunate Gambian tribesman (right) who became odd as a young man, moved to an abandoned anthill outside his village, and never spoke to anyone.

frequency of *nuthkavihak* and *were* behaviors were roughly the same as prevalence figures for schizophrenia in comparable studies of Sweden and Canada. Overall, she concluded that mental illness is not an arbitrary category defined idiosyncratically by each culture but rather that "symptoms of mental illness are manifestations of a type of affliction shared by virtually all mankind" (Murphy, 1976, p. 1,027).

Anthropological field studies of this sort must, by their very nature, rely on the perceptiveness of individual observers. They are thus unusually susceptible to the criticism of observer bias. Nevertheless, they do provide valuable information about human nature and the range of behaviors in vastly different cultural settings.

Deviation from Ideal Mental Health. A third approach involves defining normality as some ideal pattern of behavior and feeling—which may or may not be statistically common—then defining abnormality as a deviation from this ideal. A number of ideals have been proposed. For example, Jahoda (1958) stressed the importance of insight into one's own motivations, resistance to stress, autonomy, competence, accurate perception of reality, and self-actualization. Lists like this tend to be difficult to apply to a specific individual. For example, exactly what constitutes a healthy level of autonomy and independence? Further, the criteria are so demanding that virtually everyone is considered abnormal to some degree. After all, Maslow's studies of several thousand people located only a small number whom he considered self-actualized (see Chapter 11).

Just as cultural norms are limited to a certain time and a certain place, lists of ideal characteristics depend on society's value judgments. For example, Jahoda's definitions of autonomy and independent choice might be rejected by a communal society that emphasized group cooperation rather than individual choice. Nevertheless, notions of ideal characteristics have had some influence on the mental-health field, particularly for the many affluent Americans who have gone into psychotherapy not because they were overwhelmed by their problems but rather because they wanted to realize their full human potential.

Failure to Function Adequately. Of the four approaches to abnormality described here, this last criterion is the closest to common sense and is perhaps the most useful single approach. It assumes that every human being should achieve a sense of personal well-being and make some contribution to a larger social group. Specifically, we would say that an individual fails to function adequately and is therefore abnormal if she experiences great personal distress, disturbs others, or is unable to care for herself in society.

A troubled salesman may seem fine to his co-workers if he meets all his quotas. But if he is deeply unhappy with his job and a victim of chronic and overwhelming anxiety, we would say that this high level of personal distress makes him at least somewhat abnormal. On the other hand, a highly disturbed individual who tries to assassinate a rock star may experience no personal distress whatever. Nevertheless, the fact that he is a threat to other individuals constitutes a failure to function in society. Finally, some people may present no danger to anyone but themselves. A woman who is so obsessed with dirt that she must clean her apartment compulsively for 12 hours each day would be considered abnormal because this ritualistic behavior interferes with her ability to care for herself or contribute to society.

Given the differences in the four major approaches to defining abnormality, it should come as no surprise that there is sometimes controversy over whether particular patterns of behavior should be considered abnormal.

Some theorists have taken the extreme position that the line between normality and abnormality is entirely arbitrary and a matter of convention. However, there is cross-cultural evidence that some patterns of behavior that are considered highly disturbed in our culture are also labeled "abnormal" in primitive non-Western societies very different from our own (see "How Do They Know?") Consequently, most psychologists believe that the label "abnormal" is not entirely arbitrary.

FROM WITCH HUNTS TO THE MEDICAL MODEL

To some extent, a culture's conception of abnormal behavior always reflects its larger beliefs about human nature and mankind's place in the cosmos. In ancient times, when earthquakes, eclipses, and outbreaks of disease were seen as messages from the gods, abnormal behavior was often taken as a sign of possession by demons or evil spirits.

The Old Testament, for example, recounts some bizarre behavior on the part of King Saul in the eleventh century B.C. In one incident, he stripped off all his clothes in a public place; in another, Saul tried to kill his son Jonathan. The Bible attributes these actions to an evil spirit (1 Sam. 16). Modern commentators believe that Saul may have been mentally ill (Coleman, Butcher, & Carson, 1980); Saul has been tentatively diagnosed as suffering from a bipolar affective disorder, also known as manic-depressive psychosis.

Similarly, in the Middle Ages abnormal behavior was sometimes taken as a sign of possession by a devil or evil spirit who must be driven from the body. In the witch hunts of the fifteenth, sixteenth, and seventeenth centuries, as many as 100,000 people were executed for this reason. Some historians have cited tales of flying to secret meetings with the devil and similar confessions as evidence that most "witches" were actually mentally ill (Zilboorg & Henry, 1941). While critics have challenged this idea, there can be no doubt that superstitious cultures interpreted abnormal behavior very differently from the way we do.

The roots of the twentieth century's scientific approach can be traced back at least as far as Hippocrates, the Greek physician who looked for natural causes of mental illness 400 years before the birth of Christ. In an empirical study of epilepsy, Hippocrates noted, "If you cut open the head, you will find the brain humid, full of sweat and smelling badly. And in this way you may see that it is not a god which injured the body, but disease" (quoted in Zilboorg & Henry, 1941, p. 44).

In the Middle Ages, many people believed that mental illness was caused by evil spirits. In this fifteenth-century painting, St. Catherine of Siena is pictured driving a Satanic imp from the head of a disturbed woman.

During the Renaissance, some thought that mental illness was caused by movements of the stars and moon. This seventeenth-century engraving shows a group of dancing women crazed by the moon. The word *lunatic* comes from the Latin word *luna* which means "moon."

Even during the witchcraft trials of the Middle Ages, some physicians called for a more rational approach, treating the emotionally disturbed as victims of illness rather than sinners in league with the devil. Many of these theories of mental illness now seem quaint, as in the case of the Swiss physician Paracelsus's (1493–1541) theory that madness was caused by the movements of the stars and the moon. But the notion that abnormal behavior was a type of illness gradually evolved into today's medical model.

According to the **medical model,** abnormal behavior is caused by physical disease. In 1883, Emil Kraepelin published his influential *Textbook of Psychiatry,* in which he argued that abnormal behavior was based on dysfunction in the brain and proposed the first comprehensive system for classifying mental disorders. We have already introduced one of his most important categories, dementia praecox. For Kraepelin, this was a disease analogous to the measles or the mumps and was thus best understood by studying its symptoms, course, causes (or, in medical terminology, its *etiology*), and treatment. According to the medical model, dementia praecox was to be diagnosed on the basis of a specific set of symptoms, and all cases of this disease could be expected to develop in the same predictable course, with about the same chance of recovery. It was assumed that it was caused by a particular organic problem, although the actual etiology of this and other mental illnesses was not yet known. Finally, it was assumed that all cases of dementia praecox would respond to the same form of treatment, once a cure was discovered.

Around the turn of the century, researchers did indeed discover an organic basis for several syndromes of abnormal behavior, most notably *general paresis*, a gradual breakdown of mental and physical function that was proved to be an advanced case of the venereal disease syphilis. In 1906, August von Wassermann developed a blood test that could diagnose syphilis before its most dramatic symptoms appeared, and in 1917, Julius Wagner von Jauregg discovered a partial cure. This was the first time in history that medical science was able to prove the link between a mental disorder and a physical disease; many believed that bodily cures for all mental disease would soon be found. There were other dramatic discoveries during this period into the nature of such problems as senility and mental retardation. But the medical model's promise of early cures was never fulfilled, and researchers do not yet fully understand the causes of such common disorders as schizophrenia and depression.

Throughout the twentieth century, some mental-health professionals have rejected the medical model completely. For example, in his 1961 book *The Myth of Mental Illness*, psychiatrist Thomas Szasz argued that most behaviors that are considered symptoms of illness are merely deviations from society's norms. He prefers the expression "problems in living" and argues that the illness label encourages us to think that people are not responsible for their actions. We may tend to consider a sexual criminal a sick man who cannot help himself rather than an adult who should take full responsibility for his choices.

Despite these and other criticisms, medical notions have shaped most approaches to abnormal behavior throughout the twentieth century. As Brendan Maher (1966) has noted, the very words we use in everyday discussions of deviant behavior reveal this medical orientation: clinicians *diagnose* mental *illness* on the basis of its *symptoms* and treat *patients* in mental *hospitals* with *therapies* that are designed to *cure* them. Therefore, our overview of abnormal behavior focuses on the most basic goal of the medical model—diagnosing separate diseases on the basis of their symptoms.

The Controversy over Classification

The classification of abnormal behavior into discrete categories is a major part of the current mental-health system. When one person is diagnosed as schizophrenic and another is diagnosed as phobic, these labels have important consequences for the way these people are treated. (Schizophrenia, phobia, and other diagnostic categories are defined later.) But some critics of the current system argue that labels like schizophrenia do more harm than good.

CRITICISMS OF DIAGNOSTIC LABELS

Some mental-health workers emphasize that diagnosis can be dehumanizing; instead of perceiving John Smith as a unique and complex individual, we dismiss him as simply a schizophrenic. Such labels may also become self-fulfilling (see Chapter 1); a person diagnosed as schizophrenic may have trouble getting a job, for example, or may even perceive herself as sick and act differently as a result.

To support the argument that labels are misleading, critics of psychiatric diagnosis often cite a study by David Rosenhan (1973) in which people who had no history of psychiatric problems were admitted to mental hospitals. Eight pseudopatients—Rosenhan himself, four other mental-health professionals, a housewife, a painter, and a pediatrician—went to the admissions offices of different mental hospitals and falsely reported that they had been hearing voices. Except for hiding their true identities, these pseudopatients answered all other questions about their experiences and backgrounds truthfully.

All were admitted to the mental hospitals, and almost all were diagnosed as schizophrenic. (There were 12 admissions, since some patients went to more than one hospital. Eleven were diagnosed as schizophrenic, the twelfth was labeled a manic-depressive psychotic.) After they were admitted, the pseudopatients acted normally and no longer reported hearing voices. Yet they were hospitalized for an average of 19 days (the shortest stay was 7 days, the longest 52 days). In that time, not one single staff member accused a pseudopatient of faking his symptoms. Many observers interpreted this as a damning indictment of psychiatric diagnosis.

Others, however, questioned the basic rationale of Rosenhan's study. One provided the following analogy (Kety, 1974): If you swallowed a quart of blood, then went to an emergency room vomiting blood, you would probably be diagnosed as having a bleeding peptic ulcer. The fact that a physician failed to notice your deception would not imply that medical science is unable to diagnose an ulcer. Another critic (Spitzer, 1976) noted that when Rosenhan's pseudopatients were released, their diagnoses were qualified with the phrase "in remission," implying that they no longer showed signs of illness. This is an unusual diagnostic label and implies that the psychiatrists knew there was something different about the pseudopatients.

Rosenhan's (1973) study probably says more about the nature of United States mental hospitals than it does about psychiatric diagnosis. Due to understaffing, paperwork, and other factors, doctors and nurses spend little time with patients. In the hospitals in this study, staff members spent virtually all their time in a glassed-in area that the patients called "the cage." Systematic measurements revealed that attendants spent 89% of their workday with other staff members inside the cage. Pseudopatients were not able to measure the amount of time nurses and doctors spent with patients because it "was too brief" (Rosenhan, 1973, p. 254). Instead, they simply counted the number of times senior staff members emerged from the cage—about 10 times per eight-hour shift for nurses, about 7 times for doctors.

Interestingly, the only people who spent a lot of time with the pseudopatients—namely, the real patients—did notice that something was wrong. In three of the wards, the pseudopatients kept track of exactly how many of their fellow patients voiced suspicions. Some 35 of the 118 real patients actually approached the experimenters, saying things like, "You're not crazy. You're a journalist or a professor. . . . You're checking up on the hospital" (Rosenhan, 1973, p. 252). Ironically, then, Rosenhan's study might be interpreted as showing that there really is "something different" about people who are mentally ill.

However Rosenhan's study is interpreted, there is no doubt that psychiatric classification is a critical part of the current mental-health system. In the view of most professionals, any disadvantages of classification are outweighed by its advantages in promoting the understanding and treatment of abnormal behavior. If every patient is treated as an entirely new and unique case, it is difficult to predict how to treat any new patient. Classifying a person as a manic-depressive, for example, will probably lead a psychiatrist to prescribe the drug lithium rather than another drug. Diagnosis is useful not only for finding the most effective treatment for a particular individual but also for research into the nature of specific illnesses. By starting with a group of patients who have certain well-defined symptoms in common, researchers may be able to identify the cause and cure of a distinct mental illness. For these and other reasons, considerable attention has been devoted to developing a complete and comprehensive system for classifying mental illness.

THE RATIONALE OF DSM-III

Throughout the first half of the twentieth century, no single system for classifying all types of abnormal behavior was universally accepted. In 1952, the American Psychiatric Association filled this gap by publishing its *Diagnostic and Statistical Manual* (DSM). This complete and official list of syndromes of abnormal behavior was based on a scheme developed for the U.S. Army in World War II. Advances in theory and research have led to two major revisions of this influential system; the second version (DSM-II) was published in 1968, and the third revision (DSM-III) was adopted by the American Psychiatric Association in 1980.

To be scientifically acceptable, any system for classifying abnormal behavior must meet the same basic criteria as a psychological test: It must be reliable and valid (see Chapter 12). Briefly, the *reliability* of a test score or a diagnosis is a measure of its consistency across repeated measurements; *validity* involves the more difficult issue of estimating the accuracy of a particular measurement.

Before one can ask whether a diagnosis is valid, it must first be shown to be reliable. If clinicians cannot agree on the disorder of a specific patient, their different opinions cannot possibly all be correct. Therefore, the most fundamental problem for any diagnostic scheme is to establish reliability. One reason psychiatrists decided to revise DSM-II was that research revealed that its diagnostic categories were not sufficiently reliable (Spitzer & Fleiss, 1974); the single most important goal of the architects of DSM-III was to develop a more reliable system.

They attempted to accomplish this by specifying the criteria for each diagnosis precisely and in great detail. The value of this approach was demonstrated in an elaborate set of field trials conducted while DSM-III was being developed. A total of 12,667 patients were evaluated by 550 different clinicians using early drafts of DSM-III. In one pretest of DSM-III reliability, 770 patients were diagnosed by two different clinicians who interviewed them independently. When their diagnoses were compared, the agreement between judges (one form of reliability) was generally higher than had previously been found for DSM-I and DSM-II (American Psychiatric Association, 1980).

That does not mean that every patient received a single label from both clinicians; abnormal behavior takes a wide variety of forms, and some cannot easily be fit into any diagnostic scheme. However, the agreement was quite good for most diagnostic categories.

This improved reliability does not guarantee the validity of diagnosis, but it does make it possible. Several other changes were also introduced into DSM-III in the hope of increasing validity. Categories were redefined in the light of research findings, and theoretical constructs of questionable value were eliminated.

For example, the most important and most controversial change in DSM-III eliminated neurosis as a major diagnostic category. At least since Freud, clinicians have defined **neurosis** as an enduring set of symptoms that bother an individual or

TABLE 13.2
The Range of Abnormal Behavior—
A Partial List of DSM-III Categories

Diagnosis	*General Description*	*Example*
Disorders usually first evident in infancy, childhood, or adolescence	A wide variety of developmental problems ranging from mental retardation (see Chapter 12) to attention deficit disorder with hyperactivity (see Chapter 8) to excessive sleepwalking or stuttering. The major common feature of these problems is appearance before adulthood.	Anorexia nervosa: An eating disorder characterized by serious weight loss, and intense fear of becoming obese, and refusal to eat enough to maintain normal body weight. Particularly common among adolescent females. Most cases involve a single episode with complete recovery, but anorexia sometimes leads to death by starvation.
Organic mental disorders	A psychological or behavioral abnormality known to be associated with brain dysfunction. Range from transitory drug-induced states of inebriation to chronic brain disease.	Senile dementia: Degeneration of brain tissue produces a gradual loss in intellectual abilities such as memory and judgment; may also produce personality changes. Occurs in 2% to 4% of the population over the age of 65.
Substance-use disorders	Involves undesirable behavioral changes associated with the regular use of such drugs as alcohol, heroin, barbiturates, and marijuana.	Alcohol dependence: Physical addiction to alcohol, including tolerance (increasingly larger doses are needed to produce same effect) and withdrawal (physical symptoms occur when the drug is stopped) (see Chapter 3).
Schizophrenic disorders	Serious disturbances of thought, perception, and emotion. By definition, these must involve deterioration from a previous, more adequate state and must be maintained for at least six months before the age of 45.	Process schizophrenia: The young widow who "noticed poison in her food," described at the beginning of this chapter.

interfere with healthy functioning while the person remains in contact with reality. Traditionally, this was distinguished from the more dramatic impairment of **psychosis,** a serious mental disorder involving obvious disturbances in thought, emotion, and behavior. As one old psychiatric joke put it: "A psychotic thinks that two plus two equals five. A neurotic knows that two plus two equals four, but it really bothers him." While this whimsical distinction should not be taken too literally, it does convey the flavor of an important difference in the degree and kind of disturbance.

Freud's category of psychoneurosis included a number of different behavioral

Diagnosis	General Description	Example
Affective disorders	A prolonged and fundamental disturbance of mood and emotion, including severe depression and mania.	Mania: Euphoria is associated with hyperactivity, distractibility, loud and rapid speech, inflated self-esteem, and a decreased need for sleep.
Anxiety disorders	Anxiety becomes so severe that it interferes with the normal ability to function in everyday life.	Social phobias: Involve a fear of situations in which one might be observed by others, such as eating in public.
Somatoform disorders	Physical symptoms (such as pain or stomach distress) seem to be based on psychological conflicts rather than an organic disease.	Glove anesthesia: Loss of sensation in the hand caused by psychological conflicts (see Chapter 11).
Dissociative disorders	Sudden, temporary, and dramatic changes in memory, identity, and other complex psychological functions.	Multiple personality: An extremely rare syndrome in which a single individual is dominated by several distinct personalities at different points in time. One such case was popularized in the book and movie *Sybil*.
Psychosexual disorders	Problems in sexual function or adjustment that are related to psychological factors.	Fetishism: Nonliving objects (such as shoes or underwear) are the preferred or only source of sexual excitement.
Psychological factors affecting physical condition	Patients suffer from a disease or a physical condition in which psychological problems play an important role.	High blood pressure: In most cases caused by psychological stress (see Chapter 3).
Personality disorders	Inflexible patterns of behavior and enduring personality traits that interfere with social or occupational functioning or cause personal distress.	Narcissistic personality disorder: A grandiose sense of self-importance leads a person constantly to seek admiration and become preoccupied with success.

symptoms, ranging from excessive fears, or phobias (defined more formally later), to physical symptoms of hysteria such as glove anesthesia, a loss of feeling in the hand that is not based on physical damage. (See the description of Freud's case of Anna O. in Chapter 11.) Although phobias and hysterias may superficially seem to have little in common, Freud believed that both were caused by similar unconscious conflicts in which anxiety led to the maladaptive use of defense mechanisms.

Some clinicians question Freud's theory of neurosis, and no definitive proof of its validity has been uncovered by research. The DSM-III classification pays more attention to concrete behavior and less to unverified theory. Therefore, the major category of neurosis was eliminated, and phobia and hysteria (now called "conversion disorder") are no longer grouped together.

Another difference from earlier systems is that in DSM-III, a complete diagnosis of an individual includes the systematic evaluation of five different dimensions of behavior, called *axes*. For example, the problem of a businessman who was afraid to fly might have been diagnosed under DSM-II as simply "phobic neurosis." The DSM-III diagnosis might look something like this:

Axis I (Psychiatric Syndrome): Simple phobia
Axis II (For adults, Personality Disorders): Narcissistic personality disorder
Axis III (Physical Disorders): High blood pressure
Axis IV (Severity of Stress in Past Year): Moderate; began new job
Axis V (Highest Level of Functioning in Past Year): Very good

Even without understanding all the details, you can see that this assessment of five separate axes provides a more detailed picture of the person's condition than the older approach of a single label. (The terms *phobia* and *narcissistic personality disorder* are explained later in this chapter.)

Like other changes in DSM-III, the introduction of five separate axes was designed to make diagnosis as specific and unambiguous as possible. But, as you might anticipate, this new system did not satisfy everyone, and critics attacked everything from its political and economic implications to its basic philosophy. Many of these arguments have merit, and there is little doubt that future research and discussions will lead to further refinements in DSM-IV and DSM-V. DSM-III is not the ultimate system for classifying abnormal behavior, but it is the official system now used for everything from hospital files to insurance claims, so the remainder of this chapter is organized in terms of its categories.

DSM-III accepts the medical model's notion that there are separate mental diseases, each with its own symptoms, course, cause, and treatment. It lists 17 major categories of disorder and over 200 subcategories. Obviously, an introductory chapter of this sort cannot begin to cover all of them. Table 13.2 lists the most important categories to provide a concrete feeling for the wide range of possible abnormal behavior patterns. The rest of this chapter focuses on four of the most common and familiar diagnoses—personality disorders, anxiety disorders, affective disorders, and schizophrenic disorders. They are presented in this order, in a rough progression from the most ordinary and least pathological category—personality disorders—to perhaps the most frightening and bizarre syndrome of all—schizophrenia.

Personality Disorders

AN OVERVIEW

A **personality disorder** is an inflexible behavior pattern or enduring personality trait that significantly interferes with a person's occupation or social life or causes personal distress. Note that this definition stresses disturbance of one's feelings or relationships with another; only when a trait causes a problem is it considered a personality disorder.

DSM-III distinguishes between 12 different types of personality disorders. Although some of the terms sound familiar—such as paranoid, dependent, or histrionic personality disorders—each is defined by a specific list of behavioral symptoms. For example, the term **antisocial personality disorder** refers to a behavior pattern of violating the rights of others that begins before the age of 15 and interferes with adult responsibilities such as holding a job. More specifically, this diagnosis demands at least four of the following nine habitual patterns of behavior after the age of 18: problems with the law, aggressiveness, failure to plan ahead, lying, recklessness, ignoring financial obligations, inability to hold a job, inability to maintain an enduring sexual relationship, and irresponsibility as a parent. DSM-III further defines each of these nine patterns, as well as other criteria that a person must meet to be diagnosed as having an antisocial personality disorder.

People with personality disorders generally function reasonably well in society and often seek therapy only when faced with another problem, such as a crisis in the family or a criminal conviction. Compared to other more serious forms of abnormal behavior, very little is known about the causes or effective treatment of personality disorders.

To provide a more concrete understanding of this category, consider the case of one man with a **narcissistic personality disorder,** a grandiose sense of uniqueness or self-importance that leads a person to constantly seek admiration and to become preoccupied with fantasies of success.

A CASE HISTORY: NARCISSISTIC PERSONALITY DISORDER

Peter, a graduate student in English literature, believed that his PhD thesis would provide a revolutionary breakthrough in his field. For some reason, Peter's mentor failed to recognize his brilliance, so he had trouble getting past the third chapter. He blamed his professor for his difficulties and complained that his mentor should help more by doing some of the research. Peter resented other students who made faster progress through his program and referred to them as "dull drones" who were jealous of his brilliance and creativity.

Peter also had trouble relating to friends and lovers. He often became infatuated with women, but soon after actually getting involved he realized that this person failed to meet his high personal standards. Before he had sex with a woman for the first time, he would have powerful and persistent fantasies about her; afterward, each woman seemed dumb, clinging, and physically repugnant (Spitzer, Skodol, Gibbon, & Williams, 1981, p. 52).

In Greek myth, Narcissus was a beautiful youth who fell in love with his own image in a pool and died pining away for love of himself. Narcissistic personality disorders take their name from this myth.

Peter had many narcissistic traits: an exaggerated sense of the importance of his thesis, a feeling that he was entitled to more help from his mentor, and a pattern of first overidealizing and then devaluing women. His relationships with male friends were equally shallow and transitory. Because these traits interfered with his work at school and his social life, Peter was given the diagnosis of narcissistic personality disorder. This leads to the question of etiology: How did Peter develop this unpleasant and socially maladaptive pattern of behavior?

CAUSES OF NARCISSISM

Much remains to be learned about the causes of abnormal behavior; therefore, when we discuss the etiology of any syndrome we shall present several different lines of theory and research. Each explanation will be based on the five theoretical paradigms introduced in Chapter 1 (psychoanalytic, behavioral, humanist, cognitive, or biological). On the simplest level, the psychoanalytic approach looks for causes in unconscious conflicts rooted in childhood. The behavioral approach seeks environmental causes and cures based on learning. The humanistic approach emphasizes self-fulfillment in the present. The cognitive approach analyzes errors in thought and interpretation of reality. Finally, the biological approach seeks physical causes of mental disease. We shall also consider social-learning theory, which combines elements of the behavioral and cognitive approaches (see Chapter 11).

As noted throughout this text, human behavior is so complex that it is often useful to consider it from several theoretical perspectives to get a complete picture. But instead of providing five or six accounts of the etiology of each syndrome, we shall focus on two or three that have proved particularly useful for understanding that category of behavior. For narcissistic personality disorders, this implies contrasting psychoanalytic and social-learning views.

A Psychoanalytic View.   In recent years, many psychoanalysts have developed new theories regarding the development of narcissism; one of the most influential was proposed by Otto Kernberg (1975). According to Kernberg, although Peter gives a surface impression of being extremely confident or even in love with himself, this masks powerful feelings of self-hatred; unconsciously, Peter sees himself as unworthy and unlovable.

As explained in Chapter 11, psychoanalysts believe that the unconscious can deceive the conscious mind to protect the ego against threatening impulses. In this case, on a conscious level Peter seeks recognition for his revolutionary PhD thesis. But on an unconscious level, he may actually have a low opinion of his own work.

Kernberg's theory of narcissism, like other psychoanalytic theories, seeks the origins of these unconscious conflicts in childhood. Among his own narcissistic patients, Kernberg often found a mother or parent figure who seemed well adjusted to the outside world but who was cold, indifferent, or spitefully aggressive toward the child. Although we do not know the facts of Peter's childhood, Kernberg would hypothesize that such a person frustrated Peter's needs for comfort and emotional support during the oral stage of development. Thus, as an infant Peter failed to develop the healthy relationship with his mother that could provide a foundation for intimate social relationships later in life.

The early rejection by his mother produced an insatiable appetite for emotional nourishment. As an adult, Peter approaches other people with the idea that they too will fail to meet his needs. The attempts to degrade and devalue the women in his life could be Peter's way of frustrating other people so that they will not be able to frustrate him.

A Social-Learning View.   Other explanations of narcissism have also been proposed. According to one social-learning theory (Millon, 1981), Peter's parents may have seen him as "God's gift to mankind"; by indulging Peter's every whim, they made him believe that he could receive without giving and that every minor action deserved praise. According to this view, Peter's inflated sense of his own worth was a natural outgrowth of the way his parents indiscriminately rewarded every act. He came to feel that he was entitled to gratification and that other people were as solicitous as his own parents; to get what he wanted, Peter had only to ask for it. These patterns of behavior were further maintained by self-reinforcement. While most people have to learn to please others to gain the reward of approval, the narcissist can be reinforced by fantasizing about his own superior qualities; he does not need other people to the same extent.

Note that there are some points of agreement between the psychoanalytic and social-learning theories. Both predict that a child without any brothers or sisters would be more likely to become narcissistic, but they would invoke different explanations. In any case, at this time the etiology of narcissism has been the topic of more theory than research. Only when future researchers collect more data contrasting narcissists to other groups will we have a better idea of which perspective provides more useful insights.

Anxiety Disorders

AN OVERVIEW

In an **anxiety disorder,** severe anxiety interferes with the normal ability to function in everyday life. This interference can take several forms. In a **generalized anxiety disorder,** a person chronically suffers from intense anxiety and tension that do not appear to be related to any particular situation or stimulus. A more limited version, called **panic disorder,** involves unpredictable and repeated attacks of anxiety and panic. The symptoms may include shortness of breath, chest pain, dizziness, feelings of unreality, trembling, sweating, and faintness; again, these attacks are not related to any specific stimulus.

Another type of anxiety disorder is a bit more removed from the commonsense definition of nervousness. An **obsessive-compulsive disorder** involves persistent, repetitive thoughts that cannot be controlled (such as the thought of killing one's brother) or behavior patterns that are constantly repeated in a kind of ritual (such as washing one's hands over and over). Of course, everyone has thoughts and behavior patterns that are repeated; psychologists use the term *obsessive-compulsive disorder* only if they become so extreme that they cause personal distress or interfere with normal function. Although in everyday language we might speak of a person with a compulsion to drive fast cars or eat anchovy pizzas, in DSM-III a true compulsion is perceived as senseless, an external force that cannot be resisted but provides no joy. Because theory and research suggest that the ritualistic thoughts and behaviors are linked to anxiety, this rather rare condition is classified with the anxiety disorders.

Perhaps the most common type of anxiety disorder is a **phobia,** a persistent and irrational fear of a specific object, activity, or situation. Vocabulary buffs may like to list the many English words that add the suffix *phobia* (from the Greek, "to fear") to a prefix for a particular feared object. These range from the familiar (for example, *claustrophobia,* for a fear of closed places) to the ridiculous (for example, *ergasio-phobia,* for a fear of work). DSM-III recognizes only three major categories. *Social phobia* refers to a fear of situations in which one might be observed by others, such as speaking or eating in public. *Agoraphobia* refers to a fear of public places such as crowds, tunnels, or public transportation; typically, the result is that the agoraphobic restricts activities until he is afraid to leave home. All other phobias, whether to animals, heights, closed spaces, or gym clothes, are called *simple phobias.*

Table 13.3 summarizes the results of one survey of the frequency of different types of fears. Note that the everyday objects and situations most people fear—snakes, heights, flying, the dentist—differ from the sources of phobias that are strong enough to interfere with everyday life—illness, storms, death, and public places. To get a feeling for this last and most common category, consider the story of one woman who was afraid to leave her house.

A CASE HISTORY: AGORAPHOBIA

Lisa was a 28-year-old homemaker who sought professional help because she was afraid that her anxiety attacks would interfere with the care of her three young

TABLE 13.3
The Most Common Fears

Mild Fears		Intense Fears		Phobias		Phobias So Severe That People Sought Professional Help[a]
Source	Frequency (%)	Source	Frequency (%)	Source	Frequency (%)	
Snakes	39	Snakes	25	Illness	3	Public places
Heights	31	Heights	12	Storms	1	Illness
Storms	21	Flying	11	Animals	1	Death
Flying	20	Enclosures	5	Public places	0.6	Crowds
Dentist	20	Illness	3	Death	0.5	Animals

[a]Estimates of frequency in the general population are not available; listed in order of relative frequency among patients.

Note. Fears are listed in order of their frequency; percentage estimates are based on a survey of a representative sample of the population of Burlington, Vermont. Totals may exceed 100% because some people report two or more fears.

Source: Agras, S., Sylvester, D., & Oliveau, D. The epidemiology of common fears and phobias. *Comprehensive Psychiatry*, 1969, *10*, p. 152.

children. About a year earlier, she began to experience periods of nervousness in which she suddenly felt light-headed and dizzy, breathed rapidly, trembled, and felt strange and detached. Although Lisa had led an active and outgoing life before the first attack, she gradually began to restrict her activities so that she would not have an attack in public or someplace where she could not get help. For the last six months, Lisa had been comfortable leaving home only if she was accompanied by her husband or mother. When she was forced to go to a supermarket or department store, she tried to stay near the exits. She canceled her usual summer vacation because she wouldn't feel safe so far from home. Shortly before deciding to see a therapist, Lisa had asked her mother to stay with her whenever the children were home; she was worried about what would happen if there was an accident and she was not able to help because of an anxiety attack. Both Lisa and her family were confused and disturbed by these sudden odd feelings and behavior patterns (Spitzer et al., 1981, p. 268).

A year before Lisa sought help, she had all the symptoms of a panic disorder—the sudden onset of extreme signs of anxiety from no apparent cause. Like many other patients with a panic disorder, Lisa soon developed more complex problems. She began to avoid places where such attacks might occur in public. The gradual restriction of her activities, coupled with the recurrent attacks, leads to the DSM-III diagnosis of agoraphobia with panic attacks.

CAUSES OF PHOBIAS

As with other victims of mental disorders, Lisa's problems can be seen in terms of several theoretical paradigms. Two of the most influential views of phobia come from psychoanalytic and social-learning theory.

A Psychoanalytic View. For Freud, a phobia was the surface expression of a much deeper conflict. All the anxiety disorders are caused by unconscious conflicts between id, ego, and superego processes. The sexual and aggressive impulses of the id seek expression in behavior and the conscious mind. But the reality processes of the ego and the ideals of the superego oppose this expression and work to repress the impulse back into the unconscious. The final product of this unconscious conflict is intense anxiety that the id impulse will not be successfully repressed—a fear that it will force its way into the conscious mind and even lead a person to lose control.

It is impossible to understand the nature of Lisa's unconscious conflicts without knowing more about her childhood and current situation. However, since the welfare of her children seems to be one focus of the anxiety, one possibility is that they are the target of her unconscious impulses. Perhaps on rainy days, when all three children are cooped up in a small space, they act so bratty that Lisa has an unconscious desire to run away or even hurt them. According to the ideals of her superego, Lisa cannot admit these feelings even to herself. The panic attack occurred when this impulse first threatened to become conscious.

To a psychoanalyst, the fact that Lisa developed agoraphobia, rather than some other type of phobia, is no accident. Unconsciously, she fears running away and leaving the children behind. As a result, leaving her house even for a short time becomes a source of anxiety. If the unconscious aggressive impulse breaks through, she may never return.

A Social-Learning View. The roots of social-learning theories of phobia go back at least to John Watson's attempt to teach Little Albert to fear a rat by pairing movements toward the rat with a loud, frightening sound. Later learning theories stressed the role of internal cognitive processes in learning fear. In one study (Bandura & Rosenthal, 1966), subjects watched as a model apparently received a painful electrical shock whenever a buzzer was sounded. This produced observational learning; over time, these people began to experience physiological signs of anxiety whenever they heard the buzzer. Whether learned by classical conditioning or observational learning, fears may be generalized to other situations and lead to avoidance responses—actions designed to prevent the occurrence of an aversive stimulus (see Chapter 5).

In Lisa's case, it is easy to imagine a social-learning explanation of her problems. Some stimulus triggered the first anxiety attack. While it might be interesting to know what that initial stimulus was, ultimately that is less important than the continuing learning process it set into motion. At first, Lisa avoided public situations that were similar to the stimuli present at her first attack. This avoidance was designed to prevent the unpleasant symptoms from occurring again. But over time, the stimuli generalized further and further, until Lisa was avoiding any stimulus outside her familiar home base. Thus, for the social-learning theorist, Lisa's agoraphobia is a case of learning to be afraid.

As with other psychological disorders, it is not yet known whether psychoanalytic theory, social-learning theory, another approach, or some mixture of approaches presents the best explanation for anxiety disorders. However, we shall see in the next chapter that social-learning theory has developed some particularly effective techniques for treating phobias like Lisa's.

Judy Garland had a long history of depressive episodes and emotional problems. She died in 1969 after an accidental overdose of barbiturates.

Affective Disorders

AN OVERVIEW

Affective disorders involve a prolonged and fundamental disturbance of mood and emotion. Technically, they are also defined by the presence of certain symptoms of depression or mania. Of course, everyone is depressed from time to time, and it can sometimes be difficult to distinguish normal from abnormal depression. But clinicians define **depression** as a persistent and prominent loss of interest or pleasure in almost all ordinary activities, associated with such symptoms as disturbances in eating or sleeping habits, decreased energy, feelings of worthlessness or guilt, difficulty in concentrating, and recurrent thoughts of suicide or death. On the other side of the coin is **mania,** a feeling of euphoria and enthusiasm (sometimes alternating with irritability) that is associated with such symptoms as hyperactivity, loud and rapid speech, inflated self-esteem, decreased need for sleep, and distractibility.

As early as the first century A.D., physicians were aware that mania was often linked to depression and that the two might even be different manifestations of the same underlying disease. Many people experience severe depressions without mania, but most who have a manic episode "will eventually have a major depressive episode" (American Psychiatric Association, 1980, p. 216).

In DSM-III, the two major categories of affective disorders are **bipolar disorder** (formerly called manic-depressive psychosis), in which manic and depressive episodes alternate, and **major depression,** in which severe depression appears alone. Each is defined precisely in terms of a list of specific symptoms. Manic episodes usually begin suddenly and end suddenly. They last a few days to a few months, and a person's first manic episode usually occurs before the age of 30. In contrast, major depression may appear at any age, and the symptoms may begin gradually or suddenly. When mania and depression alternate in a bipolar disorder, they are usually separated by periods of at least several months in which the person's mood is relatively normal.

Estimates of the prevalence of bipolar disorder range from 0.4% to 1.2% of the population, and it occurs equally in women and men. Major depression is far more common, particularly for females. Around 20% of all women have a major depressive episode sometime in their lives, versus 10% of all men (American Psychiatric Association, 1980). At one time, critics argued that this discrepancy between the sexes reflected the bias of male mental-health professionals, that the same percentage of men and women experienced major depressive episodes but that women were more likely to be labeled depressed. There is now a large body of evidence that this is not true. No matter what definition is used, more women experience depression than men (Weissman & Paykel, 1974). No one is certain of the reason, although theories have ranged from feminist assertions that this is a by-product of unhealthy women's roles in our society to biological theories involving female hormone levels.

Again, it is important to emphasize that both mania and depression are experienced by everyone, and the line between normal and abnormal may sometimes be hard to draw. But in more severe cases, there is little doubt that something is wrong. Consider, for example, the case of an actual patient whom we shall call John.

A CASE HISTORY: BIPOLAR DISORDER

At the age of 54, John suddenly became restless and talkative. He began to send checks to friends, and even to perfect strangers, whom he said "might be in need." He was soon suspended from his office job because he was "overwrought." A few days later, he was admitted to a private mental hospital (Noyes & Kolb, 1963, p. 309).

On his arrival, John gave $5 to one patient and $1 to another. He talked quickly, loudly, and constantly. He promised several patients that he would have them released. Whenever a doctor entered the ward, John greeted him effusively, slapped him on the back or shook his hand warmly, and talked and talked. He became attracted to one woman physician and nearly drove *her* mad with his "familiar, ill-mannered, and obtrusive attentions." John was so affable that he became obnoxious, and other patients began to resent his interference in their affairs; on two separate occasions, other patients actually punched him in the face.

John was constantly and incessantly active and mischievous. He drew pictures of the doctors and nurses on his arms and wrote music on the toilet paper. He painted the face of another manic patient with Mercurochrome and played the ward piano incessantly whenever he was permitted.

At times, however, this euphoric mood seemed to shatter. In the middle of an interview, he would begin to sob audibly and bury his face in his arms. When he was first admitted, he pretended to commit suicide by poisoning himself with mercury, then drew a skull and crossbones on the wall in his room.

Interestingly, John's psychiatric history revealed three previous episodes of serious depression, lasting about six months each, at the ages of 35, 41, and 47. During his manic periods, he showed many of the classic symptoms, including excessive talkativeness and activity, a decreased need for sleep, and an inflated sense of self-esteem. In DSM-III, this patient would be diagnosed as having a bipolar disorder. More specifically, his diagnosis at the time of his hospitalization would include the adjective *mixed* to refer to the fact that he alternated quickly between periods of mania and depression.

CAUSES OF DEPRESSION AND MANIA

Research on the causes of affective disorders has focused more on depression than mania, perhaps because depression occurs far more frequently. The cognitive and social-learning theories described in this section refer only to John's depressive episodes; however, our discussion of biological theories will return to the issue of the causes of mania.

A Cognitive View. Psychiatrist Aaron Beck's therapeutic experiences with large numbers of depressed patients led him to the conclusion that depression is caused by logical errors of thought that produce excessive self-blame. This is called a **cognitive theory of depression** because it emphasizes the critical role thoughts may play in causing the disorder.

One error that Beck's patients often made when they evaluated themselves was that they *overgeneralized* from single events. For example, when John went out on one unpleasant date, he might conclude that he would never find the woman of his dreams. A related error, called *magnification*, involved exaggerating trivial occurrences. For example, if John saw a single pimple on his nose, he might decide that his face was so severely scarred that he would only find work in a freak show. In extreme cases, the logic of depressed patients may become totally distorted by *arbitrary inferences*. For example, if John invited three friends to a Milwaukee Brewers baseball game that was rained out, he might conclude that he was worthless because he couldn't even pick a clear day to go out with his friends. The common theme underlying all these errors in logic is blaming oneself and feeling guilty or worthless at times when these feelings are inappropriate.

There is considerable evidence that depressed people do indeed describe their world in precisely the ways that Beck (1967) outlined. However, we have noted many times that correlations like this do not prove causality (see Chapter 12, "How Do They Know?"). Other theorists have argued that both feelings of depression and logical errors of thought could be caused by a third factor, such as a biochemical imbalance (as described later). While Beck's theory has been useful in the treatment of depression, no one has yet been able to prove that cognitive errors actually *cause* depression.

A Social-Learning View. In Chapter 5, we introduced Martin Seligman's theory that a sense of **learned helplessness,** an organism's belief that it lacks control over a situation, can lead to depression. The animal laboratory research described there grew out of the behavioral paradigm and an attempt to understand the external stimuli that control certain forms of passive behavior. Seligman (1975) soon noticed many parallels between the behavior of animals who learned to be helpless and depressed humans. Both groups passively fail to cope with environmental demands, for example, both develop eating problems, and in both groups, levels of the neurotransmitter norepinephrine are decreased in the brain.

When researchers tried to apply this behavioral model from the animal laboratory to the real problems of human patients, however, they found that cognitive factors also seemed to play an important role. A new model of depression was therefore proposed that considered not just the feeling of lack of control but also the way people interpreted these feelings. Drawing on attribution theory (see Chapter 15), this model distinguished several kinds of conclusions a person can draw when facing failure. Its causes can be perceived as internal or external, long-term or short-term, and global or specific. Table 13.4 gives an example of the way these three types of attributions could interact as a woman interpreted the fact that a particular man rejected her. Depression is most likely to occur when attributions are global, long-term, and internal, again giving one a feeling of helplessness or lack of control.

According to Seligman, John's periods of depression could have resulted from learning that he was not in control of his life. Specifically, John probably attributed any failures in his life to internal faults that were global, long-term personality traits.

A Biological View. Since effective drugs for controlling psychotic symptoms came into wide use in the mid-1950s (see Chapter 14), there has been a revolution in both psychiatric treatment and theories of the origins of severe mental disorders. A great deal of attention had been focused on the biochemistry of neurotransmitters (chemicals released at the synapse by one neuron that influence the electrical activity of another; see Chapters 2 and 3) and their possible role in mental illness.

TABLE 13.4
Possible Interpretations of Personal Failure
(Conclusions a Woman Might Draw after Being Rejected by Her Boyfriend)

	Internal		*External*	
	Long-Term	*Short-Term*	*Long-Term*	*Short-Term*
Global	I'm ugly.	Maybe I have bad breath.	Men hate intelligent women like me.	In that mood, a man would reject Ms. Right.
Specific	Duane thinks I'm ugly.	Duane thinks I have bad breath.	Duane hates intelligent women like me.	Duane was in such a bad mood he would have rejected Ms. Right.

Source: Based on Abramson, L., Seligman, M., & Teasdale, J. Learned helplessness in humans: Critique and reformulation. *Journal of Abnormal Psychology,* 1978, 87, p. 57.

Many drugs that have proved useful in the treatment of depression increase levels of the neurotransmitter norepinephrine. The natural salt lithium decreases the symptoms of mania and decreases levels of norepinephrine. Along with other lines of evidence, this suggests that the amount of the neurotransmitter norepinephrine available at certain sites in the brain may regulate behavior and mood. Too much norepinephrine produces mania; too little produces depression. Normal behavior is associated with levels of norepinephrine that fall between these two extremes.

According to this biological view, John's manic symptoms result from a problem in the chemistry of his brain and can be corrected by drugs that alter that chemistry. His periodic bouts of depression are based on the same underlying chemical deficit.

It is important to emphasize that even if this biological theory is completely correct, psychological factors can still be important. As noted, events that produce a feeling of learned helplessness have been shown to lower brain levels of the neurotransmitter norepinephrine. Human behavior is best understood by considering how biological and psychological factors work together and by examining behavior from several theoretical perspectives.

Schizophrenic Disorders

AN OVERVIEW

In 1908, a professor of psychiatry at the University of Zurich named Eugen Bleuler argued that Kraepelin had defined the disease dementia praecox too narrowly, and as a result the diagnosis excluded too many patients with similar symptoms. He argued that the disease did not always lead to irreversible intellectual deterioration (and thus was not true dementia), and it did not always begin early in life (and thus was not praecox). Bleuler proposed a broader definition and a new name for this disorder—**schizophrenia** (from the Greek *schizein*, "to split," and *phren*, "mind"). This term has often been misunderstood. A schizophrenic is not a person with multiple personalities. (As noted in Table 13.2, multiple personality is an extremely rare form of dissociative disorder.) The splitting of the mind that Bleuler referred to is far more disabling and far more common—it involves a fragmentation of thought, perception, emotion, and other psychological processes.

Bleuler's definition was so broad that he even included a category of latent schizophrenia, for people who showed only subtle symptoms. The controversy over precisely where schizophrenia ends and other disorders begin has continued to the present day.

Traditionally, clinicians in the United States leaned toward Bleuler's more inclusive concept of the disorder, and schizophrenia was sometimes called a "wastebasket diagnosis"—if a disturbed patient was hard to classify precisely, he would probably be diagnosed as schizophrenic. In contrast, European mental-health workers generally used the term more sparingly.

As a result, studies of the prevalence of schizophrenia usually found that it was more common in the United States than in Europe. This reflects a difference in diagnostic practices rather than a true difference in the prevalence of the disorder.

When researchers directly compared the diagnoses of specific mental patients by different clinicians, for example, they found that many individuals who were called schizophrenic by New York psychiatrists would have been classified as manic-depressives or neurotics by London psychiatrists (Cooper, Kendell, Gurland, Sharpe, Copeland, & Simon, 1972).

Thus, questions about how common schizophrenia is depend on precisely how the term is defined. According to DSM-III, studies using narrow definitions of the term in Europe and Asia have found lifetime prevalence rates between 0.2% and 1%. American studies using broader definitions generally report higher rates. As a rough approximation we might say that 1 out of every 100 people in the world will become schizophrenic at some point in their lives.

A closely related issue concerns the existence of distinct subcategories or types of schizophrenia. One approach divides schizophrenia into two major categories, process and reactive. *Process schizophrenics* generally have a history of poor adjustment beginning in childhood and a low probability for recovery. This gradual deterioration suggests that some fundamental process in the brain has gone awry. This category is similar to Kraepelin's original notion of dementia praecox. In contrast, *reactive schizophrenics* have relatively normal childhood histories and a rapid onset of more severe symptoms, and their chances of returning to normal function are greater. They suffer from what laymen call a "nervous breakdown," which often appears to be a reaction to severe stress. This generalization does not imply that every patient with a long history of problems has no chance to recover; it does imply that those who are correctly diagnosed as process schizophrenics have a poor prognosis.

No one knows whether these and other differences in symptoms result from fundamentally different disease processes. This makes schizophrenia a difficult topic to study. One can hardly find the cause of a disease when no one is even sure which patients have it. Some researchers emphasize this ambiguity by using the plural term *the schizophrenias* rather than the singular *schizophrenia*, which seems to imply that all victims suffer from the same disease.

According to DSM-III, the diagnostic label **schizophrenic disorder** is reserved for people who develop serious disturbances of thought, perception, and emotion for a period of at least six months before the age of 45 and who have deteriorated from a previous, more adequate level of functioning. The detail of this definition is quite purposeful. For example, the requirement of six months' duration is meant to exclude transient psychotic episodes; the mention of deterioration excludes individuals who are born with severe mental disturbances from which they never recover.

Schizophrenia usually begins with a phase of gradual deterioration, including such symptoms as social isolation and withdrawal, severe impairment in the ability to function as a wage earner, student, or homemaker, severe decline in personal hygiene and grooming, and extremely peculiar behavior, such as talking aloud to oneself in public or collecting garbage. This is followed by an active phase characterized by psychotic disturbances of thought, perception, and emotion. In most cases, active phases of the illness alternate with calmer periods characterized by the less dramatic symptoms. According to DSM-III (American Psychiatric Association,

1980, p. 185), complete recovery is "so rare . . . that some clinicians would question the diagnosis."

We began this chapter with Kraepelin's case history of a widow who would now be classified as suffering from a schizophrenic disorder. But not one of her symptoms would apply to every schizophrenic. Indeed, the symptoms seen in the active phase of the disease are so dramatic, so varied, and so fundamental that it is difficult to characterize them systematically.

Because the schizophrenia label includes such a wide and diffuse array of problems, in this section we survey the many possible symptoms of schizophrenia in terms of their effect on thought, perception, emotion, and other psychological processes.

THE SYMPTOMS OF SCHIZOPHRENIA

Disorders of Thought.   Thought disorders can be subdivided into disturbances of form (the *way* people think) and disturbances of content (*what* people think).

Perhaps the most classic disturbance in the schizophrenic form of thought involves *loose associations* in which the person shifts quickly from one subject to another and fails to form complete and coherent thoughts. Consider, for example, this excerpt from a letter written by a patient of Dr. Bleuler's (1911):

> Dear Mother:
>
> I am writing on paper. The pen which I am using is from a factory called "Perry & Co." This factory is in England. I assume this. Behind the name of Perry Co. the city of London is inscribed; but not the city. The city of London is in England. I know this from my school-days. Then, I always liked geography. My last teacher in that subject was Professor August A. He was a man with black eyes. I also like black eyes. There are also blue and gray eyes and other sorts, too. I have heard it said that snakes have green eyes. All people have eyes. There are some too, who are blind. These blind people are led about by a boy (p. 17).

In this paragraph the reader can follow the shifts from one topic to another. But when associations become too loose, the result is incoherence, as can be seen in a sample of the speech of another patient:

> I am the nun. If that's enough, you are still his. That is a brave cavalier, take him as your husband. Karoline, you well know, though you are my Lord, you were just a dream. If you are the dove-cote, Mrs. K. is still beset by fear. Otherwise I am not so exact in eating. Handle the gravy carefully. Where is the paint-brush? Where are you, Herman (p. 21)?

The monologue continued in the same vein, jumping from one topic to the next, abruptly and without any apparent logic or plan.

Many other disturbances in the form of thought have been observed. Logic may be twisted by some personal law, as in the case of a schizophrenic patient who learned that his girlfriend had become pregnant. Since the patient had not had intercourse with her, he concluded that the conception was immaculate. This led to the further conclusion that his girlfriend must be the Virgin Mary, and he must be God (Rosen & Gregory, 1965).

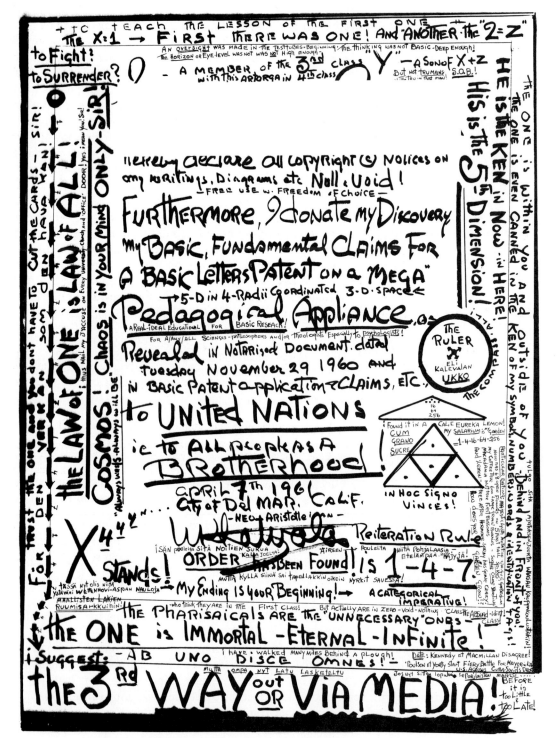

A letter written by a schizophrenic shows many signs of thought disorders.

Along with disturbances in the form of thought come disturbances in its actual content, particularly *delusions*, or false beliefs. These may involve persecution, religion, grandeur, and other issues. Whatever the theme, schizophrenic delusions tend to be bizarre, fragmented, or patently absurd. (In contrast, the delusions of patients with paranoid disorders and other psychoses may be quite coherent and logical.)

One of Bleuler's (1911) patients, for example, reported that he was being poisoned with "hydrochloric acid, hair-bread, and urine." Another complained of "human beings in her fingers who want to kill her and drink her blood." A third patient believed that if he stayed in the mental asylum "more than one year and 87 weeks, his father will have a leg torn off" (p. 119).

Delusions of grandeur are equally bizarre. One 20-year-old schizophrenic believed that he was responsible for every invention of the last 50 years and "he also possesses a remedy against spinal cord diseases. He can fly; and refuses food because he receives manna from heaven" (Bleuler, 1911, p. 120). For another, more religiously inclined schizophrenic, "A brilliant star arose which led him from his bed to the toilet and back again three times" (p. 121).

To an outsider, these beliefs may seem incredible or even laughable. To the victim of schizophrenia, such disorders of thought are all too real. They can be frightening manifestations of an entire world gone mad.

Disorders of Perception. In schizophrenia, the most common perceptual disorders involve auditory hallucinations, particularly voices coming from inside the head that threaten, curse, or provide a running commentary on a patient's behavior. Among Bleuler's (1911) examples:

> While getting ready in the morning a patient hears "Now she is combing her hair," "Now she is getting dressed;" sometimes in a nagging tone, sometimes scornfully, sometimes with critical comments. . . . [Another reports,] When I stop speaking, then the voices repeat what I have just said. . . . [A third] patient hears his leg talking . . . the voices come from various places under the skin, and constantly call out: "Don't let me out," "Don't cut it open" (pp. 98–100).

Hallucinations of the other senses are also reported, but they are less frequent. Tactile hallucinations may involve electrical, tingling, or burning sensations. Parts of the body may seem too large or small, or the body may seem so depersonalized that it feels like a machine.

Disorders of Emotion. Schizophrenia also disrupts emotional responsiveness, leading to what clinicians call *flattened affect* (a drastic reduction in the intensity of emotional experience) or inappropriate affect.

Bleuler (1911) provided an eerie portrait of the drab, emotionless atmosphere of a mental asylum at the turn of the century:

> [The patients] sit about the institutions to which they are confined with expressionless faces, hunched up, the image of indifference. They permit themselves to be dressed and undressed like automatons, to be led from their customary place of inactivity to the mess-hall, and back again without expressing any sign of satisfaction or

The English artist Louis Wain was famous for his paintings of cats in human situations, such as the tea party in the first painting in this series. In the 1920s, he developed schizophrenia and spent most of the remaining years of his life in mental institutions. This series of paintings shows how his portrayals of cats became more and more bizarre as the disease progressed.

dissatisfaction. . . . During a fire in the hospital, a number of patients had to be led out of the threatened ward; they themselves would never have moved from their places; they would have allowed themselves to be suffocated or burnt without showing an affective response (p. 40).

When emotion is shown, it may seem quite inappropriate to the situation. For example:

A patient . . . broke out into loud laughter at the news of her brother's death, because she was so pleased at receiving letters with black borders; but the loss of the brother did not seem to arouse any feeling (p. 52).

Disorders of Other Psychological Processes. DSM-III lists a number of other schizophrenic symptoms that are less central than the disorders of thought, perception, and emotion. There is almost always a disturbance in goal-directed activity that significantly interferes with everyday life; patients may be paralyzed by ambivalence regarding even such commonplace activities as getting dressed in the morning. There is sometimes a total loss of identity, as a schizophrenic comes to believe that he is controlled by an outside force. There is a tendency to become preoccupied with fantasies and withdraw from other people.

Finally, bizarre motor actions characterize a severe form of schizophrenia called *catatonia.* A catatonic patient may maintain a rigid posture and resist efforts to be moved or may engage in purposeless stereotyped movements, such as rocking back and forth, for long periods of time.

Remember, no one symptom occurs in every schizophrenic. But as the many examples in this section suggest, schizophrenic disorders are severe conditions that can dramatically interfere with or entirely destroy an individual's ability to function in the world. Fortunately, as we see in the next chapter, many of the most frighten-

A catatonic schizophrenic may remain in the same odd position for minutes or even hours.

ing schizophrenic symptoms can be reduced by drug therapy. The portrait painted here is of the untreated disease, as observed in Bleuler's asylum before the discovery of antipsychotic medications.

CAUSES OF SCHIZOPHRENIA

A Biological View. In recent years, it has become quite clear that biological predispositions play an important role in the development of schizophrenia. The most compelling evidence comes from studies of behavioral genetics.

As noted in Chapter 3, one important technique for studying the inheritance of human characteristics compares the resemblance of identical (monozygotic) and fraternal (dizygotic) twins. In the case of a continuous characteristic like IQ, we defined resemblance in terms of the correlation between twins' IQ scores. However, schizophrenia is considered discontinuous—a person is either schizophrenic or not. *Resemblance* is then defined as the **concordance rate,** the percentage of twins (or other pairs) that share the same trait. If two twins are schizophrenic, they are said to be concordant for that trait; if one twin is schizophrenic and the other is not, they are discordant.

Perhaps the most difficult part of conducting a twin study of the genetics of schizophrenia is finding a large enough number of schizophrenic twins to participate. In one classic study, Gottesman and Shields (1972) reviewed the history of every patient treated at two London mental hospitals between 1948 and 1964—a total of over 45,000 people. They found 57 schizophrenics who had a twin who could be located and agreed to participate in the study.

Given the controversy over the clinical diagnosis of schizophrenia, these researchers considered several definitions of schizophrenia. The strictest and most straightforward demanded that a person had been hospitalized and diagnosed as schizophrenic. By this conservative criterion, the concordance rate for monozygotic twins was 42%; for dizygotic twins, 9%. Although the mathematical details need not concern us here, this dramatic difference suggests that schizophrenia is highly heritable.

This conclusion is quite consistent with results from the other 10 major twin studies of schizophrenia (Rosenthal, 1971). Although precise concordance rates vary from one sample to the next, depending in part on the definition of schizophrenia, monozygotic twins consistently had a higher concordance rate than dizygotic twins, and the monozygotic concordance rate was always less than 100%.

This last point has important implications. If schizophrenia were entirely determined by genetics, two people with the same genes—such as monozygotic twins—would always be concordant for this trait. It is apparent from these studies that what one inherits is not the disease itself but rather a susceptibility or a predisposition to become schizophrenic.

Skeptics may ask whether the environments of monozygotic twins are more identical and whether this could account for the consistency. As in other areas of behavioral genetics, one answer could come from monozygotic twins who were separated at birth. In 10 of the 16 such cases reported to date, both twins were schizophrenic (a concordance rate of 62.5%).

Given the fact that this study and many others indicate that genetic predispositions do indeed play a role in the development of schizophrenia, one of the most interesting questions for future research is this: Why do some children of schizophrenic parents become schizophrenic themselves, while others do not?

Children at Risk. One way to discover why only some children of schizophrenics develop later problems would be to interview adults who were raised by schizophrenic parents. But we know that human memory often reconstructs the past to fit present beliefs (see Chapter 6) and that people are often unaware of the forces that motivate their behavior (see Chapters 1, 10, and 11). One partial solution is a longitudinal follow-up of a large group of people with a high risk of becoming schizophrenic. Although such studies are expensive and take decades to complete, this research design potentially offers so much insight that several studies of this sort are now in progress.

The first and most famous longitudinal study of the high-risk children of schizophrenic parents is still in progress; it was begun by Sarnoff Mednick and Fini Schulsinger in 1962. Around 1960, Mednick had been forced to cancel a similar study of Michigan mental patients when he found that as many as half of his subjects moved every year, making it extremely difficult to test this group repeatedly over several decades. The combination of excellent psychiatric records, low mobility, and a small geographical area made Denmark a more promising place for this type of research.

Mednick and Schulsinger began by identifying women who were hospitalized as process schizophrenics who had children between the ages of 10 and 18. Social workers then went to the homes in which these youngsters were living and enlisted the cooperation of 207 children of schizophrenic mothers for a study of the "effects of a nervous breakdown." Another 104 children—whose parents and grandparents had no psychiatric history—were also recruited as the control group. They were carefully matched on such variables as sex, age, social class, and the number of years spent in foster homes. Extensive interviews, physiological tests, and psychological tests have been conducted with each subject at regular intervals since 1962 (Mednick, 1966).

The high-risk children have indeed had more problems as they grew up. By 1974, 8 of the high-risk children had died of suicide, accidents, or other causes; all of the control group were still alive. More important, 15 of the high-risk group were themselves diagnosed as schizophrenic, versus only 1 member of the control group. An additional 55 from the high-risk group were diagnosed as suffering from milder "borderline" schizophrenic deficits; only 4 from the control group fell into this category. Similar differences were seen for other forms of psychopathology (Schulsinger, 1976).

Analyses are still continuing to identify variables that predicted the adjustment of specific groups. For example, one report (Mednick, 1970) compared two subgroups of the high-risk children—those who were disturbed as adolescents and those who were better adjusted. Interestingly, those who became disturbed in the teenage years were more likely to have had medical problems when they were born. These complications included prematurity, long labor, and a variety of other problems that may have deprived their brains of an adequate oxygen supply at birth.

It will probably be several decades before this study is complete. The continuing follow-up of this group—and others like it—may help to identify factors that cause a child with a genetic predisposition to schizophrenia actually to become schizophrenic. Perhaps the clinical psychology of the future will include preventive therapy, with specific steps that a parent can take to decrease the likelihood that a child will develop schizophrenia or other mental disorders.

Summary

1. Abnormal behavior may be defined according to four different approaches: statistical definitions, violations of cultural norms, deviations from ideal mental health, and failure to function adequately. Each approach has certain advantages and disadvantages; none is adequate by itself.

2. According to the **medical model,** abnormal behavior is caused by physical disease. This has proved useful in understanding some disorders, such as general paresis, but does not seem adequate to account for all types of abnormal behavior.

3. The leading classification scheme for abnormal behavior is called **DSM-III** (the *Diagnostic and Statistical Manual,* third edition, approved by the American Psychiatric Association in 1980). DSM-III was designed to improve psychiatric diagnosis in terms of reliability and validity.

4. A **personality disorder** is an inflexible behavior pattern or enduring personality trait that significantly interferes with a person's occupation or social life or causes personal distress. One example is **narcissistic personality disorder,** which involves a grandiose sense of uniqueness and self-importance.

5. In an **anxiety disorder,** severe anxiety interferes with the normal ability to function in everyday life. For example, a **phobia** is a persistent and irrational fear of a specific object, activity, or situation. One common type, called *agoraphobia,* involves a fear of public places that often leads a person to restrict activities to the point of being afraid to leave home.

6. According to psychoanalysts, a phobia involves the displacement of unacceptable id impulses onto a neutral object. Social-learning theorists see phobias as fears that are learned by classical conditioning and observational learning.

7. **Affective disorders** involve a prolonged and fundamental disturbance of mood and emotion. They involve either **depression**—a loss of pleasure in everyday activities associated with such symptoms as disturbances in eating or sleeping and decreased energy—or **mania**—a feeling of euphoria associated with such symptoms as loud and rapid speech, inflated self-esteem, and hyperactivity. Episodes of depression alternate with mania in **bipolar disorder** or appear alone as **major depression.**

8. Psychiatrist Aaron Beck proposed a **cognitive theory** that depression is caused by logical errors of thought that produce self-blame. A social-learning theory

holds that depression is caused by **learned helplessness**—a belief based on experience that a person lacks control over his life or situation. According to one biological theory, when brain levels of the neurotransmitter norepinephrine are too low, depression occurs; when they are too high, mania is the result.

9. The term **schizophrenic disorder** refers to serious disturbances of thought, emotion, and perception that persist for at least six months before the age of 45 in people who have deteriorated from a previous, more adequate level of function. There is a great deal of controversy over the precise definition of **schizophrenia,** but roughly 1 out of every 100 people in the world is schizophrenic. There is an important distinction between *process schizophrenics*—who have a history of poor adjustment and a poor prognosis—and *reactive schizophrenics*—who have a more rapid onset of severe symptoms and a greater likelihood of recovery.

10. The major symptoms of schizophrenia include disorders of the *form* of thought, such as *loose associations*—ideas shifting quickly from one idea to another—and disorders in the *content* of thought, such as *delusions*—false beliefs, typically about being persecuted. Also prominent are disorders of perception, such as auditory hallucinations, and disorders of emotion, such as *flattened or inappropriate affect*. Other symptoms include ambivalence and disturbances of motor activity.

11. Studies of identical versus fraternal twins strongly suggest that a predisposition to develop schizophrenia is inherited. Studies of high-risk children born to schizophrenic mothers are now trying to identify specific factors that cause a schizophrenic breakdown.

To Learn More

Vonnegut, M. *The Eden Express*. New York: Praeger, 1975. A young man's account of his own schizophrenic breakdown; excellent source on what psychosis "feels like."

American Psychiatric Association. *Diagnostic and Statistical Manual of Mental Disorders* (3d ed.). Washington, D.C.: American Psychiatric Association, 1980. Also known as DSM-III; the official list of disorders and diagnostic signs.

Davison, G. C., & Neale, J. M. *Abnormal Psychology* (3d ed.). New York: John Wiley, 1982. An excellent textbook summary; particularly strong on empirical research regarding each disorder.

14
Treating Abnormal Behavior

study

A brief history of treatment
The rise and fall of moral therapy
The growth of the helping professions

Psychotherapy
Psychoanalytic therapy
Behavior therapy
Cognitive therapy
Humanistic therapy
An eclectic approach
Is psychotherapy effective?

Biological therapies
Electroconvulsive therapy
Drug therapy

Community psychology
Mental-health services in local communities
Paraprofessionals
Prevention

Summary

HOW DO THEY KNOW?
Double-blind studies: Testing drugs to treat schizophrenia

BECOMING A CRITICAL CONSUMER
Would you believe reincarnation therapy?

On June 23, 1900, Clifford Beers tried to kill himself. Six years earlier, while attending college at Yale, Beers had become obsessed with the idea that he would be disabled by epilepsy, as his older brother had been. This fear remained secret until, filled with despair, he jumped from a fourth-story window at his home. However, instead of being killed on the concrete pavement 30 feet below, he landed feet first on a small patch of soft earth a few inches away.

Beers was rushed to a hospital, where he began to experience delusions of being persecuted. The hospital became a prison, and the hot bandages applied to his feet became tortures designed to elicit confessions for unknown crimes. Voices inside his head accused him vaguely. Then, suddenly, Beers felt he was trapped on an ocean liner that was sinking because he had accidentally left a porthole open.

These hideous delusions continued after he was sent home. Beers was convinced that he was under surveillance, surrounded by sinister actors who played the parts of his relatives. His family reluctantly decided to send him to a private mental asylum, beginning a journey through several institutions that was later chronicled in his autobiography *A Mind That Found Itself* (Beers, 1908).

For the next two years, Beers remained haunted by delusions and profoundly depressed. Except for an occasional curse or complaint, he never spoke a word. The medical staff ignored Beers, save for an occasional crude attempt to force him to speak. For example, one doctor tried to force Beers to speak by pulling him out of bed and requiring him to stand on his injured feet. This cruelly incompetent "therapy" had no effect. In a second institution, for more than a year Beers's only interaction with a mental-health professional was an occasional "Good morning" from the doctor. The staff saw that he ate three times a day, bathed regularly, and exercised by walking around the grounds in a column of men "which greatly resembled a 'chain gang.'" Meanwhile, Beers silently plotted ways to kill himself when imaginary detectives would come to take him to court for crimes he had not committed.

Ever so slowly, the patient emerged from his depression. But the pendulum swung too far, and Beers suddenly became manic and overexcited. Delusions of persecution were replaced by grandiose schemes. Beers interpreted several trifling incidents as signs that God wanted him to reform the mental-health system. He slept only two or three hours a night and wrote rambling letters on strips of manila wrapping paper 20 or 30 feet long. Then he decided to investigate rumors of serious abuse on the wards reserved for violent patients by having himself transferred there.

Beers's wish was granted after he physically assaulted an attendant. He found himself locked in a small room where the only furniture was a bed screwed to the floor. Lacking paper, he wrote long messages on the walls with a lead pencil he had hidden in his clothes and sharpened with his teeth. Frustrated by the imprisonment, he used a shoe to break a glass bulb suspended from the 12-foot ceiling. Two attendants rushed into the room, threw Beers on the bed, and "choked me so severely that I could feel my eyes starting from their sockets." After several additional incidents, Beers was tied in a straitjacket that the physician vindictively tightened until "within one hour . . . I was suffering pain as intense as any I ever endured." Although he screamed, moaned, and cried, the jacket was not loosened to make him more comfortable until the next morning, 12 hours later.

Clifford Beers (1876—1943) suffered from mental illness as a young man and was hospitalized for several years. In *A Mind That Found Itself*, he provided a vivid account of living conditions in U.S. mental institutions around the turn of the century.

Beers was moved to a small cell with little ventilation, padded walls, and only a filthy mattress on the floor. The room was often so cold he could see his breath. For three weeks, Beers was held in this room, tied into his straitjacket for about half of each day. At night, he was not even able to arrange the blankets over his body because his arms were tied.

These brutalizing experiences continued after he was transferred to another mental hospital. But, despite the incompetent actions of the staff, Beers gradually recovered. In September, 1903, he was released from the hospital. What had begun as a scheme conceived in mania gradually developed into his life work as Beers began a campaign for mental-health reform. Clifford Beers's influential autobiography, upon which this account was based, was published in 1908. In 1909, Beers formed the National Committee for Mental Hygiene to raise the standard of care for mental patients and promote research on mental illness. By the time he died in 1943, the mental hygiene movement had helped improve psychiatric treatment around the world (Deutsch, 1949).

For the contemporary reader, *A Mind That Found Itself* provides fascinating insights into mental-health care, or the lack of it, in America at the turn of the century. Brutality was not uncommon, and insensitivity and incompetence were everywhere. Patients were perceived as helpless victims of a natural disease process; the institution's role was merely to keep the patient from harming himself or others for as long as he remained ill.

It is hard to predict exactly how a contemporary Clifford Beers would fare if he had similar manic and depressive episodes in the 1980s. Unfortunately, even today the adequacy of care varies from one institution to the next, partly because of inadequate funding at some facilities. However, the hospital stay of today's patient would surely be shorter and of a far different character.

The most obvious difference in contemporary psychiatry is the widespread use of drugs that reduce psychotic symptoms. For example, in the 1980s, Beers would probably be given carefully regulated doses of the natural salt lithium carbonate to calm his manic symptoms. While today's psychiatric drugs do not cure mental illness as effectively as antibiotics can kill some infections, they do substantially relieve the behavior, thoughts, and feelings associated with mental illness.

If Beers did have to remain hospitalized for an extended period, today's institutions would have proved far more pleasant; the sort of brutality Beers encountered is now extremely rare. One of the three asylums to which Beers was committed was "considered one of the best of its kind in the country" (Beers, 1908, p. 68). A comparable institution today would probably have numerous classes, therapy sessions, and rehabilitation activities designed to encourage patients to take responsibility for their own actions and prepare for the transition back to normal life.

Thus, mental patients are considerably better off today than they once were. To appreciate just how much better off, one must go back in history, beyond the experiences of Clifford Beers at the beginning of the twentieth century, to consider the treatment of abnormal behavior throughout recorded history.

A Brief History of Treatment

In ancient times, madness was often attributed to possession by evil spirits. Many treatments of mental illness therefore involved superstitious practices designed to drive the devils out of the body. One medieval English text suggested the following cure: "In case a man be lunatic, take a skin of a [porpoise], work it into a whip, and [whip] the man therewith; soon he will be well. Amen." (Zilboorg & Henry, 1941, p. 140). Other religious treatments were less painful; Christian monks established humane asylums for the care of the mentally ill as early as the sixth century A.D.

THE RISE AND FALL OF MORAL THERAPY

Unfortunately, history has recorded numerous cases of abuse of the mentally ill. In 1547, King Henry VIII decreed that Bethlehem Hospital in London should be entirely devoted to the confinement of the mentally ill. But this institution provided no treatment; "lunatics" were simply placed in cells that lacked heat, light, and sanitation. Some of these unfortunate individuals were chained in dungeons, whipped, beaten, and ridiculed. Medical therapy was simple and the same for everyone: "Bleeding of all patients in April, purges and 'vomits' of surviving patients in May, and once again bleeding all patients in October" (Reisman, 1966, p. 10).

The popular name of this famous institution was Bedlam, which was adopted into English to refer to a place of uproar and confusion. In the eighteenth century, Bedlam was one of the most popular tourist attractions in the city of London. While the visitor to the Tower of London or Westminster Abbey saw only historic sites, presumably at Bedlam one could watch real live lunatics act crazy and strain against their chains.

Hogarth's painting "The Madhouse" shows two upper-class ladies touring Bedlam.

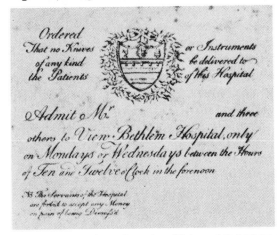

A ticket for an eighteenth-century (?) tour of Bethlehem Hospital.

The center photograph shows the Fools' Tower in Vienna in the nineteenth century. All the surrounding devices were used in the "treatment" of the mentally ill during this period. The enormous machine in the middle of the top row was used to swing lunatics until they quieted down. Troublesome inmates were also sometimes locked inside the "English coffin" at the left in the second row, and the huge wheel in the third row.

A more humane approach to treatment was favored by Philippe Pinel, a French physician who argued that mental patients were human beings who were entitled to compassion and dignity. In 1793, in the midst of the French Revolution, Pinel was placed in charge of a large mental asylum in Paris called La Bicêtre. His first official act was to order the chains removed from a small number of patients.

In some cases, the effects were quite dramatic. One man had been locked in chains 10 years earlier after taking part in a drunken brawl. Pinel approached this "lunatic" and said "give me your hand, you are a reasonable man, and if you behave well I shall take you in my employment." (Zilboorg & Henry, 1941, p. 323). The man became calm, even docile, and was later hired as Pinel's bodyguard. The favor was returned when this patient saved Pinel from a mob that wanted to lynch him for suspected anti-Revolutionary acts.

Encouraged by his success, Pinel experimented with a number of reforms. Sunny rooms replaced dungeons, and patients were permitted to wander around the grounds and exercise regularly. Staff members spent many hours talking to patients about their problems, offering both comfort and advice. Under these more positive conditions, some patients recovered and were released; others became calmer and easier to deal with. In addition, Pinel kept notes about his conversations with patients and his observations of their behavior. These were the first systematic case histories of mental patients.

Pinel's work helped to establish **moral therapy,** the treatment of mental dis-

Roger Viollet's painting of Pinel releasing the mentally ill from their chains at La Salpêtrière, a hospital he supervised after his work at La Bicêtre.

Dorothea Dix (1802–1877) crusaded for the rights of the mentally ill in the United States, Canada, and Scotland. She worked as a Boston schoolteacher, but tuberculosis forced her to retire at the age of 39. Dix then took a job teaching Sunday school to female prisoners and became aware of the gruesome conditions in many primitive institutions. She then began to tour prisons, asylums, and poorhouses to collect evidence regarding mistreatment of the insane. Her campaign led directly to the founding of 32 mental hospitals and helped establish public awareness of the problems of the mentally ill.

orders by kindness, understanding, and a pleasant environment. Moral therapy was practiced widely in European and American mental institutions early in the nineteenth century; current evidence suggests that it helped many patients to achieve more adequate adjustment (Bockhoven, 1963).

In the United States, one of the leading figures in the movement for a humane approach to mental illness was a New England schoolteacher named Dorothea Dix. Dix documented and publicized many cases of disturbed individuals who had been abused, such as Abram Simmons, a man who was imprisoned in an 8-square-foot vault for several years in a small Rhode Island town. No light or fresh air could make its way into this stone prison; in the winter, its walls were covered with half an inch of frost. Her campaign led to greater public awareness of mistreatment of the mentally ill and the establishment of many state-supported mental hospitals.

Ironically, the very success of Dorothea Dix's movement helped lead to the decline of moral therapy. When large state hospitals were built in secluded areas, mental patients were segregated from society. According to United States Census figures, the number of insane patients in hospitals and asylums rose from 2,561 in 1840 to 74,028 in 1890. (This rate of growth was about 8 times faster than the increase in the general population.) The rapid rise in the number of mental patients led to overcrowding and chaotic conditions in many hospitals; the personal attention demanded by moral therapy was no longer possible. Asylums once more assumed a custodial role, simply caring for the physical needs of those who could not care for themselves.

THE GROWTH OF THE HELPING PROFESSIONS

Traditionally, the care of the mentally ill was supervised by physicians. However, **psychiatry**—the medical specialty concerned with mental illness—was often learned by trial and error. Before the second half of the nineteenth century, medical schools barely mentioned mental illness in their formal training.

In 1844, a group of 13 physicians formed the Association of Medical Superintendents of American Institutions for the Insane, which was renamed the American Psychiatric Association in 1921. The 13 original members quickly formed themselves into 16 committees to study such issues as moral treatment, the restraint of patients, the prevention of suicide, and the construction of mental hospitals. Throughout the nineteenth century, practical issues regarding the administration of overcrowded and underfinanced asylums often seemed more pressing than theoretical questions regarding the causes and cures of insanity. Further, psychiatry was practiced almost exclusively within the walls of mental asylums (Deutsch, 1949).

All this began to change after a Viennese neurologist named Sigmund Freud introduced a number of new techniques for treating emotional illness (see Chapter 11). In the early 1900s, psychiatrists began to work in clinics and private practices to treat a wide range of mental and behavioral problems.

Other professional groups also became involved in mental-health services during this period. Of greatest interest to us here is the field of **clinical psychology**— the application of psychological principles and research to the understanding and treatment of mental illness. Although pioneer work in this field began around 1900, the profession grew slowly before World War II. The psychologists who did specialize in clinical practice during this period were employed primarily to administer tests of personality and intelligence rather than as psychotherapists, and before 1947 there was not one single training program that granted degrees specifically in clinical psychology.

The manpower demands of World War II forced many psychologists to develop clinical skills. About 1 out of every 4 American psychologists served in the military. In 1944 alone, they administered 60 million psychological tests to 20 million soldiers and civilians. In addition, many psychologists were required to perform therapy with patients for the first time (Garfield, 1965).

In 1946, the Veterans Administration provided extensive financial support for the training of new clinical psychologists to help care for the 40,000 men who were patients in neuropsychiatric VA hospitals. From this point, the profession grew rapidly. Twenty-two graduate programs in clinical psychology were established in 1947 to meet the demands of the Veterans Administration, and by 1983 the number of programs approved by the American Psychological Association had grown to 117.

Other new specialties gained in influence during this period, notably **counseling psychology,** a specialty closely related to clinical psychology that emphasizes problems in normal adjustment, such as marriage or school counseling, rather than abnormal function.

Table 14.1 summarizes the major professional groups that currently work in mental-health settings. In actual practice, the lines between the roles of these specialties are often blurred. It is easy to separate a psychiatrist from a clinical psychologist or a psychiatric social worker on the basis of training, but all three may perform similar tasks in a particular mental-health setting.

The growth of these professions in the United States reflected fundamental changes in society's perception of the nature of mental health and government's role in fostering it. In 1854, President Franklin Pierce vetoed a bill sponsored by Dorothea Dix for federal support of a mental hospital; Pierce claimed that the federal government should not be concerned with the life conditions of individuals. In contrast, in 1963, President John Kennedy signed the Community Mental Health Centers Act, which provided massive financial support to achieve two goals: the treatment of severe mental illness within the community and the prevention of future mental illness.

The fact that so many young men had been rejected from military service in World War II because of psychiatric problems had helped make the country more aware of the widespread prevalence of mental disorders. Then, in the early 1950s, psychiatry discovered several new drugs that treated psychotic behavior and thought disorders, resulting in the release of thousands of patients from mental institutions. This, in turn, created a new need for continuing programs and more trained professionals to help these individuals adjust to life within the community.

Thus, a century ago psychiatry was primarily concerned with caring for ex-

TABLE 14.1
Major Groups of Mental Health Professionals

	Typical Training	*Typical Clinical Tasks*
Psychiatrists	4 years of college 4 years of medical school (MD degree) 3 or 4 years of internship and psychiatric residency	Diagnosing and assessing abnormal behavior; providing psychotherapy; giving medical treatment and prescribing drugs
Clinical psychologists	4 years of college 4 to 6 years of graduate study of psychology (PhD or PsyD degree)	Diagnosing and assessing abnormal behavior; providing psychotherapy
Counseling psychologists	4 years of college 4 to 6 years of graduate study of counseling (PhD or EdD degree)	Providing counseling and psychotherapy for normal problems of adjustment, such as marital problems and vocational guidance
Psychiatric social workers	4 years of college 2 years of graduate study of social work (MSW degree)	Assessing social needs of psychiatric patients (work, education, etc.); providing psychotherapy
Psychiatric nurses	4 years of college (BS in nursing) 2 years of graduate study of psychiatric nursing (MA degree)	Supervising daily care of hospitalized psychiatric patients; providing psychotherapy
Paraprofessionals	Limited short-term training; college degree not necessarily required	Performing specific tasks, such as telephone counseling for suicide prevention or direct care of psychiatric patients

tremely disturbed individuals. Today, psychiatry, psychology, and related professions play a much larger role in society, providing therapy and counseling for a wide range of problems in living. In 1957, a survey of a representative sample of the United States revealed that about 3 out of every 10 people had sought help at some time from mental-health professionals; by 1976, this number had grown to nearly 6 out of every 10 (Veroff, Kulka, & Douvan, 1981). The most common and most important treatment offered to these many people was some form of counseling or psychotherapy.

Psychotherapy

People have probably sought advice from one another ever since they first started living in groups. But psychotherapy involves more than just a casual conversation between two friends or the advice a bartender gives to a regular customer. In **psychotherapy,** a trained professional employs systematic psychological procedures to help a client change troublesome thoughts, feelings, and behavior patterns.

The actual systematic procedures may vary from therapist to therapist and from client to client. Some psychotherapeutic techniques have been employed with hundreds of thousands of patients over many years. Others are relatively new, relatively untested, and sometimes even faddish.

In this short overview, it would not be useful to try to list all the many variations of psychotherapeutic technique. Instead, we focus on four theoretical paradigms in psychology (originally described in Chapter 1) to see how each has led to the development of different techniques for treating abnormal behavior: psychoanalytic, behavioral, cognitive, and humanistic. The biological approach, the fifth and final theoretical orientation described in Chapter 1, is examined separately because techniques like psychosurgery and drug therapy are not forms of psychotherapy.

PSYCHOANALYTIC THERAPY

The first patient to undergo psychotherapy might have been Anna O., a young woman whose emotional conflicts produced a variety of physical symptoms (see Chapter 11). In treating this patient, Josef Breuer laid the groundwork for the "talking cure"; when Anna talked about the roots of her psychological problems, her physical symptoms began to disappear. Starting from this observation, Sigmund Freud went on to develop the theory of psychoanalysis.

Freudian Analysis. As explained earlier, Freud believed that anxiety, neurosis, and other adult personality patterns are determined by unconscious conflicts regarding biological instincts and that early childhood experiences are particularly influential in establishing lifelong patterns of behavior.

For Freud, the treatment of inappropriate behavior patterns is based on the therapeutic power of **insight.** Once the unconscious forces that motivate behavior are consciously understood, a person can deal with reality more effectively. Insight is not simply an intellectual process; it also involves reliving intense emotional experiences. Repressed thoughts and feelings do not emerge suddenly to produce dramatic cures. Instead, psychoanalysis involves a long and repetitious process of seeing that the same underlying themes can account for behavior in many different situations. Gradually, over a period of years, the patient learns to face reality and deal with it effectively rather than unconsciously deny and distort it.

The most important therapeutic technique used throughout this long process is **free association,** in which the patient relaxes and reports every single thought as it comes to mind. Under ordinary conditions, the ego acts as a kind of editor, preventing threatening unconscious impulses from becoming conscious. In free association, the idea is to circumvent this unconscious editing by reporting every single thought, no matter how trivial or indiscreet it might seem. Indeed, Freud (1913) specifically instructed his own patients as follows:

> You will be tempted to say to yourself that this [thought] or that is irrelevant here, or is quite unimportant, or nonsensical, so that there is no need to say it. You must never give in to these criticisms, but must say it in spite of them—indeed, you must say it precisely because you have an aversion to doing so (p. 135).

Since Freud believed that restraints on the unconscious are loosened during sleep, patients in analysis are also encouraged to report their dreams. Unconscious conflicts may be revealed in symbolic form in dreams, as in the case of Freud's own dream about his father's funeral (see Chapter 11).

Any aversion or reluctance to discuss a particular dream could be a sign of **resistance,** an unconscious attempt to avoid therapeutic insights into motivation. Similarly, when a patient refuses to free-associate, it may mean that she is being defensive about important conflicts. In the same way, a patient who is habitually late for therapy, or who misses an appointment, or who refuses to pay her bill is seen as resisting the entire psychoanalytic enterprise because it may uncover threatening thoughts and feelings that have long been hidden in the unconscious mind.

As therapy progresses, the patient's relationship with the therapist becomes an important therapeutic tool and sign of progress. The term **transference** refers to some of the patient's strong positive or negative feelings toward the therapist. Freud defined this term very precisely to refer only to a repetition of emotions originally directed toward parent figures during the Oedipal period (see Chapter 11). The course of psychoanalysis expresses themes determined in childhood: A woman who hated her father may transfer these feelings to the analyst and come to hate him.

The therapist can help the patient to understand these and other reactions through **interpretation,** in which the analyst gradually guides the patient to an understanding of his thoughts and behavior. For example, if a patient becomes very angry at the analyst, he may ask whether the patient wishes he could direct this anger at his own father. Such interpretations are most likely to help only when the patient is ready for this insight; premature interpretation merely produces resistance, and the patient will deny the connection, often quite vehemently.

This is one reason why Freud believed that psychoanalysis was a long and gradual process; years of intensive therapy could be required to overcome the defenses a patient had built up. In classical Freudian analysis, the patient could expect to

Sigmund Freud's office and the first psychoanalytic couch.

continue psychotherapy two to five times each week for several years. Throughout this period, the analyst's role was passive. At each session, the patient would lie on a couch and free-associate and report his dreams for about an hour. The analyst typically sat behind the patient, to avoid giving unintentional nonverbal cues, such as nodding in encouragement or frowning at a particular theme. Interpretations were offered only when the patient appeared ready for them.

A Case History.   To get a more concrete feeling for the process of psychoanalysis, consider the case of Jim, a 37-year-old unemployed and unmarried man who came to a psychotherapist for vocational counseling. Even in the first session, "the analyst listened, doing little talking, prompting him with short, open-ended sentences" (Fine, 1973, p. 26). The analyst suggested that Jim's problems were deep-seated and that he should undergo psychoanalysis. At first Jim objected strongly, claiming that he had no serious problems. This resistance gradually lessened, and Jim agreed to come twice a week for a two-month trial period.

As Jim free-associated, it gradually became clear that he had a long history of aimlessness, drifting from job to job and dropping out from one college after another without ever completing his degree. Jim was also rather withdrawn socially; his first sexual relationship came at the age of 27 in a single homosexual experience with an older man. At the time he entered therapy, Jim's only interests in life were masturbating and going to the movies.

At this point the analyst called attention to the discrepancy between Jim's limited forms of amusement and his claim that he had no serious problems. Jim agreed that this was a type of resistance and began to seek the root of his problems. He gradually focused on his lifelong battles with his dominating mother. Jim's mother had constantly criticized him in childhood and sometimes had beaten him severely. He fought back by withdrawing; one of the "greatest victories" of his childhood was learning not to cry when his mother beat him with a strap. Early in therapy, Jim transferred this resentment to the therapist and threatened to withdraw from therapy whenever he disliked a particular interpretation.

When Jim achieved the insight that withdrawal was a lifelong pattern based on early experiences with his mother, he began to change. He gradually saw a pattern in his adult relationships of rejecting women to gain revenge on the female sex and his mother. Over the course of two years of intensive psychoanalysis, he slowly developed a healthy relationship with a woman he had known for years. He married the woman and successfully terminated pyschotherapy.

Contemporary Analysis. As noted in Chapter 11, among psychoanalysts who later revised Freud's theory, the most influential group were the *ego psychologists*, who emphasized the autonomy of the ego and its reality-based processes. Erikson, Jung, Adler, and others proposed a number of changes in Freud's classical analytic technique.

Freud's therapy had been designed to bring unconscious material into consciousness so that repressed conflicts could be resolved. Later forms of analytic therapy were developed with a somewhat different goal in mind: to promote the development and functioning of the ego in all areas of life (Kutash, 1983). The classical techniques devised to reveal unconscious conflicts—free association and dream analysis—play a less central role in contemporary analysis. Contemporary analysts also devote a great deal of attention to the way personality may be shaped by the external environment as well as internal conflicts.

On a practical basis, one of the most important sets of changes in psychoanalytic therapy is the attempt to make it more efficient. Few waitresses or college professors could afford to spend the time or money for years of classical psychoanalysis; it was generally limited to a wealthy minority. Many modifications have therefore been proposed to speed up the process.

While classical analysts often insisted on four or five therapy sessions each week, the contemporary analyst is more flexible in fitting the schedule to a patient's needs and abilities. In classical analysis, the patient typically lay on a couch while the therapist remained out of sight and the lights were dimmed to promote concentration on the inner chain of free associations. In contemporary analysis, patient and analyst sit face to face and carry on a more normal conversation. Freud believed that interpretation could not begin until transference was established; contemporary analysts argue that some types of interpretation are useful even at first analytic sessions. Thus, the contemporary analyst actively intervenes to direct discussion along the most productive path rather than wait passively for insight to occur at its own pace.

These and other changes in technique are related to changes in the psychoanalytic-patient population. Classical analysis was often limited to neurotic patients; in contemporary terminology, patients with anxiety disorders and somatoform disorders were thought to be most likely to benefit. Contemporary analysis can serve a far wider range of problems, including narcissistic and other personality disorders (see Chapter 13).

According to one recent survey of clinical psychologists, Freudian and contemporary analytic techniques are still among the most widely practiced forms of psychotherapy. However, between 1961 and 1982 the proportion who identified themselves as psychoanalysts had dropped from 41% to 14% (Smith, 1982). Much of this decline could be attributed to the growth of an alternative set of approaches known as behavior therapy.

BEHAVIOR THERAPY

In Chapter 5, we defined **behavior therapy** (or behavior modification) as a type of psychotherapy that applies scientific principles to alter observable behaviors through learning. Chapter 5 also described several basic principles of the behavioral approach: Focus on observable behaviors; identify the variables that control a problem behavior in the present; manipulate these relevant variables; and measure the behavioral effects of any intervention.

The roots of the behavioral approach are as old as mankind. Even the Old Testament includes many examples, beginning with Adam and Eve's punishment for eating the forbidden fruit. But large-scale, systematic study of behavior therapy began only around 1960.

The two types of behavior therapy described in Chapter 5—token economies and the reduction of self-destructive behavior through punishment—were straightforward applications of operant conditioning. As behavior therapy has grown in influence, it has increasingly come to recognize the importance of internal cognitive factors and observational learning. The two techniques described here—systematic desensitization to reduce fear and self-control procedures for altering one's own behavior—both recognize the way internal thoughts and feelings can influence external behavior.

Systematic Desensitization.   **Systematic desensitization** is a form of behavior therapy that reduces fear by requiring an anxious person to imagine increasingly threatening situations while remaining deeply relaxed. The therapy involves three steps: relaxation training, developing an anxiety hierarchy, and the actual desensitization. The first step is probably the simplest; as noted in Chapter 3, there are a number of forms of meditation and training that can help people to learn systematically to relax. Many therapists use a technique called progressive muscle relaxation (Jacobson, 1938) in which various muscles in the arms, in the legs, and throughout the body are tensed and then relaxed.

The second step involves constructing an **anxiety hierarchy,** a list of situations that provoke fear for that person, organized from the least threatening to the most threatening. Each anxiety hierarchy is based on some theme that evokes fear, such as traveling, giving a speech, or failing at work. Table 14.2 lists an actual anxiety hierarchy constructed in behavior therapy for a client who had an excessive fear of being criticized. Note that the order of these situations reflects this particular person's fears; another individual might place similar events in a different order.

In the actual desensitization, the client imagines each item on the list, beginning with the least threatening situation, while trying to remain relaxed. For example, after practice imagining the first item on her list, this young woman was able to think about her mother criticizing her for not sending a thank-you note without feeling anxious. Training proceeded until she could feel relaxed while imagining any of the 13 situations in the anxiety hierarchy. This learning generalized to everyday life, and her fears about criticism were reduced. For this client, training on a separate anxiety hierarchy regarding fears of travel was even more successful; after several months of therapy she bought a car, drove freely around the city, and even went on a long vacation with friends.

According to Joseph Wolpe (1958), the therapist who developed this procedure, systematic desensitization involves a process of **counterconditioning,** in which relaxation becomes classically conditioned to the same stimuli that once elicited anxiety; because the states of relaxation and fear are physiologically incompatible, through repeated practice relaxation can take the place of fear. While others disagree

---

TABLE 14.2
An Anxiety Hierarchy

In behavior therapy, a 23-year-old nurse who suffered from extreme anxiety constructed this list of situations that evoked fear. They all refer to a common theme regarding fear of criticism and are arranged from the least threatening stimulus to the most threatening.

1. Your mother reminds you that you have not yet sent a thank-you letter to a relative from whom you received a gift.
2. Your uncle wonders out loud why you don't visit him more often.
3. Your mother notes that you haven't been to church with her in quite a while.
4. Your mother comments that it has been a long time since you have visited your grandmother.
5. Your mother criticizes a friend: She just makes herself at home!
6. Your stepfather says that he can't understand how anyone could be so stupid as to be a Catholic.
7. You return an overdue book to the library; the librarian looks at you critically.
8. A physician making rounds discovers a baby in convulsions. He comments to a colleague: "You see what I mean about having to make rounds."
9. Bill [her fiancé] looks over your shoulder as you are writing, and comments that it doesn't look very neat.
10. Bill comments that you are too heavy in the waist and should exercise.
11. Bill criticizes you for being quiet on a double date.
12. You are at a party given by one of Bill's friends. You mispronounce a word and Bill corrects you.
13. Your mother comes into a room and finds you smoking.

Source: P. J. Lang. "Behavior therapy with a case of nervous anorexia." In L. P. Ullman & L. Krasner (Eds.), *Case Studies in Behavior Modification.* New York: Holt, 1965, p. 217.

about the underlying process, there is a large body of evidence that systematic desensitization is an effective way to change a wide range of behaviors, from snake and insect phobias to lack of assertiveness and anxiety about dating (Rimm & Masters, 1979).

Self-control.   Behavior therapy techniques for **self-control** provide clients with active coping strategies to deal with specific problems. While the person who undergoes systematic desensitization learns new behaviors rather passively, self-control programs require very active commitment and participation on the patient's part. Indeed, in some cases, one might be able to develop a self-control program with little or no help from a therapist by following behavioral principles regarding self-control.

For example, Williams and Long (1983) described a model for self-control that consists of six steps:

1.   Select a goal.
2.   Monitor target behaviors.
3.   Alter setting events.
4.   Establish effective consequences.
5.   Focus on contingencies.
6.   Use covert control.

Williams and Long's book outlines the most important elements for each step and shows how the model can be applied to such problems as losing weight, quitting smoking, developing athletic skills, or managing anxiety.

For example, Williams and Long (1983) described a model for self-control that
Let us consider one example. A student who wanted to improve her study habits would start by selecting a concrete and achievable goal; a college student who had not cracked a book since *Winnie the Pooh* might start with a modest goal, such as studying for 15 minutes every afternoon. The second step consists of monitoring the target behavior—in this case, studying—for some reasonable period of time. Detailed records could include the starting time, finishing time, place, and emotional state on each study occasion for a week. Baseline estimates of this sort are often surprising; many people have misconceptions about their own habits. These techniques are examples of the first principle of behavior therapy: Focus clearly on concrete, observable behaviors.

Setting events are the types of situations that promote or interfere with the target behavior. Detailed records may reveal that in the library you spend all your time people-watching but that you can study for long periods in the privacy of your room. The conclusion is obvious: Plan to study in your room, perhaps at the same time each day. Note that if you follow these instructions you will identify the variables that control a problem behavior.

Establishing effective consequences could mean reinforcing the desired behavior. You might decide that you were not allowed to watch your favorite soap opera or telephone your girlfriend until the 15 minutes of study are completed. Once this behavior is established, you could gradually increase the study time—reinforce yourself only for 30 minutes of study, then 45 minutes, and so on. In this way, you can manipulate relevant variables and apply the operant principle of shaping (see Chapter 5).

To maintain this learning, you should focus on the contingencies—tape today's assignment to your pillow, so you can't avoid looking at it if you're tempted to rest your eyes for a few hours. Anything that makes you more aware of your specific new commitment to study could help.

Finally, covert control involves using thoughts and images to alter your behavior. For example, you might allow yourself to fantasize about a loved one only after completing a certain study assignment. Or you might reduce some of the anxiety associated with studying by trying some relaxation exercises. Cognitive strategies like these have become an increasingly used strategy not just in self-control programs but in behavior therapy in general.

COGNITIVE THERAPY

Cognitive therapy traces the roots of emotional and behavioral problems to particular thought patterns; psychotherapy therefore aims to change the way people think. This idea can be traced back at least 2,000 years to the philosopher Epictetus, who wrote, "Men are disturbed not by things, but by the view which they take of them." Shakespeare expressed this notion more gracefully in Hamlet: "There's nothing either good or bad but thinking makes it so."

Cognitive approaches first began to have a major impact on psychotherapy in the 1950s, when Albert Ellis developed a system called **rational-emotive therapy.** According to Ellis, many psychological problems are caused by irrational thoughts that a particular event is awful, horrible, or catastrophic. These "foolish thoughts" can lead to feelings of "worthlessness, guilt, anxiety, depression, rage and inertia" that can drive a person "to whine and rant and to live less enjoyably" (Ellis, 1973, p. 200).

For example, imagine the cognitive processes involved in a typical dating-rejection scenario. A young man spends several days building up his courage, then telephones the woman of his dreams to invite her to a Wednesday-night all-you-can-eat fish fry at the local Howard Johnson's. She replies coolly that on Wednesday nights she always washes her hair. Stung by this rejection, our hero thinks to himself, "What a tragedy. This woman has turned me down. I'm worthless. I'll probably spend the rest of my life at Howard Johnson's alone."

A rational-emotive therapist would point out the irrational nature and self-defeating effects of these thoughts. Perhaps the woman really enjoys Wednesday hair washes. And even if this was an excuse and she did think our hero was an ugly fool, so what? That doesn't mean she's right. Unhappiness is caused not by her beliefs but by the young man's beliefs about himself. It is his irrational conclusion of worthlessness that produces the crippling fear that he will never find someone to share his flounder with.

The role of the therapist, then, is to teach a person "how to accept reality even when it is pretty grim" (Ellis, 1973, p. 182). Some cognitive therapists take a very active and aggressive approach to correcting irrational thought patterns. While the humanist Carl Rogers believes that the client is the only expert on his own problems,

Albert Ellis believes that the therapist is the expert who can efficiently identify irrational thoughts and tell a person how to act.

Ellis tries to provide emotional support by regarding the total person in a positive and supporting light. But the rational-emotive therapist does not hesitate to criticize faulty thought patterns.

Other cognitive approaches to therapy have been mentioned earlier in this text, such as Aaron Beck's cognitive theory that depression is caused by logical errors of thought that produce self-blame (see Chapter 13). Just as cognitive approaches to basic research have become increasingly influential in recent years (see Chapters 6 and 7), so cognitive approaches to therapy have also grown in impact.

Some psychologists now use the term *cognitive behavior therapy* to include Ellis's approach, covert behavior therapies, and a variety of other techniques. Though there may be some doubt about whether cognitive and behavior therapies belong in the same category, there is no doubt that they are currently attracting a great deal of theoretical and research attention. According to one recent survey of trends in pyschotherapy, cognitive behavior therapy is "one of the strongest, if not the strongest theoretical influence today" (Smith, 1982, p. 808).

HUMANISTIC THERAPY

In Chapter 11, we noted that the humanistic approach to personality emphasizes positive human qualities, such as the ability freely to pursue rational and spiritual goals. Similarly, **humanistic therapy** assumes that every person who seeks help in psychotherapy has the freedom and the capacity to choose her own goals and to fulfill her human potential. While the psychoanalyst tries to guide the patient to gain insight into motivation, and the behavior therapist attempts to modify the patient's behavior, the humanistic approach seeks a genuine encounter in which two human beings try to understand each other.

Humanistic therapy, first proposed in the early 1940s by Carl Rogers, has strongly influenced the development of psychotherapy to the present day. Rogers called his approach *client-centered therapy*. His use of the word *client* rather than *patient* emphasizes the essential dignity of the person who seeks help. Rogers also sometimes used the word *facilitator* instead of *therapist* to emphasize that the client is the real expert on herself. The professional's goal is to facilitate progress, to make it easier for the client to find her own solutions.

Rogers's technique is also called **nondirective therapy** because, unlike many other therapists, he refuses to tell people what to do or what to think. Instead of directing, Rogers tried to clarify feelings by rephrasing the client's statements and repeatedly asking the client what *she* really believes and feels. This process usually focused on the present, rather than seeking the source of a person's problems in childhood or the past.

At first, some people may be frustrated when the psychotherapist refuses to offer expert advice. In 1964, Carl Rogers was filmed in a half-hour interview with a divorced woman named Gloria who sought advice on what to tell her 9-year-old daughter about her own relationships with men. In this film *(Three Approaches to Psychotherapy)*, Gloria repeatedly asks what she should do, and Rogers repeatedly

Carl Rogers (1902–   ) developed humanistic psychotherapy and had a major influence on current approaches to mental health. Rogers was raised in a religious fundamentalist atmosphere, which was opposed to such activities as smoking, drinking, playing cards, or expressing interest in sex. In a short autobiography, Rogers even recalled a "slight feeling of wickedness when I had my first bottle of (soda) 'pop'" (Rogers, 1961, p. 5).

He attended the University of Wisconsin to major in agriculture but switched first to religious studies and then to psychology. A strong believer in the basic goodness of every human being, Rogers went on to develop a "client-centered" approach to psychotherapy to provide a supportive atmosphere in which each person could find his own answers to any problem.

asks Gloria what *she* thinks. Finally, after several direct questions, Rogers replies: "I feel that this is the kind of very private thing that I couldn't possibly answer for you. But I sure as anything will try to help you work toward your own answer" (Meador & Rogers, 1973, p. 161). Although it may seem frustrating at first, in the final analysis many people come to accept nondirective therapy that forces them to look inside themselves for the answers.

Rogers believes that to encourage personal growth, the psychotherapist must adopt three related attitudes: genuineness, unconditional positive regard, and empathy.

Genuineness refers to a real human relationship in which the therapist honestly expresses his own feelings. According to Rogers, if a therapist tries to manufacture phony concern or hide his own beliefs, ultimately this dishonesty can impede true personal growth. For example, at one point in their filmed encounter, Gloria says, "All of a sudden while I was talking to you, I thought, 'Gee, how nice I can talk to you and I want you to approve of me and I respect you, but I miss that my father couldn't talk to me like you are.' I mean, I'd like to say, 'Gee, I'd like you for my father.'" A psychoanalyst could not resist analyzing this statement as a sign of transference. But Rogers does not interpret the statement in terms of some abstract theoretical system; rather, he treats this as a legitimate human expression of emotion and responds without pretense, "You look to me like a pretty nice daughter" (Meador & Rogers, 1973, p. 161).

Of course, genuineness by itself is not enough for an effective encounter. A therapist who was insensitive might do considerable damage by genuinely expressing his feelings and telling an insecure client, "You're the most miserable excuse for a human being I've ever met. I can't believe anybody could be so stupid. And ugly too."

Along with genuineness, Rogers insists that a therapist must express *unconditional positive regard* by caring about each client as a person, totally accepting him and his ability to solve his own problems. The therapist should not judge the client's worth by his behavior—for example, condemning a man who abandoned his wife and children. Instead, he recognizes the essential dignity of this person and believes that he is able to choose the best path.

Finally, the therapist should have *empathy*, the ability to perceive the world as the client does. This should not be confused with sympathy. The therapist who says, "I'm sorry you feel insecure," may genuinely express a kind feeling, but that is not empathy. Empathy involves an attempt to "get inside the client's head" to try to understand fully why the client lacks security.

These three attitudes are very closely interrelated. To maintain a deep empathy for the moment-to-moment changes in another person's feelings, the therapist must accept and value the client; that is, empathy is best built on a foundation of unconditional positive regard. And the attitude of genuineness is the most basic of all, because a meaningful relationship demands that these feelings be honest and real.

AN ECLECTIC APPROACH

A recent survey of the actual practices of clinical and counseling psychologists indicates that 41% of all clinicians do not identify themselves with a single theoretical orientation (Garfield & Kurtz, 1976; Smith, 1982). Instead, they take an **eclectic approach,** choosing different therapeutic techniques to meet the needs of different clients. An eclectic therapist might use systematic desensitization to treat a person with a phobia and client-centered psychotherapy to help a depressed executive find joy in his work. In fact, several different techniques might be used with the same patient to resolve different problems.

Along with various forms of psychotherapy that fall easily under one of the four theoretical orientations described here, eclectic therapists also employ "mixed models" that cut across theoretical boundaries. For example, there are many different types of **group therapy,** in which one or more therapists meet with several patients at the same time. Group therapy first became popular during World War II for a very practical reason: There were simply not enough therapists available to treat all the psychological casualties of wartime. However, many experienced therapists came to believe that group therapy had a number of advantages beyond efficiency. Patients acted as therapist to others in the group, subjecting one another to social pressures, learning how to interact effectively, and comforting one another with the knowledge that other people face similar problems.

Group therapy has grown rapidly in popularity and influence over the last few decades, and many different forms of group therapy have been developed. **Sensitivity training groups** (sometimes called T-groups) promote personal growth by encouraging participants to focus on their immediate relationships with others in the group. Their goals and techniques are closely related to the humanistic paradigm. A more behavioral approach is taken in **assertiveness training groups,** in which thera-

Figure 14.1
Under the proper conditions, group therapy with several patients and one or more therapists can provide increased social support and other advantages over individual psychotherapy.

pists demonstrate specific ways of standing up for one's rights and participants practice these behaviors. Many other types of group therapy are eclectic combinations that borrow techniques from several theoretical paradigms.

Another recent development is the growth of **family therapy,** in which all the members of a family meet together for psychotherapy. A family may enter therapy because one member appears to have behavioral or emotional problems, but family therapists often find that this problem is caused by, or aggravated by, patterns of interaction among all family members. Here, the goal is to improve the workings of the family unit as well as the functioning of individual members.

Even the family therapy category can be further broken down into several theoretical approaches. Our point here is to emphasize that there are many different kinds of psychotherapy that clinicians use to treat different problems. Given this tremendous diversity, it is not surprising that the question of evaluating psychotherapy has proved to be complex and controversial.

IS PSYCHOTHERAPY EFFECTIVE?

For the first decades after Freud "invented" psychotherapy, few questioned its value or effectiveness. Therapists observed that many patients seemed to improve, and patients too seemed satisfied with the results. But in 1952, Hans Eysenck published a controversial article in which he argued that psychotherapy was "unsupported by any scientifically acceptable evidence" (p. 323).

Eysenck's basic idea was that many of the problems that bring people to therapy will disappear with the simple passage of time. Along with this type of spontaneous recovery, many psychotherapy patients may be helped by the power of suggestion or a placebo effect (see "How Do They Know?" p. 538). The fact that a therapy seems effective to both patients and doctors does not necessarily imply that it *is* effective (see "Becoming a Critical Consumer").

Previous studies had often claimed that psychotherapy worked because 50% or 60% or 70% of a particular group of patients improved by some criterion. Eysenck argued that such statistics could not prove anything until they were compared with the improvement rate for a control group of similar patients who did not undergo psychotherapy.

Eysenck located two studies of neurotics who did not receive any psychotherapy but whose problems were assessed over the course of several years. By his count, 72% of these people were classified as improved, much improved, or cured after one or two years in which they received no professional treatment. In other words, the ordinary steps people take to solve their problems—talking to friends, going on a vacation, or buying a hot tub—were quite effective. Time may not heal all wounds, but in Eysenck's survey it cured 72% of them.

In contrast, the recovery rate in 24 studies of 8,053 neurotics who received psychotherapy were distressingly low. Eysenck computed recovery rates of 64% for eclectic psychotherapy and only 47% for psychoanalysis. Although noting several qualifications, Eysenck's conclusion was quite provocative: "There thus appears to be an inverse correlation between recovery and psychotherapy; the more psychotherapy, the smaller the recovery rate" (1952, p. 322).

Many psychotherapists were not thrilled to be told that all their professional efforts had been either ineffective or harmful. A lively controversy began, and it took nearly three full decades for the smoke to clear. Although Eysenck's criticisms are still quoted by critics of psychotherapy, most experts now agree that his conclusions have been disproved. A later review of the studies cited by Eysenck (Bergin, 1971) argued that he had underestimated the recovery rate among psychoanalytic patients and made a number of errors. More important, a large body of new research (partly generated by Eysenck's challenge) proved that psychotherapy does have positive effects.

One widely cited study (Sloane, Staples, Cristol, Yorkston, & Whipple, 1975) compared the effects of psychoanalysis and behavior therapy with improvement in a control group of people who were assessed in interviews and placed on a waiting list for later therapy but never received any treatment. The patients were 90 people who came to the Temple University Outpatient Clinic with a typical range of complaints. The therapists were all highly experienced and recognized as experts in either psychoanalysis or behavior therapy. Patients were divided into three groups of 30, matched for age, sex, and the severity of their problems, and randomly assigned to psychoanalysis, behavior therapy, or the waiting-list control group.

After four months, all three groups were assessed on a number of standard tests (such as the MMPI) and in interviews. Perhaps the most straightforward criterion for improvement was based on an interview by another clinician who did not know the patient or which group each belonged to. In the judgment of these unbiased

Would You Believe Reincarnation Therapy?

One of the most difficult problems in evaluating the effects of psychotherapy is the fact that almost every type of therapy can point to the testimonials of patients who have been "cured." As you read the following account of one extremely unusual type of therapy, try to answer the following question: Does this patient's recovery prove the value of this unorthodox approach? (For an answer, see the discussion after the "Summary" at the end of this chapter.)

> Nancy S., 33, a California writer, always had trouble finishing books and articles. But unlike most authors bedeviled by blocks, she now knows where her troubles began: in the 17th century. During a session with . . . a Los Angeles therapist, she had a vision of herself as a woman on trial in America in 1677 for heresy and trying to hide an incrim-

inating diary from her inquisitors. Three hundred years later she was still "hiding the book." But no more. After . . . therapy she says: "I seem to have very little problem finishing up things now, as if the pattern were erased."

> [Nancy S.] is one of many devotees of a growing fad known as "past-lives therapy." Essentially, its practitioners take a conventional Freudian idea—that much adult behavior is unconsciously guided by early traumas—and apply it to the concept of reincarnation. Although the treatment has had a following in the U.S. and Europe for at least 15 years, more and more Americans are experimenting with the notion that their psychological problems arose during previous existences as, say, Shinto priests, Roman guards, citizens of Atlantis or even another planet (*Time*, October 3, 1977, p. 53).

observers, 80% of the psychoanalytic patients improved or recovered, along with 80% of the behavior-therapy patients and 48% of the no-treatment group. Thus, the precise type of treatment did not seem to matter, but psychotherapy did make a difference for many individuals, at least over this time period.

Of course, no single study, no matter how well designed and executed, could be expected to resolve an issue of this complexity. The most compelling conclusions to date come from a review by Mary Lee Smith, Gene Glass, and Thomas Miller (1980) of 475 different studies that compared the effects of psychotherapy with a control group of some type. The criteria for improvement in these studies included ratings by both patients and clinicians of such characteristics as self-esteem, anxiety, and social competence, as well as more objective behavioral and physiological variables. Since many studies included more than one criterion of improvement, a total of 1,776 outcome measures were considered in this review.

When this massive body of data was systematically quantified, the overall conclusion was clear and unambiguous:

> The evidence overwhelmingly supports the efficacy of psychotherapy. . . . Psychotherapy benefits people of all ages as reliably as schooling educates them, medicine cures them, or business turns a profit (Smith, Glass, & Miller, p. 183).

More precisely, the authors stated, "The average person who receives therapy is better off at the end of it than 80 percent of the persons who do not" (p. 87).

When these researchers compared different theoretical orientations, including psychoanalysis, behavior modification, client-centered therapy, rational-emotive therapy, cognitive behavioral therapy, and 13 others, they found that all produced similar effects. These researchers believe that the similarities between various schools of psychotherapy are more important than the differences.

Given the long history of controversy regarding psychotherapy, it is not surprising that this review has been criticized. However, reanalysis of the data by independent investigators (Landman & Dawes, 1982) has thus far supported their strong conclusions. Three decades after Eysenck's challenge, psychotherapists can finally rest easy knowing that there is objective proof that they do indeed help many people. Further research should help them to refine clinical techniques so that they can become even more efficient in helping all patients as fully, and as quickly, as possible.

Biological Therapies

An entirely different approach to treatment is based on a biological model that stresses the importance of brain processes in abnormal behavior. In Chapter 2, we discussed one such therapeutic technique: psychosurgery to alter thought and behavior patterns. Here we describe two other biological therapies, electroconvulsive therapy and drugs.

ELECTROCONVULSIVE THERAPY

Almost as controversial as psychosurgery is the concept of **electroconvulsive therapy,** a treatment for severe mental illness (particularly depression) in which an electric current is passed through the brain to produce a convulsion. In the 1930s, several researchers believed that schizophrenia and epilepsy were mutually exclusive diseases. Thus, they reasoned, the artificial induction of an epileptic-type seizure could relieve mental illness. Scientists now know that this theory is wrong. However, despite the disproof of its theoretical basis, and the lack of a widely accepted theory explaining why electroconvulsive therapy *should* work, it does seem to help some types of patients.

These days the patient is anesthetized and given various muscle-relaxant drugs to minimize the physical effects of the seizure. Electroconvulsive therapy typically begins by placing two electrodes on the right side of the head (the idea is to stimulate the right cerebral hemisphere because it is less involved in speech; electrodes might be applied to the left side of the head for left-handed patients whose right hemisphere controls language—see Chapter 2). An electric current of about 100 volts is then passed through the electrodes for a few fractions of a second to produce an epileptic-type convulsion. Typically, about 10 treatments are given over a period of several weeks.

Later, the patient remembers nothing about the shock or the convulsion. After regaining consciousness, the person will probably be somewhat confused and disoriented. There is also some loss of memory, particularly for events minutes before and after the treatment.

The controversy over electroconvulsive therapy was partly based on the side effects of more primitive techniques used in its early days. Anesthesia and drug treatment have now substantially reduced the risk of bruises and bone fractures, and electrical stimulation of only the nondominant hemisphere has reduced memory loss.

A review of 60 studies that evaluated the effects of electroconvulsive therapy (Scovern & Kilmann, 1980) concluded that it is the most effective treatment available for certain types of severely depressed patients, including those with bipolar disorders or a major depressive episode in late middle age. It is particularly useful for suicidal patients because it acts very quickly and thus reduces the risk that they will harm themselves. Its effects on some other conditions are more controversial, although it is now clear that electroconvulsive therapy is *not* useful in the treatment of anxiety or personality disorders.

According to the report of a special committee appointed by the American Psychiatric Association (1978) to study electroconvulsive therapy, a survey in the mid-1970s revealed that about 2 out of 3 American psychiatrists favored the use of electroconvulsive therapy with some patients, while the remaining third were generally opposed. However, only 2% of these psychiatrists felt that electroconvulsive therapy should never be used with any patient. After reviewing all available research data, this committee concluded that electroconvulsive therapy is an appropriate treatment for several specific patient groups, including severely depressed suicidal individuals who are a threat to themselves and violent patients who are a threat to others. In general, the committee recommended that electroconvulsive therapy be considered a treatment of last resort that should only be attempted when drugs do not work or cannot be used for medical reasons.

DRUG THERAPY

Of all the changes that have occurred in the treatment of mental illness over the past century, the single most influential event may have been the "drug revolution" that began in the mid-1950s. For nearly 100 years before that time, the number of patients in United States public mental institutions had slowly and steadily increased, at a rate of about 2% a year. In 1956, shortly after effective drugs became widely available, the patient population declined for the first time in modern history (see Figure 14.2).

Despite the fact that the number of people being admitted to mental hospitals has risen steadily over the past decades, their average stay has shortened considerably. Consequently, the total number of patients confined in mental hospitals at any given time has declined dramatically since effective drugs were introduced into psychiatric practice.

Table 14.3 lists the major categories of drugs currently used to treat mental

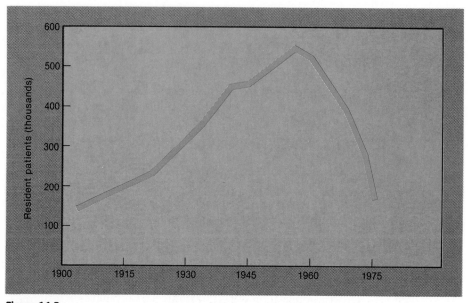

Figure 14.2

The number of inpatients in state and county mental hospitals rose steadily from 1900 to about 1955. After drugs were introduced to treat psychosis, the number of inpatients declined sharply. Although the number of people admitted for mental illness continued to increase, the average length of time they stayed in these hospitals became much shorter.

disorders. In this short overview, we discuss the first type of drug therapy to have a major impact: phenothiazine treatment of schizophrenia.

Although phenothiazines were first synthesized in 1883, it was only in 1952 that a French researcher reported that one member of the phenothiazine family, a drug now sold under the trade name Thorazine, reduced psychotic symptoms. The effects

TABLE 14.3
Drugs Commonly Prescribed for Mental Disorders

Mental Disorder	*Drug Type*	*Chemical Group (Common Trade Names)*
Schizophrenia	Antipsychotic	Phenothiazines (Thorazine, Stelazine, Mellaril) Butyrophenones (Haldol) Thioxanthenes (Taractan)
Depression	Antidepressant	MAO inhibitors (Nardil, Parnate) Tricyclics (Tofranil, Elavil)
Mania Depression (some cases)	Mood regulators	Lithium carbonate (Lithium)
Anxiety	Tranquilizers	Dicarbamates (Miltown, Equanil, Soma) Benzodiazepines (Valium, Librium, Dalmane)

Note. Drugs listed here may also be prescribed for other conditions and purposes.

were so immediate and so dramatic that within a few years phenothiazine drugs were being used throughout the world to treat psychosis, particularly schizophrenia.

Phenothiazine drugs have wide-ranging effects; they reduce hallucinations, delusions, confusion, agitation, irritability, hostility, indifference, social withdrawal, and other psychotic symptoms. Their efficacy has been repeatedly demonstrated under the most carefully controlled conditions (see "How Do They Know?") The widespread use of phenothiazines and related drugs has changed the very nature of mental institutions around the world. Physical restraint and straitjackets for violent patients were no longer necessary, and institutions were no longer expected to house most severely disturbed patients until they died.

However, the drug revolution has not abolished mental illness, and it has created some new problems of its own. Some patients are not helped by available drugs, and others improve only marginally. Many patients must continue to take the drug indefinitely to prevent the reappearance of psychotic symptoms. Even when the drug is maintained, relapses occur in about 1 out of every 3 patients (Davis, Gosenfeld, & Tsai, 1976). This is preferable to the 2 out of 3 patients who relapse when taking placebos, but it indicates that many setbacks will occur with any form of treatment.

These figures also highlight our ignorance in another way. The 1 out of every 3 patients who do *not* relapse when they take placebos obviously do not need to continue to take powerful drugs. However, there is currently no precise way to tell which patients need to continue to take antipsychotic drugs and which can get along without them.

On a theoretical level, the success of drug treatments has led many investigators to search for physiological causes and correlates of mental illness. As explained in Chapter 3, many drugs are believed to affect the brain and the body by influencing the action of neurotransmitters. There are several separate lines of indirect evidence that phenothiazines work by blocking drug receptors for the neurotransmitter dopamine (Berger, 1978). Since the technology does not yet exist for precisely charting neurotransmitter chemistry in the living human brain, this hypothesis must remain somewhat tentative.

You may remember that a lack of dopamine in the brain produces Parkinson's disease, a syndrome involving severe muscular tremors of the limbs, hands, neck, and face. Since phenothiazines block dopamine receptors, they often produce as a side effect muscle problems that resemble Parkinson's disease.

After long-term treatment with phenothiazines and chemically related drugs, about 15% of patients develop a similar syndrome called **tardive dyskinesia,** which produces frequent and involuntary muscle movements including lip-smacking, sucking, and chin-wagging motions. Aside from the social embarrassment, this syndrome can interfere with speech and eating.

Research continues with other drugs that can reduce psychotic symptoms without producing tardive dyskinesia. In the meantime, physicians must weigh the relative costs and benefits of phenothiazine treatment for each individual patient.

Motor problems are the most obvious side effect of phenothiazines, but these drugs may also lead to such disagreeable symptoms as grogginess, constipation, and

Double-Blind Studies: Testing Drugs to Treat Schizophrenia

Throughout this text, we emphasize the fact that bias and expectations can influence observations of behavior. In medicine, this is seen in the **placebo effect**: A patient's condition may improve as a result of the expectation that a particular treatment would work rather than as a result of the treatment itself.

In the centuries before medicine became a modern science, folk healers and physicians treated diseases they did not understand with drugs made of crocodile dung, swine's teeth, flyspecks, powder of precious stones, and human perspiration (Shapiro, 1971). Despite the fact that these and other ingredients had no inherent medicinal value, the placebo effect kept physicians in business as some patients improved after swallowing these bizarre concoctions.

Modern drugs may also benefit from the placebo effect in that many patients will im-

prove even if a drug has no specific effect on the illness for which it is prescribed. To compensate for this, the actual therapeutic power of a drug is generally tested in a **double-blind study** in which the effects of expectations are minimized by keeping both subjects and experimenters ignorant of the precise treatment being tested. Some patients in a double-blind study of a drug would receive a placebo, while others would receive the drug to be tested; neither the patients nor their immediate physicians would know which drug they had received. Sometimes, for practical reasons, it is only possible to perform a single-blind study, in which patients do not know which drug they receive but their doctors do.

One of the most convincing studies of drug treatment of schizophrenia was a double-blind test comparing the drug Thorazine to a placebo (Cole, 1964). (Two chemically related drugs

dryness of the mouth. These side effects contribute to patients' unwillingness to continue to take the drugs on a long-term basis. Many patients now stay in mental hospitals until their psychotic symptoms have been controlled by drugs, then stop taking medication after they leave the institution, and eventually they are forced to return once more to the hospital. This "revolving door" effect is one of the most fundamental problems faced by mental-health workers who hope to help former patients establish themselves in their local communities.

Community Psychology

Beginning in the mid-1960s, a large number of psychologists became involved in trying to bring mental-health services directly into the community. This was not limited to serving the needs of former mental patients after their release; it included

were also analyzed in this study. Their results were virtually identical to those for Thorazine. For simplicity's sake, however, we ignore them in this discussion.)

The patients in this study were newly admitted schizophrenics in nine different mental institutions. Each new patient was assigned a code number and was given drugs that came in number-coded containers several times a day for the next six weeks. All the pills looked the same, and the doctors and nurses who treated a particular patient did not know whether that person was receiving Thorazine or lactose, a sugar pill that served as the placebo.

At regular intervals, doctors, nurses, and ward attendants rated the behavior of each patient. Questionnaires and interviews permitted the assessment of 21 specific symptoms. In addition, each patient was regularly rated by staff members on a scale from 1 to 7 on the following general questions: "Considering your total clinical experience, how mentally ill is this patient at this time?" and "Compared to his condition at admission to the project, how much has he changed?"

The results were clear and unambiguous: 75% of the patients taking Thorazine were rated "much improved" or "very much improved," versus 23% of the placebo group. The placebo did seem to have some effect, but the Thorazine effect was much stronger. After six weeks of treatment, 16% of the schizophrenics who had received Thorazine were judged "normal," and another 30% were considered only "borderline mentally ill."

For 13 of the 21 specific symptoms measured in this study, the Thorazine group improved significantly more than the placebo group. For example, patients who received Thorazine were less confused, took better care of their physical needs, participated more in social activities, were less agitated and tense, had fewer auditory hallucinations and ideas of persecution, and had more coherent speech.

This experiment provided conclusive proof that Thorazine was effective in treating a broad range of schizophrenic symptoms. Double-blind studies of this sort can provide the most powerful test of the effectiveness of any new drug or medical treatment.

the potential to help every individual in our society to cope more effectively with a wide variety of problems in living. Before the community-psychology movement, most clinical psychologists limited their activities to diagnosing mental disorders and to treating problems with psychotherapy. But community psychologists assumed a far broader role: They established telephone hotlines to prevent suicide; they trained paraprofessionals to intervene in family crises; they evaluated correctional systems for prison and parole; they even organized rent strikes and demonstrations for public assistance. Thus, **community psychologists** have attempted to make mental-health services available to every person in their local communities.

The radical new approaches of community psychology, and its political activism, made this wide-ranging movement quite controversial. Here, we can only briefly describe three of the most important goals of this approach: providing mental-health services in local communities, training paraprofessionals, and preventing mental illness.

MENTAL-HEALTH SERVICES IN LOCAL COMMUNITIES

In 1963, the Community Mental Health Centers Act provided federal funding for establishing one comprehensive mental-health-care center for every community of 75,000 to 200,000 people in the United States. These centers were designed so that every citizen could receive mental-health care without leaving the community in which he or she lived and worked. Services were to include short-term hospitalization, therapy available on a walk-in basis, and 24-hour-a-day emergency services such as counseling and suicide prevention.

This federal support and the new emphasis on a mental health presence in the community helped lead to the development of many novel programs. For example, a number of rape crisis centers have been established to provide help for victims of sexual assaults. Professional and paraprofessional staff members, including some volunteers who have themselves been victims of rape, may accompany a woman to the hospital and the police station to provide medical and legal advice as well as emotional support.

But despite some notable success stories, community mental-health centers have generally failed to live up to their original promise. One very practical problem is money. The original idea was that these centers would become self-supporting, largely through insurance payments for patient services. But most of the people who came for help were poor and lacked the insurance or the personal funds to pay for the services they needed. Also, government support was reduced as national priorities shifted. By the mid-1970s, community mental-health centers were supposed to be established to meet the needs of the entire United States; in fact, centers were available to serve only about 40% of the U.S. population. Many of these were inadequately staffed and supported (Bassuk & Gerson, 1978).

One result of the failure of community mental-health centers is that former mental patients often face very unpleasant living conditions. For example, in 1978, about 40,000 chronically mentally ill patients lived in New York City. Only 424 of these lived in true halfway houses that provided a transition from the hospital to city life; about another 2,000 could be cared for in sheltered workshops. The remainder had been "dumped" by city agencies into whatever housing was available (Koenig, 1978).

One example is the Hotel Continental, a seedy hotel on Manhattan's Upper West Side with 192 residents, nearly half of whom are former mental patients. Robberies and assaults inside the hotel were regularly reported to the police. Counseling consisted of an "advice bureau" in the hotel lobby staffed by a single harried social worker, and 20 minutes of psychotherapy each month. Neighbors who lived near the hotel did not care about integrating these unfortunate people into their community; indeed, several political groups formed to urge the city to move such patients somewhere else.

Thus, while the idea of providing mental-health services in local communities sounds good in theory, the reality is often grim. Adequate financial support could improve matters considerably, but a true integration of mental patients into local communities would also require changes in social attitudes and the public's percep-

Figure 14.3
The Hotel Continental, described in one article (Koenig, 1978) on the unfortunate living conditions of de-institutionalized mental patients who are "dumped" into high-crime areas.

tion of mental illness. In the meantime, some experts have begun to wonder publicly whether certain chronic groups might be better off living in humane mental asylums.

PARAPROFESSIONALS

One chronic problem faced by community psychology is that there simply are not enough trained professionals to work with all the people who need help. One economical solution is to rely on **paraprofessionals,** mental-health workers with more limited training to perform specific tasks.

In one study (Lick & Heffler, 1977), college students were trained to teach certain relaxation techniques that have proved useful in the treatment of insomnia. One group of patients were taught the techniques by these paraprofessionals, while a second group of patients were taught the same techniques by a clinical psychologist. In this study, the professional and paraprofessional therapists were equally successful in helping insomniacs to improve their sleep.

Some paraprofessionals have received far more intensive training to perform more complex tasks. Margaret Rioch (1967) supervised a carefully selected group of women who had given up their jobs after marriage for two years of training in mental-health counseling. Elaborate training of this sort may be almost as intensive as a professional degree program.

Many community mental-health centers have recruited and trained local residents to perform interviews, home visits, and counseling. Because these paraprofessionals have an intimate knowledge of local problems, they may be particularly sensitive to the needs of clients. Further, studies of observational learning have revealed that models are perceived as more believable and relevant when they resemble learners in age and background (Rosenthal & Bandura, 1978).

A review of 42 studies that directly compared the effectiveness of professional and paraprofessional helpers found that the paraprofessionals consistently achieved well-defined clinical results that were equal to those of professionals, and in some cases even better (Durlak, 1979).

The issue of why paraprofessionals sometimes produce better results is a provocative one for research. Perhaps it results from their greater resemblance to patients, or a more careful selection of people whose personality traits are suited to a particular task, or greater enthusiasm and interest on the part of the paraprofessional. Whatever the answer proves to be, it may have important implications for the future training of mental-health professionals as well as the training of their assistants.

PREVENTION

By far the most ambitious goal of community psychology is the prevention of future cases of mental illness. This idea was first championed by none other than Clifford Beers, the turn-of-the-century mental patient whose experiences were described at the beginning of this chapter. The National Committee for Mental Hygiene, founded by Beers, was inspired partly by the victories of medical science over such diseases as typhoid and tuberculosis. They hoped to discover an analogous form of mental "inoculation" that could prevent people from becoming mentally ill in the first place.

In the 1960s, this goal was adopted by the community-psychology movement. Several levels of prevention are possible. One type of program attempts to locate individuals who have a high risk of developing a disorder and then quickly provide help at an early stage. For example, the Primary Mental Health Project used various screening procedures to identify elementary school children with behavioral and educational problems. Paraprofessionals then worked with these children to develop new skills. The behavior of the children did indeed improve as a result (Cowen & Schochet, 1973).

Although there have been some successful programs at this level, the ultimate goal of community psychology is even more ambitious: to reduce the frequency of mental illness in society and, ultimately, eliminate it altogether. Many believe that such prevention must begin with political programs that will change the very nature of society and produce more equitable opportunities for all citizens.

Critics have charged that "community psychology's greatest failure is in the area where it sought its greatest success: primary prevention" (Bernstein & Nietzel, 1980, p. 459). The reason is not surprising to anyone who has studied abnormal psychology: At this time, psychologists simply do not know enough about mental illness and its causes to effectively prevent future cases from developing.

Depending on personal preference, one may choose cynically to emphasize the current failure or optimistically view this challenge as a tremendous opportunity for future research. In either case, if you decide to go on to a career in mental health, there undoubtedly will be times when you are frustrated by the limitations of current knowledge and wish that psychology and psychiatry knew more. At such moments, it may be useful to remember the unpleasant experiences of Clifford Beers in one of the best mental asylums in the United States in the year 1900. Today's institutions and therapies are certainly not perfect, but they are a tremendous improvement over some of the practices and beliefs that were common just a few decades ago.

Summary

1. At the end of the eighteenth century, Philippe Pinel proposed **moral therapy,** which treated mental disorders through kindness, understanding, and a pleasant environment. Ironically, calls for reform of the mental health abuses led more patients to be hospitalized, and overcrowding led to chaotic conditions under which therapy was replaced by custodial care.

2. Throughout the twentieth century, several groups of professionals have specialized in the treatment of mental disorders, including **psychiatrists,** medical doctors who specialize in mental illness, and **clinical psychologists,** who are trained in psychological principles and research and apply this knowledge to the treatment of mental illness.

3. In **psychotherapy,** a trained professional employs systematic psychological procedures to help a client change troublesome thoughts, feelings, and behavior patterns.

4. Classical **Freudian analysis** attempts to provide **insight** into the unconscious forces that motivate behavior, in the belief that once these conflicts become conscious, a person can deal more effectively with reality. The most important therapeutic technique is **free association,** in which a patient reports every single thought as it comes to mind. **Contemporary analysis** involves a more active role for the therapist and places more emphasis on external constraints and ego development.

5. **Behavior therapy** applies scientific principles to alter observable behavior through learning. One example is **systematic desensitization,** which requires an anxious person to imagine increasingly threatening situations while remaining deeply relaxed. Another application of behavior therapy teaches clients **self-control** by providing them with active coping strategies to deal with specific problems.

6. **Cognitive therapy** tries to solve human problems by changing people's thought patterns. One example is Albert Ellis's system of **rational-emotive psychotherapy,** which tries to teach people actively to avoid irrational thoughts that unpleasant events are tragic or catastrophic.

7. **Humanistic therapy** seeks a genuine human encounter in which a therapist can help guide a client to find his own solutions. For example, in Carl Rogers's **nondirective therapy,** the therapist refuses to tell the client what to do and instead tries to clarify the client's own feelings. This involves genuineness, unconditional positive regard, and empathy.

8. Many therapists take an **eclectic approach** in which different therapeutic techniques are used to meet the needs of different clients. In **group therapy,** one or more therapists meet with several patients at the same time. In **family therapy,** all members of a family meet in a group for simultaneous counseling.

9. Beginning in the 1950s, some researchers questioned whether people who received psychotherapy were more likely to improve than control groups who simply waited for their problems to be resolved. According to the most recent review of 475 different outcome studies, psychotherapy is indeed quite effective in changing behavior. However, there do not appear to be important differences in the effectiveness of different types of psychotherapy.

10. In one biological treatment called **electroconvulsive therapy,** an electric current is passed through the brain to produce a convulsion and relieve depression and other mental disorders.

11. Beginning in the mid-1950s, drug treatment substantially decreased the patient population in mental institutions. **Phenothiazines** and other antipsychotic drugs reduce such psychotic symptoms as hallucinations, delusions, confusion, agitation, and social withdrawal. However, they do not "cure" mental illness; many patients must continue to take maintenance doses indefinitely. Unfortunately, many of the drugs produce serious side effects.

12. **Community psychologists** have attempted to make mental health services available to every U.S. citizen on a local level. **Paraprofessionals** are mental health workers with limited training to perform specific tasks. Outcome studies have revealed that in some settings paraprofessionals are at least as effective as professional therapists.

Discussion of "Becoming a Critical Consumer"

The answer is no. The positive effect on the woman whose writer's block was removed could equally well be accounted for by the placebo effect, expectations, or the simple passage of time.

Past-lives therapy is likely to strike many people as so outrageous that they will be skeptical of this patient's claims. But would you be equally skeptical if a friend told you that his anxiety was cured by taking massive doses of vitamin E or if you saw a celebrity on TV who said her therapist had cured her of alcoholism?

As noted in the text, systematic research has revealed that psychotherapy has positive effects. But the testimony of satisfied customers often proves only that, in the words of one expert quoted in the same Time *article, "suckers are born every minute and customers can be found for anything."*

To Learn More

Williams, R. L., & Long, J. D. *Toward a Self-Managed Lifestyle (3d ed.).* Boston: Houghton Mifflin, 1983. A guidebook of behavioral techniques of self-control, designed for those who would like to change their own behavior.

Corsini, R. J. (Ed.). *Current Psychotherapies* (2d ed.). Itasca, Ill.: Peacock Publishers, 1979. Leading proponents of different approaches to psychotherapy contributed chapters organized in a format that facilitates comparison.

Bernstein, D. A., & Nietzel, M. T. *Introduction to Clinical Psychology.* New York: McGraw-Hill, 1980. Particularly useful for students who might consider a career in this field.

15
Social Psychology

On March 13, 1964, Kitty Genovese arrived home from work at about 3:20 a.m. She parked her red Fiat in a lot about 100 feet from her apartment house in a quiet residential neighborhood in Queens, New York. As she walked toward her door, she noticed a man suspiciously standing in her path. She stopped, turned, and first walked, then ran, toward a streetlight. The man chased her and caught up quickly. He jumped on her back and stabbed her four times.

Miss Genovese screamed, "Oh my God, he stabbed me! Please help me! Please help me!" Several lights went on in the 10-story apartment building opposite the scene of the attack. One neighbor opened a window on one of the upper floors and yelled down, "Let that girl alone!"

The assailant hurried back to his car, and Miss Genovese staggered away. But, the attacker later reported, "I had a feeling this man would close his window and go back to sleep, and sure enough he did."

Moments after the first stabbing, Miss Genovese had only managed to round the corner a few yards away. The attacker quickly caught up and stabbed her again. Miss Genovese screamed, "I'm dying. I'm dying." Again windows were opened and lights went on. This time, the assailant went to his car and drove away.

Miss Genovese crawled to the entryway of her apartment house but didn't have the strength to open the door. A few minutes later the man returned for a third attack. He looked for his victim through the windows of a coffee shop and a railroad station and tried the doors of several apartment houses. Finally, he found Miss Genovese lying on the floor. He stabbed her again until she was quiet, then sexually molested her. During this final fatal attack, the killer later reported that he "heard the upstairs door open at least twice, maybe three times."

Finally, 30 minutes after the first attack, a neighbor called the police. They arrived within minutes, but Miss Genovese was dead and the killer had escaped.

The police later concluded that parts of the attack had been witnessed by at least 38 neighbors. The man who actually called the police later explained that he had done so only after telephoning a friend for advice and then going to the apartment of another neighbor to convince her to call so that he wouldn't get involved (Gansberg, 1964, p. 38; *Time,* June 26, 1964, p. 22).

The tragic story of the death of Kitty Genovese became a national scandal as the experts debated the reasons for her neighbors' callous indifference.

Some editorial writers saw the event as a sign of alienation or moral decay; others claimed that it proved that urban life had dehumanizing effects. One group of experts, however, avoided such facile explanations and empty slogans; instead, social psychologists set out to perform systematic studies to identify the causes of this disturbing event (described later in this chapter).

Social psychology studies the way people respond to other human beings and how they interact with one another. The focus is generally on the individual and how she is affected by a particular social group. As this definition implies, the problems studied by social psychologists are also of interest to experts in other fields, particularly sociology. In general, sociologists take a somewhat different approach, studying groups such as the family or a political party as self-contained units.

The first study in social psychology was published in 1898, when Norman

Figure 15.1
The scene of attacks on Kitty Genovese in March 1964. After parking her car near the Kew Gardens railroad station (1), she noticed a suspicious man and walked along Austin Street toward a police telephone box. The man caught and attacked her at (2). She got away but was attacked twice more at (3) and (4) within full sight of at least 38 neighbors—who failed to notify the police.

Triplett reported that people generally performed a task better when they were in direct competition with others than when they worked alone. He began by analyzing thousands of performances from the 1897 bicycle-racing season of the League of American Wheelmen. Triplett found that average times were considerably faster in paced races (in which two or more men raced simultaneously over the same course) than in timed races (in which each man tried independently to beat the clock). He went on to develop a laboratory device that timed how quickly a person could turn a fishing reel. Most of the 40 children he tested on this task did better when they were in direct competition with another.

Much of the history of research in social psychology involved uncovering the complexities of social stimuli. In the case of Triplett's discovery, later researchers used the term **social facilitation** to refer to an improvement in performance associated with the presence of other people. However, attempts to replicate and extend Triplett's findings were contradictory; some researchers found social facilitation effects, and others did not. In 1965, Robert Zajonc reviewed this literature and explained the contradictions: Social facilitation occurred in the performance of tasks that had already been mastered; new learning occurs more slowly if others are present. Zajonc's explanation was based on Tolman's distinction between learning and performance (see Chapter 5) and other concepts from learning theory. In this context, the most important point is that in Triplett's case and many others, continued research has permitted social psychologists to specify the factors that determine when a particular response will occur.

The first textbooks of social psychology appeared 10 years after Triplett's study. They were highly speculative in nature. Empirical research grew more slowly over the next several decades. In World War II, many psychologists began to study such practical issues as discovering more effective ways to motivate work groups, to identify potential leaders, and to improve civilian morale. This research on social stimuli, which began as part of the war effort, generated tremendous enthusiasm, and social psychology emerged as an important field in its own right.

The next 25 years were an exciting period for social psychologists as their numbers grew rapidly, and advances in research methods and theory led to great optimism and, in the words of one social psychologist, "seemed to promise dramatic advances in the understanding of human behavior" (Elms, 1975, p. 967). But somewhere around 1970, social psychology entered a period that this same writer termed a "crisis of confidence," in which the methods, the relevance, the biases, and the conclusions of social psychology were widely questioned.

Throughout this text, we have seen how over the course of its short history psychology has become more modest in its claims; instead of promising immediate solutions to global problems, it now offers a more realistic attempt to chip away at specific problems. Social psychology too reflects this larger trend. In this chapter, we see how it has emerged into the 1980s with a renewed respect for the complexity of social behavior and a continuing commitment to a systematic and empirical approach.

It is probably impossible to count all the ways that people interact with one another and all the possible forms of social behavior. The diversity of these topics has led various researchers in a number of different directions, as can be seen in the wide range of issues considered in this chapter.

Every chapter in an introductory textbook like this represents a kind of whirlwind tour; this may seem particularly true of our discussion of research in social psychology. Each of the major topics described here is worthy of a chapter of its own, or perhaps a book, or a lifetime of research.

Social Groups

Since Triplett noted that the presence of others influenced performance, psychologists have been fascinated by the effects of social groups on behavior. To provide a concrete feeling for the process of social psychological research, we begin by considering how psychologists analyzed the social stimuli in the tragic case of the young woman whose neighbors failed to help.

HELPING IN AN EMERGENCY

After analyzing the details of the Kitty Genovese case, social psychologists John Darley and Bibb Latané (1968) came up with several possible explanations for her neighbors' failure to call the police. According to the most promising theory, one important factor was **diffusion of responsibility:** When many observers are present during an emergency but cannot directly observe one another, each can rationalize doing nothing by assuming that someone else must be taking action. The social responsibility to help someone in trouble is diffused across the entire group. The larger the group, the less responsibility any particular individual will feel, and the more slowly he will react.

Darley and Latané (1968) devised an experiment to test this prediction by observing people's reactions to an artificially staged emergency. The subjects were college students who were told that they were participating in a group discussion of personal problems associated with school. To avoid embarrassment and preserve anonymity, they were told, the discussion would be held over an intercom system, each participant isolated in a separate room with a microphone that would be turned on for only two minutes at a time. Some subjects were told that there were five others in the group, some were told that there were two others, and some were told that they were discussing their problems with only one other person.

In fact, all the other "participants" were prerecorded tapes that were played through the intercom. The first "participant" hesitantly admitted that he was prone to epileptic-type seizures when he was under stress. Subjects in the two-person groups were then given two minutes to describe their own problems; those in larger groups heard one or four more voices before they got their turn. On the second round of discussion, the first tape-recorded voice grew first louder, then incoherent as he said he was actually having a seizure and needed help.

The independent variable (see Chapter 1) was the size of the group; one dependent variable was the number of people who left the isolation room within six minutes to look for help for the seizure victim. Just as Darley and Latané had predicted, larger groups led to more diffusion of responsibility and less help. As Figure 15.2 shows, only 31% of those who thought that five other people were present tried to help by the end of the two-minute fit, compared to 62% for the three-person group and 85% for the two-person discussion.

Interestingly, the people who failed to help did not seem apathetic, callous, or indifferent. "If anything, they seemed more emotionally aroused than did the subjects who reported the emergency" (Darley & Latané, 1968, p. 382). The authors argued that these observers were caught in a conflict between their own guilt and shame at doing nothing and the fear of making fools of themselves and ruining the experiment by overreacting.

Latané and Darley (1970) later provided a more complete account of several separate decisions an observer must make before coming to a victim's aid: The bystander must notice the event and interpret it as an emergency, feel personal responsibility for acting, and possess the proper skills and resources to act. In a series of experiments involving different sorts of emergencies, they found little sup-

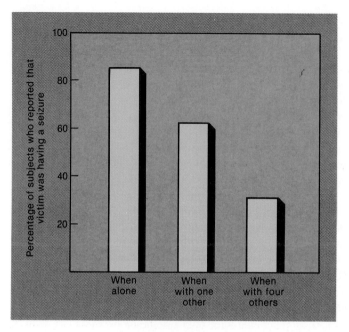

Figure 15.2
In a study of "diffusion of responsibility," subjects were less likely to report an apparent epileptic seizure when they thought it was witnessed by others.

port for the idea that there is "safety in numbers." On the contrary, larger groups seemed less likely to help for several different reasons.

Along with the diffusion of responsibility, two other processes were involved in the social inhibition of helping. **Audience inhibition** refers to the fact that a bystander runs the risk of embarrassment if she decides to help in a situation that turns out not to be an emergency. If you see someone lying on the beach gasping for breath and you immediately begin mouth-to-mouth resuscitation, you will feel pretty silly if a crowd gathers and learns that your "victim" was just breathing heavily after a long swim.

Another factor is **social influence:** In trying to decide whether an ambiguous event is indeed an emergency, a bystander tends to follow the reactions of other people. If you see a well-dressed man staggering as he walks down the street and holding one hand on his chest, he could be having a heart attack, or he could be feeling the aftereffects of a four-martini business lunch. If other people calmly step around the staggering executive, you are likely to decide that they are correct in assuming that the man does not need help, and ignore him.

These social effects on the perception of an ambiguous situation were dramatically demonstrated in another study with a phony emergency. As college students sat in a waiting room filling out questionnaires, a stream of smoke began to puff through a wall vent. Subjects who were alone in the room typically went to the vent, sniffed around, and then left to find someone to report the problem to.

But some people were left in the room with two other subjects who were actually hired by the experimenter to remain calm throughout this false emergency. Fully 90% of the people who were left with these passive confederates stayed in the waiting room as it filled up with smoke, "doggedly working on the questionnaire and waving the fumes away from their faces. They coughed, rubbed their eyes, and opened the window—but they did not report the smoke" (Latané & Darley, 1968, p. 218).

When questioned later, these passive subjects gave a variety of explanations for the smoke—it might have been steam or air-conditioning vapors or, in the eyes of two particularly imaginative subjects, a "truth gas" that would make them answer the questionnaire honestly. But all agreed that the smoke did not come from a fire and thus was nothing to worry about. The presence of other people produced audience inhibition and social influence that led these subjects to decide that the ambiguous situation was not a threat.

Later research verified that these effects were quite general and easily observed in many different settings. In 48 separate studies of over 6,000 individuals, groups consistently helped less than a single person (Latané & Nida, 1981). This large body of research also enabled social psychologists to identify factors that increased—and decreased—helping behavior. For example, bystanders were more likely to help in an emergency when the situation was less ambiguous or when others at the scene affirmed the seriousness of the situation and the desirability of taking action.

Aside from the inherent interest of this phenomenon, the classic studies described here provide several insights into the character of social psychology. According to the data summarized in Figure 15.2, in every experimental condition there were some people who did help and some who did not. Social psychologists typically do not focus on the personality traits that might distinguish these individuals. They have traditionally been more interested in demonstrating the average effects of different types of social stimuli than in exploring individual differences.

Further, in both studies described in this section, subjects were at first deceived about the actual nature of the experiment.

This research strategy raises some very difficult ethical problems (see "How Do They Know?" p. 578), and a concern over the ethics of experimentation was one of the factors that led to the reevaluation of social psychology and the "crisis of confidence" in the 1970s.

Finally, it is important to note that this research examined how individuals responded to a larger group. Many of the classic studies in social psychology described later in this chapter (such as Asch's studies of conformity and Milgram's research on obedience) share this orientation. However, an influential minority of social psychologists have explored group processes, such as the way group members interact and how groups related to each other.

GROUP PROCESSES

Beginning in the 1930s, many social psychologists became interested in the processes involved when groups reach decisions and the relative merits of individual versus group decision making. Their methods ranged from laboratory studies of groups formed strictly for the purposes of an experiment to more naturalistic studies of already existing juries and committees.

In one of the most naturalistic investigations to date, Irving Janis (1972) studied historical documents to reconstruct President John F. Kennedy's ill-fated decision to send a group of CIA-trained Cuban exiles to invade Cuba at the Bay of Pigs in 1961. The invasion was a colossal failure from start to finish. Janis later cited it as a prime example of **groupthink**—the suspension of critical thought that can lead to poor decisions when highly cohesive groups become preoccupied with seeking unanimity. Janis identified several symptoms of groupthink, including an illusion of invulnerability produced by high morale, an illusion of morality produced by shared values, and an illusion of unanimity produced by members' reluctance to express nonconformist doubts.

Groupthink is just one example of the many kinds of decision-making processes that have been analyzed by social psychologists. As a result of this large body of research, we now know a great deal about the conditions that maximize—and minimize—group productivity.

Another line of research has examined the relationships between groups that can lead to cooperation or conflict. In one classic field study (Sherif, Harvey, White, Hood, & Sherif, 1961), researchers divided boys at a summer camp into two groups. The Eagles and the Rattlers, as the groups later nicknamed themselves, lived in separate cabins, and their major contact came in contests that pitted the two groups against each other, including baseball games and a tug of war. By minimizing contact and emphasizing competition rather than mutual enjoyment, the investigators developed a strong differentiation between the *in-group* (the group a particular boy belonged to) and the *out-group* (the other). Mutual hostility was seen when the boys were asked to describe members of the out-group; more than half used terms like *weak, sneaky,* and *stinkers.* Occasional acts of hostility occurred, as when the Eagles burned the Rattlers' flag after they had lost an athletic event.

To reconcile the groups, the investigators first provided an opportunity for pleasant interactions by having them go to movies and other events together. This was a dismal failure; the Eagles and the Rattlers called each other names and threw paper plates around the room. Appeals to ethical values and good sense were equally unsuccessful. Finally, the researchers discovered a tactic that worked: They created common crises. In one instance, a rag "got stuck" in the water line to the camp; when the two groups were forced to work together to solve this mutual problem and other problems, the level of hostility was gradually reduced.

Later studies supported the idea that common goals can bring together the warring factions of a larger group. Nevertheless, the ease with which these groups of 11- and 12-year-olds formed themselves into in-groups and out-groups was quite disturbing. Many social psychologists have built upon this foundation to study how prejudice, stereotyping, and discrimination arise in the real world and what can be done about them. Although there are no simple answers, the application of that knowledge could make a difference to the future of society.

Again, an overview as brief as this can only hint at what we know. But the wide range of procedures reviewed thus far—from historical analyses of foreign policy decisions to laboratory studies of artificial emergencies—should serve as a reminder that social psychology is an unusually broad discipline. The remainder of this chapter is devoted to three of the most important issues in this field: How do people perceive each other, how do we influence each other, and how is social behavior influenced by the physical environment?

Social Perception

When we perceive a physical object such as an Apple computer or a box of Wheaties, the human brain actively constructs a coherent mental image from incomplete and sometimes ambiguous information (see Chapter 4). Similarly, **social perception**—the process of perceiving other people and interpreting their actions—is an active mental process that involves making inferences and drawing conclusions. But social perception is more complicated than object perception because the observer is called upon to draw many more conclusions: What is that person feeling? What are her intentions? What is she really like?

Further, social perception can influence later behavior. In one classic study (Kelley, 1950), college students were given brief written descriptions of a guest instructor before he began teaching. Half the written statements described the man as a "rather cold" person, while the other half said that he was "very warm." These casually constructed first impressions strongly influenced the way students evaluated his teaching. Although both groups sat through the same class, those who had been told that the teacher would be warm rated him as less formal and more considerate, sociable, popular, and humorous. More important, they actually treated him differently: 56% of the students who expected a warm teacher participated in class discussions, versus 32% of those who expected him to be cold. Several other examples of self-fulfilling prophecies—in which social perception changes behavior—were described in Chapter 1. Taken together, this evidence suggests that if we ever hope to understand human relationships, we must consider how people form opinions of one another.

FORMING IMPRESSIONS

As in the case of the warm or cold teacher, we often form impressions of people on the basis of small fragments of data. For another example, see the two men in Figure 15.3: Which man would you lend $100 to? Most people would probably pick the man in the suit and tie because he looks more respectable and reliable. Of course, he may have put on a tie because he is posing as an insurance salesman to cheat a 69-year-old widow out of her life savings. And the other fellow may actually be a suburban dentist with three children who likes to sit around in an undershirt sipping beer on weekends. In reality, Figure 15.3 shows the same man in different situations. Despite the fact that impressions can be quite misleading, they often influence the way we treat people and the way they treat us in return.

Physical Appearance. Although the cliché warns us not to judge a book by its cover, research suggests that much of the time we do judge others primarily by their physical appearance. For example, people who wear glasses are frequently considered more intelligent, reliable, and industrious than those who don't wear them (Manz & Lueck, 1968). Similarly, obese teenaged girls were judged to be less disciplined and more self-indulgent than girls of normal weight (De Jong, 1977). In another study, bearded college students were perceived as more masculine, mature, self-confident, dominant, courageous, and liberal (Pellegrini, 1973)—not to mention hairier.

Figure 15.3
The importance of physical appearance—Which man would you lend $100 to?

One factor that is especially influential in shaping impressions is physical attractiveness. In one typical study (Dion, Berscheid, & Walster, 1972), college students were asked to rate the personal characteristics of photographs of people who had been classified by other judges as physically attractive, unattractive, or average. The attractive people were perceived as happier, more successful, having a better personality, and more likely to get married.

This bias against "uglies" extends to childhood. In one study (Dion, 1972), women were asked to evaluate the actions of various children who had misbehaved. In some cases, the written account was accompanied by a photograph of an attractive child; other adults read the same account but saw a picture of a less attractive child. The women tended to make excuses for the attractive children and blame the unattractive ones.

Although this positive bias for physically attractive people has now been observed by many researchers, there is one fascinating exception: It may not apply to American blacks. In a study of 662 elementary school children, Muruyama and Miller (1981) found that among whites and Mexican-Americans, physically attractive children (identified by raters who did not know them) were indeed likely to be rated more favorably by interviewers, teachers, parents, and peers. But this was not true for black children; physical attractiveness did not lead to higher ratings on other qualities. These cultural differences could also be seen in the children's concepts of themselves; self-esteem was highest among the most physically attractive children for whites and Mexican-Americans but not for blacks. If this finding is replicated, it may provide fascinating insights into cultural differences between these groups. In the next section, a comparable difference in the nonverbal behavior of blacks and whites serves to remind us of the complexity of social stimuli; they never act in a vacuum but always derive their meaning from a particular context.

Nonverbal Behavior. Ordinarily, our conscious communication with other people is based on language. But nonverbal cues help to form impressions: how close another person stands or whether she looks you in the eye, lightly touches your arm, gestures, or maintains a certain posture.

Although some authors have published dictionaries of body language describing what many different postures and gestures "really mean" (see "Becoming a Critical Consumer"), these systems are more often based on creative imagination than on factual research. Like words themselves, nonverbal cues may have many different meanings depending on the precise context.

One form of nonverbal behavior that has been extensively studied involves gaze and eye contact. In a number of situations, people who avert their gaze and fail to look others in the eye are perceived as more formal, nervous, or less friendly (Le Compte & Rosenfeld, 1971). But in religious confession and some types of psychotherapy, eye contact may be avoided to minimize embarrassment.

The impression created by eye contact may depend not just on the physical

Gazing into another's eyes is often a nonverbal sign of attraction, as in this scene from the film *Gone with the Wind*.

Reading Body Language

Several guidelines are available to reading the nonverbal messages unconsciously sent by body language. As you read this short selection from *How to Read a Person Like a Book* (Nierenberg & Calero, 1972), evaluate the quality of the evidence upon which the claims are based. Should you believe it? (A brief discussion appears after the "Summary" at the end of this chapter.)

> We have observed in our recordings that quite frequently during the stage of the negotiation when issues are being presented and discussed or when a heated argument is taking place, one or both of the negotiators have their legs crossed. . . . We observed that the number of negotiations where settlements were reached increased greatly when both negotiators had uncrossed their legs and moved toward each other. In our recordings of such confrontations, we cannot recall one situation that resulted in a settlement where even one of the negotiators still had his legs crossed. Individuals who cross their legs seem to be the ones who give you the most competition and need the greatest amount of attention. In further verification, we discussed the crossed-leg, leaning-away position with numerous salesmen. None could recall being able to close a sale with the prospect in that position. If crossed legs are coupled with crossed arms, you really have an adversary (pp. 49–50).

situation but also on what is being said. During interviews about pleasant matters, interviewers who looked the subject right in the eye received more positive ratings. But when the same interviewers raised unpleasant topics, more eye contact led to less positive ratings (Ellsworth & Carlsmith, 1968).

Further, the meaning of eye contact can vary for different social groups and sometimes create misunderstandings. LaFrance and Mayo (1976) compared the gaze patterns in conversations between two white people or two black people in such natural settings as cafeterias, fast-food outlets, and airport waiting rooms. They found that whites tended to look at their conversational partner as they listened, while blacks tended to look away while listening.

Some disturbing implications of this cultural difference emerged when they went on to film an extended conversation between a black graduate student and a white corporation executive. As in earlier studies, the white person tended to look at his partner when he listened and look away when he spoke. But the black participant did just the opposite. As a result, when the white speaker paused and looked directly at the black, this nonverbal cue to take over the conversation was sometimes misinterpreted and both remained silent. Similarly, when the black speaker paused and stared at his partner, sometimes both began to speak at once. In this case, cultural differences in the meaning of nonverbal cues produced some uncomfortable moments that interfered with communication.

Our first impressions of people are shaped by factors like physical appearance and nonverbal behavior that can easily mislead the observer. Let us now systematically review some typical errors in person perception after discussing social relationships that are deeper and longer-lasting than first impressions.

ATTRACTION

When people describe how they became involved with their friends or lovers, they often refer to "love at first sight" or a kind of "natural chemistry" that attracted them. According to social psychologists, the truth is often far duller. For example, after reviewing several studies of how married couples first met, Kephart (1961) concluded:

> Cherished notions about romantic love notwithstanding, it appears that when all is said and done, the "one and only" may have a better than 50–50 chance of living within walking distance! (p. 269).

And indeed, many researchers have found that one of the most important factors in both liking and loving is sheer physical proximity.

Proximity.   People who have lived their whole lives in St. Louis, Missouri, are not likely to have many friends in Albuquerque, New Mexico. But on a far more immediate level, you are likely to be most friendly with people who live or work nearby. For example, department store clerks are more likely to become friendly with a salesperson who works right next to them than to a person who works a few feet farther away (Gullahorn, 1952).

Perhaps the most convincing evidence regarding proximity comes from a classic study of friendships in housing for married graduate students at the Massachusetts Institute of Technology (Festinger, Schachter, & Back, 1950). Since students were randomly assigned apartments as they became available, researchers simply asked each resident to name the three people in the building whom they saw most frequently on a social basis. Next-door neighbors were named most often, then people two doors away, three doors away, and so on (see Figure 15.4).

Interestingly, seemingly minor physical features of the housing had a major impact on the social lives of its occupants. People whose apartments were next to mailboxes, entrances, and stairways came into contact with a larger number of residents and formed more friendships. Further, the building was designed in such a way that the doors of a few apartments opened on the opposite side of the building from all the others; presumably, the architect felt that this produced a more attractive exterior. The couples assigned to these apartments rarely came into contact with other residents and became socially isolated. This study was one of the first to suggest that architectural design could have a major impact on social relationships (see "Applied Psychology").

Another demonstration of the power of proximity came from a study of 44 men who went through a training program for the Maryland State Police (Segal, 1974). Here, the single most important factor in predicting friendships was their place in

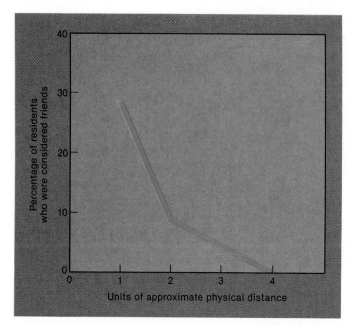

Figure 15.4

In a classic study of friendship in graduate student housing, the most important factor was physical proximity. The closer two people's apartments were, the more likely they were to become friends (Festinger, Schachter, & Back, 1950).

alphabetical order! Men whose last names were close in the alphabet sat near each other in classes and were assigned nearby rooms in the barracks. This physical proximity was a better predictor of who became friends than religious or ethnic background, age, marital status, parents' education, leisure activities, or a variety of other common interests and attitudes.

Although in some situations proximity can intensify hostile feelings, it more often leads to attraction. The reasons are not entirely understood, but they may be related to the fact that familiarity seems to increase liking (rather than contempt, as the proverb would have us believe). Further, other sources of evidence suggest that most human interactions are rewarding. As a result, the more frequent contact brought on by physical proximity is likely to produce positive feelings (Berscheid & Walster, 1978).

Similarity.   The possible importance of another factor in human attraction is mentioned in two contradictory clichés: "Opposites attract," but "birds of a feather flock together." Social psychological research has supported the idea that similarity promotes friendship, but little evidence has been found for the idea that people who are very different from each other are likely to end up together.

Theodore Newcomb (1961) studied male college students who lived in a cooperative house at the University of Michigan. Attitudes and values were first measured before the students came to school; friendship patterns and attitude changes were monitored throughout the semester. In the first few weeks, physical proximity was the only factor that correlated with friendships. But as these men had more opportunity to get to know one another, similar attitudes played an increasingly large role in the friendships they formed.

Donn Byrne (1971) has established the precise effects of similarity in a careful series of laboratory studies. To eliminate the complications introduced by such variables as physical appearance, chance encounters, mannerisms, and personality, he developed a procedure based on evaluating a "phantom other." After filling out a series of questionnaires describing his own attitudes, the typical subject in these studies read questionnaires filled out by "a stranger" and predicted how much he would like this person. In fact, the questionnaires were completed by the experimenter to construct a "phantom other" who resembled the subject in very specific ways. Similar studies have been performed in several countries, with such varied groups as elementary school children, surgical patients, Job Corps trainees, and alcoholics. The results have been remarkably consistent: The more similar a stranger's attitudes, the more a person expects to like him.

Byrne explains this relationship in terms of reinforcement theory: It is rewarding to have someone agree with you. Therefore, the more someone agrees with your attitudes (specifically, the higher the proportion of agreement), the more that stranger will reinforce you, and the greater will be your attraction. When other complications are eliminated in the controlled world of the "phantom other," there is a direct numerical relationship between the degree of attraction and the proportion of shared attitudes (Clore & Byrne, 1974).

Attempts to evaluate the idea that opposites attract have been less promising. Some researchers (Winch, 1958) have claimed that people seek mates to fulfill complementary needs (for example, a dominant male looks for submissive females). However, most studies have failed to support this idea. Nevertheless, according to one review of the literature (Berscheid & Walster, 1978), the notion of complementary needs "sounds so reasonable" that "psychologists are reluctant to abandon the hypothesis" (p. 80).

Perhaps future research will demonstrate that under some conditions, opposites do indeed attract. In any case, there is little doubt that similarity of attitudes and values is a far more potent factor in human attraction.

Intimate Relationships. You cannot have an intimate relationship with someone you've never met. Thus, variables that influence initial attraction are relevant to deeper relationships, as in the case of the large number of married couples who lived within walking distance before they met. However, several researchers have noted that as a relationship develops, different factors grow in importance.

For example, as our review of first impressions might suggest, in the early stages of a potential sexual relationship, people tend to choose partners on the basis of physical attractiveness (Walster, Aronson, Abrahams, & Rottman, 1966). However, studies of couples who are engaged or "going steady" have found that these couples tend to be matched on physical attractiveness; external ratings of the beauty of the two partners are highly correlated. There is even some evidence that couples who are mismatched in this respect are more likely to break up; a beauty and a beast may be attracted to each other in some cases, but it is less likely to last than a more even match (Hill, Rubin, & Peplau, 1976).

It was only in the 1970s that social psychologists began to study the nature of intimate relationships between friends and lovers. One of the most interesting issues explored in this research regards **self-disclosure,** the degree to which people are willing to reveal information about themselves and their feelings. Table 15.1 lists one scale for assessing self-disclosure in various relationships.

Several studies have shown that self-disclosure is often regulated by *reciprocity;*

TABLE 15.1
Measuring Self-disclosure

Check off the topics you would be willing to discuss with three specific people you know.

A casual acquaintance	An intimate friend of your sex	An intimate friend of the opposite sex	Value	
————	————	————	2.85	1. Whether or not I have ever gone to a church other than my own
————	————	————	5.91	2. The number of children I want to have after I am married
————	————	————	10.02	3. How frequently I like to engage in sexual activity
————	————	————	3.09	4. Whether I would rather live in an apartment or a house after getting married
————	————	————	9.31	5. What birth control methods I would use in marriage
————	————	————	8.56	6. What I do to attract a member of the opposite sex whom I like
————	————	————	5.28	7. How often I go on dates
————	————	————	8.56	8. Times that I have lied to my girlfriend or boyfriend
————	————	————	7.00	9. My feelings about discussing sex with my friends
————	————	————	9.50	10. How I might feel (or actually felt) if I saw my father hit my mother
————	————	————	5.39	11. The degree of independence and freedom from family rules that I have (had) while living at home
————	————	————	2.89	12. How often my family gets together
————	————	————	5.83	13. Who my favorite relatives (aunts, uncles, and so on) are and why

people tend to match each other's levels of self-disclosure. The development of an intimate relationship is usually a process of revealing oneself little by little. Violation of this norm may lead to negative feelings. In one study, people observed a video-taped conversation between two actresses. In some cases, the women purposely mismatched the level of self-disclosure: One described such intimate matters as her mother's nervous breakdown, while the other limited her conversation to the problems of commuting and her college courses. When others rated the two women in the tape, they were best liked when they both had the same degree of self-disclosure

A casual acquaintance	An intimate friend of your sex	An intimate friend of the opposite sex	Value	
_____	_____	_____	6.36	14. How I feel about getting old
_____	_____	_____	6.88	15. The parts of my body I am most ashamed for anyone to see
_____	_____	_____	4.75	16. My feelings about lending money
_____	_____	_____	6.88	17. My most pressing need for money right now (outstanding debts, major purchases that are needed or desired)
_____	_____	_____	7.17	18. How much I spend for my clothes
_____	_____	_____	3.08	19. Laws that I would like to see put into effect
_____	_____	_____	8.94	20. Whether or not I have ever cried as an adult when I was sad
_____	_____	_____	5.33	21. How angry I get when people hurt me
_____	_____	_____	3.44	22. What animals make me nervous
_____	_____	_____	9.37	23. What it takes to hurt my feelings deeply
_____	_____	_____	8.25	24. What I am most afraid of
_____	_____	_____	7.29	25. How I really feel about the people I work for or with
_____	_____	_____	8.85	26. The kinds of things I do that I don't want people to watch

Scoring instructions: The values listed next to each topic were based on judges' ratings of intimacy; high values reflect greater intimacy. The degree of self-disclosure for each person is the average value for the statements you have checked off. For example, if you checked off only statements 12, 16, 19, and 22 for a casual acquaintance, the self-disclosure score would be the average of the values of these four statements [(2.89 + 4.75 + 3.08 + 3.44) ÷ 4 = 3.54]. In all probability, your lowest score will be for the casual acquaintance. More interesting is the comparison between the two intimate friends: Which has a higher score for self-disclosure?

Source: D. A. Taylor & I. Altman. "Intimacy-scaled stimuli for use in research on interpersonal exchange." Naval Medical Research Institute, 1966.

at either a high or low level of intimacy. When they were mismatched, the woman who disclosed little was perceived as cold; the woman who bared her soul was seen as maladjusted.

In self-disclosure, as in so many other aspects of life, timing may be critical. In a similar study, a male confederate of the experimenter revealed that his girlfriend was pregnant near the beginning or near the end of a staged conversation. The person who revealed this intimate information was rated more highly when the disclosure came near the end of the conversation, perhaps because too much too soon can make a person seem nondiscriminating and thus reduce the value of the disclosure (Wortman, Adesman, Herman, & Greenberg, 1976). In all social relationships, the way a person actually behaves is often less important than how that behavior is perceived by another.

INTERPRETING BEHAVIOR: ATTRIBUTION THEORY

In recent years, one of the most active areas in research on social perception has involved **attribution theories,** which describe how people interpret and explain behavior in everyday life.

The first attribution theory was published by Fritz Heider in 1958. In his book *The Psychology of Interpersonal Relations*, Heider was concerned with the way people use common sense to try to understand and explain the events of everyday life. How, for example, does a woman decide what it really means when her husband refuses to take out the garbage? Or how does a teenager decide what his best friend is really like?

Heider was one of the first to call attention to the problem of *social perception—*the processes involved in understanding other individuals and even ourselves. He attempted to discover some of the rules people use to comprehend the actions of those around them.

As psychologists have become increasingly concerned with cognitive processes in recent years, many have built upon Heider's foundations. For example, in Chapter 13 we described how *learned helplessness* may play a role in depression. Although this theory was originally derived from studies of animal learning, we saw that researchers now believe that social perception plays an important role. Depression is most likely to result when failure is attributed to internal, global, and long-term factors.

Similarly, in Chapter 11 we described how critics of trait theories of personality have emphasized the importance of the **fundamental attribution error:** Observers consistently underestimate the power of external forces that influence others' behavior and overestimate the importance of internal personal dispositions. Thus, when a student fails a first quiz, the teacher is far more likely to believe that this was caused by internal factors (such as failure to study or a lack of ability) than by external factors (such as a distracting crisis at home).

Note that the fundamental attribution error applies to observations of other people's behavior. Another line of research has analyzed the process of **self-perception,** how people sometimes draw conclusions from observations of their own behav-

Fritz Heider (1896–   ) is best known for his development of attribution theory. Born in Vienna, Austria, Heider studied in Berlin in the 1920s with such Gestalt psychologists as Köhler and Lewin. He emigrated to the United States in 1930 to work at Smith College and the Clarke School for the Deaf. Although Heider's early work focused on the perception of physical stimuli, his most influential research focused on the social processes involved in perceiving other human beings.

ior. The conclusions may be equally erroneous, but in the opposite direction: When people explain their own behavior, they tend to overestimate the power of external factors and underestimate the importance of internal factors. Thus, the student who failed the quiz is more likely to blame external factors (such as the fairness of the test) than internal factors (such as failure to prepare adequately).

You may note that this type of analysis of self-perception is related to Schachter and Singer's cognitive theory of emotion—that the particular emotion a person experiences depends on how he perceives and interprets a situation (see Chapter 10). As you may remember, in their original experiment some subjects misattributed the cause of their physiological arousal; it was actually caused by an injection of adrenaline, but they attributed it to the happy or angry situation they were in. This led to a series of studies of the misattribution process in which people were purposely given false information about internal states to see how they would interpret it.

In one misattribution study, Valins (1966) asked college males to rate the attractiveness of women in sexually provocative pictures while they listened to the beating of their hearts through a special electronic circuit. Subjects sometimes got false feedback—they heard their hearts beat faster even though there was no change. The pictures they saw during those periods were rated as more attractive (presumably, on some unconscious level they thought: Since my heart is beating faster, I must be excited by this picture). The most general conclusion is that external information can indeed lead people to draw conclusions about their own internal states. Later studies revealed that this type of self-perception is most likely to occur when reactions are mild, ambiguous, or uncertain.

COMMON ERRORS IN SOCIAL PERCEPTION

This brief overview of attributions and errors in social perception has returned us to a theme raised in the section of Chapter 1 titled "When Common Sense Fails." The examples described there are also relevant to this discussion. Expectations and bias often influence perception, as in the case of Dartmouth and Princeton football fans who perceived the same game in very different ways (see page 17). Stereotypes can also change what people remember, as when the childhood of the fictional character Betty K was described as tranquil by people who thought she was heterosexual and stormy by people who thought she was homosexual (see page 18). People also tend to be overly influenced by vivid, concrete information, as in the example of the smoker who was convinced that cigarettes are not dangerous because he knew one three-pack-a-day man who lived to be 86 (see page 19).

Other examples are implicit in some of the phenomena described in this chapter. Consider the fact that physically attractive people create an impression of being happy and intelligent. This false conclusion is one instance of a more general phenomenon called the **halo effect:** Observers assume that a person with one or two positive traits will also possess many other positive qualities.

There are many other examples of systematic bias in common sense that have not been described here. We tend to assume that most other people are like us (Schiffenbauer, 1974). The sociable extravert assumes everyone will love his loud parties, while the inhibited introvert assumes that most people would prefer an evening at home reading. There is also a rather pleasant bias toward evaluating others positively and giving them "the benefit of the doubt" (Sears & Whitney, 1973).

In an introductory text, we cannot list all the sorts of errors people make, any more than we could provide a complete list of the factors involved in attraction or impressions. Instead, this overview is one last attempt to convince you that common sense is not the best key to understanding human behavior. A greater awareness of the pitfalls of trusting common sense can lead us to more accurate perceptions of other people and even of ourselves.

Social Influence

What is the best way to persuade a friend to accompany you to a Swedish film about alienation instead of going bowling? How can you convince a potential employer that you are the best woman for the job? How do advertisers motivate us to buy a particular brand of snow tires?

One of the most important themes in social psychology is the study of how people influence one another. Much of this research has focused on the nature of attitudes—how they are first formed and how they can later be changed.

ATTITUDES

An **attitude** may be defined as a relatively lasting tendency to react to a person, object, or event in a particular way. This reaction includes three major components:

cognitive, affective, and behavioral tendencies. The *cognitive component* involves intellectual beliefs, such as the idea that a mango is a tropical fruit. The *affective component* involves emotional evaluations, as when you like tropical fruits. Finally, an attitude involves a *behavioral component*, such as being likely to order the mango cocktail in a fruit bar.

All three components—cognitive, affective, and behavioral—must be present in an attitude. In contrast, psychologists use the word *belief* to refer to information that does not have affective implications. For example, the fact that the human eye can distinguish between 7.5 million different colors (see Chapter 4) is a belief. Whether this belief is factually correct or not, most people are not likely to get too upset if someone else came along to argue that the eye can really only see 6.4 million different colors.

The relationships of the three components of attitudes can be quite complex.

One technique for inducing attitude change is called propaganda. This Nazi pamphlet which was distributed to American soldiers during World War II is one example.

Social psychologists have been particularly interested in the extent to which behavior can be predicted from emotional feelings and cognitive beliefs.

One of the first researchers to tackle this problem was a psychologist named La Piere (1934) who was interested in the nature of prejudice. In the 1930s, many Americans were prejudiced against Orientals. When LaPiere went on a cross-country tour with a Chinese couple during this period, he kept notes about the service at 66 hotels and 184 restaurants they went to. During the entire vacation, only one establishment refused to serve the Chinese couple. But when LaPiere sent a questionnaire to these very same hotels and restaurants, 92% of the 128 places that responded said that they would not serve Chinese guests. Clearly, there was a tremendous discrepancy between intolerant attitudes and tolerant behavior.

Psychologists now know that the strength of the relationship between verbal attitudes and overt behavior varies with such factors as the strength of the attitude, its relevance in a particular situation, and the length of time between the attitude and behavior measurements. For example, Davidson and Jaccard (1979) interviewed 244 married women about their attitudes toward birth control, then interviewed them again two years later about their own behavior. Actually using birth control pills was only very weakly correlated with general attitudes toward birth control ($r = .08$). However, the correlation was much higher when the question asked specifically about attitudes toward birth control pills ($r = .32$). And an even more specific question about using birth control pills during the next two years was most strongly correlated with behavior ($r = .57$). Thus, when questions were phrased so that they related specifically to the particular behavior, the relationship was quite strong.

PERSUASION AND ATTITUDE CHANGE

Four centuries before Christ, Aristotle identified three ways an effective speaker could be persuasive: by convincing his listeners he was credible, by stirring the emotions of his audience, or by the speech itself. When social psychologists began systematically to study attitude change nearly 24 centuries later, they focused on these same three factors: the *source*, the *audience*, and the *message*.

The most influential figure in pioneer research on persuasion was Carl Hovland, a psychologist who was assigned during World War II to study ways to maintain military morale. Table 15.2 provides an overview of the major factors Hovland and later researchers found to be important. Here, we focus on some typical studies to provide a concrete feeling for the nature of this research.

Fear-inducing Messages.   In everyday life, people often try to persuade others by inducing fear. The minister who tells his flock that sinners will burn in Hell, the parent who threatens a child with cutting off his allowance, and the drug agency that tells us that speed kills all assume that these fears will affect attitudes and behaviors.

Not surprisingly, researchers have learned that the effects of a threatening message depend in part on other variables. In one study (Dabbs & Leventhal, 1966), several groups of college students were warned about the seriousness of tetanus and urged to get inoculations. Subjects in the high-fear condition heard vivid, explicit, and frightening descriptions of the disease. A milder description of the physical problems produced low fear for another group. The results were extremely clear-cut: The high-fear message produced more attitude change regarding tetanus shots, and more people from the high-fear group actually went to the college health service and received inoculations.

However, other studies have revealed that if the message unintentionally produces a feeling of vulnerability, people may be "paralyzed by fear" and actually be less likely to change their attitudes or take action to cope with the threat (Leventhal, 1970). To be effective, a threatening message must provide strong evidence that very unpleasant consequences are likely, as well as concrete recommendations for action that will almost certainly avoid these consequences. In other words, if a fire-and-brimstone preacher overdoes it and makes people feel that they are almost certainly going to Hell, many may become worse sinners as a result.

TABLE 15.2
How to Be Convincing

The following general guidelines are based on a large body of systematic research on the process of attitude change (Zimbardo, Ebbesen, & Maslach, 1977; Middlebrook, 1980). As explained in the text, more precise predictions are possible from the interactions between several variables.

For maximum effect, the *source* of a message should:

1. Be perceived as having expertise (relevant knowledge and judgment).
2. Be perceived as trustworthy (unbiased).
3. Be perceived as likable and powerful.
4. Begin by expressing views that agree with those of the audience.

For maximum effect, the *message* should:

1. Repeat important arguments.
2. Invoke fear only if explicit action is recommended that is guaranteed to reduce unpleasant consequences.
3. Support a position that is *moderately* different from that of the audience.

For maximum effect, the message should be tailored to the *audience*.

1. Present only one side of an argument if the audience is basically in agreement and will not soon hear a speaker for the other side; present both sides of the argument if the audience disagrees substantially with the speaker or will soon hear the other side from someone else.
2. Simple messages are more likely to convince audience members low in self-esteem; complex messages are more likely to convince audience members high in self-esteem.
3. Draw explicit conclusions for most audiences; if the audience is very intelligent, let them draw their own conclusions.
4. Direct arguments at the reasons this particular audience holds an attitude.

Mark Waters was a chain smoker. Wonder who'll get his office?

Too bad about Mark. Kept hearing the same thing everyone does about lung cancer. But, like so many people, he kept right on smoking cigarettes. Must have thought, "been smoking all my life... what good'll it do to stop now?" Fact is, once you've stopped smoking, no matter how long you've smoked, the body begins to reverse the damage done by cigarettes, provided cancer or emphysema have not developed.

Next time you reach for a cigarette, think of Mark. Then think of your office—and your home.

American Cancer Society

An advertisement based on fear. Research suggests that this particular ad should be effective because it explains one cause of lung cancer and offers a concrete solution: Stop smoking.

Audience Self-esteem.   One of the most important personality characteristics known to be related to persuasion is **self-esteem,** the value a person places on her own worth. According to McGuire (1968), because people with low self-esteem are less confident of their own abilities, they tend to yield more easily to other people's arguments. On the other hand, people with high self-esteem have been shown to be more interested in the external world and therefore more attentive to complex messages and more capable of understanding them. If this reasoning is correct, simple messages should produce more attitude change for people who are low in self-esteem, while complicated messages should produce more attitude change for people who are high in self-esteem.

To test this idea, Nisbett & Gordon (1967) administered a test of self-esteem to 152 undergraduates and then provided them with a number of statements about health. Some statements were simple and direct claims that did not cite supporting evidence. Others were more complicated and included a great deal of documentation which was rather involved. These complex messages did indeed produce the greatest attitude change for the high–self-esteem group. In contrast, the simpler messages were most influential for people whose self-esteem was somewhat lower.

COGNITIVE DISSONANCE.

While some social psychologists have studied the influence of characteristics of the source, message, and audience, others have developed more general theories of attitude change. Leon Festinger's (1957) theory of cognitive dissonance has been particularly influential, in part because its predictions often contradict common sense.

For example, suppose two teenagers are hired one summer by a large suburban cinema complex to scrape bubble gum off the bottom of the theater seats. One teenager earns $3 an hour for this menial task, but the other is a nephew of the owner and is paid $12 an hour for the same work. If neither worker knows what the other earns, who will have a higher opinion of his summer job? The $12-an-hour employee will be more content with his work, your common sense probably replies without hesitation. Wrong, wrong, wrong says Festinger's theory. In a few pages, we shall see why.

Festinger uses the expression **cognitive dissonance** to refer to a contradiction (dissonance) between two different thoughts (cognitions) or a thought and behavior. He further argues that people find such contradictions unpleasant; therefore, when faced with a logical conflict, a person will try to reduce the cognitive dissonance by changing attitudes or behavior.

Consider the cognitive dissonance faced by a woman who smokes a pack of cigarettes every day even though she knows cigarettes cause heart disease, lung cancer, and bad breath. Unless this woman is suicidal and enjoys bad breath, she is faced with a logical discrepancy between the attitude "Cigarettes are harmful" and the behavior "I smoke cigarettes." There are two major ways to reduce the unpleasantness associated with this cognitive dissonance: Change the behavior or change the attitude.

Quitting smoking may seem the most rational course, but it is so difficult that many people will reduce the cognitive dissonance by changing the attitude. They may seek out information that questions the negative effects of smoking, or they may argue that "I could be hit by a bus tomorrow," so it's more important to eat, smoke, and be merry in the meantime.

In one of the first studies of cognitive dissonance, Festinger, Riecken, and Schachter (1956) followed the progress of a small religious cult that had predicted that much of the world would be destroyed by earthquakes, tidal waves, and floods on December 21. This claim was based on messages a suburban housewife named Marian Keech had received from superior beings from the planet Clarion. Cynics that they were, these social psychologists assumed that the world would still be intact on December 22. But they joined the cult anyway to study the massive cognitive dissonance that would result when this prophecy failed.

In the early evening on December 21, a group of about 15 believers met in Mrs. Keech's home to wait for a flying saucer that would arrive at midnight to transport the faithful to Clarion, or possibly Venus. While a skeptical Mr. Keech slept soundly through the night, Mrs. Keech and the others followed the instructions they had received from the aliens. Since metal is not allowed on flying saucers, they removed all metal buttons, clasps, buckles, and zippers from their clothing. Just to be on the safe side, one man even threw away the aluminum foil wrapper from his gum. After everyone had memorized the secret password needed to enter the flying saucer ("I left my hat at home"), they sat around to wait.

Midnight came and went without any sign from the aliens. After several hours of unbearable tension, Mrs. Keech finally received another message at 4:45 a.m.: God had decided to spare the earth because of the faith of this special group. There would be no flood and no flying saucer.

Intuitively, one might expect the others to slink quietly home and hope their neighbors would forget the prediction. But instead this message marked the beginning of a new phase for the group. Previously, they had tried to avoid all publicity; now they called reporters and agreed to television interviews to let everyone know of their victory and to seek new members. Festinger and his colleagues explained this surprising reaction by their theory of cognitive dissonance. A member who abandoned the sect would be faced by a massive contradiction; some had even quit their jobs or squandered their savings in anticipation of leaving the Earth. But this dissonance could be reduced by the new explanation and bolstered by the support of other members of the small group "whose faith had saved the world."

In a more systematic study of cognitive dissonance, Festinger and Carlsmith (1959) required subjects to perform such dull tasks as removing spools from a tray, placing them back, removing them again, and so on for an hour. Afterwards, a control group of one-third of the subjects were simply asked to rate the interest value of these "measures of performance"; as expected, their ratings suggested that the experiment was duller than watching vanilla ice cream melt.

The remaining people were asked to tell a waiting subject that the experiment they had just completed was "exciting and fun." The researcher claimed that his assistant had failed to show up to provide this positive introduction and that he was willing to pay for the help. Half the subjects were paid $1 for describing the deadly dull task as exciting; the other half were paid $20. After giving their little pep talks, all of these subjects were later asked for an honest rating of just how exciting removing all those spools had really been. According to the theory of cognitive dissonance, describing a dull experiment as exciting involved a logical contradiction that people will find unpleasant. The people who were given $20, however, had a rational explanation for the lie: They were well paid. In contrast, those who earned only $1 did not

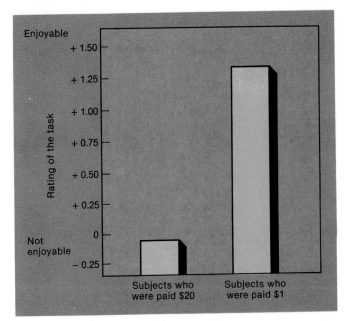

Figure 15.5

In Festinger & Carlsmith's classic study of cognitive dissonance (1959), subjects who were paid only $1 to describe a boring task as interesting later rated the task more favorably than did those who had been paid $20.

have a logical excuse. In order to reduce their dissonance, Festinger predicted that the low-paid subjects would justify the "exciting" description by convincing themselves that it was not a complete lie; the experiment was not really *that* boring.

The results confirmed this prediction: People who had been paid $1 later described the study more favorably than those who had been paid $20. Festinger argued that these results supported a more general proposition: The less justification one has for behavior, the more favorably it will be perceived. The implication for the two teenagers described at the beginning of this section is obvious. The worker who is paid only $3 an hour to remove chewed gum will have less external justification for the job than the person who is paid $12 an hour. Thus, the poorly paid worker will experience greater dissonance; one way to reduce it is to develop a more favorable attitude toward his work.

In another study that led to the same conclusion, college women went through mild or severe initiations to join a discussion group about sexual behavior. The severe initiation consisted of an "embarrassment test" that involved reading aloud 12 obscene words that nice girls didn't use when the study was conducted, and also two vivid sexual scenes from novels; the mild initiation involved reading far less offensive material. The actual group the women were allowed to join after "passing this test" was a dull, dry, banal discussion of a book on sex-related habits of lower animals in which participants spoke haltingly, contradicted themselves and one another, and "in general conducted one of the most worthless and uninteresting discussions imaginable" (Aronson & Mills, 1959, p. 179).

As expected, those who went through a mild initiation or none at all later rated

A freshman who hopes to join the marching band at Georgia's Young-Harris High School is initiated by having an egg cracked over her head. According to the theory of cognitive dissonance, this unpleasant experience should increase her later commitment to the marching band.

the discussion as stupid and boring; those who went through the more severe initiation consistently gave the discussion higher ratings. Thus, the theory of cognitive dissonance has important implications for fraternities, sororities, and social groups everywhere: The more foolish and insignificant a group, the more severe an initiation may be required to make people think that membership is worthwhile.

While virtually all social psychologists agree that insufficient justification for an act produces more favorable attitudes, some have questioned the idea that this is caused by cognitive dissonance. Daryl Bem (1965) presented evidence that the results were better explained by *attribution processes of self-perception.* According to this view, if a person is paid $20 to exaggerate the interest value of an experiment, he will conclude that the money caused him to tell this lie. But if there is no convincing external cause—as in the case of the subject paid only $1 to tell the same lie—he will attribute the action to internal causes and decide that he must have liked the experiment at least a little, or he would not have told the lie.

Self-perception is not the only theoretical rival to cognitive dissonance. **Impression management theory** emphasizes the importance of the appearance of an act to outside observers. Each of us seeks approval from others, and sometimes we may act in a certain way to create a particular impression on others. In this view, it is not a feeling of inconsistency that bothers people but the potential effects that appearing inconsistent might have on other people's opinions of us (Tedeschi, Schlenker, & Bonoma, 1971).

Research to evaluate the relative merits of these and other theories has made it clear that each theory is useful to explain certain types of behavior. Self-perception theory seems especially applicable to vague, ambiguous, and minor attitudes; cognitive dissonance seems to apply to more controversial issues in which a person feels committed to a particular point of view by choice. Given the fact that there are so many different types of attitudes and so many ways to try to change them, it is not surprising that several processes are involved. The question for future research is not to decide which theory is "right" but rather what are the situations in which a particular theory will apply?

CONFORMITY AND OBEDIENCE

While some psychologists have focused on social influences on attitudes, others have studied the way social groups directly influence behavior through two closely related processes, conformity and obedience. **Conformity** refers to behavior motivated by pressure from other members of a group. Conformity is one example of a more general phenomenon called **obedience** (or compliance) in which people follow the suggestions or orders of another person, even when they prefer not to.

Conformity. In 1951, Solomon Asch published an elegant study of the extent to which judgment could be influenced by social pressure from the members of a group. He devised a simple and unambiguous task for his experimental groups: They would be shown cards displaying four lines of various lengths and simply be asked to pick out the two lines that were equally long, as in Figure 15.6. This comparison would be performed by each member of a group of seven to nine people; each person would take a moment to look at the cards, then announce his decision aloud so that it could be recorded by an experimenter.

All but one of the group members were confederates who had been hired to behave in a certain way. On 5 of the 12 sets of lines used in this experiment, they

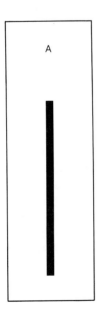

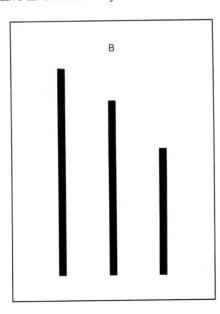

Figure 15.6

Stimuli similar to those from Asch's study of conformity. The line in (*A*) is obviously equal in length to the middle line in (*B*). But when five or six group members said that it matched one of the other lines, some subjects conformed to the majority view.

A   B   C

Actual photos of Asch's experiment. The sixth man from the left in photograph *A* is the subject; all other group members purposely give some wrong answers. In photo *B*, the subject leans forward to look at the cards when all the others give an obviously incorrect response. In photo *C*, this particular subject resists the group pressure and gives the correct answer.

provided the correct answer. But on the other 7 trials, all the confederates chose the same wrong answer. The actual subject was carefully seated at the end of the group, so that he heard everyone else agreeing on the wrong answer before it got to his turn. Asch's question was this: Would the subject have the backbone to give the answer that was obviously correct, or would he simply go along with the crowd and provide the same wrong answer everyone agreed with?

Of the 217 trials in which the group chose the wrong answer, the subject went along with this incorrect opinion on 72 trials. Subjects fidgeted, looked bewildered, smiled foolishly, and even walked over to look more closely at the lines, but in the end they went along with the group's clearly incorrect opinion about 33% of the time.

Asch also noted that some of his subjects seemed far more susceptible to this social influence than others. Only 6 of the 31 participants gave the right answer on every trial, no matter what the group thought. At the other extreme, 2 subjects gave in on all 7 trials and repeatedly agreed with the majority opinion even when it was quite clearly wrong.

Asch and other researchers went on to specify the precise conditions that produced the greatest conformity. Unanimity was one important factor; when just one other group member gave the right answer, the percentage of answers conforming to the majority opinion dropped dramatically (Asch, 1951). Ambiguity was another critical variable: When the test lines were closer in length, the subject was even more likely to accept the judgment of others.

For our purposes, the most important lesson of Asch's classic study is quite straightforward: Group members can exert powerful pressures to conform to their beliefs simply by agreeing with one another.

Obedience.   A more dramatic and controversial example of social influences involves obedience, people's willingness to follow orders. Stanley Milgram (1963) posed the problem this way:

From 1933–45 millions of innocent persons were systematically slaughtered on command. Gas chambers were built, death camps were guarded, daily quotas of corpses were produced with the same efficiency as the manufacture of appliances. These inhumane policies may have originated in the mind of a single person, but they could only be carried out on a massive scale if a very large number of persons obeyed orders (p. 371).

To bring obedience into the laboratory, Milgram told subjects that they were participating in a study of the effects of punishment on learning. The learner was a 47-year-old accountant who was really an accomplice of the experimenter. Through a rigged drawing, each subject who reported to the laboratory was "randomly" assigned to the role of the "teacher" who would administer electric shocks to punish mistakes the learner made on a memory task. The front panel of the shock generator had a series of 30 switches for increasingly intense shocks, as shown in Figure 15.7. Each time the learner made an error, the teacher was to administer a stronger shock.

In fact, of course, the study was not really concerned with punishment or memory, and the learner received no shocks at all. Instead, errors were made in a prearranged sequence to see how many shocks these subjects would administer. The victim was out of sight in another room, and in later versions of the study, as the shocks increased in intensity he began to complain: grunting aloud at 75 volts, shouting that it was becoming painful at 120 volts, then at 150 volts crying out, "Experimenter, get me out of here! I won't be in the experiment any more! I refuse to go on!" (Milgram, 1974, p. 23)

If the subject who was delivering the shocks stopped, the experimenter told him sternly to continue. If he did continue, the victim's response would increase to an agonized scream at 270 volts; at 300 volts the victim refused to provide any more answers.

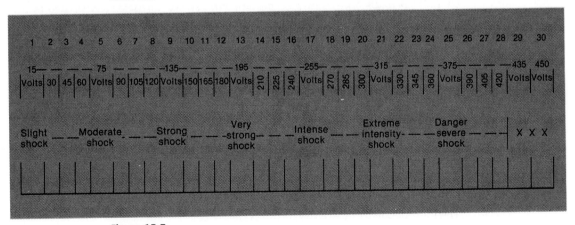

Figure 15.7
Diagram of the shock generator in Milgram's study of obedience. Subjects were required to administer increasingly stronger shocks when a "learner" made mistakes on a memory task. If the "learner" complained about the shocks, at what point would you refuse to give any more shocks?

Ethical Issues in Psychological Research:
The Case of the Obedient Subjects

Diana Baumrind (1964) argued that the rights and feelings of Milgram's subjects in the obedience study had been abused. She believed that people who had administered high levels of shock would have trouble justifying their actions and as a result would lose respect for themselves and lose the ability to trust authority figures. In Baumrind's opinion, a deceptive procedure as emotionally charged as Milgram's would be ethically justified only if it provided clear and immediate benefits to humanity, such as a cure for cancer.

Milgram (1964) replied that he had taken several steps to protect the welfare of his subjects. After the experiment was concluded, each subject was given a complete explanation of the nature and purpose of the research and was reassured that many others had administered high levels of shock to the learner. At this time, subjects were also given an opportunity to work through their feelings. Fully 92% of the original subjects later returned a questionnaire that was mailed to them; 84% of these said they were glad they had participated in the study. A year after the study had ended, a psychiatrist interviewed 40 subjects whom he judged to have the greatest risk of experiencing long-term effects. In his professional judgment, none of these subjects showed signs of having been harmed by the experiment.

Some critics were not satisfied by this reply and continued to debate the ethical values of Milgram's procedure. This was not the first debate among psychologists over the ethics of a research project, but it did help stimulate widespread discussion within the profession about a variety of ethical issues, and the American Psychological Association (APA) appointed a committee to review these problems. After several years of study and consultation, in 1973 the APA adopted a list of 10 ethical principles to regulate research with human participants. (Other principles have also been adopted to regulate animal research.)

According to these principles, participation in an experiment must be totally volun-

Under these conditions, how far do you think the average person would go? Take a moment to look back to Figure 15.7 and predict which switch would be the maximum shock delivered by the typical subject.

When Milgram (1974) asked a group of 39 psychiatrists this question, the average prediction was that people would stop around 120 volts. Separate groups of college students and middle-class adults made similar predictions; even the most cynical respondents believed that the average person would stop at 300 volts. When asked how many people would go all the way to 450 volts, the psychiatrists said that only about 1 person out of 1,000 would deliver this maximum shock.

In his first study with 40 adult men, every single one of them went beyond the average prediction of 120 volts. At 300 volts, 5 subjects refused further cooperation; no one stopped before that point. Fully 26 out of the 40 subjects, or 65%, went all

tary, and subjects must be aware of their right to withdraw from any study at any time. Before a study begins, each subject should sign a statement of informed consent that outlines the nature of the study and the agreements between experimenter and subject. Subjects must be protected from physical and mental discomfort, harm, and danger, and procedures that are likely to cause serious and lasting harm are never permitted.

Psychologists who violate any of the 10 principles outlined in this document can be suspended or expelled from the APA after a complaint is investigated by its Committee on Scientific and Professional Ethics. In addition, universities and research institutions now have committees of their own to review the implications of research proposals, and only ethically acceptable research is allowed to proceed. The United States government requires this type of review for all federally funded programs.

However, the existence of these guidelines and procedures does not imply that debate over the ethics of research is now a thing of the past. The question of deceiving subjects has been particularly complex. According to one principle of the APA (1973) code:

Openness and honesty are essential characteristics of the relationship between investigator and research participant. When the methodological requirements of a study necessitate concealment or deception, the investigator is required to ensure the participant's understanding of the reasons for this action and to restore the quality of the relationship with the investigator (p. 1).

The problem is that even with the best of intentions, psychologists may disagree about when deception is required and what steps will actually restore the quality of the relationship. The APA's code of conduct is only 2 pages long, but it was published with over 100 pages of commentary and explanations to show how it applies in specific cases.

Human societies have debated the relative merits of various ethical codes for several thousand years. It is not surprising that psychologists sometimes disagree about whether a particular experimental procedure is right or wrong. In the final analysis, we psychologists can only promise openly to debate ethical issues as they arise and to try our best to choose the right course.

---

the way to the end and delivered the 450-volt shock. These subjects showed considerable conflict and anxiety, and they did not seem to take sadistic pleasure in the suffering of the mild-mannered learner they had met a few moments before. But the firmness of the experimenter's repeated commands was enough to motivate most subjects to administer shocks they believed to be dangerous. After all, they were "just following orders." (Some of the ethical implications of this study are described in "How Do They Know?")

This basic pattern of results was repeated in other studies of over 1,000 subjects at several universities. Some factors were found to lower obedience, such as being placed in the same room with the learner or being inspired to feel personal responsibility.

Even aside from these qualifications, the results of any psychological study

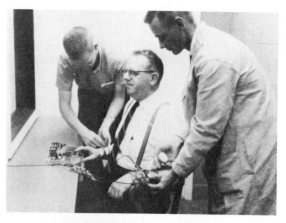
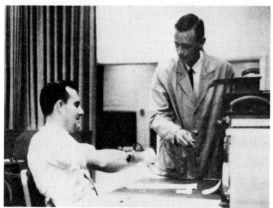
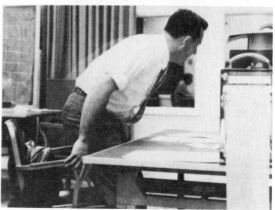

Scenes from Milgram's study of obedience: (upper left) the shock generator; (upper right) the "victim" is strapped into his chair; (lower left) a subject receives a sample shock; (lower right) this subject later refuses to continue administering shocks.

should be generalized cautiously. Other social psychologists have studied how people sometimes resist social pressure. For instance, **reactance theory** analyzes how certain types of restraints on freedom can lead a person to assert her rights (Brehm, 1966). (In everyday language this tendency is sometimes called "reverse psychology.") Asch's and Milgram's results do not mean that people are like sheep, just waiting for someone to lead them astray. They do suggest, as Milgram (1974) put it, that under some conditions, "ordinary people, simply doing their jobs, and without any particular hostility on their part, can become agents in a terrible destructive process" (p. 6). The challenge for social psychology is to specify the types of situations in which this destructive pattern is most likely to appear.

Social Behavior and the Physical Environment

Traditionally, social psychologists have focused on the way behavior is shaped by the social environment of other human beings. In the late 1960s, an influential group of researchers became interested in the way physical environments influence our work and play, our lives and loves, giving birth to a new specialty, **environmental psychology,** which studies the interrelationships between social behavior and the physical settings of everyday life.

In Chapter 4, we described the way environmental psychologists investigated one important physical reality in modern life, how noise affects behavior and experience. Other researchers have studied temperature, air pollution, urban stress, and how people perceive their surroundings. Here we introduce two of the most influential lines of research in this young specialty: the effects of crowding and the effects of architectural design.

CROWDING

In 1975, the world population passed 4 billion. If it continues to grow at the present rate, there will be 8 billion human beings packed on our planet by the year 2010. (Freedman, Sears, & Carlsmith, 1981). Although there are signs that the rate of population growth is beginning to slow, it is likely that the world of tomorrow will be more crowded than today.

There seems to be a widespread perception that this crowding helped create many of the problems of our troubled world. When two psychologists reviewed popular articles listed in the *Readers' Guide to Periodical Literature* over a 10-year period, they found writers who blamed crowding for everything from disease and pollution to crime, war, mental illness, drug addiction, and the breakdown of the family (Zlutnick & Altman, 1972). Many of these articles helped substantiate their claims by describing a classic study by John Calhoun that showed how overcrowding can lead to chaotic conditions in a rat colony.

Calhoun (1962) had devised a special environment by dividing a 10-by-14-foot room into four pens set off from each other by an electrified fence, with ramps for the rats to move from one pen to another. By his estimate, about 48 rats could live in this room comfortably. But Calhoun allowed the population to grow to 80 rats so that he might observe the effects of overcrowding.

Two of the four pens were purposely constructed with fewer connecting ramps and other features to make them less accessible. Each of these two pens was usually taken over by a dominant male rat and his harem of six or seven females; most of the remaining rats would congregate in one of the more central and accessible pens; as many as 60 rats might jam themselves into one pen to eat, although other pens were accessible. Calhoun used the term **behavioral sink** to refer to the pattern of bizarre and antisocial behavior that occurred in the overcrowded pens. Female rats had trouble reproducing and failed to care for the offspring that did survive. Male disturbances included sexual deviation, cannibalism, wild overactivity, and total social withdrawal.

While some experts quickly claimed that overcrowded human slums produced similar "behavioral sinks," those who studied Calhoun's procedures warned that it was not legitimate to generalize from a specially designed rat colony to the real world of human cities. Direct studies of human environments led to very different conclusions. For example, Freedman, Heshka, and Levy (1975) examined the correlations between the crime rate in 97 cities and the population per square mile as well as other possibly relevant variables, such as income, education, and race. Even if they

The psychological perception of crowding is determined not just by population density (the number of people per square foot) but also by situational and cultural variables.

had found that crime and population density were correlated, that would not prove that crowding *causes* crime (see "How Do They Know?" in Chapter 12), only that the two variables were somehow related. As it turned out, this qualification proved unnecessary. A careful statistical analysis revealed that, by itself, population density was not particularly related to crime. Sociological studies of this sort generally have found very few negative effects that are directly related to crowding.

Laboratory studies in which groups are confined in small rooms under crowded conditions have been somewhat less consistent. Some studies report that crowded conditions can lead to poorer performance on difficult tasks, increase later frustration and hostility, raise blood pressure, and sometimes even produce aggression (Sherrod, 1972).

Many environmental psychologists now believe that it is important to distinguish between population density—as measured by the number of square feet per person in a given situation—and the psychological perception of crowding (Stokols, 1972). People may feel quite comfortable if they are jammed into a small space at a concert, a football game, or a party. But precisely that same amount of space per person may feel more crowded on a bus ride or while waiting in line for a license.

There are several major theories regarding the way the psychological perception of crowding can sometimes produce stress and negative effects. One of the most influential theories is that crowding can reduce a person's feeling of control by restricting her movement and forcing her to interact with other people (Cohen & Sherrod, 1978). This idea is related to Martin Seligman's notion of *learned helplessness*—that when people lack a feeling of control, they give up easily when frustrated and become depressed (see Chapter 13). Some environmental psychologists have applied this theory to help architects design living spaces that maximize feelings of control and thus increase the satisfaction of the people who live in them.

APPLIED PSYCHOLOGY

Architectural Design

According to one old architects' joke, "A doctor can bury his mistakes, but an architect can only advise his clients to plant ivy." To some, this may suggest that old architects are not very funny. But it does call attention to the fact that architects have traditionally been primarily concerned with exterior appearance and that buildings last a very long time. In the past, if an architect was concerned with the way the interior design of a building might influence social behavior, he had only his own intuition as a guide.

To fill this gap in knowledge, environmental psychologists are now systematically investigating the way different sorts of living spaces affect human interaction. One of the most careful studies of this subject compared the psychological effects of living in two different types of dormitories at the State University of New York at Stony Brook (Baum & Valins, 1977). Incoming freshmen who did not know one another were randomly assigned to either a traditional corridor dormitory or a dorm arranged into suites. As illustrated in Figure 15.8, each corridor consisted of 17 double bedrooms, a bathroom, and a lounge; the suites grouped 3 bedrooms with a bath and a lounge. The actual number of square feet per person was almost identical for these two types of dormitories; however, as you might guess, the psychological sensation of crowding was not.

On a series of questionnaires, people who lived on the corridor dorm reported feeling more crowded and less satisfied with college life; they also reported more negative feelings about other students who lived in their dorm. Other questions revealed that corridor residents felt less control over their personal lives; they were more often forced into inconvenient or unwanted interactions with others, and over the course of the seven weeks of living in the dorm they increasingly agreed with statements like "It is not worthwhile trying to change things."

These feelings of helplessness and alienation were not limited to life in the dormitory itself. When corridor residents came to a psychology experiment, they sat farther away from others in the waiting room and looked at them less than students who lived in the suite dormitories. Finally, corridor residents performed more competitively on a laboratory task, even when a cooperative approach would have been more productive (Baum, Aiello, & Calesnick, 1978).

A later study revealed how minor changes in the use of physical space could improve the quality of life in a corridor dorm (Baum & Davis, 1980). The dormitory

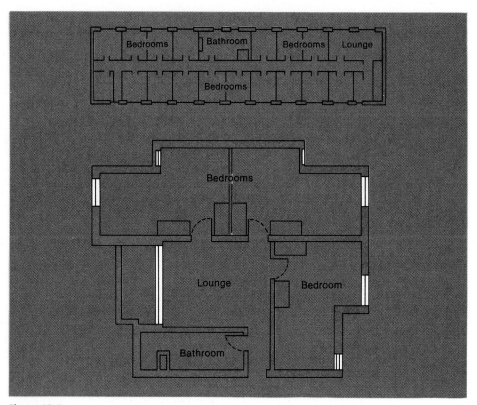

Figure 15.8
Floor plans for corridor and suite-style dormitories studied in Baum & Valin's (1977) explorations of the effects of architecture on behavior.

floor chosen for study had 27 single and double bedrooms arranged along a corridor. The design change could not have been simpler: 3 bedrooms in the middle of the floor were converted into a lounge. This effectively divided the corridor in half; instead of housing a single group of 43 students, the same floor now seemed to house two separate groups of 19 and 20 students. The attitudes and behavior of students living on the redesigned corridor were then compared with others who lived on an unmodified corridor in the same dorm and with a third group of students living in a dorm designed to house about 20 students along a short corridor.

In general, students who lived on the unmodified long corridor were least satisfied with their housing; they reported feeling more crowded, had fewer friends in their dorm, and described dormitory life as more hectic and less controllable. As in the earlier study, over the course of several weeks, long-corridor residents increasingly agreed with general statements of helplessness like "It is often not worth the effort to try to change the way things are."

In this study, an experimenter who was not aware of these predicted effects periodically observed behavior on the three dormitory floors. As the semester wore on, fewer groups of people were observed talking to each other on the long-corridor floor, and fewer doors were left open to encourage contact. Effects were also observed on laboratory behavior. Long-corridor residents acted more withdrawn than the short-corridor groups: they sat farther away from others in a waiting room, looked at others less often, and later reported feeling more uncomfortable during this period.

In the future, environmental psychologists hope to continue to contribute to the quality of life by making changes like these, one small step at a time.

Summary

1. **Social psychology** studies the way people respond to other human beings and how they interact with one another.
2. Studies of responses to emergencies have focused on three major variables: **diffusion of responsibility** (when many observers are present during an emergency, and they cannot observe each other, each can rationalize doing nothing by assuming that someone else must be taking action), **audience inhibition** (a bystander may be inhibited by fear of looking ridiculous if he mistakenly concludes that a situation demands help), and **social influence** (people tend to follow the actions of other bystanders).
3. **Groupthink** is a suspension of critical thought that can lead to poor decisions when highly cohesive groups seek unanimity. This is just one of the many processes identified in studies of group interaction.
4. **Social perception**—the process of perceiving other people and interpreting their actions—is an active mental process of making inferences and drawing conclusions. Among the factors involved in forming impressions of people are physical appearance and nonverbal behavior. *Proximity* and *similarity* are two of the most important variables in initial stages of attraction. Intimate relationships may be determined by other variables such as *reciprocity* of **self-disclosure;** people tend to match the degree of information they reveal about their actions and feelings.
5. **Attribution theories** describe how people interpret and explain behavior in everyday life. For example, the **fundamental attribution error** implies that most people tend to overestimate the importance of the internal dispositions and traits of a person who performs a particular act and to underestimate the influence of external constraints. Another common error in social perception is the **halo effect:** Observers assume that a person with one or two positive traits will also possess many other positive qualities.
6. An **attitude** is a relatively lasting tendency to react to a person, object, or event in a particular way. This reaction includes cognitive, affective, and behavioral tendencies. Three major classes of variables can influence attitude change: the *source*, the *message*, and the *audience*.

7. According to Leon Festinger's theory of **cognitive dissonance,** a contradiction between two different thoughts, or between a thought and behavior, is unpleasant, and so people try to reduce cognitive dissonance by changing the attitude or the behavior. This theory leads to several predictions that contradict common sense, such as the idea that the less justification a person has for a particular act, the more favorably she will evaluate the behavior.

8. This general proposition of cognitive dissonance has been verified in many different contexts, but some researchers have challenged Festinger's interpretation. According to Daryl Bem, these results can be explained by a **self-perception** process in which a person attributes his own behavior to external causes. Another approach, **impression management theory,** emphasizes the importance of the appearance of an act to outside observers. Each of these theories applies particularly well to some types of situations.

9. **Conformity** refers to behavior motivated by pressure from other members of a group. Solomon Asch demonstrated the power of conformity when people agreed to perceptual errors simply because they were accepted by other group members.

10. **Obedience** involves following the suggestion or orders of another person even when one prefers not to. Stanley Milgram showed how easily people will obey orders in a dramatic and controversial study in which subjects administered painful and dangerous shocks to a stranger as part of a "study of learning."

11. **Environmental psychology** is the study of interrelationships between social behavior and the physical settings of everyday life. John Calhoun's studies of rats suggested that overcrowding could lead to a pattern of bizarre and antisocial behavior that he called a **behavioral sink.** However, studies of humans have shown that crowding itself does not necessarily produce harmful effects. A more important issue is the psychological perception of being crowded, rather than a physical definition based on the number of square feet per person. Environmental psychologists have applied these findings and other knowledge about the way living spaces affect behavior to the design of better buildings.

Discussion of "Becoming a Critical Consumer"

The "evidence" cited for these claims consists of casual observations that are questionable. (Chapter 1 describes some of the errors of untrained observers, including selective attention, selective memory, and self-fulfilling prophecies.)

As explained in the text, systematic studies of behavior have revealed that the meaning of nonverbal communication is determined by the situation, the cultural context, and other variables. Schemes like this that promise to reveal the "real meaning" of a particular posture or gesture are far too simpleminded to be accurate.

To Learn More

Walster, E., & Walster, W. *A New Look at Love.* Reading, Mass.: Addison-Wesley, 1978. This introduction to research on "the most elusive of all emotions" won an award from the American Psychological Association as the best popular book of that year.

Perlman, D., & Cozby, P. C. *Social Psychology*. New York: CBS College Publishing, 1983. There are many excellent textbook overviews of social psychology; this one was sponsored by the Society for the Psychological Study of Social Issues, a group of researchers particularly concerned with applying social scientific knowledge to society.

Holahan, C. J. *Environmental Psychology*. New York: Random House, 1982. One of the first comprehensive textbooks of research in this emerging area.

Appendix
Statistics

Descriptive statistics
   The frequency distribution
   Measures of central tendency
   Measures of variability
   Types of frequency distributions

Inferential statistics

Somewhere in the world, there may be a college that does not require psychology majors to learn something about statistics. But I've never heard of it, and you probably don't go there.

Statistics is a vital ingredient in any psychology curriculum. The reason should be obvious to anyone who has read a chapter or two of this book: Statistical analysis provides powerful tools for evaluating claims about behavior. This type of evaluation and critical analysis lies at the very heart of the scientific method.

When a psychologist systematically studies behavior or experience, she typically begins by quantifying such variables as learning, color perception, aggression, or introversion. For example, in his pioneer studies of human memory, Hermann Ebbinghaus began by counting the number of nonsense syllables he was able to remember after various intervals (see Chapter 6). Mathematical procedures were then required to summarize his data and specify the time course for this memory task.

Some people break into a cold sweat when they hear the word *statistics* and may require treatment if asked to compute the probability of a coin coming up tails. This type of math anxiety can lead a student who would like to major in psychology to concentrate on Sanskrit or medieval agriculture instead, simply to avoid a course requirement in statistics.

But, as for most fears, the imagination is usually worse than the reality. Anyone who has ever played cards or tried to decide whether to trust a weatherman's forecast has applied intuitive notions of statistics and probability. This appendix is designed to review some basic concepts of statistical reasoning and to reassure the worriers that statistics is quite straightforward. True, statistical calculations can get involved at times. But even a person who has trouble balancing his checkbook can learn to compute a standard deviation or a correlation coefficient if he just takes the calculations one small step at a time.

Descriptive Statistics

Descriptive statistics provides techniques for summarizing groups of numbers. Several examples are explained throughout this book, ranging from arithmetic averages to correlation coefficients (see "How Do They Know?" in Chapter 3). Here, we review several basic techniques for summarizing a set of data.

THE FREQUENCY DISTRIBUTION

Suppose a test of reading comprehension is given to the entire fifth-grade class at Wayne Newton Memorial Elementary School. The test has 25 multiple-choice questions, and scores could theoretically range from 0 to 25 correct. The scores for the 22 girls in the class are as follows: 18, 19, 16, 21, 17, 20, 20, 19, 22, 21, 19, 19, 18, 17, 21, 20, 19, 18, 18, 20, 17, 19. How would you characterize the performance of this group?

To make sense out of this confusing list, a statistician might begin by grouping the scores into a **frequency distribution,** which summarizes the number of scores that fall into different intervals or segments. The simplest frequency distribution for the fifth-grade girls would simply count the number of students who had earned each score, as shown in Table A.1.

This summary table obviously presents a far clearer picture of the group's performance than the original list. Clearer still are graphic representations of the frequency distribution. Figure A.1 shows a *frequency histogram* of the scores in which each frequency is represented by a bar. Alternatively, each value could be represented by a point on a graph in a *frequency polygon,* as shown in Figure A.2. These two graphs summarize the same information.

To keep this example simple, each interval in Table A.1 consists of a single

TABLE A.1
Frequency Distribution of Reading Comprehension
Scores for 22 Fifth-Grade Girls

Test Score	Number of Students
22	1
21	3
20	4
19	6
18	4
17	3
16	1

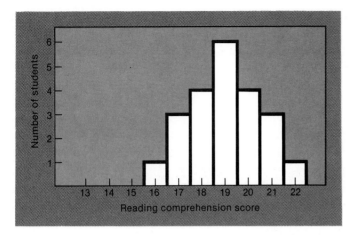

Figure A.1
Frequency histogram of reading comprehension scores for 22 fifth-grade girls.

score. But if you wanted to draw a frequency histogram summarizing the distribution of income in the United States, it would be very confusing to have a separate category for each individual income; people who earned $15,127.64, $15,127.65, and $15,127.66 would be placed in three different categories. Therefore, frequency distributions often classify cases together into larger classes or intervals. Categories of income might be $0 to $10,000, $10,001 to $20,000, $20,001 to $30,000, and so on. The precise intervals would depend on the researcher's interests and data.

Many frequency polygons and histograms appear throughout this book. For example, Figure 12.5 is a frequency polygon of the distribution of IQ in a representative sample of the U.S. population. Figure 3.4 is a frequency histogram of the number of illnesses reported by groups of men who had experienced differing levels of stress in the preceding six months.

Frequency distributions, polygons, and histograms can be very informative, but they are only the first step in a statistical description. To describe a set of data more succinctly, statisticians compute summary statistics of two sorts: measures of central tendency and measures of variability.

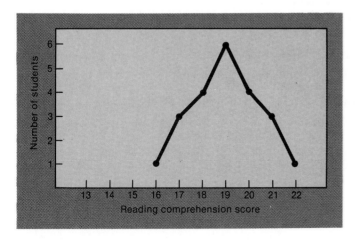

Figure A.2
Frequency polygon of reading comprehension scores for 22 fifth-grade girls.

MEASURES OF CENTRAL TENDENCY

Three different statistics are commonly used to measure the central tendency of a distribution: the *mean*, the *median*, and the *mode*.

The **mean** is the arithmetic average of a group of numbers, computed by summing the values and dividing by the number of values. If we added the 22 scores in Table A.1, the sum would be 418; dividing by 22 yields a mean score of 19.

The **median** is the middle number in a set of values that has been arranged from the smallest to the largest. Thus, to find the median in the series 10, 2, 4, 8, 6, begin by ranking the numbers in order: 2, 4, 6, 8, 10. The middle number, or median, can be identified easily as 6 because there is an odd number of values (five) in this series; two of the numbers are larger and two are smaller.

The median is slightly more difficult to compute if there is an even number of values, as in the series 2, 4, 6, 8. In this case, the median is the average of the two central values:

$$\frac{4 + 6}{2} = 5$$

The same procedure can be used to identify the median of our fifth-graders' reading scores. When the scores are ranked in order, the series reads: 16, 17, 17, 17, 18, 18, 18, 18, 19, 19, 19, 19, 19, 19, 20, 20, 20, 20, 21, 21, 21, 22. The computation of the median is often more complex when the central value is repeated, but in this case it is the average of the two values:

$$\frac{19 + 19}{2} = 19$$

Finally, the **mode** is the value that occurs most frequently in a set of numbers. Since six students scored 19 on our test and no other score occurred more frequently, the mode is 19.

Thus, in this hypothetical sample, the mean, median, and mode are identical. In the section below on "Types of Frequency Distributions," we shall see that this often occurs in symmetrical distributions like this one.

MEASURES OF VARIABILITY

Two very different distributions can easily have the same measure of central tendency. Consider two hypothetical families with a mean income of $20,000. In one, three adult brothers work as policemen and earn $19,000, $20,000, and $21,000 per year. In the other family, two adult males work only occasional odd jobs and earn $2,000 and $3,000, respectively. The third brother owns a health and diet spa and earns $55,000. Clearly, the mean income of $20,000 has very different implications for the two families. Statisticians therefore characterize distributions not just by their central tendencies but also by their spread, or variability.

The simplest such statistic is the **range,** or difference between the highest and lowest values in a distribution. For our three policemen, the range in income is

$$\$21,000 - \$19,000 = \$2,000$$

Similarly, the family of the prosperous spa owner has an income range of $53,000, and the fifth-grade-girls' reading scores have a range of 6 points.

More frequently, statisticians compute a more revealing figure called the **standard deviation,** which is a particular mathematical measure of the amount of variability, spread, or dispersion in the scores of a distribution. More formally,

$$\text{Standard deviation} = \sqrt{\frac{\text{sum of diff}^2}{N}}$$

where diff = difference between each score and the mean
and N = number of values

Thus, to compute the standard deviation of a set of scores, compute the mean, subtract each score from the mean, and square each of these differences. Then add these squared differences and divide by the number of scores. The square root of this value is the standard deviation.

While this formula may seem intimidating at first, in fact the computations are quite straightforward. Consider how this formula could be applied to the reading comprehension scores in Table A.1:

Score	Difference from Mean (Mean = 19)	Difference Squared
22	+3	9
21	+2	4
21	+2	4
21	+2	4
20	+1	1
20	+1	1
20	+1	1
20	+1	1
19	0	0
19	0	0
19	0	0
19	0	0
19	0	0
19	0	0
18	−1	1
18	−1	1
18	−1	1
18	−1	1
17	−2	4
17	−2	4
17	−2	4
16	−3	9
	Sum of diff^2 =	50

$$\text{Standard deviation} = \sqrt{\frac{\text{sum of diff}^2}{N}}$$
$$= \sqrt{\frac{50}{22}}$$
$$= \sqrt{2.27}$$
$$= 1.51$$

This formula can be used to compute the standard deviation of any distribution. As this example suggests, the calculations are more likely to be tedious than to be confusing or mysterious.

TYPES OF FREQUENCY DISTRIBUTIONS

The hypothetical reading scores we've focused on to this point provide an example of a **symmetrical distribution** in which the same number of values are equally distributed on either side of the central point and the mean, median, and mode are identical or close together. The most important symmetrical distribution for psychology was described in Chapter 12; many physical and psychological characteristics conform to a *normal distribution,* as illustrated in Figure 12.2.

However, many measurements conform to a **skewed distribution,** which is asymmetrical, with more scores falling at one end than at the other. Consider other hypothetical data: the reading comprehension scores for 22 fifth-grade boys shown in Table A.2. As you can see in the frequency histogram for this distribution (Figure A.3), these scores are not evenly distributed around a central point.

This distribution is said to be *skewed to the left* because the most deviant scores (that is, those farthest from the central tendency) fall to the left. The mirror image of this distribution, with the most deviant scores to the right of the central tendency, would be *skewed to the right.*

In symmetrical distributions, the mean, the median, and mode fall close together. Indeed, for the data in Table A.1, they were identical. However, these three measures of central tendency have different values for the skewed distribution of the boys' scores in Table A.2.

TABLE A.2
Frequency Distribution of Reading Comprehension
Scores for 22 Fifth-Grade Boys

Test Score	Number of Students
20	2
19	2
18	6
17	4
16	3
15	2
14	2
13	1

Confusion over the differences between the mean, median, and mode of skewed distributions may lead to many misunderstandings. Consider, for example, how the mean and median could be used to describe the skewed distribution of salaries in a four-person firm that stuffs pimentos inside cocktail olives. The three laborers who do all the stuffing earn $10,000, $14,000, and $16,000. But the owner-president of the firm pays himself $40,000 annually to drop by once a week, check the pimento inventory, and make sure that "everything is under control."

This distribution of salaries is skewed to the left, with a mean of $20,000 and a median of $15,000. These two figures provide different types of information. A stockholder in the company who wants to monitor the total payroll would probably be more interested in the $20,000 mean, while a labor organizer who wondered whether the workers were underpaid would learn more from the $15,000 median.

To see how misleading these figures can be, suppose that the company prospers. The president attributes this success to the fact that he always keeps the right number of pimentos in the warehouse and gives himself a raise to $60,000 per year. If the salaries of the three workers remained unchanged, the mean salary in this firm would increase to $25,000. In his annual report to the stockholders, the president might cite this 25% increase in average salary to prove that the firm rewards productivity. But the laborers would probably argue that this figure proves nothing of the sort. The more relevant figures, they might say, are the median income (which held constant at $15,000) and the income range (which increased from $30,000 to $50,000, showing a widening gap between labor and management).

Examples of this sort are sometimes cited to show that "you can prove anything with statistics." People who hate math may argue that since statistical calculations can be misleading, they can safely be ignored. In fact, the real lesson of this example is precisely the opposite: You can prove anything with statistics only to people who do not understand statistics. Thus, to avoid being misled, an educated person must become sophisticated about the appropriate uses of statistics to describe data and to infer conclusions.

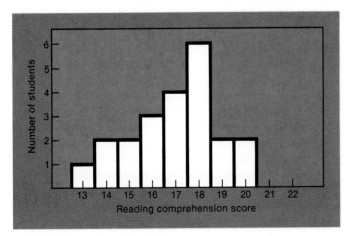

Figure A.3
Frequency histogram of reading comprehension scores for 22 fifth-grade boys.

Inferential Statistics

Inferential statistics are techniques for drawing conclusions (or making inferences) from a particular set of data. The basic concepts of inferential statistics are described in "How Do They Know?" boxes throughout this book.

For example, in Chapter 9 the discussion of "Surveys of Sexual Behavior" distinguished between a *population* (the full group of people that a researcher hopes to understand or generalize to) and a *sample* (the small subgroup of a population that actually participates in a given study). For obvious reasons, researchers can never study the entire population if they want to generalize to such large groups as human females or even United States citizens who weigh more than 300 pounds. Inferential statistics are therefore used to reach accurate conclusions about large populations on the basis of studies of relatively small samples. As explained in Chapter 9, only samples that accurately represent relevant features of the population lead to trustworthy conclusions.

Another key concept was explained in Chapter 1: *Tests of statistical significance* determine whether a particular mathematical result is likely to have occurred by chance. The vast majority of the empirical results described in this text were statistically analyzed and found to meet predetermined levels of significance.

For example, many psychological studies are designed to compare the mean scores of two or more groups that differ in terms of key variables. The Chapter 1 "How Do They Know?" box described Rosenthal and Jacobson's (1968) study of teacher expectations. In one analysis, inferential statistics compared the mean change in IQ in an experimental group of first-graders (whose teachers had been told to expect a sudden burst of intellectual growth) with the mean IQ change in a control group (whose teachers had been given no special expectations). As explained there, a *t* test revealed that there was a statistically significant difference between these two means, thus supporting the more general conclusion that expectations made a difference in this situation.

The details of the calculations involved in *t* tests and other inferential statistics can be found in any introductory statistics text. Learning more about them may not be everyone's idea of a good time, but this experience is essential for anyone who wants to understand the nature of current research in psychology.

Summary

1. **Descriptive statistics** are techniques for summarizing groups of numbers. For example, a **frequency distribution** summarizes the number of scores that fall into different intervals. Graphically, this may be summarized by bars in a *frequency histogram* or by points in a *frequency polygon*.

2. There are three major measures of central tendency. The **mean** is the arithmetic average of a group of numbers. The **median** is the middle number in a set of values that has been arranged from the smallest to the largest. The **mode** is the value that occurs most frequently in a set of numbers.

3. Two major measures of variability are the range and the standard deviation. The **range** is the difference between the highest and lowest values in a distribution. The **standard deviation** is a particular mathematical measure of the amount of variability, spread, or dispersion in the scores of a distribution, based on the squared differences of each score from the mean.

4. The *normal distribution* is one example of a **symmetrical distribution** in which the same number of values are equally distributed on either side of the central point. In a **skewed distribution,** more scores fall at one end than at the other.

5. **Inferential statistics** provides techniques for drawing conclusions (or making inferences) from a particular set of data. For example, *tests of statistical significance* determine whether a particular result is likely to have occurred by chance.

To Learn More

Weiss, N., & Hassett, M. *Introductory Statistics.* Reading, Mass.: Addison-Wesley, 1982. There are many excellent introductions to statistical inference. I think you should buy this one, which happens to have been written by my brother.

Huff, D. *How to Lie with Statistics.* New York: Norton, 1955. An entertaining classic on the misuses of descriptive statistics.

Glossary

ablation study A type of study in which surgical removal or destruction of brain tissue is followed by observation of the effects on behavior.

absolute threshold The minimum physical energy that causes a given sensory system to respond.

accommodation Changes in the shape of the lens of the eye that provide information about distance for objects that are relatively close to the eyes.

adrenal glands Two small endocrine glands that lie just above the kidneys.

aerial perspective The slight blurring and tinge of blue perceived in distant objects.

affective disorder A condition characterized by a prolonged and fundamental disturbance of mood and emotion.

afferent neuron (sensory neuron) A neuron that conveys information from sensory receptors to the spinal cord and brain.

afterimage The sensory impression that remains after a stimulus is taken away.

alcohol abuse The presence of a pattern of pathological use of alcohol, as well as an impairment of social or occupational function, for at least one month.

alcohol dependence A syndrome involving withdrawal symptoms and tolerance.

algorithm A procedure or formula that guarantees the solution to a given problem.

all-or-none principle The principle that states that at any given moment a neuron transmits its maximum electrical charge or transmits nothing at all.

amnesia A loss of memory, usually caused by damage to the brain.

amniocentesis A medical procedure in which fluid is withdrawn from the amnion, the sac surrounding the fetus, to diagnose chromosome abnormalities.

anal stage According to Freud, a psychosexual stage that usually begins around the second year of life, in which the child's major source of irritation and gratification involves processes of elimination.

androgyny A personality pattern that combines traditionally masculine and feminine traits in the same person.

anterograde amnesia A lack of ability to remember new information for more than a few seconds.

anthropology The study of the origins and characteristics of different cultures.

antipsychotic drug Any drug used primarily to decrease the hallucinations and disordered behavior of psychotic individuals.

antisocial personality disorder A behavior pattern of violating the rights of others that begins before the age of 15 and interferes with adult responsibilities such as holding a job.

anvil A bone in the middle ear that transmits vibrations from the hammer to the stirrup.

anxiety disorder A condition in which severe anxiety interferes with the normal ability to function in everyday life.

anxiety hierarchy In systematic desensitization, a list of situations that provoke fear of a particular person, organized from the least threatening to the more threatening.

aphasia A disturbance in the ability to speak or understand language caused by damage to the brain.

applied research Research that tries to solve specific problems by applying scientific principles and knowledge.

arousal A general pattern of bodily response in which several physiological systems are activated at the same time, including heart rate, sweat gland activity, and EEG.

artificial intelligence The ability of machines to perform tasks that require intelligence, such as recognizing a pattern, responding to a sentence, or solving a problem.

assertiveness training groups A behavioral form of psychotherapy in which therapists demonstrate specific ways of standing up for one's rights and participants practice these behaviors.

association areas Cortical areas of the brain that are not specifically involved with simple sensory or motor reactions.

associationism The belief that even the most complex memories are ultimately based on associations between simple ideas.

attitude A relatively lasting tendency to react to a person, object, or event in a particular way.

attribution theory A social perception theory that describes how people interpret and explain behavior in everyday life.

audience inhibition A process involved in the social inhibition of helping. A bystander runs the risk of embarrassment if he or she decides to help in a situation that turns out not to be an emergency.

auditory canal A tube that carries sound waves from the external ear to the eardrum.

autonomic nervous system Regulates the activity of smooth muscles, which control internal bodily processes such as heart rate and contraction of the bladder. Includes the sympathetic and parasympathetic branches.

autoshaping Automatic shaping that eliminates the need for step-by-step shaping of the first response.

avoidance response A response that prevents or avoids an unpleasant stimulus before it begins.

axon A nerve-cell process that transmits electrical impulses away from the cell body to other neurons.

babble Alternating consonant and vowel speech sounds that an infant exhibits, beginning at the age of approximately 4 months.

basic research Research that uses the scientific method to try to understand fundamental laws of the mind and behavior.

basilar membrane A membrane that translates physical vibrations in the ear into a pattern of electrical activity in the nervous system.

behavioral approach A theory of human behavior that focuses on the systematic study of observable behavior.

behavioral genetics The study of the inheritance of behavioral characteristics.

behavioral medicine The study of the role of psychological factors and behavior patterns in physical illness, and the application of this knowledge.

behavioral sink A pattern of bizarre and antisocial behavior that may occur in an overcrowded environment.

behaviorist A psychologist who emphasizes systematic studies of observable behavior.

behavior therapy (behavior modification) A type of psychotherapy that applies scientific principles to alter observable behavior through learning.

binocular disparity The difference between the retinal images of the two eyes.

biofeedback The technique of providing precise physiological information about internal states in order to learn to control them.

biological approach A theory of human behavior that analyzes the physiological events associated with behavior and experience.

bipolar disorder A condition in which manic and depressive episodes alternate.

blind spot An area in the retina near the fovea that has no receptor cells because nerve fibers are gathered here to form the optic nerve.

blood-brain barrier The circulatory system structures that prevent certain large molecules from reaching brain cells.

brain stem The part of the brain that contains such structures as the medulla, the pons, the reticular formation, and the midbrain.

Cannon-Bard theory of emotion The theory that the brain responds to external events, simultaneously producing both physiological and emotional experience.

case history A detailed description of the life experiences and behavior patterns of a single individual.

case study Intensive study of a single individual.

catharsis According to Freud, the relief of symptoms of mental illness by bringing unconscious emotional conflicts into conscious awareness.

CAT scan A scanning device that takes X-rays from many different angles and uses computer analysis to generate a three-dimensional picture of the brain.

cell body The main part of the nerve cell; it controls basic biochemical processes and links the dendrite to the axon.

central nervous system The spinal cord and the brain.

cerebellum A brain structure that extends out toward the back of the skull from either side of the pons and is primarily responsible for the coordination of muscle movements.

cerebral asymmetry Differences between the two sides or hemispheres of the brain.

cerebral cortex The thick layer of nerve cells that covers the brain.

cerebral hemisphere The two symmetrical sides of the brain.

cerebral localization The theory that different areas of the brain are responsible for different psychological functions.

chemical study A type of study in which a chemical is introduced into the brain to determine its behavioral or physiological effects.

chromosomes Long, thin structures in the nucleus of every cell that contain many genes.

cingulotomy A type of brain surgery in which certain fibers connecting the frontal lobes to the limbic system are cut.

circadian rhythm A cyclical change in behavior or physiology that repeats itself once every 24 hours or so.

clairvoyance A controversial process by which physical stimuli may be identified without using the known senses or telepathy.

classical conditioning A type of learning that involves repeated pairing of a stimulus that naturally elicited a reflex response with a second neutral stimulus; in time, the neutral stimulus comes to elicit a response similar to the original reflex.

clinical psychology The application of psychological principles and research to the understanding and treatment of mental illness.

closure According to Gestalt psychologists, the phenomenon whereby an incomplete pattern will often be perceived as a complete whole.

cochlea The major auditory portion of the inner ear.

cognitive approach A theory of human behavior that emphasizes the active internal nature of higher mental processes involved in such areas as attention, perception, memory, language, imagery, and reasoning.

cognitive dissonance The condition that results when there is a logical contradiction between thoughts and behavior or between two different thoughts. According to one theory, people find such contradictions unpleasant; therefore, when faced with a logical conflict, a person will try to reduce the cognitive dissonance by changing attitudes or behavior.

cognitive psychology The study of the way observers gain knowledge about the world and of how that knowledge is represented, stored, retrieved, transformed, and related to overt behavior.

cognitive theory of depression The idea that depression is caused by logical errors of thought that produce excessive self-blame.

cognitive therapy A form of psychotherapy that concentrates on changing thought patterns.

cohorts Groups of people who were born at approximately the same time.

color constancy The tendency to see an object as remaining the same color under a variety of lighting conditions.

concept A mental category of objects or events, grouped together on the basis of certain common features.

concordance rate In studies of behavioral genetics, the percent of pairs of people that share the same trait.

concrete operational stage According to Piaget, the stage of development in which a child becomes capable of logical thought, but only regarding concrete observable objects; roughly, ages 7 to 11.

concurrent schedule A complex schedule of reinforcement involving two or more different responses that are reinforced simultaneously according to independent schedules.

conditional response In classical conditioning, a learned response that resembles the original unconditional response.

conditional stimulus In classical conditioning, a neutral stimulus that is repeatedly presented with the unconditional stimulus and gradually comes to elicit the conditional response.

conditioned suppression Slowing down or stopping a response after a stimulus that signals an oncoming punishment.

cone A receptor cell in the eye that is primarily responsible for color vision.

conformity Behavior motivated by pressure from other members of a group.

conjunctive concept An item must possess two attributes at the same time to be an example of a conjunctive concept.

conservation According to Piaget, the recognition that certain basic properties (such as volume and number) remain constant even when appearances change.

constructive memory An observer's tendency to rebuild pictures of past events from the few details the observer remembers by filling in the details that have been forgotten.

constructive replication A process whereby an experimenter repeats a study but systematically changes the procedure to gain further insight into the result.

control group The group within an experiment that does not receive any special experimental treatment.

conventional level According to Kohlberg, a level of moral reasoning in which society's standards are totally adopted as one's own.

cornea The curved, transparent window that helps focus light as it enters the eye.

correlation coefficient A precise statistical expression of the relationship between two variables.

corpus callosum   A large band of nerve fibers that connects the two hemispheres of the brain.

counseling psychology   A specialty closely related to clinical psychology that emphasizes normal adjustment (such as marriage or family problems) rather than abnormal function.

counterconditioning   A process that may occur during systematic desensitization, in which relaxation becomes classically conditioned to a stimulus that formerly elicited anxiety.

criterion   In signal detection theory, the rules and guidelines an observer uses in labeling or classifying sensory events.

critical period   A developmental stage in which an organism is ready to learn certain response patterns.

cross-cultural study   A systematic comparison of patterns of behavior and experience among people from different cultural settings.

cross-sectional method   An analytical approach that compares groups of different ages at one point in time.

cue-dependent forgetting   The theory that forgetting is caused by a failure to retrieve information from storage due to inadequate memory cues.

cultural bias   A statistical difference in the validitiy of a test for different cultural groups.

cultural-familial retardation   A family pattern of mild mental retardation with no evidence of organic brain damage.

dark adaptation   The process by which the sensitivity of the retina gradually increases after a period in the dark.

decay theory   The theory that physical memory trace gradually fades as time passes by.

deep structure   According to Chomsky, the underlying organization and intent of sentences.

defense mechanism   According to Freud, an unconscious denial, distortion, or falsification of reality to protect the ego from excessive anxiety.

dendrite   A part of a neuron that usually receives electrical and chemical messages from other neurons.

dependent variable   The factor in an experiment that may be affected by manipulations of the independent variable.

depression   A persistent and prominent loss of interest or pleasure in almost all ordinary activities; associated with such symptoms as disturbances in eating or sleeping and decreased energy.

determinism   The idea that every event is the inevitable product of a series of natural forces.

developmental psychology   The study of how and why people change physically, intellectually, and emotionally as they grow from infancy to old age.

Diagnostic and Statistical Manual   A complete and official list of syndromes of abnormal behavior designed to improve diagnosis in terms of reliability and validity. Currently in its third edition, commonly known as DSM-III.

diffusion of responsibility   A phenomenon that occurs when many observers are present during an emergency who cannot directly observe each other; each can rationalize doing nothing by assuming that someone else must be taking action.

discrimination   Learning to respond only to a specific kind of stimulus.

discriminative stimulus   A stimulus that signals that a particular response will be reinforced.

disjunctive concept   An item may possess one or both of two attributes to be an example of a disjunctive concept.

displacement   According to Freud, a process by which instinctual energy is rechanneled from one object to another.

dizygotic twins   Twins that develop from two different eggs which happen to be fertilized by two different sperm at the same time. (Also called *fraternal twins.*)

double-blind study A study in which the effects of expectations are minimized by keeping both subjects and experimenters ignorant of the precise treatment being used.

Down's syndrome A biologically caused, severe form of mental retardation characterized by certain physical abnormalities. (Formerly called *mongolism.*)

drive A motivational force that incites an organism to action.

drug addiction A medically defined syndrome that includes physical dependence and tolerance.

drug receptor The part of a neuron that responds to a specific type of chemical.

eardrum A tissue in the ear that vibrates in response to sound waves.

echoic memory The retention in memory of an auditory stimulus for several seconds after it is presented.

eclectic approach In psychotherapy, choosing different therapeutic techniques to meet the needs of different clients.

educational psychologist A psychologist who works within a school system and tends to be concerned with ways of increasing teacher effectiveness.

efferent neuron (motor neuron) A neuron that transmits the commands of the spinal cord and the brain to the muscles.

ego According to Freud, an aspect of personality that develops from the id to distinguish between the subjective world of the mind and the objective world of physical reality.

ego psychology Psychoanalytic theories that propose an autonomous ego with its own reality-based processes that can be independent of purely instinctual aims.

electrical recording study A study in which one measures the normal electrical activity of the brain.

electrical stimulation study A study in which

brain tissue is stimulated by an electric current while the effects on behavior are observed.

electroconvulsive therapy A treatment for severe mental illness in which an electric current is passed through the brain; most often used for depression.

electrode A conductor of electrical activity that is placed in contact wth biological tissue.

electroencephalogram (EEG) A recording of the electrical activity at the surface of the brain or on the skull.

elicited behavior Behavior that is a response to a specific stimulus.

embryo Prenatal organism from 2 to 8 weeks old.

emitted behavior Spontaneous acts that are not responses to any known stimuli.

emotions Physical reactions that are experienced as strong feelings.

encoding The transformation of a physical stimulus into a form that human memory accepts.

encoding-specificity principle The principle that recall improves if the same cues are present during recall as during the original learning.

endocrine glands Glands that secrete special chemical messengers (hormones) directly into the bloodstream.

endorphin A natural brain chemical that is structurally similar to opiates like morphine and heroin. It is believed to be involved in the regulation of pain and other psychological functions.

environmental psychology The study of the interrelationships between social behavior and the physical settings of everyday life.

episodic memory A record of an individual's past experiences, the episodes of daily life.

epistemology The philophical study of the nature of knowledge or how we come to know about the world.

erogenous zones According to Freud, areas of

the body that are very sensitive to feelings of both irritation and pleasure.

escape response A response that ends an aversive stimulus that is already under way.

ethologist A researcher who studies the behavior patterns of a particular species in its natural environment.

eustachian tube A tube from the middle ear cavity to the throat designed to equalize pressure on the two sides of the eardrum.

experiment A scientific study in which a researcher tries to establish a causal link between two variables by manipulating one variable (the independent variable) and observing changes in the other (the dependent variable).

experimental group The group in an experiment that receives a particular treatment.

experimental psychologist A psychologist who typically conducts laboratory studies in such areas as learning, human memory, and sensation and perception.

expressive aphasia A syndrome that occurs when brain tissue in Broca's area is damaged—the person understands what others say but has difficulty speaking himself.

extinction The gradual disappearance of a learned response.

extrasensory perception A controversial process that may provide awareness of external events without the use of known sensory receptor organs.

face validity An evaluation of the accuracy of a test based on the misleading criterion of superficial appearances or what it seems to measure.

fairness The justice (or injustice) of using some psychological test to select individuals for a particular purpose.

family therapy Group psychotherapy for all the members of a family.

fear of success The fear that doing well in competitive situations will have a negative consequence, such as unpopularity.

fetus The prenatal organism from 8 weeks to birth.

fight or flight reaction A mobilizing of the body for an emergency; this reaction is a major function of the sympathetic nervous system.

figure According to the Gestalt psychologists, the object of attention, usually seen as a distinct shape in front of the ground.

fixed-interval schedule A schedule of reinforcement that reinforces the first correct response emitted after a specific amount of time has elapsed.

fixed-ratio schedule A schedule of reinforcement in which an organism is rewarded after a specific number of responses.

formal operational stage According to Piaget, a stage of development (which can begin as early as age 11) in which the person is able to solve abstract problems and deal with hypothetical possibilities.

fovea A slight depression precisely in the center of the retina. It consists entirely of cones and is very sensitive to fine visual detail.

free association In psychoanalysis, a therapeutic technique in which a patient relaxes and reports every single thought as it comes to mind.

free will The idea that people are free to choose what they will do.

frequency theory of hearing The theory that differences in the frequency of sound waves are directly coded by changes in the frequency of electrical firing in the auditory nerve.

Freudian analysis A type of psychotherapy designed to bring unconscious material into consciousness so that repressed conflicts can be resolved.

frontal lobe One of the major lobes of the brain, located at the front of the brain.

frontal lobotomy Destruction of the connections between the frontal lobes and other brain structures.

functional analysis Specification of the external variables that cause an organism to behave in a certain way.

fundamental attribution error The tendency to overestimate the importance of the internal dispositions and traits of a person who performs a particular act and to underestimate the influence of external constraints.

general adaptation syndrome According to Selye, the body's physiological response to stress. It is divided into three stages: alarm, resistance, and exhaustion.

generalization Responding in a similar way to stimuli that resemble each other; the greater the similarity, the closer the response.

generalized anxiety disorder A condition in which a person chronically suffers from intense anxiety and tension that do not appear to be related to any particular situation or stimulus.

genes Physical structures that transmit characteristics from parent to child.

genetics The study of the transmission of inherited characteristics.

genital stage According to Freud, a psychosexual stage that begins around puberty, when the physical changes of adolescence reawaken sexual urges.

gerontology The scientific study of the elderly.

gonads Sexual glands: testes in men and ovaries in women.

grammar The complete system of rules that relates sounds to meanings in a specific language.

group therapy Psychotherapy in which one or more therapists meet with several patients at the same time.

groupthink The suspension of critical thought that can lead to poor decisions when highly cohesive groups become preoccupied with seeking unanimity.

growth spurt A sudden increase in the rate of growth for both height and weight.

hallucinogenic drug A chemical substance that causes hallucinations and alters sensory perception.

halo effect The tendency to assume that a person with one or two positive traits will also possess many other positive qualities.

hammer A bone in the middle ear that is connected to the eardrum and vibrates with it.

heritability A mathematical estimate of the relative importance of genetics and environment in determining a particular trait for a specific population.

heuristic A general solution strategy, usually derived from experience (rule of thumb).

heirarchy of needs According to Maslow, a series of biological and psychological needs that motivates normal human behavior and which must be satisfied in the following order: physiological needs, safety needs, belongingness and love needs, esteem needs, and self-actualization needs.

high blood pressure (hypertension) Abnormally high levels of the average force of the blood moving away from the heart, pushing against the artery walls.

holism The theory that claims that each psychological function is controlled by a wide variety of cells through the entire brain, rather than being concentrated in a few discrete areas.

holophrase A single word a young child uses to express an entire message.

hospices Institutions that are specifically designed to meet the needs of patients who are dying.

human engineering The application of scientific principles to the design of equipment and machines so as to maximize human efficiency.

humanistic approach A theory of human behavior that is concerned with human values, subjective experience, and the uniqueness of each individual.

humanistic theory The assumption that every person who seeks psychotherapy has the freedom and the capacity to choose personal goals and to fulfill his or her human potential.

humanistic therapy Therapy in which the therapist guides the client to find his or her own solutions.

hyperactivity (hyperkinesis) A common form of learning disability characterized by extreme restlessness and a short attention span that lead to impulsive and disorganized behavior.

hypothalamus A brain structure that lies between the thalamus and the midbrain and seems to be involved in a wide variety of complex behaviors, including eating, drinking, temperature regulation, sexual behavior, and aggressive behavior.

iconic memory The retention in memory of a literal image of a visual stimulus for a fraction of a second after it is presented.

id According to Freud, an aspect of personality composed of innate biological instincts that seek immediate satisfaction.

identity crisis The crisis of establishing a strong sense of personal identity.

idiographic approach An approach to personality that attempts to understand the behavior and experience of a single individual.

impression management theory A theory of attitude change emphasizing the importance of the appearance of an act to outside observers.

incentives External stimuli that increase the likelihood of behavior.

independent variable The factor in an experiment that the experimenter manipulates.

industrial psychologist A psychologist who applies research findings to the world of work.

information-processing approach Attempts to analyze thought processes into a series of separate steps.

infradian rhythm A cyclical change in behavior or physiology that repeats itself at intervals of more than a day.

insight In psychoanalysis, the conscious understanding of the unconscious forces that motivate behavior.

instincts Inborn forces that direct an organism toward a certain goal.

intelligence quotient (IQ) A unit of measurement for intelligence. In children, this score is based on the ratio between mental age and chronological age multiplied by 100.

interference theory The theory that people forget information because one memory prevents another from being recovered.

interposition A phenomenon in perception whereby, if one object blocks the view of another, the partially obscured object will seem more distant.

interpretation A part of some psychoanalytic therapies in which the therapist gradually guides the patient to an understanding of his or her thoughts and behavior.

interview A systematic discussion of a person's experiences and feelings.

introspection The careful, rigorous, and disciplined analysis of one's own thoughts by highly trained observers.

iris In the eye, a circular arrangement of muscular cells that controls the diameter of the opening that admits light.

James-Lange theory of emotion The theory that an event automatically triggers a particular pattern of bodily changes and that the brain then identifies each emotion on the basis of a particular physiological pattern.

jet lag Discomfort or decreased efficiency caused by traveling across time zones.

kinesthetic sense A sense of body movement and position based on feedback from the muscles, joints, and tendons.

latency period According to Freud, a period beginning around the age of 6 when children of both sexes are relatively unconcerned with psychosexual conflicts and are more involved in refining ego processes for dealing with the environment.

lateral hypothalamus An area on the sides of

the hypothalamus that is believed to be a feeding center that signals an animal to start eating.

law of effect A theory that holds that rewards "stamp in" learned connections between actions and their responses; thus, behavior is shaped by its consequences.

learned helplessness An organism's belief, based on prior experience, that it is helpless or lacks control over a particular situation.

learning A relatively permanent change in behavior that occurs through experience.

learning disabilities Problems in school learning that are not caused by any known physical, intellectual, or emotional deficit.

lens A body of tissue in the eye that changes shape to focus light on the retina.

lesion A wound or injury.

levels of processing The theory that information does not pass from one storage system to another but rather is encoded in a particular way during input, depending largely on the person's intentions.

life instincts According to Freud, inborn mental representations of physical needs that help the individual and the species to survive, including hunger, thirst, and sex.

limbic system A series of structures located near the border between the cerebral hemispheres and the brain stem. It is involved in the regulation of such "animal instincts" as fighting, fleeing, feeding, and reproduction.

linear perspective The tendency for distant objects to seem closer together than near objects.

linguistic competence Abstract knowledge of a language.

linguistic performance The way people apply knowledge when they produce and comprehend language.

linguistic relativity hypothesis Whorf's belief that language determines the content of thought or the way a person perceives the world.

linguistics The study of the fundamental nature and structure of human language.

literal replication A process whereby an experimenter tries to repeat a study as precisely as possible.

longitudinal study Observations made repeatedly of the same individual over a long period of time, sometimes through an entire life.

long-term memory (LTM) The memory system that stores large amounts of information for long periods of time.

loudness The psychological dimension corresponding to the intensity of a sound, primarily determined by the amplitude of sound waves.

major depression A severe depression that appears without a history of mania.

mania A feeling of euphoria and enthusiasm; associated with such symptoms as hyperactivity, loud and rapid speech, inflated self-esteem, decreased need for sleep, and distractibility.

maturation Sequences of growth and internal bodily changes that are primarily determined by biological timing.

mean The arithmetic average.

means-end analysis In cognitive psychology, repeatedly comparing the current state of affairs with the final goal state and taking steps to reduce the difference between the two.

medical model A theoretical model of abnormal behavior that argues that abnormality is caused by physical disease.

meditation A technique that produces a relaxed physiological state characterized by decreased heart rate and oxygen consumption and specific EEG changes.

medulla The first brain structure that emerges from the spinal cord as it widens upon entering the skull; it contains nerve fibers that connect the spinal cord to the brain.

method of constant stimuli A method for measuring absolute thresholds whereby a number of stimuli of different physical intensities are presented in random order. After each trial, the subject indicates whether or not he or she has sensed anything.

method of loci Visualizing images of the things to be memorized in an orderly arrangement of locations.

microelectrode A wire small enough to record the electrical activity of a single nerve cell at a time.

midbrain A brain structure that relays information from the eye and ear to higher centers for visual and auditory processing.

midlife crisis A period of severe stress, a questioning of goals, and progress that occurs roughly between ages 40 and 45.

mnemonic devices Techniques used for organizing information so that it can be remembered more easily.

monozygotic twins Twins that develop from the division of a single fertilized egg. (Also called *identical twins*.)

moral therapy The treatment of mental disorders by kindness, understanding, and a pleasant environment.

morpheme The smallest unit of speech that has meaning.

motive A force that influences the strength or direction of behavior.

motor strip A primary projection area that lies inside the frontal lobe of the brain and is responsible for certain muscle movements.

narcissistic personality disorder A grandiose sense of uniqueness or self-importance that leads a person constantly to seek admiration and to become preoccupied with fantasies of success.

narcotic antagonist A drug that is known to block the effects of opiates.

narcotics Opiates that relieve pain and induce sleep.

naturalistic observation The careful observation, recording, and analysis of behavior.

need A physiological requirement of the organism, such as a need for food, water, or oxygen.

need for achievement (nAch) The attempt to excel and surpass others and to accomplish difficult tasks as rapidly and independently as possible.

negative reinforcer Any stimulus that increases the probability of behavior when it is removed after the behavior.

neuroanatomical study A study that focuses on the structure of the nervous system.

neuron An individual nerve cell, the fundamental building block of the nervous system.

neurosis An enduring set of symptoms that bothers an individual or interferes with healthy functioning while the person remains in contact with reality. Under the current system, this is a descriptive term rather than a formal diagnostic category.

neurotransmitter A chemical released at the synapse by the electrical action of one neuron that influences the electrical activity of another neuron.

nomothetic approach An approach to personality that attempts to understand the behavior and experience of people in general or the average case.

nondirective therapy A type of humanistic therapy in which the therapist refuses to tell people what to do or what to think.

normal distribution A particular mathematical distribution in which cases are symmetrically arranged around the average.

norms Standard figures that describe the performance of the average person in relation to some larger group.

obedience Following the suggestions or orders of another person even when one prefers not to.

object permanence According to Piaget, the awareness that objects continue to exist even when they are not present to be seen, touched, or sensed.

observational learning Learning by observation, which involves modeling or copying the behavior of another person.

obsessive-compulsive disorder A disorder that involves persistent repetitive thoughts that cannot be controlled or behavior patterns that are constantly repeated in a kind of ritual.

occipital lobe One of the major lobes of the brain, located at the back of the head.

Oedipus complex In Freudian theory, a critical conflict in the phallic stage involving a young boy's sexual attraction to his opposite-sex parent and a sense of jealousy and rivalry with his same-sex parent. The conflict is resolved when the boy identifies with his father by adopting his values, beliefs, and habits.

operant conditioning A type of learning in which the probability of a response changes when reinforcement or punishment is presented following that response.

operations According to Piaget, the mental actions that organize a person's view of the world.

opponent-process theory of color vision The theory that there are three systems for color vision, each responding to two colors: red and green, blue and yellow, and black and white.

opponent-process theory of motivation The theory that many acquired motives arise from the interplay of two opposing processes in the brain, such as pleasure in response to pain.

oral stage According to Freud, a psychosexual stage, which lasts roughly for the first year of life, in which an infant derives satisfaction primarily through the mouth.

oval window A part of the cochlea that transmits sound waves from the middle ear to the basilar membrane by displacing the cochlear fluid.

overlearning Practice beyond the point of mastery.

overregularization The tendency of children to force every utterance to conform to grammatical rules, even when inappropriate.

panic disorder A condition in which recurrent attacks of anxiety and panic are not related to any specific stimulus.

paradigm A common set of beliefs and assumptions shared by a particular group of scientists.

paraprofessionals Mental health workers with limited training in performing specific tasks.

parapsychology Research on occult or psychic phenomena.

parasympathetic nervous system A part of the autonomic nervous system that maintains appropriate internal states in times of relaxation; its nerve fibers originate at either end of the spinal cord.

parietal lobe One of the major lobes of the brain, located at the top rear of the brain.

peak experience According to Maslow, a mystical feeling of happiness, peace, and contentment that a self-actualized person frequently experiences.

perception The process of actively interpreting a pattern of stimuli as an organized mental image.

perceptual constancy The tendency of observers to perceive an object as stable even when its sensory image changes.

peripheral nervous system All nerve fibers outside the brain and spinal cord.

personality An individual's characteristic pattern of thought, behavior, and emotions.

personality disorder An inflexible behavior pattern or enduring personality trait that significantly interferes with a person's occupation or social life or causes personal distress.

personality inventory A standard list of questions about an individual's behavior and feelings to assess personality traits.

personality psychologist A psychologist who focuses on the problem of individual differences, how we come to be different from one another.

phallic stage According to Piaget, a psychosexual stage that occurs roughly from ages 3 to 6, when a child first becomes fully aware of the genital differences between males and females.

phenothiazine drugs A group of antipsychotic drugs that reduces hallucinations, delusions, confusion, agitation, social withdrawal, and other psychotic symptoms.

pheromone A chemical substance that provokes a specific reaction in another organism of the same species.

phobia A type of anxiety disorder characterized by a persistent and irrational fear of a specific object, activity, or situation.

phonemes The distinct sounds that make a difference in meaning in a particular language.

phonology The rules that govern the use of sounds in a language.

phrenology The outdated theory that claims that the brain consists of a number of separate organs, each responsible for a specific human trait.

physical dependence A syndrome in which withdrawal from a drug produces physical symptoms.

physiological motives Internal bodily states that direct an organism's behavior toward a goal, such as food, water, or sex.

physiological psychologist A psychologist who studies the biological bases of behavior—how the structure of the brain is related to experience, for example, and how genetics influences behavior.

pitch The psychological sensation that a sound is high or low, primarily determined by the frequency of vibrations.

pituitary gland A gland that controls the secretions of other endocrine glands and is itself under the control of the hypothalamus.

placebo effect The phenomenon whereby medical treatments of no value in themselves seem to cure patients by the power of suggestion.

place theory of hearing The theory that sounds of different frequencies activate different places on the basilar membrane.

pleasure principle According to Freud, the tendency of the id to reduce instinctual tension and return the organism to a comfortable state.

Poggendorf illusion An optical illusion in which a continuous line seems to be misplaced when it is partially obscured.

pons A brain structure that continues out of the medulla and contains fibers connecting the brain and spinal cord.

positive reinforcer Any stimulus that increases the probability of a behavior when it is presented after the behavior.

postconventional level According to Kohlberg, a level of moral reasoning that involves applying universal principles of right and wrong that are more fundamental than the laws of any specific society.

preconventional level According to Kohlberg, a level of moral reasoning in which people accept society's commands primarily to gain rewards and avoid punishments.

Premack principle The principle that a more preferred behavior will reinforce a less preferred behavior.

preoperational stage According to Piaget, the stage in which symbolic thought first appears. The 2- to 7-year-old child gradually learns to use speech, play, gestures, and mental images to represent the world.

primary projection areas Cortical areas of the brain that receive input from the sense organs or control the movement of particular muscle groups.

proactive inhibition The process by which information is forgotten as a result of interference from material that was presented before the learning task.

productive thinking According to Gestalt psychologists, a type of thought in which one solves a problem by reorganizing its elements.

projective test A test in which a person projects his or her inner feelings and conflicts by responding to an ambiguous stimulus such as a picture of an inkblot.

proximity According to Gestalt psychologists, the tendency of stimuli that are physically close together to be perceived as belonging together and forming a group.

psychiatrist A licensed physician trained in medicine before specializing in the treatment of mental and emotional problems.

psychiatry The medical specialty concerned with mental illness.

psychoactive drug A chemical substance that influences behavior or subjective experiences by altering responses in the nervous system.

psychoanalytic approach A theory of human behavior that stresses the importance of unconscious conflicts and biological instincts in the determination of complex human behavior.

psycholinguistics The study of how people actually speak and use language.

psychological dependence A compulsion to use a drug that is not based on physical factors.

psychophysics The study of the systematic relationship between the physical attributes of stimuli and the psychological sensations they produce.

psychosexual stages According to Freud, periods of life during which sexual instincts associated with different erogenous zones are particularly important.

psychosis A serious mental disorder involving obvious disturbances in thought, emotion, or behavior.

psychosocial stage According to Erikson, a period during which all individuals must confront a common crisis, caused in part by the new demands posed by different phases of life.

psychosomatic disease A physical illness that is partly caused by psychological factors.

psychosurgery Brain surgery aimed at changing a person's thought or behavior patterns.

psychotherapy The application, by a professional, of systematic psychological procedures to help a client change troublesome thoughts, feelings, and behavior patterns.

puberty The period when sexual maturation begins.

punisher Any stimulus that, when paired with a particular behavior, decreases the probability of that behavior.

punishment A process that reduces the likelihood that a response will be continued.

pupil In the eye, a hole in the center of the iris.

questionnaire A written list of questions to which people must respond.

radical behaviorism A position that accepts the existence of internal events such as thoughts and ideas but continues to emphasize the relationships between environmental events and observable behavior.

rational-emotive therapy A cognitive approach to therapy developed by Albert Ellis that argues that many psychological problems are caused by irrational thoughts that a particular event is awful, horrible, or catastrophic.

reactance theory A theory that analyzes how certain types of restraints on freedom can lead a person to assert his or her rights.

reality principle According to Freud, the ego tries to delay the discharge of instinctual energy until an appropriate object is present.

recall Remembering information spontaneously or on the basis of certain cues.

receptive aphasia A syndrome that occurs when brain tissue in Wernicke's area is damaged, characterized by difficulties in understanding speech.

recognition The process of deciding whether information being presented has been encountered before.

reflexes Involuntary acts automatically elicited by certain stimuli.

reinforcer Any stimulus that, when paired with a particular behavior, increases the probability of that behavior.

relative size The phenomenon whereby larger objects are generally perceived as closer.

relaxation response A state physiologically distinct from more casual states of relaxation. Four basic elements are required to elicit the relaxation response: a quiet environment, a comfortable position, a mental device, and a passive attitude.

relearning A comparison between learning material once (perhaps measured by time or the number of repetitions required) and relearning the same material on a second occasion.

reliable Consistent and reproducible. *Test-retest reliability* is the correlation between pairs of test scores based on repeating precisely the same test on two different occasions. *Alternate-form reliability* is the correlation between pairs of test scores achieved by the same person on two different forms of the same test.

REM Rapid eye movements that occur during sleep and are associated with dreaming.

reorganization According to Gestalt psychologists, solving a problem by perceiving new relationships among its elements.

replication The repetition of a study to see whether similar results are found.

representative sample A group in which subjects are systematically chosen to represent some larger population.

repression According to Freud, a defense mechanism that reduces anxiety by preventing an anxiety-producing object or feeling from becoming conscious.

reproductive thinking According to Gestalt psychologists, a type of thought in which a person applies past solutions to new problems.

resistance In psychoanalysis, an unconscious attempt to avoid therapeutic insights into unconscious motivation.

reticular formation A complex network of neurons and fibers in the brain that passes through the medulla, pons, and other structures and is particularly involved in sleep, waking, alertness, and attention.

retina The light-sensitive surface at the back of the eye.

retrieval Recovering information from storage in memory.

retroactive inhibition The process by which information is forgotten as a result of other information presented after the learning task.

retrograde amnesia An inability to recall events that occurred before some trauma to the brain.

reversibility According to Piaget, a mental operation in which a person can think of a transformation that would restore an original condition.

rod A receptor cell in the eye that is primarily responsible for night vision.

sample A relatively small number of cases taken from a larger population.

Schachter and Singer's cognitive theory of emotions The theory that the specific emotion a person experiences will depend on how he perceives and interprets his situation, while its intensity will be determined by the degree of physiological arousal.

schedules of reinforcement Different patterns of reinforcement and punishment that influence learning.

schema An area in the memory network that contains information and expectations about familiar events.

schizophrenic disorder A diagnostic label reserved for people who develop serious disturbances of thought, perception, and emotion for a period of at least 6 months prior to the age of 45 and who have deteriorated from a previous, more adequate level of functioning.

school psychologist A psychologist who provides advice and guidance in the school system.

sclera The tough outer covering of the eye that protects the delicate structures within.

script A schema that summarizes general knowledge about particular situations.

sedative A drug that depresses the activity of the central nervous system.

self-control In behavior therapy, active coping strategies used by an individual to deal with his own problems.

self-disclosure The degree to which a person is willing to reveal information about herself and her feelings.

self-efficacy An individual's belief in his own competence or ability to achieve a goal through certain actions.

self-esteem The value a person places on her own worth.

self-fulfilling prophecy An expectation that comes true partly because the person believes it will.

self-perception The process by which a person sometimes draws conclusions from observations of his own behavior.

semantic memory The abstract knowledge of words, symbols, and ideas and the rules for relating them.

semantics The rules governing the meaning of sentences, words, and morphemes.

semicircular canals A portion of the inner ear that helps regulate the sense of balance.

sensation The process of responding to a simple physical stimulus, such as a spot of light or a musical note.

sensitivity In signal detection theory, a true measure of the response of sense organs.

sensitivity training groups A form of group therapy that attempts to promote personal growth by encouraging participants to focus on their immediate relationships with others in the group.

sensorimotor stage According to Piaget, a stage of development that lasts roughly from birth to age 2, when infants directly discover the relationship between their own sensations and motor acts.

sensory neurons Neurons, also known as *afferent neurons,* that convey information from sensory receptors to the spinal cord and brain.

sensory stage The period during which the eye maintains a vivid and complete image of sensory impressions, from about 0.25 second to 2 seconds.

sensory storage The component of human memory that maintains a vivid and complete image of sensory impressions for about 0.25 second to 2 seconds.

separation anxiety Profound distress occurring when a child is separated from its mother or primary caretaker.

set effect A tendency to solve problems in terms of old habits and assumptions, even when they no longer apply.

shape constancy A tendency to perceive objects as maintaining the same shape regardless of the view from different angles.

shaping The technique of teaching a complex behavior by reinforcing successive approximations of the desired activity.

short-term memory (STM) The memory system that stores a limited amount of information for no more than 30 seconds.

signal detection theory Attempts to account for both psychological and sensory factors that influence psychophysical judgments; precise mathematical procedures have been proposed to separate true sensory limits (sensitivity) from more psychological factors (criteria).

similarity According to Gestalt psychologists, the tendency of stimuli that resemble each other to be perceived as belonging together and forming a group.

size constancy The tendency to see objects as constant in size even when the visual image changes.

Skinner box A soundproofed box with a lever (for a rat to push) or a key (for a pigeon to peck) and a device to deliver food. A Skinner box may also include an electrified floor to deliver shocks or a series of colored lights to serve as stimuli.

social cognition The understanding of the social world, including other people's behavior, thoughts, and feelings.

social facilitation An improvement in performance associated with the presence of other people.

social learning theory A theory that holds that internal cognitive processes are an important factor in determining behavior, along with other types of learning.

social motives Forces that direct human behavior toward certain patterns of relationships with other people, such as autonomy and affiliation.

social perception The process of perceiving other people and interpreting their actions. It is an active process that involves making inferences and drawing conclusions.

social psychology The study of the way people respond to other human beings and how they interact wth one another.

sociology The study of society, groups, and social institutions.

somatic nervous system Connects the brain and spinal cord with sensory receptors and voluntary muscles.

somatosensory strip Located at the front of the parietal lobe of the brain and across the central fissure from the motor strip; electrical stimulation of this strip produces specific sensations.

sound Wave motion generated by physical vibrations through a material medium (such as air).

species-specific behavior Behavior patterns that are characteristic of a particular species.

spinal cord A long, thin column of neurons that emerges from the bottom of the brain and runs down the back next to the spinal vertebrae, the bony structure that protects the spinal cord from injury.

split-brain surgery Surgery that involves cutting the corpus callosum, the fibers connecting the left and right hemispheres of the brain.

spontaneous recovery The reappearance of an extinguished response in a weaker form after a rest period.

standard deviation A mathematical measure of the amount of variability, spread, or dispersion of a particular set of scores.

statistically significant Unlikely to have occurred by chance according to some predetermined criterion, usually a probability of less than .05.

stimulant A drug that increases the activity of the central nervous system.

stirrup A bone in the middle ear that connects the anvil to the oval window.

storage The physical retention of a memory.

stranger anxiety The phase in infancy when children seem anxious when strangers are near; they may cry, fret, or try to move away.

stress The perception of a threat to physical or psychological well-being with which the individual is unable to cope.

stroke A cerebrovascular accident that occurs when a blood vessel in the brain is blocked or broken and brain tissue is damaged.

successive approximations Behavior that increasingly resembles a desired activity.

superego According to Freud, an aspect of personality that represents moral ideals and strives to perfection rather than pleasure.

surface structure According to Chomsky, the actual words in a sentence and the relations between them.

survey A summary of information drawn from many interviews or questionnaires in order to measure the behavior of large groups of people.

sympathetic nervous system A part of the autonomic nervous system that activates the glands and smooth muscles of the body in periods of emotional excitement.

synapse The point at which the axon of one neuron is connected to the dendrite or cell body of another neuron.

syntax The collection of rules specifying the

way words can be combined to form sentences.

systematic desensitization A form of behavior therapy that reduces fear by requiring an anxious person to imagine increasingly threatening situations while remaining deeply relaxed.

tardive dyskinesia A syndrome that occurs after long-term treatment with phenothiazines and other chemically related drugs, producing involuntary muscle movements including lip-smacking, sucking, and chin-wagging motions.

taste buds Structures in the tongue that contain the receptor cells responsible for taste sensation.

telegraphic speech A form of speech characteristic of children, beginning around age 2 and consisting of shortened sentences that drop "unnecessary" words such as articles, prepositions, and adjectives.

telepathy A controversial process of possible thought transmission from one person to another.

temperament An underlying energy level or other factor that helps produce a consistent style of responding in many different situations.

temporal lobe One of the major lobes of the brain, located just over the ear.

terminal drop The tendency of IQ to decline in the five years or so preceding death, perhaps as a result of a general decline in health and physical abilities.

test of statistical significance A test to determine whether a particular mathematical result is likely to have occurred by chance.

thalamus A structure in the brain through which information from the eye, ear, and skin senses passes on its way to be analyzed by higher processing centers in the cerebral cortex.

Thematic Apperception Test (TAT) A test in which a person is asked to use imagination to make up stories about a series of ambiguous pictures; used to reveal the hidden forces that motivate behavior.

token economy A setting in which behavior is changed by rewarding specific actions with tokens that can be exchanged for reinforcers.

tolerance A phenomenon whereby increasingly large doses of a drug are required to produce the same effects.

trait A predisposition to respond to a variety of situations in similar ways.

transference In psychoanalysis, a patient's inappropriate strong positive or negative feelings toward the therapist.

trichromatic theory The theory that there are separate color receptors in the eye for red, green, and blue.

type theory An approach to personality that sorts people into separate personality categories or types.

ultradian rhythm A cyclical change in behavior or physiology that repeats itself more than once a day.

unconditional response In classical conditioning, a natural reflex response elicited by an unconditional stimulus.

unconditional stimulus In classical conditioning, a stimulus that automatically elicits a natural reflex called the *unconditional response.*

valid Accurately measuring a particular trait. *Criterion validity* implies that performance on a test accurately predicts some external and independent measure. *Content validity* involves a systematic analysis of a particular skill; test items are designed to measure the relevant knowledge and abilities. *Construct validity* implies that the trait measured by a test is systematically related to a conceptually meaningful pattern of behavior.

variable-interval schedule A schedule of reinforcement that varies the amount of time that must elapse before a response is reinforced.

variable-ratio schedule A schedule of reinforcement that varies the number of responses required for each reward.

variables   Factors that are measured or controlled in a scientific study.

ventromedial hypothalamus   An area in the front and central portions of the hypothalamus that is believed to be a satiety center that signals animals to stop eating.

vestibular sense   Sensations that provide information about the pull of gravity and help maintain balance.

visceral sense   Feedback from internal organs.

Yerkes-Dodson law   The theory that there is an optimal level or most desirable amount of arousal for any activity; too much arousal or too little produces inferior performance.

zygote   A fertilized egg.

Credits *(continued)*

Bibliography

The boldface numbers in brackets following each entry refer to the pages on which you will find the study cited.

Abelson, R. P. Psychological status of the script concept. *American Psychologist*, 1981, *36*, 715–729. **[250]**

Abramson, L. Y., Seligman, M. E. P., & Teasdale, J. D. Learned helplessness in humans: Critique and reformulation. *Journal of Abnormal Psychology*, 1978, *87*, 49–74. **[498]**

Agras, S., & Jacob, R. Hypertension. In O. F. Pomerleau & J. P. Brady (Eds.), *Behavioral medicine: Theory and practice*. Baltimore: Williams & Wilkins, 1979. **[113]**

Agras, S., Sylvester, D., & Oliveau, D. The epidemiology of common fears and phobia. *Comprehensive Psychiatry*, 1969, *10*, 151–156. **[493]**

Ainsworth, M. D., & Bell, S. M. Attachment, exploration, and separation: Illustrated by the behavior of one-year-olds in a strange situation. *Child Development*, 1970, *41*, 49–67. **[310]**

Allport, G. *Pattern and growth in personality*. New York: Holt, Rinehart and Winston, 1961. **[422]**

Allport, G. W. *Letters from Jenny*. New York: Harcourt Brace Jovanovich, 1965. **[425]**

American Psychiatric Association. *Electroconvulsive therapy*. Washington, D.C.: American Psychiatric Association, 1978. **[535]**

American Psychiatric Association. *Diagnostic and statistical manual of mental disorders* (3d ed.). Washington, D.C.: American Psychiatric Association, 1980. **[79, 100, 457, 485–488, 489, 492, 493, 495, 496, 500–501, 505, 509]**

American Psychological Association. *Ethical principles of psychologists*. Washington, D.C.: American Psychological Association, 1973. **[578–579]**

Anand, B. K., & Brobeck, J. R. Hypothalamic control of food intake in rats and cats. *Yale Journal of Biological Medicine*, 1951, *24*, 123–140. **[371]**

Anastasi, A. *Psychological testing* (5th ed.). New York: Macmillan, 1982. **[450, 471]**

Anrep, G. V. Pitch discrimination in the dog. *Journal of Physiology*, 1920, *53*, 367–385. **[164–166]**

Anrep, G. V. The irradiation of conditioned reflexes. *Proceedings of the Royal Society B*, 1923, *94*, 404–426. **[167]**

Arieti, S. *Interpretation of schizophrenia*. New York: Basic Books, 1974. **[475]**

Arkes, H. R., Wortmann, R. L., Saville, P. D., & Harkness, A. R. Hindsight bias among physicians weighing the likelihood of diagnoses. *Journal of Applied Psychology*, 1981, *66*, 252–254. **[20]**

Aronow, E., & Reznikoff, M. *Rorschach content interpretation*. New York: Grune & Stratton, 1976. **[466]**

Aronson, E., & Mills, J. The effects of severity of initiation on liking for a group. *Journal of Abnormal and Social Psychology*, 1959, *59*, 177–181. **[573]**

Asch, S. E. Effects of group pressure upon the modification and distortion of judgment. In H. Guetzkon (Ed.), *Groups, leadership and men*. Pittsburgh: Carnegie, 1951. **[575–576, 580]**

Aserinsky, E., & Kleitman, N. Regularly occurring periods of eye motility and concomitant phenomena during sleep. *Science*, 1953, *118*, 273–274. **[90, 92]**

Atkinson, J. W. *Motives in fantasy, action and society*. Princeton: Van Nostrand, 1958. **[380]**

Atkinson, J. W., & Litwin, G. H. Achievement motive and test anxiety conceived as motive to approach success and motive to avoid failure. *Journal of Abnormal and Social Psychology*, 1960, *60*, 52–63. **[378]**

Atkinson, J. W., & McClelland, D. C. The effect of different intensities of hunger on thematic apperception. *Journal of Experimental Psychology*, 1948, *38*, 643–658. **[377]**

Atkinson, R. C., & Shiffrin, R. M. Human memory: A proposed system and its control processes. In K. W. Spence & J. T. Spence (Eds.), *The psychology of learning and motivation: Advances in research and theory* (Vol. 2). New York: Academic Press, 1968. **[214–215, 218]**

Atwood, M. E., & Polson, P. G. A process model for water jug problems. *Cognitive Psychology*, 1976, *8*, 191–216. **[248]**

Ax, A. F. The physiological differentiation between

anger and fear in humans. *Psychosomatic Medicine*, 1953, *15*, 433–442. **[386]**

Ayllon, T., & Azrin, N. *The token economy*. Englewood Cliffs, N.J.: Prentice-Hall, 1968. **[10t, 197, 199]**

Azrin, N. H., & Holz, W. C. Punishment. In W. K. Honig (Ed.), *Operant behavior: Areas of research and application*. Englewood Cliffs, N.J.: Prentice-Hall, 1966. **[183, 194]**

Azrin, N. H., Hutchinson, R. R., & Hake, D. F. Extinction-induced aggression. *Journal of the Experimental Analysis of Behavior*, 1966, *9*, 191–204. **[179]**

Bahrick, H. P., Bahrick, P. D., & Wittlinger, R. P. Fifty years of memory for names and faces: A cross-sectional approach. *Journal of Experimental Psychology: General*, 1975, *104*, 54–75. **[208]**

Baker, J. P., & Christ, J. L. Teacher expectancies: A review of the literature. In J. D. Elashoff & R. E. Snow (Eds.), *Pygmalion reconsidered*. Worthington, Ohio: Charles A. Jones, 1971. **[29–30]**

Bandura, A. Influence of models' reinforcement contingencies on the acquisition of imitative responses. *Journal of Personality and Social Psychology*, 1965, *1*, 589–595. **[196]**

Bandura, A. *Social learning theory*. Englewood Cliffs, N.J.: Prentice-Hall, 1977. **[414]**

Bandura, A., Adams, N. E., & Beyer, J. Cognitive processes mediating behavioral change. *Journal of Personality and Social Psychology*, 1977, *35*, 125–139. **[414–417]**

Bandura, A., & Rosenthal, T. L. Vicarious classical conditioning as a function of arousal level. *Journal of Personality and Social Psychology*, 1966, *3*, 54–62. **[494]**

Bandura, A., Ross, D., & Ross, S. Imitation of film-mediated aggressive models. *Journal of Abnormal and Social Psychology*, 1963, *66*, 3–11. **[194]**

Bandura, A., & Walters, R. H. *Adolescent aggression*. New York: Ronald Press, 1959. **[325]**

Bartlett, F. C. *Remembering: A study in experimental and social psychology*. London: Cambridge University Press, 1932. **[10t, 224–225]**

Bassuk, E. L., & Gerson, S. Deinstitutionalization and mental health services. *Scientific American*, 1978, *238*, 46–53. **[540]**

Baum, A., Aiello, J. R., & Calesnick, L. E. Crowding and personal control: Social density and the development of learned helplessness. *Journal of Personality and Social Psychology*, 1978, *36*, 1000–1011. **[583]**

Baum, A., & Davis, G. E. Reducing the stress of high-density living: An architectural intervention. *Journal of Personality and Social Psychology*, 1980, *38*, 471–481. **[583]**

Baum, A., & Valins, S. *Architecture and social behavior: Psychological studies in social density*. Hillsdale, N.J.: Lawrence Erlbaum Associates, 1977. **[583, 584f]**

Baumrind, D. Some thoughts on ethics of research: After reading Milgram's "Behavioral study of obedience." *American Psychologist*, 1964, *19*, 421–423. **[578]**

Beck, A. T. *Depression: Clinical, experimental and theoretical aspects*. New York: Harper & Row, 1967. **[497]**

Beers, C. W. *A mind that found itself: An autobiography*. Garden City, N.Y.: Doubleday, 1908. **[512–514]**

Bell, A. P., Weinberg, M. S., & Hammersmith, S. K. *Sexual preference*. Bloomington, Ind.: Indiana University Press, 1981. **[350]**

Beloff, J. Historical overview. In B. B. Wolman (Ed.), *Handbook of parapsychology*. New York: Van Nostrand Reinhold, 1977. **[157]**

Belvedere, E., & Foulkes, D. Telepathy and dreams: A failure to replicate. *Perceptual and Motor Skills*, 1971, *33*, 783–789. **[157]**

Bem, D. J. An experimental analysis of self-persuasion. *Journal of Experimental Social Psychology*, 1965, *1*, 199–218. **[574]**

Bem, D. J., & Allen, A. On predicting some of the people some of the time: The search for cross-situational consistencies in behavior. *Psychological Review*, 1974, *81*, 506–520. **[427]**

Bem, S. L. The measurement of psychological androgyny. *Journal of Consulting and Clinical Psychology*, 1974, *42*, 153–162. **[429, 430]**

Bem, S. L. Sex-role adaptability: One consequence of psychological androgyny. *Journal of Personality and Social Psychology*, 1975, *31*, 634–643. **[429]**

Bem, S. L. On the utility of alternative procedures for assessing psychological androgyny. *Journal of Consulting and Clinical Psychology*, 1977, *45*, 196–205. **[430]**

Benson, H. *The relaxation response*. New York: Avon Books, 1975. **[110–111]**

Berger, P. A. Medical treatment of mental illness. *Science*, 1978, *200*, 974–981. **[537]**

Bergin, A. E. The evaluation of therapeutic outcomes. In A. E. Bergin & S. L. Garfield (Eds.), *Handbook of psychotherapy and behavior change: An empirical analysis*. New York: Wiley, 1971. **[532]**

Berland, T. *The fight for quiet*. Englewood Cliffs, N.J.: Prentice-Hall, 1971. **[139]**

Berndt, T. J. Relations between social cognition,

nonsocial cognition, and social behavior: The case of friendship. In J. H. Flavell & L. D. Ross (Eds.), *Social-cognitive development: Frontiers and possible futures.* New York: Cambridge University Press, 1981. **[300]**

Bernstein, D. A., & Nietzel, M. T. *Introduction to clinical psychology.* New York: McGraw-Hill, 1980. **[543, 545]**

Berscheid, E., & Walster, E. H. *Interpersonal attraction* (2d ed.), Reading, Mass.: Addison-Wesley, 1978. **[560, 561]**

Bever, T. G., & Chiarello, R. J. Cerebral dominance in musicians and nonmusicians. *Science,* 1974, *185,* 137–139. **[71]**

Bigelow, H. J. Dr. Harlow's case of recovery from the passage of an iron bar through the head. *American Journal of the Medical Sciences.* 1850, *39,* 14–22. **[43]**

Blackwell, H. R., & Schlosberg, H. Octave generalization, pitch discrimination, and loudness thresholds in the white rat. *Journal of Experimental Psychology,* 1943, *33,* 407–419. **[180]**

Blasi, A. Bridging moral cognition and moral action: A critical review of the literature. *Psychological Bulletin,* 1980, *88,* 1–45. **[333]**

Bleuler, E. Dementia praecox or the group of schizophrenias (J. Zinkin, trans.). New York: International Universities Press, 1950. (Originally published, 1911.) **[501–505]**

Block, T. C., & Balloun, J. L. Behavioral receptivity to dissonant information. *Journal of Personality and Social Psychology,* 1967, *6,* 413–428. **[16]**

Bockhoven, J. S. *Moral treatment in American psychiatry.* New York: Springer-Verlag, 1963. **[517]**

Bolles, R. C. Species-specific defense reactions and avoidance learning. *Psychological Review,* 1970, *77,* 32–48. **[190]**

Borgida, E., & Nisbett, R. The differential impact of abstract vs. concrete information on decisions. *Journal of Applied Social Psychology,* 1977, *3,* 258–271. **[19]**

Boring, E. G. *A history of experimental psychology* (2d ed.). Englewood Cliffs, N.J.: Prentice-Hall, 1950. **[48]**

Botwinick, J. Intellectual abilities. In J. E. Birren & K. W. Schaie, (Eds.), *Handbook of the psychology of aging.* New York: Van Nostrand Reinhold, 1979. **[353]**

Bousfield, W. A. The occurrence of clustering in the recall of randomly arranged associates. *Journal of General Psychology,* 1953, *49,* 229–240. **[232]**

Bower, G. H. Analysis of a mnemonic device. *American Scientist,* 1970, *58,* 496–510. **[231]**

Bower, G. H., Clark, M. C., Lesgold, A. M., & Winzenz, D. Hierarchical retrieval schemes in recall of categorized word lists. *Journal of Verbal Learning and Verbal Behavior,* 1969, *8,* 323–343. **[232]**

Bowlby, J. *Attachment and loss* (Vol. 1): *Attachment.* New York: Basic Books, 1969. **[309–310, 311]**

Bradley, C. The behavior of children receiving benzedrine. *American Journal of Psychiatry,* 1937, *94,* 577–585. **[302]**

Bradshaw, J. L., & Nettleton, N. C. The nature of hemispheric specialization in man. *Behavioral and Brain Sciences,* 1981, *4,* 51–91. **[71]**

Brainerd, C. J. Training and transfer of transitivity, conservation, and class inclusion of length. *Child Development,* 1974, *45,* 324–334. **[299]**

Bransford, J. D., & Johnson, M. K. Considerations of some problems of comprehension. In W. G. Chase (Ed.), *Visual information processing.* New York: Academic Press, 1973. **[233–234]**

Breasted, J. H. (Ed.). *The Edwin Smith surgical papyrus* (Vol. 1). Chicago: University of Chicago Press, 1930. **[58]**

Brehm, J. W. *A theory of psychological reactance.* New York: Academic Press, 1966. **[580]**

Breland, K., & Breland, M. A field of applied animal psychology. *American Psychologist,* 1951, *6,* 202–204. **[177]**

Breland, K., & Breland, M. The misbehavior of organisms. *American Psychologist,* 1961, *16,* 681–684. **[190]**

Brennan, J. G. *Thomas Mann's world.* New York: Columbia University Press, 1942. **[12]**

Breuer, J., & Freud, S. *Case studies in hysteria.* In J. Strachey (Ed.), *The standard edition of the complete psychological works of Sigmund Freud* (Vol. 2). London: Hogarth Press, 1955. (Originally published, 1893–1895.) **[10t, 403]**

Brothers, J. *How to get whatever you want out of life.* New York: Simon & Schuster, 1978. **[379]**

Brown, F. M. Rhythmicity as an emerging variable for psychology. In F. M. Brown & R. C. Graeber (Eds.), *Rhythmic aspects of behavior.* Hillsdale, N.J.: Lawrence Erlbaum Associates, 1982. **[90]**

Brown, J. S. Motivation. In E. Hearst (Ed.), *The first century of experimental psychology.* Hillsdale, N.J.: Lawrence Erlbaum Associates, 1979. **[362]**

Brown, P., & Jenkins, H. M. Autoshaping of the pigeon's keypeck. *Journal of the Experimental Analysis of Behavior,* 1968, *11,* 1–8. **[188]**

Brown, R., & McNeil, D. The "tip of the tongue" phenomenon. *Journal of Verbal Learning and Verbal Behavior,* 1966, *5,* 325–337. **[223]**

Bruner, J. S., Goodnow, J., & Austin, G. A. *A study of thinking.* New York: Wiley, 1956. **[251]**

Buckhout, R. Nearly 2000 witnesses can be wrong. *Social Action and the Law,* 1975, *2,* 7. **[227]**

Buros, O. K. (Ed.). *The eighth mental measurements yearbook.* Lincoln, Neb.: University of Nebraska, Buros Institute of Mental Measurements, 1978. **[460, 471]**

Burtt, H. E. An experimental study of early childhood memory: Final report. *Journal of Genetic Psychology,* 1941, *58,* 435–439. **[207–208]**

Burwen, L. S., & Campbell, D. T. The generality of attitudes toward authority and non-authority figures. *Journal of Abnormal and Social Psychology,* 1957, *54,* 24–31. **[426, 427]**

Byrne, D. *The attraction paradigm.* New York: Academic Press, 1971. **[561]**

Calhoun, J. B. Population density and social pathology. *Scientific American,* 1962, *206,* 139–146. **[581]**

Camp, D. S., Raymond, G. A., & Church, R. M. Temporal relationship between response and punishment. *Journal of Experimental Psychology,* 1967, *74,* 114–123. **[182]**

Campos, J. Heart rate: A sensitive tool for the study of emotional development. In L. Lipsitt (Ed.), *Developmental psychobiology: The significance of infancy.* Hillsdale, N.J.: Lawrence Erlbaum Associates, 1976. **[288]**

Cannon, W. B. The James-Lange theory of emotions: A critical examination and an alternative theory. *American Journal of Psychology,* 1927, *39,* 106–124. **[55, 384–385, 386]**

Cannon, W. B., & Washburn, A. L. An explanation of hunger. *American Journal of Physiology,* 1912, *29,* 441–454. **[368–369]**

Carroll, J. B., & Horn, J. L. On the scientific basis of ability testing. *American Psychologist,* 1981, *36,* 1012–1020. **[450]**

Cartwright, R. D. *A primer on sleep and dreaming.* Reading, Mass.: Addison-Wesley, 1978.

Catania, A. C. *Learning.* Englewood Cliffs, N.J.: Prentice-Hall, 1979. **[184]**

Chomsky, N. *Syntactic structures.* The Hague: Mouton, 1957. **[260]**

Chomsky, N. *Aspects of the theory of syntax.* Cambridge, Mass.: M.I.T. Press, 1965. **[259]**

Clark, B., & Graybeil, A. Linear acceleration and deceleration as factors influencing nonvisual orientation during flight. *Journal of Aviation Medicine,* 1949, *20,* 92–101. **[146]**

Clark, H. H., & Clark, E. V. *Psychology and language.* New York: Harcourt Brace Jovanovich, 1977. **[219]**

Clarke, A. M., & Clarke, A. D. B. *Early experience: Myth and evidence.* New York: Free Press, 1976. **[317]**

Clark-Stewart, K. A. Popular primers for parents. *American Psychologist,* 1978, *33,* 359–369. **[312]**

Clore, G. L., & Byrne, D. A reinforcement-affect model of attraction. In T. L. Huston (Ed.), *Foundations of interpersonal attraction.* New York: Academic Press, 1974. **[561]**

Cobb, S., & Rose, R. M. Hypertension, peptic ulcers, and diabetes in air traffic controllers. *Journal of the American Medical Association,* 1973, *15,* 489–492. **[104]**

Cohen, L. B. Our developing knowledge of infant perception and cognition. *American Psychologist,* 1979, *34,* 894–899. **[285, 286, 287]**

Cohen, S., Evans, G. W., Krantz, D. S., & Stokols, D. Physiological, motivational, and cognitive effects of aircraft noise on children. *American Psychologist,* 1980, *35,* 231–243. **[142]**

Cohen, S., Glass, D. C., & Singer, J. E. Apartment noise, auditory discrimination and reading ability in children. *Journal of Experimental Social Psychology,* 1973, *9,* 407–422. **[140]**

Cohen, S., & Sherrod, D. R. When density matters: Environmental control as a determinant of crowding effects in laboratory and residential settings. *Journal of Population: Behavioral, Social, and Environmental Issues,* 1978, *1,* 189–202. **[583]**

Colby, C. Z., Lanzetta, J. T., & Kleck, R. E. Effects of the expression of pain on autonomic and pain tolerance responses to subject-controlled pain. *Psychophysiology,* 1977, *14,* 537–540. **[395]**

Cole, J. O. Phenothiazine treatment in acute schizophrenia. *Archives of General Psychiatry,* 1964, *10,* 246–261. **[538]**

Coleman, J. C., Butcher, J. N., & Carson, R. C. *Abnormal psychology and modern life* (6th ed.). Glenview, Ill.: Scott, Foresman, 1980. **[481]**

Collins, A. M., & Qullian, M. R. Retrieval time from semantic memory. *Journal of Verbal Learning and Verbal Behavior,* 1969, *8,* 240–247. **[221–222]**

Conger, J. J. *Adolescence and youth: Psychological development in a changing world.* New York: Harper & Row, 1977. **[359]**

Cooper, J. E., Kendell, R. E., Gurland, B. J., Sharpe, L., Copeland, J. R. M., & Simon, R. *Psychiatric diagnosis in New York and London.* London: Oxford University Press, 1972. **[500]**

Coren, S., & Girgus, J. S. *Seeing is deceiving: The psychology of visual illusions.* Hillsdale, N.J.: Lawrence Erlbaum Associates, 1978. **[153, 154]**

Corkin, S. A prospective study on cingulotomy. In

E. S. Valenstein (Ed.), *The psychosurgery debate.* San Francisco: Freeman, 1980. **[66]**

Cowen, E. L., & Schochet, B. B. Referral and outcome differences between terminating and nonterminating children seen by nonprofessionals in a school mental health project. *American Journal of Community Psychology*, 1973, *1*, 103–112. **[542]**

Cowles, M., & Davis, C. On the origins of the .05 level of statistical significance. *American Psychologist*, 1982, *37*, 553–558. **[31]**

Craik, F. I. M., & Lockhart, R. S. Levels of processing: A framework for memory research. *Journal of Verbal Learning and Verbal Behavior*, 1972, *11*, 671–684. **[228, 229]**

Craik, F. I. M., & Tulving, E. Depth of processing and the retention of words in episodic memory. *Journal of Experimental Psychology: General*, 1975, *104*, 268–294. **[229]**

Crichton, M. *Five patients: The hospital explained.* New York: Knopf, 1970. **[19]**

Cronbach, L. J. Five decades of public controversy over mental testing. *American Psychologist*, 1975, *30*, 1–14. **[470]**

Czeisler, C. A., Moore-Ede, M. C., & Coleman, R. M. Rotating shift work schedules that disrupt sleep are improved by applying circadian principles. *Science*, 1982, *217*, 460–463. **[95]**

Dabbs, J. M., & Leventhal, H. Effects of varying the recommendations in a fear-arousing communication. *Journal of Personality and Social Psychology*, 1966, *4*, 525–531. **[568]**

Darley, J., & Latané, B. Bystander intervention in emergencies: Diffusion of responsibility. *Journal of Personality and Social Psychology*, 1968, *8*, 377–383. **[551, 553]**

Darwin, C. *The expression of the emotions in man and animals.* London: Murray, 1872. **[393]**

Darwin, C. A biographical sketch of an infant. *Mind*, 1877, *2*, 286–294. **[279]**

Davidson, A. R., & Jaccard, J. J. Variables that moderate the attitude-behavior relation: Results of a longitudinal survey. *Journal of Personality and Social Psychology*, 1979, *37*, 1364–1376. **[568]**

Davis, J. M., Gosenfeld, L., & Tsai, C. C. Maintenance antipsychotic drugs do prevent relapse: A reply to Tobias and MacDonald. *Psychological Bulletin*, 1976, *83*, 431–447. **[537]**

Davis, K. Final note on a case of extreme isolation. *American Journal of Sociology*, 1947, *52*, 432–437. **[316]**

De Casper, A. J., & Fifer, W. P. Of human bonding: Newborns prefer their mothers' voices. *Science*, 1980, *208*, 1174–1176. **[290]**

DeJong, W. *The stigma of obesity: The consequences of naive assumptions concerning the causes of physical deviance.* Unpublished doctoral dissertation, Stanford University, 1977. **[555]**

De Mause, L. (Ed.). *The history of childhood.* New York: Psychohistory Press, 1974. **[313]**

Dement, W. C. *Some must watch while some must sleep.* New York: Norton, 1974. **[91]**

Deutsch, A. *The mentally ill in America* (2d ed.). New York: Columbia University Press, 1949. **[513, 518]**

de Villiers, J. G., & de Villiers, P. A. *Language acquisition.* Cambridge, Mass.: Harvard University Press, 1978. **[266]**

Devlin, Hon. Lord Patrick (chair). *Report to the secretary of state for the Home Department of the departmental committee on evidence of identification in criminal cases.* London: Her Majesty's Stationery Office, 1976. **[266]**

Dewan, E. The programing (P) hypothesis for REM sleep. In E. Hartmann (Ed.), *Sleep and dreaming.* Boston: Little, Brown, 1970. **[92]**

Dion, K. Physical attractiveness and evaluations of children's transgressions. *Journal of Personality and Social Psychology*, 1972, *24*, 207–213. **[556]**

Dion, K., Berscheid, E., & Walster, E. What is beautiful is good. *Journal of Personality and Social Psychology*, 1972, *24*, 285–290. **[556]**

DuBois, P. H. *A history of psychological testing.* Boston: Allyn & Bacon, 1970. **[438, 446, 449, 457]**

Durlak, J. A. Comparative effectiveness of paraprofessional helpers. *Psychological Bulletin*, 1979, *86*, 80–92. **[542]**

Dworkin, B. R., & Miller, N. E. Visceral learning in the curarized rat. In G. E. Schwartz & J. Beatty (Eds.), *Biofeedback: Theory and research.* New York: Academic Press, 1977. **[188]**

Ebbinghaus, H. [*On memory*] (H. A. Ruger & C. E. Bussenves, trans.). New York: Teachers College, Columbia University, 1885. **[205–207]**

Eddington, A. G. A new tabulation of statistical procedures used in APA journals. *American Psychologist*, 1974, *29*, 25–26. **[31]**

Edwards, B. *Drawing on the right side of the brain.* Boston: Houghton Mifflin, 1980. **[69]**

Ekman, P. Face muscles talk every language. *Psychology Today*, September 1975, pp. 35–39. **[393]**

Ekman, P., & Friesen, W. V. Constants across cultures in the face and emotion. *Journal of Personality and Social Psychology*, 1971, *17*, 124–129. **[394, 397]**

Ekman, P., Sorenson, E. R., & Friesen, W. V. Pancultural elements in facial displays of emotion. *Science*, 1969, *164*, 86–88. **[393]**

Elashoff, J. D., & Snow, R. E. (Eds.). *Pygmalion reconsidered*. Worthington, Ohio: Charles A. Jones, 1971. **[29]**

Ellis, A. Rational-emotive therapy. In R. Corsini (Ed.), *Current psychotherapies*. Itasca, Ill.: Peacock Publishers, 1973. **[527–528]**

Ellsworth, P. C., & Carlsmith, J. M. Effects of eye contact and verbal content on affective response to dyadic interaction. *Journal of Personality and Social Psychology*, 1968, *10*, 15–20. **[558]**

Elms, A. C. The crisis of confidence in social psychology. *American Psychologist*, 1975, *30*, 967–978. **[550]**

Emrick, C. D. A review of psychologically oriented treat-ment of alcoholism. *Journal of Studies on Alcohol*, 1975, *36*, 88–108. **[101]**

Endler, N. S. The role of person-by-situation interactions in personality theory. In D. Magnusson & N. S. Endler (Eds.), *Personality at the crossroads: Current issues in interactional psychology*. New York: Halsted Press, 1977. **[428]**

Epstein, S. The stability of behavior: I. On predicting most of the people much of the time. *Journal of Personality and Social Psychology*, 1979, *37*, 1097–1125. **[428]**

Epstein, W. The influence of syntactical structure on learning. *American Journal of Psychology*, 1961, *74*, 80–85. **[262]**

Erikson, E. *Childhood and society* (2d ed.). New York: Norton, 1963. **[328, 359]**

Erlenmeyer-Kimling, L., & Jarvik, L. F. Genetics and intelligence: A review. *Science*, 1963, *142*, 1477–1478. **[454]**

Etaugh, C. Effects of nonmaternal care on children. *American Psychologist*, 1980, *35*, 309–319. **[316]**

Eysenck, H. J. The effects of psychotherapy: An evaluation. *Journal of Consulting Psychology*, 1952, *16*, 319–324. **[531–532]**

Fancher, R. E. *Pioneers of psychology*. New York: Norton, 1979. **[6, 35]**

Fantz, R. L. The origin of form perception. *Scientific American*, 1961, *204*, 66–73. **[154, 286]**

Farber, S. L. Telltale behavior of twins. *Psychology Today*, January 1981, pp. 58–62, 79–80. **[84]**

Feigl, H. Quoted in J. R. Anderson. *Cognitive psychology and its implications*. San Francisco: Freeman, 1980, p. 383. **[241]**

Festinger, L. *A theory of cognitive dissonance*. Stanford, Calif.: Stanford University Press, 1957. **[571]**

Festinger, L., & Carlsmith, J. M. Cognitive consequences of forced compliance. *Journal of Abnormal and Social Psychology*, 1959, *58*, 203–210. **[572–573]**

Festinger, L., Riecken, H. W., & Schachter, S. *When prophecy fails*. Minneapolis: University of Minnesota Press, 1956. **[571–572]**

Festinger, L., Schachter, S., & Back, K. *Social pressures in informal groups: A study of a housing community*. New York: Harper & Row, 1950. **[559, 560f]**

Fincher, J. *Sinister people*. New York: Putnam, 1977. **[72]**

Fine, L. J. Psychodrama. In R. Corsini (Ed.), *Current psychotherapies*. Itasca, Ill.: Peacock Publishers, 1973. **[522]**

Fisher, S., & Greenberg, R. P. *The scientific credibility of Freud's theories and therapy*. New York: Basic Books, 1977. **[410, 411]**

Flavell, J. On cognitive development. *Child Development*, 1982, *53*, 1–10. **[299]**

Fleming, J. D. Field report: The state of the apes. *Psychology Today*, January 1974, pp. 31–46. **[271]**

Ford, C. S., & Beach, F. A. *Patterns of sexual behavior*. New York: Harper & Row, 1951. **[350]**

Frank, L. K. Projective methods for the study of personality. *Journal of Personality*, 1939, *8*, 389–413. **[463]**

Frankenburg, W. K., & Dodds, J. B. The Denver Developmental Screening Test. *Journal of Pediatrics*, 1967, *71*, 181–191. **[282]**

Freedman, D. G. Ethnic differences in babies. *Human Nature*, January 1979, pp. 36–43. **[304]**

Freedman, J. L., Heshka, S., & Levy, A. Population density and pathology: Is there a relationship? *Journal of Experimental Social Psychology*, 1975, *11*, 539–552. **[581]**

Freedman, J. L., Sears, D. O., & Carlsmith, J. M. *Social psychology* (4th ed.). Englewood Cliffs, N.J.: Prentice-Hall, 1981. **[581]**

Freud, S. The interpretation of dreams. In J. Strachey (Ed.), *The standard edition of the complete psychological works of Sigmund Freud* (Vols. 4 and 5). London: Hogarth Press, 1953. (Originally published, 1900.) **[405]**

Freud, S. The psychopathology of everyday life. In J. Strachey (Ed.), *The standard edition of the complete psychological works of Sigmund Freud* (Vol. 6). London: Hogarth Press, 1953. (Originally published, 1901.) **[409]**

Freud, S. Leonardo da Vinci: A study in psychosexuality. In J. Strachey (Ed.), *The standard edition of the complete psychological works of Sigmund Freud* (Vol. 11). London: Hogarth Press, 1957. (Originally published, 1910.) **[405]**

Freud, S. On beginning the treatment. In J. Strachey (Ed.), *The standard edition of the complete psycho-

logical works of Sigmund Freud (Vol. 12). New York: Norton, 1958. (Originally published, 1913.) **[521]**

Freud, S. Beyond the pleasure principle. In J. Strachey (Ed.), *The standard edition of the complete psychological works of Sigmund Freud* (Vol. 17). London: Hogarth Press, 1955. (Originally published, 1920.) **[405, 410]**

Friedman, M., & Rosenman, R. H. *Type A behavior and your heart*. Greenwich, Conn.: Fawcett, 1974. **[431]**

Friedman, M. I., & Stricker, E. M. The physiological psychology of hunger: A physiological perspective. *Psychological Review*, 1976, *83*, 409–431. **[371]**

Fromkin, V. A. Slips of the tongue. *Scientific American*, 1973, *229*, 110–117. **[240]**

Fuerst, R. E. Inference peddling. *Psychology Today*, March 1979, pp. 92–96. **[453]**

Fuller, J. L., & Thompson, W. R. *Foundations of behavior genetics*. St. Louis: Mosby, 1978. **[80, 115]**

Galanter, E. Contemporary psychophysics. In R. Brown et al. (Eds.), *New directions in psychology I*. New York: Holt, Rinehart and Winston, 1962. **[121*t*]**

Galton, F. *Hereditary genius: An inquiry into its laws and consequences*. London: Macmillan, 1869. **[81–82]**

Galton, F. *Inquiries into human faculty and its development*. London: Macmillan, 1883. **[136]**

Galton, F. Supplementary notes on "prehension" in idiots. *Mind*, 1887, *12*, 79. **[219]**

Gansberg, M. 37 who saw murder didn't call the police. *New York Times*, March 27, 1964, pp. 1; 38–39. **[548]**

Gantt, W. H. Reminiscences of Pavlov. *Journal of the Experimental Analysis of Behavior*, 1973, *20*, 131–136. **[164]**

Garcia, J., & Koelling, R. A. The relation of cue to consequence in avoidance learning. *Psychonomic Science*, 1966, *4*, 123–124. **[190]**

Garcia, J., McGowan, B. K., & Green, K. F. *Biological restraints on boundaries of learning*. Englewood Cliffs, N.J.: Prentice-Hall, 1972. **[190]**

Gardner, A. R., & Gardner, B. T. Teaching sign language to a chimpanzee. *Science*, 1969, *165*, 664–672. **[269–271]**

Gardner, B. T. Project Nim: Who taught whom? *Contemporary Psychology*, 1981, *26*, 425–426. **[273]**

Gardner, H. *The shattered mind*. New York: Random House, 1974. **[38]**

Garfield, S. L. Historical tradition. In B. B. Wolman (Ed.), *Handbook of clinical psychology*. New York: McGraw-Hill, 1965. **[518]**

Garfield, S. L., & Kurtz, R. Clinical psychologists in the 1970's. *American Psychologist*, 1976, *31*, 1–9. **[530]**

Garnes, S., & Bond, Z. S. *Slips of the ear: Errors in perception of casual speech*. In Papers from the Eleventh Regional Meeting, Chicago Linguistic Society, 1975, 214–225. **[265]**

Gates, A. Recitation as a factor in memorizing. *Archives in Psychology*, 1917, *40*. **[235]**

Gates, A., & Bradshaw, J. L. The role of the cerebral hemispheres in music. *Brain & Language*, 1977, *4*, 403–431. **[71]**

Gazzaniga, M. S. The split brain in man. *Scientific American*, August 1967, *217*, 24–29. **[68]**

Gibson, E. J., & Walk, R. D. The "visual cliff." *Scientific American*, 1960, *202*, 65–71. **[288–290]**

Gilligan, C. *In a different voice: Psychological theory and women's development*. Cambridge, Mass.: Harvard University Press, 1982. **[334]**

Gittelman, R., Abikoff, H., Pollack, E., Klein, D., Katz, S., & Mattes, J. A controlled trial of behavior modification and methylphenidate in hyperactive children. In C. K. Whalen and B. Henker (Eds.), *Hyperactive children*. New York: Academic Press, 1980. **[303]**

Glass, D. C., & Singer, J. E. *Urban stress: Experiments on noise and social stressors*. New York: Academic Press, 1972. **[140]**

Gleason, J. Do children imitate? *Proceedings of the International Conference on Oral Education of the Deaf*, 1967, *2*, 1441–1448. **[268]**

Gol, A. Relief of pain by electrical stimulation of the septal area. *Journal of Neurological Sciences*, 1967, *5*, 115–120. **[46]**

Goldbeck, N., & Goldbeck, D. *The dieter's companion*. New York: Signet, 1975. **[374]**

Goldberg, P. Are women prejudiced against women? *Trans-action*, 1968, *5*, 28–30. **[335]**

Goldstein, A. Endorphins as pain regulators—reality or fantasy? Speech presented to the American Pain Society, 1980. **[103]**

Goldstein, A., & Grevert, P. Placebo analgesia, endorphins, and naloxone. *Lancet*, 1978, *II*, 1385. **[103]**

Goleman, D. Split-brain psychology: Fad of the year. *Psychology Today*, October 1977, *11*, pp. 89–90; 149–151. **[69]**

Goodenough, D., Shapiro, A., Holden, M., & Steinschriber, L. A comparison of "dreamers" and "non-dreamers." *Journal of Abnormal and Social Psychology*, 1959, *59*, 295–302. **[92]**

Gottesman, I., & Shields, J. *Schizophrenia and genet-*

ics: A twin study vantage point. New York: Academic Press, 1972. **[506]**

Gough, P. B. Grammatical transformations and speed of understanding. *Journal of Verbal Learning and Verbal Behavior,* 1965, *4,* 107–111. **[263]**

Green, D. M. *An introduction to hearing.* Hillsdale, N.J.: Lawrence Erlbaum Associates, 1976. **[136, 139]**

Gregory, R. L. *Eye and brain* (3d ed.). New York: McGraw-Hill, 1978. **[119, 159]**

Gregory, R. L., & Wallace, J. G. Recovery from early blindness: A case study. *Experimental Psychology Society Monograph No. 2,* Cambridge, Mass., 1963. **[118]**

Gullahorn, J. Distance and friendship as factors in the gross interaction matrix. *Sociometry,* 1952, *15,* 123–134. **[559]**

Guttman, N. Operant conditioning, extinction, and periodic reinforcement. *Journal of Experimental Psychology,* 1953, *46,* 213–224. **[365]**

Guttman, N., & Kalish, H. I. Discriminability and stimulus generalization. *Journal of Experimental Psychology,* 1956, *51,* 71–88. **[179]**

Hall, G. S. Notes on the study of infants. *Pedagogical Seminary,* 1891, *1,* 127–138. **[281]**

Hall, G. S. *Adolescence: Its psychology and its relations to physiology, anthropology, sociology, sex, crime, religion, and education* (Vol. 1). Englewood Cliffs, N.J.: Prentice-Hall, 1905. **[325]**

Hall, M. H. A conversation with Abraham H. Maslow. *Psychology Today,* July 1968, 34–37, 54–57. **[417]**

Harlow, H. F. Love in infant monkeys. *Scientific American,* 1959, *200,* 68–74. **[306–308]**

Harlow, H. F. *Learning to love.* New York: Ballantine Books, 1971. **[309]**

Harlow, H. F., & Harlow, M. Effects of various mother-infant relationships on Rhesus monkey behaviors. In B. M. Foss (Ed.), *Determinants of infant behavior* (Vol. 4). London: Methuen, 1969. **[309]**

Harlow, J. M. Passage of an iron bar through the head. *Boston Medical and Surgical Journal,* 1848, *39,* 390–393. **[43]**

Harlow, J. M. Recovery from the passage of an iron bar through the head. *Massachusetts Medical Society Publication,* 1869, *2,* 329–347. **[43]**

Harris, S. L. Teaching language to nonverbal children, with emphasis on problems of generalization. *Psychological Bulletin,* 1975, *82,* 565–580. **[177]**

Harrower, M. Were Hitler's henchmen mad? *Psychology Today,* July 1976, pp. 76–80. **[465]**

Hassett, J. *A primer of psychophysiology.* San Francisco: Freeman, 1978. **[111, 143]**

Hassett, J. But that would be wrong . . . *Psychology Today,* November 1981, pp. 34–50. **[333]**

Hastorf, A. H., & Cantril, H. They saw a game: A case study. *Journal of Abnormal and Social Psychology,* 1954, *49,* 129–134. **[16]**

Hathaway, S. R., & Meehl, P. E. *An atlas for the clinical use of the MMPI.* Minneapolis: University of Minnesota Press, 1951. **[462]**

Hayes, C. *The ape in our house.* New York: Harper & Row, 1951. **[269]**

Hearnshaw, L. S. *Cyril Burt, psychologist.* Ithaca, N.Y.: Cornell University Press, 1979. **[454]**

Heider, E. R., & Olivier, D. C. The structure of the color space in naming and memory for two languages. *Cognitive Psychology,* 1972, *3,* 337–354. **[255]**

Heider, F. *The psychology of interpersonal relations.* New York: Wiley, 1958. **[564]**

Held, R., & Bossom, J. Neonatal deprivation and adult rearrangement: Complementary techniques for analyzing plastic sensory-motor coordinations. *Journal of Comparative and Physiological Psychology,* 1961, *54,* 33–37. **[155]**

Herrnstein, R. J. On the law of effect. *Journal of the Experimental Analysis of Behavior,* 1970, *13,* 243–266. **[176]**

Herron, J. (Ed.). *Neuropsychology of left-handedness.* New York: Academic Press, 1980. **[72]**

Hess, E. *The tell-tale eye.* New York: Van Nostrand Reinhold, 1975. **[125]**

Hetherington, A. W., & Ranson, S. W. The spontaneous activity and food intake of rats with hypothalamic lesions. *American Journal of Physiology,* 1942, *136,* 609–617. **[371]**

Hill, C. T., Rubin, Z., & Peplau, L. A. Breakups before marriage: The end of 103 affairs. *Journal of Social Issues,* 1976, *32,* 147–168. **[15, 562]**

Hite, S. *The Hite report.* New York: Dell, 1976. **[347]**

Hoffman, D. M., & Fidell, L. S. Characteristics of androgynous, undifferentiated, masculine, and feminine middle-class women. *Sex Roles,* 1979, *5,* 765–781. **[429]**

Hoffman, F. J. *Freudianism and the literary mind.* Baton Rouge, La.: State University Press, 1945. **[12]**

Hoffman, L. W. Fear of success in males and females: 1965 and 1971. *Journal of Consulting and Clinical Psychology,* 1974, *42,* 353–358. **[382–383]**

Hoffman, L. W. Fear of success in 1965 and 1974: A follow-up study. *Journal of Consulting and Clinical Psychology,* 1977, *45,* 310–321. **[383]**

Hohmann, G. W. Some effects of spinal cord lesions on experienced emotional feelings. *Psychophysiology,* 1966, *3,* 143–156. **[385–386]**

Holmes, T., & Rahe, R. The social readjustment rating scale. *Journal of Psychosomatic Research,* 1967, *11,* 213–218. **[105]**

Horner, M. Fail: Bright women. *Psychology Today,* November 1969, pp. 36–38; 62. **[380–383]**

Hubel, D. H. The brain. *Scientific American,* 1979, *241,* 44–53. **[73]**

Hubel, D. H., & Wiesel, T. N. Brain mechanisms of vision. *Scientific American,* 1979, *241,* 150–163. **[146]**

Hunt, M. *Sexual behavior in the 1970's.* Chicago: Playboy Press, 1974. **[347, 348, 349, 350]**

Hunt, M. *The universe within.* New York: Simon & Schuster, 1982. **[249, 251, 263, 275]**

Hyde, J. S. How large are cognitive gender differences? *American Psychologist,* 1981, *36,* 892–901. **[338]**

Ingvar, D. H., & Lassen, N. A. (Eds.). Brain work: The coupling of function, metabolism, and blood flow in the brain. Munksgaard, 1975. **[47]**

Isaacs, M. B. Sex role stereotyping and the evaluation of the performance of women: Changing trends. *Psychology of Women Quarterly,* 1981, *6,* 187–195. **[335]**

Isaacson, R. L. Relation between N achievement, test anxiety, and curricular choices. *Journal of Abnormal and Social Psychology,* 1964, *68,* 447–452. **[380]**

Izard, C. E. *The face of emotion.* Englewood Cliffs, N.J.: Prentice-Hall, 1971. **[393]**

Jacob, R. G., Kraemer, H. C., & Agras, W. S. Relaxation therapy in the treatment of hypertension: A review. *Archives of General Psychiatry,* 1977, *34,* 1417–1427. **[113]**

Jacobs, J. Experiments on "prehension." *Mind,* 1887, *12,* 75–79. **[218]**

Jacobson, E. *Progressive relaxation.* Chicago: University of Chicago Press, 1938. **[524]**

Jahoda, M. *Current concepts on positive mental health.* New York: Basic Books, 1958. **[479–480]**

James, W. *The principles of psychology.* New York: Holt, Rinehart and Winston, 1890. **[285, 364]**

Janis, I. *Victims of groupthink: A psychological study of foreign-policy decisions and fiascoes.* Boston: Houghton Mifflin, 1972. **[553–554]**

Jenkins, J. G., & Dallenbach, K. M. Obliviescence during sleep and waking. *American Journal of Psychology,* 1924, *35,* 605–612. **[210]**

Jensen, A. R. How much can we boost IQ and scholastic achievement? *Harvard Educational Review,* 1969, *39,* 1–123. **[456]**

Jensen, A. R. *Bias in mental testing.* New York: Macmillan, 1980. **[452]**

Jones, E. *The life and work of Sigmund Freud* (3 vols). New York: Basic Books, 1953–1957. **[404]**

Jones, E. E. The rocky road from acts to dispositions. *American Psychologist,* 1979, *34,* 107–117. **[427]**

Jones, M. C. The elimination of children's fears. *Journal of Experimental Psychology,* 1924, *7,* 382–390. **[169]**

Jones, R. A. *Self-fulfilling prophecies.* Hillsdale, N.J.: Lawrence Erlbaum Associates, 1977. **[18]**

Juel-Nielsen, N. Individual and environment: A psychiatric-psychological investigation of monozygotic twins reared apart. *Acta Psychiatrica Scandinavia,* 1965, *183,* 152–292. **[454]**

Julien, R. M. *A primer of drug action.* San Francisco: Freeman, 1975. **[96t]**

Kagan, J., Kearsely, R. B., & Zelazo, P. R. *Infancy: Its place in human development.* Cambridge, Mass.: Harvard University Press, 1978. **[311, 315]**

Kamin, L. J. *The Science and politics of IQ.* Hillsdale, N.J.: Lawrence Erlbaum Associates, 1974. **[468]**

Kanter, J. F., & Zelnick, M. Sexual experience of young unmarried women in the United States. *Family Planning Perspectives,* October 1972, pp. 9–18. **[347]**

Kaplan, A. G. Androgyny as a model of mental health for women: From theory to therapy. In A. G. Kaplan & J. P. Bean (Eds.), *Beyond sex-role stereotypes.* Boston: Little, Brown, 1976. **[429]**

Kaplan, A. G., & Bean, J. P. *Beyond sex-role stereotypes.* Boston: Little, Brown, 1976. **[430]**

Kaplan, R. M. Nader's raid on the testing industry. *American Psychologist,* 1982, *37,* 15–23. **[467]**

Kastenbaum, R., & Weisman, A. D. The psychological autopsy as a research procedure in gerontology. In D. P. Dent, R. Kastenbaum, & S. Sherwood (Eds.), *Research planning and action for the elderly.* New York: Behavioral Publications, 1972. **[356]**

Katchadourian, H. A., & Lunde, D. T. *Fundamentals of human sexuality.* New York: Holt, Rinehart and Winston, 1975. **[347, 350]**

Katz, M. *The people of Hamilton, Canada West: Family and class in a mid-nineteenth-century city.* Cambridge, Mass.: Harvard University Press, 1975. **[325]**

Kelley, H. The warm-cold variable in first impressions of persons. *Journal of Personality,* 1950, *18,* 431–439. **[555]**

Kephart, W. M. *The family, society, and the individual.* Boston: Houghton Mifflin, 1961. **[559]**

Keppel, G., & Underwood, B. J. Proactive inhibition in short-term retention of single items. *Journal of Verbal Learning and Verbal Behavior,* 1962, *1,* 153–161. **[212]**

Kernberg, O. F. *Borderline conditions and pathological narcissism.* New York: Aronson, 1975. **[491]**

Kessen, W. The American child and other cultural inventions. *American Psychologist,* 1979, *34,* 815–820. **[314]**

Kety, S. S. From rationalization to reason. *American Journal of Psychiatry,* 1974, *131,* 957–963. **[484]**

Kimble, G. A. *Hilgard and Marquis' conditioning and learning.* Englewood Cliffs, N.J.: Prentice-Hall, 1961. **[182]**

Kimble, G. A. *Foundations of conditioning and learning.* Englewood Cliffs, N.J.: Prentice-Hall, 1967. **[194]**

Kinsey, A. C., Pomeroy, W. B., & Martin, C. E. *Sexual behavior in the human male.* Philadelphia: Saunders, 1948. **[346]**

Kinsey, A. C., Pomeroy, W. B., Martin, C. E., & Gebhard, P. H. *Sexual behavior in the human female.* Philadelphia: Saunders, 1953. **[346, 348, 349]**

Klein, K. E., & Wegmann, H. M. Circadian rhythms in air operations. In A. N. Nicholson (Ed.), *Sleep, wakefulness and circadian rhythms* (Vol. 105). Neuilly-sur-Seine, France: NATO Advisory Group for Aerospace Research and Development, 1979. **[94]**

Knittle, J. L. Early influences on the development of adipose tissue. In G. A. Bray (Ed.), *Obesity in perspective.* Washington, D.C.: U.S. Government Printing Office, 1975. **[373]**

Koenig, P. The problem that can't be tranquilized. *New York Times Magazine,* May 21, 1978, pp. 15–17; 44–50; 58. **[540, 541*f*]**

Kohlberg, L. *The development of modes of moral thinking and choice in the years 10 to 16.* Unpublished doctoral dissertation, University of Chicago, 1958. **[330]**

Kohlberg, L. Moral stages and moralization. In T. Lickona (Ed.), *Moral development and behavior: Theory, research and social issues.* New York: Holt, Rinehart and Winston, 1975. **[330–334]**

Kohler, I. Experiments with goggles. *Scientific American,* 1962, *206,* 62–73. **[155]**

Köhler, W. *The mentality of apes* (E. Winter, trans.). New York: Harcourt Brace Jovanovich, 1925. **[191–192]**

Kraepelin, E. *Clinical psychiatry: A textbook for physicians* (A. Diffendorf, trans.). New York: Macmillan, 1902. (Originally published, 1883.)

Kraepelin, E. *Lectures on clinical psychiatry* (2d ed.) (T. Johnstone, trans.). London: Bailliere, Tindall & Cox, 1912. **[474–475]**

Kripke, D. F. Ultradian rhythms in behavior and physiology. In F. M. Brown & R. C. Graeber (Eds.), *Rhythmic aspects of behavior.* Hillsdale, N.J.: Lawrence Erlbaum Associates, 1982. **[90]**

Kryter, K. D. *The effects of noise on man.* New York: Academic Press, 1970. **[140]**

Kübler-Ross, E. *On death and dying.* New York: Macmillan, 1969. **[354–356]**

Kuhn, T. S. *The structure of scientific revolutions.* Chicago: University of Chicago Press, 1970. **[7]**

Kutash, S. B. Modified psychoanalytic therapies. In B. B. Wolman (Ed.), *The therapist's handbook: Treatment methods of mental disorders* (2d ed.). New York: Van Nostrand Reinhold, 1983. **[523]**

Lacey, J. I. Somatic response patterning and stress: Some revisions of activation theory. In M. H. Apley & R. Trumbull (Eds.), *Psychological stress.* Englewood Cliffs, N.J.: Prentice-Hall, 1967. **[388]**

Lachman, R., Lachman, J. L., & Butterfield, E. C. *Cognitive psychology and information processing: An introduction.* Hillsdale, N.J.: Lawrence Erlbaum Associates, 1979. **[12, 21]**

LaFrance, M., & Mayo, C. Racial differences in gaze behavior during conversations: Two systematic observational studies. *Journal of Personality and Social Psychology,* 1976, *33,* 547–552. **[558]**

Lamal, P. A. College students' common beliefs about psychology. *Teaching of Psychology,* 1979, *6,* 155–158. **[16]**

Land, E. H. The retinex theory of color vision. *Scientific American,* 1959, *200,* 84–99. **[133]**

Landman, J. T., & Dawes, R. M. Psychotherapy outcome. *American Psychologist,* 1982, *5,* 504–516. **[534]**

Lang, A. R., Goeckner, D. J., Adesso, V. J., & Marlatt, G. A. Effects of alcohol on aggression in male social drinkers. *Journal of Abnormal Psychology,* 1975, *84,* 508–518. **[98]**

Lang, P. J. Behavior therapy with a case of nervous anorexia. In L. P. Ullman, & L. Krasner (Eds.), *Case studies in behavior modification.* New York: Holt, Rinehart and Winston, 1965. **[525]**

LaPiere, R. Attitudes versus actions. *Social Forces,* 1934, *13,* 230–237. **[568]**

Latané, B., & Darley, J. M. Group inhibition of bystander intervention in emergencies. *Journal of Personality and Social Psychology,* 1968, *10,* 215–221. **[553]**

Latané, B., & Darley, J. M. *The unresponsive bystander: Why doesn't he help?* Englewood Cliffs, N.J.: Prentice-Hall, 1970. **[551]**

Latané, B., & Nida, S. Ten years of research on group size and helping. *Psychological Bulletin*, 1981, *89*, 308–324. **[553]**

Lazarus, R. S. Little hassles can be hazardous to health. *Psychology Today*, July 1981, pp. 58–62. **[106]**

LeCompte, W., & Rosenfeld, H. Effects of minimal eye contact in the instruction period on impressions of the experimenter. *Journal of Experimental Social Psychology*, 1971, *7*, 211–220ff. **[557]**

Lenneberg, E. H., Rebelsky, F. G., & Nichols, I. A. The vocalizations of infants born to deaf and hearing parents. *Human Development*, 1965, *8*, 23–37. **[265]**

Lenney, E. Concluding comments on androgyny: Some intimations of its mature development. *Sex Roles*, 1979, *5*, 829–840. **[429, 430]**

Lerner, M. When, why and where people die. In E. S. Schneidman (Ed.), *Death: Current perspectives*. Palo Alto, Calif.: Mayfield, 1976. **[322]**

Leventhal, H. Findings and theory in the study of fear communications. In L. Berkowitz (Ed.), *Advances in experimental social psychology* (Vol. 5). New York: Academic Press, 1970. **[569]**

Levine, J. D., Gordon, N. C., & Fields, H. L. The mechanism of placebo analgesia. *Lancet*, 1978, *II*, 654–657. **[103]**

Levinson, D. *The seasons of a man's life*. New York: Knopf, 1978. **[322, 339–341]**

Levy, J., & Reid, M. Variations in writing posture and cerebral organization. *Science*, 1976, *194*, 337–339. **[72]**

Lick, J. R., & Heffler, D. Relaxation training and attention placebo in the treatment of severe insomnia. *Journal of Consulting and Clinical Psychology*, 1977, *45*, 153–161. **[541]**

Linden, E. *Apes, men, and language*. New York: Saturday Review Press, 1974. **[270]**

Lockard, R. B. Reflections on the fall of comparative psychology. *American Psychologist*, 1971, *26*, 168–179. **[190]**

Loehlin, J. C., Lindzey, G., & Spuhler, J. N. *Race differences in intelligence*. San Francisco: Freeman, 1975. **[455, 456, 471]**

Loehlin, J. C., & Nichols, R. C. *Heredity, environment, and personality: A study of 850 sets of twins*. Austin, Tex.: University of Texas Press, 1976. **[84, 86–87]**

Loftus, E. F. Reconstructing memory: The incredible eyewitness. *Psychology Today*, December 1974, *8*, 116–119. **[226]**

Loftus, E. F. *Eyewitness testimony*. Cambridge, Mass.: Harvard University Press, 1979. **[226, 237]**

Loftus, E. F., & Loftus, G. R. On the permanence of stored information in the human brain. *American Psychologist*, 1980, *35*, 405–420. **[224]**

Loftus, E. F., & Palmer, J. C. Reconstruction of automobile destruction: An example of the interaction between language and memory. *Journal of Verbal Learning and Verbal Behavior*, 1974, *13*, 585–589. **[227]**

Logue, A. W. Taste aversion and the generality of the laws of learning. *Psychological Bulletin*, 1979, *86*, 276–296. **[190–191]**

Logue, A. W., Ophir, I., & Straus, K. E. The acquisition of taste aversions in humans. *Behavior Research and Therapy*, 1981, *19*, 319–333. **[190]**

London, M., & Bray, D. W. Ethical issues in testing and evaluation for personnel decision. *American Psychologist*, 1980, *35*, 890–901. **[466]**

Lorayne, H., & Lucas, J. *The memory book*. New York: Stein & Day, 1974. **[232, 237]**

Lorenz, K. *On aggression*. New York: Harcourt Brace Jovanovich, 1966. **[368]**

Lovaas, O. I., & Simmons, J. Q. Manipulation of self-destruction in three retarded children. *Journal of Applied Behavior Analysis*, 1969, *2*, 143–157. **[182–183]**

Lubin, B., Wallis, R. R., & Paine, C. Patterns of psychological test usage in the United States: 1935–1969. *Professional Psychology*, 1971, *2*, 70–74. **[465]**

Luchins, A. S. Mechanization in problem-solving: The effect of Einstellung. *Psychological Monographs*, 1942, *54* (Whole no. 248). **[245, 247]**

Lush, J. L. Genetics and animal breeding. In L. C. Dunn (Ed.), *Genetics in the twentieth century*. New York: Macmillan, 1951. **[79]**

Lykken, D. T. Statistical significance in psychological research. *Psychological Bulletin*, 1968, *70*, 151–159. **[382]**

Lykken, D. T. The detection of deception. *Psychological Bulletin*, 1979, *86*, 47–53. **[390]**

Lynch, S., & Yarnell, P. R. Retrograde amnesia: Delayed forgetting after concussion. *American Journal of Psychology*, 1973, *86*, 643–645. **[216]**

McCarley, R. W. Where dreams come from: A new theory. *Psychology Today*, December 1978, pp. 54–65; 141. **[93]**

McClelland, D. C. Risk-taking in children with high and low need for achievement. In J. W. Atkinson (Ed.), *Motives in fantasy, action, and society*. Princeton: Van Nostrand, 1958. **[378]**

McClelland, D. C. N achievement and entrepreneurship: A longitudinal study. *Journal of Personality* and *Social Psychology*, 1965, *1*, 389–392. **[378]**

McClelland, D. C. Managing motivation to expand human freedom. *American Psychologist*, 1978, *33*, 201–210. **[380]**

McClelland, D. C., Clark, R. A., Roby, T. B., & Atkinson, J. W. The effect of the need for achievement on thematic apperception. *Journal of Experimental Psychology*, 1949, *37*, 242–255. **[377]**

McClelland, D. C., & Winter, D. G. *Motivating economic achievement*. New York: Free Press, 1971. **[379]**

Maccoby, E. E. *Social development: Psychological growth and the parent-child relationship*. New York: Harcourt Brace Jovanovich, 1980. **[314, 319, 336]**

Maccoby, E. E., & Jacklin, C. N. *The psychology of sex differences*. Stanford, Calif: Stanford University Press, 1974. **[337–338]**

Maccoby, E. E., & Jacklin, C. N. Sex differences in aggression: A rejoinder and reprise. *Child Development*, 1980, *51*, 964–980. **[337–338]**

McDowell, J. J. The importance of Herrnstein's mathematical statement of the law of effect for behavior therapy. *American Psychologist*, 1982, *37*, 771–779. **[177]**

McGeoch, J. A. The influence of associative value upon the difficulty of nonsense-syllable lists. *Journal of Genetic Psychology*, 1930, *37*, 421–426. **[232]**

McGuire, W. J. Personality and susceptibility to social influence. In E. F. Borgatta & W. W. Lambert (Eds.), *Handbook of personality theory and research*. Chicago: Rand McNally, 1968. **[570]**

McNeill, D. *The acquisition of language*. New York: Harper & Row, 1970. **[266]**

Maher, B. A. *Principles of psychopathology: An experimental approach*. New York: McGraw-Hill, 1966. **[483]**

Malinowski, B. *The sexual life of savages in north-western Melanesia*. New York: Harcourt Brace Jovanovich, 1929. **[477]**

Manz, W., & Lueck, H. Influence of wearing glasses on personality ratings: Cross-cultural validation of an old experiment. *Perceptual and Motor Skills*, 1968, *27*, 704. **[555]**

Marcia, J. E. Identity in adolescence. In J. Adelson (Ed.), *Handbook of adolescent psychology*. New York: Wiley, 1980. **[330]**

Margerison, J. H., St. John-Loe, P., & Binnie, C. D. Electroencephalography. In P. H. Venables & I. Martin (Eds.), *A manual of psychophysiological methods*. New York: Wiley, 1967. **[73]**

Marshall, G. D., & Zimbardo, P. G. Affective consequences of inadequately explained physiological arousal. *Journal of Personality and Social Psychology*, 1979, *37*, 970–988. **[392]**

Marslen-Wilson, W. D., & Teuber, H. L. Memory for remote events in anterograde amnesia: Recognition of public figures from news photographs. *Neuropsychologia*, 1975, *13*, 353–364. **[204]**

Martin, G. B., & Clark, R. D. Distress crying in neonates: Species and peer specificity. *Developmental Psychology*, 1982, *18*, 3–9. **[290]**

Marx, M. B., Garrity, T. F., & Bowers, F. R. The influence of recent life experience on the health of college freshmen. *Journal of Psychosomatic Research*, 1975, *19*, 87–98. **[107t]**

Maslow, A. *Motivation and personality*. New York: Harper & Row, 1954. **[419]**

Maslow, A. *The psychology of science: A reconnaissance*. Chicago: Henry Regnery, 1969. **[418]**

Maslow, A. *Motivation and personality* (Rev. ed.). New York: Harper & Row, 1970. **[419–420]**

Maslow, A. *The farther reaches of human nature*. New York: Penguin Books, 1971. **[420–421]**

Masters, W. H., & Johnson, V. E. *Human sexual inadequacy*. Boston: Little, Brown, 1970. **[344]**

Matarazzo, J. D. *Wechsler's measurement and appraisal of adult intelligence* (5th ed.). Baltimore: Williams & Wilkins, 1972. **[452]**

Mathews, K. E., & Canon, L. K. Environmental noise level as a determinant of helping behavior. *Journal of Personality and Social Psychology*, 1975, *32*, 571–577. **[140]**

Mayer, J. *Overweight: Causes, cost and control*. Englewood Cliffs, N.J.: Prentice-Hall, 1968. **[373]**

Meador, B. D., & Rogers, C. R. Person-centered therapy. In R. Corsini (Ed.), *Current psychotherapies*. Itasca, Ill.: Peacock Publishers, 1973. **[529]**

Meddis, R., Pearson, A. J. D., & Langford, G. An extreme case of healthy insomnia. *Electroencephalography and Clinical Neurophysiology*, 1973, *35*, 213–224. **[92]**

Mednick, S. A. A longitudinal study of children with a high risk for schizophrenia. *Mental Hygiene*, 1966, *50*, 522–535. **[507]**

Mednick, S. A. Breakdown in individuals at high risk for schizophrenia: Possible predispositional perinatal factors. *Mental Hygiene*, 1970, *54*, 50–62. **[507]**

Meehl, P. E., & Hathaway, S. R. The K factor as a suppressor variable in the MMPI. *Journal of Applied Psychology*, 1946, *30*, 525–564. **[461, 462]**

Melton, A. W., & Irwin, J. McQ. The influence of degree of interpolated learning on retroactive inhibition and the overt transfer of specific responses. *American Journal of Psychology*, 1940, *53*, 173–203. **[211]**

Melzack, R. *The puzzle of pain.* New York: Basic Books, 1973. **[144]**

Menyuk, P., & Bernholtz, N. Prosodic features and children's language production. *Quarterly Progress Report* (Research Laboratory of Electronics, M.I.T.), 1969, *93,* 216–219. **[267]**

Metzner, R., Litwin, G., & Weil, G. M. The relation of expectation and mood to psilocybin reactions: A questionnaire study. *Psychedelic Review,* 1965, *5,* 3–39. **[99]**

Miale, F. R., & Selzer, M. *The Nuremberg mind.* New York: Quadrangle, 1976. **[465]**

Michaels, R. H., & Mellin, G. W. Prospective experience with maternal rubella and the associated congenital malformations. *Pediatrics,* 1960, *26,* 200–209. **[281]**

Middlebrook, P. N. *Social psychology and modern life.* New York: Knopf, 1980.

Miele, F. Cultural bias in the WISC. *Intelligence,* 1979, *3,* 149–164. **[471]**

Milgram, S. Behavioral study of obedience. *Journal of Abnormal Psychology,* 1963, *67,* 371–378. **[576–577]**

Milgram, S. Issues in the study of obedience: A reply to Baumrind. *American Psychologist,* 1964, *19,* 848–852. **[578]**

Milgram, S. *Obedience to authority: An experimental view.* New York: Harper & Row, 1974. **[577–580]**

Miller, G. The magical number seven, plus or minus two: Some limits on our capacity for processing information. *Psychological Review,* 1956, *63,* 81–97. **[219]**

Miller, G. A., & Buckhout, R. *Psychology: The science of mental life* (2d ed.). New York: Harper & Row, 1973. **[165]**

Miller, N. E. Learning of visceral and glandular responses. *Science,* 1969, *163,* 434–445. **[187–188]**

Millon, T. *Disorders of personality; DSM III: Axis II.* New York: Wiley, 1981. **[491]**

Milner, B. The memory defect in bilateral hippocampal lesions. *Psychiatric Research Reports of the American Psychiatric Association,* 1959, *11,* 43–52. **[204]**

Milner, B., Corkin, S., & Teuber, H. L. Further analysis of the hippocampal amnesic syndrome: 14-year follow-up study of H. M. *Neuropsychologia,* 1968, *6,* 215–234. **[204]**

Mischel, W. *Personality and assessment.* New York: Wiley, 1968. **[426, 427, 428]**

Mischel, W. On the interface of cognition and personality. *American Psychologist,* 1979, *34,* 740–754. **[428]**

Moore, B. R. The role of directed Pavlovian reactions in simple instrumental learning in the pigeon. In R. A. Hinde & J. S. Hinde (Eds.), *Constraints on learning.* London: Academic Press, 1973. **[188]**

Moore-Ede, M. C., Sulzman, F. M., & Fuller, C. A. *The clocks that time us.* Cambridge, Mass.: Harvard University Press, 1982. **[93, 95]**

Moray, N., Bates, A., & Barnett, T. Experiments on the four-eared man. *Journal of the Acoustical Society of America,* 1965, *38,* 196–201. **[218]**

Moskowitz, B. A. The acquisition of language. *Scientific American,* 1978, *239,* 92–108. **[265]**

Moulton, J., Robinson, G. M., & Elias, C. Psychology in action: Sex bias in language use. *American Psychologist,* 1978, *33,* 1032–1036. **[256–257]**

Mowrer, O. H., & Jones, H. M. Extinction and behavior variability as functions of effortfulness of task. *Journal of Experimental Psychology,* 1943, *33,* 369–385. **[178]**

Muntz, W. R. A. Vision in frogs. *Scientific American,* 1964, *210,* 110–119. **[52]**

Murphy, J. M. Psychiatric labeling in cross-cultural perspective. *Science,* 1976, *191,* 1019–1028. **[478–479]**

Murray, F. In search of Albert. *Professional Psychology,* 1973, *4,* 5. **[169]**

Murray, H. A. *Explorations in personality.* New York: Oxford University Press, 1938. **[376]**

Muruyama, G., & Miller, N. Physical attractiveness and personality. In B. A. Maher (Ed.), *Progress in experimental personality research.* New York: Academic Press, 1981. **[556]**

Muson, H. The lessons of the Grant Study. *Psychology Today,* September 1977, pp. 42; 48–49. **[342]**

Naitoh, P. Chronobiologic approach for optimizing human performance. In F. M. Brown & R. C. Graeber (Eds.), *Rhythmic aspects of behavior.* Hillsdale, N.J.: Lawrence Erlbaum Associates, 1982. **[89, 95]**

Nathan, P. E., & Goldman, M. S. Problem drinking and alcoholism. In O. F. Pomerleau & J. P. Brady (Eds.), *Behavioral medicine: Theory and practice.* Baltimore: Williams & Wilkins, 1979. **[101]**

Nauta, W. J. H., & Feirtag, M. The organization of the brain. *Scientific American,* 1979, *241,* 88–111. **[60, 73]**

Nelson, K. Structure and strategy in learning to talk. *Monographs of the Society for Research in Child Development,* 1973, *38*(Nos. 1 and 2). **[267]**

Neugarten, B. L. Adult personality: Toward a psychology of the life cycle. In W. C. Sze (Ed.), *Human life cycle.* New York: Aronson, 1975. **[338]**

Newcomb, T. *The acquaintance process.* New York: Holt, Rinehart and Winston, 1961. **[560]**

Newell, A., & Simon, H. A. *Human problem solving.*

Englewood Cliffs, N.J.: Prentice-Hall, 1972. **[247, 248]**

Newman, H. H., Freeman, F. N., & Holzinger, K. J. *Twins: A study of heredity and environment.* Chicago: University of Chicago Press, 1937. **[454]**

Nickerson, D., & Newhall, S. M. A psychological color solid. *Journal of the Optical Society of America*, 1943, *33*, 419–422. **[130]**

Nickerson, R. S., & Adams, M. J. Long-term memory for a common object. *Cognitive Psychology*, 1979, *11*, 287–307. **[223]**

Nierenberg, G. I., & Calero, H. H. *How to read a person like a book.* New York: Cornerstone Library, 1972. **[558]**

Nisbett, R., & Ross, L. *Human inference: Strategies and shortcomings of social judgment.* Englewood Cliffs, N.J.: Prentice-Hall, 1980. **[19, 35, 426]**

Nisbett, R., & Wilson, T. D. Telling more than we can know: Verbal reports on mental processes. *Psychological Review*, 1977, *84*, 231–259. **[362]**

Nisbett, R. E., Borgida, E., Crandall, R., & Reed, H. Popular induction: Information is not always informative. In J. S. Carroll & J. W. Payne (Eds.), *Cognition and social behavior.* Hillsdale, N.J.: Lawrence Erlbaum Associates, 1976. **[19]**

Nisbett, R. E., & Gordon, A. Self-esteem and susceptibility to social influence. *Journal of Personality and Social Psychology*, 1967, *5*, 268–276. **[571]**

Notterman, J. M. Force emission during bar pressing. *Journal of Experimental Psychology*, 1959, *58*, 341–347. **[178]**

Noyes, A. P., & Kolb, L. C. *Modern clinical psychiatry* (6th ed.). Philadelphia: Saunders, 1963. **[496]**

Nuckolls, K. B., Cassel, J., & Kaplan, B. H. Psychosocial assets, life crisis and the prognosis of pregnancy. *American Journal of Epidemiology*, 1972, *95*, 431–441. **[108]**

Occupational Safety and Health Administration. Occupational safety and health standards. *Federal Register*, 1971, *36*, 105. **[140]**

Ogle, J. W. On the diurnal variations in the temperature of the human body in health. *St. George's Hospital Report*, 1866, *1*, 220–245. **[88]**

Olson, D. R., & Filby, N. On the comprehension of active and passive sentences. *Cognitive Psychology*, 1972, *3*, 361–381. **[263]**

Olton, D. S., & Noonberg, A. R. *Biofeedback: Clinical applications in behavioral medicine.* Englewood Cliffs, N.J.: Prentice-Hall, 1980. **[109]**

Orlofsky, J. L., Marcia, J. E., & Lesser, I. M. Ego identity status and the intimacy vs. isolation crisis of young adulthood. *Journal of Personality and Social Psychology*, 1973, *27*, 211–219. **[330]**

Orme-Johnson, D. W., & Farrow, J. T. (Eds.). *Scientific research on the transcendental meditation program* (Vol. 1). New York: Maharishi European Research University Press, 1977. **[111]**

Ostberg, O. Circadian rhythms of food intake and oral temperature in "morning" and "evening" groups of individuals. *Ergonomics*, 1973, *16*, 203–209. **[89]**

Pagano, R. R., Rose, R. M., Stivers, R. M., & Warrenburg, S. Sleep during transcendental meditation. *Science*, 1976, *191*, 308–310. **[111]**

Parlee, M. B. The sexes under scrutiny: From old biases to new theories. *Psychology Today*, November 1978, pp. 62–69. **[89]**

Pavlov, I. P. *Conditioned reflexes* (G. V. Anrep, trans.). London: Oxford University Press, 1927. **[164]**

Pellegrini, R. Impressions of male personality as a function of beardedness. *Psychology*, 1973, *10*, 29. **[555]**

Perry, D. K. *Evaluation of tests for improvement of programmer trainee selection.* SDC Technical Memorandum 3570, System Development Corporation, 1967. **[440]**

Pert, A., Pert, C. B., Davis, G. C., & Bunney, W. E. Opiate peptides and brain function. In H. M. van Praag (Ed.), *Handbook of biological psychiatry* (Vol. 2). New York: Dekker, 1982. **[103]**

Peterson, L. R., & Peterson, M. J. Short-term retention of individual verbal items. *Journal of Experimental Psychology*, 1959, *58*, 193–198. **[212]**

Pfungst, O. *Clever Hans.* New York: Holt, Rinehart and Winston, 1911. **[25–27]**

Pheterson, G. I., Kiesler, S. B., & Goldberg, P. A. Evaluation of the performance of women as a function of their sex, achievement, and personal history. *Journal of Personality and Social Psychology*, 1971, *19*, 114–119. **[335]**

Piaget, J. *The child's conception of the world.* Totowa, N.J.: Littlefield, Adams, 1960. (Originally published, 1926.) **[295–296]**

Piaget, J. *Play, dreams and imitation in childhood.* New York: Norton, 1962. **[225]**

Piaget, J. Intellectual evolution from adolescence to adulthood. *Human Development*, 1972, *15*, 1–21. **[298]**

Plomin, R., & DeFries, J. C. Genetics and intelligence: Recent data. *Intelligence*, 1980, *4*, 15–24. **[454]**

Pocs, O., Godow, A., Tolone, W. L., & Walsh, R. H. Is there sex after 40? *Psychology Today*, June 1977, pp. 54–56; 87. **[350]**

Pollack, I., & Pickett, J. M. Intelligibility of excerpts from fluent speech: Auditory vs. structural context. *Journal of Verbal Learning and Verbal Behavior*, 1964, *3*, 79–84. **[264]**

Pollock, G. H. The possible significance of childhood

object loss in the Josef Breuer–Bertha Pappenheim (Anna O.)–Sigmund Freud relationship: I. Josef Breuer. *Journal of the American Psychoanalytic Association*, 1968, *16*, 711–739. **[403]**

Pomeroy, W. B. *Dr. Kinsey and the Institute for Sex Research*. New York: Harper & Row, 1972. **[345, 347]**

Porac, C., & Coren, S. The assessment of motor control in sighting dominance using an illusion decrement procedure. *Perception and Psychophysics*, 1977, *21*, 341–346. **[154]**

Porter, R. H., & Moore, J. D. Human kin recognition by olfactory cues. *Physiology and Behavior*, 1982, *27*, 493–495. **[143]**

Premack, D. Reinforcement theory. In M. R. Jones (Ed.), *Nebraska Symposium on Motivation: 1965*. Lincoln, Neb.: University of Nebraska Press, 1965. **[173]**

Premack, D. Language in the chimpanzee? *Science*, 1971, *172*, 808–822. **[271]**

Rabkin, J. G., & Struening, E. L. Life events, stress, and illness. *Science*, 1976, *194*, 1013–1020. **[108]**

Rahe, R. H. Subjects' recent life changes and their near-future illness in susceptibility. *Advances in Psychosomatic Medicine*, 1972, *8*, 2–19. **[105–106]**

Raskin, D. C., & Hare, R. D. Psychopathology and detection of deception in a prison population. *Psychophysiology*, 1978, *15*, 126–136. **[389]**

Raskin, D. C., & Podlesny, J. A. Truth and deception: A reply to Lykken. *Psychological Bulletin*, 1979, *89*, 54–59. **[390]**

Rathbun, C., McLaughlin, H., Bennett, O., & Garland, J. A. Later adjustment of children following radical separation from family and culture. *American Journal of Orthopsychiatry*, 1965, *35*, 604–609. **[317]**

Ray, O. *Drugs, society, and human behavior* (2d ed.). St. Louis: Mosby, 1978. **[98, 99, 115]**

Reisman, J. M. *The development of clinical psychology*. Englewood Cliffs, N.J.: Prentice-Hall, 1966. **[514]**

Rensberger, B. Can a pill be mightier than the sword? *New York Times*, September 12, 1971. **[51]**

Reschly, D. J., & Sabers, D. L. An examination of bias in predicting MAT scores from WISC-R scores for four ethnic-racial groups. *Journal of Educational Measurement*, 1979, *16*, 1–9. **[468]**

Rescorla, R. A. Pavlovian conditioned fear in Sidman avoidance learning. *Journal of Comparative and Physiological Psychology*, 1968, *65*, 55–60. **[193]**

Rescorla, R. A., & Wagner, A. R. A theory of Pavlovian conditioning: Variations in the effectiveness of reinforcement and non-reinforcement. In A. H. Black & W. F. Prokasy (Eds.), *Classical condition-*

ing II. Englewood Cliffs, N.J.: Prentice-Hall, 1972. **[193–194]**

Rhine, J. B. *Extrasensory perception*. Boston: Boston Society for Psychic Research, 1934. **[156]**

Rice, B. The new truth machines. *Psychology Today*, June 1978, pp. 61–78. **[120]**

Riegel, K. F., & Riegel, R. M. Development, drop, and death. *Developmental Psychology*, 1972, *6*, 306–319. **[353]**

Rife, D. C. Handedness, with special reference to twins. *Genetics*, 1940, *25*, 178–186. **[72]**

Rimm, D. C., & Masters, J. C. *Behavior therapy: Techniques and empirical findings* (2d ed.). New York: Academic Press, 1979. **[526]**

Rioch, M. J. Pilot projects in training mental health counselors. In E. L. Cowen, E. A. Gardner, & M. Zax (Eds.), *Emerging approaches to mental health problems*. Englewood Cliffs, N.J.: Prentice-Hall, 1967. **[542]**

Robinson, M. F., Freeman, W., & Watts, J. W. Personality changes after psychosurgery. In N. Bigelow (Ed.), *Proceedings of the First Research Conference on Psychosurgery, 1949*. Bethesda, Md.: National Institutes of Health, U.S. Public Health Service, Publication No. 16, 1951, 159–162. **[65]**

Rodin, J. Current status of the internal-external hypothesis for obesity. *American Psychologist*, 1981, *36*, 361–372. **[373, 375]**

Rodin, J., & Langer, E. Long-term effects of a control-relevant intervention with the institutionalized aged. *Journal of Personality and Social Psychology*, 1977, *35*, 897–902. **[354]**

Rogers, C. R. *On becoming a person*. Boston: Houghton Mifflin, 1961. **[529]**

Rosch, E. Cognitive representation of semantic categories. *Journal of Experimental Psychology: General*, 1975, *104*, 192–233. **[252–253]**

Rosen, E., & Gregory, I. *Abnormal psychology*. Philadelphia: Saunders, 1965. **[501]**

Rosen, P. L. *The Supreme Court and social science*. Urbana, Ill.: University of Illinois Press, 1972. **[12]**

Rosenhan, D. L. Reply to letters to the editor. *Science*, 1973, *180*, 365–369. **[484]**

Rosenkrantz, P., Vogel, S., Bee, H., Broverman, I., & Broverman, D. M. Sex role stereotypes and self-conceptions of college students. *Journal of Consulting and Clinical Psychology*, 1968, *32*, 287–295. **[334]**

Rosenman, R. H., Brand, R. J., Jenkins, D., Friedman, M., Straus, R., & Wurm, M. Coronary heart disease in the Western collaborative group study. *Journal of the American Medical Association*, 1975, *233*, 872–877. **[431]**

Rosenman, R. H., Brand, R. J., Shultz, R. I., & Friedman, M. Multivariate prediction of coronary heart disease during the 8.5-year follow-up in the Western collaborative group study. *American Journal of Cardiology*, 1976, *37*, 903–910. **[432]**

Rosenthal, B., & McSweeney, F. K. Modeling influences on eating behavior. *Addictive Behavior*, 1979, *4*, 205–214. **[371]**

Rosenthal, D. *Genetics of psychopathology.* New York: McGraw-Hill, 1971. **[506]**

Rosenthal, R., & Jacobson, L. *Pygmalion in the classroom.* New York: Holt, Rinehart and Winston, 1968. **[27–29, 30–31, 32]**

Rosenthal, R., & Rubin, D. Interpersonal expectancy effects: The first 345 studies. *Behavioral and Brain Sciences*, 1978, *3*, 377–415. **[30]**

Rosenthal, T. L., & Bandura, A. Psychological modeling: Theory and practice. In S. L. Garfield & A. E. Bergin (Eds.), *Handbook of psychotherapy and behavior change: An empirical analysis* (2d ed.). New York: Wiley, 1978. **[542]**

Roskies, E., Spevack, M., Surkis, A., Cohen, C., & Gilman, S. Changing the coronary-prone (Type A) behavior pattern in a nonclinical population. *Journal of Behavioral Medicine*, 1978, *1*, 201–216. **[433]**

Ross, J., & Lawrence, K. A. Some observations on memory artifice. *Psychonomic Science*, 1968, *13*, 107–108. **[231]**

Ross, L., Turiel, E., Josephson, J., & Lepper, M. R. *Developmental perspectives on the fundamental attribution error.* Unpublished manuscript, Stanford University, 1978. **[427]**

Rubin, J. Z., Provenzano, F. J., & Luria, Z. The eye of the beholder: Parents' view on sex of newborns. *American Journal of Orthopsychiatry*, 1974, *44*, 512–519. **[336]**

Rubovits, P. C., & Maehr, M. L. Pygamalion analyzed: Toward an explanation of the Rosenthal-Jacobson findings. *Journal of Personality and Social Psychology*, 1971, *19*, 197–203. **[29]**

Rumbaugh, D. M. (Ed.). *Language learning by a chimpanzee: The Lana project.* New York: Academic Press, 1977. **[271]**

Russell, W. R., & Nathan, P. W. Traumatic amnesia. *Brain*, 1946, *69*, 280–300. **[216]**

Sackett, G. P., Ruppenthal, G. C., Fahrenbruch, C. E., & Holm, R. A. Social isolation rearing effects in monkeys vary with genotype. *Developmental Psychology*, 1981, *17*, 313–318. **[309]**

Samelson, F. J. B. Watson's Little Albert, Cyril Burt's twins and the need for a critical science. *American Psychologist*, 1980, *35*, 619–625. **[170]**

Savage-Rumbaugh, E. S., Rumbaugh, D. M., & Boysen, S. Symbolic communication between two chimpanzees (Pan troglodytes). *Science*, 1978, *201*, 641–644. **[272]**

Savage-Rumbaugh, E. S., Rumbaugh, D. M., & Boysen, S. Do apes use language? *American Scientist*, 1980, *68*, 49–61. **[272]**

Scarr, S., & Salapatek, P. Patterns of fear development during infancy. *Merrill-Palmer Quarterly*, 1970, *16*, 53–90. **[288]**

Scarr, S., & Weinberg, R. A. IQ test performance of black children adopted by white families. *American Psychologist*, 1976, *31*, 726–739. **[456]**

Schachter, S. *Emotion, obesity, and crime.* New York: Academic Press, 1971. **[386]**

Schachter, S. Recidivism and self-cure of smoking and obesity. *American Psychologist*, 1982, *37*, 436–444. **[374]**

Schachter, S., Goldman, R., & Gordon, A. The effects of fear, food deprivation, and obesity on eating. *Journal of Personality and Social Psychology*, 1968, *10*, 91–97. **[372]**

Schachter, S., & Gross, L. Manipulated time and eating behavior. *Journal of Personality and Social Psychology*, 1968, *10*, 98–106. **[372]**

Schachter, S., & Singer, J. E. Cognitive, social, and physiological determinants of emotional state. *Psychological Review*, 1962, *69*, 379–399. **[365, 391–392, 565]**

Schaie, K. W., & Labouvie-Vief, G. Generational versus ontogenetic components of change in adult cognitive behavior: A fourteen-year cross-sequential study. *Developmental Psychology*, 1974, *10*, 305–320. **[353]**

Schank, R. C., & Abelson, R. P. *Scripts, plans, goals, and understanding.* Hillsdale, N.J.: Lawrence Erlbaum Associates, 1977. **[250]**

Schiffenbauer, A. Effect of observer's emotional state on judgments of the emotional state of others. *Journal of Personality and Social Psychology*, 1974, *30*, 31–35. **[566]**

Schrag, P., & Divoky, D. *The myth of the hyperactive child and other means of child control.* New York: Pantheon Books, 1975. **[302]**

Schulsinger, H. A ten-year follow-up of children with schizophrenic mothers. *Acta Psychiatrica Scandinavica*, 1976, *63*, 371–386. **[507]**

Schultz, T., & Horibe, F. Development of the appreciation of verbal jokes. *Developmental Psychology*, 1974, *10*, 13–20. **[279]**

Schwartz, G. E., Fair, P. L., Salt, P., Mandel, M. R., & Klerman, G. L. Facial muscle patterning to affective imagery in depressed and nondepressed subjects. *Science*, 1976, *192*, 489–491. **[395]**

Schwartz, G. E., & Weiss, S. What is behavioral medicine? *Psychosomatic Medicine*, 1977, *36*, 377–381. **[112]**

Sclafani, A., & Springer, D. Dietary obesity in adult rats: Similarities to hypothalamic and human obesity syndromes. *Physiology and Behavior,* 1976, *17,* 461–471. **[374]**

Scovern, A. W., & Kilmann, P. R. Status of electroconvulsive therapy: Review of the outcome literature. *Psychological Bulletin,* 1980, *87,* 260–303. **[535]**

Sears, D. O., & Whitney, R. E. Political persuasion. In I. deS. Pool et al. (Eds.), *Handbook of communication.* Chicago: Rand McNally, 1973. **[566]**

Sears, R. R., Whiting, J. W. M., Nowlis, V., & Sears, P. S. Some child-rearing antecedents of aggression and dependency in young children. *Genetic Psychology Monographs,* 1953, *47,* 135–234. **[411]**

Segal, M. W. Alphabet and attraction: An unobtrusive measure of the effect of propinquity in a field setting. *Journal of Personality and Social Psychology,* 1974, *30,* 654–657. **[559]**

Seligman, M. E. P. *Helplessness: On depression, development, and death.* San Francisco: Freeman, 1975. **[186, 498]**

Seligman, M. E. P., & Hager, J. L. (Eds.). *Biological boundaries of learning.* Englewood Cliffs, N.J.: Prentice-Hall, 1972. **[188]**

Selye, H. *The stress of life.* New York: McGraw-Hill, 1956. **[104]**

Sexton, M. M. Behavioral epidemiology. In O. F. Pomerleau & J. P. Brady (Eds.), *Behavioral medicine: Theory and practice.* Baltimore: Williams & Wilkins, 1979. **[112]**

Shapiro, A. K. Placebo effects in medicine, psychotherapy, and psychoanalysis. In A. E. Bergin & S. L. Garfield (Eds.), *Handbook of psychotherapy and behavior change: An empirical analysis.* New York: Wiley, 1971. **[538]**

Shapiro, D. Preface. In D. Shapiro, T. X. Barber, L. V. Di Cara, J. Kamiya, N. E. Miller, & J. Stoyva (Eds.), *Biofeedback and self-control.* Chicago: Aldine, 1973. **[109]**

Sheehy, G. *Passages: Predictable crises of adult life.* New York: Dutton, 1976. **[339, 359]**

Sherif, M., Harvey, D., White, B., Hood, W., & Sherif, C. *Intergroup conflict and cooperation: The Robber's Cave experiment.* Norman, Okla.: Institute of Group Relations, University of Oklahoma, 1961. **[554]**

Sherrod, D. The physical environment and social behavior. In D. Sherrod (Ed.), *Social psychology.* New York: Random House, 1982. **[582]**

Shields, J. *Monozygotic twins.* London: Oxford University Press, 1962. **[454]**

Siffre, M. *Beyond time* (H. Briffault, Ed. & trans.). New York: McGraw-Hill, 1964. **[89]**

Silverman, J. Shamans and acute schizophrenia. *American Anthropologist,* 1967, *69,* 21–31. **[478]**

Silvern, L. E., & Ryan, V. L. Self-rated adjustment and sex-typing on the Bem Sex-Role Inventory: Is masculinity the primary predictor of adjustment? *Sex Roles,* 1979, *5,* 739–763. **[435]**

Siqueland, E. R., & De Lucia, C. A. Visual reinforcement of nonnutritive sucking in human infants. *Science,* 1969, *165,* 1144–1146. **[290]**

Skinner, B. F. *Walden two.* New York: Macmillan, 1948. **[8, 181, 200]**

Skinner, B. F. *Science and human behavior.* New York: Macmillan, 1953. **[412]**

Skinner, B. F. A case history in scientific method. *American Psychologist,* 1956, *11,* 221–233. **[174]**

Skinner, B. F. *About behaviorism.* New York: Knopf, 1974. **[413]**

Skinner, B. F. *The shaping of a behaviorist.* New York: Knopf, 1979. **[178]**

Sloane, R. B., Staples, F. R., Cristol, A. H., Yorkston, N. J., & Whipple, K. *Psychoanalysis versus behavior therapy.* Cambridge, Mass.: Harvard University Press, 1975. **[532]**

Slobin, D. I. *Psycholinguistics.* Glenview, Ill.: Scott, Foresman, 1971. **[267]**

Smedslund, J. The acquisition of conservation of substance and weight in children. *Scandinavian Journal of Psychology,* 1961, *2,* 11–20. **[299]**

Smith, M. L., Glass, G. V., & Miller, T. I. *The benefits of psychotherapy.* Baltimore, Md.: Johns Hopkins University Press, 1980. **[533–534]**

Smith, S. Trends in counseling and psychotherapy. *American Psychologist,* 1982, *37,* 802–809. **[524, 528, 530]**

Smith, S. M., Brown, H. Q., Toman, J. E. P., & Goodman, L. S. The lack of cerebral effects of d-tubercurarine. *Anesthesiology,* 1947, *8,* 1–14. **[241]**

Snyder, F., & Scott, J. The psychophysiology of sleep. In N. S. Greenfield & R. A. Sternbach (Eds.), *Handbook of psychophysiology.* New York: Holt, Rinehart and Winston, 1972. **[92]**

Snyder, M. Self-fulfilling stereotypes. *Psychology Today,* July 1982, pp. 60–67. **[18]**

Snyder, M., & Uranowitz, S. W. Reconstructing the past: Some cognitive consequences of person perception. *Journal of Personality and Social Psychology,* 1978, *36,* 941–950. **[17]**

Snyder, S. H. Brain peptides as neurotransmitters. *Science,* 1980, *209,* 976–983. **[53]**

Solomon, R. L. The opponent-process theory of acquired motivation: The costs of pleasure and the benefits of pain. *American Psychologist,* 1980, *35,* 691–712. **[366–367]**

Solomon, R. L., Kamin, L. J., & Wynne, L. C. Traumatic avoidance learning: The outcomes of several extinction procedures with dogs. *Journal of*

Abnormal and Social Psychology, 1953, *48*, 291–302. **[184]**

Speisman, J. C., Lazarus, R. S., Davidson, L., & Mordkoff, A. Experimental reduction of psychological stress based on ego defense theory. *Journal of Abnormal and Social Psychology*, 1964, *68*, 359–380. **[393]**

Spelt, D. K. Conditioned responses in the human fetus in utero. *Psychological Bulletin*, 1938, *35*, 712–713. **[166]**

Spence, J. T., & Helmreich, R. L. *Masculinity and femininity: Their psychological dimensions, correlates and antecedents.* Austin, Tex.: University of Texas Press, 1978. **[430]**

Sperling, G. The information available in brief visual presentations. *Psychological Monographs*, 1960, *74*(No. 11). **[217–218]**

Spitzer, R. L. On pseudoscience in science, logic in remission, and psychiatric diagnosis: A critique of Rosenhan's "On being sane in insane places." *Journal of Abnormal Psychology*, 1976, *84*, 442–452. **[484]**

Spitzer, R. L., & Fleiss, J. L. A reanalysis of the reliability of psychiatric diagnosis. *British Journal of Psychiatry*, 1974, *125*, 341–347. **[485]**

Spitzer, R. L., Skodol, A. E., Gibbon, M., & Williams, J. B. W. *DSM III Case Book.* Washington, D.C.: American Psychiatric Association, 1981. **[475, 489, 493]**

Spock, B. *Baby and child care.* New York: Pocket Books, 1976. **[312, 319]**

Springer, S. P., & Deutsch, G. *Left brain, right brain.* San Francisco: Freeman, 1981. **[72, 75]**

Sroufe, L. A., & Waters, E. Attachment as an organization construct. *Child Development*, 1977, *48*, 1184–1199. **[310]**

Sroufe, L. A., & Wunsch, J. C. The development of laughter in the first year of life. *Child Development*, 1972, *43*, 1326–1344. **[278]**

Sternbach, R. A., & Tursky, B. Ethnic differences among housewives in psychophysical and skin potential responses to electric shock. *Psychophysiology*, 1965, *1*, 241. **[145]**

Sternberg, R. J., Conway, B. E., Ketron, J. L., & Bernstein, M. People's conceptions of intelligence. *Journal of Personality and Social Psychology*, 1981, *41*, 37–55. **[449]**

Stewart, D. N., & Wisner, D. M. de R. Incidence of perforated peptic ulcer during the period of heavy air raids. *Lancet*, 1942, *1*, 259–261. **[104]**

Stokols, D. On the distinction between density and crowding: Some implications for future research. *Psychological Review*, 1972, *79*, 275–278. **[582]**

Stratton, G. M. Vision without inversion of the retinal image. *Psychological Review*, 1897, *4*, 341–481. **[154–155]**

Stunkard, A. J. Behavioral medicine and beyond: The example of obesity. In O. F. Pomerleau & J. P. Brady (Eds.), *Behavioral medicine: Theory and practice.* Baltimore: Williams & Wilkins, 1979. **[374]**

Stunkard, A. J., & Koch, C. The interpretation of gastric motility: I. Apparent bias in the reports of hunger by obese persons. *Archives of General Psychiatry*, 1964, *11*, 74–82. **[372]**

Suomi, S. J., & Harlow, H. F. Social rehabilitation of isolate-reared monkeys. *Developmental Psychology*, 1972, *6*, 487–496. **[309]**

Szasz, T. *The myth of mental illness.* New York: Harper & Row, 1961. **[478, 483]**

Szucko, J. J., & Kleinmuntz, B. Statistical versus clinical lie detection. *American Psychologist*, 1981, *36*, 488–496. **[390]**

Tanke, E. D., & Tanke, T. J. Getting off a slippery slope: Social science in the judicial process. *American Psychologist*, 1979, *34*, 1130–1138. **[12]**

Tavris, C., & Offir, C. *The longest war.* New York: Harcourt Brace Jovanovich, 1977. **[335]**

Tedeschi, J. T., Schlenker, B. R., & Bonoma, T. V. Cognitive dissonance: Private ratiocination or public spectacle? *American Psychologist*, 1971, *26*, 685–695. **[574]**

Teitelbaum, P. Sensory control of hypothalamic hyperphagia. *Journal of Comparative and Physiological Psychology*, 1955, *43*, 156–163. **[371]**

Teitelbaum, P., & Epstein, A. N. The lateral hypothalamic syndrome: Recovery of feeding and drinking after lateral hypothalamic lesions. *Psychological Review*, 1962, *69*, 74–90. **[371]**

Terrace, H. *Nim: A chimpanzee who learned sign language.* New York: Knopf, 1979. **[272–273]**

Teuber, H., Corkin, S., & Twitchell, T. E. A study of cingulotomy in man. In *Psychosurgery*, a report of the National Commission for the Protection of Human Subjects of Biomedical and Behavioral Research. Washington, D.C.: U.S. Government Printing Office, 1976. **[66]**

Thomas, A., & Chess, S. *Temperament and development.* New York: Brunner/Mazel, 1977. **[305, 306–307]**

Thomas, A., Chess, S., & Birch, H. G. The origin of personality. *Scientific American*, 1970, *223*, 102–109. **[304–305, 306]**

Thompson, R. F. *Introduction to physiological psychology.* New York: Harper & Row, 1975. **[61, 73, 367]**

Thorndike, E. L. Animal intelligence. An experimental study of the associative processes in animals.

Psychological Review, Monograph Supplement, 1898, *2,* 1–109. **[170]**

Thorndike, E. L. Sex in education. *Bookman,* 1906, *23,* 211–214. **[430, 435]**

Thorndike, R. L. Review of Pygmalion in the classroom. *American Educational Research Journal,* 1968, *5,* 708–711. **[129]**

Tieger, T. On the biological basis of sex differences in aggression. *Child Development,* 1980, *51,* 943–963. **[337–338]**

Timberlake, W. A molar equilibrium theory of learned performance. In G. H. Bower (Ed.), *The psychology of learning and motivation* (Vol. 14). New York: Academic Press, 1980. **[173]**

Tolman, E. C. The nature of instinct. *Psychological Bulletin,* 1923, *20,* 200–216. **[364]**

Tolman, E. C. *Drives toward war.* Englewood Cliffs, N.J.: Prentice-Hall, 1942. **[365]**

Tolman, E. C., & Honzik, C. H. Introduction and removal of reward, and maze performance in rats. *University of California Publications in Psychology,* 1930, *4,* 257–275. **[193]**

Tomkins, S. S. *Affect imagery consciousness* (Vol. 1): *The positive affects.* New York: Springer-Verlag, 1962. **[395]**

Tresemer, D. *Fear of success.* New York: Plenum, 1977. **[382]**

Triplett, N. The dynamogenic factors in pacemaking and competition. *American Journal of Psychology,* 1898, *9,* 507–533. **[548–550]**

Tulving, E. Episodic and semantic memory. In E. Tulving & W. Donaldson (Eds.), *Organization of memory.* New York: Academic Press, 1972. **[220–221]**

Tulving, E. Cue-dependent forgetting. *American Scientist,* 1974, *62,* 74–82. **[213, 214, 223]**

Tulving, E., & Thompson, D. M. Retrieval processes in recognition memory. *Journal of Experimental Psychology,* 1971, *87,* 116–124. **[213–214]**

Turnbull, C. Some observations regarding the experiences and behavior of the BaMbuti Pygmies. *American Journal of Psychology,* 1961, *74,* 304–308. **[154]**

Ullman, M., Krippner, S., & Vaughan, A. *Dream telepathy.* New York: Macmillan, 1973. **[157]**

Underwood, B. J. Interference and forgetting. *Psychological Review,* 1957, *64,* 49–60. **[211]**

U.S. Congress. Use of polygraphs and "lie detectors" by the federal government (House Report No. 198, 89th Congress, 1st session). Washington, D.C.: U.S. Government Printing Office, 1965. **[390]**

Vaillant, G. E. *Adaptation to life.* Boston: Little, Brown, 1977. **[342–344]**

Valenstein, E. S. *Brain control: A critical examination of brain stimulation and psychosurgery.* New York: Wiley, 1973. **[50, 65, 75]**

Valenstein, E. S. Historical perspective. In E. S. Valenstein (Ed.), *The psychosurgery debate.* San Francisco: Freeman, 1980. **[64, 66]**

Valins, S. Cognitive effects of false heart-rate feedback. *Journal of Personality and Social Psychology,* 1966, *4,* 400–408. **[565]**

Vandenbos, G. R., DeLeon, P. H., & Pallak, M. S. An alternative to traditional medical care for the terminally ill. *American Psychologist,* 1982, *11,* 1245–1248. **[357]**

Vane, J. R. Relation of early school achievement to high school achievement when race, intelligence, and socioeconomic factors are equated. *Psychology in the Schools,* 1966, *3,* 124–129. **[453]**

Vaughan, E. D. Misconceptions about psychology among introductory psychology students. *Teaching of Psychology,* 1977, *4,* 138–141. **[15–16]**

Veroff, J., Kulka, R. A., & Douvan, E. *Mental health in America.* New York: Basic Books, 1981. **[520]**

Wahba, M. A., & Bridwell, L. G. Maslow reconsidered. *Organizational Behavior and Human Performance,* 1976, *15,* 212–240. **[421]**

Wallace, R. K. Physiological effects of transcendental meditation. *Science,* 1970, *167,* 1751–1754. **[110]**

Wallace, R. K., Benson, H., & Wilson, A. F. A wakeful hypometabolic physiological state. *American Journal of Physiology,* 1971, *221,* 795–799. **[110]**

Wallace, W. L. Review of the Scholastic Aptitude Test. In O. K. Buros (Ed.), *The seventh mental measurements yearbook.* Lincoln, Neb.: University of Nebraska, Buros Institute of Mental Measurements, 1972. **[440]**

Walster, E., Aronson, V., Abrahams, D., & Rottman, L. Importance of physical attractiveness in dating behavior. *Journal of Personality and Social Behavior,* 1966, *4,* 508–516. **[561]**

Walters, G. C., & Grusec, J. E. *Punishment.* San Francisco: Freeman, 1977. **[180, 181, 184, 194, 314]**

Ward, M. H., & Baker, B. L. Reinforcement therapy in the classroom. *Journal of Applied Behavior Analysis,* 1968, *1,* 323–328. **[197]**

Watson, J. B. *Psychological care of infant and child.* New York: Norton, 1928. **[314]**

Watson, J. B. *Behaviorism* (Rev. ed.). New York: Norton, 1930. **[162–163, 171, 241]**

Watson, J. B., & Rayner, R. Conditioned emotional reactions. *Journal of Experimental Psychology,* 1920, *3,* 1–14. **[168–170, 187]**

Waugh, N., & Norman, D. A. Primary memory. *Psychological Review*, 1965, *72*, 89–104. **[219]**

Wechsler, D. *The measurement and appraisal of adult intelligence.* Baltimore, Md.: Williams & Wilkins, 1958. **[450–452]**

Weissman, M., & Paykel, E. *The depressed woman.* Chicago: University of Chicago Press, 1974. **[496]**

White, B. L. *The first three years of life.* Englewood Cliffs, N.J.: Prentice-Hall, 1975. **[316]**

White, R. W. Ego reality in psychoanalytic theory: A proposal regarding independent ego energies. *Psychological Issues*, 1963, *3*, 1–210. **[411]**

Whorf, B. L. Science and linguistics. In J. B. Carroll (Ed.), *Language, thought and reality: Selected writings of Benjamin Lee Whorf.* Cambridge, Mass.: M.I.T. Press, 1956. **[254]**

Wilkinson, R. T. The relationship between body temperature and performance across circadian phase shifts. In F. M. Brown & R. C. Graeber (Eds.), *Rhythmic aspects of behavior.* Hillsdale, N.J.: Lawrence Erlbaum Associates, 1982. **[89]**

Williams, D. R., & Williams, H. Automaintenance in the pigeon: Sustained pecking despite contingent non-reinforcement. *Journal of the Experimental Analysis of Behavior*, 1969, *12*, 511–520. **[188]**

Williams, R. L., & Long, J. D. *Toward a self-managed lifestyle* (3d ed.). Boston: Houghton Mifflin, 1983. **[526, 545]**

Wilson, G. T., & Lawson, D. M. Expectancies, alcohol, and sexual arousal in male social drinkers. *Journal of Abnormal Psychology*, 1976, *85*, 587–594. **[99]**

Winch, R. F. *Mate selection: A study of complementary needs.* New York: Harper & Row, 1958. **[561]**

Wingerson, L. Hypertension compliance. *Medical World News*, 1977, *18*, 20–28. **[113]**

Winter, R. *The smell book: Scents, sex and society.* Philadelphia: Lippincott, 1976. **[144]**

Wittner, D. A boy who shut everyone out. *Life*, May 26, 1972, pp. 32–35. **[16]**

Wollen, K. A., Weber, A., & Lowry, D. H. Bizarreness versus interaction of mental images as determinants of learning. *Cognitive Psychology*, 1972, *3*, 518–523. **[231, 232, 237]**

Wolpe, J. *Psychotherapy by reciprocal inhibition.* Stanford, Calif.: Stanford University Press, 1958. **[525]**

Woodworth, R. S. *Experimental psychology.* New York: Holt, Rinehart and Winston, 1938. **[217]**

Wortman, C. B., Adesman, P., Herman, E., & Greenberg, R. Self-disclosure: An attributional perspective. *Journal of Personality and Social Psychology*, 1976, *33*, 184–191. **[564]**

Wundt, W. *[Outlines of psychology]* (C. H. Judd, trans.). New York: Stechert, 1907. **[280]**

Zaidel, E. The split and half brains as models of congenital language disability (NINCDS Monograph No. 22, U.S. Public Health Service Publication No. 79-440). Washington, D.C.: U.S. Government Printing Office, 1978. **[68]**

Zajonc, R. B. Social facilitation. *Science*, 1965, *149*, 260–274. **[549–550]**

Zelazo, P. R., Zelazo, N. A., & Kolb, S. Walking in the newborn. *Science*, 1972, *176*, 314–315. **[283, 285]**

Zelnick, M., & Kanter, J. F. Sexual activity, contraceptive use and pregnancy among metropolitan-area teenagers: 1971–1979. *Family Planning Perspectives*, 1980, *12*, 230–237. **[348]**

Zilboorg, G., & Henry, G. W. *A history of medical psychology.* New York: Norton, 1941. **[481, 514, 516]**

Zimbardo, P. G., Ebbesen, E. B., & Maslach, C. *Influencing attitudes and changing behavior* (2d ed.). Reading, Mass.: Addison-Wesley, 1977. **[569]**

Zlutnick, S., & Altman, I. Crowding and human behavior. In J. F. Wohlwill & D. H. Carson (Eds.), *Environment and the social sciences: Perspectives and applications.* Washington, D.C.: American Psychological Association, 1972. **[581]**

Zubin, J., Eron, L. D., & Schumer, F. *An experimental approach to projective techniques.* New York: Wiley, 1965. **[464]**

Index

Note: Italic *f* or *t* following page number indicates subject will be found in *figure* or *table*. Page numbers for studies cited in the text are given in the bibliography.

85 86 9 8 7 6 5 4 3 2